Two week loan

Please return on or before the last date stamped below.
Charges are made for late return.

EUI – Series A–7
Daintith (ed.), Law as an Instrument of Economic Policy:
Comparative and Critical Approaches

European University Institute
Institut Universitaire Européen
Europäisches Hochschulinstitut
Istituto Universitario Europeo

Series A

Law/Droit/Recht/Diritto

7

Badia Fiesolana – Firenze

Law as an Instrument of Economic Policy:
Comparative and Critical Approaches

edited by
Terence Daintith

1988

Walter de Gruyter · Berlin · New York

UWCC LIBRARY

Library of Congress Cataloging-in-Publication Data

Law as an instrument of economic policy : comparative and critical
approaches / edited by Terence Daintith.
VIII, 432 p. 15,5 × 23 cm. -- (Series A--Law = Series A--Droit ; 7)
Based on papers presented at a colloquium held in Florence,
Mar. 1985.
Includes index and bibliography.
ISBN 0-89925-417-9 (U.S.) : $ 116.00 (est.)
 1. Economic policy--Congresses. 2. Industrial laws and legisla-
tion--Congresses. I. Daintith, Terence. II. Series: Series
A--Law ; 7.
K3820.A55 1985a
343'.07--dc 19
[342.37]

CIP-Kurztitelaufnahme der Deutschen Bibliothek

Law as an instrument of economic policy : comparative
and crit. approaches / ed. by Terence Daintith.
– Berlin ; New York : de Gruyter, 1987.
 (European University Institute : Ser. A, Law ; 7)
 ISBN 3-11-011430-5
NE: Daintith, Terence [Hrsg.]; Istituto Universitario
Europeo <Fiesole>: European University Institute / A

Dust Cover Design: Rudolf Hübler, Berlin. – Setting: Kösel, Kempten
Printing: Gerike, Berlin; Binding: Verlagsbuchbinderei Dieter Mikolai, Berlin.
Printed in Germany.

Foreword

Under the less-than-elegant title "Law and Economic Policy: Alternatives to De-legalisation", a programme of research was conducted from 1982 to 1985 at the European University Institute by my colleague Gunther Teubner and myself, culminating in a colloquium held in Florence in March 1985. Reproduced in this volume in revised and developed form are thirteen of the papers presented at that colloquium. Some of these papers represent the final product of a collective research endeavour by the members of a working group which set out to study the legal implementation of economic policy in France, Germany, Hungary, Italy, the Netherlands and the United Kingdom through a systematic comparative examination of recent legal developments in the fields of energy and manpower policy. Underlying this collective research was the sense of a need to test and perhaps to respond to a current of criticism of the way in which and the extent to which law is used as an instrument of State policy, criticism which, in our view, threatened to be destructive of the positive contribution which legal ordering could make in the field of policy implementation. "Legalisation" is the term used by some of these critics to describe what they see as an overburdening of the social and economic system with detailed legal regulation. As well as furnishing some modern data on legal implementation by reference to which such claims may be judged, our research has also been designed to offer a comparative perspective through which the influence on legal implementation of different legal systems, and of the characteristics of the different policy fields involved, may be discerned.

Of the seven working group papers here presented, six are accompanied by papers prepared by colloquium participants not involved in the working group but who were made aware of its objectives and methods and were invited to offer, on the basis of their own outlook and experience, an alternative treatment of the same topic. Our hope is that in this way the empirical work the group has done can be readily situated in an appropriate critical context. Also relevant, perhaps, to an appreciation of our investigation are the results of the parallel inquiry conducted within the general project framework under the direction of Gunther Teubner, an inquiry which examined the concept of legalisation (Verrechtlichung, which Teubner now translates as "juridification") in the four fields of labour law, competition law, company law and social security law. The papers read on these themes at the March 1985 colloquium were published in 1987 in a companion volume edited by Gunther Teubner under the title *Jurification of Social Spheres*.

This book does not contain the whole of the results of the working group's activities. Members of the group also produced detailed inventories of measures in the fields of energy and manpower policy in their respective countries, along with comparative reports of an interim nature which have served as the basis of the thematic papers presented here. These documents, which are on file at the European University Institute, are listed in detail in Appendix 4 to the Methodological Note which follows my introductory paper, where there are also listed the names and activities of members of the working group who participated in the early stages of its work but who do not appear here as authors of the final studies: Giuliano Amato, Jean-Michel de Forges, Jacqueline Dutheil de la Rochère, Patrick Nerhot, Claudio Franchini and Tony Curran. Their contributions were essential and are much appreciated. A first attempt, within a limited compass, to apply the methodology of the project in the field of energy policy in Europe may be found in a companion volume, Daintith and Hancher, *Energy Strategy in Europe: The Legal Framework*, published in 1986.

As editor, I am deeply conscious of my debt to the contributors to this volume, both the members of the working group whose papers appear herein – Brian Bercusson, Attila Harmathy, Leigh Hancher, Hans Jarass, Kamiel Mortelmans and Dietrich von Stebut – all of whom also participated in the burdens of the preliminary work above described; and the "external" commentators, some of whom have furnished us with major contributions on their appointed themes. Special thanks also go to Anne-Lise Strahtmann for her efficient typing and secretarial work, Iain Fraser for his translations of the papers by Fromont and Ost, Tony Curran for editing and referencing, Ralf Rogowski for preparing the index, and Brigitte Schwab for seeing the book through a complex publication process.

Terence Daintith
San Domenico di Fiesole
October 1986

Table of Contents

Part One

Introduction

Law as a Policy Instrument: Comparative Perspective

Terence Daintith

Firenze

Contents

I. Introduction

To formulate and operate an economic policy is generally accepted to be a necessary and legitimate responsibility of European governments. Law is a powerful social guidance mechanism: those governments enjoy, at the least, a highly privileged position in their State's law-making process,[1] and may often have independent if constitutionally circumscribed law-making powers of their own.[2] It would be surprising, therefore, if such governments did not deliberately set out to use law as a means to the achievement of their ends in the economic policy field – and, indeed, in all other policy fields. And in fact, ever since governments have had "policies" in the modern sense, they have supported them with laws. Yet many lawyers still react with unease or even distaste when invited to view law as an instrument of policy, and even those who find nothing strange about the notion will readily admit that the relationship between law and policy remains a problematical one. What problems lawyers perceive seems to depend a lot on where they come from. For the English – to start at home – the main problem is of law's use as a vehicle of arbitrary power,[3] or of "policy without law".[4] The Germans – or some of them – worry about "Verrechtlichung", and assume that everyone else does too.[5] Among Francophones, one's allegiance as a public or private lawyer appears to be an important factor: while public lawyers are concerned about law's inefficiency as a control mechanism,[6] private lawyers are more inclined to fear "legislative inflation"[7] or the decline of "droit" in the face of "loi":[8] a decline which appears to correspond to Weber's "materialisation of law". American concerns focus on the regulatory process, which some hold to be in "crisis"[9] and others would restrict or dismantle,[10] though there remain voices asking for more extended legal ordering of governmental action.[11] This variety may reflect subjective differences among academic lawyers of different nations – their propensity to anxiety, for example – but it may also suggest the existence of a

---

[1] Thus while the United Kingdom government has negligible powers of extra-parliamentary law making, it enjoys commanding procedural advantages in the parliamentary legislation process: see D. Miers and A. C. Page, *Legislation* (1982, London), ch. 5.

[2] As in France, under the 1958 Constitution, art. 37.

[3] See e.g. Viscount Hailsham of St. Marylebone, *Elective Dictatorship* (1976, London), H. W. R. Wade, *Constitutional Fundamentals* (1980, London), ch. 4.

[4] J. T. Winkler, "Law, State and Economy: The Industry Act 1975 in Context", (1975) 2 *Brit. Jl. of Law and Society* 103; Wade, *supra*, note 3, esp. at pp. 55–57.

[5] G. Teubner, "Juridification: Concepts, Aspects, Limits, Solutions" in G. Teubner, ed., *The Juridification of Social Spheres* (1987, Berlin) (hereinafter cited as Teubner, "Juridification").

[6] See e.g. M. Fromont, "Le contrôle de aides financières publiques aux enterprises privées", *Actualité Juridique Droit Administratif* (A. J. D. A.) 1979.3; D. Loschak, "Le principe de légalité: mythes et mystifications" A. J. D. A. 1981.387; R. Savy, *Droit Public Economique* (1977, Paris); G. Farjat, *Droit Economique* (2d ed., 1981, Paris), at pp. 757–766.

[7] N. Nitsch, "L'inflation juridique et ses conséquences", *Arch. Philos. Dr.* 1982.161.

[8] B. Edelman, "La dejuridicisation du fait de la loi (regards un peu sombres sur les lois Auroux" *Droit Social* 1984.290.

[9] See D. Trubek, ed., *Reflexive Law and the Regulatory Crisis* (1984, Madison).

[10] See text at notes 23–25 *infra*.

[11] Though these are mostly to be found in the legislature, rather than among academics: see R. Stewart, "'Reform' of American Administrative Law; The Academic vs. the Political Agenda" (1984, mimeo).

series of different national sets of problems with the law/policy relationship, and the futility of grand generalisations about it.

These expressions of concern about instrumental law, and the sense of national differences of intensity and emphasis, prompted the comparative empirical enquiry, into law's use as an instrument of economic policy, whose results are presented in the six thematic papers[12] which form the bulk of the present volume. Three of these papers take as their subject matter a type of instrument of economic management (regulations, subsidies, manipulation of the public sector), the others address issues which affect the entire field of economic policy implementation: private, as opposed to state, ordering of the economy; the significance of the time-scale of policy for legal implementation; and the influence of different legal systems on modes of implementation of policy. On their specific themes, these papers speak for themselves, as also do the related critical papers and comments prepared by scholars outside the group. The thematic papers all result, however, from an extended period of work which has had an important collective, as well as individual, dimension. The tasks of this introductory paper, therefore, are to identify, explain, and so far as possible justify the collective approach chosen; and to point to some results of the enterprise as a whole. This involves explaining the background to the investigation, the choice of the fields which have been the subject of detailed study and from which the data analysed in the succeeding papers have been drawn, the concepts and methods used, and the working hypotheses which have structured the analysis as a whole.

II. Background

Our questions[13] about the problematic relationship between law and economic policy have been three. First, what forms of law are used for the implementation of economic policy? Second, what factors determine whether law is invoked for the resolution of policy problems and, if invoked, the forms of law that are used? In particular, are the characteristics and demands of the national legal system as important, in shaping such choices, as the nature of the problem or of the policy field concerned? Third, can one differentiate between countries in terms of the quality or intensity of legal implementation of policy, so as to explain some of the varied reactions to the law/policy relationship to which I referred at the beginning

---

[12] *Viz*, H. Jarass, "Regulations as an Instrument of Economic Policy" (hereinafter "Jarass"), below pp. 75–96; D. von Stebut, "Subsidies as an Instrument of Economic Policy" (hereinafter "von Stebut"), below pp. 137–152; L. Hancher, "The Public Sector as Object and Instrument of Economic Policy" (hereinafter "Hancher"), below pp. 165–236; A. Harmathy, "The Influence of Legal Systems on Modes of Implementation of Economic Policy" (hereinafter "Harmathy"), below pp. 245–266; K. Mortelmans, "Short and Long-term Policy Objectives and the Choice of Instruments and Measures" (hereinafter "Mortelmans") below pp. 283–321; B. Bercusson, "Economic Policy: State and Private Ordering" (hereinafter "Bercusson") below pp. 359–420.

[13] In this paper, the plural pronoun is used to refer to the work and opinions of the study group as a whole, the singular pronoun to express the personal views of the writer.

of this chapter? To explain this choice of questions I begin by looking at the kinds of problems which others have identified in the relationship: in particular, in the use of law as an instrument of policy. Such an examination forms the object of this section. By way of preliminary, however, it will be helpful to explain exactly what I mean by "economic policy".

A. "Economic Policy"

What is policy? The Oxford English Dictionary gives as its chief sense "a course of action adopted as advantageous or expedient". This definition implies action guided by deliberation, purpose and choice. There are common uses of the term "policy" which imply no action (as when a government's statements about its objectives and the means it proposes to use for attaining them are referred to as its "policy") or little deliberation (as when any sequence of government actions is retrospectively called its "policy" in a given field). *Purposeful activity*, however, expresses the essence of the term's use here. The adjective "economic" is used in a broad sense, and is not intended to confine discussion to the area of actions which are explicitly directed to the attainment of macro-economic policy objectives such as high and stable employment levels, balance of payments equilibrium, price stability or economic growth.[14] By way at least of a general definition (I discuss later the considerations that led to the selection of the particular policy areas and objectives that figure in the comparative study) economic policy includes *all purposeful governmental action whose actual or professed primary objective is the improvement of the economic welfare of the whole population for which the government is responsible or of some segment of that population*. This definition is broad enough to subsume government's attempts both at more nearly optimal allocation of resources and at fairer distribution of wealth, while at the same time acknowledging that a government's descriptions and justifications of its economic policy measures may sometimes lack truth or candour. That it is broad enough to subsume much (but probably not all) of what is also termed "social policy" does not matter: clear distinctions between what is economic and what is social may be important for some purposes, but there is nothing to suggest that analysis of the law/policy relationship is one of them.

It will be seen that the definition refers to the *governmental* origin of economic policy. In a sense it goes without saying that economic policy will be governmental, in that the State, today, assumes explicit responsibility for the economic welfare of its citizens.[15] In another sense, however, this State connection has to be seen as part of the problem, for if the legal structures common to most Western democracies embody or reflect *any* guiding principle of economic welfare, it is that of the "invisible hand" of the market rather than State direction, and I shall argue that this bias both shapes the instrumental role of law and creates unease

---

[14] See e.g. A. K. Dasgupta and A. J. Hagger, *The Objectives of Macroeconomic Policy* (1971, London).

[15] E.g., in the United Kingdom Government's White Paper on Employment Policy (1944), Cmd. 6527; or the German Stabilitätgesetz of June 8, 1967.

about this role. A second point to keep in mind is that departures from the market principle of economic organisation do not lead ineluctably to substantive State control or guidance. The last hundred years have witnessed the steady development of private, usually associational centres of economic power, to some extent free to determine and pursue their own economic objectives. Companies and trade unions are the obvious examples. The State may adopt a variety of strategies in relation to such private power-centres, combining in different proportions *control,* on the one hand, and *reliance* – for policy input, for policy implementation, or, at the extreme, for policy-*making and* implementation, on the other. Brian Bercusson's contribution to this volume represents a sustained attempt to apply the general methodology of this study to the deployment of private economic power, and thereby to cast further light on the choice of forms and occasions for implementation of policy through State law. Every strategy save that of pure control demands that we pay some attention to the "private" dimension of economic policy.

Notwithstanding these important possible variations, the State today remains at the centre of the economic policy stage in Western no less than in Eastern Europe, and it is the legal instrumentalisation of its actions that accordingly form our primary focus. The State, however, is not monolithic: at any given time there exists a diffusion of power, both territorial and functional, among its various organs. Territorial diffusion involves not only the constitutional division of competences in a federal state like West Germany, but also the diffusion of powers and functions to regional and local levels, strongly marked in Italy and not absent even in the most centralising of States. Some economic policy functions, whether of formation or, more commonly, of execution, may be discharged at these sub-State levels. We have not attempted any systematic analysis of sub-State competences in the economic sphere, nor have we chosen our fields for detailed study with this issue in mind. I should signal here, however, that the way in which competences are divided could have an important influence on the choice of legal means for the implementation of policy.[16]

Functional diffusion takes two forms. Within the executive branch, power may be diffused through the use of specialist executive organs falling outside the departmental framework of central government, charged with the running of public enterprises and with a variety of regulatory and public service functions. While such bodies will not normally occupy a privileged role in policy-making, their functions in relation to implementation are important and complex. In particular we may encounter them both as objects of economic policy on a similar footing to private bodies, and as instruments through which central government seeks to carry out its policy aims.[17]

Power is also functionally diffused across the dividing line between the executive and non-executive organs of the State, between the central government on the one hand, and Parliament and the courts on the other. This type of

[16] See below, p. 39, and R. Stewart, "Regulation and the Crisis of Legalisation in the United States", below pp. 100–102.
[17] Below, p. 27.

dispersion of power is obviously of importance to an investigation of the law/
policy relationship, but does not operate to diminish the executive's role as the
lead policy player. Parliaments, it is suggested, should not be viewed as the makers
or possessors of economic policies.[18] Their role is rather one of scrutiny, discussion and legitimation of policies formed elsewhere – usually within the executive.
In the formation of such policies groups of members of Parliament, or even
individual members, may exercise some influence, but it is clear that, in general,
Parliaments today carry less weight in the formation of policy than do a variety of
other bodies, from the political parties to the trade unions, employers' associations and other major interest groups.

The possible role of the courts as policy-makers cannot be so readily dismissed.
Courts do, after all, take decisions with binding effect, not only for the individual
parties before them but also, through the operation of doctrines of judicial
authority and precedent, for all parties who now or in the future find themselves in
similar situations. In the civil sphere, the decisions are usually reached without the
help or intervention of any other organ of government. Courts may, in arriving at
their decisions, be seeking, consciously or unconsciously, to arrive at goals in the
nature of economic objectives. In developing the common law of restraint of trade
in the United Kingdom, for example, the courts may be seen as attempting to
inhibit, through a judicial policy of non-enforcement, the use of contractual
devices to create or consolidate dominant positions in local and national markets.[19] While codification, and the vigour of executive-inspired legislative activity,
have left the courts little space in which to play such a role, the possibility of
judicial decisions figuring as a significant feature of instrumental law in a given
country and policy area cannot be wholly discounted.[20] Current debates about the
relationship of law and policy, however, treat policy as a matter of executive
inspiration and legislative expression, and judicial activity as falling wholly within
the legal system with which policy implementation is problematically related.[21]

B. The Tensions in the Law/Policy Relationship

To recapitulate, therefore, economic policy here normally connotes purposeful
activity on the part of central government whose primary objective is the
improvement of economic welfare. From the very beginnings in the nineteenth
century of the development of such a systematic State approach to economic
improvement, the instrumentalisation of law in its service has provoked concern

---

[18] This is a Eurocentric remark. For a transatlantic contrast see, again, Stewart, below.
[19] For an account of the common law of restraint of trade see J. D. Heydon, *The Restraint of
Trade Doctrine* (1971, London); *Chitty on Contracts* (25th ed., 1983, London), vol. I,
paras. 1082–1142.
[20] See P. Del Duca, *Legitimating Bureaucratic Decisionmaking: A Comparative Investigation of Air Pollution Control Policies* (unpublished Ph. D thesis, EUI, Florence, 1985), at
pp. 219–238, explaining how judicial activism has compensated for administrative inertia
in this field in Italy.
[21] Below, esp. at pp. 8–10. In fact our inquiry has not turned up any major judicial contributions to policy-making or implementation.

which, as already noted, still persists. I need to spend a few moments in analysing these expressions of concern, because dissatisfaction with the terms in which some of the principal arguments are posed has helped to shape the present inquiry.

A key to these arguments may be obtained by substituting for "economic policy" the more suggestive term "State intervention in the economy". This familiar image is based on the liberal conception of a separation of the State from the economy, which constitute distinct worlds operating according to different principles: commandment for the State, market exchange for the economy. The State is seen as coming into the economy – from the outside. Law normally enters the scene in two guises: as public law, organising the structure of the State and expressing its command functions, and as private law, underpinning the system of market exchange with a structure of rights and duties whose observance is ultimately guaranteed by State power. Most, if not all, of the modern critiques of "instrumental law" draw directly or indirectly upon this conception. This should not surprise us, in the light both of the continuity of the liberal tradition in modern times and of the reflection in Roman law of a similar image of State/law/economy relations. Both West and East European legal scholars have pointed out that the threefold distinction of the Roman Digest between ownership, obligations and public law had an ideological significance in so far as it recognised the existence of a set of principles and concepts governing the acquisition and keeping of property flowing not from national law but from the *ius gentium* of mankind. The rules – of private law – operative in this sphere thus formed a separate corpus isolated from politics and linked with public power essentially through the category of *actions*, within which the enforcement machinery of the State could be called in aid to vindicate claims based on independently derived rights of property.[22] In the modern-dress version of these ideas the courts appear as the only organ of the State properly concerned with the protection of these property rights.

Against this background the instrumental deployment of law at the instigation of central government in aid of its economic policies is said to lead inevitably, or to have led in fact, to a variety of negative results. These arguments may be ordered according to whether they are more concerned with negative effects on the economy or on the law itself, though this distinction is far from clear cut.

At one extreme the laissez-faire position is very simple: State interference in the economy will lead to misallocation of resources, economic inefficiency, and a net wealth loss; any law which is the vehicle of such interference must be bad. This argument has been elaborately reworked in legal terms by the lawyer-economists of the Chicago School, who conduct detailed analyses of legislative regulation of economic activity to show its inefficient character, and similarly detailed analyses of common law rules and principles to show how the judges, perhaps without knowing it or even in spite of themselves,[23] have plodded steadily along the golden

---

[22] G. Samuel, "Roman law and modern capitalism", (1984) 4 *Legal Studies* 185, 187–8; G. Eorsi, *Comparative Civil (Private) Law* (1979, Budapest), pp. 85–88.

[23] P. H. Rubin, "Why is the Common Law Efficient?", (1977) 6 *Journal of Legal Studies* 51; G. L. Priest, "The Common Law Process and the Selection of Efficient Rules", *ibid.*, at 65. For the subsequent development of these ideas see J. Hirshleifer, *Evolutionary*

road to allocative efficiency. In its extremer forms[24] this argumentation would deny any place for redistributive legislation, and even where a place is seen for law to promote ends other than efficiency, or to cope with market failures, there is suspicion of the regulatory style of legislation (fears of "agency capture") and of legislation generally (legislators as personal, rather than social, utility maximisers).[25] Appropriate adjustments of common law rights and duties are thus preferred where possible.

A similar position is reached via a different route by Hayek. His key point is that the dynamics of the market are too complex and variable to be grasped by the policy-maker who, continually erring in his appreciations of market malfunctions, enacts "corrective" legislation which leads sooner or later to visibly inefficient results and calls for further "correction". A properly functioning economy can therefore only be attained by avoiding this kind of intervention and relying on the free play of competition guaranteed by appropriate permanent legal rules. Hayek, however, joins to this essentially economistic approach[26] a concern with State power in general, and with the risks of its "arbitrary" use, which links him to the broad preoccupations of many modern public lawyers confronted with the instrumental use of law. In the interests of freedom, he propounds the idea that the only rules of law that are acceptable are general and abstract, at least in the sense that any legal discrimination between groups (as between, say, men and women, old and young) is equally recognised as justified by those within and those outside the favoured group.[27] The necessary characteristics cannot be possessed by interventionist laws, such as laws for the regulation of prices. Unless the rules for price determination are constantly changed in response to the ever-changing circumstances of the market (which implies individual decisions and a lack of essential generality), they will produce legal prices which are out of line with market prices. Supply and demand will not then balance, and if price control is to be maintained some form, of rationing system, itself involving arbitrary discretionary decisions, will need to be introduced.[28]

In effect, Hayek purports to identify, and to explain the operation of, the disease whose legal symptoms had for decades been the anxious concern of what Harlow and Rawlings term "red light" theorists,[29] guided by Dicey's dictum that the "rule of law" required the absence of wide, arbitrary or discretionary powers

Models in Economics and Law (1982, Greenwich) vol. 4 of *Research in Law and Economics).*

[24] See R. Posner, "Utilitarianism, Economics and Legal Theory" (1978) 8 *Journal of Legal Studies* 103; "The Ethical and Political Basis of the Efficiency Norm in Common Law Adjudication", (1980) 8 *Hofstra Law Review* 487.

[25] R. Posner, "Theories of Economic Regulation", (1974) 5 *Bell Journal of Economics and Management Science* 335; G. Stigler, "The Sizes of Legislatures" (1976) 5 *Journal of Legal Studies* 17; R. E. McCormick and R. D. Tollison, *Politicians, Legislation and the Economy: An Inquiry into the Interest-Group Theory of Government* (1981, Boston).

[26] For which he is criticised by Teubner, "Juridification", at pp. 31–33.

[27] F. von Hayek, *The Constitution of Liberty* (1960, London), p. 154.

[28] *Ibid.* pp. 227–228.

[29] C. Harlow and R. Rawlings, *Law and Administration* (1984, London), ch. 1.

of constraint in persons of authority.[30] Law in the age of the welfare State, however, exhibits constant departures from these requirements. British commentators have been particularly exercised by rule-less laws (which simply make broad grants of decision-making power to administrators), laws explicitly or impliedly excluding judicial review of administrative decisions,[31] the shifting of powers of substantive rule-making from Parliament to central government departments through legal delegation,[32] and the detailed and pettifogging nature of many of the rules so made.[33] The way in which these complaints are expressed is strongly influenced by a conception of Parliament as the only legitimate law-maker under the United Kingdom constitution[34], but the same essential concerns find expression in systems which recognise in the executive a broad capacity of implementation of laws[35] or even an independent regulatory capacity.[36] Recent writings like those of Ost and Loschak resemble those of British public lawyers in the sense that they are likewise concerned about the amount of discretionary power detained by the executive as a result of its assumption of broadening economic and social responsibilities, and concerned also about the difficulty of judicial control of such power.[37] There is, however, an important difference of emphasis. British writers, obsessed by the sovereignty of Parliament, tended to see the problem as one of improper abnegation or delegation by Parliament of its responsibility for the enactment of substantive law. They wrote as though they would have had no complaint had Parliament itself laid down all the substantive rules needed to give effect to economic and social policy (the unstated premise being that if this were impossible – as proponents of discretion and delegated legislation claimed it was – the remedy was to drop the interventionist policies). Modern Continental writing attributes these effects to the combination of a much wider range of factors, which includes not only delegation (within as well as to the executive) and discretion[38] but also multiplication of laws and sources; instability of laws; diminution of the binding force of laws by reason of ineffective or selective enforcement, or the deliberate creation of laws without sanctions; and the use of laws not as binding

---

[30] A. V. Dicey, *Introduction to the Study of the Law of the Constitution* (10th ed., by E. C. S Wade, 1950, London), pp. 187–196.

[31] S. A. de Smith, *Judicial Review of Administrative Action* (4th ed., 1980, London, by J. M. Evans), ch. 7.

[32] G. Hewart, *The New Despotism* (1929, London).

[33] The *locus classicus* is C. K. Allen, *Law and Orders* (3d ed., 1965, London).

[34] As to whether this is a correct deduction from sovereignty of Parliament doctrine, see T. C. Daintith, "Public Law and Economic Policy" (1974) *Journal of Business Law* 9, at pp. 11–16.

[35] See e.g. A. Jacquemin and B. Remiche, "Le pouvoir judiciaire entre l'opportunité et la légalité économiques", and F. Ost, "Entre jeu et providence, le juge des relations économiques", in A. Jacquemin and B. Remiche, eds., *Les magistratures économiques et la crise* (1984, Brussels) at pp. 9–36 and 37–90 (Belgium).

[36] See references at note 6, *supra*.

[37] Loschak, *supra* note 6, at p. 392; Ost, *supra* note 35, at pp. 54–58.

[38] Loschak, *ibid.* Farjat, *supra* note 6, at pp. 761–762.

rules but as negotiating counters.[39] This wider range of questions is now being addressed in Britain as well.[40]

Most of this recent writing is less concerned about the unbalancing of the constitution by inappropriate legislative practice, than with the changes in the character of law that are said to be occurring as a result of the attempt to use it for complex instrumental ends. These changes are not necessarily seen as bad. For Farjat they are the essence of "economic law", which he terms the antithesis of the liberal model of law;[41] Ost speaks of them as characterising "la justice normativetechnocratique", which he contrasts with "la justice légaliste-liberale".[42] For Teubner, however, such changes, at least if carried too far, will produce a deformation or even disintegration of law, by threatening its essential characteristic of normativity.[43] Following Luhmann[44] Teubner picks out as particularly worrying the volume and rapidity of change of legislation (Luhmann also makes a remarkably sweeping attack on legislation as "bad law" by reason of defective conceptualisation and drafting),[45] and the introduction of purposive criteria into law, placing on judges the burden of "controlling results".[46]

These anxieties – or at least those which are concerned with the qualities of instrumental law, as opposed to its very existence[47] – are expressed as if the function of instrumental law must necessarily be to alter, by commandment, the

---

[39] See references in notes 6 and 35 *supra*.

[40] Winkler, *supra* note 4; Daintith, "The Executive Power Today", in J.Jowell and D.Oliver, eds., *The Changing Constitution* (1985, Oxford) at pp. 174–197.

[41] Farjat, *supra* note 6, pp. 701–716.

[42] Ost, *supra* note 35, pp. 46–90.

[43] "Juridification" at pp. 25–27.

[44] N. Luhmann, *The Differentiation of Society* (1982 English ed., New York) ch. 6; "The Self-reproduction of Law and its Limits", in G.Teubner, ed., *Dilemmas of Law in the Welfare State* (1986, Berlin) at pp. 111–127.

[45] *The Differentiation of Society*, at p. 132.

[46] "Juridification" p. 26. This complaint, it may be said in passing, sounds odd to a public lawyer, particularly in the British context, where legislation regularly confers powers on the executive without any mention of the purposes for which those powers are to be exercised. In recent years courts have become readier to infer a legislative purpose in such cases from an examination of the statue as a whole, thus enabling them to check whether the relevant powers have in fact been exercised with this purpose: see e.g. Padfield v. Minister of Agriculture, Fisheries and Food [1968] A.C. 997. Checking purpose in this way does not, of course, necessarily lead to checking results; where the law *does* explicitly ask for the checking of results (take, for example, the EEC Treaty provision forbidding "measures having an effect equivalent to a quantitative restriction on imports", article 30), the tendency of courts has been to develop rules of thumb by reference to which such measures may be recognised, without the necessity for a case-by-case examination of actual effects. (See, e.g. European Court of Justice, Case 8/74, Dassonville [1974] E. C. R. 837). There is no evidence that this has led either to the ineffectiveness of these provisions or to judically-induced distortions of trade. Perhaps this would be seen by Luhmann as a self-defence mechanism on the part of the legal system; the interesting thing is that it appears to work.

[47] See text at notes 23–25 *supra*.

operation of an economy which has been comprehensively organised by private law. The property rights, and liabilities, created and ordered by private law are taken to regulate all actual and potential economic relations, with the consequence that in a State which subscribes to the rule of law, any State policy seeking to influence the economic operations of the private sector – other than by pure exhortation – must operate by imposing changes in the private law set of property rights and liabilities. There are a number of familiar ways in which such changes may be effected: specific adjustments of property rights or civil liabilities (which affect only the content, not the scope of the private law system); new or revised criminal prohibitions, policed in the ordinary way, which restrict some property rights and may reinforce others; the installation of regulatory systems placing areas of economic life under State supervision and thus imposing detailed restrictions on the play of private law rights and duties therein. It is hard to trace clear boundaries between these categories, though some have tried.[48] What I would stress here is not the possible differences between the categories, but what links them: the actually or potentially[49] mandatory character of the legal dispositions involved. The assumption that economic life is exhaustively ordered by private law, to which the State is linked principally through its courts, thus furnishes an explanation of both the *need* to use law as an instrument of economic policy, and the mandatory *character* of that law.

If the use of law as an instrument of policy necessarily involves the unilateral alteration of private law rights, and the changing of the landscape of legal coercion, it is natural to expect it to assume a similar shape to the law (be it code or case law) which maintains those rights: to be general in coverage, precise in form, abstract in expression, individual in focus, long-standing in duration. When instrumental law fails to take this shape, holders of these expectations accuse it of deformity and talk of excessive burdening with detail,[50] of purely technical content,[51] of excessive mobility,[52] of lack of standards and conferment of arbitrary power,[53] of badly drafted legislation.[54] There is no doubt that much of the law through which the State alters private rights is open to criticism of this kind. The scope of "instrumental law" cannot, however, be properly restricted by reference to laws of this type. There exist, and have long existed, types of law which are not concerned with the alteration of private rights, but which are no less capable of being put to use as an instrument of policy. They stem not from the State's concern with the

---

[48] *E.g.* R. S. Summers, "The Technique Element in Law", (1981) 59 *California Law Review* 733.

[49] Potentially, in that changes to civil rights or liabilities may only operate with mandatory effect when invoked by one of the parties to a transaction. In many cases a party may be allowed by the other to contract out of a liability, or the liability may simply not be enforced.

[50] Teubner, "Juridification", at pp. 37–38.

[51] A. Supiot, "Délégalisation, normalisation et droit de travail", *Droit Social* 1984.296.

[52] Loschak, *supra* note 6.

[53] Hewart, *supra* note 32.

[54] Luhmann, *supra* note 45.

definition and protection of the legal position of *individuals,* but from the desire to provide formal recognition and protection for collective interests, in particular to interests of the whole collectivity as expressed through democratic or other representational procedures. Such interests might include the proper management of State funds and property and, more generally, of "public" goods in which private rights cannot (e.g. national defence) or do not (e.g., in the United Kingdom, roads) exist.[55] Such laws, whose mandatory effect is either indirect, or is confined to organs or individuals within the State apparatus, may assume shapes which differ considerably from that associated with laws for the maintenance or alteration of private rights.

Consider the case of laws relating to public finance; in particular, that of annual budget laws. Apart, perhaps, from the precision with which they are normally expressed, such laws do not stand up too well against the criteria mentioned earlier in the previous paragraph. They are neither general nor abstract, but express a variety of specific decisions; in their spending provisions, at least, they focus upon aggregates, not on individuals; they are of short duration. It is difficult to deny that they are law, however:[56] seen from the standpoint of the public administration, the spending limits they impose imply precise prohibitions – there is no lack of normativity. What accounts for their existence is a desire not to protect private rights, but to assure democratic control over the public purse by resort to solemn means. Their link with private rights is slender, being confined to the alteration, by their tax provisions, of the level or incidence of the taxes which private persons are legally obliged to pay to government. It is possible to assimilate those obligations to private law obligations insofar as they constitute one among a number of legal constraints on the free disposition of income and capital, others among which are furnished by rules of private law. Tax laws, are, however, distinctive in that they involve a purely bilateral "vertical" relationship between individual and State, as opposed to the "horizontal" relationships with other

---

[55] It is of course true that there may be a collective interest in the protection of individual rights. There is also an "individual" aspect to the task of managing public goods, in the sense that an element of management may consist in forbidding or controlling individual behaviour which damages those goods or the enjoyment of them by others (e.g. spying in relation to defence, dangerous driving in relation to roads). Lawyers tend, however, to emphasise the individual impact, rather than the collective inspiration, of such legal prohibitions, and they are here treated as examples of our "private rights" model.

[56] Note, though, that German doctrine might allow them to be "formal" law, but not law in a substantive sense, the latter referring only to measures authorising interference with the life, liberty or property of citizens. See M. Rheinstein, ed., *Max Weber on Law in Economy and Society* (1954, Cambridge, transl. by E. Shils and M. Rheinstein from M. Weber, *Wirtschaft und Gesellschaft* [2d ed., 1925]), at p. 47, n.14, explaining Weber's classification of the State budget as administrative rather than legislative in character. The distinction, or at least its use to mark off separate areas of activity for legislature and administration, was not absorbed by the Grundgesetz and is now not observed in practice, Parliament legislating regularly and in detail in such areas as state aids, temporary laws, "action programmes" and so on: see M. Fromont and A. Rieg, *Introduction au Droit Allemand,* tome 1 (Les fondements) (1977, Paris), at pp. 175–177.

private parties that are the normal material of private law.[57] On the spending side, however, private rights are neither reduced nor enlarged by the attribution of spending power to the executive, though the use of that power may well involve legal arrangements such as contracts, gifts or loans. The fact that the legal interface between annual budget laws and private legal rights is minimal in no way prevents such laws from having massive effects on economic activity, by way of a process of diffusion through the economy effected, almost entirely, through the transmission mechanism of private contracts. In this way taxes are passed on, distributed or absorbed; the effects of public expenditures are multiplied as the funds are disseminated through contract payments, contractors' wage payments, employee savings payments, building society investments, and so on. The understanding of these processes (though not necessarily of their legal articulation) permitted the transformation of the budget from an enactment of State "housekeeping" to an instrument of economic policy, but this instrumentalisation has involved no change in the structure of budget laws (though it has had important effects on the procedures through which they are discussed). By reason of this change of function, such laws may today be seen as a form of instrumental law which uses the private law relations of the economy without their unilateral alteration.

Budget, laws, which present, by their form, the most striking contrast with laws altering private rights, cannot simply be dismissed as a quirk of Parliamentary procedure, a fortuitous borrowing of the clothes of the law for essentially financial decision-making. Were this so, new names would need to be found for a great part of what today fills the statute books. Budget laws are, after all, only the most general and short-term sub-class within a class of laws whose function it is to order the management and distribution of the patrimony of the State: its financial wealth, its land, goods and manpower and the public services it provides therewith. These are the laws that provide for grants and subsidies to farmers and to industrialists; that organise State systems for the provision of health care, education, professional training, defence; that constitute and control State enterprises; that regulate the award of social security and social assistance payments. Such laws are explained not by the need to alter existing private rights – they do not do so – but by the need to furnish a formal and binding organisation for the performance of public functions. They may create new private rights vis-à-vis government, in the way that tax laws create new private duties, but they are not to be explained by reference to such creation. Social security payments, for example, are normally available as of right in the United Kingdom, but it is extremely rare for subsidy payments to industry and agriculture to be other than wholly discretionary. Yet the legal provisions regulating the award of such subsidy payments, particularly in the agricultural sector, are almost as detailed as those for social security. This ceases to be puzzling when it is realised that the function of the law here is not to ensure that payments are made to those who qualify for them (the interest of the government in ensuring the success of the policy of which the payments are an instrument is thought to be sufficient for that), but rather to ensure that payments

---

[57] Third-party involvement in tax administration (e.g. of employers in PAYE) does not belie this distinction.

are not made to those who do not qualify for them. There may well be a case for extending, in countries such as the United Kingdom or the United States, the range of payments, goods or services obtainable as of right, on a variety of grounds such as institutionalised reliance, equality of opportunity, and so on.[58] The award of such rights would change the content and function of such legislation; but not the reasons for its existence in the first place. The key to these reasons remains the collective interest in the correct, regular and efficient organisation of the tasks of the State.

This interest, of course, exists independently of any particular line of government economic policy. So far as the constitutional rules which underpin this democratic preference require, rules of law will be promulgated to express, or authorise, schemes of government spending, to prescribe the structure of public bodies and to provide for their mode of operation, whatever the importance of such measures to government policy objectives. One may therefore speak, as in relation to the law affecting private rights, of the instrumentalisation of an independently-existing body of law. The functions of that body of law are, however, different, reflecting as it does the need for collective control of the non-coercive action of the State as opposed to that for protection of the individual against its coercive action.

By reason of these differences, what I will here call "collective interest" law could offer a rather different set of standards for judging legal developments connected with economic policy. The presumptions about the impersonality, dynamism and circumstantial variety of market relations which have helped to shape the preferences for generality, abstractness and stability as characteristics of private law rules apply with much less force to the highly organised public sector. Moreover, where the legal rights of individuals are not directly affected, the rationale for formulating all legal rules in terms of the position and conduct of individuals (whether these be natural or legal persons) is greatly weakened, and legal rules expressed in aggregative terms (budget ceilings, etc.) can perform a legitimate function. At the same time, the concern of collective interest law with the structure, competences and behaviour of organisations in the public sector still demands that it share the capacity of private law for the effective resolution of conflict, and hence be sufficiently precise to afford guidance to those involved in this process. It must be normative and not just descriptive: but this does not mean that to be effective it need look anything like private law. An illustration, from United Kingdom law relating to public enterprise, may help to make the point.

When transport was nationalised in 1947, the industry was placed in the hands of a statutory public corporation, the British Transport Commission. The Transport Act 1947, its constitutive statute (which was of course neither abstract nor general, being concerned solely with the Commission and its functions) provided that it should be

---

[58] As argued by C. Reich, "The New Property", (1964) 73 *Yale Law Journal* 733. For a critical review of the case, in the context of the extension of fourteenth amendment protection in the United States, see S. Williams, "Liberty and Property: The Problem of Government Benefits" (1983) 12 *Journal of Legal Studies* 3.

the general duty of the Commission so to exercise their powers under this Act as to provide, or secure or promote the provision of, an efficient, adequate, economical and properly integrated system of public inland transport and port facilities within Great Britain for passengers and goods with due regard for safety of operation; and for that purpose it shall be the duty of the Commission to take such steps as they consider necessary for extending and improving the transport and port facilities within Great Britain in such manner as to provide most efficiently and conveniently for the needs of the public, agriculture, commerce and industry.[59]

Here, it appears, is purposive law with a vengeance. Hearing across the years, perhaps, the pre-echo of modern concern about the ability of the judge to engage in the sort of controlling of results that appears to be envisaged by such legislation, Parliament went on to provide that nothing in the foregoing provision should be

construed as imposing on the Commission, either directly or indirectly, any form of duty or liability enforceable by proceedings before any court or tribunal to which they would not otherwise be subject.[60]

In *Fife C. C. v. Railway Executive* [61] a Scottish court held that this exclusionary provision meant exactly what it said, so that the court could not entertain a complaint on behalf of railway users that certain actions of the Commisssion were inconsistent with this statutory duty. So what is the nature of the Commission's statutory duty? Is this merely "soft", sanctionless law? or law with a purely symbolic function? Private law paradigms make it hard to think otherwise. In fact, provisions of this type, which are to be found in all public enterprise statutes – sometimes with, sometimes without, an express judicial ouster clause – have an important legal function in regulating conflicts between the enterprises and the central government departments which enjoy legal powers of "general direction" of their activities.[62] The provisions operate as standards by reference to which public corporations may seek to resist formal directions or, more often, informal pressures, which they see as inconsistent with the proper discharge of their functions. In elevating to the status of law the targets and orientations of the public enterprise, they legally restrict the ability of government to determine policy through the exercise of its directive power. Even in this context, the courts have not been called upon, but on several occasions public corporations have pressed their resistance to the point of requiring government to secure the enactment of new legislation to authorise changes which might otherwise have been seen as in conflict with these statutory duties.[63]

---

[59] S. 3(1). The Act was repealed and replaced by the Transport Act 1962, installing a new organisational structure, but one regulated according to the same legal principles.

[60] S. 3(5).

[61] 1951 S. C. 499.

[62] E.g Transport Act 1947, s. 4(1): "The Minister may, after consultation with the Commission, give to the Commission directions of a general character as to the exercise and performance by the Commission of their functions in relation to matters which appear to him to affect the national interest, and the Commission shall give effect to any such directions." There are many other "direction" provisions in similar form.

[63] Examples include the Civil Aviation (Declaratory Provisions) Act 1971 arising out of

As between powerful actors, therefore, this kind of law operates to determine the space within which highly political arguments about the discharge of economic functions will take place, and to require that if the boundaries of that space are to be altered without the consent of one of the participants, this be done in an overt and solemn way. The fact that this can be effectively done by law which is at once vague, purposive and not suitable for judicial enforcement[64] suggests that one needs, in order to judge fairly the quality of legal rules, to develop a second set of criteria, based on the organisational functions of collective interest law. Just what such criteria might be I am not presently equipped to indicate in detail, but their *general* inspiration, given the collective and democratic origins of this body of law, might not be very different from the demand for public law to guarantee and structure a more participatory democracy which is today voiced by British critics of "traditional" public law scholarship.[65] The function of such criteria should not, in my view, be to replace the set derived from the private law model. Such a claim would imply an absolute pre-eminence of State organisation, as a basis for economic relations, over economic actor rights. This seems an unattractive goal; we might feel unhappy if the above-quoted terminology of the Transport Act 1947,[66] and no more, applied to regulate the activities of a State body with *coercive* powers over the property of individuals. West European States do not seem to be moving in this direction, and even in Eastern Europe, where the idea has been enthusiastically embraced, the private law foundations of economic activity have in most places survived the switch to socialist ownership. Despite the challenge of a radical conception of economic law as a mass of legal means attached to economic-technological processes, wholly internal to a comprehensive mechanics of State organisation of the economy ("staatliche Leistungspyramide"),[67] private law concepts have continued to furnish criteria for the design of economic law.[68]

In evaluating instrumental law today, therefore, there should be a place for both sets of criteria. This is not simply to say that some laws alter private rights and

---

governmental attempts to transfer route licences from the nationalised airlines to private competitors; and the Oil and Gas (Enterprise) Act 1982, ss.9–11, arising, in part, out of attempts to divest the British Gas Corporation of its oil interests.

[64] F. Cassese, "Public Enterprises and Economic Policy: A Comment", below p. 238, seems less optimistic about the effectiveness of the constitutive statutes of public enterprise, but is there treating such statutes only as a potential vehicle of governmental control, not as a means of structuring, and hence constraining, it. See also p. 240.

[65] See e.g. J. P. W. B. McAuslan, "Administrative Law, Collective Consumption and Judicial Policy", (1983) 46 *Modern Law Review* 1; T. Prosser, "Towards a Critical Public Law", (1982) 9 *Journal of Law and Society* 1; A. Hutchinson, "The Rise and Ruse of Administrative Law and Scholarship", (1985) 48 *Modern Law Review* 293.

[66] See text at note 59 *supra*.

[67] Eorsi, *supra*, note 22, pp. 213–225. Note how Eorsi's comments on the "thinning" of law in the Leistungspyramide model (pp. 223–224) ("which might prove to be a healthy trend") parallel Luhmann's anticipations of the "de-differentiation" of law (*op.cit.* note 45 *supra*, p. 135).

[68] For numerous examples see J. N. Hazard, "Socialism, Legalisation and Delegalisation", below, pp. 267–279.

should therefore be judged according to the "private rights" set of criteria, while others do not and should therefore be judged according to the collective interest set. Life is more complex than that. Over the past hundred years or so in Western Europe the State has steadily become a more important participant in the economy, operating as often as not according to the forms of private enterprise; at the same time, through concentration of economic power, the economy has become ever less atomistic and ever more "organised".[69] In consequence the difference between large private organisations and State organisations, both in terms of internal structure and of relations with other economic actors, is sometimes hard to perceive,[70] and their relations with each other are hard to classify in terms of any public/private dichotomy.[71] This process of assimilation and interpenetration of public and private suggests at least that it may sometimes be appropriate for laws changing existing private rights to be structured according to collective interest criteria, and for laws which do not have this effect to meet the standards of the private rights model.[72]

In order, therefore, to give sensible answers to the sorts of questions asked in the debate about instrumental law, such as whether modern economic management can be structured and controlled by law, or whether law is being dangerously deformed by the attempt to adjust its structure to the task of economic regulation, we need to undertake an analysis which differentiates between types of law, explores their characteristics when used in an instrumental fashion, and relates that use to the characteristics of economic policy itself. We cannot assume that economic policy will necessarily be implemented through law at all, still less that that law will be "regulatory" law.[73] Such an analysis ought to be such as to enable us to explain when and why law is used as a policy instrument, and why it takes on particular shapes (in terms of detail, source, duration and so on) in response to given policy stimuli. If we understand why the instrumental law of the economy takes the shape it does, we might be in a position to say whether there is, in fact, inadequate legal control or serious instrumental deformation; and if so, whether this can be cured by adopting different alternatives among available legal choices, or only by changes in the substance or style of policy itself.

III. The Design of the Inquiry

To answer the initial question – what forms of law are used for the implementation of economic policy, and why? – in a way which has any pretensions to accuracy, requires a first-hand and comprehensive study of relevant legal materials. Secondary sources, though more manageable, are likely to date quickly and to distort

---

[69] Farjat, *supra* note 6, *passim*.

[70] Cf. M. Horwitz, "The History of the Public/Private Distinction", (1982) 130 *University of Pennsylvania Law Review* 1423.

[71] G. Poggi, *The Development of the Modern State* (1978, London), ch. VI.

[72] The scope for, and means for the exercise of, private economic power are extensively explored in Bercusson, below.

[73] Cf. Teubner, ("Juridification", pp. 36–37).

perceptions by concentrating on problematical cases. A first-hand study, however, poses serious problems of selection of material and method of working. Our
approach to questions of selection has effectively been determined as a consequence of the decision to pursue a comparative approach, and in this section I look
first at its promise and constraints. As to method, it is implicit in the foregoing
argument that a scheme of analysis and classification of legal measures must be
developed, by reference to which the incidence of given types of law can be
measured, and the incidence of significant characteristics (stability, source, sanctions etc.) likewise assessed. These observations, however, need to be made by
reference to the substance and style of the economic policies to which the legal
measures are instrumental. So that this may be done in a systematic way, economic
policy itself must be broken down into a series of component elements to which
relevant legal measures can be directly or indirectly related. These processes of
analysis are described in the succeeding parts of this section.

A. The Comparative Approach

I have already noted[74] the suspicion that perhaps there do not exist any general
problems in the use of law as an instrument of policy, only a series of local
difficulties occasioned by specific characteristics of national legal systems. Our
investigation tests this hypothesis, and even if it shows that similar problems in
legal implementation occur in several countries, may also permit the identification
of ways in which differences in national systems affect the use or shape of
instrumental law. Such comparative findings have at least two kinds of practical
applications.

First, comparative findings, by clarifying the relationship between legal system
characteristics and features of instrumental law, can indicate what is involved, in
terms of adaptations to the system, in securing "improved" legal implementation
of policy.[75] "Improvement" may be in terms of effectiveness (though it should
immediately be acknowledged that unambiguous indicia of effectiveness are hard
to find in the economic policy sphere), or of the reduction or elimination of the
various disfigurements of instrumental law to which the commentators have
pointed. Some such improvements may be shown to be easy, others to require the
displacement of deeply enracinated system values.

Secondly, a comparative approach to the legal implementation of economic
policy may make specific contributions to an understanding of the possibilities
and difficulties of the European Community enterprise of policy harmonisation
or convergence in the economic field. Particularly by illuminating the complex
relationship between laws and legal structures on the one hand, and economic
policy implementation on the other, and showing to what extent inconsistent
national implementation choices are shaped by ephemeral or incidental factors on
the one hand, and by ingrained and hard-to-alter legal structures on the other, a
comparative inquiry may suggest both promising directions for harmonisation

---

[74] Above, pp. 4–5.
[75] See Mortelmans, below, pp. 317–320.

(towards the most deeply enracinated positions), and areas where harmonisation is unlikely to succeed. It is noteworthy that in one key area, that of energy policy, the Community has already abandoned harmonisation on the ground that there is too much diversity in the relevant situations of the Member States.[76] Investigation along the lines here described has shown that an important element of that diversity is expressed through the relevant legal structures of the Member States.[77]

While offering these advantages, the comparative approach also imposes constraints. Most important of these is the need to ensure that the variables compared have adequate explanatory power. If we assemble a cross-national set of legislative enactments at random and trace each back to its policy origins, we encounter differences – of political, economic and legal circumstances – at every step of the way. Not least among these will be differences of perception among governments as to *what* their problems are, as distinct from how to solve them. As we are primarily concerned here with the instrumental functions of law, examination of differences in problem situations is not likely to help us much. We seek, therefore, to get rid of this element of diversity by concentrating the investigation on some restricted *fields of policy*, in which the States whose law is subject to comparison see their problems as similar and are pursuing similar policy objectives under constraints which, if not the same, differ in well-known and -understood ways. For this reason also the starting point must be fields of policy and not fields of law: the general recognition of a substantive field of law, such as social security law or competition law, carries no guarantee that States will confront similar problem situations, or will pursue similar policy objectives through their instrumentalisation of law in these fields.[78]

The choice of policy fields obviously has to be related to the choice of countries for inclusion in the comparison. Located as we are, it seems natural to focus the inquiry within the framework of the European Community: the question then becomes that of how many countries one needs to examine. The four major countries, France, Germany, Italy and the United Kingdom, not only provide an irreducible minimum for a study which would have some significance from the point of view of Community policy: earlier studies have also shown that these countries exhibit interesting contrasts in their approaches to the choice of policy instruments in the economic sphere, the relative dirigisme of France and Italy contrasting with a more relaxed or market-oriented approach in Germany and the United Kingdom,[79] so that a study of this small group of countries should ensure that a reasonable range of policy experience is examined. All this experience,

[76] EC Commission, The *Development of an Energy Strategy for the Community* (1981), COM (81)540 final.
[77] T. C. Daintith and L. Hancher, *Energy Strategy in Europe: The Legal Framework* (1986, Berlin).
[78] K. Hopt, "Restrictive Trade Practices and Juridification: A Comparative Law Study" in G. Teubner ed. *supra* note 5 at pp. 291–332.
[79] P. VerLoren van Themaat, *Economic Law of the Member States of the European Communities in an Economic and Monetary Union: An Interim Report* (1974, Luxembourg), ch. 2.

however, may be shaped by the basically mixed character of their economies. There seems to be no reason why the study should not also offer insights about whether the debate about instrumental law is in some way tied to the circumstances of mixed economies or whether it may also be relevant to socialist economies, as is in fact suggested by the long-running arguments in Eastern Europe about the proper structure and scope of "economic law".[80] The scope of the inquiry has therefore been extended to include Hungary, whose relatively open system of economic management suggested that it may present the fewest problems of non-comparable variables to which I have already alluded.

Relating countries to policy areas, two such areas emerge as offering the strongest possibilities for useful comparison: energy policy, and manpower policy, in each case, over the period since 1973. The energy crisis that occurred in late 1973 created, for all European Community countries, a profound "energy shock", and caused a major reappraisal of energy policies hitherto in force (or of the absence of such policies) and intensive co-ordination activities among consumer States, both in the context of the Community and of the Organisation for Economic Co-operation and Development (OECD). There consequently exists a high degree of similarity between the policy objectives pursued by Community Member States since 1973 for the general purpose of reducing oil import dependence, notwithstanding their significantly different energy endowments and energy use patterns. Hungary, though cushioned from the violent swings of the world oil market by the availability of Soviet supplies, has also adopted similar energy policy objectives. In the context of an inquiry which thus has energy policy as an important focus, it seems sensible to add, as a representative of the smaller Community countries, the Netherlands, a major energy producer which, in the period under review, was also encountering re-adaptation problems as a result of the fast depletion of its domestic resources of natural gas.

The second area is that of manpower policy. Here again, the recession, triggered by the oil crisis has forced a concentration of attention by policy-makers on a fairly coherent set of objectives which presently vary little from place to place and are pursued with similar degrees of intensity; creation and maintenance of jobs, and manpower adjustment policies which smooth the working of the labour market and facilitate its adjustment to changes in the international division of labour. Some comparable policies, it is clear, are pursued in Hungary, though against an economic and social background which is more distinctive than was the case in the energy policy field. Despite this problem, manpower policy is an attractive object of investigation, not least because it presents a major economic contrast with energy policy. Energy policy may be described as sectoral in the sense that much policy activity is directed towards the energy industries themselves. Its instruments, and even its objectives, may thus be strongly shaped by the characteristics of that particular sector. Even though other areas of energy policy – energy conservation, for example – affect the whole economic population, it is desirable to select, as a second policy area, one which is cross-sectoral in character

---

[80] Eorsi, *supra* note 22, at pp. 213–225 and see the reports from East European countries in G. Rinck, ed., *Begriff und Prinzipien des Wirtschaftsrechts* (1971, Frankfurt and Berlin).

in order to have a fair representation of types of economic policy within the inquiry.

Apart from this coverage of both sectoral and cross-sectoral policy, there is no sense in which the fields chosen are designed to be *representative* of the whole of a State's economic policy activity. Comparability, not representativity, is the key criterion. The search for comparability may, indeed, have led us to policy areas that are a little unusual, in that the pressures dictating common approaches to the problems have been closely associated (at least in the case of the five Community Member States) with a sense of a *crisis,* experienced on a *regional scale;* and this cannot be said for most national policy areas. The sense of crisis under which government has acted in these fields should however strengthen rather than weaken the significance of our comparative findings on the way in which law has been used, in that one might expect governmental attention to the niceties of proper relationships between law and policy to be at its lowest at such times. Solutions developed here to problems in the policy/law relationship should be capable of generalisation to areas of less rapid policy change.

B. Policy Objectives

So far I have simply defined economic policy as "purposeful activity on the part of central government whose primary objective is the improvement of economic welfare"[81] and have specified a concern with energy and manpower as fields of policy. Some further analysis and specification is necessary if we are to be able to explain the incidence and shape of instrumental law by reference to the characteristics of policy, and to determine with precision exactly what examples of instrumental law we need to look at.

It is implicit in what I have already said about policy fields that we are operating on the basis of a distinction between the ends and the means of economic policy and are taking the ends as given. We do not seek to criticise them here nor to explain how they are adopted or amended. This is not to deny the existence of organic links between policy implementation and the possible reformulation of policy ends, as well as of policy means, on the basis, *inter alia,* of feedback from affected actors.[82] The ability to make contributions to this feedback process may, indeed, be a relevant criterion of assesment of instrumental law, but is not one that we have been able to apply systematically in the course of our investigation. The distinction does, however, imply that we are treating the *ends* of economic policy as being extra-legally determined. This is a conventional instrumentalist position, but it is criticised by Summers on the ground that law may itself be a source and definer of the very goals which it exists, as a means, to service.[83] Obviously law may be used to express, and thereby perhaps to solemnise, policy goals, as my

---

[81] Above, p. 6.
[82] For an example within our field of investigation see Hancher, below p. 230.
[83] R. S. Summers, *Instrumentalism and American Legal Theory* (1982, Ithaca and London), pp. 60–61, 74–78.

example from the United Kingdom Transport Act shows,[84] but if it could
determine them the analysis here would be defective in so far as it ignored the
possibility of legal system influences on the choice of policy goals (which we shall
be calling "objectives"), no less than on means to attain them. The difficulty raised
by Summers is, however, essentially semantic, in that he treats as the "immediate
goal" of a law compliance with its own prescriptions,[85] a usage which simply
forces us back to look for the higher-level goals – in whose formation legal
influence is hard if not impossible to discern – which are capable of explaining the
content of those prescriptions, and which are the subject of our concern here. One
might also ask, however, what if anything it can mean to say that a law (as opposed
to a legislator, an administrator, or other user of the law) "has a goal".[86] one
should certainly not assume that any of these people actually desires the situation
which would come about as the result of the perfect implementation of the law.[87]

In order, therefore, to define our field of inquiry, we begin by identifying two
sets of policy objectives, in the energy and manpower sectors respectively, which
(subject to certain qualifications for Hungary) all States in our study appear to
have pursued over the ten-year period starting in 1973. In energy the main selected
objectives are short-term management of disturbances in energy supply,[88] alteration of the structure of energy demand (through conservation and changes in
consumption patterns), and alteration of the structure of supplies, through
development of domestic (especially nuclear), and diversification of overseas,
supplies.[89] In manpower policy we distinguish the objectives of job maintenance,
job creation, and manpower adjustment through the efficient movement of
workers into, within and out of the labour market.[90] These objectives, further
broken down for convenience of investigation, are set out in tabular form below.[91]

---

[84] Above, pp. 16–18. Other examples are furnished by the expression of national planning
    objectives in the form of legislation, as in Hungary, see Harmathy, below, pp. 245–266,
    and by the enunciation of general economic principles in the German Stabilitätsgesetz of
    1967.

[85] Summers, *supra* note 83, at pp. 75–76.

[86] *Ibid.*, pp. 76–77.

[87] See further below, p. 30.

[88] See Council Directive 73/238/EEC, O.J. 1973, L 228/1. In Hungary the availability
    throughout the 1970s of Soviet energy supplies made the problem of short-term market
    disturbance much less important than in the West: see Hancher, Comparative Report on
    the Management of Short-term Energy Disturbances (1984) pp. 4–6, on file at EUI.

[89] See EEC Council Resolutions of September 17, 1974, O.J. 1975, C 153/1, and May,?
    1980, O.J. 1980, C 149/1. For a systematic substantive treatment of the policies of the
    five EC Member States here in question, arranged according to this schema, see Daintith
    and Hancher, *supra* note 77, chapter 5.

[90] See O. E. C. D., *Ministers of Labour and the Problems of Employment* (1976, Paris), vol.
    I, pp. 85–88 (Employment, Manpower Policy Measures: Appendix to the Recommenda-
    tion of the Council on a General Employment and Manpower Policy). Again, higher
    levels of employment in Hungary have meant a different emphasis, with objectives in the
    job maintenance and creation areas being related more precisely to the needs of specific
    groups.

[91] See Methodological Note, pp. 47–50.

Governmental pursuit of such objectives is attested by their adhesion to collective policy statements,[92] by explicit commitments in policy and planning documents,[93] and in some cases by inference from the nature of implementation measures actually adopted.

C. Legal Measures and Their Analysis

Settling this list of detailed policy objectives in the two fields has enabled us to proceed to the identification of the legal and other formal measures adopted by States for the achievement of the objectives over the period covered by our investigation (1973–82), or adopted previously and in active operation during the period. These measures provide the basic data for analysis and comparison. Analysis has been conducted according to a standard scheme with six main elements: the general or specific character of the measure; its duration; its source in the legal hierarchy (broadly conceived to include not only Parliament, government, Ministers etc., but also courts, regional or local authorities, the European Communities, as well as non-legal measures); its unilateral or bilateral character; its content (in terms of whether it is purely declaratory, whether it creates duties and how it sanctions them, whether it creates powers, transfers funds or property etc.); and finally the procedures associated with its operation. A full table of the headings and subheadings in the analysis is set out below.[94] Together, these headings are designed to pick up most of the characteristics which have been said to be sensitive from the point of view of the debates on the instrumental role of law.

On the basis of this analysis we are able to say what is the incidence of general as against specific legal measures, of short-term as against long-term ones, what is the frequency of amendment and substitution of legal measures (at least over our rather restricted period of inquiry), what is the incidence of "high-source" (Parliament) as against "low-source" (departments, Ministers) measures, and so on; and to compare these profiles of legalisation as between one country and another.

D. Policy Instruments

This information has considerable intrinsic value in so far as it provides up-to-date empirical evidence to support or refute the various impressionistic descriptions of trends in instrumental law which have fed the debates on this subject. By itself, however, it can do little to explain why instrumental legislation should assume particular forms or why particular sources should be favoured, nor why such preferences should vary from one country to another. To obtain such explanations we need to introduce into our analysis a typology of *means* of economic policy (here termed economic policy *instruments*). Such instruments form the link

---

[92] As cited in notes 89 and 90 *supra*.

[93] For a collection of such commitments relating to energy, see Daintith and Hancher, *supra* note 77, ch. 3 and appendix 3.

[94] See Methodological Note, below, pp. 50–54.

between the objectives of economic policy, on the one hand, and the specific legal measures of implementation, on the other. Only by introducing some such intermediate concept can we take account of the fact that the very existence of *legal* measures of implementation of economic policy results not from economic policy alone but from the fact of pursuing such a policy *within the framework of a given legal system* – that framework being understood to include both the constellation of legally protected private rights, duties and freedoms, and a constitutional structure for the exercise of all State power. If we are to understand how such a legal system determines the incidence of legal, as opposed to non-legal, implementation of policy, and how it shapes the relevant legal measures, we need some non-legal standard by reference to which we may observe and compare national variations in legal implementation. This we do by making each legal measure appear as the operationalisation, according to the demands of the national legal system, of one of a range of possible instruments of policy.

A variety of typologies of policy instruments have been offered, both by economists[95] and by political scientists.[96] Mayntz's classification, in particular, into regulative norms, financial transfers and incentives, public provision, procedural regulation, and persuasion, has considerable intuitive appeal.[97] Rather than simply adopt it, however, it seems desirable to attempt to trace out the steps through which a typology of instruments can be derived *a priori*, without relying on inferring a categorisation from examination of the characteristics of implementing measures: we need to avoid the circularity implicit in defining instruments by reference to legal measures and then comparing measures by reference to instruments. We may then check our results against the categories already proposed by others.

The first step is to consider the nature of the economic objectives which form our starting point. Kirschen has defined such objectives as "the economic translations of political aims into concepts which can be given some quantification".[98] While he had in mind objectives of a more general character than those we have picked out here, quantifiability remains a key characteristic even of such highly specific objectives as development of domestic energy supplies, or job maintenance or creation. Performance in relation to these objectives is likewise quantitatively assessed. Progress in job maintenance or creation will obviously be measured by the number of jobs created or maintained; in domestic energy development, by quantities of production or reserves. Even for objectives which might seem harder to quantify, such as diversification of imported energy supplies or

---

[95] The most elaborate is perhaps that of Kirschen, developed in E. S. Kirschen et al., *Economic Policy in our Time* (3 vols., 1964, Amsterdam), and in E. S. Kirschen, ed., *Economic Policies Compared: West and East* (2 vols., 1974, Amsterdam). See also VerLoren van Themaat, *supra* note 79, using a classification derived from Zijlstra.

[96] R. Mayntz, "The Conditions of Effective Public Policy: A New Challenge for Policy Analysis" (1983) 11 *Policy and Politics* 123; C. Hood, *The Tools of Government* (1983, London).

[97] Mayntz, *supra* note 96, pp. 127–128.

[98] See *Economic Policy in Our Time* (1964), vol. 1 at p. 17.

efficient manpower adjustment, some numerical measures are normally available and used, such as the number of suppliers of a given energy source and the proportion of needs met by the largest supplier; or for manpower, the composition of the labour force, particularly by reference to age, the length of waiting periods between jobs, and so on. Non-quantifiable elements are in most cases relegated to a secondary position.

Without too much distortion, therefore, one can treat the essence of economic policy as being the attempt by government to influence the movement of a range of economic quantities or indicators, by promoting movement in a preferred direction or toward specified targets. Though the popular vocabulary of economic management suggests the capacity of government, by itself, to secure such results – we speak of government "creating jobs", "restricting imports", "boosting investment" – its ability to do this by direct action is in fact restricted by reference to the economic resources and activities which it has under its immediate control. Outside this area its means of influencing economic quantities must be indirect, in the sense that they operate on the actions and decisions of persons outside the government, whose aggregated results determine the level of the relevant economic indicators. This distinction between direct and indirect action forms the first element of an instrument typology.

Governmental self-management is clearly an instrument of policy in so far as government uses its direct control over its own finances, labour, property, equipment and so on for the purpose of advancing policy objectives. Government may, for example, be able to make a worthwhile contribution to energy saving by ordering a reduction of working temperatures in its offices, schools and barracks. The size of the contribution will depend on the extent to which central government *directly* controls the provision of public sector activities; where there has been diffusion of responsibility for such activities to separately-constituted bodies, even within the public sector, such changes may be beyond the reach of government managerial power, and may require the use of the same kinds of instruments as are used to affect the behaviour of actors in the private sector. The public character of the bodies may, however, lead to those instruments being operationalised in such cases in a distinctive way. At the same time non-government public sector bodies may be made the object of legal (or non-legal) measures simply in order that they may serve as a transmission mechanism, through which the aim of affecting the behaviour of private sector actors is attained. The position of public sector banks and credit institutions offers an example of this type. This means that delineation of the instrumental role of the public sector as a whole is a highly complex matter.[99] On balance it seems best to take, as an instrument-type, the whole phenomenon of "public sector management", understood as comprising both governmental self-management in the strict sense of direct, hierarchical control, and the distinctive application of policy instruments to public sector bodies outside central government.

[99] See Hancher, below.

Outside the scope of its managerial powers, government action in pursuit of economic policy goals involves attempting to change other people's behaviour,[100] the "others", in the public sector as well as in the private, who charge prices, pay wages, export and import goods, invest capital, borrow and lend money, make take-over bids, purchase goods and services. It is their actions which in aggregate or on average make up the greatest part of all the quantities which government is trying to manipulate; their actions, therefore, which must be made different from what they would have been in the absence of the policy. More precisely, *some* of those actions, *some* of that behaviour, must be different: zero and 100 per cent are not necessarily the only quantities that government aims at. A government that wants a rising birthrate for economic reasons may not wish every wife to bear an extra child. Government would appear to possess a bewildering variety of means for use in this enterprise, ranging from criminal sanctions to mentions in the Honours List, but it is possible to order their discussion and inter-relation by resort to two reference concepts: of the *costs* of behaviour, and of the *resources* of government.

All behaviour choices involve a weighing of the costs of the alternative courses of action, measured not just in money but also in terms of time, of satisfactions foregone, of self-esteem, of reputation and so on. Government's aim is that such choices should, so far as is possible and necessary, be compatible with its policy objectives. This involves changing choices, either by showing the decision-makers that they are misguided as to their own balance of costs, or by altering those balances. The first approach will be realised simply by the presentation of appropriate information to those confronted with choices – as by indicating to householders how much in heating bills they may save by installing roof insulation. To change the relative costs of different choices requires stronger measures, which may be aimed either at increasing the costs of the choices which are incompatible with the government's programme – as by fining builders who do not install roof insulation – or reducing the costs of choices which are compatible with it – as by offering subsidies to householders who do install insulation. All government measures which are addressed to third parties, whether legal or non-legal, formal or informal, can be analysed in terms of this relative cost concept. To be sure, the kinds of costs imposed or relieved will vary: a criminal prohibition backed by imprisonment creates costs in terms of loss of liberty and reputation, while heavy taxes impose money costs. This difference in nature does not, however, make them non-comparable. In their daily decision-making economic actors balance bundles of costs including these different elements; they may discount such costs by reference to the likelihood of detection, prosecution and conviction for a criminal offence no less than they may calculate the likelihood of successful evasion of taxes.

---

100 With the arguable exception, on the margins of our subject, of social welfare policy for such ends as the relief of poverty, where transfer payments by government may *in themselves* meet the policy goal, without any need for behavioural change on the part of recipients. But even social assistance schemes usually have *some* elements designed to affect behaviour, to encourage obtaining of work, retraining, etc.

Viewing policy implementation, including legal implementation, in terms of the relative costs of economic actors' decisions helps to elucidate two important points, which tend to be disguised by differences in legal technique.

First, it is implicit in the relative costs concept that the individual decision-maker always retains a choice as to whether he will align his conduct with the demands of government policy, no matter what instrument government deploys. One may imagine – though it is much harder actually to find – situations in which the physical control and supervision exercised by governmental agents is so tight as to eliminate even the possibility of non-compliance, so that choice is absent and non-compliance beyond price. The rarity of such cases, however, serves essentially to emphasise the element of choice existing in all normal cases, even in the face of express prohibitions. The point is worth stressing, not least because there is a tendency among writers who set out to assess the costs and benefits of using different kinds of instruments, in fields such as pollution policy, to assume that people always obey mandatory legal rules.[101] On this basis regulatory standards are argued to be inflexible and productive of sub-optimal results, in contrast to "market-type" instruments such as taxes, subsidies, or tradeable pollution entitlements. These are said to leave sufficient discretion to the individual to permit him to adjust his activity in a way which is capable of achieving the best available balance of compliance costs and policy benefits. Behaviour in response to mandatory rules is in fact much more complex than this model allows for: in the economic sphere, at least, calculated and negotiated non-compliance are common phenomena, and are based on the same kind of cost-benefit analysis as is explicitly demanded by the use of "market-type" instruments.[102] There may still be very good reasons for preferring, in a given case, a tax-based to a regulation-based scheme (for example, greater economic transparency or the reduction of administrative discretion): but the evaluation must take account of the individual's "discretion to disobey",[103] as well as the capacity of regulatory schemes to offer more satisfying protection to certain kinds of non-economic values than can taxation.[104]

---

[101] For an example see S. Breyer, "Analyzing Regulatory Failure: Mismatches, Less Restrictive Alternatives, and Reform", (1979) 92 *Harvard Law Review* 549, at 581: "The very fact that taxes do not prohibit an activity, or suppress a product *totally,* means that those with special needs and willingness to pay may obtain it. Taxes thus lessen the risk, present with standard setting, of working serious harm in an unknown special case."

[102] For some evidence in a United Kingdom context see D. Storey, "An Economic Appraisal of the Legal and Administrative Aspects of Water Pollution Control in England and Wales", in T. O'Riordan and G. D'Arce, ed., *Progress in Resource Management and Environmental Planning,* vol. 1 (1979, New York), ch. 9. For a contrary view of the general point made here see R. Cooter, "Prices and Sanctions", (1984) 84 *Columbia L. Rev.* 1523.

[103] The phrase, but not the thought, is borrowed from M. R. Kadish and S. H. Kadish, *Discretion to Disobey: a study of Lawful Departures from Legal Rules* (1973, Stanford). For the contrary view see Jarass, below, p. 81. As he points out, in the fields covered by our investigation the practical significance of this classificatory issue is limited.

[104] See Stewart, below, pp. 113–115.

Second, and in some sense a corollary to the above point, the idea that all government measures work by changing relative costs reminds us of the essential imprecision of much government action. If government is dealing with small numbers of actors, it may acquire the necessary information about the effect of proposed measures by such means as bilateral discussion and negotiation, and operate with some degree of precision. The attractiveness of working in this way is an obvious reason for government encouragement of private interest associations. But many areas of economic life obstinately remain as unorganised, large-number situations. Here government moves in a fog: it cannot know the individual cost balances of the large numbers of economic actors it addresses, and can only judge the likely impact of its measures by observation of the effects of past measures, by sampling, and other aggregative techniques. In consequence it is unrealistic for government to think in terms of obtaining precise results from its measures, and in fact it seldom does so; yet if it uses legal measures shaped by the private rights model – such as criminally sanctioned prohibitions – precise and uncompromising drafting will be required. Thus what appears from a reading of the statute book or the Official Gazette to be a clear and unqualified prohibitory measure may from the standpoint of government policy be the means of effecting a reduction of uncertain extent in the incidence of the prohibited behaviour, an element of an implementation programme which may yield different results depending upon such variables as the strength of economic counter-forces and the resources devoted to enforcement. The persistence of prohibited conduct does not, there-fore, *necessarily* denote a failure of implementation or the "symbolic" character of the prohibition; government may be satisfied with the results it is getting. There is here an important but seldom-remarked conflict between lawyers' and policy-makers' pictures of instrumental law. Lawyers see hard-edged individual obliga-tions, which should be uniformly observed and impartially applied;[105] policy-makers see a change in the general conditions of decision-making, whose aggre-gate results can be guessed at but whose effects on any given individual are both unknowable and uninteresting. The conflict disappears only when individuals get big enough to matter to policy-makers.

Turning back to the development of an instrument classification, then, the relative costs concept suggests a broad division into cost-revealing instruments (information), and cost-altering instruments. For the moment we may simply divide the latter group into cost-increasing instruments, directed to the reduction or elimination of behaviour incompatible with policy, and cost-reducing instru-ments, directed to the promotion of compatible behaviour. To break the group down further, we need to take into account the different *resources* on which government may be able to rely for the purpose of effecting changes in relative costs.

Three types of resources may be distinguished. First, there is the physical force which is at the disposal of government; normally, the threat of exercise of such

---

[105] This expectation does not, of course, extend to instrumental changes to private law rules, where the discretion of the right-holder to invoke, or not to invoke, the (changed) rule is assumed: cf. D. Black, "The Mobilization of Law" (1973) 2 *Journal of Legal Studies* 125.

force in response to undesired behaviour – as by imprisonment or confiscation of property – is all that is needed to induce its renunciation. Second, there is the wealth of government, in the sense of its capacity to use offers of money or other forms of property as an inducement to economic actors to behave in desired ways. Third, there is the respect it may enjoy as a recognised or duly constituted government, as a legitimate repository of secular authority. Each of these resources may be possessed in varying degrees by different governments; their possession and use are not dependent upon the existence of any particular form of legal or constitutional system, though obviously their deployment is shaped by the characteristics of the legal system actually obtaining in any given State. In relating these resources with the alteration of economic actors' costs, one might at first sight assume a pairing between force and the increasing of costs (the paradigm case being a force-backed prohibition of undesired behaviour), and between wealth and cost-reduction (through grants and subsidies for desired behaviour). In fact, if one considers not a hypothetical initial position, but the situation of economic actors within an existing policy framework at a given moment, one sees that each resource may be used either "positively", for cost-reducing purposes, or "negatively", for cost-increasing purposes. Thus a threat to withdraw government benefits previously enjoyed may discourage undesired behaviour as may a new prohibition; a reduction of taxes, or the relaxation of a prohibition, may encourage a specific course of desired behaviour just as may a financial reward. From the standpoint of the economic actor, in fact, government's resources appear as positive and negative sanctions.[106]

Instruments appear within this framework of impacts and resources as distinctive ways of employing resources to produce impacts. The threat of force is used to increase costs both through regulations (including prohibitions) and through taxes, both through the unilateral imposition of regulations and through their consensual acceptance. As well as underpinning different instruments in this way, resources may be recombined within a given instrument: thus the incentive to make consensual arrangements with government which are restrictive of private behaviour may derive both from the fear of imposed regulations backed by force, or from the fear of withdrawal of existing benefits, or both. In the light of these possibilities of differentiation and recombination, and of the need to be able to relate specific legal and other implementing measures to instrument-types in an unambiguous way, the following typology of instruments has been adopted for the study:

1. Unilateral regulation
2. Taxation
3. Consensual constraints, i.e. control of activity through contractual and other agreements with government
4. Removal or relaxation of regulations
5. Removal of taxation or the granting of tax exemptions

---

[106] Cf. V. Aubert, *In Search of Law: Sociological Approaches to Law* (1983, Oxford), at pp. 159–169.

6. Public benefits, e.g. subsidies and other financial assistance, provision of public services and other forms of assistance in kind
7. Public sector management
8. Information.

The similarity to Mayntz's list[107] is obvious. Apart from some differences of grouping of instruments, which are not important here, the main element in her scheme not represented is that of procedural regulation, which she defines as "norms establishing decision and conflict resolution procedures for private parties".[108] She argues that particular significance attaches today to this instrument by reason of the degree to which the State relies upon private organisations for participation in the formulation and implementation of policy, under the banner of self-regulation. Procedural regulation is the means by which the State creates or ratifies the structures of internal decision-making within, and of inter-relationship between, such organisations. Self-regulation is undoubtedly an important modern phenomenon: for Schmitter and Streeck it is an element of an "associative" model of social order equal in significance to the established "community", "market" and "State" models;[109] for Teubner it is part of a style of "reflexive" law which offers *the* way out of an otherwise unavoidable "regulatory trilemma".[110] Why then does it not figure in our analysis?

The short answer is that self-regulation *does* figure; but it appears as an area for discovery, rather than as a tool for analysis. Our perspective is that of the way in which the State deploys its resources in aid of policy implementation: and the resources which the State may use to create, and then to control, self-regulatory capacity are not different in kind from those which it may use for purposes of "direct" policy implementation. Regulation, benefits, bargains all play their part. What is distinctive is the content of the measures employed (conferment of competences structured by procedural limitations) in conjunction with the nature of the actors addressed (economically powerful organisations). An empirical enquiry like this, whose starting point is the analysis of measures, may therefore enable us to discover the extent of the complex phenomenon of self-regulation in the fields examined and to understand its supports, by identifying the occasions on which competences are conferred on private bodies or rules promulgated for the discharge of such bodies' functions and powers. It appears, in fact, that explicit reliance upon self-regulation as a vehicle of policy is almost unknown in the field of energy policy,[111] but much commoner in the manpower field, where collective agreements, sometimes with regulatory extension, play a major role in the

---

107 See above, p. 26.
108 *Supra* note 96, at p. 128.
109 W. Streeck and P. C. Schmitter, *"Community, Market, State – and Associations? The Prospective Contribution of Interest Governance to Social Order* (EUI Working Paper No. 94, 1984, Florence).
110 Teubner, "Juridification", esp. pp. 33–40.
111 See Jarass, below, p. 79.

furtherance of particular policy objectives or sub-objectives[112] and where labour subsidy programmes may be confided to autonomous bipartite or tripartite organisations.[113] Explicit reliance, however, by no means exhausts the scope and significance of self-regulation in these sectors, as Brian Bercusson's wide-ranging study in this volume convincingly shows.[114]

Two further remarks may be made about self-regulation in the context of this study. First, the measures employed by the State to create and structure self-regulatory capacity offer the clearest example of the determination and revision of "private" legal rights by means adopted from public law: the determination of competences, and the creation of decisional structures for their exercise, are key functions for public law. The self-regulation phenomenon is one of deliberate and explicit organisation or ratification by the State of a diffusion of economic power. It is precisely where economic power is accumulated within private sector organisations (whether by reason of such diffusion, of industrial concentration, of trade unionism or any other cause) that we may expect to encounter legal implementation which draws in some measure on "collective interest" as opposed to "private rights" legal models.

Second, the instrument typology here can be linked with self-regulation in the sense that it is no less applicable to the implementation functions of the organisation than to those of the State itself.[115] Its basic concepts are equally relevant to private power holders, who may also deploy a range of resources in order to change the relative costs of behaviour by others – normally their individual members – the results of whose actions are of concern to them. Essentially the same kinds of resources are available, though the monopoly of legitimate force reserved to the State by most modern legal systems means that the threat of force will usually be available only by delegation from the State or on an illegitimate basis. Both kinds of situation are common. Further pursuit of this application is beyond the scope of this study, but the typology could serve, among other things, to facilitate comparison of the operation of private interest organisations of widely differing types, or to identify ways in which different legal systems affect the governance capacities of similar organisations in different countries.

IV. Hypotheses and Results

The elaboration of a typology of instruments completes the methodological apparatus of our inquiry. The triple typology of measures, instruments and objectives immediately engenders a series of questions, essentially about the relationships of these three elements of policy, among themselves and with national legal systems, which have structured our examination of the mass of legal

---

[112] For example, their use for the purpose of creating job opportunities in particular areas or sectors, or for facilitating early retirement from the labour market.

[113] See von Stebut, below, p. 150.

[114] Below, pp. 359–420.

[115] As Bercusson demonstrates, below pp. 359–420.

and other data collected and whose answers may help to pinpoint the key elements in the law/policy relationship and to indicate the extent and seriousness of the problems present there. In the following paragraphs of this section I look at these relationships and attempt to draw together a number of specific findings reported in the thematic contributions to this volume.

A. The Design of Measures

I consider first the influences bearing on the design of measures. The key question is whether the shape of legal measures varies according to the nature of the instrument that they operationalise. To some extent this is bound to be so, in that certain characteristics of instruments are replicated in the typology of legal measures we use: thus consensual constraints will obviously be operated by bilateral legal norms, regulations by unilateral ones; measures implementing subsidy instruments will have as their substantive content the transfer of funds or property, those implementing regulations the imposition of duties; and so on. But there are many points in which the measures operationalising the same instrument might vary (as to scope, or period, or source, for example), and the process of tracing such variations should permit the making of empirically-based comments about assertions of the changing shape of instrumental law, of its move away from the "private rights model", both in general terms – is this true? – and in a more discriminating way, by indicating in relation to which instruments, if any, the phenomenon is particularly marked. We might guess that if there are such correspondences, then it is measures which implement the instruments least likely to bear on private rights – relaxations of regulations and taxes, public benefits, information, maybe public sector management also – which are most likely to be temporary, non-general, low level, etc. We might be wrong. Among other things, the guess is dependent upon there in fact being regularities in the relationship between instruments and measures across a number of legal systems. It cannot be assumed, *ex ante,* that these will be found. It may be that demands of the national legal system are a stronger determinant of the shape of legal measures than are the characteristics of the instruments they implement, and that these demands are diverse enough to make all measures from a given system resemble each other more than they resemble the measures from each other system operationalising the same instrument. Despite the fact that Western European legal systems, at least, are said to resemble one another greatly in fundamentals,[116] and that the Hungarian system has abandoned less of its private law underpinnings than one might at first sight assume,[117] the variety of approach to the instrumental law issue by scholars of different nationalities gives some initial credence to this latter hypothesis.[118]

---

[116] See e.g. R. David, *Les Grands Systèmes du Droit Contemporain* (8me ed. 1982, Paris, by C. Jauffret-Spinosi), pp. 25–26.

[117] Hungary has not, for example, adopted a code of economic law, as have Czechoslovakia and the German Democratic Republic.

[118] Above, pp. 4–5.

The ways in which national legal systems may bear upon the shape of legal measures, and the general significance of system differences in our fields of inquiry, are examined in detail in Attila Harmathy's contribution.[119] In thinking about possible legal system effects, we have had in mind not only the formal and explicit constitutional requirements of the system, but also two other sources of influence which, while properly labelled "legal" as opposed to "political" or "economic", are not capable of such precise expression. The first may be termed legal *style:* the historical evolution of a given legal culture may dictate or encourage certain choices – in terms of "ways of doing things" – which are not easily referable to the effects of constitutional or other rules. One example might be the Anglo-Saxon preference for procedural rules and safeguards as a guarantee of fair administrative action, contrasted with the French reliance on judicial review of administrative action on substantive grounds. Another example, which emerges from the investigations of Leigh Hancher into public sector management, is afforded by the contrast between the German and Dutch preference for the use of general rules of corporation law as the means of structuring and controlling public enterprise activity, and that of the French, Italians and British for a specialised legal regime for this purpose.[120]

The second influence, which might be termed legal *substance,* is that furnished by the existence, at the time when policy is being formulated, of relevant bodies of substantive law, whose adaptation or development may provide one means of achieving the objective at hand. In such a situation the policy-maker may be more likely to resort to an instrument which draws on such a body of law than to one which requires the creation of quite new legal arrangements; and if he does, the shape of the measures he uses will be dictated by the terms in which the existing legal scheme is expressed. In so far as such substantive norms are seen as accidental, as responses to past policy needs rather than as core elements of the legal system, their influence, or lack of it, tells us little about the relationship between a given legal system and modes of implementation of policy therein; but a demonstration of the relevance of existing substantive provisions to the policy-maker's choice of instruments and measures would provide support for incrementalist theories of policy formation and implementation.[121]

Having set out these considerations, let me try to assess their influence by looking briefly at some of the characteristics of the measures examined which seem important from the point of view of a critical evaluation of instrumental law: principally their scope, temporal dimension, source, and certain features of their contents. The task is simplified by the fact only a part of the instrument range needs to be taken into account: taxation measures, relaxations of regulations, and pure information measures were all encountered too rarely in our survey to permit

---

[119] Below, pp. 245–266.
[120] See Hancher, below, pp. 225–226. In France and Italy, though not in the United Kingdom, this preference is reinforced by formal constitutional requirements: French Constitution, art. 34; Italian Constitution, art. 43.
[121] Leading exponents include D. Braybrooke and C. E. Lindblom: see their *A Strategy of Decision* (1963, New York), esp. ch. 5.

the making of significant findings about them. I consider below the possible reasons for this. In relation to the remaining instrument-types – regulations, consensual constraints, subsidies, and public sector management – it has been hard to identify consistent cross-national relationships between instrument-types and characteristics of measures. At some times legal system influences seem to prevail, at others the characteristics of the policy field may have a direct influence on the shape of measures.

One thing at least is clear: that the law is not dissolving into a "wilderness of single instances", of individual measures of limited duration. Outside the field of public sector management, individual measures are rare,[122] and are even then often connected to the foundation of public bodies which will carry on activities like subsidy distribution.[123] The finding requires qualification in that instruments may be operationalised by a series of measures, issued at descending levels of the legal hierarchy, of increasing degrees of particularity,[124] and individual measures at the lowest level may be invisible to the reviewer of formal or published acts of government; but it is still important to notice the determination of lawmakers to express their precepts – even in fields like territorial or sectoral job creation or maintenance – very largely in general and objective terms.

As for the temporal element, the complexity of the demands addressed by policy-makers to the legal system in this respect is well brought out by Kamiel Mortelmans' contribution to this volume.[125] Different time-scales are involved in the attainment of the various objectives examined, varying between the need to be permanently ready to act quickly and (if possible) briefly to cope with energy supply disturbances, and the need to make steady efforts over a long but not necessarily indefinite period of time to attain a satisfactory national standard in fields like energy conservation. The nature of the time element in measures may therefore depend more on the character of the objective pursued than on either the type of instrument involved or the demands of a particular national legal system, so that it may be misleading to generalise about this particular instrument-measures relationship. Some specific remarks can however be made.

The first is that measures expressed to be of permanent or indefinite duration predominate over the whole field of our inquiry. The most important usage of temporary measures occurs in the field of response to energy disturbances, where substantial numbers of short-term regulatory measures are found; these, however, are normally second-level measures, whose authorisation is found in permanent legislation containing broad powers for dealing with energy crises. (The exception is Italy, which has relied largely on the constitutional emergency power to introduce, by governmental fiat, *decreti-leggi* which lapse after 60 days unless converted into Parliamentary legislation.) The explicit time-limitation in this

---

[122] Note though that in the nuclear field, individual measures dominate even where the industry is privately run, as in Germany. This seems to result from governmental pursuit of subsidy policies in an industry with few actors.

[123] Cf. von Stebut, below, p. 143.

[124] See Mortelmans, below, pp. 299–304, 308–310.

[125] Below, pp. 287–298.

sphere should be seen rather as an expression of respect for democratic concerns about unusually broad delegations of regulatory power to cope with crisis conditions, than as a simple reflection of the expectation that those crisis conditions will sooner or later cease. Temporary measures also predominate in the field of manpower (but not energy) subsidies,[126] though even here we frequently encounter open-ended measures, notwithstanding the fact that the conditions attacked may be expected to be of temporary duration.[127] This is true, for most countries, of subsidy policy in the areas of job maintenance and facilitation of movement between jobs. This preference for open-endedness perhaps reflects the fact that schemes in these fields are *reactive,* offering a response to a situation whose duration government cannot predict, as opposed to *pro-active* (as in the job creation field), seeking to secure a once-and-for-all shift in behaviour, a shift whose period of accomplishment can be estimated (not necessarily accurately, of course) in advance. Yet while a contrast of this kind also appears in the energy sector between the objectives of energy conservation (reactive) and alteration of consumption patterns (pro-active), open-ended subsidy schemes dominate in both these fields.

A second, perhaps obvious remark is that measures expressed to be permanent, or of indefinite duration, have no guarantee of a lifespan greater than that of temporary measures. Relevant here is the distinction used by Mortelmans between ordering polices and process policies.[128] Frequent variation of measures expressing ordering policies might give us more cause for concern than equivalent variation of process policy measures, but we did not in fact find much evidence of such variation outside the field of process policies like price control in the energy sector. Frequent variation is most widespread in Hungary, doubtless because regulation assumes much of the burden elsewhere carried by flexible market relations.

A characteristic of measures which, we thought, might correspond in a more regular way with different instrument-types is that of their source (Parliament, central government, individual Ministers etc.), since national constitutions may allot these bodies law-making competences which vary in some degree with the characteristics of different instruments.[129] In fact, subsidies and regulations, the instrument-types to which the great majority of measures refer, do not appear very distinctive in terms of sources. In the Western states examined,[130] parliamentary participation in the process of making regulations appears in general to be rather more regular and intensive than is the case with subsidies. Subsidies, in their

---

[126] See von Stebut, below, pp. 143–144.
[127] Note that though a scheme may be of indefinite duration, the period for which assistance may be enjoyed by any particular recipient is likely to be limited.
[128] See Mortelmans, below, pp. 296–297.
[129] See T. C. Daintith, "Legal Analysis of Economic Policy – I" (1982) 9 *Journal of Law and Society* 191, and compare note 56 *supra.*
[130] In Hungary parliamentary involvement is limited to legislative approval of medium term plans, which are implemented by collective or individual ministerial decrees.

turn, have a higher legal profile, in terms of formal legal expression and the source thereof, than do measures of public sector management.[131]

The more striking differences, however, relate to the practice of individual states and to the subject-matter treated. As to national differences, Jarass notes that Germany is three times as likely to use Parliamentary legislation as a vehicle for regulation as is France, and that this sort of discrepancy can be found between the two countries in relation to subsidies also.[132] In this respect a fairly consistent ordering appears among countries, with the United Kingdom next following Germany in "Parliament-mindedness" and the Netherlands and Italy occupying an intermediate position above France and Hungary. Less easy to predict, perhaps, is the significance of subject-matter in this respect. Particularly in the field of regulatory measures, Parliament, in all the Western states, holds a much more important position, as law-maker, in the manpower sector than in the energy sector. This greater involvement in one of the two sectors examined may be explained by reference to three factors, which overlap: the greater constitutional or political importance attached to the situation of workers than to energy problems; the fact that labour law and relations are (unlike energy) a recognisably distinct subject matter in terms of established law, which is unlikely to be capable of regulation by the use of executive powers (e.g. of price control or rationing) conferred by legislation for use in a variety of sectors; and, finally, the fact that, among regulatory techniques, the adjustment of individual rights is much more important in the manpower sector than in the energy field.

This third factor is directly evidenced by the data collected in this study about the content of measures. An important dichotomy, within the instrument of regulation, is that which opposes regulation by the adjustment of individual rights, legally enforceable on the initiative of the holders of those rights, and regulation through the conferment of control powers on government, utilisable on the initiative, and often at the discretion, of government itself. In the first case the task of securing compliance with regulatory policy is left to interested individuals, in the second government keeps it in its own hands.[133] The former approach predominates in such fields as job maintenance and labour market adjustment, through the legislative conferment of basic or supplementary employment security rights on employees. (There are of course exceptions, such as the long-established administrative control of dismissals operating in the Netherlands, more recently introduced in France also.) The second is much more frequently encountered in areas like energy conservation, and typically takes the form of legislation empowering administrative authorities to lay down rules or standards breach of which may be visited with criminal or, more commonly, administrative penalties. The contrast is not surprising: there is a high degree of

---

[131] See Hancher, below, p. 224.
[132] Below, p. 95.
[133] Legal systems vary in the extent to which they offer facilities for concerned individuals and groups to compel, through legal process, the due exercise of governmental control powers of this type, or to act themselves in the event of governmental default: see Jarass, below, p. 92, Stewart, below p. 114.

congruence between individual interests in job security and a State policy of job maintenance, and a high capacity for effective enforcement of individual worker rights based on trade union support. Both of these factors are absent in the energy sector. While long-term similarity of interest may exist as between the State and the large enterprises which make up the supply side of the industry, it is only rarely that such interests may be furthered by the enlargement of the enterprises' "private" rights, and even where this is the case (in relation, for example, to the compulsory acquisition of land for oil terminals, pipelines, generating stations etc.) the State will normally exercise some control, *ex ante,* of the use of these rights.

The influence of characteristics of the policy field is also reflected in a complex way in the extent to which measures *confer powers* on central government or other public authorities. The conferment of *regulatory* powers is, as noted above, the antithesis of the direct adjustment of individual rights, and we consequently find many more examples of such power-conferment in the energy sector than in the manpower sector. At the same time there is a high degree of centralisation of such control powers in the energy sector: delegation of rule-making power to local, regional, or functionally specialised bodies is unusual, occurring only where (as in Italy in relation to aspects of energy conservation) a group of functions touching on one of the objectives is constitutionally confided to a sub-national level of government. The exercise of policing functions at the local level may, of course, be more common. Centralisation of power in the hands of a politically responsible government seems appropriate to the situations of disturbance, or even crisis, which will trigger many of the regulatory schemes in the energy sector; but in relation to less dramatic objectives, such as energy conservation or development of domestic resources, we may find the explanation rather in the domination of energy supply by powerful enterprises (or even monopolies) operating on a national scale, and a relative lack of organisation of consumer interests.[134]

In the manpower sector, the conferment of powers is notable rather in the operation of *subsidy* schemes than of regulation. Here, however, it is associated with a decentralisation of the administration of such schemes, normally through bodies with a specialised competence in this sector like the Manpower Services Commission in the United Kingdom, the *Bundesanstalt für Arbeit* in Germany.[135] This diffusion of power to often tripartite (workers/employers/State) quasi-autonomous bodies reflects the same congruence of policy goals between State and economic actors as is manifested in the strength of individual rights enforcement in the regulatory mode. The decentralised approach to policy implementation in this field is emphasised and extended by the occurrence of collective agreements, at various levels, which may interlock with or substitute for State action, and under which benefits may be made available to particular groups of workers in aid of objectives similar to those of State policy: examples are afforded by agreements favouring early retirement of workers in the Netherlands, or redistribution of industrial investment in Italy.

[134] For details see Daintith and Hancher, *supra* note 77, ch. 3.
[135] See von Stebut, below, p. 144.

B. The Choice of Instruments

The extent to which instrument choices are determined by idiosyncracies of
national legal systems, as opposed to being a function of objectives and of the
social and economic context in which they are pursued, is again a question for
which an answer may be suggested by the empirical enquiries we have pursued. At
the same time hypotheses about cross-national regularities in relationships between objectives and instruments can be tested. Mayntz, for example, suggests
that problems whose solution depends on the positive motivation and voluntary
collaboration of the target population – the people whose behaviour the policy-
maker wants to change – are better tackled through incentive (benefit) or
information instruments than through regulation.[136] A number of the energy and
manpower policy objectives picked out in the study are responses to problems of
this type – energy conservation and job creation, for example – so that the data
should show how far governments follow out this logic.

Jarass in fact points out that a strong negative motivation, on the part of the
population, towards the behaviour desired by government is not a necessary
condition for the use of regulations, but agrees that where innovative behaviour is
required, regulations are much less likely to be employed: the relative incidence of
regulations, in the manpower sector, for job creation as opposed to job maintenance, and in the energy sector, for alteration of consumption patterns as opposed
to restriction of consumption, alike attest to this.[137] Jarass further suggests that the
difficulty of using regulations in situations where innovation or initiative are
needed is one of sufficiently specifying the behaviour which is required. This
thinking reflects the "private rights" model of instrumental law, whereby hard-
edged rules, not vague precepts, are sought after in cases where private rights are to
be affected.[138]

At this point the earlier discussion of the apparent interpenetration of the public
and private sectors within State and economy, occasioned by the concentration of
economic power in State and private enterprise and other organisations,[139]
suggests the introduction of another hypothesis, relating to the size and degree of
organisation of the target population. Does the private rights model, as represented by formal general regulations or subsidy schemes containing clearly
formulated rules of application or eligibility, assume greater importance where the
State addresses a large and unorganised population? The study offers evidence in
support of this possibility: on the supply side of the energy industry, where a few
powerful actors are involved, regulations are encountered less frequently than on
the generally less well organised demand side, being replaced by more flexible and
individualistic instruments such as consensual constraints, public sector management, and individualised subsidies.[140] By such means the State may oblige
individually powerful actors, as a matter of contractual or statutory duty, to

[136] Cf. Mayntz, *supra* note 96, at p. 138.
[137] Below, pp. 88–90.
[138] Above, pp. 12–13.
[139] Above, p. 18.
[140] See Jarass, below pp. 86–87.

undertake courses of innovative behaviour to which it may only encourage larger groups (like employers, or house-owners, or builders) by means of general subsidy schemes of uncertain effect.

Another idea which receives support from the study data is that of the variable impact of different instruments. The heavy preponderance of regulations in the field of short-term responses to energy supply difficulties is mainly attributable to the desire of governments to achieve a rapid effect and to manifest a strong and incisive governmental reaction to crisis; these needs are not present to the same degree in any other area we have investigated.[141] A different kind of point about impact is made by von Stebut in relation to subsidies in the manpower sector, when he points out that by reason of their indirect or non-coercive impact they correspond better than do regulations to a fundamental characteristic of the policy field, that is, the idea of freedom to choose one's work,[142] which in some of the countries studied is the object of constitutional guarantee.[143]

The relationship between regulations, in general, and public benefits, in general, is a complex one, in that a variety of factors appear to combine together to affect the the policy-maker's choice as between these two types of instrument. The difficulty of drawing broad distinctions is indicated by the fact that regulations and subsidies are often found in close proximity, occupying complementary or mutually reinforcing roles in relation to a given objective. An example from the energy sector is the promotion of energy conservation by regulatory standards for the construction of new buildings, coupled with subsidies for the conversion of old ones; from the manpower sector, that of the provision of a public service of job placement, coupled with the regulation of private employment agencies, where these are permitted at all. Overall, however, the incidence of regulations, in relation to that of subsidies, is much greater in the energy sector than in manpower. To explain this Jarass points most strongly to the idea of innovation, probably of greater general importance in manpower policy and especially significant in the field of job creation (where regulations are very few), while von Stebut, as already noted,[144] emphasises the different kinds of impact of the two instruments, the impact of subsidies on the choices of actors (especially individual workers or unemployed) being – legally speaking at least – non-coercive whereas that of regulations is coercive.

As between subsidies and regulations the size of target population does not seem to be an important variable, in that general subsidy schemes are frequently encountered in both sectors. There are, however, limits to the capacity of such schemes: von Stebut asserts that they respond rather to situations of local or sectoral difficulty, than to needs for global economic adjustments.[145] Clearly a problem the State confronts in the latter type of situation is that of the sheer cost – and of the highly visible nature of such cost – of national subsidies which are not

[141] Ibid., pp. 84–85.
[142] See below, p. 141.
[143] See art. 12 of the German Basic Law, art. 4 of the Italian Constitution.
[144] Above, p. 142.
[145] Below, pp. 137–143.

tightly defined in terms of their beneficiaries or of the occasions of benefit. In such circumstances it may be easier to load the costs of behaviour changes on to the actors concerned by means of regulation – so long as they have the capacity to bear such costs. Considerations of how best to allocate the costs of compliance with policy may do much to explain the rarity of tax measures in the fields we have examined, and even the relative rarity of tax exemptions which, to work effectively, require that the target population be in good enough economic health to be actually paying the relevant tax.[146] Differing capacities to bear regulatory costs may also explain some national variations in the use of instruments in particular policy fields: thus only in the United Kingdom and the Netherlands, with successful indigenous oil and gas industries, do we find regulations (or consensual constraints), as opposed to public benefits, used to guide indigenous energy development along the paths preferred by the State.

With the occasional exception of situations of this type, which are attributable more to variations in social or economic context than to legal systems, the factors we have identified as relevant to instrument choices appear to operate in much the same way in all West European legal systems.[147] One should not deduce from this that the demands of the legal system cannot influence the choice of instruments: feedback from the legal system is certainly possible, in that it may install links between particular kinds of instruments and particular characteristics of implementing measures, which may make some instruments more attractive to the policy maker and some less so, other things being equal. An example will illustrate the point. If regulation to restrict the level of wage increases would require Parliamentary legislation, a government which is short of Parliamentary time or of a stable majority may prefer to achieve the same purpose by threatening withdrawal of public benefits from firms granting excessive increases, if this can be done by simple decree.[148] The example also demonstrates the error of assuming

---

[146] Such tax exemptions as have been encountered often relate to non-progressive taxes like social security payments or fuel duty, rather than to variable income or corporation taxes.

[147] More important variations from the general pattern observed in the use of subsidies and regulations occur in Hungary. Not only is there a higher incidence of regulations than in any West European State, which may be readily assumed to reflect a more dirigiste style of economic management, there are also a few interesting inversions of this tendency, as where subsidies are used to encourage firms to employ handicapped workers, whereas several Western States impose quotas or other regulatory obligations (United Kingdom, France, Italy). In both the general and the special case economic structures and situations appear to be at the root of the difference. Notwithstanding recent moves towards the diffusion of market-type incentives, the highly structured and centralised nature of the Hungarian economy and the overwhelming predominance of State and co-operative enterprise therein continue to call for regulatory measures where less centralised economies may rely on market forces or, in dealing with their public sector enterprises, on less formal measures. Instrument choices in the manpower sector need to be seen against the background of labour shortages and output targets faced by firms.

[148] As occurred in the United Kingdom: for details see Ganz, Comment, 1978 *Public Law* 333; R. Ferguson and A. C. Page, "Pay Restraint: The Legal Constraints" (1978) 128 *New Law Journal* 515.

that the choice of an instrument to attain an objective, and of a measure to put that instrument into operation, are necessarily separate and independent steps. While the concept of a policy instrument is more than a mere analytical construct, but reflects real choices about ways of achieving policy ends, the policy-maker may often pass directly from objectives to a specific type of measure which seems "natural", without perceiving that quite different instrument choices are in principle available.[149]

What emerges, therefore, from our survey is that West European legal systems are, at least in terms of their broad effects,[150] similar enough not to cause, through the operation of this kind of mechanism, significant discrepancies in instrument choices between the different States involved. Far more important are the differing characteristics of the policy fields which, as already noted, also may have a direct influence on the shaping of legal measures.[151] That this is not a trite or trivial finding is shown by the strong contrast that the United States case offers us. There, legal system factors seem strongly determinative both of instrument choices and of their realisation in the shape of legal measures, and produce profiles of instrument choice and measure design which differ from the European ones. Among instruments, at least at Federal level, regulation dominates. While drawing attention to the existence in the United States of economic and political pressures for regulation which reflect concerns similar to those voiced in Europe, Stewart also lays heavy stress on the influence of the special constitutional features of the American polity: the separation of Executive and Legislature, which deprives Congress of direct concern with the implementation of the measures it enacts, and the Federal-State separation, which limits the scope of Congress to use direct modifications of private rights as a means of policy implementation.[152] The first feature helps to explain Congressional preferences for broad regulatory standards to be implemented and enforced by agency action, even to serve functions, like the promotion of new technology, which in Europe would more readily be assigned to other instruments like subsidies: Congressmen get the political credit and the agency, beset on every side by interest groups, courts, and budget officials, does the detailed and ungrateful implementation work. The second separation operates directly on the content of regulation: since adjustment of rights as between individuals is seen as primarily and traditionally the concern of the States, direct modification of such rights by Congress as a tool of policy is ruled out in all but a

---

[149] Cf. Mayntz, *supra* note 96, at pp. 129–131.
[150] Obviously, specific instances of legal system feedback can be found. A good case is furnished by the different ways in which the European Community obligation to hold certain levels of oil stocks has been translated into the national laws of Member States: see G. P. Levy, "The Relationship between Oil Companies and Consumer State Governments in Europe 1973–82", (1984) 2 *Journal of Energy and Natural Resources Law* 9, at pp. 14–17; and for legislative references Daintith and Hancher, *supra* note 77, at pp. 99–100.
[151] Above, pp. 41–42.
[152] See Stewart, below, pp. 101–102, 113–122.

few established areas, leading to the dominance of control-type regulation (termed "administrative" by Stewart) even in areas where the congruence of private interests and public policy might suggest other methods.

V. Conclusion

At this point it might be safest to leave the reader to draw his own conclusions as to the lessons of the study, not least because any attempt at broad findings here will certainly need to be read in the light of the exceptions and qualifications which emerge from the detailed findings and opinions in the papers that follow. Nonetheless, since the material reviewed does suggest to me some directions in which answers to the general questions posed in this introductory paper might be sought, I propose to state them here.

The study has postulated three interlinked determinants of the ways in which law might be used in implementation of policy: the characteristics of the policy field (here subdivided by sector and by objective); the nature and mode of operation of the resources available to government (here represented by the notion of instruments); and the demands of the national legal system itself. Of these three, it is the first that appears the most powerful: patterns of legal implementation, as traced by our scheme of analysis of measures, vary more strongly according to the policy field – energy or manpower – in which measures are deployed than according to the legal system which deploys them.[153] Cross-national generalisation across a number of policy fields thus appears unpromising. Together, the influence of these two factors, policy field and legal system, leaves relatively little scope for regularities between instruments and measures (other than necessary ones like the relationship between the subsidy instrument and measures transferring funds) across the boundaries of legal systems and broad policy sectors. In West European countries at least, legal systems appear to be a rather weak cause of differentiation of legal implementation of policy, producing, outside the area of *sources* of law (where they are important), only occasional significant disparities which correspond mainly to differences in pre-existing bodies of national law. This finding offers some encouragement to further comparative reflection on instrumental law. Before considering what kind of contribution the study makes to such reflections, a puzzle must be confronted: why should national perceptions of the problems and virtues of instrumental law vary so, if different national law-makers respond in largely consistent ways to policy stimuli?

The subjective differences between academic lawyers evoked at the beginning of this paper may provide a part of the answer, but it hardly seems satisfactory to stop at that. In terms of specific countries, the study, in conjunction with Stewart's paper, does suggest that there are major system-related differences between legal implementation in the United States and in Western Europe, which

---

[153] Cf. R. Mayntz, "Political Intentions and Legal Measures: the Determinants of Policy Decisions", below, at pp. 69–71.

might (subject to what is said in the next paragraph) go some way to explain distinctive American attitudes to instrumental law and which should, in any event, counsel caution about the transposability of American experience and solutions into the European context.[154] Examination of the Hungarian case shows that comparisons with socialist experience are likewise risky, not because the legal profile of implementation is necessarily radically different,[155] but because the background against which economic objectives are formulated may, in some cases at least, offer little resemblance to that in the West.

These points apart, it should in general be remembered that this study has concentrated on the formal, *ex ante* aspects of legal implementation, taking as its primary data the laws and other published measures through which policy instruments have been put into operation. Equally important, however, to the observer's sense of how the legal system operates may be the government's capacities for administrative operation and enforcement of the rules it makes. Excessively detailed legal regulation may be much more irksome in Germany, where it is likely to be efficiently enforced, than in Italy, where this is less likely. Another factor, not considered in the study save in so far as it might feed back into implementation strategies, is that of judicial power to review and correct legally defective measures. This may cut both ways. Where such powers are limited, as in the United Kingdom, broad delegations of rule-making or administrative power are treated with concern as occasions of arbitrariness and excessive discretion.[156] Where such powers are strong, their application in relation to similar kinds of general implementing measures may induce a spiral of regulatory complexity of the kind described in this volume, in relation to the United States, by Professor Stewart.[157] Complaints of excessive legalisation result.[158]

While these possibilities may deserve further investigation, they remain on the margins of our inquiry. Having suggested that one can, in Western Europe, generalise about legal implementation of policy, across legal systems but within, rather than across, well-defined fields like energy policy and manpower policy, the more important question is what principle, or principles, should be adopted as a guide for further comparative investigation, whether of a purely critical or of a policy-oriented kind. Two relationships suggested by the study's findings seem to be particularly powerful in this respect.

The first is that of *congruence of public policy and private interest.* This is an hypothesis worthy of use by lawyers both for the purpose of understanding why they are confronted with particular phenomena of instrumental law, such as regulation (or why it should be absent), and for that of evaluating and criticising the specific legal arrangements that are made. It manifests itself not only in Bercusson's explanation of why and how governments resort to industry self-

---

[154] Compare A. Harden and N. Lewis, "Regulation, De-Regulation and Privatization: Some Anglo-American Comparisons", (1983) 34 *N. Ireland Legal Qly* 207.

[155] See Harmathy, below pp. 245–266.

[156] Above, p. 11.

[157] Below, pp. 97–133.

[158] Ibid., p. 125, and Teubner, *supra* note 5, esp. at pp. 6–7.

regulation as an instrument of policy,[159] but also in Jarass' examination of the
relative attractiveness of regulation,[160] and in my own remarks on the choice
between public and private initiative in regulatory enforcement.[161] Consideration
of exactly what congruence exists, what is the nature of the relevant private
interests, who holds or represents those interests and how great is their economic
power, may permit the researcher to determine where schemes of self-regulation
represent mere abnegation of authority on the part of government, or where they
are cosmetic devices to hide a loss of control; or to say what legal devices should be
sought for the protection of those whose interests conflict with the ones enjoying
this happy state of congruence. It may also help to explain contrasting national
choices between, say, control-type regulation and regulation through the adjustment of individual rights, and to suggest what consequences might follow from a
switch from one to the other.

   The second relationship may be barely stated as that between *the size of a target
population and the form of the legal (and other) measures directed at it.* The study
shows that there is no straightforward correspondence between regulatory
measures and respect for what I have called the "private rights" model of law. In
particular, as pointed out by von Stebut,[162] public benefit laws may, at least in
form, answer just as well to the demands of this model as may their regulatory
counterparts, especially where general subsidy schemes are concerned. But there
is a correspondence, cutting across the categories of instruments we established,
between all (or most) instruments as applied to small groups of actors, or large
individual actors like public enterprises, and legal forms which are more individualised, more variable, more flexible, more like what I call the "collective
interest" model of legislation. In studies, whether national or comparative, of
specific policy fields, the detailed tracing of this relationship may elucidate just
what functions law is fulfilling in such "small numbers" situations: whether, in
particular, the legal forms used for the various instruments deployed – tax
exemptions, for example, or public sector management – are anything more than
expressions of an essentially contractual or bargained arrangement between
government and the economic actors involved, or whether they do offer additional protection for the public interest through the procedures for decision and
opportunities for review which are associated with their use.[163] In this way we may
be able to develop a constructive critique of the use and design of law in such
situations, one which takes account of its potential for new applications such as the
promotion of values like openness in discussion, rather than being limited to
envisaging, with the aid of a traditional but partial model of law, a bleak
dichotomy of tighter regulation or the withdrawal of law.

[159] Below, pp. 359–420.
[160] Below, pp. 75–96.
[161] Above, pp. 38–39.
[162] Below, pp. 137–152. Note, however, the doubts expressed by Fromont, "State Aids:
     Field of Operation and Legal Regime", below, p. 161.
[163] For a demonstration, based on some randomly chosen United Kingdom examples, see
     Daintith, *supra* note 40, especially at pp. 188–197.

Given that a bargaining approach may be easiest where there is some congruence of public policy and private interest, and that this congruence may be most easily perceived where small numbers of powerful actors, like trade unions or banks, operate as representatives of or intermediaries for large numbers of individuals, there may clearly be an overlap between these two relationships. Each, however, seems to me to be worthy of exploration, in both national and comparative contexts, as a means of comprehending the bewildering variety of legal expressions of economic policy, and of determining in which cases the more unusual among these expressions represent unfortunate distortions of law as opposed to ingenious adaptations to its modern control tasks.

Methodological Note

While the main elements in the design of this research, and in particular the concepts and classifications employed, have been described in the foregoing introductory chapter, it seems useful to set out in a separate note the common scheme adopted in this investigation for the collection and analysis of data, in order to permit readers to evaluate the empirical or quantitative observations made from time to time in the different chapters. For this purpose the investigation may be divided into four phases:

1. Planning

At this stage the research group as a whole (for members at different times, see below pages 54–55), on the basis of an introductory paper by Professor Daintith and a number of short surveys of different policy fields prepared by members, selected the fields of policy for investigation, agreed classifications of objecives within those fields which could be used in all countries to be covered (set out in full in Appendix A hereto), and settled the classifications of instruments and of legal measures which have been described in the introductory chapter and are set out in full as appendices B and C hereto.

2. Data Collection

The basic unit of data collection has been the (legal) measure. Data has been compiled in the form of two sets of national inventories of measures, one set for energy policy, one for manpower policy. Each inventory has been designed to be a comprehensive listing of legal and other formal (i.e. publicly acknowledged) measures taken for the achievement of the listed policy objectives over the period from 1973 to the date of compilation of the inventory (normally early 1983). Also included, however, are measures taken prior to 1973 which have been employed for the pursuit of these objectives since that date.

Each inventory has been prepared by a member of the group familiar with the law and legal system of the country in question, normally a national of that country.

The group agreed a standard form of reporting of each measure, including

   (i) the objective (or objectives) promoted;
  (ii) the official title;
 (iii) the law or other formal source (if any) authorising the making of the
       measure;
  (iv) a summary of its contents;
   (v) the type of instrument brought into operation by the measure;
  (vi) analysis of the measure in terms of the coded classification of measures;
 (vii) available information on the performance of the measure;
(viii) links with other measures (e.g. those replaced by or replacing this measure;
       those applying or applied by this measure) and
  (xi) bibliographical information on the measure.

In identifying and analysing measures the compilers of inventories were asked to
concentrate on substance rather than on form. Thus the statute, or regulation,
would not necessarily be treated as a single measure, but might in many cases be
treated as containing several distinct measures, each operationalising a different
kind of instrument. A variety of objectives, however, might be promoted by a
single measure, and in such cases, the measures were listed under more than one
kind of objective.

   While the uniform reporting of measures provides the basis for quantitative
observations on the incidence of different kinds of measures and instruments and
their relationship with objectives, the data is not of a kind which lends itself easily
to quantified comparison. Two broad types of problem may be distinguished:

(a) difficulties in the consistent classification of data: attribution of measures to
    given objectives or instruments depends in considerable measure on the
    subjective appreciation of the reporter. Particular problems were encountered
    with the treatment of collective agreements and of measures addressed to
    public sector bodies.

    (i) collective agreements: these may be an instrument of government policy
        either in the strong sense that government specifically encourages or
        recognises them, or attaches binding legal force to them, in relation to a
        given objective; or in the weaker sense that government, by reason of
        satisfaction with the processes or results of collective bargaining, uses its
        own policy instruments either not at all or only in an interstitial or
        supplementary way. In the first case classification was by reference to the
        instrument used by government in relation to collective agreements (e.g.
        regulatory extension, triggering of subsidy, etc.); in the second, the
        practice of making collective agreements was treated as part of the
        background to the implementation of the given objective. The line
        between these two types of treatment has not been easy to draw. Where
        government itself appears as a party to collective agreements (other than
        with its own employees) the "consensual constraint" or "public benefits"
        instrument categories have usually been appropriate.
   (ii) Public sector: Here the problem is that instruments of a given type

(regulations, subsidies, etc.) may be either addressed specifically to public sector bodies, or addressed to a wider group of economic actors within which some public sector bodies fall. Only the first kind of application has been coded as public sector management, the second being treated as an example of the general instrument type.

Other, less important problems of the same type were identified and, so far as possible, eliminated in group discussion.

(b) Difficulties of meaningful quantification: the importance of measures relating to different kinds of instrument cannot simply be measured by counting their frequency, by reason of the very differences of function that are discussed in the introductory chapter (see especially pages 34–39). For example, subsidies may be given either on the authority of an annual budget line only, or also on that of a "permanent" law or order, but in the latter case annual budget funding remains necessary. For this reason we have not treated such budget authorisations, even in the former case, as *separate* measures; conversely, since regulations generally do not fall for annual renewal, we treated renewals or regular amendments of regulations as such separate measures. Great caution is therefore needed in the interpretation of an observation of, say, relative numbers of regulatory and subsidy measures in a given country, though the validity of cross country comparisons relating to the *same* instrument is, of course, not impaired by this factor.

Another problem of the same kind arises from the fact that formal (but non-legal) measures may have different degrees of visibility in the different states examined, so that there exists the risk of under-reporting where such measures are hard to identify. The mix of legal and non-legal measures may likewise vary from instrument to instrument, so that the under-reporting problem may also occur differently according to the instrument in question.

3. Data Evaluation

Besides group review and analysis of the separate inventories, identifying and to some extent solving the problems set out above, evaluation was conducted on a systematic basis by means of the preparation, by a member of the research group, of a comparative report on the treatment in the inventories of a given objective or group of objectives. Each report reviews the relevant measures from the inventories under such headings as:

(i) the objective: its importance in different countries in terms of number and content of measures, with particular reference to significant variations;

(ii) the incidence of the different kinds of instruments, both generally and in particular countries;

(iii) any patterns observable in the profile of measures employed, whether in relation to particular instruments, in particular countries or both.

It then goes on to point to any difficulties or anomalies in the treatment of problems by different rapporteurs, and to apply to these materials some working hypotheses developed in the planning stage of the investigation. The hypotheses

which emerged as most significant are those discussed at pages 33–44 of the introductory chapter above. Reports once prepared were circulated to compilers of the
inventories in order further to reduce anomalies in inventories and to check the
accuracy of the preparatory reports. Indications of authors and subjects of comparative reports are to be found in Appendix D; copies of these reports are on file
at the EUI.

4. Final Studies

On the basis of research group discussions of the inventories and comparative
reports, the six themes addressed in the current volume were selected as the subject
matter of definitive studies. Most of these are qualitative in approach; the studies
on regulation and subsidies offer tentative conclusions on the utilisation of these
instruments and on the manner of their legal operationalisation, based on broad
aggregations of the study data, but, in the light of the difficulties described above,
do not purport to offer precise quantification of the incidence of instruments of a
given type or of measures with particular characteristics. Such indications are
provided in a number of the comparative reports. The same approach has been
followed in the conclusions to the introductory chapter, above. The studies, along
with an introductory paper and contributions on the same themes by contributors
from outside the research group (who were, however, made aware of its methods
of working), were presented at the colloquium "Law and Economic Policy:
Alternatives to Delegalisation" at the European University Institute, Florence,
from 26 to 29 March 1985, and have since been revised in the light of discussion
there.

Appendix A

Energy Policy Objectives

Short-term responses to disturbances in energy supply

Code
10. Restriction of consumption
11. Preservation of the pattern and level of supply
12. Stabilisation of prices and profits in energy markets

Alteration of the structure of energy demand

Code
20. Promotion of economy in energy use ("energy saving" or "conservation")
21. Alteration of energy consumption patterns

Alteration of the structure of energy supply

Code
30. Development of nuclear energy supplies
31. Development of other domestic energy resources
32. Diversification of supplies of imported energy

Manpower Policy Objectives

Job creation

Code
10. In general
11. In specific territorial areas
12. In specific industrial sectors

Job maintenance

Code
20. In general
21. In specific territorial areas
22. In specific industrial sectors

Manpower adjustment

Code
30. Access of potential workers to the labour market
31. Movement between jobs
32. Exit from the labour market

Appendix B

Instruments

1. Unilateral regulation
2. Taxation
3. Consensual constraints, i.e. control of activity through contractual and other agreements with government
4. Removal or relaxation of regulations
5. Removal of taxation or the granting of tax exemptions
6. Public benefits, e.g. subsidies and other financial assistance, provision of public services and other forms of assistance in kind
7. Public sector management
8. Information

Appendix C

Coding of Measures

1. Scope
   10. General
   11. Individual
2. Temporal validity
   20. Permanent
   21. Temporary
      210. Limited by reference to a specified date or period
      211. Limited by reference to the occurrence (or non-occurrence) of a specified event
3. Source
   30. State constitution
   31. Parliament
      310. Legislation
            3100. Ordinary
            3101. Budgetary
            3102. Other special types
      311. Other acts (e.g. resolutions)
   32. Central government
      320. Formal acts
         3200. Authorised by Parliament
            32000. Collective acts
            32001. Acts of individual Ministers
         3201. Not authorised by Parliament, i.e. taken in pursuit of independent powers
            32010. Collective acts
            32011. Acts of individual Ministers
      321. Informal acts (e.g. circulars)
   33. Other territorial authorities
      330. Regional authorities (e.g. Italian regions, W. German Länder)
         3301. Acts of legislative assemblies
         3302. Other acts
      331. Communes, municipal authorities, etc.
   34. Judicial decisions (developing and applying common law principles or advancing new interpretations of statutory rules)
   35. Other bodies (e.g. regulatory organs distinct from central government and other territorial authorities)
   36. European Community organs
      360. Acts of the Council and Commission having direct effect within the national legal system
         3600. Regulations
         3601. Decisions
         3602. Other

    361. Other acts
        3610. Of the Council
        3611. Of the Commission
        3612. Of the Parliament
        3613. Of the Court
  37. Acts of international organs
    370. Having direct effect within the national legal system
    371. Not having direct effect
4. Nature of relation created
  40. Unilateral
  41. Bilateral (e.g. contracts) and legally binding
  42. Bilateral, not legally binding
5. Substantive Content
  50. Declaratory
    501. Of legal rules or situations
    502. Of policy objectives or plans
    503. Of intentions
  51. Imposing duties
    510. Sanctioned by criminal penalties
    511. Sanctioned by adminstrative penalties
    512. Sanctioned by civil penalties
    513. Without sanctions
  52. Granting powers to
    520. Central government
    521. Other public bodies
    522. Other persons
  53. Removing or relaxing general duties
  54. Granting exemptions from, or making exceptions to, general duties (e.g. tax exemptions)
  55. Transferring
    550. Funds
    551. Property
  56. Constituting
    560. Public bodies
    561. Other bodies
6. Procedural conditions (i.e. for the performance of any of the operations under 5. above)
  60. No special procedures
  61. Obligation to inform
    610. Parliament or a parliamentary body
    611. Central government or a central government organ
    612. Other territorial authorities
    613. Other public bodies
    614. Specified private bodies or individuals
    615. The general public or a part of it
  62. Obligation to consult or seek the opinion of

620. Parliament or a parliamentary body
621. Central government or a central government organ
622. Other territorial authorities
623. Other public bodies
624. Specified private bodies or individuals
625. The general public or a part of it
63. Obligation to obtain the approval of
630. Parliament or a parliamentary body
631. Central government or a central government organ
632. Other territorial authorities
633. Other public bodies
634. Courts or other judicial bodies
635. Specified private bodies or individuals
636. The general public or a part of it
64. Obligation to hold a public inquiry or investigation
65. Other special procedures

Appendix D

Research Group Participation

Name and Institution	Planning	Inventory	Comparative Report	Final Study (this volume)
Professor *Giuliano Amato* Facoltà di Scienze Politiche, Istituto Giuridico, Università degli Studi di Roma	yes	Energy: Italy (joint)		
Professor *Brian Bercusson* Department of Law EUI	yes	Energy: UK (part) Manpower: UK	Manpower adjustment: movement between jobs	Public and private ordering
Tony Curran Research Assistant Department of Law EUI		Manpower: Italy		
Professor *Terence Daintith* Department of Law EUI	yes		Economy in energy use Job maintenance general	Introduction
Professor *Jean-Michel de Forges* Faculté de Droit Université René Descartes (Paris V)	yes	Manpower: France		

Dr. *Franchini* Facoltà di Scienze Politiche, Istituto Giuridico, Università degli Studi di Roma		Energy: Italy (joint)	Development of non-nuclear domestic energy resources	
Leigh Hancher International Instituut voor Energierecht Rijksuniversiteit Leiden	yes	Energy: France (part) Energy: UK (part)	Short-term energy objectives: Manpower adjustment exit from labour market	Public sector management
Professor *Attila Harmathy* Institute for Legal & Administrative Sciences of the Hungarian Academy of Sciences Budapest	yes	Energy: Hungary Manpower: Hungary	Alteration of energy consumption patterns and job maintenance in specified territorial areas	Comparative legal systems
Professor *Hans Jarass* FB Rechtswissenschaft Universität Bochum	yes	Energy: Federal Republic of Germany	Development of nuclear energy supplies	Regulation
Professor *Kamiel Mortelmans* Europa Instituut Rijksuniversiteit Utrecht	yes	Energy: Netherlands Manpower: Netherlands	Stabilisation of energy prices and profits Manpower adjustment access to labour market	The temporal element
Dr. *Patrick Nerhot* Assistant, Department of Law, EUI		Energy: France (part)		
Professor *Jacqueline de la Rochère* Faculte de Droit, Université René Descartes (Paris V)	yes			
Professor *Dietrich von Stebut* FB Rechts- u. Wirtschaftswissenschaft, Freie Universität Berlin	yes	Manpower: Federal Republic of Germany	Job creation objectives	Subsidies

Political Intentions and Legal Measures: The Determinants of Policy Decisions

RENATE MAYNTZ

Köln

Contents

Introduction

The research reported in this volume and its companion publication[1] pursues two different objectives which are both covered by the formula "law as instrument of economic policy". The latter volume is concerned with the process of legalisation (or juridification) taking place over time in such areas as wage determination, industrial relations and corporate structure. The perspective of these studies is longitudinal, and the major questions concern changes in the intensity, specificity and objectives of legal regulation. A second set of studies is more concerned with specific policy instruments such as regulation, financial incentives, and public provision, and the way these instruments are used in different countries. Here the perspective is largely comparative, making use of the data collected on the objectives, instruments, and legal measures of energy and of manpower policy in different European countries. These observations are addressed to the second of these two concerns as represented specifically by Terence Daintith's contribution[2] and therefore take the formula "law as policy instrument" as a starting point. After briefly discussing what this formulation implies and how it relates to the cognitive interests of different disciplines, I will go on to consider what inferences a comparative analysis of legal measures permits with respect to the major determinants of policy decisions. For this purpose I will outline a causal model of policy

---

[1] G. Teubner, ed., *Juridification of Social Spheres* (1987, Berlin).
[2] Terence Daintith, "Law as Policy Instrument: A Comparative Perspective," above, at pp. 3–55.

decisions and will ask how an international comparison can help make inferences from explicitly formulated policy decisions to the factors that have shaped them.

I. Law as a Policy Instrument: What is the Issue?

To talk about law as policy instrument implies that there are other kinds of instruments which might be used instead. The question is then why law rather than some other policy instrument is being chosen, and what effects this particular choice has:

Figure 1

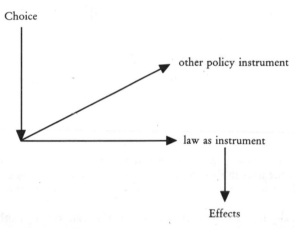

"Legalisation" would here be the consequence of an increasing reliance on law *in state intervention*, a meaning that must be distinguished from legalisation in the sense of a *general increase* of legal norms (as distinct from social custom, convention, or informal social norms) in society.[3] Of course, the growing inclination of the state to formulate legal norms for policy purposes may be an important cause of legalisation in the second sense, but sociologists at least have tended to emphasize other reasons which have to do with the changing integration needs of society. This line of reasoning, which can be traced back to Durkheim, finds clear expression for instance in the work of Kaupen, for whom a multiplication of legal norms reflects the dominance of the problem of social integration, one of Parsons' four functional imperatives.[4] In the present context, however, "legalisation" is of interest as a reflection of different political intervention styles.

[3] This is the meaning which R. Voigt gives to the term; "Verrechtlichung in Staat und Gesellschaft", in: R. Voigt (ed.) *Verrechtlichung*, (1980, Königstein) at p. 16.
[4] Wolfgang Kaupen, "Über die Bedeutung des Rechts und der Juristen in der modernen Gesellschaft", in: Kaupen/Werle (eds) *Soziologische Probleme juristischer Berufe*, (1974, Göttingen) at pp. 23–25.

Focusing, then, on the choice of law as a policy instrument, it seems important to clarify the nature of the alternatives which this formulation implies. Figure 2 may be helpful in this regard.

Figure 2

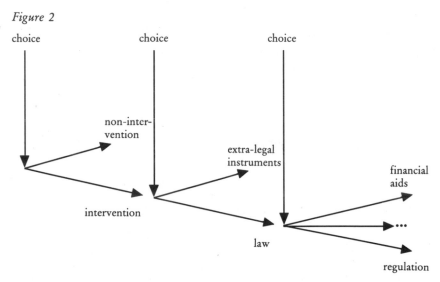

The first alternative is between state intervention and non-intervention. Many economists see the issue in these terms, with de-legalisation becoming the battle-cry of the advocates of laissez-faire and of the self-regulation powers of the market.

The second alternative is between intervention through law or by other, extra-legal means. Such extra-legal means can be bargaining, informal pressure, or the threat of resorting to legislation – alternative political strategies which the continental European scholar with his ingrained legalism tends to overlook but which are occasionally highlighted by British colleagues.[5] Another policy instrument which is sometimes considered as an alternative to law is money.[6] This distinction, as well as the singling out of law as one policy instrument among others, makes a lot of sense in a historical perspective, where rulers have often used money (as well as other gifts, and even their daughters) to further their political intentions and to obtain compliance. In such an historical perspective, legalisation describes the emergence of Max Weber's legal-rational type of political order and of the modern constitutional state. However, when we deal with present societies and speak of policy, the distinction between law and other policy instruments

---

[5] See e.g. T. Daintith, "The Executive Power Today: Bargaining and Economic Control", in J. Jowell and D. Oliver, eds., *The Changing Constitution* (1985, Oxford) at pp. 174–197.

[6] Niklas Luhmann, *Politische Theorie im Wohlfahrsstaat*, (1981, München/Wien) at pp. 94 ff.

undoubtedly loses much of its importance. Today, there is very little really discretionary giving of public money to private actors. The big spending programmes in the fields of social welfare and industrial policy (subsidies) are normally couched in the form of a law; even the procurement of weapons has a legal basis in the budget. Similar arguments could be made with respect to other possible alternatives to "law as policy instrument", such as the public provision of services, and self-regulation, which, if it does not mean simply non-intervention, is usually based on legally conferred rights and procedural norms. It certainly makes a big difference whether modern governments try to reach policy goals by the normative regulation of the behaviour of private parties, by offering incentives for the same purpose or by having public agencies do directly what they wish to be done – but these are not *alternatives* to law. The interesting question with respect to the use of law in public policy is today not *whether* it is involved or not, but how.

In fact, in his most recent paper, Daintith himself has reformulated the research question in this way.[7] In the classification of policy instruments, law does not appear as a separate category. Trying to keep the type of policy instrument and the "shape" of legal measures which are intended to put them into effect analytically distinct, Daintith now asks what is the empirical relationship between them (see Figure 3).

Obviously, legal norms can play quite different roles when it comes to putting a policy into effect. They may prescribe the behaviour of a target group, entitle private actors to receive public money, authorise a public agency to engage in certain activities or confer the power upon it to formulate binding standards. Furthermore, the measures "implementing" a policy can differ considerably in their legal status. Here the distinction between law and alternative legal forms, such as ministerial decrees, cabinet orders, administrative guidelines, or standards formulated by an independent regulatory agency, is meaningful even in a narrow sense.

Figure 3

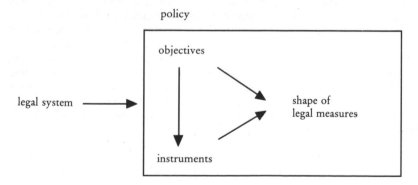

[7] T. Daintith, *supra* note 1.

The status of legal norms and their specific function in a given policy context are largely determined by the choice of policy instrument, i.e. of how to bring about what the policy-makers want to achieve, with the scope for choice as to the "shape" of legal measures getting narrower as the mode of intervention is formulated in growing detail. Having chosen to try and control the behaviour of private actors instead of resorting to public provision, in the attempt say, to abate pollution, and having further decided to do this not by moral exhortation or through offering financial incentives, but by constraining potential polluters to observe certain emission standards, there may still be the alternative to do this directly by having parliament formulate the corresponding standards or indirectly by setting up an independent regulatory agency to do so, but from this point on very little choice remains as to the status and the function of the legal norms involved. To the extent that this is so, observable relationships between the "instrument" and "legal measure" categories are logical rather than empirical, i.e. the latter appear largely as operationalisation (or specification) of the former. The relationship between objectives and instruments is of a somewhat different nature. Legal restrictions on the central government's scope for authoritative intervention are an important factor of instrument choice, especially where a given choice would interfere with constitutionally guaranteed spheres of autonomy and areas of personal freedom. However, within these constraints there are also other factors at work. Some of the empirical analyses of the incidence of specific instruments (and measures) in different policy areas and with respect to different policy goals suggest implicitly that effectiveness considerations play a major role in making instrument choices.[8] Thus, a higher incidence of instrument X in a given context is explained by reference to some characteristic of the target population which renders this particular instrument more effective than other possible alternatives. Apart from the fact that such a (rather rationalistic) interpretation of the behaviour of policy-makers would need ulterior empirical evidence, the many cases where the empirical findings do not lend themselves easily to such an interpretation suggest that there are other factors involved in policy design which need closer attention. In fact, this is where the research interest of political science comes into the picture. By and large, the political scientist is less interested in the *nexus* which obtains between policy objectives, instruments, and the specifics of legal measures than he is in the *choice* of goals and instruments, and in what observable preferences can tell him about the character of a given political system, particularly about the distribution of effective decision-making power between the different branches, organs, and levels of government, about the basic orientations of policy-makers, and about the political (rather than legal) constraints under which they operate. I will come back to these questions in section III of this paper.

---

[8] See especially the contributions by Hans Jarass and Dietrich von Stebut to this volume.

II. The Analytical Dimensions of Programmes

Policy decisions have many different aspects. They have a substantive content, and they have formal properties. They are about objectives (or ends) and about instruments (or means). Together, they constitute what is sometimes called a "programme" – the output of the policy formation process and the basis of subsequent routine implementation. To the extent that policy decisions are explicitly formulated and set down in writing, programmes can be empirically analysed independently of the process of their development.

Comparative legal studies have customarily worked with analytical schemes to describe the relevant norms in a given field in detail. In contrast, classical studies of comparative policy analysis have concentrated so much on the substantive content of – for instance – educational or housing policy that no need was felt for a more formalised description of governmental interventions.[9] But this has changed, and more recently various analytical schemes for the description of programmes have been proposed, some deriving from an interest in the process of legislation,[10] some stemming from an interest in policy implementation and evaluation.[11] Some of these schemes are quite elaborate; Jann for instance distinguishes between (1) outcome goals (or policy objectives), (2) various programme elements relating to the desired effects (including choice of policy instrument and definition of the target group), and (3) several programme elements relating to implementation (including definition of implementation agents, funding etc.) – a total of ten analytical dimensions.[12]

The different cognitive interests of legal scholars and political scientists are clearly reflected in the analytical dimensions singled out for the description of programmes. The six dimensions of the scheme for coding legal measures described by Daintith[13] reflect on the one hand an interest in the question how the use of legal norms for policy purposes comes to influence the character of law: its scope, its temporal validity, and the nature of the relation it creates. On the other hand, the dimensions "substantive content" and "source" express the interest in the different roles that legal norms can play in translating policy objectives into action, and in the legal status of these norms.

---

[9] Quite characteristic in this respect is the book by Arnold J. Heidenheimer, Hugh Heclo, Carolyn Teich Adams, *Comparative Public Policy – The Politics of Social Choice in Europe and America*, (2nd ed., 1983, New York).

[10] Ludwig Göbel, "Probleme der Regelungsform und der Institutionalisierung", in: C. Böhret ed., *Gesetzgebungspraxis und Gesetzgebungslehre*, (1980, Wiesbaden), at p. 84.

[11] See for instance Peter Knoepfel and Helmut Weidner, "Normbildung und Implementation: Interessenberücksichtigungsmuster" in *Programmstrukturen von Luftreinhaltepolitiken*, in: R. Mayntz ed., *Implementation politischer Programme*, (1980, Königstein/Ts.) at pp. 88f.

[12] Werner Jann, *Kategorien der Policy Forschung*, Speyerer Arbeitshefte, (1981, Wiesbaden) at pp. 49ff.

[13] For full details, see the Methodological Note, esp. Appendix C, above, at pp. 47–55.

In contrast, analytical schemes developed in the context of research policy implementation put great emphasis on a detailed categorisation of operative rules which influence the behaviour of the implementation agents and hence the concrete "output" of the programmes in terms of acts or decisions (see Figure 4).[14]

Figure 4

Programme elements

I. Core elements
   explicit objectives, whether these relate to the behaviour of the target group or the
   intended effect of this behaviour
   definition of target group
   choice of policy instrument

II. Elements which operationalise the core
   designation of implementation agents
   administrative procedures
   due process rules (complaints etc.)
   participation rules
   adaptive or self-correction mechanism
   internal control procedures
   temporal validity

If one is specifically interested in those programme characteristics which presumably influence either the behaviour of implementation agents or the reactions of the target group and interested third parties, the legal properties of concrete measures seem less relevant. In particular I would suggest the hypothesis that the legal status of a given state intervention (as operationalised in the dimension "source") and the role of legal norms within a programme (as operationalised in the dimension "substantive content") are only of minor importance as to its effects, especially for the extent to which it is able to realise policy objectives and to avoid "implementation deficits". To the citizen it probably does not matter much whether what he receives or is asked to do is the content of a law passed by parliament, of a ministerial decree, or of a standard formulated by an independent regulatory agency. In fact, the average citizen is often not familiar with these distinctions and ignores the legal status of norms he is expected to comply with. Provided the content is the same, the legal status *per se* should not make much of a difference – except perhaps for the chances of successfully opposing or avoiding compliance, since due process norms will differ with the legal status of the

---

[14] Renate Mayntz, Christa Lex, *Voraussetzungen und Aspekte administrativer Praktikabilität staatlicher Handlungsprogramme. Wissenschaftliche Ausarbeitung im Auftrag des Bundesministeriums des Innern*, (1982, Köln) at pp. 22f.

substantive norm. It is for such reasons that implementation research has generally paid very little attention to *legal* programme characteristics.

Where interest shifts from the possible effects to the determinants of policy decisions, the nature of the determinant one is trying to assess again tends to be reflected in the analytical dimensions singled out for coding policy measures or describing programmes. If the legal system is the major factor of interest, other formal and substantive properties of programmes seem relevant than would be the case in a study which attempts for instance to trace the influence of national culture (or political intervention style). In both cases, it is important to identify and focus on those programme characteristics which are likely to be influenced by – and hence reflect – a particular determinant. Thus, in one recent study which sought to test the effect of national culture on social and economic regulation, the intensity (scope, density, and specificity) of the regulation of target group behaviour was used as one of the major formal properties for which programmes were coded.[15]

III. The Determinants of Policy Design – A Causal Model

Whereas it is quite evident that it is impossible to infer the effects which a given programme will actually have from its observable characteristics, it seems much less problematic to infer its major determinants from them. In fact, programmes are sometimes analysed because their characteristics are taken to be an indicator of some factor that presumably shaped them. This was true for instance with respect to the determinant "national political and administrative culture", which played the central theoretical role in the comparative study just referred to. To use programme characteristics as an indicator of important factors which played a role in its development appears on first sight plausible enough, considering they have shaped its content and form – much as geological and archeological research interprets sediments and remnants to infer what or who produced them, how, and why. The very use of this parallel, however, alerts us to the theoretical assumptions which must be made in such an interpretation. What, then, are the important determinants of policy decision, and to what extent can they be inferred from observable programme characteristics?

There is no need to argue at length that the legal system, even in the very wide meaning this term is given by Daintith, is only one among many factors which shape the policy decisions incorporated in a given programme. Nor is it very difficult to list the major factors and combine them into a master model, as Figure 5 tries to do.

---

[15] Renate Mayntz, J. Feick, L. Klaes, Ch. Lex, R. Seebach, *Regulative Politik und politisch-administrative Kultur – Ein Vergleich von fünf Ländern und vier Interventionsprogrammen,* Forschungsbericht, (1982, Köln).

Figure 5: Major Determinants of Policy Output

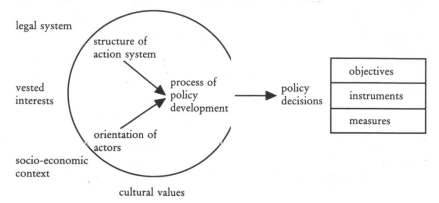

The major components of this model have all been objects of political science, though they were not necessarily seen as linked to policy outcomes. In fact, interest in policy decisions is relatively recent, and, at least in the Federal Republic of Germany, political scientists are currently debating whether or not policy analysis is a basically new approach that is changing the traditional understanding of the discipline.[16] In particular, scholars of comparative government, the "in-stitutionalists" with their detailed and historically informed descriptions of political structures, have traditionally not linked their analyses of the polity to policy – maybe because (as v. Beyme suggests) the functions of government were an unproblematical datum for them.[17] The two policy determinants which have been most intensively discussed are the societal power structure (structure of vested interests) and the ideology of governing parties. Very often, the discussion is framed in terms of some alternative, contrasting for instance the relative influence of socio-economic context with that of politics, or of institutions with that of individual attitudes. These debates and the empirical data that have been collected in their support are at times very instructive, but they do not add up to an integrated theory or dynamic explanatory model which would be able to account for observable programme characteristics. Nor is it possible to develop such a model fully in this paper, but it is worthwhile to spell out some of the require-ments such a model would have to fulfill.

The plurality of factors which can plausibly be argued to have an influence on the form and content of policy decisions raises the issue of their relative weight. Instead of discussing this by arguing for (or against) the dominant influence of one particular factor, it seems more fruitful to ask how these different factors combine.

---

[16] In November 1984, the German Professional Association of Political Scientists, DVPW, held a symposium on the topic "Zum Verhältnis der Policy-Forschung/Policy Studies zu den 'Kernbereichen' des Faches", where this issue was debated.

[17] Klaus v. Beyme, *Policy Analysis und traditionelle Politikwissenschaft,* paper presented at the symposium mentioned in footnote 16.

Some of the factors in the model have a direct, some an indirect effect. If one thinks in terms of a concrete policy-making process, the most direct or proximate causes of a given programme design are the decisions taken by specific actors in a specific sequence. These individual decisions are primarily influenced by a number of subjective factors (interests, value orientations, ideological conviction, cognitive models etc.), but the way these individual contributions are aggregated, the amount and kind of influence which individual actors have, are shaped by structural features of the political-administrative system. Many context features become effective by impinging on the action system by determining who participates in the process, and by influencing the choices of policy-makers. Constitutional norms, for instance, general cultural value orientations, or the availability of resources, first become effective when they are taken into consideration in the making of policy decisions in order to avoid such anticipated consequences as the later revision of a statute by the constitutional court, widespread popular resistance to a policy, or the inability to finance a programme. Thus, all background or context factors must be linked to the decisions of individuals in order to shape policy measures. But it is evident that the indirect nature of the influence which such factors have says nothing about their relative weight in determining policy output.

It is also important to recognise that some factors influence policy output by shaping it substantively, while others merely constrain or limit the choice of policy-makers. The preferences of decision-makers have an immediate shaping influence, while constitutional norms and the institutional framework are constraining rather than shaping factors. They narrow the range of feasible choices, but there is no point-by-point correspondence between them and the substantive content of specific policy decisions. While largely constraining, the legal system can also occasionally have a shaping influence, as when for example existing legal norms require certain substantive objectives to be pursued or procedural rules in implementation to be observed, which must therefore be written into a programme.

Most important of all, it should be recognised that not all factors influence the various programme elements to the same extent. At least part of the fruitless debate about the major or minor importance of specific factors results from the neglect of this differential importance of a given factor for different programme elements. In particular, the elements in the programme core, especially the impact goals, the intended distribution of costs and benefits (who receives what or is asked to do what) are likely to be influenced most strongly by other factors than those which affect the design of the operative elements. Nor are these elements decided on at the same time, or by the same actors, which also means that different criteria may structure the relevant decisions. This conjunction of sequence and orientational differences is important because it may lead to internal contradictions between various programme elements, notably policy goals and their "operationalisation" in specific rules and measures.

If these remarks have served to "dynamise" the static causal model represented in Figure 5 and to clarify somewhat the nature of the relationships between different factors, we can now turn to some of the factors in more detail.

Socio-economic variables exert an indirect influence on policy outputs, but are generally considered to be very influential. Two schools of thought in particular have concentrated on these determinants: neo-marxists, who have focused on the macro-social power structure (or structure of vested interests), and welfare state theorists, who have focused instead on the stage of socio-economic development which a country has reached. Neo-marxists tend to assign a merely instrumental role to political institutions and to deny political actors the power of effecting real choices. For them, policy content is shaped by the dominant class interests which are reflected in particular in the substantive policy goals and in the cost/benefit implications of the measures for the major socio-economic groups.[18] Welfare state theorists focus on the substantive content of social policy decisions, especially the introduction of social security measures. Their view is less deterministic, in that they recognise that in addition to socio-economic variables such as the degree of industrialisation, political variables like democratisation or the existence and strength of labour parties also play a role, and the relative weight of these two kinds of variables is one of their major research interests.[19] In both analytical traditions, formal programme properties are generally not considered, and it is indeed difficult to construe relationship which could plausibly link them to socio-economic background variables.

As we move from the socio-economic context to the political action system which produces the policy decisions, three sets of factors which influence their form and content can be distinguished: the structure of the political action system, the preferences, orientations, and attitudes of the individual political actors, and the process of policy development, in which various political actors within a given institutional framework participate over time in a collective decision process.

The structure of the political action system is a favourite research object of political scientists, but scholars in the field of comparative government have in general not tried to identify the policy consequences of specific institutional arrangements.[20] The neo-corporatist school of thought is a notable exception, even though the emphasis is here less on the form and content of policy decisions than on their effects.[21] Still, it is highly plausible that structural features of the political action system such as a country's party system, the role which the head of government plays, or the relative weight of parliament and ministerial bureaucracy in drafting legislation, will, if indirectly, affect policy decisions. Overall structural properties such as the relative openness of a political action system to

[18] Joachim Hirsch, *Staatsapparat und Reproduktion des Kapitals*, (1974, Frankfurt) is a good illustration of this approach as applied to German science and technology policy.

[19] See for instance H. L. Wilensky, *The Welfare State and Equality. Structural and Ideological Routes of Public Expenditures*, (1975, Berkeley); also Peter Flora, Arnold J. Heidenheimer (eds.), *The Development of Welfare States in Europe and America*, (1981, New Jersey), esp. chapts. 2, 4 and 5.

[20] A typical example is R. Rose, E. Suleiman (eds.) *Presidents and Prime Ministers*, (1980, Washington D.C.).

[21] G. Lehmbruch, Ph. C. Schmitter, *Patterns of Corporatist Policy-Making*, (1982, Beverly Hills/London).

the demands of organised and unorganised interests, or the relative concentration or dispersion of decision-making power, can influence such general characteristics of policy outputs as their responsiveness, timeliness, coherence, and reactive or proactive nature. Of course, this kind of relationship can only be identified if the programme output of several countries is compared, and if a larger number of programmes is considered, which may be one reason why there are no systematic empirical tests of such hypotheses.

The structural features of the political action system have also an – indirect – influence on the content of specific policy decisions, because they determine the relative power of different political actors and their specific functions in the collective decision process. However, institutions only provide the framework within which action takes place, and in order to predict a specific policy output, it would be necessary to know not only the involvement and relative power of particular actors, but also their substantive preferences, which are the factors that find the most direct expression in policy decisions. These preferences, incidentally, do not only relate to policy goals (or the intended distribution of costs and benefits), but also to such programme characteristics as the type of instrument or the choice of implementation agents. That the ideological orientation of policy-makers influences their decisions has always been assumed, though expectations that their social origin might find a direct expression in the public policy adopted have been largely disappointed.[22] The simple truth that only the *combination* of the – facilitating and restricting – structure of the action system with the specific orientations of given actors produces whatever effect politics have on policy is neglected by pure "institutionalists" and pure "behaviourists" alike.

An attitudinal factor which has recently attracted a growing amount of attention is summarily designated by the term national (political, administrative) culture. These attitudinal factors presumably characterise the policy-makers in a given country by virtue of their belonging to a specific national culture. In the United States for instance this would be a pronounced individualism and a general preference for reliance on individual self-help and free market forces rather than the state. It seems obvious that different intervention philosophies, different "ways of doing things", can grow out of different cultural value orientations, but they can also be influenced by the social background, training, and the career experience of policy-makers, factors which produce a specific sub-culture. It may even be meaningful to break down the cultural factor further by distinguishing between the sub-cultures of bureaucrats and of politicians. Cultural factors should not so much influence the choice of policy objectives as the choice among different types of instruments and among potential implementation agents, as well as a number of formal characteristics such as the generality or specificity of legal norms or the scope for discretionary action left to implementation agents.[23] Again, however, national intervention philosophies or "ways of doing things" do not

---

[22] See for instance the various contributions to the volume edited by Moshe M. Czudnowski, *Does Who Governs Matter?* (1982, Illinois).

[23] This is suggested by a study of Werner Jann, *Staatliche Programme und 'Verwaltungskultur'*, (1983, Opladen).

only derive from attitudinal factors, but are likewise shaped by structural constraints, such as the cooperative or antagonistic relationship between central and local governments and the existence or non-existence of administrative courts.

When process features were mentioned as a final major set of factors, reference was made not only to "politics", i.e. the power struggle between opposing parties, organised interests etc., but also to properties of the *collective decision process* in which policy is being developed. Process features are dealt with in a number of studies and theories which basically try to show that the reality of policy-making differs from the normative model of rational decision, and just how it does so. Some, but not all of these studies have explicitly pointed to the impact which the nature of the collective decision process has on substantive policy output. Already in 1959, Lindblom thus saw that the incrementalist character of policy was related to the pervasive bargaining and compromising which characterise the political decision process in a highly pluralistic society.[24] On the basis of an empirical study, Mayntz and Scharpf have later argued that the short-term, small-scale, and reactive (rather than long-term, comprehensive, and proactive) nature of the programmes generated in the German federal bureaucracy is the outcome of what was described as a dialogue process linking together in a collective decision process policy-makers located in different parts of the system.[25] Another approach called "bureaucratic politics" has emphasised how the power struggle between organisations, domain interests, and procedural routines shapes the strategic choices of decision-makers. It is evident that this must have an effect on the decisions produced; in fact, Allison, who first developed this approach, started with the attempt to explain the specific set of decisions taken by the US government in the Cuban missile crisis.[26] The assumed relationship of process to specific output features is weaker in March and Olson's "garbage" can model of decision processes, or Nedelmann's model of conflict transformation in processes of policy development.[27] A basic thesis of these models is that in the course of the collective decision process, the initial problem (or conflict) becomes dissociated from the decision output. The decisions which are finally produced do not only reflect the – often non-issue-related – interests and strategies of a fixed set of actors, but the sequence in which different participants have entered and maybe left the process again. It may be, however, that the most important influence of the process characteristics considered in these models, i.e. how closely policy development

[24] Charles Lindblom, "The Science of 'Muddling Through'", in: PAR 2/1959; later extended in the book: *The Intelligence of Democracy. Decision-Making Through Mutual Adjustment*, (1965, New York).

[25] Renate Mayntz, Fritz W. Scharpf, *Policy-Making in the German Federal Bureaucracy*, (1975, Amsterdam/New York).

[26] Graham T. Allison, *Essence of Decision. Explaining the Cuban Missile Crisis*, (1971, Boston); Graham T. Allison, Morton H. Halperin, "Bureaucratic Politics. A Paradigm and Some Policy Implications", in: Raymond Tanter, Richard H. Ullmann eds., *Theory and Policy in International Relations*, (1974, Princeton) at pp. 40–79.

[27] J. G. March, J. P. Olsen, *Ambiguity and Choice in Organisations*, (1976, Bergen); B. Nedelmann, *Rentenpolitik in Schweden*, (1982, Frankfurt/New York).

approximates to a rational decision process, is not on the form and content of programmes, but on a property that cannot be derived from programme characteristics themselves: their potential effectiveness or problem-solving capacity.

IV. The Theoretical Potential of Comparative Policy Research

The plurality of factors which shape policy decisions and the complexity of their interactions present an obvious problem when it comes to making inferences from programme characteristics which can be studied by documentary analysis. Since the effects of various factors may combine, overlap, reinforce, or cancel each other out, it is impossible to derive the major factors which shaped a programme from its observable features with anything approaching certainty. In fact, one and the same substantive decision can easily result from a variety of different power constellations, bargaining processes, and sets of preferences. By adopting a comparative design in which some factors are varied while others are held constant, this confusing complexity can be somewhat reduced. In order to vary socio-economic context, the legal system, the institutional framework, and an attitudinal factor such as national culture, an international comparison is necessary. The major problem in such a design is to make a country selection which does not vary all of these factors at the same time (and in different directions), though this is what normally happens. It is also possible to focus the comparative design by selectively coding observable measures for those features on which the chosen explanatory variable should exert a particularly strong influence. In this way, the problem of causal attribution can be somewhat mitigated, but it can hardly be solved. For purposes of illustration let me refer to some results of the five-country-comparison referred to before, a study which I initiated and where we attempted to identify the influence of national culture or intervention styles, on regulatory programmes – in particular on the intensity (scope, density, and precision or specificity of rules) of regulation.[28]

As in the case of Daintith and Teubner's research, our data consisted largely of written documents containing the various measures, which we analysed for a number of formal characteristics including intensity of regulation, but also for their manifest objectives, their source and legal status, and details of the instrument (the general type being a constant). If there really is anything like a "national intervention style", this should become visible as a kind of common denominator of the policies adopted in a given country. We chose therefore three different regulatory problems – the containment of epidemic diseases, drug regulation, and commercial freight traffic regulation – and analysed these for each of the five countries covered. As in the study which is the subject of this volume, we attempted to select policy problems which by and large could be considered as constants, i.e. that did not vary from country to country. In the attempt to order the rich detail of our findings we adopted rough scales (high-medium-low) for our major formal dimensions and aggregated the results by country and by policy

[28] *Supra*, note 15.

field. Figure 6 gives an example. As can be seen, the results are anything but conclusive. There are differences between countries in what we have called intensity of regulation, and by and large they confirm what national stereotypes would have led one to expect. However, the differences are not very pronounced, and there is considerable variance within countries from policy field to policy field, so that in the aggregate, the intensity of regulation varies as much between policy fields as it does between countries.

Considering this result, the question arises of what is it that we have varied by selecting these different policy fields. To begin with, each policy field has a different structure: a different kind of target group, different vested interests, a different problem-solving technology. Also, different sets of policy-makers may be involved, and different sets of implementation agents may be available. In the regulation of drug production and commercial freight traffic, for example, powerful and organised interests are involved who may have resisted very strict measures, while in the containment of epidemic diseases, there may have been a more widespread consensus as to the necessity of strict measures, and this may be reflected in the different scores in Figure 6. Thus, any attempt to explain the residual variance not accounted for by the major determinant singled out for analysis inevitably draws attention to additional factors which, however, have not been systematically controlled. It is likely that the comparative analysis of manpower and of energy policy in different European countries will lead to similarly inconclusive results, both with respect to explaining the links between objectives, instruments, and legal measures which go beyond mere logical implications, and to the shaping influence of the legal system.

Figure 6: Intensity of Regulation of Target Group Behaviour
(3 = low, 9 = high for scope, density, and specificity)

	Belgium	Germany	France	Great Britain	Italy	Average score
Containment of epidemic diseases	9	9	9	7.5	9	8.7
Drug regulation	6	3	6	8.25	8.25	6.3
Commercial freight traffic	4	9	8	4	9	6.8
Average score	6.3	7	7.7	6.6	8.8	

The discussion in the previous section alerts us to yet another methological limit which confronts comparative policy studies that are based merely on documentary evidence. Some of the most salient effects of the main policy determinants cannot be inferred from observable programme characteristics alone. This holds for instance for the timeliness, the responsiveness, the reactive or proactive nature and the cost/benefit implications of a policy, which presuppose extensive contextual information (e.g. about the nature of a problem, the interests actually involved, etc.) before they can be attributed to a given programme.

To point to the inherent methodological limits of attempts to infer what shaped a policy from its directly observable characteristics should not be regarded as an unfair criticism of the approach chosen in this research. For one thing, documentary analysis can be very helpful in the process of legalisation (or de-legalisation) in a longitudinal perspective. It is well to remember also that Daintith himself is not primarily interested in the *determinants* of the characteristics for which he is coding the policies selected for analysis. The attempt to ask what these factors are and how far they *might* be inferred from observable programme characteristics, though stimulated by the work of Teubner and Daintith, goes at least partly beyond the scope of their present research – without, I hope, therefore seeming irrelevant.

Part Two

Regulation

Regulation as an Instrument of Economic Policy

HANS D. JARASS

Bochum

Contents

I. Introduction

The growing interest in the implementation of public policy focuses on different aspects and problems of the process by which public policy programmes are realized. In particular, the kind of instruments used, their relative functions and disfunctions, is given attention.[1] Among the different implementation instru-

---

[1] On implementation research see R. Mayntz ed., *Implementation politischer Programme II*, (1983, Heidelberg); P. Sabatier and D. Mazmanian, *Effective Policy Implementation*, (1981, New York).

ments regulation has a specific place. It is often regarded as the classic or main implementation instrument. In quite a different way the use of regulations is also a topic in another current debate – the debate on de-regulation and de-legalisation.[2] There regulation is not so much an instrument of state policy, but a result of a growing, probably of a too extensively expanding state sector. In spite of that two-fold interest in regulation we know relatively little about the conditions under which and the objectives for which the instrument of regulation is generally used.[3] This paper therefore tries to offer some help in answering these questions. It encompasses a comparative evaluation of the use of regulations in two policy fields and in six European countries from 1973 to 1982. The policy fields are energy policy and manpower policy and the countries studied are France, Germany, Great Britain, Hungary, Italy and the Netherlands. An attempt is made to clarify the relationship between the conditions and the objectives which are characteristic of the instrument of regulation.

The comparative evaluation is based on extensive material collected within the context of the "Legal Implementation of Economic Policy" research project at the European University Institute in Florence. The material consists primarily of inventories, listing all energy policy and manpower policy measures in the above mentioned countries since 1973. The second, less important part of the underlying material consists of brief comparative studies each of which relates to a specific objective of energy and manpower policy, and which together provide a summary and initial evaluation of the inventories.

A comparative analysis, dealing with several countries generally encounters great difficulties.[4] Additional problems arose from the way the underlying data have been collected, as will be discussed later in more detail.[5] Therefore the following evaluation is intended to provide suggestions rather than real answers to the questions under discussion.

II. The Meaning of "Regulation"

A. The Characteristics of Regulation

At first glance it seems quite clear what is meant when we speak of "Regulation". In the discussion on de-regulation for example, the term is usually not defined more closely, but is simply assumed to be understood. A more careful examination however shows that the term can mean, and be taken to mean, quite different things.

[2] See W. Hoffmann-Riem, "Die Reform staatlicher Regulierung in den USA" (1984) 23 *Der Staat* at 17; R. Voigt ed., *Abschied vom Recht*, (1984, Stuttgart); H. Zacher, et al., *Verrechtlichung von Wirtschaft, Arbeit und sozialer Solidarität*, (1985, Stuttgart).
[3] Yet see the presentation by R. Mayntz, "Implementation von regulativer Politik", in: Mayntz supra note 1 at p. 50.
[4] On the difficulties of comparative implementation research see J. Feick, "Internationale Vergleichbarkeit staatlicher Interventionsprogramme – Konzeptionelle und methodische Probleme", in: Maintz supra note 1 at p. 197.
[5] See section III, below.

Regulation of the economy is often taken as a synonym for state activities with respect to the economy. Conversely, when de-regulation is demanded the objective is that of leaving this activity to private enterprises; the state is requested to give up its activities related to the economy. In that sense all economy activity of the state means regulation.[6] A somewhat more restricted meaning of the term regulation is used, if regulation and public enterprises are separated.[7] By this definition regulation is taken to mean state intervention into the economic conduct of private enterprises, and this contrasts with the use of public enterprises by the state itself to carry out economic activities.

Even with that restricted meaning regulation comprises quite different instruments, like commands and prohibitions, taxes, subsidies, information etc., instruments which vary greatly in character. It is therefore understandable, that in many cases the term regulation is used with an even more limited meaning. Regulation is then neither a synonym for activities of the state related to the economy nor a synonym for state intervention into the private economy, but merely one kind of instrument the state uses for the implementation of its economy policy. That is the sense in which the term regulation was employed by the inventories on which this paper is based. They classified the economic measures with respect to the following categories:[8]

- Unilateral regulation of private activity
- Taxation of private activity
- Consensual constraints
- Removal or relaxation of unilateral regulations
- Other public benefits
- Public sector management
- Information

Regulation in that sense means statutory or other rules laid down by the state to govern the economic conduct of private business.[9] The standards laid down may either prohibit certain activities of private enterprises or prescribe a certain course of action. Most of the measures categorized as regulations in the inventories contain such standards of conduct.

---

[6] Cf. E. Gellhorn and R. Pierce, *Regulated Industries*, (1982, New York) at p. 7; J. Müller and I. Vogelsang, *Staatliche Regulierung*, (1979, Baden-Baden) at p. 341.

[7] See S. Cassese, "Public Enterprises as Instrument and Object of Economic Policy", below, at pp. 237–242.

[8] Other categories of instruments are given by F. Kaufmann and B. Rosewitz, "Typisierung und Klassifikation politischer Maßnahmen", in: Mayntz *supra* note 1 at p. 37.

[9] See J. Hucke and E. Bohne, "Bürokratische Reaktionsmuster bei regulativer Politik", in: Wollmann ed., *Politik im Dickicht der Bürokratie*, (1979, Stuttgart) 183 f.; Klaes, et al., *Regulative Politik und politisch-administrative Kultur*, (1982, Frankfurt) 16; R. Mayntz *supra* note 3 at p. 51; R. Stewart, "Regulation Innovation and Administrative law: A Conceptual Framework", (1981) 69 *California Law Review* at p. 1264; W. Jann, *Kategorien der Policy-Forschung*, (1981, Wiesbaden) at p. 62.

The standards established by regulations can vary greatly in type. An important distinction must be made with respect to how the standards are enforced. On the one hand public authorities may be entrusted with the implementation of the rules, as is typical in the sphere of public law. On the other hand the implementation of the rules may be left to private persons who are given the legal rights to enforce the regulation through the courts. This is typical of the private law approach.[10]

From the standpoint of state economic policy, public law regulations are perhaps the more obvious choice. The economic conduct desired by the state is made obligatory, or, more often, undesirable economic conduct is forbidden. If those concerned do not conform, the administrative bodies impose negative sanctions. They may make use of such means as administrative compulsion and execution, or seek to impose a legal penalty or fine etc. Not infrequently the economic activity is made subject to a licence, i.e. before it can be exercised it must be authorized. This permits an a priori control by the state in relation to compliance with regulations.[11]

Influencing economic behaviour by public law regulation is often accomplished in several steps. The first step consists of a substantive rule which is rather vague. In addition administrative bodies are supplied with the appropriate powers to give concrete form to the substantive rule, whether in the context of a specific case or for all the relevant cases. This may go so far that the first step of regulation essentially consists of an authorization. Thus, in various countries the government or a minister is authorized to take whatever measures necessary in the case of an oil shortage. The second step consists of the general or particular directives issued by the government through the responsible minister, which contain the actual regulation.

In cases where the first step contains no more than a broad authorization one may doubt whether this step can still be qualified as a regulation. Is it not more to the point to classify this step as "Public sector management", provided that public sector management means, in accordance with the inventories, the use not only of public enterprises for the implementation of economic policy, but also the use of administrative agencies? In spite of that, the inventories have generally classified these authorisations as regulations. And this seems to be reasonable: on the one hand they are closely related to the regulatory measures originating in these authorisations, and in many cases the authorizations provide at least some standards, even thought they may be extremely vague. On the other hand, one has to concede that the boundary line between regulations and the alternative instrument of public sector management is often flexible at that point.

A similar effect often arises from those standards which are intended to control not only private companies but also, and perhaps primarily, public enterprises. As a result the precise boundary between regulations and public sector management becomes more blurred, particularly since in many cases it is not possible to tell from the measures the extent to which they also in fact concern public enterprises.

[10] See H. Jarass, *Wirtschaftsverwaltungsrecht,* (2nd ed. 1984, Frankfurt) at p. 30.
[11] For further discussion see Jarass *supra* note 10 at p. 167.

Rules and standards designed to govern conduct under private law are characterised by the fact that their enforcement is left to private persons, to whom the law gives the legal right to have these rules enforced by the courts. An example of this is the measure giving the employee the legal right to paid leave for training in order to improve his professional mobility. Whether use is made of this right depends in each case on the employee. If he does not make use of it, or if he is reluctant to go to court in order to enforce his right, professional mobility is not promoted.[12]

Private enforcement of regulations can also be achieved through public law regulations. In these cases the private persons have the right to sue the administration if it does not enforce a public law standard. The implementation of environmental policy in the United States and in Germany relies heavily on this approach,[13] and it should not be confused with private law regulations and their "enforcement".

While in the cases considered so far the instrument of regulation serves the purpose of prescribing the economic conduct of individuals in certain ways, this instrument can also be used to define spheres of influence, respectively to create rights of influence. This means that the solution of certain disputes is left to the private participants. The state refrains from providing substantive standards for the conflicts in that way. It merely determines the method of conflict resolution.[14] The classic example is the introduction by the state of workers' co-determination in certain enterprises. In doing this the state merely prescribes the spheres of influence of the owners and workers within an enterprise. Other forms of procedural regulations are found in the cases of genuine economic self government,[15] where the state provides an institution, as for example the professional (public law) chambers, where the liberal professions can handle their own affairs.

Such measures, which might be described as "procedural",[16] occur comparatively rarely in the inventories. In the area of energy policy they play practically no role at all. In the area of manpower policy their significance is somewhat greater. The relative absence of procedural regulations (in that sense) may be related to the fundamental design of the inventories which assumes that the instruments of economic policy are oriented towards certain substantive objectives. This is not the case with procedural regulations which leave the substantive goals flexible. On the other hand, it must be noted that in most cases procedural regulations are combined with substantive regulations which prescribe desired conduct. The

---

[12] R. Stewart, *Regulation and the Crisis of Legalization in the United State*, EUI-Paper (1985, Florence) at p. 7 seems to deny the regulatory character of private law rules.
[13] S. H. Jarass, "Der Rechtsschutz Dritter bei der Genehmigung von Anlagen", (1983) NJW at p. 2844; H. Jarass, "Effektivierung des Umweltschutzes gegenüber bestehenden Anlagen", (1985) DVBl at pp. 193 and 195.
[14] See C. Offe, *Berufsbildungsreform*, (1975, Frankfurt) at 85; A. Windhoff-Héritier, *Politikimplementation*, (1980, Königstein) at p. 44.
[15] See Jarass *supra* note 10 at p. 96.
[16] Cf. Mayntz *supra* note 3 at p. 52; Windhoff-Héritier *supra* note 14 at pp. 42 and 44, speaks of "entscheidungsprozedurale Programme" (decision procedural programmes).

statutes establishing professional associations for example, provide some substantive standards for the decisions of the associations. In addition the procedural regulations can be understood as modes of implementation of the substantive regulations as is exemplified by the German "Erdölbevorratungsverband", an independent public law corporation consisting of the oil product importers and producers, which is obliged to maintain a certain level of oil reserves.[17]

In defining regulations, the question generally arises whether only the content is relevant or whether the form should also be taken into account. The typical *content* of a regulation, as already discussed, consists in prohibiting or prescribing certain activity, whereas its typical *form* is that of a statute or a rule. There is often a tendency to speak of regulations if a statute or a rule is the subject of interest. In its most extreme form this tendency regards every statute or rule as a regulation irrespective of whether it establishes substantive standards of conduct, creates possibilities for exercising influence, concerns internal administrative structures, distributes subsidies etc. Such a definition cannot be considered appropriate in our context, since it would invalidate the classification of instruments which is the basis of the research project. Every instrument can use the form of a statute. Even if one has to concede that statutes are especially important in the case of regulations, other/every instrument may appear in the form of a statute.

B. Related Instruments

The instruments used by the state to implement economic policy can be classified according to the criteria of whether or not they mean a loss or a gain for the addressees, i.e. whether they are cost-increasing or cost-reducing.[18] Accordingly, the inventories, which form the basis of the study, make a distinction between "Unilateral regulation of private activity" and "Removal or relaxation of unilateral regulation". This distinction appears to be important, even though it is rarely used in the literature relating to regulations. Yet, assigning certain measures to one of the two categories can become quite difficult. For example, it is quite conceivable that at the same time a regulation may either directly or indirectly intensify obligations for some people and reduce obligations for others. Furthermore the introduction of a regulation which is regarded as burdensome in itself may have a liberalising effect because it replaces an even more burdensome regulation, a fact which can be easily overlooked in considering a specific measure. Conversely, the lifting of a burdensome rule is not necessarily favourable in effect for those concerned. If as a result a more general and less favourable regulation comes into effect, the opposite is the case. It is therefore problematic to assign a measure to the category "Unilateral regulations" or to "Removal or relaxation of unilateral regulations". This difficulty may perhaps explain why cases of the latter category are found only rarely in the inventories and why their occurrence is limited to a

---

[17] See §§ 2 ff. Erdölbevorratungsgesetz v. 25. 7. 1978 (BGBl I S. 1073) and Jarass *supra* note 10 at p. 276.
[18] See T. Daintith, Law as Policy Instrument: A Comparative Perspective, EUI-Paper (1985, Florence) at p. 41.

few countries.[19] To avoid these problems the two categories have been combined for the purpose of this paper.[20]

The second category of instruments which shows similarities with the instrument of regulation is the "Taxation of private activity", i.e. the imposition of taxes designed to control economic activity. Therefore we also have to ask whether this category should not be linked with "Regulation". "Taxation", like regulations, imposes statutory obligations on those subject to them. To combine the two categories would indeed be justified if the category of "Regulation" is defined formally, since in that case the nature of taxation as a unilaterally imposed regulation would be the conclusive factor. In substance however a tax, as far as its influence on economic behaviour is concerned, works quite differently from regulations.[21] Regulations result in binding obligations which cannot be influenced by those subject to them, while a tax only means a financial burden if those towards whom it is directed do not conform to the behaviour required by the state. Take the example of an embargo on the import of certain goods compared with the imposition of a duty on imports. The former prevents the import, the latter merely increases the price of the goods. The duty is only a factor in the economic calculation, whereas an embargo on imports excludes any further economic considerations. One has to concede that this difference is on the one hand reduced the larger the duty is; and on the other hand a regulation may allow for some degree of calculation, if there is a good chance that infringements of it will not be prosecuted. In specific cases every difference between the two may disappear: if we have a totally binding regulation which is only sanctioned by a very limited administrative fine then the measure is more a (control) tax than a regulation in the technical sense; while a prohibitive tax on the other hand functions like a regulation. But in the typical case the difference remains and because of its analytical value should not be overlooked.[22]

In the following comparative evaluation it is not very important whether we include taxation with regulation or not, since the inventories list very few taxation measures.[23] Therefore, the relationships described below would be practically the same whether or not we include tax measures.

[19] In the energy policy sector this instrument is used mainly by Great Britain, in the manpower policy area mainly by Italy and the Netherlands.

[20] In a different context the answer can be different; see D. v. Stebut, Subsidies as an Instrument of Economic Policy, EUI-Paper (1985, Florence) at p. 8.

[21] See Jarass *supra* note 10 at 193. Correspondingly subsidies and taxes are often put into a single category; see S. Breyer, "Analyzing Regulatory Failure: Mismatches, Less Restrictive Alternatives, and Reform"; in: (1978/79) 92 *Harvard Law Review* 581; R. Mayntz, *Soziologie der öffentlichen Verwaltung*, (1978, Heidelberg) 58; F. Scharpf, "Theorie der Politikverflechtung", in: F. Scharpf et al., *Politikverflechtung*, (1976, Frankfurt) at p. 15; see also Mayntz *supra* note 3 at p. 52. The opposite view is taken by T. Daintith *supra* note 17 at p. 43.

[22] The difference between taxes and regulations relates to the different implementation process; the existence of a bargaining process before the enactment of a regulation is therefore no counter argument.

[23] With all objectives and countries there are less than two measures. Only for one objective in Great Britain are more tax measures used.

Problems of definition also arise with respect to the instrument of "Consensual constraints", though it may appear that there are no similarities between it and the instrument of regulation. Yet at least those consensual constraints, which are of a general nature, i.e. those that concern a great number of persons, can be functionally equivalent to regulations. Take the example of self-restraint agreements in the area of environmental policy which are used as substitutes for equivalent regulations.[24]

Yet there are important differences. Most obvious are the different ways of enforcing a consensual constraint on the one hand, and a regulation on the other. A consensual constraint is in many cases a gentlemen's agreement, as is in the case of the Century Treaty by which the German electric utilities industry has agreed to use coal until the end of the century. And even if the consensual constraint consists of a binding agreement the adherence to the agreement is practically never enforced by administrative or judicial execution. Whether binding or not, consensual constraints are observed because otherwise the state could withdraw an advantage or promise given to the private partners. For this reason consensual constraints are probably more similar to subsidies or control taxes, which are similarly implemented by incentives and not by force.

III. Basis of Comparative Evaluation

The inventories which form the basis for this paper list all energy policy and manpower policy measures in France, Germany, Great Britain, Hungary, Italy and the Netherlands since 1973 in a standardised form, each measure being classified with respect to objective, type and form. The data contained in the inventories are extraordinarily varied and stimulating, particularly since in each case an effort is made to give a complete picture. Yet the evaluation of this data for the purpose of this paper presented considerable difficulties. In particular, the relative importance to be attached to the individual measures presented a problem. For example, what is the relative weight of an amendment to a law with potentially only minimal consequences and the enactment of the complete law; what importance does a subsidy have compared with the setting up of a public enterprise, etc.? In the following discussion all the measures listed in the inventories are granted equal weight,[25] although it should not be forgotten that they vary greatly in terms of their practical importance. For these and other reasons the figures given below provide no more than rough points of reference and it is not suggested that they meet the standards of empirical social science.[26]

To avoid excessive distortions, relationships between the factors under consideration which include less than six measures have been omitted. This was of

---

[24] S. H. Jarass *supra* note 10 at p. 154.

[25] Where several objectives have been assigned to a measure, corresponding fractions resulted. A similar procedure has been used with the categories differentiating measures.

[26] The wide variations in subsidy classification and the lack of complete uniformity of temporal scope (some measures dating from before 1973 being included) give rise to further reservations.

practical importance only for relationships which concern one single country. Finally the figures covering all the countries do not include the figures for Hungary. The Hungarian economic system differs too greatly from the systems in the other countries to permit us to collate the figures together.

A further problem was that the material has not been assembled with a view to answering the specific questions examined in this contribution. As a consequence a number of measures had to be redefined or completely excluded.[27] Taking all these aspects into consideration it should be borne in mind that the following observations are to be understood as suggestions for further studies rather than as specific results.

The instrument of regulation may be used because this instrument appears to be particularly efficient in given circumstances. Conversely, it may not be used because of its specific weaknesses as an instrument. In both cases, the reason is related to the nature of regulations. On the other hand, regulations may not be used because another type of instrument is particularly efficient. Or the instrument of regulation may be chosen because the other instruments are inefficient in the given circumstances. In these cases, the explanation lies in the nature of the alternative instruments. Therefore the nature of instruments other than regulations, in particular subsidies (direct as well as indirect), cannot be completely disregarded, despite the fact that this study is limited to regulations. Nevertheless only cursory attention will be given to those other instruments, since specific studies on them are included in this volume.

IV. Influence Exerted by the Type of Objectives

A. Categorisation of Objectives

The use of the different instruments of economic policy is intended to achieve certain objectives. One may therefore ask whether the instrument of regulations occurs more often in context with certain objectives or types of objectives than with others. Since the objectives regularly involve the solving of certain problems, the formulation of the question aims at the same time at relating the instrument use to the functional or political problems which are addressed by the instruments.

In the following pages the categories of objectives used by the inventories which form the basis of this paper are employed. With respect to energy policy, the different measures have been assigned to three groups of objectives:

(1) Short-term responses to disturbances in energy supply
   - Restriction of consumption
   - Preservation of the pattern and level of supply
   - Stabilization of prices and profits in energy markets
(2) Alteration of the structure of energy demand
   - Promotion of economy in energy use
   - Alteration of energy consumption patterns

---

[27] Excluded have been mainly the many measures taken by private organizations in the area of manpower policy.

(3) Alteration of the structure of energy supply
   - Development of nuclear energy supplies
   - Development of other domestic energy resources
   - Diversification of supplies of imported energy

For manpower policy measures, the following classification of objectives has been used:

(1) Job creation
   - In general
   - In specific territorial areas
   - In specific industrial sectors
(2) Job maintenance
   - In general
   - In specific territorial areas
   - In specific industrial sectors
(3) Manpower adjustment
   - Access of potential workers to the labour market
   - Movement between jobs
   - Exit from the labour market

B. Temporal Scope

In the field of energy policy the influence of the type of objective is particularly pronounced if one compares the differences between the first group of objectives, i.e. "Short-term responses to disturbances in energy supply", and the two other groups "Alteration of the structure of energy demand" and "Alteration of the structure of energy supply". While at least two thirds of the measures are classified as regulations in the first group of objectives, the corresponding proportions in the other groups are much lower.[28] Even when the countries are individually considered, this remains the case. The proportion of regulatory measures in the group of "Short-term responses" is without exception clearly higher than in the group dealing with the alteration of energy demand and energy supply.[29] Only in Hungary is the difference, although present, less marked.

The cause of these differences could possibly be traced to the fact that the objectives of the first group deal with the provisional handling of a sudden shortage of goods, i.e. the functioning of a rationing system. Such a massive intervention in the functioning of the market can probably best be achieved by means of direct regulation. This explanation is however contradicted by the fact that short-term responses to disturbances of energy supply are also achieved

---

[28] The proportion of two thirds for the objective "Stabilization of prices and profits" is probably too low, since there is some doubt whether the categorization in the inventories as non-regulatory is always correct. If we take that into account the difference described is even bigger.

[29] In the Netherlands the number of measures for the objective "Development of other domestic energy resources" is higher than for the objective "Stabilization of prices and profits".

by much less dramatic measures than by full rationing, as for example by car-free weekends or lighting restrictions.

Probably of more importance is therefore the fact that all objectives of the first group are short-term, while the "Alteration of the demand structure" like the group "Alteration of the supply structure" consists of rather long-term objectives. In the first group the economic policy has to deal with direct reaction to a sudden crisis in the energy supply, whereas the objectives of the two other groups consist of long-term aims relating to structural changes in energy supply and energy demand. To put it in more concrete terms: regulatory measures like car-free weekends or lighting restrictions, which are intended to reduce energy consumption in the short-run, are replaced by other measures, often of a non-regulatory character, as for example by subsidies or tax reductions, if long-term restrictions of energy consumption are intended.

There are substantive reasons to explain why the instrument of regulation is much more frequently used with short-term objectives than with long-term objectives. When rapid effect is desired, the instrument of regulation may well be superior in most cases to the other instruments with the possible exception of unconditional payments as used in disaster situations. Regulations take effect immediately on the enactment and publication of the related laws while the main alternative, i.e. the granting of (real) subsidies by which the behaviour of private persons is to be changed, depends for its effect on attracting the co-operation of those concerned, and this generally takes time.[30] Furthermore subsidies have to be applied for and granted. With long-term objectives on the other hand, time is less important. Therefore in such cases it is easier to do without regulations with their specific disadvantages.[31]

Another factor which may have furthered the use of regulations instead of other measures in the case of short-term reactions to energy disturbances was probably the crisis situation produced by the sudden and enormous rise in the price of oil. In such a situation the government is expected to react actively and strongly. Since the public often believes that regulations are more effective than other instruments like subsidies, consensual constraints etc., regulations have at least a symbolic advantage. One could suggest that they have a greater impact on public attention as compared to other instruments.

On the whole the temporal scope of the objectives probably has considerable influence on the choice of instruments. But it should be borne in mind that it is a question of the temporal scope of the objectives and not of the measures. Whether the measures themselves have in any sense a time limit is unimportant in this connection.

---

[30] See, J. Hucke, "Implementation von Finanzhilfeprogrammen in: Mayntz *supra* note 1 at p. 89; F. Scharpf, "Interessenlage der Adressaten und Spielräume der Implementation bei Anreizprogrammen", in: Mayntz *supra* note 1 at p. 106.

[31] Concerning specific implementation problems, see R. Mayntz, in: *Implementation politischer Programme I*, (1981, Königstein) at p. 244.

C. Number of Persons Directly Affected

In the field of energy policy there is a second point which should be noted. In order to achieve the objective of the "Development of nuclear energy supplies" regulations are only rarely used. There is a marked difference between the the the use of regulation for this objective and how it is employed in the attainment of other energy-related objectives. This also applies for the most part in the individual countries, although the difference is sometimes less pronounced.[32] An explanation for this could be that the development of the use of nuclear energy is promoted mainly by public enterprises, and not by private companies. But this is not true for all the countries under consideration.[33]

In all the countries studied the development of nuclear energy is in the hands of a few companies, whether public or private.[34] Consequently the implementation of the objective "Development of nuclear energy supplies" only directly affects a small number of persons. Their number is clearly smaller than the number of persons directly affected by the other objectives of energy policy. This supports the argument that objectives of economic policy whose implementation affect relatively few persons are more often pursued using instruments other than regulations. The decisive point here is that the actual number is small. It is of no significance whether legal measures of general or individual application are used.[35] Furthermore it is a question of those *directly* concerned, i.e. persons whose conduct is to be directly modified by state action.[36]

The tendency to prefer other instruments to regulations when it is a question of influencing the conduct of a few persons is understandable. The small number of those involved permits agreements and informal contacts between the government and those concerned. Thus instruments other than regulations can be effectively employed. Conversely the instrument of regulation is probably more efficient than agreements and informal influence when in the pursuit of a political objective it is necessary to influence the conduct of a relatively large number of persons, at least if the behaviour to be regulated is homogeneous.[37]

One objection to this explanation might be that state nuclear policy must be active on two different levels. On the one hand there are technological and economic difficulties, which have to be overcome. On the other hand there are, at least in some countries, problems with the public opinion: nuclear energy in these countries has to be defended against considerable public resistance, which necessitates the adoption of appropriate measures to cope with this resistance. The

---

[32] In two countries another objective shows a slightly lower proportion of regulations.

[33] Above all in Germany and the Netherlands private companies play an important role.

[34] For the situation in Germany see H. Jarass, "Formen staatlicher Einwirkung auf die Energiewirtschaft", (1978) 17 *Der Staat* at p. 514.

[35] The classification of measures according to their scope thus permits no firm conclusions concerning this question.

[36] In general also Mayntz *supra* note 3 at p. 53.

[37] Interestingly regulations seem to work less efficiently the more diverse the proscribed behaviour is; see P. Sabatier and D. Mazmanian, "The Implementation of Public Policy: A Framework of Analysis", in: Sabatier and Mazmanian *supra* note 1 at p. 8.

statutes in Germany and Italy which provide the opportunity for the public to participate in the decisions on the location of nuclear energy plants are an example for that. Yet these measures are addressed to a great number of persons. But the basic argument still holds. Remarkably, the German and Italian measures which deal with public resistance are regulations. And the low over-all percentage of regulations used for the development of energy supply is simply the consequence of the fact that most of the reported measures which are adopted to further this objective try to overcome the technological and economic problems (or other problems where the energy suppliers are the target group) and not the public opinion problem.

Indications that the number of those directly concerned by a certain policy is influential in policy choice can also be found in the field of manpower policy. Here the two groups of objectives "Job creation" and "Job maintenance" are each divided into three sub-groups, the first of which covers the objective pursued in a general manner,while the second and third sub-groups relate to the objectives pursued in particular territorial areas or certain sectors of the industry. Measures in the first sub-group probably affect in each case larger numbers of persons than measures in the territorial or sectoral sub-groups. And in fact, the instrument of regulation is in both cases more frequently used with the first sub-group than with the other two sub-groups. This tendency is particularly marked in the group "Job maintenance", where in the first sub-group over half of the measures are regulations, whereas in the two other sub-groups regulations make up less than a quarter of the measures.[38]

D. Supply and Demand

In the field of energy policy the instrument of regulation is also used to a differing extent in the two groups consisting of long-term objectives. With respect to the "Alteration of the structure of energy demand", nearly half of the measures are regulations. For the "Alteration of the structure of energy supply" the figure is however slightly under 25 per cent. The trend is roughly the same in all the countries.[39] Regulations thus appear to be called on to a greater extent to control demand rather than to control supply.

The reason for this relationship is not clear. Presumably the factor, already mentioned, of the number of persons directly concerned plays a role here too, since the number of energy suppliers and thus of persons directly affected by control of supply is probably considerably smaller than the number of consumers and thus of those affected by control of demand. An explanation for the difference might however also be found in the factor of innovative activities, a factor to which we shall return later.[40]

---

[38] In one country the figures in the group "Job creation" are the same.
[39] In two countries the situation is the reverse.
[40] See below IV F.

E. Motivation of Those Affected

Among all the objectives of energy policy, as well as of manpower policy, the energy objective "Restriction of consumption" shows the highest proportion of regulations. This is also true for the individual countries; this objective always shows the highest or second highest proportion of regulations. The means used to achieve it include speed limits, heating restrictions, a ban on display lighting, encouragement of car pooling, no-driving weekends etc. With most of these measures it can be assumed that those affected by the implementation of the measures are completely disinterested. Therefore does the lack of motivation on the part of those affected tend to increase the necessity to employ the instrument of regulation, as is assumed in the literature?[41] This hypothesis appears to be somewhat exaggerated, since in particular the alternative instrument of subsidies can create motivation and therefore may well be used where there is a lack of motivation. On the other hand, a marked motivation against the measure is difficult to overcome by the instrument of subsidy and therefore to this extent recourse must be made to regulations.

On the basis of our data what can we say in answer to this question? With respect to the short-term objective "Restriction of consumption", strong objection on the part of those affected is quite plausible, while similar objections are less probable with respect to the objective with the next-highest proportion of regulations, i.e. short-term "Preservation of the pattern and level of supply". In the individual countries this objective also shows the second-highest, or even the highest, proportion of regulations. This argues against the idea that strong objection by those affected encourages the use of the instrument of regulation. With the other objectives, it is rather difficult to determine whether those affected show strong objection to the particular policy or not. Taking all these aspects into consideration, on the basis of our data it is not possible to draw a definite conclusion concerning this factor.

F. Innovation and Commitment

In the field of manpower policy, the instrument of regulations is much less frequently used in the first group of objectives dealing with "Job creation" than in the other groups of objectives "Job maintenance" and "Manpower adjustment". For the two latter groups the proportion of regulatory measures is about one-third, while the proportion of regulations in the "Job creation" group is extremely low. In the individual countries, the objectives of "Job creation" are also pursued by measures with the lowest proportion of regulations.

This raises the question of the way in which the "Job creation" group differs from the two others. New jobs can only be created by innovative, committed and independent activities on the part of the economic actors. Consequently it is a question of motivating these persons to take such innovative action. In contrast, in

---

[41] See R. Mayntz, "The Conditions of Effective Public Policy", (1983) 11/2 *Policy and Politics* at 128; Windhoff-Héritier *supra* note 14 at p. 51 even requires conformity between the objectives of both the state and those affected.

the "Job maintenance" and the "Manpower adjustment" groups the conduct of those affected needs to be influenced only to a limited extent and in a compara- tively clearly describable way: the objectives of job maintenance involve the preservation of existing conditions – i.e. the prevention of change of conduct and the objectives of manpower adjustment involve bringing about rather limited changes in conduct. The influence exercised by the state can therefore be termed incremental.[42]

The very limited use made of the instrument of regulations in the area of "Job creation", and thus in an area where it is a matter of promoting innovative activities, is understandable. Such action cannot be produced by order. The state can only stimulate it, induce it by incentives or carry out the activity by itself through public enterprises.[43] On the other hand, it is much more possible to prevent changes of conduct by regulatory prohibitions, or to prescribe specific aspects of conduct by instructions. Taken together there is much to support the argument that innovative, committed behaviour can only be achieved by incen- tives, especially by subsidies, or by public enterprises, while regulations are more efficient with incremental changes and the prevention of change.[44] A certain exception is possible if the objective can be described precisely, as for example by emission standards. In that case regulations can be used to enhance innovative behaviour as well. But such precise objectives cannot comprise a pattern of economic behaviour in its totality; they are necessarily restricted to certain aspects. We may therefore assume that the instrument of regulation is more suitable if the objective is to *constrain* private behaviour rather than to *shape* it, a difference which is the basis of the distinction between "Wirtschaftsaufsicht" and "Wirtschaftslenkung".[45]

Further confirmation of the assumption that innovative behaviour is less effectively achieved by regulation is obtained if we compare within energy policy the objectives of "Alteration of energy supply structure" with the other objective groups "Short-term responses to supply disturbances" and "Alteration of energy demand structure". Changing the structure of energy supply probably requires a higher degree of active and positive behaviour on the part of those affected than coping with short-term disturbances of energy supply and changing the structure of energy demand. Therefore, it is quite interesting that the measures to alter the energy supply show a relatively low proportion of regulations, while in the two

[42] On the difference between innovative and incremental economic actions, see Windhoff-Héritier *supra* note 14 at p. 64.

[43] S. Cassese *supra* note 7 at p. 3.

[44] Further discussion in Stewart *supra* note 9 at p. 1288; Mayntz *supra* note 41 at p. 138; also K. Lange, "Normvollzug und Vernormung", in: *Jahrbuch für Rechtssoziologie und Rechtstheorie VII*, (1980, Stuttgart) 275; R. Bender, "Einige Vorschläge zur Implemen- tierung von Verfahrensgesetzen", in: *Jahrbuch für Rechtssoziologie und Rechtstheorie VII*, (1980, Köln) at p. 293 f.

[45] See P. Badura, "Wirtschaftsverwaltungsrecht", in: v. Münch (ed.), *Besonderes Verwal- tungsrecht*, (7. Aufl. 1985) at p. 292; Jarass *supra* note 10 at p. 107; E. Steindorff, *Einführung in das Wirtschaftsrecht der Bundesrepublik Deutschland*, (1977, Darmstadt) at p. 100.

other groups of objectives dealing with "Short-term responses to disturbances of energy supply" and the "Alteration of energy demand" considerably higher proportions are to be found. The difference specifically between the alteration of energy supply and the short-term responses may well be due to the different temporal scope of the objectives.[46] But the difference between the two long-term objective groups "Alteration of the structure of energy supply" on the one hand, and "Alteration of the structure of energy demand" on the other hand, continues to argue in favour of the relationship between non-regulation and innovative activities, particularly since this difference applies to each individual country too.[47]

G. Preservation and Change

Related to the above-mentioned factor there is another aspect, which deals with the question whether the main purpose of a measure is to preserve established structures and modes of conducts or to change them. This aspect is not the same as the factor of innovative behaviour. Innovative behaviour requires change in any case, but not every change is innovative. In the field of manpower policy, the aim of preservation is most characteristic of the objectives of "Job maintenance". The objectives of "Job creation" mean the opposite of preservation, while the objectives "Manpower adjustment" can be classified rather as intermediate cases. The relative proportion of measures classified as regulations is in conformity with this. Thus where the purpose of preservation is dominant the instrument of regulation appears to be used more often than where the purpose of change is in the foreground. This difference however exists mainly between the "Job creation" group on the one hand and the "Job maintenance" and "Manpower adjustment" groups on the other hand. Accordingly the relationship between the two latter groups of objectives is partially reversed in the individual countries. This would seem to indicate that the factor of innovating activities, which makes up for the essential difference between the "Job creation" group on the one hand and "Job maintenance" and "Manpower adjustment" groups on the other hand,[48] is more important than the change/preservation factor.

In the field of energy policy there are also some indications that policies of change mainly use instruments other than regulations. For the objectives dealing with the alteration of energy demand structure or energy supply structure, which by definiton involve aiming at change, far fewer regulations are employed than is the case for the short-term objectives "Preservation of the pattern and level of supply" and "Stabilization of prices and profits in energy markets", which are concerned with preservation. But the difference may well be due to the differing temporal scope of the measures, since the objective "Restriction of consumption" which is designed to bring about short-term changes, shows as great a proportion of regulations as do the other above-mentioned short-term objectives whose main characteristic is stability.

[46] See above IV. B.
[47] With the exception of the Netherlands.
[48] See above IV. F.

V. Influence of Policy Fields

A. Overall Difference

Most people would agree that energy policy and manpower policy are quite different fields of economic policy. So we should ask what kind of use is made of the instrument of regulation in these two areas.[49] The difference is striking, i.e. half of the energy policy measures are classified as regulations, but less than a quarter of the manpower policy measures.

How can this difference be explained? Is it due to the particular characteristics of the two areas, or to the different attitudes of those involved in the two areas, or to different structures of administrative organization and procedure? It appears to be quite difficult to answer this question. Closer analysis of the difference shows however that it cannot be traced to the general dissimilarities between energy policy and manpower policy. The reason has more probably to do with the above-mentioned factors influencing the use of regulatory or non-regulatory measures, for these factors have a different importance in each of the two policy areas. Thus in the energy policy field the first group of objectives, which comprises short-term measures, shows an unusually high percentage of regulations.[50] This is a result of the fact that since 1973 energy policy has had to cope with two sudden severe shortages. Manpower policy has not been confronted with comparable problems. Certainly unemployment became a more and more severe problem in the 70s; but the problem did not develop within a couple of weeks as was the case with the oil prices. If we exclude the short-term measures from energy policy, the proportion of regulations in that policy comes closer to that in the field of manpower policy. With respect to the choice of instruments in energy policy and manpower policy they have much more in common than might at first be thought, provided we exclude the sudden energy shortages which occurred in the 1970s.

The remaining difference can be explained by the fact that in the manpower policy field innovative and positive activities are relatively more important than in the energy policy area. While in manpower policy such activities are without doubt essential for the three objectives of "Job creation", in the energy policy area this is clearly the case for only one of the objectives (Development of nuclear energy supplies). The increase in the importance of innovative activities however leads to a reduction of the proportion of regulations, as already shown above.[51]

B. Type of Regulation

Even if the proportion of regulations is similar in the area of energy policy and manpower policy, the kind of regulations used may be different. And indeed with

---

[49] Thus A. de Laubadère, *Droit public économique*, (3rd ed. 1978, Paris) at p. 109, considers that in the economic policy area the instrument of imperative regulation plays a smaller role than in other areas.

[50] See above IV. B.

[51] See above IV. F.

respect to that question we find important deviations; these differences will be examined below.[52]

The first factor which differentiates between the two areas is the kind of enforcement used. There are basically three possibilities of enforcement: administrative, penal and private. Administrative enforcement is enforcement by administrative agencies using the different means of administrative execution like administrative penalities or substitute performance (to be paid by the addressee). Penal enforcement is enforcement by a public prosecutor and the courts. The third alternative leaves the "enforcement" to private persons who have the right to sue others for not obeying the regulations. The first two alternatives can be characterized as public enforcement and the third as private enforcement, since administrative and penal enforcement is characteristic of public law regulations, whereas private "enforcement" is characteristic of private law regulations.[53] To avoid misunderstandings it should be added that the major difference between the two kinds of enforcement is not so much the mobilization point, i.e. *who* activates the enforcement process. As mentioned above public law enforcement can be activated by private persons too if they have the right to sue the administration for not enforcing a regulation.[54] The major difference between public law and private law enforcement is whether a public entity like an administrative agency or a public prosecutor is involved or not.

If we ask what role public and private enforcement plays in the two fields of energy policy and manpower policy we find significant differences. While in the former the enforcement is dominated by administrative and penal means, in the latter the corresponding proportion is much lower. The enforcement of energy policy regulations thus takes place almost exclusively through public law, while in manpower policy private law and public law are represented in approximately equal proportions. With respect to the individual countries the difference is especially significant in Germany and Great Britain, but it is also to be found in the other countries. Only in France is there no great difference between the two policy fields.

A further difference between the two fields of energy and manpower policy can be found with respect to the relative importance of the parliament on the one hand and the government or a minister on the other hand. In the energy policy field, barely one quarter of the regulatory measures originate from parliament whereas in the manpower policy area over half of all regulations are enacted by parliament. The difference is also reflected in the tendencies in each individual country. These findings are not surprising considering the above-mentioned difference. Regulations enforced by administrative or penal sanctions, i.e. public law regulations, are enacted by parliament, but in many cases also by the government or an individual minister, whereas private law regulations are nearly always enacted by parliament.

A similar tendency is shown by the fact that the granting of powers is much more common with energy policy regulations than in the case of manpower policy

---

[52] See above VI. B.
[53] See above II. B.
[54] See above p. 79.

regulations. A considerable proportion of the measures of energy policy gives powers to central government or other public bodies, while in manpower policy such cases can scarcely be found. This is in line with the fact that, as pointed out, government and ministers are more active in energy policy, while in manpower policy parliament has a bigger role. Parliament needs no authorisations whereas government and ministers often do.

VI. Other Factors

A. Influence of National Differences

One factor which should have considerable importance for the choice between regulations and other instruments is the difference among the individual countries. The traditions and administrative structures characteristic of the respective states could easily explain different uses of instruments.[55] The deviations are however rather limited compared with other differences. Only Hungary proves to be something of an exception to the rule and, as might be expected, has by far the greatest proportion of regulations: over half of all measures are regulations. Conversely, Germany is the country with the smallest proportion of regulations, about half as many as Hungary. The difference between Germany and the other countries, where the percentages of regulations remain relatively close together, is however not great. The difference might even be due to specific technical reasons such as the structure of the inventories, which included a large number of subsidies for Germany. This in turn led to a reduction in the German proportion of regulations.

Taken as a whole, the differences between the various countries are surprisingly slight and less marked than is the case with the factors discussed above relating to the type of objectives. Correspondingly, the discussion of the influence of objectives showed that the characteristics specific to individual countries play a minor role in the choice of instruments: the general differences are nearly always found in the individual countries too. Only Hungary has a special position, although the difference is less marked than might have been expected.[56] As will be shown below, differences specific to individual countries are not related to the choice of instruments, but rather to the legal nature of the measures respective to the kind of regulation.[57]

Moreover caution must be exercised in interpreting the figures for individual countries. Because of the fairly small number of measures, errors are more quickly magnified in this context. This is also relevant to the problem mentioned above of

[55] See D. Ashford, *Comparing Public Policies – New Concepts and Methods*, (1978, London) p. 2; R. Mayntz, "Political Intentions and Legal Measures: The Determinants of Policy Decisions" above, at pp. 119–149.

[56] Besides that the proportion of regulations in Hungary may be a bit oversized, because in that country measures may be classified as regulations which are in other countries classified as public sector management.

[57] See below VI. B.

providing and interpreting the basic inventories. In addition the proportion of regulations in the individual countries varies greatly according the whether we consider either energy policy or manpower policy. Particularly significant is the difference in the case of Great Britain, which is one of the countries most in favour of regulations in energy policy, while the opposite seems to be the case as far as manpower policy is concerned. Apart from Hungary, it is difficult to identify those countries which prefer regulation in general.

B. Legal Nature of Measures

The material found in the inventories permits another quite different level of comparison, since it relates each measure not only to objectives and categories of instruments, but also to different kinds of measures. This means a classification of a markedly juridicial nature which is based on the (legal) scope of application, the source, the substantive content and other aspects. What conclusions can be drawn as to the functions of regulations from correlating these aspects with the relative use made of regulations?

A clear positive relationship exists between the use of regulations and the legal content "Imposing duties" in energy policy as well as in manpower policy. Conversely, there is a clearly negative correlation between the use of regulations and the legal content of "Transferring of funds and property" in the two policy fields. The same is true in all of the individual countries under study. Nevertheless, we cannot infer very much from that. These links are probably to a large extent a result of the fact that in these cases the categories of measures and of instruments are relatively close. To put this another way, regulations are defined essentially as a superimposition of duties, while the transfer of resources and property is linked closely with the instrument of subsidy and public sector management. The positive or negative correlations are therefore not surprising. They are the consequence of the categories employed and are in line with our definition of regulation.[58]

Another aspect of the measures is the scope. Measures can be of a general or an individual scope. One might expect that with measures of a general character the proportion of regulations is higher than with measures of an individual character because after all the classical form given to regulations, a statute, is typically of a general nature. And indeed among general measures the proportion of regulations is twice as high as among individual ones. But if we examine the two policy fields we find that the difference comes more or less exclusively from energy policy, whereas in manpower policy the proportions of regulations are quite similar. It seems therefore that the policy areas are of great importance for the scope of the measures. But caution is necessary. The differences between "general" and "individual" are drawn differently. In manpower policy many of measures, which are restricted to certain regions or sectors, are classified as individual though they regularly concern a great number of people whereas in energy policy measures classified as individual concern only a few people; measures restricted to the

[58] See above II. A.

"sector" of coal or of oil for example are classified as general if they concern more than a few people.

The differences between the individual countries cannot be explained in this way. There we find for example that in Germany the proportion of regulations with individual measures is zero. In Great Britain the proportion of regulations with general measures is a good deal higher than with individual measures, whereas in France even the opposite is the case. Here the national peculiarities have a significant impact.

The sources of the measures, i.e. the bodies enacting them, may also be an important factor. Most measures are enacted by parliament on the one hand and government or a minister on the other hand. Which of the two bodies uses regulations more often than other instruments?[59] The inventories show that, taking both policy fields together, government and ministers are a little more regulation-prone than parliaments; but the difference is small. If we restrict the analysis to one of the two policy areas, the picture changes drastically. In energy policy government and ministers are clearly more regulation-prone, whereas in manpower policy it is the parliament which makes use of a higher proportion of regulations.

Within the individual countries the differences are not that significant, but we can find the tendencies described above in the two policy areas here also. If we change our question and ask what proportion of the regulations is enacted by parliament or government/ministers,[60] we get great differences from country to country. In Germany nearly half of the regulations are enacted by parliament, in Great Britain more than a third, whereas in France only about half of the proportion in Britain is enacted by parliament. Yet this difference can also be found with other instruments than regulations. Obviously the decisive factor is that certain countries assign more tasks to parliament or to government irrespective of the type of instrument.

The latter point can be generalised. The difference between individual countries is much more pronounced with respect to the kind of measures (which are primarily legally differentiated) than with respect to the kind of instruments. The decision whether to use regulations or other instruments seems to be mainly influenced by factors independent of national peculiarities and the political and administrative culture of the different countries. But these factors become quite important, when the kind of regulation, especially its legal character, is at stake.[61]

---

[59] This question should not be mixed up with the one discussed above under V. B. There the question was what part of the regulations originates from parliament and what part from government and ministers. Here we are dealing with the relative tendency of these bodies to use regulations or other instruments, independent of the factor what part of all regulations they enact.

[60] This formulation of the question corresponds to the one under V. B.

[61] Not unsimilar are the results of Klaes, et al. *supra* note 9 at p. 246.

C. Impact on Public Attention

One explanation of the above average use of regulations in crisis situations was the fact that regulations let the state appear more active in solving the crisis than other instruments.[62] A similar argument is presented when a major cause for the use of regulations is seen in the fact that a moral condemnation is desired which can only or most effectively be provided by regulations.[63] There are many examples for this in the context of environmental policy, where incentive instruments are not used, even if they are more effective, because only a strict prohibition satisfies the public. The use of regulations in these cases is not the consequence of their higher functional efficiency compared to other instruments but the consequence of their political efficiency and rationality. Regulations have on the average a stronger impact on public attention and therefore have other political consequences which differ from those of other instruments. And one can speculate that regulations are less often used in circumstances where the government prefers to avoid public attention. In a more general way it is an open question as to the degree the choice of policy instruments depends also upon elements of political rationality, i.e. upon the aims of the politicians with regard to their position, and not only upon factors of substantive or functional rationality which were in the foreground of this paper.

---

[62] See above IV. B.
[63] Stewart *supra* note 12 at p. 19.

Regulation and the Crisis of Legalisation in the United States

RICHARD B. STEWART

Harvard

Contents

I. Introduction

This paper examines the current debate in the United States over the use of administrative regulation and alternative instruments to achieve economic objectives, and the relation between regulation and legalisation. It will consider the reasons why administrative regulation has been the dominant instrument and administrative rulemaking the dominant legal measure for implementing economic policy; the choices made among various types of regulatory instruments; the role of administrative regulatory controversies in the development of administrative law and the crisis of legalisation in the U.S.; and current movements toward deregulation and use of alternative instruments in response to this crisis.

Such a paper will necessarily be summary and impressionistic. Unfortunately, there is not available a standardised inventory of U.S. instruments and measures in energy and manpower policy comparable to that prepared for this project on selected European nations. This paper accordingly cannot directly compare U.S. experience with the European experience, insightfully analysed by Hans Jarass. It offers more general hypotheses and observations, some drawn from the U.S. experience in energy policy, in the hope that they will be of comparative interest.

During the period 1965–1980 there was a very large increase in the number, scope, and intensity of economic policy instruments deployed by the U.S. government in response to political demands for new economic and social programmes. This growth was especially pronounced in administrative regulatory programmes. Congress during the 1960–1980 period doubled the number of major federal regulatory programmes, creating by statute some thirty new programmes. The characteristic measure used to implement these programmes consisted of administrative regulations adopted by federal agencies through rulemaking. The number of pages in the Federal Register, where such regulations are published, increased from 14,000 pages in 1960 to over 87,000 pages in 1980.[1] These regulations sought to impose uniform and often rigid requirements on a vast, diverse, and dynamic nation. Centralised controls were imposed not only on private business activity but also on the practices of and services provided by state and local governments and universities, hospitals, and other non-profit organisations.[2]

Beginning about 1975, strong adverse reactions to these developments appeared, culminating in President Reagan's election in 1980. Federal administrative regulatory programmes were condemned as excessively centralised, overly uniform and rigid, unduly costly and burdensome, and destructive of liberty, diversity, and initiative. One can thus speak of a crisis of regulation.

The growth of administrative regulation was associated with a sharp increase in

---

[1] See generally S. Breyer & R. Stewart, *Administrative Law and Regulatory Policy*, Chapter 3, (2d ed. 1985, Boston).

[2] These controls were imposed not only by coercive regulatory commands but also by the impositions of requirements as a condition of receipt of federal grants and financial assistance. See generally R. Cappalli, *Federal Grants and Cooperative Agreements: Law, Policy and Practice* (1982, Wilmete, Ill.).

litigation. The new regulations were generated through complex rulemaking proceedings lasting several years, followed in many instances by years of litigation in the federal courts and remands for still further agency proceedings. Firms seeking to market new products or construct new facilities would encounter a maze of regulatory requirements and licensing proceedings.The delay, expense, constraints, inconsistencies, burdens, and uncertainties generated by adversary legal proceedings led to sharp criticism of the legal system which had developed in order to control administrative regulation. Thus a crisis of legalism became associated with the crisis of regulation, merging into a crisis of legalisation.[3] This paper considers the reasons why this crisis arose and the solutions to it that have been proposed.

There has during the past fifteen years been a tremendous increase in academic studies of regulation in the U.S., not only by legal scholars but also by economists, political scientists, policy analysts, and historians. This paper will provide a highly selective overview of what we do and do not know, giving some examples from energy policy as a case in point. (It will, for the sake of economy, deal only with the federal government.) The paper will then examine the current political debate over regulation and economic policy. President Reagan has effectively exploited popular dissatisfaction with administrative overregulation and legalisation to initiate a far-reaching but highly incomplete effort to relax or eliminate regulatory requirements. Some critics of this effort advocate "reregulation": reinstatement, expansion, and strengthening of administrative regulatory programmes. Others, while believing that deregulation is appropriate in some sectors, assert that where government intervention is needed it should take the form of decentralised market-type incentives. Still others believe that the entire system of economic policies must be coordinated and rationalised through a new "industrial policy". Still others advocate radical political and economic decentralisation. Each of these alternatives responds to the crisis of legalisation.

II. Regulation and Other Instruments of Economic Policy

This paper deals with microeconomic policy – government progammes designed to correct problems occurring in particular sectors or aspects of the economy – rather than macroeconomic policies designed to manage aggregate demand, investment, employment, money supply, interest rates, and trade balances.[4] Administrative regulation is the characteristic instrument of microeconomic policies in the U.S., and it is with respect to such policies that legal controls are most fully developed. Indeed, macroeconomic policy as such is barely subject to

[3] See generally S. Breyer, *Regulation And Its Reform* (1981, Cambridge, Mass.); R. Litan and W. Nordhaus, *Reforming Federal Regulation* (1981, Yale); R. Stewart, "Regulation, Innovation and Administrative Law: A Conceptual Framework," (1981) 69 *California Law Review* 1263.

[4] Tariffs, export subsidies, quotas, and other measures dealing with external trade, capital, and monetary flows are also used as a means of indirect domestic economic policy (favouring or protecting certain industries, etc.).

control through formal agency procedures and judicial review. To be sure, the line between "micro" and "macro" is often hazy, and the aggregate effects of microeconomic policies on macroeconomic performance can be profound. This section examines the principal instruments of microeconomic policy in the U. S., examining first regulation and then alternatives.[5]

A. The Dominance of Administrative Regulation in the U. S.

Regulation consists of governmental standards or commands, backed by coercive sanctions, requiring private persons to undertake or refrain from specified conduct. Regulation may take the form of statutory commands enforced in the ordinary courts through criminal prosecutions or through civil actions initiated by the government or private plaintiffs. Alternatively, statutes may delegate the task of issuing and enforcing regulatory rules and order to administrative agencies. The latter has been the dominant approach to regulation in the U. S., particularly at the federal level. It is widely accepted that criminal enforcement must play an essentially supplementary role in regulation in advanced industrial societies. But the extent to which the U. S. has relied upon administrative rules and orders as the primary instruments of regulation is striking. Civil actions play a distinctly subordinate role in most areas of social and economic regulation.

The reasons for the U. S. pattern are several. The U. S. regulatory experience has, as developed further below, been powerfully shaped by the early experience in regulating particular sectors of the economy: railroads; public utilities distributing electricity, water, and natural gas; banking; etc. Regulating prices, profits and entry in a given industry requires a considerable degree of coordination and consistency. For example, in regulating railroad rates it is important to ensure that all shippers pay the same rate for the same commodity and also to ensure that the aggregate revenues produced by all rates are sufficient to allow the railroad to cover its costs without earning a monopoly profit. Such coordination and consistency would be very difficult to achieve through case-by-case adjudication, particularly if the action were a private one for damages, which would be tried to a jury.[6] Centralised and specialised administrative bodies can achieve the needed coordination and consistency. A related factor favouring the creation of administrative bodies was the expense of litigation, the relatively small individual

---

[5] In order to reflect some of the special features of economic policy in the United States, the classification used below does not precisely follow that developed by Terence Daintith in connection with this project: see above, pp. 51–54.

[6] Such coordination and consistency would also be proportionately more difficult to achieve in a system of federal regulation (which became necessary with the spread of interstate railroads, energy distribution systems, and so on) because of the more extended federal court system. Recognising the problems of achieving needed coordination and consistency through court adjudication of rate controversies, the Supreme Court in Texas and Pacific R. R. Co. v. Abilene Cotton Oil Co., 204 U. S. 426 (1907), held that notwithstanding an express provision in the Interstate Commerce Act saving common law actions, a private action for damages based on the asserted unreasonableness of a railroad rate fell within the "primary jurisdiction" of the Interstate Commerce Commission and must be tried by it.

economic stake of the many consumers affected, and the unavailability of class actions in the courts. An administrative agency could initiate action to protect consumers as a group by issuing regulations and taking enforcement action. In some instances consumers might also obtain damages through an administrative proceeding, such as a shipper's action for reparations before the Interstate Commerce Commission. Administrative proceedings were often less encumbered by procedural formalities and therefore cheaper than court actions. In Europe, by contrast, government ownership rather than regulation was typically the response to the need for social control in particular sectors such as transportation and communications. In the absence of an administrative regulatory scheme, the interactions between these new government enterprises and consumers and other market actors would often be governed by the law applied in private court actions.

The need for coordination, consistency, and self-starting capacity in environmental, health, safety, and other social regulatory programmes is also great. Controls must be coordinated in order to avoid competitive distortions and ensure, for example, that emission restrictions on all pollution sources in an air basin are sufficient to ensure healthy air. The stake of an individual in cleaner air is generally too small to justify his incurring the costs of a lawsuit, and judicial devices for pooling collective non-economic interests are limited. These considerations all favour the use of administrative regulation.

A second set of factors favouring administrative regulation in the U.S. stem from the politics of a congressional as opposed to a parliamentary system of government. As discussed more fully below, Congress has important political incentives to respond to a perceived economic or social problem by enacting a regulatory statute and delegating its implementation and enforcement to an administrative agency. Congress gets political credit for dealing with the problem, but shifts to the executive branch the political costs involved in resolving particular controversies over regulatory policy and taking enforcement action. By contrast, if Congress dealt with the problem by enacting a new statute to be enforced in private civil litigation, it would be forced to assume more responsibility for the precise content of regulatory policy and its results. In the past twenty years, in which a combination of Republican Presidents and Democratic Congresses have predominated, the congressional approach to credit-claiming and blame-shifting has changed, particularly in the context of environmental health and safety regulation. Congress, responding to fears that the executive will not vigorously enforce vague administrative regulatory statutes, has enacted quite detailed but often impossibly ambitious statutes, shifting to the executive the onus for not achieving unrealistic goals and deadlines.

A third set of factors favouring administrative regulation in the U.S. grows out of its federal institutional structure. Most of the private law governing social and economic relations is state law, and the overwhelming proportion of private adjudication occurs in the state courts. Federal law and jurisdiction is exceptional and requires special justification. For Congress to deal with regulatory problems by federal statutes creating federal rights of action in federal courts would be resisted as an intrusion on state prerogatives, It would also be resisted as an unwarranted expansion of federal court jurisdiction by those, within the federal judiciary and without, who believe that the federal courts are already overloaded with business and fear that a further expansion of the federal judiciary would impair its cohesiveness and distinctive authority. By contrast, federal administrative regulatory programmes generally do not displace state private law. Also, the increase in the federal court workload created by proceedings to review the decisions of a new federal agency is not as large nor as salient as that created by the authorisation of new civil actions.

There are, however, several important areas of regulation where civil court actions play a major role: antitrust actions brought both by the federal government and by private plaintiffs, private actions to redress violations of the federal securities laws, and private actions dealing with important aspects of labour law. The reasons for this pattern have not been studied, but there are several suggestive factors. The need for close coordination and consistency in these fields is less acute than in sectoral economic regulation of particular industries or in many areas of environmental and other social regulation. The need for self-starting administrative capacities is also less in these areas, either because plaintiffs consist of organised economic interests (competitors, industrial and commercial consumers, unions or employers) or because it is easier to aggregate the purely economic interests of consumers and purchasers or sellers of securities and monetise their injury for remedial purposes. With respect to congressional and federal politics, it is notable that in two of the three areas where civil actions play a major role (securities law and labour), the relevant federal statutes created a federal administrative authority but did not explicitly authorise private actions. Private rights of action were "implied" by the federal courts.[7] Also, it would not be tolerable from the viewpoint of federalism that multistate enterprises and stock exchanges be governed, at least with respect to basic structures, by different antitrust and securities laws in different states.

B. Different Types of Administrative Regulation

There are many different types of administrative regulatory instruments; the principal ones used in the U.S. may be summarised as follows:[8]

1. Cost of service ratemaking is designed to limit the prices charged by a business to the costs (including capital costs) of providing commodities to consumers. It is often combined with limitations on entry and regulation of service quality. This system of regulation was originally developed to prevent monopoly pricing and restriction of output by natural monopolies (railroads, pipelines, water, gas and electricity distributing companies) but it has also been applied to competitive industries (natural gas production, airlines, trucking). Administrative agencies have used both adjudicatory and rulemaking procedures to set rates.

[7] See, e.g., J.I. Case Co. v. Borak, 377 U.S. 426 (1964) (labour law); Textile Workers v. Lincoln Mills, 353 U.S. 448 (1957) (labour law). See generally, R. Stewart and C.R. Sunstein, "Public Programs and Private Rights," (1982) 95 *Harvard Law Review* 1193.

[8] For a comprehensive review of regulatory instruments in the U.S., see S. Breyer, *supra* note 3.

2. *Historically-based price controls* limit the prices charged by enterprises to a historical "base price" charged in the past plus increased costs. Such controls have been used in wartime to control inflationary demand for domestic goods. Such price controls have been used on a selective basis in peacetime to control rents in housing and natural gas production. They are generally implemented through administrative rulemaking.

3. *Standards* consist of specific, generally applicable rules (typically formulated by administrative agencies through rulemaking) specifying required or prohibited characteristics of the products sold, the production processes used, or the employment and procurement practices followed by firms. Examples include a wide range of environmental, occupational health and safety, consumer product, and anti-discrimination regulation.

4. *Screening* involves the use of general criteria, such as "unreasonable risk", that are applied through agency adjudication on a case-by-case basis to determine whether particular products should be sold or proposed projects (such as a new energy facility) should be permitted. Examples include regulation of pesticides and other chemicals, many aspects of professional licensing, and licensing of new facilities under environmental statutes.

5. *Public interest allocation* requires administrative agencies to decide which of several competing applicants will receive valuable government franchises, such as broadcast licenses, or other benefits. It has also been used to ration regulated commodities such as natural gas. Traditionally such allocation was accomplished through adjudicatory proceedings using vague statutory "public interest" standards, although agencies today are increasingly resorting to general rules.

6. *Historically based allocation* resolves the question of how scarce benefits should be distributed by allocating them on the basis of past receipt or usage. This technique has been widely used to ration consumer goods in wartime and regulated commodities such as natural gas. Rulemaking is the principal mode of implementation.

7. *Mandatory disclosure* and other regulation of information include the financial disclosure requirements of the Securities and Exchange Commission and regulation of advertising by the Federal Trade Commission. Both rulemaking and adjudication have been used to formulate such requirements.

C. Alternatives to Administrative Regulation

Various instruments other than administrative regulation have been used in U. S. economic policy. There is, as developed below, increasing interest in expanded use of some of these alternatives in lieu of existing approaches.

1. *Competitive markets, structured by antitrust law,* can be regarded as the basic instrument of economic policy in the U.S., the norm against which other government "interventions" must be justified. As already noted, the basic structure of markets is regulated through public and private actions brought under the

federal antitrust laws. "Deregulation," in effect, proposes to substitute this instrument for administrative regulation. Prevailing antitrust law has, however, been attacked as not permitting economically efficient combinations and preventing joint research and other cooperative arrangements assertedly needed to bolster the international competitiveness of U. S. firms.

2. *Economic-based incentives* use money transfers, rather than specific commands, to influence behaviour in the desired direction. They have long been preferred to regulation by economists on the ground that they promote economic efficiency by allowing for decentralised flexibility in conduct.[9] Such incentives can be sub-categorised as follows:

a) *Taxes or fees* can be imposed to discourage the conduct upon which a tax is imposed (cigarette smoking, pollution). Differential tax rates can be used to channel investment into activities enjoying lower tax rates.

b) *Subsidies,* in the form of grants, loans, loan guarantees, credits or deductions or credits against taxes otherwise due ("tax expenditures"), or in-kind transfers can be used to encourage particular forms of activity. Moreover, regulatory conditions can be imposed on grants or subsidies. The recipient must comply with the conditions in order to be eligible for continued funding, but the basic sanction for non-compliance is withdrawal of funding rather than coercive sanctions. This hybrid technique is widely used by the federal government to achieve compliance by state and local governments and non-profit organisations receiving federal funds with a wide range of anti-discrimination, minimum wage, environmental protection, and other requirements.[10]

c) *Government contracts or services* (such as education or research) are another means of stimulating desired activity. The imposition of conditions in such contracts is another widely-used means whereby the federal government obtains compliance with regulatory requirements.

d) *Marketable rights* are a means of allocating resources or benefits for which there is excess demand. Potential examples include broadcast licenses, airport landing rights, and pollution permits. In these situations there are no pre-existing competitive markets because the resource in question (e.g., the air) is a collective one not subject to appropriation though traditional private law property rules or because the government has created the resource or benefit. In order to create

---

[9] However, as pointed out by Daintith, above, pp. 30–31 the difference between regulation and taxes or other economic incentives is one of degree because the sanctions imposed on business firms for violating regulations are monetary or can generally be translated into a monetary cost. Hence firms may, using a cost-benefit calculus, decide that partial regulatory compliance is economically rational. See Roberts, *The Complexity of Real Policy Choice* (1975). However, regulations – as opposed to economic incentive systems – may call into operation norms of law-abidingness that will lead firm managers to obey them even though compliance is not cost-effective for the firm. *Cf.* S. Kelman, *What Price Incentives? Economists and the Environment* (1981, Dover, Mass.).

[10] See generally, R. Cappalli, *supra* note 2.

market mechanisms for allocation of such resources or benefits, the government must establish a system of transferrable property rights in them.

3. *Government ownership and management* of enterprises has played a relatively small role in the U.S. compared to most other countries. Rather than assuming public management over transportation, communications, banking, and so on, the U.S. has tended to opt for regulation. However, government ownership and management is significant in the area of natural resources.

4. *Government information and persuasion* may be used to influence conduct. It may be used as a substitute for compulsory disclosure by private firms or regulation of their advertising (for example, the government may itself disseminate information about the health effects of smoking). Such instruments have been little used in the U.S. because of industry opposition and fears of paternalism.

5. *Private law rules* may be modified by legislation or (exceptionally) by administrative action in order to encourage, discourage, or redirect private litigation. This technique is widely used at the state but rarely at the federal level.

6. *Negotiation* leading to consensual constraints is a technique that assumes many forms, but two categories may be roughly distinguished:

a) *Dependent bargaining* occurs between government and private parties in situations where the government has the power to use some independent policy instrument, such as regulation or the award of a government contract, in order to impose a sanction or withhold a benefit. This independent power of the government gives the private parties an incentive to agree to consensual constraints. Both sides may prefer informal agreement because of the speed, flexibility, certainty, and lower cost it can afford. Bargaining occurs in the shadow of the alternative instruments available to the government.

b) *Constitutive bargaining* occurs when the government establishes a decision-making procedure and structure within which private interests can reach consensual constraints. The distinctive features of this technique are i) relatively formalised procedures or structures, often established by law; ii) the bargaining occurs entirely or principally among private parties rather than between such parties and the government; iii) government intervention is at best remote. Examples include corporation law; labour-management collective bargaining (structured through regulatory requirements designed to encourage or protect unionisation); the self-regulation of the securities industry fostered by the Securities and Exchange Commission; and various government steps to encourage industry-wide agreement on safety or similar standards.

Recent proposals to provide systemic encouragement of negotiation in agency rulemaking[11] represent a hybrid of these two approaches, as did the corporatist system of interest representation employed by the National Recovery Administration in the early New Deal.

---

[11] See Harter, "Regulatory Negotiation: A Cure for Malaise," (1982) 71 *Georgia Law Journal* 1.

III. The Relation Between Economic Policy Instruments and the Legal Order

The liberal distinction between public and private, between government and the market, has played and continues to play a very powerful role in legal and political thought in the United States. The lack of a feudal or mercantilist past, the absence of any strong tradition of centralised administration, the geographical and cultural heterogeneity of the nation and its continental scale, and the common law tradition and the dominant position of lawyers and courts have all contributed to this phenomenon.

Government "intervention" in the market (which is, however, itself an artifact of legal "intervention" by government) through administrative regulation has been viewed as exceptional and in need of special justification, legislative author-isation, and legal control. The courts have assumed the responsibility, often on constitutional grounds, for ensuring that such interventions have been legisla-tively authorised. To this end, they have imposed formal hearing requirements on the administrative agencies responsible for carrying out these interventions. These hearings are used by adversaries to generate a trial-type record forming the basis for agency decision and judicial review of both the facts and the law underlying the agency's action. In recent decades judicial review has extended beyond the issue of legal authority to also consider whether the agency has exercised discretion in an informed, considered, and reasonable way.[12]

Traditionally these legal controls applied only to coercive regulation and taxation; they did not extend to the various other instruments of economic policy catalogued above. In large part this distinction reflected the common law origins of American administrative law, which was (particularly in the case of federal administrative law) built upon the private law tort suit or injunction action. Government officers were treated, provisionally, as private citizens who could, like other citizens, be sued if they infringed the plaintiff's common law rights by seizing his person or property. The officer might then offer as an affirmative defence the claim that his act had been legally authorised, and in this way the legality of official action would be reviewed. Coercive regulation and taxation could be judicially reviewed under this approach, but government withholding of grants, contractual opportunities, and the like generally could not because they would not amount to a common law wrong. These "proprietary" and related activities could not be reconceptualised as a common law tort.[13]

This distinction reflected history, legal conceptualisms, and the hostility of common law judges to displacement of the common law by administrative regulation.[14] But a distinction in the extent of judicial control over the deployment of different instruments may to some extent be justified on functional grounds, at least in the U. S. context. Because of the political salience of budget decisions and

[12] See generally S. Breyer & R. Stewart, *supra* note 1., Chapters 4, 6.

[13] See generally, J. Vining, *Legal Identity: The Coming of Age of Public Law* (1978, Cambridge, Mass.); R. Stewart, "The Reformation of American Administrative Law,« (1975) 88 *Harvard Law Review* 1675.

[14] See T. C. Daintith, above pp. 8–19.

the importance to Congress of fiscal control over the executive, Congress normally keeps a tight rein on spending decisions. In the case of administrative regulation, credit-claiming and blame-shifting incentives noted above have often resulted in broad regulatory delegations to administrators. Hence the need for judicial checks on administrators is often much greater in the case of regulation. Coercion is a dinstinctly powerful and focused form of government intervention. The allocation of grants and contracts tends to involve managerial judgments not easily reduced to litigation.

In the past two decades the sharp difference between legal control of regulation and taxation and control of other economic policy instruments has in some respects blurred. Liberalised doctrines of standing, reviewability, and ripeness, and the expansion of procedural rights have made other instruments, such as grants and contracts, and even negotiation and deregulation, subject to various degrees of procedural formality and judicial review.[15] Nevertheless, the legal controls applicable to administrative regulation (and, to a lesser extent, taxation) continue to be more extensive than those applicable to other instruments.

The legalisation of administrative regulation has changed and in some respects intensified in the past twenty years because of changes in the character of regulatory programmes. Most administrative regulatory programmes prior to 1960 dealt with particular sectors of the economy – airlines, railroads, broadcasting, banking, telecommunications, pharmaceuticals, and so on. Legal rights to agency hearings and judicial review were generally restricted to members of the regulated industry. While litigation was not infrequent, a great many policy questions were negotiated between the agency and the industry that it was charged with regulating.

After 1960, Congress created many regulatory programmes – most notably health, safety, environmental, and anti-discrimination programmes – that apply to many or all industries or employers. Faced with the necessity of regulating very large numbers of firms, agencies shifted from case-by-case adjudication (the traditional procedure for making and enforcing regulatory policy) to adoption of highly specific regulations of general applicability. These regulations – almost inevitably overinclusive or otherwise arbitrary in many applications – were a fertile source of controversy. At the same time, the large numbers of firms and industries affected, and the conflicts of interest among them, made negotiated solutions much more difficult.

Several other developments occurring at the same time contributed to the increased incidence and complexity of litigation attending administrative regulation. Courts, responding to claims that agencies had failed adequately to protect environmental, consumer, and other "public" interests, extended to advocacy groups representing such interests the right to participate in formal agency procedures and seek judicial review. At the same time, concerns that agencies were too often biased or careless led courts to increase the rigour of procedural requirements (particularly in rulemaking) and develop less deferential approaches to review (particularly with respect to agency exercise of discretion). These

---

[15] See generally S. Breyer & R. Stewart, *supra* note 1., Chapters 4, 9, 10.

developments have simultaneously increased the length and complexity of administrative proceedings (more parties and issues), the number of judicial review proceedings (greater likelihood of invalidating the agency's actions on procedural or substantive grounds), and reduced the chances for successful bargaining (greater number of parties).[16]

The further legalisation of regulation that has occurred in recent decades can be understood as an effort to ameliorate some of the problems and characteristics associated with the new generation of regulatory programmes: the proliferation of regulation; the greater reliance on centralised, uniform, and therefore inevitably overinclusive or arbitrary standards; the high social and economic stakes involved in the new environmental health and safety programmes; the serious implementation gaps that attend society-wide efforts at regulatory transformation; the displacement of political decision-making mechanisms by bureaucratic and technocratic ones. These are the ingredients of the crisis of regulation, and the courts stepped in, often with Congress' endorsement, to cure the crisis. This intervention can be ultimately understood as an effort to legitimate the exercise of new administrative powers unprecedented since the 1933 National Recovery Administration, which the Supreme Court had struck down on constitutional grounds.[17]

However, the courts' attempted cure of the regulation crisis has itself created a crisis of legalism. Its manifestations are sharply increased litigation: delay, cost, uncertainty, and complexity in regulatory decision-making; the devotion of considerable resources to "zero-sum" adversary struggles of questionable social utility; division and diffusion of responsibility for regulatory policy; and accretion of power to politically non-accountable judges.

This dual crisis of legalisation ultimately stems from the heavy use, in the U.S. regulatory welfare state, of command strategies of law as contrasted with constitutive strategies.[18] Constitutive strategies of law are procedural and structural: they create a framework within which interests recognised as legally empowered determine substantive outcomes through their individual decisions about the use of their factor endowments and through joint decisions reached through specified transaction rules – such as rules for voting or contracting. The legal order does not itself attempt to specify or control, save within rather broad bounds, specific outcomes.[19] Examples of constitutive legal orders in the U.S. include the federal Constitution,[20] the common law, the conglomerate or m-form corporation,[21] and

---

[16] See R. Stewart, "The Discontents of Legalism: Interest Group Relations in Administrative Regulation," (1985) *Wisconsin Law Review* 665.

[17] A. L. A. Schechter Poultry Co. v. United States, 295 U. S. 495 (1983).

[18] For a European perspective on what I term command law and its discontents, see G. Teubner, *After Legal Instrumentalism?: Strategic Models of Post-Regulatory Law* (EUI Working Paper No. 100) (1984, Florence).

[19] See F. Hayek, *Law, Legislation, and Liberty* (1973–75, London).

[20] See J. Ely, *Democracy and Distrust: A Theory of Judicial Review* (1981, Cambridge, Mass.).

[21] See A. Chandler, *The Visible Hand: The Managerial Revolution in American Business* (1977, Cambridge, Mass.).

the system of collective bargaining law created by the National Labor Relations Act and the federal courts.

Administrative regulation, by contrast, is unabashedly command-oriented and instrumental: it coercively specifies conduct in order to achieve particular substantive ends. As centralised regulation has increasingly displaced constitutive strategies of law, the problems of overload, erosion of normativity, and cumulative substantive irrationality and ineffectiveness become more and more apparent.[22] The courts have not been able to cure the problem; the effort to alleviate some symptoms has only created others. Despite efforts to develop general procedures to structure the rulemaking process, reviewing courts are inevitably drawn into ad hoc consideration of the instrumental rationality of each regulation, a task for which they are ill-qualified. Moreover, each regulatory decision is legally compartmentalised in separate adversary rulemaking and review proceedings. Furthermore – this process tends to fragment further a decision-making process that is already highly disaggregated because of the dispersion of responsibility among agencies and the difficulties of gathering and processing information to coordinate the thousands of particular commands issued by the government. This further fragmentation compounds the tendency towards aggregate substantive irrationality and ineffectiveness.[23]

The increasing recognition that regulatory decisions are interdependent and have aggregative and synergistic consequences for particular industries[24] and for the economy as a whole[25] has produced a counter-reaction. Each President since Nixon has exercised central executive review, through the Office of Management and Budget, of new agency regulations with major economic consequences.[26] President Reagan has extended this review process by requiring agencies to prepare and use (to the extent permitted by relevant programme statutes) cost-benefit analysis in developing new regulations.[27] But such review, unless it is to duplicate the work of the line agencies (and replicate the problems of acquiring and processing the information needed to coordinate thousands of commands) can only have a limited effect. The only real solution to the crisis of legalisation associated with regulation may be a shift to constitutive strategies of economic policy.

---

[22] See G. Teubner, *supra* note 18; cf. F. Hayek, *The Constitution of Liberty* (1946, London).

[23] See, e.g., S. Melnick, *Regulation and the Courts: The Case of the Clean Air Act* (1983, Cambridge, Mass.).

[24] See, e.g., F. Grad et al., *The Automobile and the Regulation of its Impact on the Environment* (1975, Oklahoma).

[25] See, e.g., M. Weidenbaum, *Cost of Regulation and Benefits of Reform* (1980), (estimating the annual costs of administering federal regulatory programs at $6 billion, and annual compliance costs at $120 billion); R. Stewart, *supra* note 3.

[26] See H. Bruff, "Presidential Power and Administrative Rulemaking," (1979) 88 *Yale Law Journal* 451.

[27] Executive Order 12, 291, 46 Fed. Reg. 13193 (1981).

IV. Identifying Problems Requiring Intervention and Selecting Instruments: Functional Approaches

A. Introduction

The U. S. experience poses two basic questions: why has administrative regulation been used as a dominant instrument of economic policy, and why is it only now that its use is so sharply criticised?

One approach to these questions is a functional one. The use of economic policy instruments may be understood as responses (and potential solutions) to perceived societal needs or problems. Thus the use of a particular instrument follows the identification of an economic problem, a diagnosis of its causes, and the selection of an instrument that will address the cause and cure the problems. This analysis assumes, of course, some functional capacity, political or otherwise, in the social system, to carry out these tasks. On this view, the current widespread perception of legal-regulatory failure presumably reflects serious errors in the process of identification, diagnosis, and prescription, or a basic change in circumstances.

The closest approximation to a fully developed functionalist theory is the analysis of economic policy instruments developed by economists and academic lawyers over the past two decades.[28] This analysis assumes that the purpose of institutional arrangements is to maximise economic welfare in the face of limited resources; that market arrangements are presumptively best able to achieve this goal; that government intervention through other policy instruments is justified only when failures in market arrangements lead to serious losses of economic welfare; and that the particular type of corrective instrument to be chosen depends upon the nature of the market failure in question and the costs of deploying alternative instruments to correct it.

This economic framework is relatively congenial in the U. S. context where, as noted above, there is a traditionally sharp distinction between public government and private economic activity, a strong presumption in favour of market ordering of the economy, and a political burden of justification on government "intervention". The economic framework also provides a useful set of conceptual tools for analysing the nature of asserted market defects and the consequences of using different policy instruments in response. But it often fails to explain why as an historical matter administrative regulation has been a dominant economic policy instrument; in many cases such regulation has seriously reduced economic welfare. Nonetheless, the economic framework can help to identify such cases and direct inquiry into the reasons why economically inefficient policies were adopted.

---

[28] For a lucid summary of this work, see S. Breyer, *Regulation and Its Reform* (1981, Boston).

B. Market Failures

The following are the principal types of market failures traditionally recognized by economists: 1) market power of natural monopolies leading to restriction of output and excessive prices; 2) external costs (e.g. pollution); 3) external benefits (e.g., worker training, basic research); 4) imperfect consumer information; 5) "moral hazard" (e.g., decreased incentives for care on the part of those who have insurance); 6) Rationalisation to achieve economies of scale that may not be achieved on a decentralised basis (e.g., electric utility interconnection and capacity pooling); 7) severe inflation caused by short-term shortages (e.g., consumer durables in wartime; 8) distributional failures. The last occurs because the wealth accruing to factor owners under market arrangements may not result in an equitable distribution of income.

The existence of such market failures presents only a *prima facie* case for government intervention. For it may be that the use of even the best-suited instrument will cost society more (or cause greater distributional inequities) than the market failure.

C. The Economic Critique of Administrative Regulation: False Failures and Mismatches

From the economist's perspective, there are two basic reasons for the crisis of administrative regulation experienced by the U.S. in recent years. First, regulation has been used to attack alleged problems that do not represent market failures at all. This is the "false failure" problem. Second, even when serious market failures have occurred, the regulatory instrument used to deal with it is often not the appropriate corrective instrument. Other instruments would be more successful in correcting the market failure or do so at less cost. Indeed, in many cases the regulatory instrument selected has led to a net loss in economic welfare. This is the "mismatch" problem.

False failures are of three types. First, some asserted market failures – such a price increases reflecting resource scarcity, or the bankruptcy of inefficient competitors – do not represent failures but are rather the economically healthy consequences of the price system and competition. The appropriate solution in these cases is to do nothing.

Second, many economic problems are caused by misguided governmental economic policies rather than market failures. For example, much inflation is due not to natural monopolies but to government fiscal and monetary policies and government-sponsored cartels. Natural gas shortages in the U.S. were caused by government price controls. The appropriate solution in these cases is to undo the misguided government policy rather than compounding the problem by adopting new regulations, such as price controls or rationing.

The third component of the false failure problem is more subtle. Markets may appear to fail because they create waste and fail to anticipate needs. The scrapping of investment that results from competition in times of excess capacity is waste. Failures to anticipate trends in energy demand that result either in inadequate or excessive supply also reduce social welfare. But failure is a relative concept. Even if the market is far from perfect, it may perform better, on average, than the alternatives, including various forms of regulatory government planning. Government itself "fails" for a variety of reasons, including skewed incentives and diseconomies of centralised decisionmaking. All of the available evidence strongly suggests that the market would have performed far better than U. S. government efforts to "plan" and manage energy supply and demand in the post-OPEC embargo period. Television advertising may not provide viewers with the economically optimum amount of information, but the efforts of the Federal Trade Commission to correct the problem through regulation may well make the problem worse.[29] If so, the market could not be said to have failed.

The mismatch problem arises when the wrong instrument – one that is unduly costly and clumsy – is used to deal with a genuine market failure. Administrative regulation is, from the economic viewpoint, a presumptively disfavoured instrument because it tends to centralise determination of prices, outputs, and production processes in the government, displacing decentralised decisions by producers and consumers. This leads to inefficiencies because government agencies cannot generate and process all of the information employed by the market price system. Nor can it duplicate the cost minimising, information-seeking and innovation incentives of the market system. Government central planning of outputs through command and control regulation by regulatory bureaucracies is accordingly likely to result in higher production costs and reduced consumer satisfaction. It is also less likely than more decentralised, constitutive processes of decision to cope satisfactorily with uncertainty, adapt to changing conditions or preferences, and stimulate innovation.

Other economic policy instruments – instruments such as taxes or subsidies, or government provision of information – have less of these "central planning" drawbacks than administrative regulation. They make greater use of market incentives and allow for greater decentralised flexibility. They are accordingly presumptively preferred. For the same reasons, less intrusive forms of regulation – such as required disclosure of hazards – are presumptively to be preferred to more intrusive ones – such as outright bans of products that present some hazard. In some cases this presumption in favor of decentralised incentives is outweighed by other considerations. If a chemical is seriously toxic and there are ready substitutes for it, the appropriate solution may be a regulatory ban. But in many other cases economic analysis suggests that there would be large economic benefits in switching from regulation to other instruments.

For example, negative externalities, such as pollution, could more appropriately be dealt with by taxes or the creation of transferrable pollution permits, rather than through regulations that specify the permitted degree of pollution by each facility. Economic incentives are superior because they promote a least-cost allocation of abatement efforts (firms that can control pollution cheaply will do more abatement and pay less in fees or for permits, while firms with high abatement costs will control less and pay more). They reward firms that develop environmentally superior processes and products. They ensure that the prices of

---

[29] See S. Breyer and R. Stewart, *supra* note 1., Chapter 8.

products whose production or use involves environmental degradation reflect such degradation, giving consumers an incentive to purchase environmentally superior products.

Similarly, economic analysis suggests that the problem of economic rents earned by favourably situated producers in competitive industries such as natural gas production should not be dealt with by price controls, which discourage new investment and production and require the government to engage in allocational rationing. Excess profit taxes are the more appropriate response.[30]

D. Values other than Economic Efficiency

How are we to account for the frequent use of administrative regulation to deal with asserted problems that are not market failures at all or that could be handled more appropriately by other instruments? On economic premises, it would seem that the answer must either be a) ignorance or analytic error, or b) political institutions that allow some interests to exploit government power to redistribute wealth in their favour while imposing a net economic loss on society as a whole. As we develop in the next section, these explanations have considerable empirical power. But it is also clear that the norms which citizens believe should govern the selection and deployment of different instruments of economic policy are broader than economic efficiency. An adequately rich functional account of economic policy would have to incorporate these norms, which would include the following:

1. *Moral condemnation.* If the private conduct sought to be altered is viewed as morally reprehensible, then the instinctive response is to prohibit the conduct with the force of law. Other instruments, such as taxes or subsidies, do not to the same extent convey, and indeed may negate, moral condemnation. In order to arouse public concern and develop political support for economic policy initiatives, it may be necessary to generate moral condemnation of "polluters", "monopolistic" energy companies, and so on. Such condemnation in turn makes selection of regulatory instruments more likely.

2. *Distributional equity.* The use of economic incentives, such as taxes, and market-type allocational systems, such as auctions, promotes economic efficiency but also allows those with greater wealth to obtain more of a scarce resource or engage in more of a disfavoured activity. Concerns about distributional equity may lead to use of less economically-efficient alternatives, such as uniform regulatory prohibitions or allocations, that are perceived as distributionally fairer. Hence, for example, U.S. use of gasoline rationing rather than taxes or price increases to deal with supply shortages during the OPEC embargo. Other conceptions of distributional equity may be reflected in energy regulation designed to preserve small refiners, and manpower programmes targeted to various minority groups.

---

[30] For discussion of additional examples, see S. Breyer, *supra* note 29.

3. Non-commodity values. Market or market-type allocations or incentives may also be resisted because it is believed to be morally or socially inappropriate to treat the resource or conduct in question as a commodity.[31] Many believe that broadcasting should educate citizens; simply auctioning off broadcast licences and letting audience ratings govern programming would be inconsistent with this goal. In these and other contexts regulation may be selected to ensure that non-commodity values, including "need" and "merit", are given weight. Others oppose the use of economic incentives, such as pollution taxes, to deal with environmental problems, on the ground that it tends to debase and undermine environmental values by reducing them to market terms.[32]

4. Assuring control over outcomes. The response of private actors to instruments such as taxes, subsidies, information and the like is uncertain. Command and control regulation may assure greater certainty in outcomes because the conduct required or prohibited is specified and the specification can be coercively enforced.[33] Hence in those cases where greater certainty in outcome is desired – for example, to ensure that pollution is kept controlled below some threshold above which serious damage may be caused – regulation may be preferred even though it is more costly than other instruments.

5. Access to judicial remedies. The U.S. has traditionally put a high value on the availability of hearing rights and judicial review in order to test the legality of administrators' actions and control their discretion. Judicial remedies are most fully developed and are better suited for controlling the power when it is exercised through regulatory instruments. Hence a concern to limit and control the power of the executive may lead Congress to prefer regulatory instruments, buttressed by provisions for judicial review. This concern is quite explicit in "action-forcing" citizen suit provisions in many federal environmental statutes, empowering any person to sue the agency in court to mandate performance of protective statutory duties.

6. Honouring expectations created by past regulation. Once initially established, a regulatory system may be difficult to change or eliminate because it has created strong expectation interests that society is reluctant to destroy. Trucking regulation, broadcast licence allocations, and even pollution permits have lead to investments and capitalisations premised on their continuance. Even if, as is usually the case, the letter of the law negates any entitlement, government officials will be reluctant to destroy the economic values thus created.[34] Once begun, administrative regulatory systems may thus be hard to abandon.

---

[31] See R. Stewart, "Regulation in a Liberal State: The Role of Non-Commodity Values," (1983) 92 *Yale Law Journal* 1537.

[32] See S. Kelman, *supra* note 9.

[33] However, implementation gaps, monitoring and enforcement failures, and the monetization of sanctions undermines the control assurance which regulation provides. *Supra* note 8.

[34] Other regulatory instruments, such as subsidies, may create similar expectations, but the property-like character of regulatory permits or allocations makes the expectational

These norms have played a substantial role in U. S. economic policy and help to explain the dominance of administrative regulatory insruments. However, they introduce considerable indeterminacy into the analysis. It is often difficult to say how they should apply in a given context or be weighed against each other. Moreover, not all non-economic norms favour regulation. Belief in the political virtues of decentralisation, for example, has been a powerful factor in the deregulation efforts of recent years. Even if these complexities were resolved through more detailed and complete analysis of particular economic policies, these various norms would not provide a complete account of why economic policies have developed as they have. Inadequate knowledge and interest-group politics have also played an important role; they are considered in the following section.

V. The Identification of Problems Thought to Require Intervention and the Selection of Instruments: The Role of Limited Knowledge and Interest-Group Politics

The evolution of economic policy results from the interplay between changing social norms and changing conditions. This interplay, however, is powered by political struggle, structured by legal and political institutions, and conditioned by a societal learning process. Because of changes in conditions and in norms, this learning process – a cycle of diagnosis, prescription and evaluation – is always incomplete.[35] Economic policy is thus inevitably made under conditions of limited knowledge. This circumstance in turn heightens the impact of interest-group politics on policy choices.

A. Limited Knowledge and Structural Constraints

The particular administrative regulatory instruments most often used in the U. S. have been of two basic types: 1) sectoral regulation of competition in a given

claims associated with regulation especially strong. Such expectations are most powerful and explicit in sectoral economic regulation designed to exclude entry and maintain the existing allocation of market shares (as in transportation) or where licences are regularly renewed, inviting a massive investment of capital in reliance upon continuation of the practice (as in broadcasting). But certain forms of social regulation also create expectations that impede needed flexibility. For example, if an environmental regulatory agency issues a regulation requiring a pollution source to make substantial capital investments of operating changes in order to achieve a particular level of pollution control, the source will strongly resist the later imposition of additional controls to allow new industry to be built within an air shed or water basin. For this reason, the use of economic incentives such as transferrable pollution rights is a better instrument for maintaining environmental quality while accommodating new development.

[35] See J. Krier & E. Ursin, *Pollution and Policy: A Case Essay on California and Federal Experience with Motor Vehicle Air Pollution 1940–1975* (1978, California) (analysing the evolution of policy as a process of "exfoliation"); R. Stewart, "History and Policy Analysis," (1979) 31 *Stanford Law Review* 1159.

industry through some combination of entry, service, and price controls ("sectoral economic regulation") and 2) environmental, health, safety, anti-discrimination, and consumer protection regulation through uniform standards that often apply to many or all industries ("social regulations").[36]

Sectoral economic regulation began in the United States in the second half of the nineteenth century with administrative regulation of railroads, grain elevators, and other enterprises that had at least some natural monopoly characteristics. The diagnosis of newly perceived problems and the prescriptions adopted for them has tended to follow pre-existing diagnoses and prescriptions. The cost-of-service ratemaking system of railroad regulation adopted in the 1887 Interstate Commerce Act was modelled closely on British statutes enacted several decades earlier. Later this model was extended, with various modifications, to the administrative regulation of trucking, barge transport, airlines, banks, pipelines, natural gas production and sales, petroleum allocations, maritime shipping, broadcasting, interstate telecommunications, and other industries. Most of these industries are very different from the nineteenth century railroad industry. But there has been a strong "satisficing" tendency, in the face of limited information and weak theory, to assimilate newly perceived problems and solutions to past ones. This tendency is also reflected in the proliferating use of uniform standards in social regulation.

Today, hindsight informed by experience and stronger theory enables us to see that many of these regulatory interventions were unwarranted or inappropriate and have caused serious economic losses to no good purpose.[37] However, the wisdom of Minerva's owl often comes too late, because regulatory interventions create powerful economic interests that would be harmed by deregulation and will exert political effort to prevent it.[38]

The tendency to persist with regulatory instruments has been reinforced by structural-political factors that have discouraged resort to alternative instruments of economic policy. Outside the natural resource area, there has traditionally been strong public antipathy to government ownership and management of any substantial sector of the domestic economy. Private law rules have traditionally been recognised as the preserve of the states. Any effort to federalise private law would inevitably be accompanied by a dramatic increase in federal court jurisdiction that would be strongly opposed. The creation of new neo-corporatist frameworks within which social interests could reach negotiated solutions is impeded by fractioned and decentralised character of interest group association in

---

[36] There are of course important programmes such as SEC regulation of the securities industry, that do not fit either pattern.

[37] See, e.g., S. Breyer & P. MacAvoy, *Energy Regulation by the Federal Power Commission* (1974, Cambridge, Mass.) (natural gas price regulation); Civil Aeronautics Board Practices and Procedures, Report of the Subcommittee on Administrative Practices and Procedures of the Senate Committee on the Judiciary, 94th Cong. 1st Sess. 6 (1974) (airline regulation). See generally A. Kahn, *The Economics of Regulation* (1966, New York).

[38] See R. Noll & B. Owen, *The Political Economy of Deregulation* (1983, Washington).

the U.S. There would be strong antipathy to federal government creation of authoritative interest group representatives.[39]

B. Interest Group Politics

Limited information and weak theory have important political implications. The ways in which different affected groups interpret a perceived economic "problem" tend to reflect their interests. Consider the role of cognitive dissonance in the diagnosis of the "the railroad problem" in the last two decades of the nineteenth century. From the view of some shippers, the problem was excessively high rates. For others, it was price discrimination. For some railroads, the problem was "ruinous competition". For others, it was unduly burdensome state regulation. Each such interest group will seek to persuade officials and the public to adopt its definition of the problem – a definition calculated to invite a policy response favourable to that group.

Besieged with multiple definition and often lacking powerful economic theory or adequate evidence to resolve the controversy, legislators often are unable to agree on any single diagnosis. They nonetheless face strong political pressure to act by setting one or more instruments in motion. In the case of broadcasting, for example, Congress created the Federal Communications Commission, gave it power to allocate frequencies and issue licences, and told it to regulate in "the public interest, convenience and necessity".

The technique of giving administrators considerable discretion to use specified regulatory instruments to deal with an ill-defined economic "problem" has been widely used by Congress. It enables legislators to sidestep politically controversial choices,[40] and can be defended on the ground that "expert" administrators will be better able to develop the information and understanding needed to better define the problem and the appropriate solution. In many cases selection of other instruments, such as taxes, would force Congress to choose a particular solution rather than delegate the task.

Affected private interests may, for a variety of reasons, also prefer regulatory instruments. Economic regulation, involving as it does controls on entry, service, and prices, provides the regulated industry with a ready mechanism for cartelisation and exclusion of new competitors. Regulation of social externalities can also be bent to this purpose.[41] Adverse regulatory decisions can be blocked or delayed by industry use of rights to hearings and judicial review.

---

[39] The federal promotion of collective bargaining through unions enjoying the exclusive right to represent workers and the promotion of securities industry self-regulation are important exceptions to this generalisation. It should be noted, however, that the proportion of the business workforce that is unionised has now dropped below twenty per cent.

[40] See T. Lowi, *The End of Liberalism* (2d ed. 1979, New York).

[41] Government subsidies would provide an alternative way for an industry to enrich itself through the political process, but subsidies may be harder to justify as an appropriate response to an asserted market failure, are likely to attract new entrants, and are subject (unlike regulatory statutes) to annual review through the budget process.

Consumer, environmental, and similar advocacy groups also have reason to favour regulatory instruments. Regulation evokes and responds to moral condemnation. Such condemnation tends to depreciate the significance of compliance costs, which are in any event less visible under a regulatory approach than they would be if tax or subsidy instruments were used. Such advocates accordingly believe that a regulatory approach is likely to result in stronger measures than if other instruments were used. In contrast to many other instruments, regulation requires a large federal bureaucracy to administer and implement programmes. Such bureaucracies can be powerful political allies. In addition, hearing rights and judicial review can be used by advocacy groups (which are often run by lawyers) to force the pace of implementation.

Accordingly, politicians, industry, and environmental and consumer advocates all have reasons to prefer regulatory instruments, even though the use of such instruments in many cases imposes a net welfare loss on the public as a whole by restricting competition and innovation, and imposing higher compliance costs than other instruments. The public as a whole is not politically organised to fight congressional or administrative battles over what should be done about particular economic "problems".[42]

C. Ripples and Linkages

A final set of reasons for the dominant use of regulatory instruments in the U. S. is the tendency for regulation to ripple and spread. Regulation of one sector or aspect of the economy creates side effects that are in turn thought to require intervention. Use of regulation for the initial intervention makes it more likely that regulation will be used for the second intervention, which itself may create additional ripple effects provoking yet further regulatory interventions.

A classic example of the ripple effect in sectoral economic regulation is the extension of ICC regulation of railroads to include barges and then trucking. ICC efforts to "manage" the railroad industry were disrupted by barge and truck competition. The regulatory system was therefore extended to include them, without much thought to whether the very fact of competition should bring into question the need for regulation. As a result, a largely competitive transportation industry was substantially cartelised, imposing large welfare losses on consumers. Similar anticompetitive consequences ensued when the FCC extended its regulation over broadcasting to include cable television.

---

[42] The two economic policy instruments, other than regulation, that have enjoyed the greatest growth over the past twenty-five years are subsidies and the imposition of conditions on federal grants or contracts. Subsidies often take the form not of appropriations, which are subject to regular budget scrutiny, but of deductions from or credits against taxes otherwise payable (tax expenditures) or "backdoor" forms of spending such as loans or loan guarantees. The use of conditions on federal grants or contracts reduces the saliency of regulatory costs. The costs of complying with grant or contract conditions is not an item in the federal budget, while the "carrot" of federal money can be used to "buy off" opposition that would arise if such conditions were directly enforced through regulation.

The ripple effect often operates somewhat differently in the context of social regulation. Initially regulation is directed at the most visible or compelling aspect of a perceived problem. As implementation of the initial regulatory response is undertaken and new information is generated, it is perceived that the problem is far more extensive than initially thought. Moreover, the initial effort to deal with one aspect of the problem may exacerbate other related aspects. Consider, for example, pollution regulation. Regulation of air and water pollution initially focussed on common, large-volume residuals such as SO_2 or organic wastes. But it then became apparent that other pollutants, including toxic metals and organic compounds, also pose a serious threat. Regulation was therefore extended to include these pollutants. Regulation of one aspect of an industrialised ecosystem may make other aspects worse. Regulation to reduce SO_2 concentrations has encouraged the use of tall stacks to disperse emissions, causing acid rain. The regulatory effort to reduce air and water pollution has exacerbated the solid waste problem. New regulatory programmes are then created to deal with these ripple effects.

The ripple effects of particular regulatory interventions are often obscure, and the functional linkages between regulatory programmes that are perceived as independent but are in fact functionally interdependent are often not well understood. The proliferation of nominally independent and unrelated regulatory programmes creates pervasive distortions of substantial areas of the economy.

A brief sketch of energy policy in the U.S. since 1930 provides a good example of this process.[43] At that time natural gas pipelines and local distribution systems, and electric generating, transmission, and distribution systems were subject to federal and state regulation as natural monopolies. Energy production and other aspects of distribution were substantially unregulated.[44] During the 1930s, domestic production of petroleum was partially cartelised, largely through state regulation, in response to excess capacity. This step resulted in relatively high prices that made domestic oil companies particularly vulnerable to competition from the new low-cost supplies discovered in the Middle East during the 1950s. In order to protect domestic companies, petroleum import quotas were imposed, supposedly on grounds on national security. These quotas, allocated on an historical basis, became economically valuable entitlements that helped to maintain the existing structure of the domestic industry and impeded for a considerable time federal efforts to respond to the 1973 OPEC boycott and subsequent price increases.

Gasoline taxes (and net retail prices) had long been lower in the U.S. than in other industrialised nations, in part because the quotas masked the fact that the U.S. would become increasingly become dependent on imported supplies as it ran down its own reserves, and in part because such taxes could reduce the value of the quota entitlements. Faced with serious supply shortages resulting from the OPEC

---

[43] For further detail, see A. Aman, *Energy and Natural Resources Law* (1983); D. Zillman and L. Lattman, *Energy Law* (1982, St. Paul).

[44] However, the public lands have been an important source of energy resources, and hydroelectric facilities have been subject to federal licensing requirements.

boycott, the Congress was unwilling, in large part because of distributional concerns, to restrain demand by enacting sharp tax increases or allowing prices to rise to the market-clearing level. Instead, an elaborate system of price controls was introduced, together with an intricate system of internal quotas, entitlements, and rationing. Throughout most of the rest of the 1970s the U. S. attempted to hold the domestic U. S. price below the world price (a process that, ironically, subsidised imports through a rolled-in pricing system at the same time that the Congress was promoting other steps to reduce imports). A mammoth regulatory bureaucracy was established to control almost every aspect of the industry, and regulations and litigation mushroomed. These controls discouraged investment in new domestic exploration and production.

At the same time, production from other U. S. energy sectors was hampered by the side-effects of other regulatory programmes. In 1954 the Supreme Court construed the Natural Gas Act's price control provisions to include not only natural gas transmission (where some pipelines had a monopoly position justifying cost-of-service ratemaking) but natural gas production (a generally competitive sector of the industry.[45] The resultant extension of price controls made for cheap interstate natural gas prices, encouraging consumers to run down existing supplies, and simultaneously discouraged producers from investing in new exploration and development. The result by the 1970s was a severe domestic natural gas shortage and an elaborate federal rationing scheme.[46] Federal rationing of interstate natural gas gave preference to residential and commercial consumers, causing industrial customers to relocate to Louisiana and Texas in order to secure access to unregulated intrastate gas.

In the case of nuclear energy, a fateful decision was made in the 1950s to promote private ownership and management of nuclear electric generating plants. In order to make nuclear plants no less attractive to private utilities than alternative fossil fuel facilities, location of nuclear plants within local utility service areas relatively near population centres was allowed. This decision triggered increasingly strong demands for safeguards and shielding to protect those populations against the risk of an accident. Anti-nuclear activists exploited regulatory hearing and judicial review processes to force tightened and more expensive regulations and drag out the licensing process, with the result that the growth of the industry was substantially retarded.

The response of the federal government in the mid-1970s to these cumulative and interacting developments was the attempted creation of a national energy plan to forecast and manage supply and demand. Supply was to be encouraged by a large variety of subsidies, demand restrained through a complex series of regulatory controls on automobiles, space heating, and other energy-consuming activities. This effort in many respects proved a clumsy failure. In the late 1970s and early 1980s, under presidential leadership, the U. S. eventually turned to deregulation of energy prices and the use of a strategic petroleum reserve as the basic response to energy problems.

---

[45] Philipps Petroleum Co. v. Wisconsin, 347 U. S. 672 (1954).
[46] See S. Breyer and P. MacAvoy, *supra* note 37.

D. Instruments, Measures, and Institutions

What is the relation between the instruments selected to carry out economic policy and the legal measures and institutions that authorize and execute those instruments? In the context of this paper it is possible to offer only a few observations (including some comparative ones) on this large topic.

In the U. S. system of separated powers, the role of Congress is of paramount importance. In the context of domestic economic policy, the executive wields few if any inherent powers.[47] Powers to tax, spend, and regulate must be granted by Congress. Congress' role is important not only for legal but also political reasons. Reversing the precedence established in the New Deal, when it was the executive who proposed new economic policies and programmes, Congress has during the past twenty years become the prime generator of new initiatives, particularly with respect to administrative regulation, subsidies, and conditional grants. This pattern reflects the increasingly decentralised character of congressional politics and the incentives of members to propose and secure the enactment of new programmes that serve organised interest groups. As previously noted, this shift has occurred within an historical context of Republican Presidents and Democratic Congresses, which has given Congress an incentive to write detailed, overly ambitious social regulatory statutes in order to control tightly executive discretion and shift to the executive responsibility for implementation failures.

There is no well-developed analytic inventory of statutory law, and it is still a largely unexplored question why Congress legislates in considerable detail on some subjects but leaves great discretion to agencies of courts in others. As a rough generalisation one can say that statutes resolve policy issues more decisively and leave less to the discretion of administrators or courts when taxing and spending are the economic policy instruments selected. Otherwise, generalisations are hazardous. Regulatory statutes can, for example, run the gamut from the open-ended "public interest, convenience, and necessity" standard of the Communications Act to the prolix and detailed provisions of the Clean Air Act or Clean Water Act.

The instruments selected also fail to show an orderly pattern, although the dominance of administrative regulation is striking. Based on the European experience, both Daintith and Jarass suggest that regulation is less likely to be employed when the number of persons affected is small and more informal alternatives (such as negotiation and contract) can be employed.[48] But in the U. S. there are many instances where industries contain a relatively small number of firms, such as automobile manufacture or pharmaceuticals, but are subject to elaborate formal regulatory standards.[49] Again, Jarass and Daintith suggest that financial incentives or consensual instruments are to be preferred to regulation

---

[47] There is, however, uncertainty over the extent to which the executive can use "proprietary" powers, such as contracting, to promote policies not specifically authorised by Congress.

[48] See H. Jarass, above, pp. 86–87; T. Daintith, above, at pp. 40–41.

[49] This practice reflects, at least in part, the growing distrust of informal agency-industry cooperation that has attended the rise of public interest law.

when long term aims requiring private investment and cooperation predominate.[50] Although one sees a variety of financial incentives used in such situations in the U. S., one also encounters frequent reliance in environmental statutes on administrative regulation to "force" innovation and investment.[51]

The formulation of economic policies and their implementation is a highly disaggregated, uncoordinated process. This is particularly true in the case of regulation. The tendency, previously noted, to view functionally related economic problems as independent phenomena requiring distinct responses is accentuated by the highly decentralised character of Congress and its lawmaking process. A further degree of disaggregation and lack of coordination is introduced at the administrative level, where implementing responsibility is parcelled out to a wide variety of departments and agencies – including the multi-member "independent" regulatory commissions, whose heads are to a substantial degree legally and politically insulated from presidential control. Lack of coordination and continuity is aggravated by the lack of a strong administrative tradition in the U. S. and the fact that high agency policymaking officials are political appointees whose average tenure in office is two years. Administrative policies emerge out of a molecular process of interaction and negotiation among the responsible administrators, the relevant congressional committees, and affected interest groups, punctuated by formal hearings and judicial review proceedings.

Courts have attempted to promote rationality and equity in administrative decision-making by developing procedural requirements for agency decision-making that afford a wide variety of affected interests the right to participate and challenge the data, analysis, and policy considerations underlying proposed agency decisions, and by "hard look" judicial review of the decisions made. While these procedures have often contributed to more careful decision-making, it is debatable whether they have contributed much, if anything, to the welfare of society as a whole. In large part these developments can be understood as efforts to legitimate an interest group struggle. The policies that emerge from this process may accommodate the various participant interests but disserve the general interest.

For example, the environmental regulatory process has tended to generate a "best available technology" approach under which polluter sources are required by administrative regulation to control pollution by use of technologies that are available and are within the economic capability of the relevant industry. This approach serves administrators' interests in a control strategy that is relatively easy to implement and defend in court; environmentalists' interests in making assured progress in reducing risk without incurring the political backlash that would be generated by large-scale shutdowns or similar disruptions; and the interests of large existing plants in a predictable system that imposes disproportionate burdens on smaller competitors and potential new entrants. But the public is in many cases disserved because cleanup is far more costly than it would be if strategies (including the use of economic incentives) were followed; resources are often

[50] Jarass, *supra*, at pp. 86–87; T. D. Daintith, *supra*, at pp. 40–41.
[51] See R. Stewart, *supra* note 2.

misdirected towards less important risks; and innovation and new entry are discouraged.[52]

The consequences of economic policies are largely a function of Congress' decisions whether to intervene in a given area and what type of instrument to authorise, rather than the decisions made by agencies or courts as to the precise terms on which these instruments should be applied. Perhaps the most significant decisions by agencies and courts are those expanding or contracting the area in which a particular set of regulatory or other instruments operates. Regulatory statutes are often vague or ambigous on the question of boundaries. From the New Deal until recently, the dominant tendency was administrative and judicial expansion of boundaries, as illustrated by judicial extension of price controls on natural gas pipelines to natural gas production,[53] and administrative extension (with judicial blessing) of regulation of over-the-air broadcasting to cable operations.[54] During the past decade, the prevailing if erratic administrative and judicial tendency has been to shrink the domain of regulation.[55]

The basic tool that the executive has developed to control economic policy is the budget. In the past decade presidents have sought to extend the budget to include new forms of government subsidy, including tax expenditures and "backdoor" items such as loan guarantees. There has been talk of a regulatory budget, in which Congress would authorise the total amount of private sector compliance expenditures that various regulatory agencies could "spend" each year. There are, however, serious problems in implementing the notion of a regulatory budget, many of which revolve around the problem of quantifying regulatory costs.[56] Presidents have instead sought to control regulation through the process of OMB review of regulation described previously.[57] This process has, to a moderate degree, succeeded in producing less costly and burdensome regulations, promoting the use of less intrusive policy instruments (e.g., disclosure rather than mandatory controls) and blocking outright some ill-advised regulatory initiatives.

Significant deregulation – abolition or relaxation of existing regulatory controls – has also been achieved during the past decade. Such deregulation has generally occurred through presidential initiatives. For example, deregulation of the airline industry began when Presidents Ford and Carter appointed to the Civil Aeronautics Board chairmen committed to that policy. This deregulatory effort was supported by Senator Kennedy and others in Congress and eventually resulted in legislation abolishing the Board and the entire regulatory scheme that had existed since 1938. Presidents Carter and Reagan initiated, with eventual statutory approval by Congress, outright or phased repeal of price controls (and associated rationing schemes) over petroleum and natural gas. Other deregulatory efforts by

---

[52] See B. Ackerman & W. Hassler, *Clean Coal/Dirty Air* (1979, Cambridge, Mass.); R. Stewart, *supra* note 3.
[53] See note 42, *supra*.
[54] See the history recounted in FCC v. Midwest Video Corp., 440 U. S. 689 (1979).
[55] *Id.*
[56] See DeMuth, *The Regulatory Budget, Regulation* (1979).
[57] See p. 109 above.

the executive branch include relaxation of controls over trucking and railroads, broadcasting, telecommunications, and banking, and steps to reduce the costs or burdens associated with many forms of environmental regulation.

These deregulatory efforts, which have generally been taken by administrators within the framework of existing legislation, have stirred sharp controversy.[58] Opponents have successfully blocked some deregulatory initiatives in court, although the rulings have generally been based on procedural grounds rather than on the ground that relevant statutes preclude deregulation.[59] Many of these cases involve environmental, health and safety regulation, where courts seem to be especially sensitive to the increased risks associated with deregulation. Courts are much more ready to validate deregulation in the economic sphere.[60] The deregulatory efforts have had general public support and achieved a considerable success, saving consumers many billions of dollars.[61]

While most "regulatory reform" has consisted of straightforward abolition or relaxation of traditional administrative command and control regulation, there have also been successful efforts to introduce less intrusive forms of regulation (such as disclosure requirements in lieu of product bans) or with other policy instruments. For example, the Environmental Protection Agency has, through its "tradeoff" and "bubble" policies, created a limited system of transferrable pollution permits within the existing regulatory scheme. This system has allowed regulated firms to reallocate compliance obligations in a more cost-effective pattern, generating cost savings in excess of $750 million.[62] The Federal Trade Commission has taken steps to encourage industry self-regulation through voluntary standard setting.[63]

E. Explaining Deregulation

The deregulation initiatives described in the previous section amount to a striking reversal of the trend towards expanded administrative regulation that had ruled the previous four decades. By unleashing new competitive forces, deregulation has imposed economic uncertainty or loss on regulated firms and their employees (who were in many cases able to extract high wages from regulatory cartelisation) and incurred the ire of many consumer and environmental advocates. How and why has this seemingly improbable political innovation occurred? Three factors seem to have been decisive.

[58] See, e.g., S. Tolchin & M. Tolchin, *Dismantling America: The Rush to Deregulate* (1983, San Francisco).

[59] See, e.g., Motor Vehicle Mfrs Ass'n v. State Farm Mutual Ass'n, Inc., 103 S. Ct 2856 (U.S. Sup. Ct 1983) (repeal by Transportation Department of regulation requiring automobile manufacturers to install airbags or other passive restraints); M. Garland, "Deregulation and Judicial Review," (1985) 98 *Harvard Law Review* 505.

[60] See, e.g. FCC v. WNCN Listeners Guild, 450 U.S. 582 (1981) (upholding FCC refusal to regulate radio entertainment programming).

[61] See R. Litan & W. Nordhaus, *supra* note 3.

[62] See R. Stewart, "Economics, The Environment, and the Limits of Legal Control," (1985) 9 *Harvard Environmental Law Review* 1.

[63] See Harter, *supra* note 10.

First, new approaches to economic policy analysis pioneered by academics during the 1960s[64] provided the conceptual tools needed to criticise the performance of the existing regulatory system and provide the intellectual rationale for deregulation and other alternatives. Many of the younger professionals exerting influence during the 1970s as legislative staff, assistants to top agency and White House officials, or policy analysts within the agencies and OMB had been trained in the new analysis. This analysis demonstrated that many forms of traditional economic regulation harmed consumers and enriched the regulated industry by limiting competition. This insight was popularised by Ralph Nader and other consumer advocates as part of their claim – widely accepted by the public – that regulatory agencies had been "captured" by the regulated industry.[65]

Second, the existing regulatory system had generated conspicuous examples of failure or breakdown that convinced the public of the need for basic changes. The persistence of high fares and excess capacity in the regulated airline industry was one such example. The clumsy system of energy controls and the embarrassing failures of national energy planning was another. The high degree of legalisation attending these and other regulatory programmes was also an important factor in changing public attitudes.

The proliferation of federal rules and regulations was one manifestation of legalisation. Federal administrators, faced with limited agency resources and the need to implement ambitious regulatory programmes designed to control closely the actions of many actors in a vast and diverse nation tended to use regulatory standards as the basic policy instrument. In many cases Congress had mandated their use, but even when it had not administrators used it because alternatives – such as screening or other case-by-case approaches – would have overwhelmed limited agency resources. The need to economise on decision-making costs also exerted strong pressure to make regulations nationally uniform and to minimise the variables which they address. These factors, together with the problems of centralising and processing information about the diverse and changing conditions of a large and dynamic economy, inevitably resulted in regulations that were overly rigid, overinclusive in some important respects and underinclusive in others, and dysfunctional or arbitrary in many applications.[66] Moreover, the lack of coordination and consistency among or even within programmes resulted in imposition of inconsistent or cumulatively very burdensome requirements. These conditions generated colourful "horror stories" – striking instances of regulatory excesses – that were widely aired in the media and Congress and helped create a growing sense that the nation was being oppressed by a growing tide of arbitrary regulations. These conditions undermined the normative credibility of the entire regulatory system, and encouraged noncompliance. The problem of noncompliance was aggravated by the severe monitoring and enforcement problems inherent in any effort to enforce detailed central controls throughout a vast nation.

[64] See A. Kahn, *supra* note 37.
[65] See, e.g., R. Fellmuth, *The Interstate Commerce Commission* (1969).
[66] See E. Bardach & R. Kagan, *Going By The Book: The Problem of Regulatory Unreasonableness* (1982, Philadelphia).

A related aspect of legalisation which also helped to discredit the regulatory effort was the proliferation of agency hearings and judicial review proceedings as a result of developments previously discussed: the shift in emphasis from regulation of particular industry sectors to economy-wide social regulation; the formalisation of rule-making procedures and the intensification of judicial review; and the extension of hearing and review rights to beneficiary advocacy groups and other indirectly affected interests.

The third factor in making deregulation possible is political entrepreneurship. The powerful but latent and inchoate public dissatisfaction with "overregulation" needed to be galvanised by a political leader and transformed into usable political power in order to overcome the economic and ideological interests allied with existing regulatory programs. Ronald Reagan has played this entrepreneurial role with considerable effectiveness.

In addition, technological innovations in some sectors, such as broadcasting, telecommunications, and banking, transformed the pre-existing industry and unleashed a tide of new competition. Maintaining tight regulatory control of these industries would have required a massive extension and intensification of regulation at a time when regulation was becoming widely discredited. The fruits of competition – cable television, cheap telecommuniations via satellite, convenient banking through automated teller machines – were visible and compelling. Substantial deregulation was the alternative adopted. Moreover, in these instances and others, such as airline regulation, some important members of the regulated industry supported deregulation in the belief that it would enable them to take market share from competitors.

F. The Current Extent of Deregulation

Despite the successes of the deregulation movement, many aspects of the economy, including agriculture and the extremely large and rapidly expanding health care sector, remain subject to intensive regulation. In other sectors, such as banking, broadcasting, telecommunications, and natural gas production, only partial deregulation has occurred. The Reagan administration has largely failed in its effort to achieve a widescale rollback of environmental health and safety regulation.[67] This pattern reflects several factors. In some areas, such as environmental regulation, market failure is so serious that an analytic case for total deregulation can not be made. Various forms of social regulation continue to enjoy strong public support. Deregulation of medical care is opposed both on market failure grounds and grounds of distributional equity. Further deregulation of sectors such as banking and agriculture is resisted by many within the regulated industry.

Moreover, it would be misleading to focus solely on administrative regulation, ignoring the continuing importance of other economic policy instruments, which have been left largely untouched. Even if administrative deregulation were far more complete than it now is, the U. S. would still be far from a "free market"

---

[67] See generally G. Eads and M. Fix, *Relief or Reform? Reagan's Regulatory Dilemma* (1984, Washington D.C.)

economy. Federal fiscal and financial incentives are especially pervasive and important in sectors such as health care, transportation, agriculture, and housing. The tax laws include a great miscellany of provisions designed to steer subsidies to specific industries and activities. Tariffs and non-tariff constraints on trade have assumed growing importance in structuring the domestic economy.

These various measures are the product of the same congressional politics and ripple phenomena that produced the federal regulatory system, and they have the same disaggregated, uncoordinated, patchwork character. The federal system of financial incentives is increasingly the object of academic study and criticism on the ground that it creates perverse incentives, rewarding less productive sectors of the economy and penalising more productive ones, and transfers wealth to politically powerful groups through processes not subject to effective political accountability.[68] President Reagan's tax reform proposals represent a limited effort to rationalise this system, but the political fate of the proposals remains highly uncertain.

VI. Future Economic Policy Strategies

The partial reversal of previously dominant U. S. economic policy strategies that has occurred in recent years as a result of deregulation initiatives raises important questions about the future evolution of those strategies. Will deregulation continue and intensify? Will deregulation be replaced by reregulation, particularly when Democrats regain the White House? One must also consider the growing academic and political interest in "industrial policy." This interest is based on the belief that existing economic policies hinder the competitiveness of U. S. industry in world markets. It is argued that these policies must be rationalised and restructured in order to promote growing, high-value-added industries and cushion the adjustment for declining industries and their workers.[69] The implications of various economic policy strategies for legalisation must also be considered. The following are the principal possible alternatives:

A. Reregulation

Under this alternative, the deregulation initiatives of the Reagan administration would be halted, administrative regulation would be reintroduced in sectors (such as airlines and broadcasting) where it has been abandoned, and regulation in other areas (such as the environment) would be extended and strengthened. The premise of reregulation is that important social and economic concerns require that government intervene in markets and that administrative regulation is usually the most effective, accountable, and distributionally equitable instrument available. Even if regulation is costly, a wealthy society should be willing to take strong

---

[68] See Reich, Reflections on Boundaries: A reply to Charles Reich, (1984) 2 *Yale Law & Policy Review* 204. See also H. K. Dixit, *Tax Reform as Industrial Policy*, J. F. Kennedy School of Government, Working Papers on Industrial Policy, WP 85 1 (1985, Harvard).
[69] See R. Reich, *The Next American Frontier* (1983, New York).

measures to protect citizens against toxic health risks or the dislocations of the market. Reregulation is supported by many environmental and consumer advocates and representatives of the poor, and by unions and industries adversely affected by unrestricted competition.[70]

B. Negotiated Regulation

There is growing interest in encouraging greater use of negotiation in the rule-making process to make regulations more workable and responsive to the concerns of those affected and to reduce the resort to formal adversary procedures.[71] Such an approach would retain the existing regulatory system while seeking to minimise the adverse effects of legalisation. There is, however, considerable doubt as to how successful such a strategy would be. Important regulations affect many different interest groups. Reaching agreement among them would be difficult, particularly in light of the fact that there is no way legally to bind dissenters or those who refuse to participate. Moreover, many consumer and environmental advocates are wary of regulatory negotiation, believing that industry would have an advantage because of its superior informational, financial, and analytical resources – an advantage which formal hearing and review rights to some degree offset. On the other hand, regulatory negotiation is a new idea and recent efforts to promote such negotiation at the U. S. Environmental Protection Agency have successfully produced consensus in two regulatory rule-makings.[72] Finally, there are serious questions whether interest-group negotiation within the currently fragmented regulatory system would produce adequate coordination of regulatory policies and serve national interests in efficiency and productivity.

C. Deregulation

Another possibility is continued deregulation together with elimination of special tax and other financial incentives, in order to create, so far as possible, a "level" marketplace playing field on which all firms and industries compete on equal terms. This approach reflects a profound faith in the virtues of competitive market allocations or a deep scepticism about government's ability to deal with market failures. It is also highly sceptical of "industrial policy," believing that the capital market is the best system for identifying and supporting growth industries. Critics of industrial policy proposals assert that government efforts to "manage" growth inevitably support declining industries for a longer period than warranted, and in other ways channel resources to politically powerful groups at the expense of the general interest.

Support for sweeping deregulation is generally limited to some economists and fringe political interests, and the prospects for its realisation remote. But who in England in 1700 would have anticipated the sweeping away of mercantilism and the triumph (however brief) of Adam Smith's ideas?

[70] See S. Tolchin & M. Tolchin, *supra* note 58.
[71] See Harter, *supra* note 11.
[72] See R. Stewart, *supra* note 16.

D. Economic Incentives: Socialising the Market

An alternative strategy would end administrative regulation of price and entry in competitive industries, abandon government intervention elsewhere unless market failures were serious, and rationalise the existing sytem of tax and fiscal incentives. It would retain the existing regulation of markets through the antitrust laws. However, it would acknowledge that there are a variety of important social concerns in areas such as health, environment, safety, and consumer protection, as wells as a need to facilitate the movement of labour and other resources from declining industries into more productive ones. But it would use, wherever possible, instruments other than command and control administrative regulation to deal with these problems. In particular it would use instruments that would "socialise" decentralised market incentives rather than displacing the market through centralised regulation.

Examples would include government provision of increased information to consumers; imposition of pollution taxes or creation of transferable pollution permits to deal with environmental degradation; replacement of the current health care system, which relies on heavy regulation to offset the moral hazard created by a third-party-payment system of health care insurance, by a system of first party insurance (subsidised by government matching grants where necessary) and a competitive system of health maintenance organisations; retraining vouchers for workers displaced by import competition; and so on. These alternatives would, it is argued, meet real social needs in a far more cost-effective way than regulation and maintain strong incentives for competition and innovation. They would also eliminate much of the legalisation associated with command and control regulation. There is growing interest among economists, policy analysts, and some politicans and administrators in such alternatives, although many such alternatives are largely untested and would be opposed by the interests favouring reregulation.

E. Bureaucratic Rationality

If one believed that a considerable degree of continued administrative regulation were desirable or politically inevitable, one might seek to promote greater economic rationality in regulation by strengthening the existing system of internal executive branch controls on administrative decisionmaking.[73] Such a strategy would build on the current OMB regulatory review process, perhaps introducing review of the scientific and technical aspects of regulatory policy as well as the economic aspects. A more vigorous effort would be made to review and reform existing as well as new proposed regulations, and to coordinate regulatory and other economic policies. This managerial strategy would imply considerable delegalisation: a shift to less formal procedures for agency decisionmaking, a radical reduction in the intensity of judicial review, abolition of the special legal status of the "independent" regulatory commissions, and a substantial increase in the power of OMB. Such changes would be justified on the grounds that the

[73] Cf. J. Mashaw, *Bureaucratic Justice* (1983, Yale).

current legalisation and disaggregation of economic policy prevents needed coordination and control, and that executive branch review may be superior to judicial review as a means of ensuring that agency policies are based on adequate data and analysis and a reasonable evaluation of competing policies.[74] The ultimate implication of this approach would be a frankly managerial one, in which Congress statutorily provided a "bottom line" goal, such as the reduction of acid precipitation by twenty-five per cent, subject to an upper-limit cost constraint, and allowed the executive wide discretion to select appropriate instruments and strategies to achieve this goal.[75]

While there has been an increase in White House/OMB control of regulation in recent years, there are two basic problems in relying upon this strategy as a solution to the crisis of regulatory legalisation. First, it is questionable whether any version of the current regulatory system can be adequately controlled and coordinated on a centralised basis. Either review and control must be highly selective and therefore highly incomplete, or OMB will have to largely duplicate the existing decision process of the various agencies, creating a fresh crisis of coordination and control within OMB. It may, in other words, be functionally impossible to secure an adequate degree of overall rationality in economic policies that rely on regulatory instrumentalism.[76] A shift to constitutive strategies may be necessary. Second, the radical delegalisation and transfer of power to the President that would be involved in such a strategy would provoke strong opposition in a nation with a deeply-rooted distrust of administrative power and a strong belief in the availability of the courts as a check on arbitrary government power.[77]

F. Centralised Industrial Policy

A small but influential group of academics and business and labour leaders believe that the existing system of administrative regulation and tax and financial incentives should not be abolished but rather should be restructured and coordinated to promote the competitiveness of U.S. industry and both encourage and ease the transition of resources from declining sectors into more productive ones.[78] They are highly sceptical of the ability of market mechanisms to accomplish this goal, particularly in light of the fact the U.S. must compete in the world economy against other nations, such as Japan, that use tariff, tax, regulatory, and fiscal policies to advance their competitive position. Industrial policy advocates also argue that it is politically naive to suppose that the existing highly developed and

---

[74] Judicial review would presumably continue to be available to ensure that agencies conform to relevant statutes, but the current judicial effort to control the exercise of administrative discretion would be abandoned.

[75] See B. Ackerman and W. Hassler, *supra* note 52.

[76] See generally T. Sowell, *Knowledge and Decisions* (1982, New York).

[77] See L. Liebman and R. Stewart, "Bureaucratic Vision" (Book Review), (1983) 96 *Harvard Law Review* 1952.

[78] See, e.g., Business-Higher Education Forum, *America's Competitive Challenge* (1983); Industry Policy Study Group, *Promoting Economic Growth and Competitiveness* (1984); R. Reich, *supra* note 69.

pervasive system of federal economic policy can be eliminated or displaced by radically different alternatives. Instead, the existing system should be coordinated and gradually reformed with a view to industrial policy objectives.

Just how this coordination would occur within the existing system of statutory and other legal arrangements is quite unclear. One possibility is a system of centralised executive branch control and coordination similar to that discussed in the previous section but devoted to explicit sectoral economic planning. Such a strategy would, however, reintroduce in aggravated form the problem of central control and coordination.[79] and the problem of greatly increased presidential power.

Others propose a central industrial policy board, composed of representatives from government, business and labour unions, that would be the focal point for negotiated changes in and coordination among economic policies.[80] This approach would be similar to the "negotiated regulation" alternative, but would create a centralised macro-process that would simultaneously deal with all regulatory policies rather than a micro-process of negotiating each regulatory rule separately. What is proposed, in effect, is centralised neocorporate decision-making. But what of representation for consumer, environmental, and other politically vocal and important interests? Excluding them would seriously undermine the perceived legitimacy and public acceptability of the entire effort. But including them raises many problems, including the difficulty of providing authoritative representation for loosely organised "public interests," and the increased decision-making costs and danger of impasse if too many groups and interests must reach agreement. The relation of any such system of informal bargaining to the existing system of administrative law also raises difficult questions. Finally there is a deep tradition of distrust of centralised neocorporatism, tracing back to the dismal experience with the National Recovery Administration in the early years of the New Deal.[81]

G. Decentralised Industrial Policy

A quite different approach to industrial policy is increasingly the subject of academic interest in the United States. The basic strategy is to decentralise much economic policy-making to constitutive processes established within business firms or other production units. This strategy is sceptical of the capacity of centralised bureaucracies to identify and deploy appropriate incentives. Devolution is also seen as preferable on political grounds (increasing liberty and diversity) as well as on economic grounds.[82]

One version of this approach would make businesses responsible for aspects of economic policy now assumed by government. For example, business firms might

---

[79] See B. R. Scott, How Practical is National Economic Planning?, (1978) *Harvard Business Review* at 131 (March–April 1978).

[80] See Industry Policy Study Group, *supra* note 78.

[81] See R. Connery, *The Administration of an N. R. A. Code*, (1938, Chicago); R. Baker, *The National Bituminous Coal Commission* (1941, Baltimore).

[82] See, e.g., J. Bowles, D. Gordon & T. Weisskopf, *Beyond the Wasteland* (1983).

be directly responsible for unemployment and worker retraining, (either by requiring them to provide continued employment or by requiring them to pay for unemployment and retraining benefits) rather than simply sloughing off redundant workers and having government provide their support. Shifting responsibility to firms would give then an incentive to adopt investment and worker training and hiring decisions with an eye to shifting workers from declining sectors within a firm to growing sectors, easing the transition problem. Occupational health and safety protection might be dealt with through decentralised negotiation and enforcement systems involving worker representatives and independent health professionals. This approach would avoid the substantive arbitrariness and legalisation of the current system of uniform central regulations.

Radical versions of this approach would encourage formation of small, flexible work units, organised within larger corporations or linked through cooperative structures, with a high degree of worker control.[83] A different version would be neocorporatist in structure, providing representation for worker, environmental, consumer, and community interests within the governing structure of business and other organizations.[84]

These alternatives, which would relegalise existing economic policies through new constitutive, decentralised decision-making structures created by federal law or encouraged by federal tax and financial incentives, remain vaguely defined and face many obstacles, including the pressure of national and international product, capital, and labour markets; the low extent of unionisation in the United States; the difficulty, in a diverse and heterogenous society, of providing authoritative representation for environmental, consumer, and other loosely organised public interests; and fear of corporate cooptation of new social mechanisms. For these reasons, among others, proposals for changes in the structure of corporate government to provide representation for various economic and social constituencies which were advanced in the early 1970s as solutions to the problem of corporate social responsibility and regulatory ineffectiveness have borne little fruit. Even modest steps, such as the appointment of "independent" directors, have encountered sharp scepticism.[85]

---

[83] See Piore, The Theory of Macro-Economic Regulation and the current Economic Crisis in the United States (MIT Economics Dept. Working Paper 285, 1981; Boston) arguing that U. S. economic policy since the New Deal has been geared to nourish and maintain large, bureaucratically organized industrial production units dedicated to high-volume, standardised output of capital goods and consumer products, regulated in turn by large government bureaucracies. This system is said to be in crisis because of international overcapacity in the industrial sector and the impact of post-industrial technologies.

[84] See G. Teubner, *Corporate Responsibility as a Problem of Corporate Constitution* (EUI Working Paper No. 51 (1983, Florence); G. Teubner, *supra* note 18. See also, P. Schmitter, *Democratic Theory and Neo-Corporatist Practice* (EUI Working Paper No. 74 [1983] Florence).

[85] See generally, C. Stone, *Where the Law Ends. The Social Control of Corporate Behavior* (1976, New York); V. Brudney, "The Independent Director: Heavenly City or Potemkin Village?," (1982) 95 *Harvard Law Review* 597.

These various alternatives represent ideal types, and the actual evolution of policies and institutions will undoubtedly partake untidily of elements of each of them. The alternatives can be classified as either command or constitutive strategies. Reregulation explicitly reaffirms the dominant command approach, while the negotiated regulation, bureaucratic rationality and centralised industrial policy alternatives retain the major elements of the command approach while attempting in different ways to minimise its dysfunctions. Deregulation, economic incentives, and decentralised industrial policy represent different forms of constitutive strategies to promote regulatory welfare goals. As suggested above, excessive legalisation and other serious dysfunctions seem to be an inevitable consequence – at least in the U.S. context – of approaches that seek to use administrative regulation to achieve specific changes in conduct within a dynamic and diverse economic and social system. This suggests that constitutive strategies should be encouraged. My own personal preference is for the economic incentives strategy, believing that in the U.S. context it is the constitutive approach that best deals with market failures while avoiding the excesses of regulatory legalisation. The particular conditions which make this an attractive strategy for the U.S. include the size and diversity of the nation and its economy; the reduction in the number of particularistic administrative decisions, and attendant legalisation, which it achieves; the obstacles to centralised coordination created by the highly fragmented U.S. political and administrative system; and the relatively unfavourable conditions for centralised or decentralised neocorporatism created by the very loose and fluid type of associationalism that predominates in the U.S.

The policies and institutions that eventually emerge will, of course, be deeply affected by the play of political forces. The same conditions of uncertainty that operate at the "micro" level in determining whether serious market failures exist in particular sectors and selecting corrective instruments also characterise the "marco" level of institutions and general policy strategies. Different groups will tend to define the problems of "regulatory failure" and "legalisation crisis" from the perspective of their own interests, and advocate responses designed to favour those interests. Societal learning in the face of uncertainty and changing conditions will be heavily influenced by this interest group struggle. But regulatory legalisation is unlikely to continue to enjoy the hegemony that it has enjoyed for the past several decades.

Part Three

Subsidies

Subsidies as an Instrument of Economic Policy

Dietrich von Stebut
Berlin

Contents

I. Introduction

What follows is a look at the achievement of economic policy goals through the use of subsidies and connected instruments. The intention is to show how far economic policy goals in the areas of energy policy and labour market policy were pursued through subsidies and connected instruments in the years since 1973, what specific legal measures were taken, and what are the special features of the use of subsidies and connected instruments in comparison with other instruments of economic policy, such as regulations.

The main basis of the study is the inventories drawn up for France, Germany, Hungary, the Netherlands, Britain and Italy together with comparative reports on those inventories.[1] Those sources have been supplemented by additional information on the specific features of the legal systems studied.

How then can the various methods of legal implementation of economic policy by financial assistance be treated systematically? With an eye to the debate on legalisation and degalisation, what statements are possible on subsidies and connected instruments? Figures will not be given in this paper, since in consequence of the structure of the national inventories they do not have the requisite significance.

II. Definition and Demarcation

The object of study is the use of subsidies and connected instruments to realise economic policy goals, especially in overcoming structural crises in the area of energy supply and employment (specifically, reduction of oil dependency and of unemployment). For this it is necessary to define what exactly is meant by subsidies and connected instruments, as:

– the term "subsidy" is itself diversely defined;
– what is covered by "connected instruments" must be clarified.

For the purposes of this research project, subsidies have been treated as a form of financial assistance, under the generic term public benefits.[2] It follows that this study qualifies as subsidies all types of financial assistance by public authorities. It is harder to determine what should be included under connected instruments.

Subsidies and connected instruments are mutually exclusive of the instruments treated in our research as having essentially restrictive effect, viz. unilateral regulation of private activity, taxation of private activity, and consensual constraints, i.e. control of private activity through contractual and other agreements with the government. Only measures that from the viewpoint of those directly affected are favourable can be counted as subsidies and connected instruments. Specialised financial and other kind of assistance by public authorities to public enterprises are not considered as falling within this category.[3] In contrast, the present report will only deal with financial and other assistance of the type afforded by public authorities to private persons.

Identical economic policy goals may, however, be pursued in one country through subsidies and in another through government influence on public enterprises. In countries with a large number of public enterprises financial expenditure for the realisation of economic policy goals is hard to determine and rarely published. In such countries an economic sector may therefore receive consider-

---

[1] For details see Methodological note, above pp. 47–55.
[2] For discussion on the instrument classification, see T. Daintith, "Law as Policy Instrument: A Comparative Approach", above at pp. 25–33.
[3] On public enterprises see the contributions by L. Hancher and S. Cassese, below at pp. 165–236, 237–242.

able hidden or invisible financial support the implications of which fall outside the scope of this paper.

If all kinds of financial assistance by public authorities are considered as subsidies, connected instruments accordingly include non-financial support by public authorities. Here one may think of government advice and information. These, too, may be supplied as public benefits.[4] Secondly and more particularly, however, subsidies and connected instruments also include public benefits afforded through exemption from regulation or taxation. From an economic point of view individual exemption from regular taxation or general duties equally represent a supporting measure through the reduction of economic burdens. Removal or relaxation of unilateral regulations, and removal of taxation or the granting of tax exemptions[5] are of course not subsidies in the narrow sense. If such removals or relaxations are not general exceptions but individual support measures, they will be counted among subsidies and connected instruments at least to the extent that benefits for individual cases are involved. In contrast to regulations such exemptions do not affect everyone but only the specific beneficiaries of the individual cases. One example should clarify this demarcation: removal of taxation by tax exemption for (all) diesel generators (e.g. in Germany),[6] because of its general effect, does not come under subsidies and connected instruments, while tax exemptions for energy rationalisation investments (as in Hungary)[7] do count as such.

III. Subsidies in Relation to Objectives

It appears that there are certain objectives which cannot be effectively implemented by the subsidy instrument. In their comparative survey of implementation of energy policy objectives, Leigh Hancher and Kamiel Mortelmans have already noted that subsidies are unsuitable as short-term response to disturbances in energy supply, since they can lead neither to a short-term increase in supply, nor an immediate reduction in demand, nor a stabilisation of prices and profits in energy markets.[8] The granting of financial aid in cases of disturbances in energy

---

[4] Thus "Information", listed as a distinct instrument in the project instrument coding (see Methodological note, above at p. 51) will in these cases be assimilable to subsidies. Obligations to supply information to government bodies about economic activity, on the other hand, should by reason of the burdens they impose be assimilated rather to regulatory measures, and are outside our contemplation here.

[5] See Methodological note, *supra* note 1.

[6] See Law of July 25, 1978 (BGRI, 1 1105) which provides petroleum tax exemptions for diesel generators, in H. Jarass, *German Energy Policy – Inventory of measures*, at p. 30 (Doc. 4/83 on file at the European University Institute).

[7] See section 4 of the Decree of the Minister of Finance, No 18, July 1, 1982, in A. Harmathy, *Hungarian Energy Policy – Inventory of measures*, at p. 13 (Doc. 5/83 on file at the European University Institute).

[8] See L. Hancher, Management of Short-term Disturbances, Doc. 6/84, on file at EUI; K. Mortelmans, Comparative Policy Study: Stabilisation of Prices and Profits, Doc. 19/83, on file at EUI.

supply – not met with in any country – would not achieve the goal aimed at, the removal of such disturbances, but might be likely to intensify them.

Subsidies may well be suitable in response to local or sectoral crises to restore lost equilibrium. If, however, an increase of supply cannot be achieved, the use of subsidies and other financial assistance would lead not to restriction of consumption or stabilisation of prices, but to a rise in consumption and prices. Subsidies therefore are, at least in this case, not an instrument suitable for fast response in crisis situations affecting the whole economy and not only a few firms or particular regions.

Otherwise, subsidies are relatively frequently used as a means to influence energy demand and energy supply. The reason, already given by Terence Daintith, readily suggests itself: alterations of energy demand or energy supply "frequently involve investments in such forms as the installation of new and more effective equipment, more expensive building methods and so on".[9] In general they are connected with specific, narrowly defined economic policy aims, not widely spread ones. Either they favour only a few firms or specific measures from the outset, or they are regional or have a narrowly delimited sphere of application. This distinguishes them from the necessarily general short-term responses to disturbances in energy supply. It therefore does not matter whether the range of potential beneficiaries is wide, or narrowly delimited from the outset. The only essential point is that only a narrowly delimited number of recipients should actually be entitled.

The extent to which subsidies are used as an instrument to implement energy policy objectives seems on the other hand hardly to depend on whether the state concerned has a market-oriented or more plan-oriented economic system. For instance, in Hungary and Italy subsidies are used relatively frequently as a control instrument, whereas the French inventory very rarely mentions subsidies as a means of energy policy. It is tempting to see the reason as being France's centralised administrative structure. Since subsidies can only have specific, individual effects, the legal implementation of economic policy by subsidising is not discovered where as an expression of legal culture only general rules applying to the whole country can be issued. This does not, however, exclude the possibility of hidden or invisible subsidies which are granted at the local or regional level, not published and therefore not reported on in the national inventories.

If, however, one considers that subsidies are very important in the area of French labour market policy, this thesis loses much of its conviction. It may be safer to assume that regulations are preferred in the energy sector and are also applicable and accepted there, while in the area of labour market policy regulations either cannot be applied at all or are not considered as a suitable instrument because of the desirability of freedom of decision for those concerned. In the area of manpower policy subsidies have overwhelming importance as a means of guidance, while other instruments are used to a lesser extent. This at least applies for measures designed to influence employee behaviour directly. The decisive

[9] T. Daintith, Comparative Report on Energy Policy: Energy Conservation, Doc. 21/83, on file at EUI, at p. 9.

difference here is whether the measure in question is directed to the employers or to the employees. Subsidies are granted to employees as well as to employers, whereas regulations and the related norms setting out requirements or prohibitions are only imposed on employers.

One is tempted to assume that regulations, because of their dirigiste, freedom-limiting effect, are not used when the behaviour of workers or the unemployed is to be influenced. Whenever an instrument is to be used via measures addressed to workers or the unemployed themselves, it is almost exclusively subsidies, which act indirectly and suggest a lesser degree of governmental compulsion, that are offered. By contrast, action addressed to firms is taken through other instruments as well, notably through regulations (e.g. quota systems in favour of handicapped workers).[10]

The close links between the instruments of regulation and subsidy and their mutually complementary nature become particularly noticeable when subsidies fulfil the function of a secondary instrument. Examples for this are subsidies for enterprises to meet increases of minimum wages (the Netherlands and France);[11] reduction of social costs to maintain sex ratios in the industrial sector (Italy);[12] permission to enterprises in crisis to opt out of the compulsory obligation in respect of the employment of handicapped persons (Italy).[13] In such cases as these, subsidies are used to complement regulations or to smooth out their undesired side effects.

The notion that subsidies are preferred in states with a more market-oriented economic system, while regulations are used in planned economy states, finds no greater support in the field of manpower policy than in that of energy policy. Instead, the finding is that in all countries studied including Hungary subsidies are used to implement all the manpower objectives covered. It is striking that in Hungary subsidies are used as an instrument to implement manpower policy objectives even when regulations are used for this in other countries. For instance, the employment of handicapped workers is almost always brought about through regulations, which provide a quota system whereby the handicapped must constitute a certain percentage of all workers.[14] Only in Hungary is employment

---

[10] See for example the U. K. Disabled Persons (Employment) Act 1958 in B. Bercusson, *U. K. Manpower Policy – Inventory of Measures*, at p. 78 (Doc. 13/83 on file at EUI) and laws mentioned in von Stebut, *German Manpower Policy – Inventory of Measures* at pp. 7, 11, 33 and 111 (Doc. 16/83 on file at EUI).

[11] See Royal Decree of February 22, 1974 (Loonsuppletieregeling) in K. Mortelmans, *Dutch Manpower Policy – Inventory of Measures* at p. 62 (Doc. 15/83 on file at EUI) and Law 82–660, of July 30, 1982 (Prices and Incomes Act), Decree No 75–437 of June 4, 1975 on training employment contracts in J. de Forges, *French Manpower Policy – Inventory of Measures* at pp. 67 and 79 (Doc. 33/83 on file at EUI).

[12] See Law 502 of August 5, 1978 (Measures concerning the cost of labour and the reduction of social security costs for employers in the industrial sector) in P. A. Curran, *Italian Manpower Policy – Inventory of Measures* at p. 43 (Doc. 14/83 on file at EUI).

[13] See Law No 482, 1968 (Mandatory placement of the Handicapped) in Curran, *supra* note 12 at p. 54.

[14] See note 10 *supra*.

policy in favour of the handicapped pursued by granting firms that employ handicapped workers or home workers a subsidy.[15] However, the fact that in Hungary as well as in the other countries studied energy saving measures are boosted by subsidies contradicts the common idea that in centrally administered countries economic management is enacted by regulations or respectively infor- mal acts. Nor, in the case of Hungary, can the use of subsidies as an instrument of economic policy be explained by the existence of a small sector organised on a free enterprise basis. Subsidies are too frequently and too indifferently used for this to be an adequate explanation. A better conclusion, already mentioned above, is that economic management through the provision of financially attractive subsidies is preferred in cases where public measures of constraint in the form of regulations fail or should be avoided.

The example of Hungary permits certain cautious conclusions concerning the reasons for the more or less considerable extent to which hidden or invisible financial support is granted instead of open subsidies.

It is tempting to assume that these hidden or invisible subsidies are more frequently granted in countries with planned economies than in those organised on the basis of free enterprise. In fact, the comparatively precise and elaborate figures about subsidy practice in Hungary permit the conclusion that it is rather the necessity, or otherwise, of statutory regulations concerning the allocation of subsidies that determine whether the grant of financial aids is brought to public attention or dealt with in privacy (e.g. by negotiations). In other words, this is a reflection of the legal culture of the countries examined.

IV. Subsidies in Relation to Measures

What legal measures are taken to secure economic policy goals by using subsidies and connected instruments?

A. Scope

As legal measures usually have not individual but general effect, it is likely that most of the legal subsidisation measures are general in scope. However, individual measures are met with as well. They are based on different procedures of subsidy allocation.

(a) Firstly, there exist, for instance in the Netherlands, agreements between entrepreneurs and administrations about preferential sales conditions for public services (e.g. preferential tariffs for gas).[16]

(b) Furthermore, there are two different kinds of legal regulation of individual cases. There are, for instance, subsidy laws providing benefits for a specific

---

[15] See Decision of the Minister of Finance No 68, of December 30, 1981 in A. Harmathy, *Hungarian Manpower Policy – Inventory of Measures* at p. 17 (Doc. 17/83 on file at EUI).

[16] See Agreement between the Minister of Economic Affairs and Gasunie of April 6, 1963 in K. Mortelmans, *Dutch Energy Policy – Inventory of Measures* at pp. 7 and 24 (Doc. 7/83 on file at EUI).

enterprise, e.g. the National Coal Board in Great Britain or specific steel companies in Germany. Individual measures also include those authorising specific administrations to grant precisely assigned subsidies (e.g. in the area of energy policy in the Netherlands or connected to short-time workers support in Germany).

(c) Finally, collective agreements between associations of employers and workers about additional benefits for the creation of jobs or the settlement of outgoing employees (as for instance in France or Italy) form a third group of individual measures.

These different procedures for granting or providing for the grant of subsidies are an expression of different legal systems and procedures in the specific countries. If we leave aside the perhaps special case of collectively agreed rules on subsidisation, it is striking that such individually regulated subsidies are not encountered in France, Italy or Hungary. This suggests that in these states subsidies are either regulated through general measures or granted by public authorities using techniques of low visibility.

B. Temporal Validity

Subsidies may be based upon measures of permanent or of temporary validity. In all the countries studied both kinds of measures are implemented. This does not mean that cases of permanent support through subsidisation are frequent. We can only say whether the legal rules granting power to allocate subsidies are of permanent or of temporary validity. Individual measures of subsidy are almost inevitably of temporary validity. Subsidies based only on budgetary legislation (e.g. in France or Germany)[17] or forming part of long-term planning arrangements (e.g. of five-year plans in Hungary)[18] necessarily also represent measures of temporary validity. So also do subsidies for the support of experimental undertakings (as, for example, in the Netherlands).[19] In practice subsidy measures which result from budgetary law may often be permanent. This becomes obvious when they are repeated unchanged through several consecutive years. Repeated appearance in the budget does not necessarily require a new decision. The reason might simply be the implementation of a long-term plan or even a long-term commitment to subsidise.

There is a significant difference in the method of subsidy allocation in the area of energy policy on the one hand and of manpower policy on the other. While in the area of energy policy measures of permanent validity predominate, manpower policy is largely implemented through measures of temporary validity. A reason for these different approaches might be the implementation of adjustment subsidies on the one hand and of maintenance or social subsidies on the other. While

---

[17] For German examples see Jarass, *supra,* note 6, at pp. 21–24.

[18] See Law No. 111 of 1980 on the Sixth National Economic Five Year Plan and Government Decree No 1055 of December 24, 1980 in Harmathy, *supra,* note 7 at pp. 26 and 27.

[19] See Government White Paper No 17554. XIII, (Experiment "Ambachtspromotie Oost-Groningen") in Mortelmans, *supra* note 11, at p. 21.

in the area of energy policy public support is practically always intended to change energy consumption and production as well as the kind of energy resources used, subsidies are employed in the labour market not only for adjustment through the creation of new jobs, but also in large measure to maintain jobs acutely endangered. It can be supposed that the only reason not to give such legal measures in the area of energy policy temporary validity is the fact that as soon as the goal they were aimed at is achieved their purpose is completed automatically. The legislator does not, however, know when this moment will arrive. In the employment sector, job maintenance subsidies may be granted on the basis of a regulation of permanent validity created in anticipation of need. At the same time, where there are major shifts of economic situation which place jobs in acute danger, fast-acting temporary measures may also be created as an initial and temporary reaction. Cost considerations, however, if nothing else, prevent their being extended into permanent solutions.

C. Source

Apart from constitutional provisions nearly all types of legal measures – e.g. legislation, governmental acts, acts of territorial authorities[20] – are used as a basis for subsidy allocation. Despite the fact that subsidies, because of their tendency to distort competition, are the subject of provisions of EEC law – leading to decisions on the inadmissibility of certain measures – judicial decisions, acts of European Community organs and of (other) international organs have not figured in the national inventories. Still, this is understandable as national measures are either issued in observance of Community provisions or, where they contravene these rules, they do not, with rare exceptions, do so explicitly.

It is striking, however, that in all countries including Hungary bodies distinct from central government are authorised to make decisions about subsidy allocation in the area of manpower policy, while in the area of energy policy we find only two cases of this, one in the Netherlands, one in Hungary. First, that shows the greater degree of self-administration through largely autonomous organisations (e.g. Manpower Services Commission in Great Britain, local employment committees in France, Federal Institution for Labour in Germany) in the area of manpower policy. Second, with the exception of Hungary, a major part of economic policy concerning the labour market is shaped by non-governmental organisations, i.e. trade unions and employers' associations. In France, Great Britain, Italy, the Netherlands and Germany the autonomous organisations even reach agreements on the grant of subsidies, i.e. of socially-motivated additional benefits or improvements of working conditions for certain employees. In all countries save Hungary, where they do not oocur, these agreements may be regarded as a form of legal implementation of economic policy.

[20] For the general classification of sources of acts see Methodological note, above, at pp. 52–53.

D. Substantive Content

It is tempting to assume that the substantive content of measures which lead to the grant of subsidies will consist wholly of "granting exemptions from or making exceptions to general duties" and the "transferring of funds".[21] In fact, measures granting subsidies very often include provisions for the purposes of "granting powers to central government or other public bodies" or of "constituting public bodies". This suggests that in these cases existing organisational provisions are considered insufficient and that there is a need for additional control and supervision of subsidy allocation. Thus we find that in the allocation of subsidies to influence the labour market special or even autonomous bodies are employed to a large extent (e.g. ISFOL and CIPI in Italy, Federal Institution for Labour in Germany, MSC in Great Britain, an Interministerial Committee and Provincial Committees in France, START in the Netherlands).[22] If in connection with the grant of subsidies supervisory bodies are created or new tasks are delegated to supervisory bodies already in existence, the obviously acute need for additional supervision and control of efficiency raises the presumption that subsidies are often granted spontaneously and uncoordinatedly.

V. Reasons for the Choice of the Instrument Subsidy for Legal Implementation of Economic Policy

The presumption is tempting that subsidies are chosen as a means of economic policy when a closely defined aim is pursued or when the number of potential recipients is small.[23] A look at manpower policy and its widely distributed subsidies does not, however, confirm it. Furthermore, in the area of energy policy it is by no means the case that subsidies are only used to support the small number of energy enterprises. On the contrary, it is striking that subsidy schemes often exist where an incentive to participate in energy saving measures through changing one's source of energy supply, better insulation, and so on is to be created for a large number of persons. Accordingly, there must be different reasons to explain the use of the subsidy instrument.

We have already suggested that the use of subsidies is to be preferred where the compulsion inherent in regulations needs to be avoided or where their observance cannot be achieved or supervised. For instance, there is no enforcing the maintenance of endangered jobs if the employer is not able to pay the wages. An additional reason for preferring the subsidy instrument is that only a financial incentive is created and the desired action is taken voluntarily. Also, for measures aiming at the socially motivated maintenance of existing structures subsidies are the most effective instrument to achieve short-term goals. I therefore share Hans

---

[21] On the classification of the content of measures see above, at pp. 53–54.
[22] For legislative references see (Italy) Curran, *supra* note 12 at p. 21; (Germany) von Stebut, *supra* note 10 at p. 2; (United Kingdom) Bercusson, *supra* note 10 at p. 16; (France) de Forges, *supra* note 11 at p. 3; (Netherlands) Mortelmans, *supra* note 11 at p. 66.
[23] See Daintith, above, at p. 41.

Jarass' opinion that regulations are preferred to subsidies in the pursuit of short-term goals and immediate effects, only if it is confined to adjustment subsidies.[24] Where jobs are to be maintained through public measures, maintenance subsidies are obviously an instrument equal or even superior to regulations.

If we consider the use of socially motivated maintenance subsidies to overcome acute crises on the labour market, we can see that subsidies might in appropriate circumstances be an instrument suitable to counter short-term disturbances. Their limitations, as a response to short-term disturbances in the energy sector,[25] do not therefore necessarily apply generally, not is the key distinction one between response to failure of supply as opposed to failure of demand. This distinction applies in the energy sector only because financial incentives cannot achieve a short-term rise in energy supply. In other circumstances it may be possible to smooth out supply through financial support, and subsidies can be used accordingly.

VI. Description and Classification of Public Benefits

An evaluation of the national inventories shows that subsidies and other public benefits can be classified as follows:

A. Supporting and Easing Subsidies

Subsidies are generally granted through the allowance of financial benefits to the recipient. However, the same effect can be achieved, if obligations otherwise borne by individual beneficiaries are removed or eased. This method is met with relatively frequently. In the area of energy policy, examples are the numerous tax privileges for energy saving measures,[26] in that of labour market policy exemptions from making redundancy payments (in the United Kingdom),[27] reduction of social security contributions in order to increase salaries up to the minimum wages (in France)[28] or permission to opt out of compulsory obligations in cases of crisis (in Italy).[29] Public assistance through easing subsidies can thus either be granted as an instrument to boost adjustment measures or as a means of socially motivated support.

---

[24] H. Jarass, "Regulation as an Instrument of Economic Policy", above at p. 85.
[25] On the choice of this and other policy objectives see Daintith, above, at pp. 23–25.
[26] See e.g. Law No 368 of June 1978 (Investment Account Act) in Mortelmans, *supra* note 16, at p. 46; and Law (BGBI 1 878) of June 27, 1978 in Jarass, *supra* note 6, at p. 29.
[27] See Finance Act 1981, and in particular the Inland Revenue Circular issued under the Act, in Bercusson, *supra* note 10 at p. 63.
[28] See Youth Employment Act, Law No 77–704, of July 5, 1977 in Deforges, *supra* note 11, at pp. 6 and 7.
[29] See Law of March 27, 1983 in Curran, *supra* note 12 at p. 63.

B. Primary and Secondary Subsidies

Another possible distinction we might draw on the basis of the national inventories is one between primary and secondary subsidies. While primary subsidies are the generally current form of public support, we also encounter secondary subsidies whose aim is to equalise undesired effects of regulations in general or in individual cases. An example from the area of labour market policy is the French social security subsidy just mentioned[30] or, in the energy area, the compensation for losses arising from price control and price fixing in the United Kingdom.[31] One should not assume that secondary subsidies are always used to cancel out the market-distorting effects of regulatory interventions. This is the case only where compensatory payments are allowed to all those affected by a legal measure. Often, however, public benefits are also granted on an individual basis compensating some but not all of those concerned for the effects of a burdensome measure. While primary subsidies might be granted to achieve adjustments of behaviour as well as to maintain existing structures, secondary subsidies only have this maintenance function.

C. Maintenance and Adjustment Subsidies

The distinction already drawn between maintenance and adjustment subsidies[32] does not correspond to that between ordering policy and process policy.[33] Adjustment subsidies can be an instrument of ordering policy as well as of process policy and, conversely, maintenance subsidies may be granted not only as a possible measure of process policy, but also in the pursuit of a qualitative change of economic structures. It is rather the reaction sought to be provided by the subsidy that is essential to the classification. Adjustment subsidies incite the beneficiary to take action, to change behaviour, while maintenance subsidies discourage him from bringing about undesired changes and enable him to continue his present behaviour. As examples of adjustment subsidies in energy policy we might cite the subsidies to boost changes in energy consumption or in the kind of energy resources used.[34] In the area of manpower policy practically all of the subsidies intended to create jobs or to train employees are adjustment subsidies. Maintenance subsidies in energy policy include compensatory measures to maintain activity and employment in the coal mining industry.[35] The main use of maintenance subsidies, however, is as an instrument of labour market policy to secure endangered jobs. These examples also show that maintenance subsidies are

---

[30] *Supra* note 28.
[31] See Compensation for Limitation of Prices (Electricity Boards) Order 1974, S. I. 1774 No 1959 and similar orders.
[32] See at p. 143 above.
[33] See Mortelmans, "Short and Long-term Policy Objectives and the Choice of Instruments and Measures" below, at pp. 283–321.
[34] For details see Daintith, *supra* note 9, esp. at pp. 7–16.
[35] See T. Daintith and L. Hancher, *Energy Strategy in Europe: the Legal Framework* (1986, Berlin) at pp. 89–92.

by no means always socially motivated and that adjustment subsidies might also be granted on social grounds. Maintenance subsidies may be granted with a rather economic approach, although this is more common with adjustment subsidies.

VII. Legal Structure

The wide variety of legal measures used for granting public benefits[36] can be broadly classified as follows:

A. Announcement of Subsidies in Government Statements or Budgets

Governments, in the pursuit of economic policy goals, make announcements of public benefits which have widely differing effects. It is not only in Hungary with its five-year plans where examples are found; they are met with in most of the other countries as well.[37] It is hard to see how far the announcement of plans or the creation of authorities competent to allocate subsidies involves binding commitments for the state. At any rate, the announcement of future payments in a Hungarian five-year plan has effects different from those of the declarations of intent issued by government bodies in the other countries.

B. Creation of Legal Bases for the Grant of Subsidies

In all the countries studied, rules that themselves provide for the issue of subsidies in a quasi-automatic way exist beside those that authorise public bodies to allocate subsidies. The latter provisions apparently allow competent authorities more extensive discretion and frequently lead to a situation in which the actual subsidy allocation is made on the basis of negotiations (consensual subsidies). Such legal rules conferring authority are to be distinguished from the individual official decision on the allocation of the subsidy itself. Authorising rules may range from the very general, as with budgetary law, to those which regulate the details of the subsidy allocation connected to a specific programme (support conditions, support period, total sum and so on).

The extent of parliamentary participation in advance of the grant of subsidies (determination of allocation conditions) and in the supervision of their use thus differs widely. Parliamentary decisions about the allocation of subsidies often accompany rules of the types already discussed, concerning the creation of new authorities or the delegation of additional powers to existing bodies. The more automatic type of subsidy rules often takes the form of easing subsidies through tax reduction.

---

[36] See generally for the United Kingdom, G. Ganz, *Government and Industry* (1977, London); for France, D. H. Scheuing, *Les aides financières publiques* (1977, Paris); for Italy, G. Pericu, *Le sovvenzioni come strumento di azione amministrativa* (2nd ed. 1971, Milan).

[37] See for example the Dutch Action Plan for Energy Saving of 1979, and the Italian National Energy Plans of 1975, 1977 and 1981.

C. Public Measures for the Actual Grant of Subsidies

While our research was not designed to collect comprehensive information about the actual award of individual subsidies, so that many may remain invisible, it is at least possible to state that in addition to a legal basis for subsidy allocation further action by public authorities is very frequently necessary for the actual grant and transfer of public benefits, as is demonstrated by the occasional creation, by law, of specific public bodies entrusted with these functions.

D. Supervisory Measures

The national inventories have also shown that in subsidy policy public supervisory measures intended to verify a proper use of the benefits are necessary and usual. They may not, however, be expressly provided for in the relevant law. The need for intensive supervision and the system of supervision used are partly demonstrated by the creation of special bodies entrusted with supervisory tasks. Often, however, these tasks are performed by private or public banks on the basis of corresponding directives or guidelines.

In this connection we should distinguish control at the allocation stage and control at the utilisation stage. The former type includes control by imposing obligations which firms must meet in order to receive public benefits: presentation of annual accounts, for example, or forward planning projections. Inspections, audit and review during the utilisation process exemplify the second type.

VIII. The System of Decision-Making and Allocation

The finding that legal rules regarding the grant of subsidies often provide for the creation of supervisory bodies or delegate additional power to supervisory bodies already existent permits the conclusion that rules of procedure with general validity in relation to individual subsidy allocation and for the supervision of their proper use are lacking. Legal culture, in this respect, is, or is regarded as, insufficient. We find also that in addition to public authorities autonomous institutions, as well as public and private banks, are competent for the grant and allocation of subsidies in the individual countries.

A. Competence of Public Authorities

To identify more clearly the institutions competent for the legal implementation of economic policy in the different countries a distinction has to be drawn between competence to make general decisions on subsidies and competence to order the actual measure of subsidisation in the individual case. For fundamental decisions on the kind and extent of subsidies central bodies are nearly always competent. It is only in Germany and Italy that these decisions are also taken on the regional level (through the Länder and regioni). Here, regional legislation may be completely autonomous, but, to a certain extent, its function is to amplify and carry out central provisions and concepts. It thus represents local implementation of national laws.

The extent of delegation of decision-making power to specific autonomous organisations is striking. There is, however, a major difference between rules in the energy and manpower sectors. While in the Netherlands, France and Great Britain we almost always find central decisions in the area of energy policy, the power of decision in the area of manpower policy is – with the exception of the Netherlands – largely delegated to autonomous organisations. In the Netherlands public bodies also take all the fundamental decisions on subsidisation in the manpower policy sector. Still another peculiarity is to be found in Hungary. There, the National Bank of Hungary and the National Labour Office, with competence for general decisions on subsidies, are regarded as regulatory organs distinct from central government.

Accordingly, the significant difference between the very small number of subsidy rules reported in the area of French energy policy on the one hand and of German or Italian policy on the other can be explained by the fact that multi-stage measures are taken here. In Germany and Italy the utilisation of the subsidy instrument requires more than one measure at different levels. In France, there is no visible action taken below the central government level. If one also considers that in France the number of subsidy rules in the manpower policy area is very high, the presumption that hidden or invisible subsidies might be frequent in the area of energy policy because of the peculiarities of the French legal system is almost inevitable. M. Fromont therefore stresses that the legal technique of subsidisation often escapes notice by observers because it chiefly concerns financial aid distributed not by the public authorities but by credit institutions, which may be semi-public or even private.[38]

B. Autonomous Organisations

One peculiarity of subsidy allocation in the area of manpower policy is the employment of autonomous organisations entrusted with specifying the criteria of subsidy allocation, deciding who actually gets the subsidies and supervising their use. Public authorities thus delegate their competence to self-governing bodies among which, at least from some points of view, special funds and interministerial committees must also be counted. In addition, in all of the countries studied except Hungary, trade unions and employers' associations are also regarded as organisations competent for the legal implementation of economic policy, at least to the extent that they create legally binding rules through their agreements.

C. Public and Private Banks

The use made of public and private banks as channels for subsidy allocation and supervision is hard to determine with certainty. Beside the specialised institutions in the form of Development Banks that we find in Hungary, Germany and Italy, banks may participate in a less direct fashion through the grant of subsidies in the form of reductions of interest rates, as, for instance, in France and Great Britain.

---

[38] M. Fromont, "State Aids: Their Field of Operation and Legal Regime", below at pp. 150–160.

IX. Delegalisation

Following the evaluation of the national inventories and the comparative studies, it must be doubted whether subsidies are in general an instrument of economic policy which is less legalistic than others such as regulation. This certainly could not be said, for example, of easing subsidies in the form of tax reductions. Those who complain of "legal pollution" while only taking account of regulations in the narrower sense, should think also of the complicated systems of rules which relate to the grant of subsidies.

The classifications already developed[39] show that in almost all of the countries studied a complex legal structure is required before subsidies can actually be allocated and received. This starts with the making of plans and the adoption of corresponding laws providing means and delegating power to the central administration, to regions or regional parliaments or to autonomous bodies. Frequently, legal framework regulations still have to go through a further procedure of specification before their implementation by public authorities or other institutions is possible. Furthermore, an approval procedure and, last but not least, the supervision of subsidy use are still required. Finally, if subsidies are granted in the form of credits, their repayment still has to be regulated and supervised. On this basis it is hardly possible to make global statements about the "low" or "high" legal profile of subsidies and other public benefits as an instrument of policy. The only exceptions are perhaps public support through exemption from general duties, or public benefits allocated at the discretion of public authorities where few if any legal regulations are to be observed. Here it is clear that no complex legal procedure is necessary. Such measures however are for obvious reasons poorly represented in the inventories.

In any event, legal implementation of economic policy through subsidies and other public benefits is not a suitable means for combatting "legal pollution". Delegalisation in the area of subsidy allocation does not even seem to be desirable. The current trend is toward judicial enforcement of claims to the grant of subsidies and toward judicial control of public allocation practice.[40] At the same time, at least in some countries, a closer legal regulation of these instruments of economic

---

[39] See Methodological note, above, at pp. 50–54.

[40] Cf. for the United Kingdom, Ganz, *supra* note 36 at pp. 32–39, 46; for France, M. Fromont, *Rapport sur le Droit Economique Français* (1973, Brussels) at pp. 39–40, Scheuing, *supra* note 36 at pp. 102, 215 ff., 244 f., M. Auby et M. Fromont, *Recours contre les Actes Administratifs dans les Pays de la Communauté Economique Européenne* (1971, Paris) at pp. 239 ff.; for Italy, M. Sacchi Morsiani, *Report on Italian Economic Law* (1973, Brussels) at pp. 45 ff., Pericu, *supra* note 33 at pp. 148 ff., Auby et Fromont, at p. 303; for the Netherlands, P. Verloren van Themaat, *Report on the Economic Law of the Netherlands* (1973, Brussels) at pp. 55, 57; Reinders, *Subsidering van instellingen*, (1981) as well as B. Boerner and M. Bullinger, *Subventionen im Gemeinsamen Markt* (1978, Köln); concerning control through the EEC, cf. Commission Decision of July 22, 1982 no. 82/653/EEC in OJ 1982, L 277/15.

policy is considered necessary and is demanded more and more frequently.[41] There is no tendency towards delegalisation. The recent debate on additional legal guarantees concerning subsidy allocation rather shows the opposite trend: that more, rather than less, legalisation is regarded as necessary in the interest of the rule of law and of orderly procedure.

A warning must finally be given to avoid a tempting misinterpretation. Even if rules concerning subsidy allocation are to be regarded as a very legalistic instrument of economic policy, they can still simultaneously preserve a high degree of voluntariness and self-regulation as they hardly represent public compulsion. Accordingly, even if subsidy rules are criticised as "legal pollution", their abolition would not necessarily lead to more voluntariness and self-regulation, in that the economic policy goal pursued through their allocation might still require to be achieved by some other no less legalistic means. Delegalisation therefore is an alternative to legalistic rules concerning subsidy allocation only where other interventionist measures are at the same time abandoned.

---

[41] Cf. Bleckmann, "Ordnungsrahmen für das Recht der Subventionen", *Gutachten für den 55. Deutschen Juristentag,* (1984) at D 57 with reference to corresponding tendencies in Austria and Switzerland.

State Aids: Their Field of Operation and Legal Regime

MICHEL FROMONT

Dijon

Contents

In our view, there are four legal instruments of economic policy: supervision of the private economy, i.e. regulation of the behaviour of firms and verification of observance (one may even use the term economic policing): financial levies on the private economy, i.e. fiscal and parafiscal levies on firms, to which should probably be added certain aspects of monetary policy; support for the private economy, i.e. aid given to firms; and participation by public enterprise in economic activity, whether on a monopoly basis or in competition with private enterprises.

Among the aids given to firms, financial aid is the most important form of support to the private economy.[1] The other forms of aid have only a secondary

---

[1] General bibliography: French law: D. H. Scheuing, *Les aides financières*, (1974, Paris); P. H. Cassou, *Les aides financières aux entreprises*, (1977, Paris); R. Savy, *Droit public économique*, (second edition, 1977, Paris), at pp. 63 ff.; A. de Laubadère, *Droit public économique*, (4th ed. (with the collaboration of P. Delvolvé), 1983, Paris), at pp. 453 ff.; Savy and M. Fromont, *L'intervention des pouvoirs publics dans la vie économique*, in vol. 1, Institutions et politiques, (1978, Paris). German law: Bleckmann, *Subventionsrecht*, 1978; Ipsen and H. Zacher, *Verwaltung durch Subventionen*, VVDStRL) 25, (1967, Berlin); K. H. Friar, *Ordungsrahmen für das Recht der Subventionen*, 25. Juristentag, (1984, Munich); H. Jarass, *Wirtschaftsverwaltungsrecht und Wirtschaftsverfassungsrecht*, (2nd., ed., 1984, Frankfurt/M.), at para 14; H. Goetz, *Das Recht der Wirtschaftssubventionen*, (1966, Munich). H. Maurer, *Allgemeines Verwaltungsrecht*, (fourth ed., 1985, Munich), at para 17. English law: Y. Fortin, "Le contrôle de l'administration économique

importance. This is true first of all for the many types of aid in kind, less perhaps because they are negligible from the firm's point of view, than because their impact is relatively diffuse and therefore hard to evaluate. The main types of aid in kind are the provision of information, whose importance will increase with the growing complexity of our society's organisation: the availability of land (dependencies of the public domain or industrial sites), goods, or services on favourable terms (especially in the area of transport and telecommunications), the award of certain public contracts; and finally a number of legal privileges which government normally enjoys exclusively, but may exceptionally make available to deserving enterprises (for instance, the right to exercise a monopoly or to expropriate).

By contrast, aid is sometimes hard to distinguish from other measures which in principle have to do with other types of intervention by government. One may, for example, be in doubt as to the nature of measures whereby less restrictive fiscal or social rules are applied to certain enterprises. It is indisputable that these measures relate to the application of binding rules or of levies. It may however be considered that these fiscal or social exemptions should be regarded as aid whenever entitlement to them is subject to an individual administrative decision granting them, based on economic policy considerations. One may likewise wonder what is the nature of loans and guarantees accorded by public or semi-public credit institutions. In principle, such loans and guarantees are a simple manifestation of the action of public enterprises. However, whenever such financial facilities are accorded within the framework of a financial aid programme set up by government, they should be treated in the same manner as aid is dealt with by this study; in some countries, they even constitute an important means of financial aid.

Like all legal instruments of economic policy, financial aids are the result of both a political choice and legal constraints. The relations between politics and law are not in fact unilateral: politics certainly commands the choice of legal instruments; but the legal framework, generally the outcome of a long evolution and of previously made fundamental choices, pre-dates the political decisions of the moment and imposes constraints on them: ways of thinking, existence of higher rules, political and administrative institutions, and so on. In short, while economic law includes ephemeral legal rules that vary along with the relevant political decisions and have an indisputably instrumental character, it also includes stable, if not permanent, legal rules, which government must respect and which thereby limit its freedom to choose and handle legal instruments.

This dialectic of law and politics applies particularly to aid. Though this seems to be a pure product of political decisions, it is in reality the product of a sort of marriage between law and politics. This certainly applies to the construction of the legal regime for assistance, which depends both on political choices and on the pre-existing legal framework. It is, however, equally true of the actual decision to have recourse to financial aid, and hence for determining the area of aid.

en Grand-Bretagne" (1978, Paris); H. W. R. Wade, *Administrative Law*, (5th ed. 1982, Oxford); T. C. Daintith and T. A. E. Shape, "Britisches Subventionsrecht", in *Subventionen im Gemeinsamen Markt*, (ed. by Boerner/Bullinger, (1978, Cologne) at p. 97.

I. The Area of Operation Aid Policies

Appearances strongly support the view that the field occupied by aids depends essentially on political considerations. Nevertheless, it equally depends on legal facts, which are no less real for being less apparent.

A. Political Choices

All the countries of Western Europe have chosen the same type of economic system, namely the mixed economy, characterised by the co-existence of a private sector, often preponderant, and a public sector. They also have the same type of economic policy, characterised by the endeavour to conserve the mechanisms of the market economy, while at the same time correcting them. This endeavour to correct market mechanisms leads inevitably to the favouring of those techniques of economic supervision that fall short of being actual direction of the economy by government. Hence, it leads to the development of incentive measures whose effect is limited to bringing down the relative costs of the beneficiary enterprises, leaving them both autonomy and financial responsibility.

In this connection, the political rhetoric used by national leaderships is largely irrelevant. In particular, it matters little whether this or that country stresses the social market economy, or the special economic responsibilities of government. At most, this difference in rhetoric is reflected in greater or lesser clarity, and hence greater or lesser transparency vis-à-vis Community law, in the financial aid actually granted. It should further be noted that in this area the German Federal government, like the French government, periodically issues a report on subsidies.[2]

If a distinction is to be drawn, it should rather be between those countries that favour so-called global and indirect interventions (relating principally to public levies and to a lesser extent to certain techniques for supervising the private economy, particularly credit and monetary policies), and those countries that favour interventions of a selective nature (consisting either in the promulgation of discriminatory rules, or, more especially, in the granting of various subventions and aids). In our view, however, the difference is not great, since all countries of Western Europe practise both policies concurrently. As for the choice between techniques of supervising and techniques of supporting the private economy, the research reported elsewhere in this volume shows that it does not seem to depend on an overall philosophy of the economic action of government, but instead on legal considerations.[3]

B. Elements of the Legal System

The legal elements tending to influence the choice of financial aid from amongst the various conceivable intervention procedures all seem to us to be more bound up with a certain legal tradition and a certain conception of the organisation and

[2] M. Fromont and H. Siedentopf, "Le démantèlement des aides financières publiques", *Annuaire européen d'administration publique* 1983, at p. 635.
[3] See generally the contributions of Jarass and von Stebut above pp. 75–96 and 137–152.

action of government than with the existence of inviolable legal rules that those in government have to observe.

This is true first of all for the constitutional rules in force in countries with a written constitution. To be sure, the constitutional guarantee of property and of economic freedom would certainly be against total nationalisation of the economy or its generalised authoritarian control by the State, while it does not *a priori* stand in the way of systematic use of the technique of financial aid. However, this institutional guarantee is no bar to fairly large-scale nationalisations, as shown by the decision of the French Constitutional Council of January 16, 1982,[4] nor even of fairly far-reaching guidance of the action of private enterprises, as shown, for instance, by the decisions of the German Constitutional Court regarding the laws on wine, or alcohol made from wine, or the 1965 law on stocks of oil products.[5] Likewise, the principle of equality seems *a priori* to be against any allocation of financial aid to particular firms; but the study of constitutional case-law again shows that in reality it is opposed only to particular discriminations which are considered arbitrary, especially those specifically contrary to economic policy objectives. At most, it may be noted that these constitutional rules, in countries like Germany and France, inhibit the free creation of financial aid by local bodies, which explains why these bodies often prefer to grant aid in kind, on a case by case basis, and within no precise legal framework.[6]

It is even easier to demonstrate the proposition in cases where legal rules which might prevent the institution of financial aids are contained in a legislative text or in common law, and can thus be amended by simple enactment. Paradoxically, however, the existence of a body of rules of legislative or equivalent status quite often seems to induce government to prefer the simple amendment of the rules applying to relationships among individuals or between them and the State. This temptation seems particularly strong where such rules of law organise relations between private actors whether they be individuals or collective bodies, and thus do not create direct relationships between such actors and government. The tradition of respect for private autonomy then leads government to favour the amendment of rules applying to relationships between private persons. In this connection, the example of employment policy is remarkable: before setting up schemes of financial aid aimed at saving or creating jobs, the governments in the various countries studied first of all reformed the rules relating to the termination of employment contracts. Nevertheless, as research reported in this volume has shown, the two techniques are in reality more complementary than antagonistic.

Should the legal facts able to influence the choice of aid procedure be seen as including institutional factors, more specifically, the division of powers among legislature, executive and judiciary? One might, in fact, imagine that some countries might favour action by the legislature and the courts over that by the

---

[4] Decision nr. 81–132 DC of January 16, 1982, Rec. p. 18.

[5] BVerfGE 21, 150; BVerfGE 14, 120; BVerfGE 30, 292 (see our analysis in *Revue du droit public et de la Science Politique* 1972, p. 1465).

[6] In France, local bodies can set up aid programmes only to the strict extent authorised by the decentralisation laws of 1982 and 1983. In Germany, articles 91a, 91b, 104a and 109 of the Constitution put rather strict limits on the economic action of local bodies.

executive, regarded as dangerous to freedom, and consequently would prefer certain forms of supervision of private economic activity and of financial levies to financial aids, which by their necessarily selective nature involve intervention by the administration. Conversely, one might imagine that a government unsure of its parliamentary support or doubtful of the interpretations of the laws given by the courts might prefer recourse to the technique of aid, which can often be set up without intervention by the legislature, as being above all an administrative matter. Likewise, in a federal State, in which the federation has great financial power and little legislative power, as is the case with the United States, one might imagine that financial techniques would be preferred to legislative techniques.[7] Within the framework of the present study, however, such hypotheses are hard to verify beyond dispute, though these considerations very probably play some part.

As one might have expected, the legal factors do not play a decisive role in the choice of whether to use the instrument of financial aid; by contrast, they seem to play a more important part in the legal handling of aid, as we shall now show.

II. The Legal Regime of State Aids

To be effective, financial aid must be accorded selectively, which raises a difficult problem, since all Western legal systems maintain the ideal of the greatest possible subordination of the administration to pre-existing rules of law, i.e. to general, non-discriminatory rules. This is the major problem dominating the construction of the whole legal system for financial aids, whether it has to do with their creation, their award or their use.

A. The Creation of Financial Aids

The power to create financial aids necesarily belongs to public bodies that have considerable financial resources available to them. That is why financial aid is mainly State aid: in the case of a federal state such aids may come either from the federal government, or, when tax receipts are shared among the provincial governments, from such a government. However, the trend towards decentralisation that has characterised recent developments in certain countries, notably Italy and France, and also, specifically, the idea that financial aid should be adapted as far as possible to local economic realities, explains why such aid is increasingly often accorded by regions, sometimes in a framework of pre-established State regulation, which is nevertheless capable of modification. Aid granted by local authorities (municipalities and groups of municipalities) is far from being negligible, but is most frequently accorded on a case by case basis with no pre-established programme, and is therefore difficult to find out about, even for the Community authorities who have the task ensuring that it is in conformity with the Treaty establishing the European Economic Community.[8]

---

[7] See, however, Stewart, above, p. 98.
[8] B. Boerner and M. Bullinger, eds., *Subventionen im Gemeinsamen Markt*, (1978, Cologne).

Thus we come to the second problem relating to the creation of financial aid. What should be the legal form of the decision to create it? Ought it to be normative in character, i.e. to lay down general rules of law, or may it be informal, i.e. a mere document which is internal to the administration and a declaration of intent? The choice is important: in the first case, the aid measures will use the same legal techniques as economic supervision (or economic policing) measures, and are therefore largely subject to the principle of legality; in the second case, the aid measures are closer to financial decisions of private banks than to measures taken by public authorities. In short, the first system guarantees above all protection for the rights of enterprises, and the second allows delicate economic problems to be dealt with in a framework of commercial confidence.

Looking at the various countries studied, one finds that there has not yet been a clear decision between those alternatives. To be sure, budget authorisation is always necessary if the aid is financed from budget resources, but an aid is often included, not to say submerged, in an overall budget authorisation,[9] which in any case is designed only to provide the necessary financial means. In contrast, if the aid is financed from bank resources, government authorisation is sufficient to launch a loan publicly and gather the necessary funds. Sometimes it is not even necessary.

It is particularly important to determine the conditions to be met for obtaining aid. These are rarely defined by law, and not even always by government regulation. Quite often they are defined by a mere circular, or by a letter sent to the body responsible for allocating aid, or even a letter sent to a representative organisation of the enterprises concerned. From law one passes, then, to "non-law", or more exactly from the use of legal techniques specific to the exercise of public power to the pure and simple use of legal techniques applicable to relations between private persons, which afford considerable scope for secrecy and for the autonomy of the parties' will. The choice between the two techniques is certainly influenced by the country's legal tradition, but also by the desire of government to give more or less publicity to the operation, and hence by the greater or lesser number of enterprises which may be interested by the offer of public financial support, or the amount of discretion to be accorded to the allocating bodies. The legal factors play an essential but not exclusive role.

The duration of the aid programme does not depend on the legal form given to it, since budget authorisations may be renewed, and conversely a legislative or regulatory provision may be laid down for a limited period, or simply abrogated at the end of a year. In general, programmes of aid aimed at a fairly large number of enterprises have to last several years to have appreciable incentive effects, especially where investment subsidies are concerned; on the contrary, temporary aid is conceivable only to cope with a short-term crisis or to support a few well-informed big enterprises. The legal factor here seems to play a very minor part. However, things are different in the rather rare case where a body with its own staff has been created with the specific aim of allocating financial aid; such bodies

---

[9] Decision nr. 76–73 DC of December 28, 1976 of the French Constitutional Council, on the economic and social development fund supplies an excellent example.

seek to perpetuate themselves, and the best way of doing that is to conserve their reason for existence, namely the allocation of public aid. The example of the French National Cinema Centre is a good one; others might however be cited, particularly where professional bodies have been set up for such purposes. There is, then, a certain correlation between the duration of programmes and the authority responsible for implementing them, i.e. for deciding on the grant of aid.

B. The Granting of Financial Aids

The granting of financial aids is indisputably a delicate operation. As said above, it is necessarily a matter for the administration. Precisely because of its selective nature, aid can only very rarely have an automatic character, such as to permit the self-effacement of the administration in favour of judicial regulation of the programme. Aid may in fact be granted automatically only where it is aimed at correcting market mechanisms, particularly the effects of the law of supply and demand on prices, and hence at largely removing from the laws of the market particular economic agents regarded as unable to face competition by themselves, like farmers or film-makers.

But while the granting of subventions can only be discretionary, it must still not be arbitrary. The Western legal tradition is categorically opposed to this. The aid systems are therefore handled in such a way as to reconcile the necessary selection of enterprises with their no less necessary equality vis-à-vis the public authorities.

Two major legal techniques are used to this end. The first consists in defining normatively only the broad lines of the programme, leaving it up to the public administrative authorities responsible for implementing it to define the conditions of award in a very flexible fashion. In the event of dispute, the judge finds both that the administrative authority should in principle follow the instructions given to it, and at the same time have the power and even the duty to ignore them whenever special circumstances justify this. It is remarkable that British, German and French case law are in perfect agreement on this point. In the *British Oxygen Company* case, the House of Lords found in 1970 that the administrative authority could itself limit its own discretionary power in defining its principles of action;[10] likewise, the German federal administrative court accepts that the administrative authority should not without reason ignore its previous practice and the directives it has given itself (Vergaberichtlinien); finally, the French Conseil d'Etat allows an administrative authority to define the conditions for granting aid in a directive, but to depart from it in special circumstances.[11]

The second legal technique often escapes notice by observers because it chiefly concerns financial aid distributed not by the public authorities but by credit institutions, which may be public, semi-public or even private. In general, this

[10] *British Oxygen Co Ltd.* v. *Board of Trade* (1971) A. C. 610: see the commentary by Y. Fortin, *Le contrôle de l'administration économique en Grande-Bretagne, supra* note 1, at pp. 161 and 201.

[11] Conseil d'Etat. December 11, 1970, *Crédit foncier de France v. Demoiselle Gaudillat et Dame Ader,* Rec. p. 750, concl. Bertrand.

involves loans or guarantees on favourable terms which are granted on the basis of government support. This type of aid is allocated by credit institutions as if it involved simple loans or bank guarantees, but in reality they act within a framework of government directives or recommendations, which often take the form of mere letters. The discretionary power is then complete, since it is identified with the autonomy of will that private law acknowledges every banker to have (subject to a few limitations imposed by law), and observance of the principles laid down by government is assured only by the exercise of the control powers or means of pressure it has available. Obviously, this technique is particularly developed in countries which like France have almost entirely nationalised the banking system; it is however not unknown in other countries (e.g. for housing loans in Germany).

To compensate for the extent of discretionary power to grant aid, one might imagine the fairly extensive development of rules of procedure and form, particularly of principles of publicity, motivation and even of consultation of the enterprises concerned.[12] In fact this is by no means the case, and rules of procedure and form are hardly developed at all, even in a common law country like Britain. At most, one may note participation by representatives of the professions in certain decisions, and a tendency to require aid decisions to be motivated whenever they have an automatic character (a fairly marked development in France because of the law of July 17, 1978) or where the decision is one of rejection (para. 39 of the German code of administrative procedure). In any case, no specific procedure has been developed in respect of the granting of subventions. Probably in many areas the administration, or the credit institution entrusted with the distribution of aid, has preferred to use the procedure habitually followed by the banks and financial institutions, rather than follow the public administrative procedure which is established in many countries.

C. The Use of Aid

Where the conditions for granting aid are defined by the texts creating it or by subsequent regulation, they always refer, at least in general terms, to the use to be made of it, for instance in the form of a simple indication of the purpose for which the aid is to be employed. But precisely because these conditions are often defined in the vaguest of terms, the result as we have seen is that the allocating bodies have a freedom of evaluation which is almost the same as enjoyed by a private banker.

One might expect that as a *quid pro quo* the body allocating the aid would impose precise conditions for its use when granting it. In fact, however, the relations created by decisions awarding aid escape any precise regulation, even on an individual basis. Moreover, enterprises are rarely punished. For instance, they are never given orders to reimburse badly used aid, since by definition they are poorly run and therefore without financial resources. This is, moreover, the reason for the appearance of subventions which are reimbursable in the event not

---

[12] M. Fromont, "Le contrôle des aides financières publiques", *Actualité juridique: Droit administratif,* 1979, at p. 3.

of failure, but of success, which is quite paradoxical. The most one can say is that procedures for graduated payment have multiplied, allowing payments to be cancelled when they are no longer justified. It is only for enterprises in regular receipt of aid that there are developing controls that tend to transform them into semi-public, and sometimes even public, enterprises (participatory loans, government supervision).

This shortcoming of legal systems for aid has the effect of notably restricting the effectiveness of this type of State intervention. Selective aid seems to be justified only by way of an improvised and temporary remedy, and only automatic aid allows systematic (and hence rather blind) compensation for the backwardness of certain regions or of certain types of enterprise (farming, press, cinema etc.).

Conclusion

Public financial aid is indisputably the most striking manifestation of the modern State's financial power, but this instrument of intervention has not yet secured the legal status it deserves. To be fully effective, it should borrow both the techniques of administrative law (rigorous definition of basic terms, observance of minimal procedural and basic rules) and those of banking and commercial law (particularly, guarantees of proper performance and follow-up of the use of aid).

Part Four

The Public Sector

The Public Sector as Object and Instrument of Economic Policy

LEIGH HANCHER

Warwick

Introduction

This chapter is concerned with the use of the public sector by government to achieve stated objectives in the fields of manpower policy and energy policy. Previous studies of economic law and policy in the EC countries have recognised the importance of the public sector as an instrument of economic policy. VerLoren van Themaat distinguished the use of the economic weight of the public sector, which he classified as an indirect measure, from global instruments of economic policy such as subsidies or regulation.[1] Breyer in his study of regulation com-

---

[1] VerLoren van Themaat, 1973, *Economic Law of the Member States of the EC in an Economic and Monetary Union* (1983, Brussels) at para 4.1.

mented that "nationalisation or direct participation by government in the management of an enterprise should be kept in mind as a possible, though cursorily explored, alternative to classical regulation".[2] Other writers, commenting on the failure of business regulation in Western Europe to achieve its stated aims have suggested nationalisation or some form of public ownership as an alternative mechanism for achieving desired policy goals.[3]

At the risk of over-simplifying we may argue that the difference between the regulatory and public sector strategies of economic policy implementation is that the former is a method of control without ownership, the latter of management through ownership. If regulation as a technique of economic policy implementation has failed in its task in guiding or influencing the activities of private enterprise, then control through ownership might appear as an attractive and efficient alternative. However, it seems fair to say that control through ownership has not been examined as a possible solution to the so-called "regulatory" crisis.[4] The present concerns of the various protagonists in the deregulation debate are limited to either a dismantling of all forms of state intervention on the one hand[5] or alternatively, are directed to improvements in regulatory techniques.[6]

The proximity of government by virtue of *ownership* to the initial targets of policy measures may allow for the selective deployment of alternative forms of instruments in the pursuit of specified goals, and forms may be of a legal or non-legal quality. Legal forms will be arms-length or *visible,* while non-legal forms may often be *invisible* and based on hierarchical elements inherent in the relationship between government and public enterprise. However, in certain cases hierarchical instruments may be legal in form and hence visible. In the context of our current survey on the legal implementation of energy and manpower policies, an important focus of inquiry is the legal profile of this latter category of instruments: the public nature of the enterprise *may* lead to those instruments being operationalised in a *distinctive way* from arms-length controls addressed to the private sector.

Most non-legal studies of the role of the public sector in policy implementation have focused on the use of the public sector as a tool of *macro-economic policy,*[7] while legal studies have been concerned with the form and structure of the public sector and the legal nature of their relations with government and with the private sector.[8] The theory of public enterprise in Western Europe posits a broad division between the government and the enterprise, giving the government broad powers

---

[2] S. Breyer, *Regulation and its Reform.* (1981 Cambridge, Mass.)

[3] R. Cranston, "Regulation and Deregulation" (1982) 25 *University of New South Wales Law Journal* 1.

[4] G. Teubner, "Juridification: Concepts, Aspects, Limits, Solutions" in Teubner, G., ed., *Juridification of Social Sciences* (1987, Berlin).

[5] S. Stigler, "The Theory of Economic Regulation" (1971) 11 *Bell Journal of Economics* 3.

[6] Breyer, *supra* note 2. Trubek, *Reflexive Law and the Regulatory Crisis* (1984, Wisconsin); B. Mittnick, *The Political Economy of Regulation* (1980, New York).

[7] VerLoren van Themaat, *supra,* note 1.

[8] W. Friedman ed., *Public and Public Enterprise in Mixed Economies* (1974, London).

of policy determination and the enterprise autonomy of operations.[9] By setting broad policy goals for the public sector governments may realise the goals of macro-economic policy without resort to further types of policy instrument such as regulation, taxation or subsidy. In focusing attention on the the concept of a "public sector entity", be it another level of government, a parastate agency or a public enterprise, we would wish to explore whether, if at all, central government has at its disposal a set of administrative controls or alternatively, financial power which allows it to utilise the public sector in preference to or in conjunction with other "arms-length" policy instruments.

In this context public sector management might be seen as an attractive alternative to classical regulation and other global policy instruments because it is perceived to be indirect in the sense (a) that it is less *visible:* government may use the economic powers which flow from ownership to achieve ends similar to those achieved by more overt forms of instrument without having to obtain parliamentary or popular support and (b) it is more *flexible:* government may utilise a variety of means to influence the public sector. A government may alter the levels of finance available to the public sector either in general or for specific projects. It may influence the public sector entity through its power to appoint or dismiss chairmen and members of boards; or by granting it certain privileges and concessions, or exempting it from the requirements of certain regulations. These controls are all examples of hierarchical instruments which may be legal or non-legal in *form,* depending on (i) the constitutive statutes of public enterprise, (ii) constitutional contraints on governments, (iii) national traditions of state intervention, factors to be further explored in section III below.

Obviously, the distinction between regulatory control and management is never as clear-cut as this in practice. As we shall see in section I, the term "public sector" has been divided into two distinct categories: national, regional and local bureaucracies, and public enterprises. While any global definition of a public sector firm is fraught with difficulties, its core would include criteria for distinguishing the enterprise from government departments in general. If the enterprise has some degree of autonomy from government bureaucracy it may well be that the method of control through regulation prevails over that of management. Factors influencing the initial *choice* of method will be considered in detail in sections III and IV.

In this chapter, I do not propose to attempt a comprehensive survey of the legal and economic nature of the public sector in each of the six countries but to assess its potential as a policy instrument, and the manner in which it is used in relation to a specific set of policy objectives. Assuming at least a limited degree of public sector autonomy and the problems that poses for instrumental analysis, section II goes on to inquire as to the nature of public sector management. As Professor Cassese notes in his contribution,[10]

> the weak point in the concept of public enterprise as an instrument of economic policy is that which may be called the *transitive quality* of the term publicness.

[9] *Ibid.*
[10] S. Cassese, below at p. 239.

If, in order to realise policy objectives, public enterprises are endowed with some degree of autonomy from central government and control of their activities is attempted through hierarchical instruments, tensions may develop over the concepts of 'publicness' and that of 'enterprise'. As Cassese and other commentators have pointed out, governments do not always have guidelines on which to base and implement coherent policies. Rescue operations leading to public ownership may be mounted without any clear conception of the future role these industries are expected to play. On the one hand, enterprises may be set up to pursue a specific goal but, having accomplished their task, government might feel contrained, perhaps for employment reasons, from disbanding them. On the other hand, public enterprises may well be endowed with a sufficient degree of autonomy to expand and diversify their functions. Indeed their very survival in the market, free from financial dependence on government, may make horizontal or vertical expansion an economic necessity. This process acquires its own momentum and may result in either (i) the ability of the enterprise to resist central, hierarchical controls, or alternatively, and potentially more damaging for an instrumental concept of the public sector, (ii) the ability of public enterprise to impose its own goals on government, hence transforming the nature of policy objectives.

The methodology though not the conceptual framework of our study has tended to assume the unidirectional quality of policy objectives, and the method of classifying instruments and measure has not allowed us to look behind the *form* of the measure. It is proposed partially to resolve this difficulty by attempting to identify the *purpose* of public sector management and in turn to relate that purpose to the choice of measure. In particular, as outlined in Section II, it is necessary to distinguish between the public sector as *object* as opposed to *instrument* of policy.

With these caveats in mind the aim of this chapter is to attempt to assess in two limited policy areas, energy policy and manpower policy, the relative importance of public sector management as an alternative form of economic policy implementation, the policy objectives to which this instrument seems suited and the legal profile of public sector management as compared with non-public sector instruments. From a legal perspective it is interesting to inquire how far we can explain national differences in the use of "classical regulation", taxation and subsidies by reference to variations in the *quality* and *quantity* of public sector management in the different countries under study. Having identified the extent and reasons for the choice of public sector management it must then be asked to what extent legal mechanisms aimed at public sector management vary from measures directed at the private sector. As a general hypothesis it could be assumed that where the public sector is small compared to the private sector, many of the measures will reflect patterns of control in the latter sector. This may also be true in cases where governments have traditionally refrained from using the public sector as an instrument for the achievement of macro-economic goals. If the public sector is expected to operate through the market mechanism and is endowed with considerable operational autonomy, government measures of public sector management will probably be limited to specific, narrowly defined interventions to secure particular results which would not normally result from the play of market forces.

The relevant question from our point of view is how far that intervention conforms to or deviates from legal styles of intervention in the private sector.

Conversely, in countries where the public sector is relatively large, the private sector may be a less significant model, especially if the public sector is seen as an important instrument of economic policy. In such situations it may well be the case that there is a tendency towards informal, ad hoc intervention, made possible by both the government's formal, legal powers of control and by the fact that it holds the purse strings. This may in turn influence the quality and quantity of other forms of policy instrument to be directed towards the remainder of the private sector. Alternatively the size and nature of the public sector may mean that government cannot rely on managerial or hierarchical powers alone: formal regulatory controls are required. The relevant question to be posed here is whether instruments are operationalised in a distinctive way.

It is suggested that the potential instrumentality of the public sector will depend on several factors: the legal form and structure of the public sector, its size and economic and political importance, and the traditions of state intervention and patterns of administrative and legal styles in each country. These factors may also have an impact on the legal *form* of public sector management. Section III will examine the nature and importance of the public sector in each country, and will attempt to describe the traditions and styles of state intervention. Section IV will then return to the question of the choice of public sector management as an instrument in furtherance of our lists of policy objectives. How far does that choice reflect past tradition, and how far is it a function of previously existing patterns of ownership and organisation? To what extent is the public sector used as an instrument in the attainment of sectoral (i.e. energy) as opposed to cross-sectoral (i.e. manpower) policy objectives? Can we distinguish between the resort to public sector management in the case of pro-active objectives (for example, job creation, alteration of energy supply patterns) as opposed to reactive objectives, (for example, job maintenance or short-term energy crisis management measures)?[11] Have Western European governments been able to utilise the public sector as an innovative mechanism? As Hans Jarass argued in his chapter, in Europe the regulatory instrument has not been favoured as a means of promoting innovation,[12] in marked contrast to the American experience of regulation with its emphasis on standard-setting.[13]

In section V we will examine the legal operationalisation of public sector management as an instrument of energy and manpower policy and compare the legal profile of instruments addressed to the public sector with those addressed to the private sector. If the latter is a model for public sector management we might anticipate a similarity in the legal profile of public sector management. If the private sector is a less significant model, the interesting question is not only the

---

[11] Cf. T. Daintith, "Law as Policy Instrument: A Comparative Perspective", above at p. 37.

[12] H. Jarass, "Regulation as an Instrument of Policy" above at pp. 88–90.

[13] R. Stewart, "Regulation and the Crisis of Legalisation in the United States," above at p. 103.

extent to which the legal profile of the public sector model is distinctive but also whether the forms of intervention in the private sector have been approximated to those of the public sector. It is hoped that this type of analysis will allow us to evaluate the process of assimilation and interpenetration of public and private in each of the countries under study, and so further contribute to our understanding of the nature and limits of instrumental law, and its use in the implementation of policy.

I. Problems of Definition and Delineation

A comprehensive definition of the term public sector would be problematic in a single country study, and is of course more so in a comparative one. It would seem fair to say that the term has no fixed legal or economic meaning and can be used to describe, alternatively (or at one and the same time) the state bureaucracy, (including central, rational and local bureaucracies) public expenditure and publicly owned enterprises.

In our country studies of the implementation of manpower policy and energy policy, the term "public sector management" has been taken to refer either to state bureaucracy or public enterprise. The problem of control of public expenditure has not been directly addressed. However government's concern to reduce the overall public sector deficit will obviously have an impact on the institutional, financial and economic framework within which its public sector industries and the bureaucracy operate. For example, in the *United Kingdom* government policy on the nationalised industries has been heavily influenced by the public sector spending targets introduced by the Conservative government shortly after its election in the spring of 1979.[14] The legal and institutional developments in the management of national public expenditure policy are, however, beyond the scope of this chapter.

In distinguishing between the two major components of the public sector, state bureaucracy and public enterprise, a working definition of public enterprise is necessary to separate the commercial from the administrative activities of the state sector. The term 'public enterprise' has no static meaning: public enterprise assumes a variety of legal forms and indeed a spectrum of legal possibilities exists throughout the European Community, if not in Hungary. An attempt to explore and explain these legal forms is not called for here, but in order to distinguish the private from the public and the commercial component from the 'bureaucratic' component, I will treat an enterprise as a public one if it fulfills the following economic criteria:

(a) if it sells its goods or services at a price related to costs, irrespective of whether the final price is fixed in accordance with general 'social' objectives. This serves to distinguish enterprises from the state bureaucracy whose services are financed by taxes.
(b) if the state (local or central) retains a direct or indirect share of the capital of the enterprise.

[14] See below at pp. 193–194.

I suggest that for comparative purposes it is better to focus on economic criteria as opposed to legal criteria. While French jurisprudence is virtually unanimous in regarding separate legal personality as an essential attribute of a public enterprise under French law, insistence upon this attribute would tend to falsify comparisons between countries, notably by excluding from the scope of public enterprise in France and in Italy important industries such as posts and communications.[15]

It is suggested that this working definition of public enterprise will be useful in distinguishing policy directed towards restructuring or rationalising state bureaucracies from measures addressed to particular enterprises. While both types of policy instrument have been classified as *'public sector management'* in our surveys of national implementation of manpower and energy policies, substantive changes in administrative style need only concern us in so far as they affect the framework within which policy towards public sector firms is delivered.[16]

The term 'public sector employee' also poses problems for a comparative study and is linked to the problem of establishing a clear boundary between the administration and public enterprise. Public sector employees are usually defined as those employed in various departments and agencies at central, state, provincial and local level which produce *non-market* goods and services.[17] However, in some countries, as noted above, market goods are produced by entities which have no distinct legal status, making for difficulties of comparison. Complications are added by the fact that not all of the countries studied adopt a similar division between public and private employees in terms of their legal position, if they adopt one at all. In general all employees of legally independent public corporations are classified as 'private' while all those involved in traditional public administration and defence functions are 'public'. An employee of the German railway company is a public sector employee and his or her contract of employment is regulated by separate legislation.[18] His or her counterpart in the United Kingdom would be regarded as a private employee, and even although the United Kingdom does not recognise the sharp distinction between private and public law, there are special legal rules governing certain categories of public employee.[19] Such considerations are obviously important to a legal study of the implementation of manpower policy if rights are significantly affected by this categorisation. The measures listed in the national inventories did not highlight a significant reliance on the non-commercial public sector for the pursuit of manpower policy objectives, but further study of national policies suggests that the use of the commercial public sector to achieve certain manpower policy goals may be an important alternative to other instrument forms. For these reasons, the *major focus* of this paper will be

---

[15] The French PTT is a 'régie directe' while the Italian Post and Telecommunications service is an *azienda autonoma* (RDL no 520, 23 April 1925).

[16] On administrative style see Harmathy, below at pp. 245–266.

[17] United Nations, *A System of National Accounts* (1968, New York).

[18] W. H. McPherson, *Public Employee Relations in Germany*, (1971, Ann Arbor).

[19] R. Hepple and P. O'Higgins, *Public Employee Trade Unions in the United Kingdom: The Legal Framework*, (1971, Ann Arbor).

on public enterprises, as it is suggested that a comparison between managerial techniques in the public sector and arms-length controls in the private sector constitutes the most fruitful area of study.

II. The Public Sector as Object and Instrument

Our study is concerned with a strictly delineated set of policy objectives focussing on (i) choice of instruments and (ii) the degree of legalisation in terms of the number or complexity or other characteristics of the legal measures associated with the operation of these instruments.

The collection and collation of national legal measures by individual rapporteurs reflects the rather 'catch-all' nature of the term 'public sector'. If a measure had as its target one or a number of public sector agencies, it could be labelled "public sector management". A closer examination of the national inventories reveals that the overarching category of "public sector management" is something of a black hole. In order to gain further insights into the strategic deployment of the public sector in the pursuit of policy objectives it is necessary to tease out the *rationale* behind the appearance of legal measures directed to the public sector of the economy. It is possible to imagine a number of motives:

(a) government selects the public sector because it wishes to influence its behaviour directly. This in turn relates to the point made earlier about the 'transitivity' of the term 'publicness'. Government-owned firms might have become too autonomous and so measures might be targeted at particular activities which governments consider undesirable. Alternatively measures may seek to impose new duties on public enterprises in an attempt to require them to fulfil certain tasks which they have either failed to fulfil in the past or have hitherto not been required to perform.

(b) alternatively government selects the public sector:

   (1) because it has no choice: private sector activity is either non-existent or inconsequential; for example electricity production and supply in the United Kingdom, France and Italy. In this respect, the public sector could serve as both object and instrument: a policy aimed at a public sector monopoly firm, such as a pricing policy, could make use of that firm as an instrument for promoting alteration of energy consumption patterns in the private sector, and would hence be an alternative to regulation.

   (2) because it wishes to influence indirectly the behaviour of the non-public sector: for example public sector procurement policy may be based on criteria which favour firms in particular sectors or territorial areas, and hence the objectives of job creation or job maintenance could be indirectly pursued.[20]

As this threefold classification suggests, there may be legal and non-legal reasons for the choice of the public sector as an *instrument* of policy. Legal reasons relate,

[20] For the UK, see C. Harlow, *Commercial Interdependence* (1983, Policy Studies Institute, London).

inter alia, to constitutional restrictions requiring certain activities to be performed as public services and not transferred to the private sector. A useful illustration of the way in which such a restriction might militate against the policy designs of government can be found in the legal disputes surrounding the decision of the French government to reorganise the Commissariat de l'Energie Atomique in 1976. Article 34 of the French Constitution prohibits the transfer of public services to the private sector unless such transfer is made the subject of legislation, approved by Parliament. By a decree of 1975[21] however, the Government proposed to transfer certain of the CEA's commercial interests to a wholly owned subsidiary – COGEMA, in which the CEA would be the sole shareholder. Several French trade unions challenged the legality of this decree on the grounds that COGEMA, as an enterprise at private law, would have the power to create further subsidiaries and hence attract private capital in violation of Article 34. The Conseil d'Etat was satisfied, however that overall control of COGEMA's activities would be retained by the CEA and hence it would remain in the public sector.[22]

More important, however, are the political and economic arguments which explain the choice of the public sector to achieve policy goals, including the belief that natural monopolies should not remain in private ownership, that adequate investment or risk taking initiatives will not be secured without state intervention, or that national security can only be secured through direct ownership. As we shall see, many enterprises were taken into public ownership for these reasons in the post-war period. However in the decade 1973–1983 with which we are concerned, in addition to certain enterprises being taken into some form of public ownership, we can observe two further developments.[23] First in the United Kingdom[24] and to a lesser extent the Netherlands and Germany, there has been a marked attempt to "disengage" the state from large sectors of the economy, while in Italy and more especially France the public sector has expanded in size and scope. Secondly, in Hungary, France and to a lesser extent Italy, the public sector has been identified in various national plans as a major instrument for the achievement of energy policy and manpower objectives. To secure planned manpower and energy targets, certain modifications in the relationship between the public sector firm and government on the one hand and in the relationship between the public sector firm and the remainder of the private sector have resulted. A large part of the commercial public sector and, in particular, the energy utilities were taken into public ownership at a time prior to the 1973 oil crises and subsequent economic recession. In many cases they had been legally constituted to serve a specific set of goals: to superimpose energy or manpower policy goals may require statutory amendments.

The decade 1973–1983 witnessed not only significant changes in the size and nature of the public sector but also fundamental changes in the perception of its legitimate role in the economy. Specific policies targeted at the public sector,

---

[21] Decree no. 75–1250, December 26, 1975.
[22] CE 24 Nov. 1978, *COGEMA*, AJDA, 1979. 240.
[23] Shonfield A., "The Politics of the Mixed Economy" (1980) *International Affairs* 1.
[24] For example Energy Act 1983 and Oil and Gas Enterprise Act 1982, s. 29.

whether they take the form of privatisation or of granting greater autonomy to a firm which remains in public ownership, may be part of a wider policy, aimed at restoring greater competitiveness to the economy as a whole. This form of public sector management is an indirect means of influencing private economic actors.

However public sector management as an *object* of policy retains considerable importance, even in countries with large privatisation programmes. As I will attempt to show, it is important to bring out the extent to which the style of public sector management has charged in recent years. When VerLoren van Themaat classified the public sector an indirect instrument of economic policy, he was referring to the economic power and influence that could be exerted by the sheer size of that sector of the economy that was in *public ownership* in one form or another.[25] Public ownership retains its overall importance in the energy sector, as the Tables at Appendix I show. However when we turn to other industrial sectors or to examine countries such as Germany or the Netherlands where the degree and extent of public ownership is more limited than in the United Kingdom, France or Italy, it is important to be aware firstly that *ownership* does not necessarily imply *control,* a proposition well known to company law, but secondly that even where absolute ownership is lacking, a state might use alternative legal forms to further the interests of those industries in which it has, for a variety of reasons, a stake: just as ownership does not necessarily imply control and therefore management, the converse might not be true either. A limited degree of public *participation* in an enterprise, together with effective deployment of regulation and the selective use of subsidies, might provide an effective alternative to full ownership in realising policy goals. Finally we should be aware of the significance of competition or 'anti-trust' laws in policing unregulated markets. Although it might be argued that competition law is another form of government regulation, it has been argued that "in principle (the) antitrust laws differ from classical regulation both in their aims and methods. The anti-trust laws seek to create or maintain the *conditions* of a competitive market rather than *replicate* the results of competition or correct for defects of competitive markets. In doing so, they act negatively through a few highly general provisions prohibiting certain forms of private conduct".[26] As we shall see certain countries which do not favour a high profile public sector often use competition law to protect and promote national firms, thus achieving similar results. I will term the use of regulation, subsidies and "competition law" in the context of the public sector as *supplementary* instruments, and will further subdivide this category into *supportive* and *directive* instruments.

Obviously Hungary provides a different perspective on public sector management, as the socialisation of ownership would imply that most of the legal measures adopted will bear upon the public sector. Hungary offers an interesting comparison more from the point of view of technique.

The following section will be devoted to a brief survey of the nature and development of the role of the public sector in the six countries in the ten year period 1973–1983. While changes in the level of public sector employment are

[25] VerLoren van Themaat, *supra* note 1.
[26] Breyer, *supra* note 2.

more easy to assess quantitatively, the changing economic role of public sector enterprises can only be determined qualitatively, through an examination of the evolution of specific national policy objectives over the past decade and an evaluation of the fluctuations in importance and size of the public sector, the form and structure of control of public enterprise and the major developments affecting each government's attitude to and relationship with its administration and its state-owned enterprises. Furthermore, comprehensive assessment of the present use of the public sector as policy instrument requires an understanding of the various legal forms underpinning ownership and management functions.

As our focus is on two distinct policies – manpower adjustment and energy policy – I will attempt to review recent developments from the point of view of their impact on the implementation of these two policies. This means that certain important features of public ownership are not covered and in particular the participation of government in banking, finance and credit institutions are not referred to. While such an omission would be fatal to a general survey of the public sector and state intervention in the economy, our concerns are more limited here. Secondly, focus is largely directed at public sector management on a national as opposed to a regional or local level. The use of the public sector at lower levels of government has always been of considerable importance in West Germany and the Netherlands and is becoming of greater significance in Italy and France, but a full account of its nature would be beyond our scope. Where, however, the involvement of regions or localities significantly affects the legal content of measures aimed at public sector management, the increasingly important issue of decentralisation will be touched upon. Finally public procurement policy has not been examined in any great detail, although this must surely remain an important feature of the instrumental use of the public sector. Moreover, there is evidence, at least in the United Kingdom context, that as ownership declines, managerial objectives may be at least partially secured through contracts between government and newly privatised industry.[27] Procurement policy remains an under-researched area in the various countries under study and it has not been possible even to attempt to fill that gap within the confines of this research project. However it must be acknowledged that a full appreciation of the importance of the public sector as a policy instrument will not be possible until such time as detailed research on procurement policy is completed.[28]

[27] B. Hogwood, "Regulation and Deregulation: The Instruments of Desire" (1983) 61 *Public Administration* 6.

[28] R. Williams and R. Smellie "Public Purchasing: An Administrative Cinderella" (1985) 63 *Public Administration* 23.

III. The Nature and Changing Role of the Public Sector

A. Italy

1. Size and Importance

Following VerLoren van Themaat, I will take the *Italian* situation as a point of departure.[29] The Italian public sector enterprises are recognised as an extremely important instrument of national economic policy and have in turn become a key instrument in the implementation of energy and manpower adjustment policy. The following Table illustrates the importance of the public sector and in particular the importance of state shareholdings (whose subsidiaries are classified as partly state-owned enterprises) in the Italian economy. The share of the non-market public sector in Italy in 1979 was 14.7 per cent of total employment, while the total employment in public corporations was 6.3 per cent, bringing the total to 21.0 per cent.[30]

Table 1: Principal economic data for Italian public enterprises for the period and percentages of corresponding national values.

Absolute values – '000 Million Lire unless otherwise stated)

	1977	1978	1979	1980
Gross product	9,914.4	12,271.9	14,535.3	16,741.2
Percentage of national total	24.3%	23.8%	24.0%	24.7%
Fixed investment	4,702.4	5,426.0	6,190.7	6,792.7
Percentage of national total	47.4%	46.7%	49.0%	47.1%
Personnel costs	9,168.6	11,096.0	13.029.5	14,966.4
Percentage of national total	28.5%	28.6%	28.8%	29.3%
Number of employees –'000's	1,265.3	1,283.4	1,291.6	1,276.8
Percentage of national total	23.7%	24.6%	25.0%	25.4%

Source CEEP: Public Enterprise in the European Community, Brussels 1981, p. 101.

If we refer to the Tables at Appendix I, we can see that public enterprise occupies a strategic role in the Italian energy sector, while Table 1 above indicates the overall importance of public involvement in the industrial sector.

Public ownership as a means of promoting industrial development and modernisation dates back to the Fascist era, with the creation of the Istituto per la Ricostruzione Industriale (IRI) in 1933 in response to a banking collapse.[31] The IRI is not only the oldest state holding company: it is also the largest. Through six finanziarie (financial holding companies) IRI controls several hundred operating

---

[29] *Supra* note 1.
[30] OECD, *Employment in the Public Sector,* (1982, Paris). The CEEP Study (1981) puts this figure at 25.4 per cent.
[31] R. Romeo, *Breve storia della grande industria in Italia* (4th ed., 1972, Bologna).

companies in all the vital sectors of the economy including shipbuilding, steel, shipping and telecommunications. IRI's present statute dates back to 1948 and lays down a very general objective for the company: "IRI manages the shareholdings and assets in its possession."

ENI, the second largest state enterprise controls directly and indirectly more than 200 companies in a wide range of sectors, but its multisector structure is more integrated than IRI and its activities have traditionally been concentrated in the field of oil and gas. ENI's statute of 1953, in contrast to that of IRI, lays down clear objectives for the company: "ENI should promote and carry out projects of national interest in the field of hydrocarbons and natural gases."[32] A principal point of contrast between these two major state holdings companies has been the relatively small participation of the private sector in ENI's subsidiary companies.[33]

In the mining and extraction sector private participation was practically nil, in part because the mining law of 1957 prohibited ENI from setting up joint ventures with private firms to prospect for oil and gas in the Italian mainland.[34] This law was abolished in 1967, and with the exception of the Po valley where it continues to enjoy exclusive rights, ENI is authorised to set up joint venture companies. The multi-sectoral dimension which the ENI group had acquired by the mid-1960's was legitimated by law no 1153 of 1967, which extended the companies' lawful objectives to include the chemical and nuclear sector.[35] ENI was given the task of searching for and processing uranium while IRI was to be responsible for constructing nuclear power plants. It is impossible to describe in detail here the problems of coordinating the various state-owned elements of the nuclear industry but, as we shall see, many of the measures addressed to this sector have been aimed at achieving a unified structure.[36]

ENI is also a fully integrated oil company, embracing all the various branches of the industry: exploration, extraction, transport, refining, distribution and chemicals[37] and has extensive interests in exploration and exploitation of natural gas, but unlike its French and British counterparts, has had only limited success in developing a distribution network for natural gas[38].

In recognition of ENI's powerful position the first National Plan entrusted it with the task of guaranteeing the national supply of oil and natural gas. Although the government simultaneously stated that it was not its intention to encourage concentration in the oil industry nor to increase ENI's share of the market at all

[32] Law no. 136 of February 10, 1953.
[33] F. Forte et al., I "modelli" dei gruppi a partecipazione statale (1972, Napoli) at pp. 34–35.
[34] Mining Law no. 6 of January 11, 1957 in Gazz. Uff., January 29, 1957, no. 25.
[35] Law no 1153, of November 14, 1967 in Gazz. Uff., December 13, 1967 no 340.
[36] See T. Daintith and L. Hancher, Energy Strategy in Europe: The Legal Framework (1986, Berlin) at p. 52 for background to this and below at pp. 188–191.
[37] For annual accounts of activities in these various fields, see ENI, Relazione e Bilancio, annual.
[38] D. Cozzi, Breve storia dell'ENI, at pp. 101–102 (1975, Bologna).

costs,[39] in fact ENI was to acquire, within the space of a few months, the interests of the departing multinational Shell.[40]

The remaining state-holding company EFIM was set up in 1962 in accordance with Law no. 1589 of 1956, the general statute on state holding companies to administer the state's holdings in the heavy engineering industry.[41] Although it was intended that this new Ente di Gestione's activities were to be limited to the mechanical industry,[42] EFIM was quick to expand its activities outside the engineering sector. In response to objections from the Corte dei Conti, EFIM's constitutive statute was amended, giving it the right to create new subsidiaries.[43]

The fourth state holding company, EGAM, which was formally created in 1958 to administer state holdings in the mining sector, remained dormant during the 1960s, and was only activated in 1971. The company's attempts to diversify into shipping insurance created a scandal, and it was liquidated by law in 1977,[44] its companies being distributed between ENI and IRI.

It should be noted that the national agency for electrical energy (ENEL) created in 1962[45] is not an ente di gestione, but a public agency enterprise, (ente pubblico economico), a concept used to describe legal entities which are not governed completely by the normal regulations of private law, but whose relationship with the state is regulated by their respective constitutive statutes. ENEL is charged with the function of carrying out through the national territory the activities of production, import and export, transport conversion and distribution of and sale of all forms of electrical energy. There are however three exceptions to ENEL's legal monopoly: local communes who applied for an authorisation to operate municipal companies within two years of the 1962 law coming into force: self generators, and companies producing less than 15 million kilowatts per year. These types of companies are subject to the co-ordination and control of ENEL,[46] so that the latter is usually described as an administrative, as opposed to a legal monopoly.[47]

2. Form and Structure

The fundamental provisions regulating the Italian system of state holdings are to be found in (i) the constitutive statute of each state holding company, and (ii) Law no. 1589 of 1956, as amended, which institutionalised the "IRI formula" for mixed ownership enterprise and lays down that the holdings of the state in joint-stock companies shall be organised in accordance with criteria di economicita. Control

---

[39] Mondo Economico, no 36/37, 27. September–9. October 1975, "Rapporto mese", at pp. 35–36.

[40] G. Levy, "The Relationship between Oil Companies and Consumer State Governments in Europe, 1973–72" (1984) 2 Journal of Energy and Natural Resource Law 9.

[41] Originally held by EFIM, Pres. Decree no. 38 of January 27, 1962.

[42] See G. Alzona, L'EFIM? profilo di un ente a participazione statale (CEEP, 1976).

[43] Pres. Decree no. 1284 of August 9, 1967.

[44] Law no. 267 of June 6, 1977 (in Gazz. Uff., June 7, 1977, no. 153).

[45] Law no. 1643, 1962.

[46] Law no. 452 June 27, 1969 and DPR no 342, March 19, 1965.

[47] Quadri. 6 Diritto Pubblico (2nd edition, 1980, Padova) at p. 79.

over these state holding companies was transferred to a newly created Ministry for State Participation and to a special interministerial committee. When national economic planning was introduced in 1967[48] this committee was abolished and its functions devolved to the CIPE (Comitato Interministeriale della Programmazione Economica), thereby linking the state enterprises to the organ responsible for economic planning. Thus, the institutional structure of the system of state holdings acquired a clearly defined legal structure; with private, joint-stock companies at the base, at the apex government institutions, and in between a number of state holding companies, the Enti di Gestione. As we shall see, amendments to this system have been made, but the basic pyramidic structure remains.

The CIPE presides over the system and formulates the general policy of the state enterprises. The five year sectoral plans of each state holding company have to be approved by the CIPE, as do recommendations to increase the *fondi di dotazione*, the endowment fund.[49] Any increase in the endowment funds must be approved by Parliament, after the CIPE has given an opinion, but the laws authorising increases of endowment funds are merely financial laws and in general do not allocate the funds for specific purposes.

The Minister for State Participation occupies an intermediate position between the CIPE and the holding companies, communicating the plans of the former to the latter and reporting on the financial and administrative activities of the holding companies.

The Enti di Gestione (but not the industrial companies in which they hold shares) are further subject to the scrutiny of the Corte di Conti.[50] The Court in theory presents an annual report to parliament.[51] ENEL is supervised by both the CIPE and the Ministry of Industry and Commerce. The former approves ENEL's annual and plurennial programme. In carrying out its institutional objective – the production and distribution of energy at a level suitable in quantity and price for a balanced economic development of the country[52] – the agency normally acts in accordance with the prescriptions of private law.[53] The price at which it contracts to sell industry is regulated by the CIP (the Interministerial Committee on Prices).

ENEL's capital originally consisted only of the assets transferred on nationalisation, but due to its critical financial situation, a *fondi di dotazione* similar to those established for the state holding companies was created in 1973[54] and has subsequently been increased on several occasions.

---

[48] Law no. 48 of 1967, Decree no. 554 of 1967.

[49] Any increase in the endowment funds must be approved by Parliament, after the CIPE has given an opinion, but the laws authorising increases of endowment funds are merely financial laws and in general do not allocate the funds for specific purposes.

[50] Law no. 259, March 21, 1958, implementing article 100 of the Constitution.

[51] It was only in 1975 that the Court submitted its report on the activity of IRI in the financial years 1964–1972.

[52] Article 1 of Law no 1643, 1962.

[53] Art. 3, no. 11, of Law no. 1643, 1962.

[54] Law no 253, May 7, 1973.

3. Developments

Despite the presence of this formal hierarchical system of control, there is little scope for direct control over the state holding companies' dealings or their private sector companies. Moreover the original statutes only provide for Government 'supervision' which does not imply overall control of all the acts of public sector firms. During the period of the so-called "economic miracle", the relative lack of control meant that the state holdings diversified their interests beyond their legal objectives, as in the case of ENI and EFIM, with government subsequently legitimising this action. The aggressive and expansionist policies of personalities such as Mattei at ENI and Sinigaglia at Finsider (a wholly owned subsidiary of IRI) in the 1950's and 1960's have left a legacy of 'giants with feet of clay' to the 1980's, giants now financially dependent on government and, while earlier studies of the activities of the state holding companies celebrated their dynamism and leadership in the modernisation of the Italian economy,[55] "by the end of the 1970's these appraisals appear like a description of a paradise lost".[56]

Varying explanations for the poor performance of the public sector have been advanced, none of which can be examined in any detail here.[57] The main factors held responsible for the crisis of state industry, are the sectoral composition of state industry, the expansionary strategy of the 1970's, the under capitalisation of the state holding companies, the subordination of management to political forces and the imposition of the so-called 'improper burdens' (political and social obligations imposed by Parliament and government), preventing the holding companies from operating in accordance with the *criteria di economicita*.[58]

Irrespective of the validity of these varying explanations, the distinctive feature of the state sector, 'historically the principal instrument of industrial policy' in Italy,[59] is that it is now perceived to be incapable of performing this task adequately and hence the revitalisation of public entrepreneurship has become a goal of successive governments. Policy objectives to achieve this revitalisation can be divided into three, and each has an impact on the realisation of effective manpower and energy policies:

(i) a reform of the institutional setting of state holdings; (ii) the concentration of resources by creating delimited areas and an end to the instrumental use of the state holding system for the purpose of rescue operations; (iii) the identification of the specific financial requirements of state companies and of the methods of satisfying them.[60]

These reforms have tended to take place at sectoral level. As mentioned above, while Italy possesses a public monopoly in nuclear energy production and electri-

---

[55] S. Holland, *The State as Entrepreneur* (1972, London).

[56] M. Kreile, "Crisis Management in Italy" in S. Wilks and K. Dyson eds., *Industrial Crises* (1983, Oxford).

[57] See Kreile, *supra* note 56, for an outline plus further references.

[58] R. Prodi 'Italy' in R. Vernon (ed.), *Big Business and the State* (1974, London).

[59] C. Scognamiglio, *Crisi e risanamento dell'industria italiana*, (1979, Milan).

[60] Extracted from de Michels, G. "Rapporto di sintesi: Le linee di una politica delle partecipazioni statali", reprinted in CEEP: *Public Enterprise in the EC* (1981, Brussels).

city generation, responsibility for the various aspects of the nuclear fuel cycle was divided between three public enterprises: ENEL had been given responsibility for the production of nuclear power for use in electricity generation,[61] the CNEN was responsible for research and development while ENI had been given responsibility for production and sale of nuclear fuels.[62]

Although all three bodies are subject to the supervision of the CIPE and the Ministry of Industry (and state participation in the case of ENI), it appears that there was little coordination of their respective aspirations. The 1975 National Energy Plan had drawn attention to this defect but it was only in March 1982 that the organisational functions of the CNEN were reformed and its powers increased to create a new Comitato nazionale per la ricerca e per lo sviluppo dell'energia nucleare e dell'energia alternativa.[63]

Legislation aimed at incorporating the regional authorities into the process of selecting nuclear sites had been introduced in 1975,[64] but serious delays in the nuclear power programme persist. A new law of January 1983 however has made provision for the allocation of grants to Communes and Regions operating electrical power stations fuelled by combustibles other than hydrocarbons. This law obliges ENEL to give grants to the Communes and to the Regions in whose territory plants for the production of electricity are located.[65]

In the industrial sector, Law no. 675 of 1977[66] introduced a series of innovations in the institutions and style of policy making. These included an attempt to reorganise the system of granting funds to both private and public sector industry and to eliminate political clientilism by limiting the discretionary financial powers of government, hence satisfying the third objective, outlined above. Law no. 675 also attempted to satisfy the second objective by creating the CIP (Interministerial Committee for the Co-ordination of Industrial Policy) within the CIPE. This Committee was charged with responsibility for the activities of GEPI.[67] GEPI was created as a public finance company to offer support in conjunction with a private partner, for private firms in difficulty and to restore them to self-sufficiency.[68] The Law no. 675 limited GEPI's interventions to the Mezzogiorno and the underdeveloped areas of central Italy, in an attempt to avoid further indiscriminate rescues. GEPI was also made responsible for financing public sector firms and for designating those sectors where intervention by the state holding companies was necessary. The Law obliged the Ministry of State holdings to submit a medium term investment programme of the state holding companies and determined that

[61] Pres. Decree no 185, of February 13, 1964 in Gazz. Uff., May 3, 1964, no 112.
[62] Law no 1153 of November 14, 1967 in Gazz. Uff., December 13, 1967 no 340.
[63] Law no 84 of March 5, 1982 in Gazz. Uff., March 22, 1982 no 79.
[64] Law no 393, of August 2, 1975 in Gazz. Uff., August 23, 1975 no 224.
[65] Law no 8 of January 18, 1983 in Gazz. Uff., January 14, 1983 no 13.
[66] Gazz. Uff., September 7, 1977 no 234.
[67] Societa di Gestioni e participazioni industriali.
[68] Law no 184, March 3, 1971 in Gazz. Uff., April 28, 1971 no 105. – The companies aided by the GEPI were primarily in the textile and engineering sectors. On its failure see Schoppa P.: "State, Market, Bank and Firm. Objects and Instruments of Public Intervention", in *Review of Economic Conditions in Italy*, June 1980, pp. 243–303.

the projected increases of the endowment funds were only to finance new investment or to enlarge or modernise existing funds. Additional 'soft loans' were only to be granted if plans conformed to GEPI directives.

Law 675 is considered a complete failure and rather than shielding public firms from political interference, it has only served to increase it with the result that sectoral restructuring and investment plans will only be approved if employment levels are maintained. Augmentations of the endowment funds have often been severely delayed or indeed fail to materialise at all.[69]

In conclusion, although the public sector remains a major policy instrument in Italy, governmental control and especially parliamentary control has remained weak. This has enabled public sector companies to diversify when they are financially strong but has led to their dependence on the state when they are financially weak. Measures such as those recently enacted have aimed, unsuccessfully, to put a halt to the *random* use of the public sector as a legally invisible instrument of policy.

B. France

1. Size and Importance

Public sector participation in *France* is equally of long standing tradition, dating back to Louis XIV (who nationalised the tobacco industry). The 'first wave' of nationalisation occurred under the 1936 Popular Front and the post-war governments of 1945–1946, and the 'second wave' in 1982 with the nationalisation of five major industrial groups (Saint Gobbain, CGE, Rhône-Poulenc, Thomson-Brandt, PUK), and holdings in Matra and Dassault were increased.[70] The two major steel producers Usinor and Sacilor were effectively nationalised in the previous year. Private banks with deposits of more than Fr. 1 billion were also nationalised, and the state gained control over a number of other companies via its acquisition of two holding companies, Paribas and Indosuez. The motivation behind these two 'waves' was however dissimilar. The three large energy concerns, EDF, GDF and CDF, were created with the aim of rationalising and modernising the existing industries, while certain key sectors were brought under state control (banking and insurance). The Compagnie Française des Pétroles (CFP) was created in 1924 with the dual aim of exploiting the French oil concession in Iraq and of assuring the development of the French refining industry through its subsidiary, CFR. The Régie Autonome de Pétrole (RAP) was created in 1939 to exploit gas produced in the Saint Marcet region, thus assuring state controlled exploration and development throughout the national territory. The Bureau de Recherche de Pétroles (BRP) was set up in 1945, an ordonnance of the same year established the Commissariat à l'Energie Atomique, and the Société Nationale des Pétroles d'Aquitaine (SNPA) was established to exploit hydrocarbon deposits in that region.[71]

---

[69] D. Fausto, "The Finance of Italian Public Enterprises", *Annals of Public and Cooperative Economy*, (March 1982) at pp. 19–20.

[70] Law no. February 11, 1982 in J. O. February 2, 1982.

[71] See Daintith and Hancher, *supra* note 36, Chapter 5.

If the first wave of nationalisations had been inspired by the need for post-war reconstruction, the second wave of nationalisations effected by the Law of February 11, 1982 has been motivated by the desire to rebuild the national industrial structure and to 'reconquer' the domestic market. In 1981, President Mitterand declared that "les nationalisations sont une arme de défense de la production française" qui "correspond à une certaine vue de la société moderne – et aussi à un souci d'efficacité".[72]

The entrepreneurial autonomy of the public sector was to be assured: "la nationalisation n'est pas une étatisation".[73] The means by which this goal is to be secured and the extent to which such an approach marks a break with or a continuation of past practice, and the political and legal wrangles leading up to the nationalisations of 1982 will be explored below.[74] A distinguishing feature of French public sector involvement is its presence in the so-called new technology industries.[75]

Following the 1982 nationalisations, the size of the public sector increased dramatically, especially in the industrial sector. In 1981 11.0 per cent of the active population was employed by public enterprise as opposed to 7.5 per cent in 1979, while employment in the administrative public sector stood at 14 per cent.[76] In 1981 total percentage of national production represented by the public sector in the different sectors of the economy was as follows.

Table 2: National Production and the French Public Sector[77]

Sector:	Percentage under public sector control	Sector:	Percentage under public sector control
Energy		*Finance*	
Coal	95%	Banks pre-nationalisation	59%
Electricity production	89%	post-nationalisation	91%
Natural gas production	100%	Insurance	36%
Petroleum refining and		*Industry*	
distribution	23%	pre-nationalisation	18%
Transport and Communication		post-nationalisation	32%
Rail	100%		
Air	87%		
Sea	10%		
TV, radio, post and			
telecommunications	100%		

---

[72] Quoted in A. Delion, "Les entreprises publiques et le concept d'efficacité," (1981) *Revue Française d'administration publique*, 650.

[73] A. Boubil, "Nationalisation, les conditions du succès", (1981) *Revue Française de l'Administration Publique*, 643.

[74] For a useful introduction see A. Delion and M. Durupty, *Les Nationalisations* (1982, Paris).

[75] For a detailed account of the economic importance of the public sector, see A. Delion "La place des entreprises publiques dans l'économie" (1983) 1824, *Problèmes économiques*, 18 mai, at p. 1824.

[76] OECD *supra* note 30.

[77] Source: Delion and Durupty, *supra* note 74.

Following the 1982 nationalisations, the state is now the largest employer, with approximately two million civil servants having security of tenure. With the addition of over 600,000 salaried employees following the nationalisations, France is now on a par with Austria in its level of public sector employment.[78] A reduction in the size of the civil service was a long-standing objective which the Giscard Government had intended to implement.[79] However, the size of the post-nationalisation public sector has continued to expand,[80] although the Mitterand government has attempted to create additional jobs in the public sector by reducing the working week, and by encouraging part-time work, early retirement and fixed term contracts.[81]

2. Form and Structure

In 1963, A. G. Delion noted:

> The principal theoretical difficulty preventing the development of a consistent doctrine about public enterprises as an institution is the diversity of their legal appearance. Their conditions of creation and their system of management conflict, their legal forms vary, the statutes proliferate without relationship to the facts; the several efforts to establish order, notably in 1947/48, have failed.[82]

As with the Italian public sector, French public enterprise may take a variety of legal forms; some may have no distinct legal personality (e.g. régies) while those that do may be wholly or partly state owned. Wholly state owned companies may be subject to public law (the établissements publics nationaux à caractère industriel et commercial (EPIC), such as EDF, GDF) or private law (the société nationale e.g. Banque de France). Partly owned enterprises usually have the form Société d'Economie Mixte (SEM) and are subject to private law (e.g. CNR, CFP). The newly nationalised companies have retained their private law form. As in the Italian case, subsidiaries of the various public enterprises are subject to private law.

In contrast to Italy there is no single Minister responsible for state participation: "technical" tutelle is assured by the Ministry responsible for the particular industry or economic sector to which the public enterprise belongs while responsibility for "financial" tutelle rests with the Ministry of the Economy and Finance. The legal form of the enterprise is not reflected in the allocation of an enterprise to a particular ministry. As in Italy, the government has the right to nominate the President (PDG) of public sector enterprises, although it is usually argued that these appointments are not subject to political exigencies in the way that they are in Italy.

---

[78] Mouriaux, R. Fard, "Unemployment Policy in France 1976–1982", in J. J. Richardson and R. Henning, *Unemployment Policy Responses of Western Democracies*, (1984, London) at p. 150.

[79] J. Auroux, *Les Droits des travailleurs*, (1981, Paris) at p. 13.

[80] Mouriaux, *supra* note 78.

[81] These measures were incorporated in the solidarity contracts, adopted by the Council of Ministers on October 20, 1982.

[82] A. Delion, *Le statut des entreprises publiques* (1967, Paris).

The most important method of controlling the activities of public enterprise is through the provision of funding, and as in Italy this tends to be the preserve of government, with parliament only approving general appropriations in the annual budget, of funds to cover capital and revenue subsidies, issues of additional capital and FDES (Fonds de Développement Economique et Social) loans.

Ministerial approval is theoretically required for all planning, investment and pricing decisions, but it is generally argued that the degree of control exercised in this way is uneven, varying according to the bargaining strength of the enterprise concerned, the importance which government attaches to a particular objective, the priorities of national and sectoral plans, and the extent to which these coincide with the objectives of the individual enterprises. Examples of contradictory practices abound.[83] While the Giscard government wished to accord considerable autonomy to the Elf-Aquitaine group in developing long-term oil and gas supplies, the company's proposed purchase of the American mining company, Kerr McGee, was blocked on account of the expenditure involved. Prime Minister Barre argued that the expenditure of over 16 billion francs would lead to "an indiscriminate extension of the public sector". It was perhaps exactly for this reason that the Socialist Prime Minister Mauroy authorised the purchase of Texas-Gulf the following year.[84] Nonetheless the Socialist government has been quick to intervene in activities of their public oil companies which do not accord well with foreign policy, as in the case of CFP's attempt to suspend its purchases of Mexican oil or Elf Aquitaine's proposed deal with Libya. In the latter case the government reverted to the traditional type of control over the company's activities, blocking the proposed investment in Libya on grounds of non-authorisation by the Minister.

As with the Italian case, a centralised system of indicative planning together with a theroretically extensive network of control over the public sector belies reality. However in France it is necessary to distinguish between the large public enterprise such as CFP and Elf-Aquitaine which are highly profitable and capable of raising capital to acquire foreign interests and those financially dependent on the state. CDF and to a certain extent GDF have been traditionally under-capitalised, while EDF has increasingly had to rely on the provision of state finance to fund the expansion of the nuclear programme.

3. Developments
The major characteristics in the development of the French public sector appear to be the conflicting desire of government to increase the financial and managerial autonomy of the public sector while harnessing it to the pursuit of government objectives and, secondly, the growth of participation in subsidiary companies

---

[83] See M. Durupty, "La Maitresse de l'Etat sur les entreprises publiques" (1981), Revue Française d'Administration Publique 731 for a useful sectorial breakdown of policy unconsistencies. For a review of the influence of the public enterprises in the planning process in general, see N. Lucas, *Energy: Planning, Politics and Policy in France* (1979, London).

[84] Durupty, *supra* note 83, at p. 735.

(politique de filialisation) which has de facto allowed certain public sector companies an increasing independence from their sponsoring departments. Efforts to restructure public enterprise reflect this polarisation. On the one hand, the extension of state intervention through equity holdings in private companies, the so-called "nationalisations silencieuses",[85] would seem to imply that at a time of economic crisis the public sector expands. At the same time, following the Nora Report of 1967, there has been a continued 'privatisation' of the managerial practices of numerous public firms, either as a means of granting autonomy for its own sake or to allow the enterprises to compete on the international scene.[86] The reorganisation of the state petroleum companies, commencing in 1967 with the fusion of the BRP and ERAP[87] followed in 1976 by the fusion of ERAP with SNPA to form Elf-ERAP[88] was motivated by the government's desire to compete in the international market. ERAP, constituted as an EPIC, is primarily a state holding company. As a result of the merger, it increased its holding in SNPA from 52 per cent to 70 per cent, and at first sight it would appear that the new arrangements, with the state holding company at the apex, left the public nature of the merged company unchanged.[89] In fact the 1976 reorganisation gave the SNPA, a société anonyme, the central role, thus 'privatising' the managerial arrangements.[90]

A similar process of transformation has occurred in the nuclear sector. In 1970 the CEA was authorised to diversify its field of activities from the scientific and research aspects of atomic energy into the mere commercial aspects. This process of diversification was reinforced with the creation in 1975 of COGEMA (Compagnie générale des matières premières) with responsbility for the production of nuclear fuels. As we have noted, the legality of this was challenged by the French unions.[91] In both cases, the creation of subsidiaries has allowed for greater participation of private capital and in consequence a diminishing role for direct state control.[92]

Furthermore, the creation of subsidiaries and the extent to which public enterprises have diversified their interests has led commentators to describe the French public sector as being dominated by the 'groupe public' – a concept which

---

[85] Rapport d'information, fait du nom de la Commission des Finances sur le contrôle des entreprises publiques en 1977 (Filiales et prises de participation des entreprises publiques) par E. Bonnefois, J. O. R. F. Doc. Senat, no 379, juin 16, 1977, at p. 189.

[86] Rapport (Nora) sur les entreprises publiques, Groupe de travail du comité interministeriel des entreprises publiques (avril 1967).

[87] Daintith and Hancher *supra* note 36. Chapter 5.

[88] L. Grayson, *The National Oil Companies*, chapter 4 on the S. N. E. A., (1981, Chichester) at pp. 75–106.

[89] M. Debene, 'Le redeploiement des entreprises publiques", *Droit Social*, 1978. 75, and P. Huet, "Aspects juridiques de la restructuration du secteur pétrolier d'Etat," Recueil Dalloz, 1979, Chron. 89. See also Colson J. P., "Aspects juridiques de la politique nucléaire de la République," AJDA, juin 1977, p. 290.

[90] Huet, *supra* note 89.

[91] Colson *supra* note 89.

[92] *Ibid.*

has no juridicial validity but which aptly describes the nature of the public sector in France. It is the emergence of this phenomenon which has caused a re-evaluation of the potential instrumentality of the public sector in France in the pursuit of conjunctural goals. As noted the Nora Report of 1967 recommended a move away from 'économie de commandement' to an 'économie de concertation' as far as the public sector was concerned. The initial attempts to free public sector firms from direct control took the form of *'contrats du programme'* with EDF and SNCF. However these contracts were rendered obsolete by the oil crisis of 1973–74 and the recession which followed, the government exercising strict control over tariff increases in an attempt to control inflation. However the principle of the 'politique contractuelle' was revived for both private and public sector in the process leading up to the adoption of the Eighth National Plan. A *contrat d'entreprise* was concluded with CDF in 1978, providing for a fixed rate of investment and level of subsidisation by the government. Despite the existence of this contract, CDF was required to continue the exploitation of a non-profitable mine at Ladrecht where no alternative employment was available thus putting an end to a one-year strikes.

While seeming to relax its a priori controls, the government strengthened its a posteriori scrutiny of the activities of the public sector, through the increased powers of the Cour de Comptes to investigate both the activities of the public enterprises and indirectly, their subsidiaries.[93] The Socialist Government elected in 1981 appears committed to the principle, if not the practice of managerial autonomy via the conclusion of contracts:

> il ne faut pas que les entreprises industrielles soient des appendices de l'administration. Leur autonomie de décision et d'action doit être totale. Les contrôles necessaires seront effectués a posterio. Le secteur nationalisé exercera son action en respectant les règles de la concurrence loyale.[94]

Consequently the Ninth National Plan has made extensive use of the 'politique contractuelle' in specifying goals for the newly nationalised industries and we will examine the impact of these developments in the context of energy and manpower objectives below. It should be observed that, as in Italy control over the activities of the public sector is somewhat uneven. While the statutes of the different French public utilities provide for strict control on the running of the companies, in practice these legal controls are of little consequence. The financial standing of the firm is the more important factor in determining the relationship between government and the firm. Parliamentary control remains weak, and although the process of diversification and expansion has weakened governmental control over the oil and nuclear sector, the ability of public companies to absorb troubled private sector firms has had its advantages for the government, allowing for potential use of the public sector as an invisible policy instrument.

[93] Law no. 76–539 of 22 June 1976.
[94] F. Mitterand, Press conference, February 23, 1982.

C. The United Kingdom

1. Size and Importance

If the thrust of recent developments in France has been to locate public enterprise firmly at the centre of the economic stage, their counterparts in the United Kingdom have been gently nudged into the wings, or indeed dismissed from the cast entirely. The present government's commitment to privatisation, to reducing monopoly power and to curbing public expenditure has characterised its attitude to the public sector. Appendix 2 contains a list of the public enterprises which have been sold between 1979–1984.

Prior to the 'privatisation waves of 1981–1984' the relative size of the public enterprise sector was as follows:

Table 3: The Size of the Public Sector in the UK

	1976	1977	1978	1979
% contribution of GDP	11.8	11.6	11.4	11.1
% total employment	7.9	7.7	8.0	8.1

Source: CEEP Review (1981)[95]

The OECD estimated the share of the administrative public sector in total employment in the United Kingdom to be 21.5 per cent in 1979, a level which appeared to have remained static since 1975.

Nationalisation of the three main energy industries – coal, electricity and gas – occurred in the immediate post-war period.[96] The government has had a stake in the oil industry since 1914 when it acquired a share in the British Petroleum company. The decades following the post-war nationalisations saw a period of reorganisation and concentration. In 1957 the Central Electricity Generating Board (CEGB) was created with responsibility for supplying the 12 Area Boards in England and Wales, and an Electricity Council was created with the primary duty of advising the Minister on policy and pricing.[97] The Conservative government has challenged the role of the CEGB by removing its monopoly powers of electricity generation.[98]

As with France and Italy, the development of nuclear power has been undertaken by a distinct public body. The United Kingdom Energy Authority (UKAEA) was established to produce, use and dispose of atomic energy, to conduct research and to carry out other activities.[99] Since then the UKAEA has overseen "the

---

[95] These figures include certain organisations other than the nationalised industries, such as housing corporations and passenger transport executives, but not limited liability companies which were wholly or partly owned by the government, directly or via the former National Enterprise Board.

[96] Coal Nationalisation Act 1946; Electricity Act 1947; Gas Act 1948.

[97] Electricity Act 1957, s. 2.

[98] Energy Act 1983.

[99] Atomic Energy Authority Act 1954, ss. 1 and 18.

biggest injection of public money into a single technology ever seen in Britain".[100] As in France, the military and technical aspects of the UKAEA have been separated from its more commercial activities.[101]

A similar process of rationalisation and centralisation took place in the gas industry, following the discovery of large quantities of natural gas in the southern basin of the North Sea. The British Gas Corporation (BGC) was created in 1972[102] and given all statutory responsibilities for the industry, as well as a monopoly of supply.[103] The National Coal Board (NCB) was endowed with a virtual monopoly of coal production in 1946, and its activities have been confined to coal production and distribution, although it did have some interests in North Sea oil and gas exploration prior to the creation of the British National Oil Corporation (BNOC) in 1975 when its interests were transferred to the latter.[104] The nature of BNOC and the subsequent creation of Britoil and Enterprise Oil will be dealt with below.

Following criticisms of the lack of effective oil depletion and oil revenue policies[105] and the return to power of a Labour government in 1974, a policy of a more active state participation in the exploration and production of North Sea oil was pursued. The government considered British Petroleum (BP), a multinational company in which it then held a 40 per cent shareholding, for this purpose, but anxiety over the possible reactions of foreign governments prevented any further development of this kind. Two of the existing state energy corporations had already participated in the first four licensing rounds, and presumably their interests could have been extended. However in order to compete effectively in a market dominated by the highly integrated oil majors, the government was anxious to establish a company of similar size and standing in order to establish a source of expertise and knowledge which would be at the disposal of the public sector and government. The importance the government attached to this was reflected in the 1975 Act, Section 3(3), placing BNOC under a duty to act as adviser on oil policy matters. The desire to acquire the necessary expertise to intervene effectively in the oil market also motivated the German government to encourage the merger of Veba and Deminex in 1974.[106]

Although the Government had originally intended to buy its way into commercial finds as a full licensee with a 51 per cent interest to be held by the newly created BNOC[107] the Labour government instead relied upon a policy of participation through negotiated agreements with the intention that the private companies would be left financially no better or no worse off through having entered these

[100] M. Ince, *Energy Policy* (1982, London) at p. 32.
[101] The Atomic Energy Act 1971 established two units within the authority as private companies, the Radiochemicals Centre Ltd. and British Nuclear Fuels Ltd. (BNFL).
[102] Gas Act 1972.
[103] Section 29.
[104] Coal Industry Act 1977.
[105] Public Accounts Committee, North Sea Oil and Gas, (1972–73) H. C.
[106] See Grayson *supra* note 88, Chapter 6 on Veba, at pp. 146–174.
[107] Petroleum and Submarine Pipelines Act 1975.

participation agreements, under which BNOC was to have the right to take, at market price, 51 per cent of all oil produced. All 62 companies licensed in the first four rounds, before the creation of BNOC, concluded such agreements.

When the new conservative government came to power in 1979, the Secretary of State for Energy announced that BNOC would no longer act in its role as adviser,[108] and that its privileges could be removed. The government also announced its intention to privatise the Corporation and in 1982 passed the Oil and Gas (Enterprise) Act, which privatised the exploration and production, but not the participation functions of BNOC. The former were transferred to a new Corporation, Britoil PLC, while BNOC retained its participation, trading and government agency functions. A participation agreement was then concluded between the privatised Britoil and BNOC.

Until March 1985 BNOC remained as a state corporation whose principal activity was the lifting of participation and royalty oil and its disposal in the national interest. However as a result of the heavy trading losses sustained by BNOC in its attempts to maintain North Sea oil prices, the government announced its intention to abolish BNOC and its rights to participation oil.[109] Nonetheless the government has retained its commitment to some form of state agency with access to royalty oil, hence ensuring security of supplies.

In the industrial sector, nationalisation tended to be *in* rather than *of* sectors in general decline or sudden crisis. Large sections of the steel industry were first nationalised in 1947, denationalised then renationalised by virtue of the Iron and Steel Act 1967. In the engineering industry the government was obliged to rescue Rolls Royce Ltd. in 1971 and Upper Clyde Shipbuilders the following year. The British Leyland Act of 1975 enabled the Secretary of State to buy up a large part of the equity in the ailing car manufacturing company. In 1977 the Aircraft and Shipbuilding Act transferred the assets of four engineering companies and 27 shipbuilding companies to two new public corporations, British Aerospace and British shipbuilding.

British attempts to emulate the French and Italian practices of 'state-led' approaches to industrial modernisation and to adopt the French system of indicative planning have not met with great success. The Industrial Reorganisation Corporation set up in 1966[110] was wound up by the Conservative Government in 1971.[111] However a largely similar departmental Industrial Reorganisation Executive was created in the following year.[112] The National Enterprise Board (NEB) was created in 1975[113] to fulfill a role similar to that of the IRC "to secure where necessary large scale sustained investment to offset the effects of the short-term pull of market forces".[114] As with its predecessor, the NEB has tended to be

---

[108] H. C. Debates vol. 970, cols 891–2, July 26, 1979.
[109] Financial Times, March 14, 1985.
[110] Industrial Reorganisation Corporation Act 1966.
[111] Industry Act 1971, s. 1.
[112] Industry Act 1972.
[113] Industry Act 1975.
[114] Cmnd 5710, August 1974.

saddled with 'lame ducks' and had only succeeded in fulfilling its entrepreneurial role to a very limited extent by the time its powers were substantially reduced by the Conservatives in the 1980 Industry Act,[115] and its remaining holdings finally transferred to the National Research and Development Corporation.

2. Form and Structure

As in the Italian and French case, public enterprise may take many legal forms in the United Kingdom. All those which are to be examined here are statutory corporations whose functions and purposes are determined by Parliament under the form of legislation. While it is not possible to impose such system in the various provisions as would allow for a brief discussion of the legal nature of the functions of public enterprise and the nature of ministerial powers in determining the range of activities in which each corporation may engage, two features of the legislation deserve comment. Firstly it would seem that successive labour and conservative governments have attempted to determine the permitted scope of the public sector's ancillary activities with as much precision as possible thus preventing, without a priori consent, the diversification of the enterprise.[116] In general it would appear to be the case that British public enterprise has not diversified its activities through the acquisition of shares in private companies in the way that its French counterpart has done. Where profitable subsidiaries have been set up the present government has made it its policy to transfer these to the private sector thereby confining the range of activities of public sector companies as narrowly as possible.[117]

The second of the legislative features to which we referred above, is the Minister's powers to order divestiture of assets or discontinuance of activities, a power which features in varying forms in the Acts which constituted the post-war corporations.[118] This means the process of privatisation can be achieved without the need for new global legislation. The Minister's powers to order divestiture may be restricted in that a relevant statute (for example Section 7[2] of the Gas Act 1972) may require him to be satisfied, before he exercises his powers, that the relevant activities are not necessary or that their cessation will not be prejudicial to the proper discharge of the duties of the relevant board. The very vagueness of these provisions open up the possibility of a challenge in the courts by a recalcitrant board. On the whole, British governments have tended to resort to either ad hoc legislation widening ministerial powers[119] in order to avoid the risk of their policy decisions being challenged in the courts,[120] or to informal pressure and non-renewal of posts. If a divestiture order is made under existing legislation it will often be required to be in the form of a statutory instrument, thus allowing

[115] W. Grant, *The Political Economy of Industrial Policy*, (1982, London).
[116] T. Daintith, "Public and Private Enterprise in the United Kingdom," in W. Friedman ed., *Public and Private Enterprise in Mixed Economies*, (London, 1974), at p. 195.
[117] British Rail, for example, was forced to sell its prestigious chain of hotels.
[118] See Daintith *supra* note 116, at pp. 232–233.
[119] For example the Gas Act 1972 section 7(2).
[120] For example of the latter, see R. Baldwin, "The CAA: A Quango Unleashed", (1980) 58 *Public Administration* 287.

some scope for parliamentary debate and possible disapproval.[121] The disposal of the UKAEA's interests in Amersham International was undertaken in this way.[122]

Challenges to some recent Ministerial directions have been considered by public corporations, but in the final event compliance has been secured before the matter reached the courts. The government recently announced its intention to review and update the existing statutes of the nationalised industries with the aim of setting out a common core framework to be applied to all industries remaining in the public sector.[123] These proposals which have so far met with strong disapproval from the industries concerned would, if implemented, allow government greater power to direct corporations to dispose of profitable subsidiaries, would substantially reduce the financial independence of those corporations, or parts of these corporations which remained in public ownership as well as considerably extending powers over the appointment and dismissal of chairmen.

In contrast to Italy, there is no single minister responsible for state participation but in practice three departments are primarily involved: Trade and Industry (DTI) for the industrial sector, Environment for transport (except air transport which is the responsibility of the DTI) and the Department of Energy, established in 1974 for all the industries involved in the energy sector. There is no equivalent to the French economic and technical 'tutelle', but in practice the Treasury, although seldom specified in the relevant legislation, is party to the approval of the annual investment plans which the corporations are statutorily required to submit for ministerial approval.

Strict financial discipline of the activities of the nationalised industries is assured through the setting of external financing limits (EFL's) which set a ceiling on the total of government grants, issues of Public Dividend Capital, net borrowing and leasing. Each EFL is therefore the differene between the industry's revenue and its current and capital expenditure. A negative EFL may be set, as in the case of BGC and the CEGB, who make a net contribution to the Exchequer. Hence EFL's operate in a way similar to cash limits for other non-commercial parts of the public sector, and are central to government's policy of reducing the PSBR. The nationalised industries Chairmen have argued that the process of setting strict EFL's undermines the principle that Government should set only strategic guidelines, leaving daily business to the industry.[124] Moreover individual EFL's have a direct impact on pricing, – both BGC and the Electricity Council have raised their tariffs to levels higher than annual inflation rates would require – and

---

[121] In the exercise of his powers under section 11 of the Oil and Gas (Enterprise) Act 1982, the Secretary of State for Energy has made a number of statutory instruments for the purpose of transferring to the private sector BGC's offshore interests, see e.g. BGC (Disposal of Offshore Oilfield Interests) Directions 1982. SI 1982 no 1131 and SI 1983 1096.

[122] SF: no.

[123] The Future of the Nationalised Industries, The Treasury, December 1984. These proposals have since been withdrawn, but the Government has made clear its intention to apply the same basic philosophy in future reforms to the individual statutes of the nationalised enterprises. H. C. Debates vol. 86, col 318, November 15, 1985.

[124] See Redwood J. and Hatch J., *Controlling Public Industries* (1982, Oxford).

on manpower: in an effort to improve productivity substantial staff cuts have been made by many of the big 'loss-making' corporations, e.g. British Rail.[125]

While these EFL's are incorporated into the annual Public Expenditure White Paper which is presented to Parliament, the latter usually votes on public spending plans as a block. More recently, energy pricing policies have been determined in the so-called 'star chamber', a Cabinet Committee comprising the Deputy Prime Minister and Treasury Officials. The deliberations of this committee have been criticised as Parliament has not been made sufficiently aware of expenditure objectives. Parliament does have some opportunity to scrutinise nationalised industries policies and practices in Select Committees. Between 1952 and 1979 a Nationalised Industries Select Committee had performed this function, but following the reform of the Committee system, select committees now shadow the activities of leading departments of State, so that a Select Committee on energy can review and question the policies of BGC, BNOC, CEGB and the NCB.[126] Nonetheless Parliamentary scrutiny remains weak and is largely *ex post facto*.

Ministerial control over the activities of the National Enterprise Board was secured through "Guidelines" issued by the Minister for Industry. The 1976 guidelines required the NEB to conform to directions and to seek formal approval for certain investments. In practice close collaboration between civil servants at the DTI and the officials on the NEB rendered directions and approval mere formalities.[127] The extent of control exercised by the NEB over the companies in which held shares also varied considerably. Despite its 100 per cent shareholding in Rolls Royce, control over that company's activities was minimal.[128]

3. Developments

It will appear from the above that British attempts to restructure the public sector have taken the opposite direction from the French and Italian experience. I have gone into some detail in describing the changes which have taken place since the 1979 election because in many respects the quest to reduce public sector spending and to restore the competitiveness of the British economy has profoundly influenced the institutional framework for the delivery of energy policy, energy policy goals being subordinated to revenue policy considerations, as illustrated by the government's recent announcement of its intention to privatise the British Gas Corporation.[129] At the same time, it should be acknowledged that the Conservative commitment to competition implies that energy policy ends are to be secured through stimulation of private sector activity, and the measures undertaken in the

---

125 Three White Papers have been published in an attempt to clarify the economic and financial objectives of nationalised industries and to compensate for the lack of operational guidance contained in the nationalisation statutes themselves, which merely require corporations to break even, taking one year with another. Cmnd. 1137, 1961; Cmnd 3487, 1967; Cmnd 7131, 1978.
126 See reports of the Select Committee on Energy since 1979.
127 B. Hindley, *State Development Corporations* (1983, London).
128 S. Wilks, *The Car Industry in the UK* (1984).
129 H. C. Debs, vol 78, cols 639–648 (May 2, 1985) and Gas Bill, H. C. 109, March 18, 1986.

Oil and Gas (Enterprise) Act 1982 were justified on the grounds that private sector involvement in North Sea oil and gas exploration was in jeopardy, thus threatening the long-term security of supplies. Similarly the 'landing requirement' and the various provisions restricting liquefaction of natural gas and pipeline construction, which are in effect indirect barriers to the export of gas from the United Kingdom, remain unaltered.[130]

A final development which may have implications for manpower and energy policy is section II of the Competition Act 1980, which enpowers the Secretary of State for Trade to direct the Monopolies and Mergers Commission (MMC) to investigate efficiency and costs, the services provided, or the possible abuse of a monopoly within nationalised industries. In many of its subsequent reports, the MMC has specifically examined manpower efficiency, skills and training and has made recommendations for improvements. In its investigation of the CEGB it reviewed many of the Board's practices pertaining to energy pricing, import policies, nuclear power programme investment and manpower aspects. Implementation of the MMC's recommendations is unlikely but the reports have contributed to the governments' goal of ensuring the competitiveness and efficiency of the public sector. The practice of referring to the MMC various aspects of public sector activity should not be equated with increased public accountability, however.[131]

D. The Netherlands

1. Size and Importance

The size and scope of the public sector is much more limited in the Netherlands. In 1979 the manpower employed in the major public sector firms accounted for 6 per cent of the total workforce of the entire economy, with transport and communications accounting for the highest share (43 per cent). The administrative public sector employment accounted for 14.7 per cent in 1979.[132]

There has never been a Dutch equivalent to large-scale nationalisation of vital sectors of the economy, but the motivation behind the nationalisation of several key industries reflects concerns for the public interest in securing reliable energy supplies (DSM – Dutch State Mines in 1902) or for the provision of high risk capital (Ultra Centrifuge Nederland (NV) in 1962) or strategic considerations (e.g. the Dutch Gas Union in 1953). There is a more extensive participation at provincial and municipal level than in the United Kingdom – especially in the electricity production and gas distribution sector.

[130] A. C. Page, "Competition and Monopoly in the United Kingdom Energy Supply – The Case of Gas" (1984) 2 *Journal of Energy and Natural Resources Law*, 30. The government is apparently now ready to consider such exports: Financial Times.

[131] M. Garner, "Efficiency Audits" (1982) 60 *Public Administration* 409. The Gas Bill 1980 clause 25 makes provision for the new Director General of Gas to make a reference to the MMC under the Competition Act 1980 section 24.

[132] OECD *supra*, note 30.

2. Form and Structure

The two main legal forms of public enterprise are the state enterprise and the state share holding company. State enterprises have a public law status, but do not have a legal personality distinct from the department which created them.[133]

The regulations governing the administration of state enterprises are contained in the State Accountancy Act 1927 as amended in 1976. State share-holdings, which may range from less than 1 per cent to 100 per cent participation, are subject to private law, and operate as limited companies. Government's dealings with these companies are regulated by the State Accountancy Act 1976. Parliamentary approval is needed to establish a state holding either singly or jointly with a private firm, or to participate in the equity of an existing firm if a certain sum of money over a fixed limit is involved. The Act also lays down certain rules on the role of the Government Audit Office (Algemene Rekenkamer), a financial control office which reports to Parliament on government finance. The Minister of Finance must inform this office of all loans made by the state to the public sector and the conditions on which they are made.

In addition certain enterprises operate in the form of an Association[134] or a Foundation.[135] Both forms are prevented by either common law (Burgelijk Wetboek) in the case of Associations or by statute in the case of Associations from pursuing profit-making activities.[136]

In many cases certain activities that originally took the form of a state enterprise, have been gradually re-constituted as state share holding companies in the legal form of a limited company, as in the case of Dutch State Mines (DSM) the major state holding company involved in gas production. In the case of DSM the state has a 100 per cent shareholding but many of the companies formed as 'state share holdings' have less than 50 per cent state participation, e. g. Royal Dutch Steel (35 per cent). The 'strategic sectors' such as energy, apart, it would appear that it has been the policy of successive governments to take a minority holding in enterprises in need of investment capital and this is usually done on a temporary basis. Certain state holding companies participate in a number of subsidiaries, DSM being the primary example. In certain cases the activities of the subsidiaries are constrained by a law,[137] which allows the subsidiary only to participate in a market in which other private companies do not operate in the Netherlands.[138] Although the relation between government and company is governed by public law rules under the 1976 Act, it would seem that in practice the position of the state as shareholder hardly differs from the position of a private shareholder. Mention should also be made of NEHEM, the Dutch Reconstruction Company set up in 1972 along similar lines to the British IRC, but which eventually evolved as a

---

[133] Most of the communications services take this form.
[134] For example Vegin: Vereniging van Exploitantan van Gas Bedrijven.
[135] Stichting
[136] Wet op Stichtingen 1956.
[137] Wet Autovervoer Goederen.
[138] For example Van Gend en Loos. The well known freight company is owned by the Dutch State Railways.

tripartite body which prepares sectoral structure studies and advises government on the use of subsidies. It acts as intermediary between the firms and financial institutions. The NEHEM does not have independent financial means but acts as a negotiating body. Most financial support for sectoral projects is given by the National Investment Bank under the guarantee of the State.

3. Developments

It has been observed that state enterprises and state shareholdings in the Netherlands have seldom been used as instruments of stabilisation policy, although the public sector has been used as an instrument of sectoral, industrial and regional policies. State Shareholding Companies have been established in depressed regions to stimulate investment, but it has been suggested that in general the legal structure of the enterprises, guaranteeing considerable autonomy, is not condusive to central economic planning.[139] Certain aspects of the energy industry would appear more amenable to state control however. Gas and electricity prices have been used as an instrument of economic policy, with differential tariffs being set for certain industrial producers (e.g. Dutch Chemical Industry) and for the horticulture sector. In both cases this has met with disapproval from the EC Commision.[140] It should also be noted that in general the rescue operations of the National Investment Bank, originally set up in 1963 to finance modernisation programmes are not subject to scrutiny by either the Audit Office or Parliament. State policies of support through indirect shareholdings via the NIB are largely outside the purview of Parliament and in 1978 the Van Dijk Commission found that Parliament had made insufficient use of its right to challenge the budget of the Ministry of Economic Affairs. Finally, the more decentralised and fragmented structure of Dutch public sector ownership especially in the energy sector is in marked contrast to the situation in the United Kingdom, France and Italy where the state enterprise concerned is endowed with a monopoly or near monopoly of energy supply, Private sector involvement, in particular that of the two oil majors Shell and Esso, through participation in NAM, which is engaged in natural gas production, and through Gasunie, which is responsible for wholesale gas distribution, is a further feature peculiar to the structure of public enterprise in the Dutch energy sector.

E. West Germany

1. Size and Importance

An initial glance at the statistics on public ownership in West Germany would suggest a picture of state influence not dissimilar to that of pre-nationalisation France. According to a 1983 Federal Government Report the federal government alone has directly and indirectly shares in more than 900 enterprises of a varied kind.[141] With over 430,000 employees the *industrial* concerns in which govern-

---

[139] Jan Jenrik, *State Enterprises and State Shareholdings*. PhD thesis, Leyden 1981.
[140] EC Commission. Thirteenth Report on Competition Policy (1984).
[141] Federal Industrial Holdings, 1983 Federal Minister of Finance, Bonn.

ment participates, employ about 2.7 per cent of the total number employed in manufacturing industries, trade and transport. The concentration of Federal Government participations in commercial enterprises is in transport and communications, the industrial sector, as well as banking, housing and research and development.

The major industrial shareholdings of the federal state in 1983 were:

Table 4: Federal Share Holdings

Company	Employees	State Share (%)
Veba (energy and chemicals)	83,000	43.75
Volkswagen (vehicles)	347,000	20.00
Salzgitter (steel, plant)	57,000	100.00
Viag (energy, aluminium)	26,300	86.50
Saarbergwerke (mining, energy)	33,000	74.00
IVE (Industrial management)	4,000	100.00

In addition these companies have formed numerous subsidiaries in often economically powerful important sectors of the economy. In 1979, 14.7 per cent of the total workforce was employed in the administrative public sector.[142]

The undertakings of the Länder and local authorities are more service oriented and are to be found primarily in the fields of banking, electricity, gas, water and district heat supplies.

At the federal level, much of this state involvement arose out of the first reconstruction years of the Federal Republic, although the holding in Veba is directly linked to the country's strategic oil needs.[143] While Germany never embarked on a programme of nationalisation, a certain amount of state involvement reflects regional and employment policy concerns. However the state would appear reluctant to take on national lame-ducks, as the reluctance to take a direct stake in the troubled AEG-Telefunken electronics group illustrated.[144] The commercial banks have acted as the major organisers of industrial activity, and the conception of an activist, entrepreneurial role for the state has had little support except when the structural problems of industry were perceived to be too great for the banks to handle alone, as in the case of the Ruhr coal industry in the 1960's, and the Saar steel industry and the shipbuilding industry in the 1970's.[145]

Perhaps a major distinguishing feature of German public enterprise as the Tables in Appendix I illustrate, is that no single enterprise engaged in energy production or distribution holds a complete or near complete national monopoly position.

[142] OECD *supra* note 30.
[143] See Grayson, *supra* note 88, at p. 150.
[144] Financial Times, November 18, 1982.
[145] K. Dyson, "The Politics of Economic Management" in Paterson, W. and Smith, G., *The West German Model*, (1981, London).

2. Form and Structure

Not only does the level of ownership of public enterprises vary, but the legal form of that ownership also varies. As in France, Italy and the Netherlands enterprises may be constituted in public or private law. Federal enterprises can be public law corporations which are either legally dependent or independent. The legally dependent, or so-called section 26 (of the Federal Budget Order 1969) enterprises do not have separate legal personality and so participation by public bodies at Länder or municipal level is excluded, whereas the legally independent enterprises, such as the Deutsche Bundesbahn or Salzgitter are set up by individual Acts of Establishment which lay down broad guidelines with respect to purpose and performance. There is little uniformity in the obligations contained in these acts; some specify public purposes and others incorporate strictly commercial criteria. The Deutsche Bundesbahn Act clearly directs that the German Federal Railways should be run on commercial principles and only within this framework shall it fulfill its public goals.[146] Shares in publicly owned enterprise at public law may be held by different Federal departments and alternatively at different governmental levels , i.e. with one or a number of Laender or municipalities participating, e.g. Saarbergwerke.

The majority of public enterprise in the industrial and energy sector however can be classified as *mixed economy enterprises*. Within a mixed-economy enterpries the minority partner must have a blocking share that allows a veto on decisions of the qualified majority. If such a provision does not exist the company would be termed a public enterprise with subsidiary private participation or a private enterprise with subsidiary public participation.[147] Obviously this provision can only be of value to the minority – public or private – in influencing certain fundamental decisions as opposed to actively influencing the policy of the enterprise.

Section 65 of the Federal Budget Order of 1969 and the corresponding regulations in the Municipal orders (Gemeindeordnung) of the Land – prohibits the respective tiers of government from taking shares in enterprises under private law which do not have limited liability. Therefore the mixed economy enterprise usually takes the form of the joint stock company, the Aktiengesellschaft. The majority of public enterprises in the energy and industry sector take this form – e.g. Ruhrkohle, RWG, Veba, VIAG, Ruhrgas. Responsibility for the various federal state enterprises is distributed between ll separate Ministries but the Minister of Finance is responsible for the largest and most important groups.[148]

Section 65 of the Federal Budget Order 1969 provides the main basis for the administration of public enterprise and this Act makes the Federal Minister for

---

[146] Art. 28 part 1 of German Federal Railways Act of December 13, 1951 (Bundesbahngesetz).

[147] P. Jaeger, "Der gemischtwirtschaftliche Betrieb", in *Wirtschaftswissenschaftliches Studium 1977*, (1977) vol. 6, pp. 109–114. See also Ress, G. "Government and Industry in the FRG, (1980) 29 *International and Comparative Law Quarterly* 87.

[148] For a breakdown of the direct and indirect participation of other ministries see the annual Beteiligungen des Bundes (Bundesministerium der Finanzen, Bonn).

Finance responsible for coordination of the activities of all Federal public enterprises irrespective of departmental sponsorship. His permission must be sought before shares are bought and sold, or when nominal equity, the ambit of the enterprise or the scope of influence of the Federal government is changed. Thus 'horizontal control' is assured.

Most importantly the Federal Budget Order S65 provides that the Federal government can only participate in a mixed economy enterprise if it is granted an appropriate influence, especially in the supervisory board or in a respective organ of control. This allows for 'vertical control' of the activities of the enterprise.[149] Control at Länder level is exercised in a similar way. The representation of the Federal government on the supervisory boards at the different levels within groups of federal public enterprises under private law is as follows:

(a) Holding companies: representative of the Federal government, (members of Parliament, parliamentary secretaries of state, state secretaries, department heads of federal ministers).
(b) First level subsidiaries (Tochtergesellschaften) – private members, employee representatives: representatives of the federal government (as above) and executive officers of the holding companies.
(c) Second level subsidiaries (Enkelgesellschaften): representatives of the Federal Government, and members of the executive board. Representation is dependent on the size and significance of the enterprise concerned.[150]

Financial and managerial control is assured through the Federal Audit Office.[151]

The extent to which this supervisory control can be used to pursue economic policy goals is open to debate. A broad distinction is usually drawn between those enterprises fulfilling special federal functions and those operating in the commercial field.[152] In the former the principle of economic management, i.e., an optimal use of resources is applied while in the latter, ordinary commercial goals are to be pursued. It is usually acknowledged that this commercially oriented policy of participation does not exclude these enterprises from being required to pursue Federal government's economic objectives, to the extent that this does not hamper the pursuit of enterpreneurial goals.

3. Developments

The extent and nature of state intervention in the German economy has always been a matter of debate as is the extent to which the public sector is indeed 'managed' at all. In the mid-seventies, Streit calculated the relative importance of state ownership to be similar to that of the United Kingdom.[153] While it is

---

[149] See K. Haenser, "Der Bund und seine Unternehmen", in *Öffentliche Wirtschaft und Gemeinschaft*, (1975) vol. XXV, no 2, at pp. 55–61.
[150] See annual reports on state participations.
[151] Which is given wide powers under art 114, para 23 of the Grundgesetz, and the Federal Budget Order 1969, sections 44, 48 and 53.
[152] Haenser, *supra* note 148.
[153] M. Streit in Griffiths, R. T. (ed.), *Government Business and Labour in European*

generally recognised that German public enterprises act in a commercially oriented manner, the annual reports on state participation issued by the Minister of Finance suggest that public enterprise is used as an instrument to pursue employment, regional and sectoral policy goals. The 1983 report notes that a considerably large portion of the investment of Salzgitter and Volkswagen was made in structurally weak regions. The extent to which such investment is in accordance with entrepreneurial goals is not made clear. However it would appear that some enterprises, in particular VEBA and VIAG, can offset losses incurred in the pursuit of wider policy goals against the profitability of other companies in their respective groups, and in particular the profits made in the electricity sector.

In fact the extent to which concentration in the energy sector in general had increased, and in particular manifested signs of increased vertical and conglomerate forms of concentration, as well as horizontal concentration, was the subject of a critical report by the Monopolkommission in 1976.[154] In the opinion of the Monopolkommission the substitutional element of competition is threatened by the rise of conglomerate mergers. The success of the Federal Cartel Office – the body responsible for administering the Competition Act (GWB), in controlling mergers has been mixed for two reasons. Firstly merger control was only introduced by a 1973 amendment to the GWB and it soon became apparent that the minimum size threshold for exemption from merger control (DM 50 million turnover) was on the high side.[155] In consequence, large enterprises found it possible to avoid reporting certain mergers by acquiring small and medium firms in markets formerly dominated by the latter.[156] Hence the 1980 amendment[157] included a rider to the DM 50 million exemption. This was to the effect that control could be exercised when an enterprise with a turnover greter than DM 4 million is taken over by an enterprise having a turnover of greater than DM 1 billion. It is generally argued that this control has probably come too late. Cable has shown that mergers in the industrial sector between 1958–1977 were concentrated on a small number of industries – including iron and steel and mineral products, so that these sectors already displayed a high level of concentration before the Cartel Office was equipped with its wider powers.[158]

Secondly the Federal Minister of Economics may sanction a merger prohibited by the FCO[159] if the adverse effects of the merger are considered to be compensated by overall economic advantages or an overriding public interest. Of the five applications for merger permission made between 1973 and 1980, only one has

---

Capitalism, (1977, London) at pp. 120–135, and G. Denton et al., Economic Planning in Britain, France and Germany (1968, London).

[154] Monopolkommission, Hauptgutachten I, 'Mehr Wettbewerb ist möglich' (1977).

[155] August 3, 1973 BGBL I, 917 sections 23–24b.

[156] Between 1973 and 1979 3388 mergers out of a total 13,900 were covered by this exemption. Mueller, Heidenbaum and Schneider, German Anti-Trust Law (1981, Frankfurt) at p. 85.

[157] April 24, 1980 BGBL I 458 amending sections 23–24a of the GWB.

[158] Cable J., "Economic Determinants and Effects of Mergers in West Germany. 1964–74," Zeitschrift für die gesamte Staatswissenschaft (1980), Vol. 136(2), 226.

[159] Section 24(3).

been refused. A brief examination of the reasoning behind each permission would suggest that in Germany, control of merger activity can often be used as an alternative to public ownership both in cases where there is a stated desire to build a national champion as in the VEBA/Gelsenberg and VEBA/BP mergers, which were considered to contribute to the efforts of the Federal government in securing long term energy supplies, or where the merger has preserved specialised know-how which was important for the international competitiveness of the specialised manufacturing tools industry as in the case of Thyssen/Huller. The permission in Babcock-Artos was granted because the merger avoided the failure of a company, thereby preserving employment opportunities in the textile sector.[160] These mergers have been permitted subject to certain restrictions and conditions. As Bauer points out this gives the Minister the opportunity to mould areas of activity of large enterprises according to his own ideas.[161]

The Federal Cartel Office, as Tillotson argues, has not been immune to employment considerations especially where the interests of a national champion are at risk.[162] He contrasts the FCO's handling of the Karstadt/Neckermann merger with that of the abortive attempt of GKN to take over Sachs and concludes that although Karstadt was the largest department store of Europe, it was German owned, whereas GKN was British and Sachs did not require rescuing.

A further point of interest in the use of the GWB as an alternative form of intervention relates to the exemption of public utilities from the provisions on vertical and horizontal restraints and concerted practices. In particular, S103 of the Act exempts the zoning agreements of the various public utilities supplying electricity or gas. The exemptions granted under S103 and S104 have been narrowed by the 1980 amendment and the powers of the Cartel Office to control abusive practices by a public utility strengthened, but substantial horizontal and vertical concentration already existed, especially in the electricity supply industry.[163] In considering the use of the public sector to obtain manpower and energy policy goals, the deployment of supplementary legal instruments in the form of competition policy should not be overlooked. Although no single public enterprise is endowed with a monopoly of the manufacture of strategic products, not only does the administration of the GWB provide for an alternative means of guaranteeing markets for large, part-state owned companies, but financial support, especially for vital industries such as the nuclear power development industry, is provided through project oriented assistance, especially in the form of research and development aid. A study carried out by the Institut für Weltwirtschaft[164] in Kiel in 1979 showed that five industries (computer equipment,

---

160 Federal Minister of Economics Wu W/E 147, Feb. 1, 1974, Wu W/E 165, March 3, 1979, Wu W/E 159, August 1, 1977 and Wu W/E 155, October 17, 1976.

161 J. F. Bauer, "The Control of Mergers Between Large, Financially Strong Firms in West Germany" *Zeitschrift für die gesamte Staatswissenschaft* (1980) Vol. 136(3), at p. 444.

162 J. Tillotson, "The GKN/Sachs Affair: A case study" (1980) 14 *Journal of World Trade Law* 39 at pp. 65–66.

163 See Daintith and Hancher, *supra*, note 36, at p. 50.

164 K. H. Juettemeir and K. Lammers: *Interventionen in der Bundesrepublik Deutschland*, Kiel Discussion Paper 63. (Kiel 1979).

energy, chemical industry, machinery and electrical engineering) received 77 per cent of government R + D aid in 1974. Within these industries the Federal government has revealed a distinct preference for a few large private and public companies – Veba, Ruhrkohle, Brown Boveri (nuclear construction) and Messerschmitt-Bölkow-Blohm (aircraft). The Federal Research Ministry created in 1972, remained a stronghold of the so-called 'SPD-technocrats' between 1974 and advocated the importance of labour market and structural adjustment and 'positive' R + D policies. The activities of this 'structural' ministry raised suspicions of imperialism, and favouritism towards certain firms, on the part of the FDP Economic and Interior Ministers. A rigorous energy saving programme drawn up by the Research Ministry in the wake of the second shock was blocked in Cabinet by the FDP Economics Minister Lambsdorff, on the grounds that it was too interventionist.[165]

Despite the demise of the SPD in the 1982 elections, the Research Ministry has continued to produce aggressive project-oriented R + D packages. The proposed programme for 1983 to 1985 met with the partial disapproval of the EC Commission which required certain amendments to be made before it would grant exemption under Article 92(3) of the Treaty of Rome. The Five Year Programme has a total budget of DM 13,465 million.[166]

Two further questionable implications of using public enterprises for economic policy purposes have been noted by Schatz.[167] Firstly the Federal Republic has tended to be unsympathetic if not hostile to private investors who planned to locate their production in a region where major public undertakings predominate (for example in shipbuilding) in the fear that this would increase competition on the factor markets. Secondly many public industrial and energy industries which have been operating in sectors most affected by increasing competition from abroad, have been supported by government through relatively easy access to a variety of subsidies, regional and sectoral, as well as procurement policies. The coal industry provides the most obvious example.

Finally procurement policies by public enterprises should be mentioned. While there is no explicit 'buy national' legislation in the Federal Republic[168] Schatz argues that state companies are expected to prefer West German over foreign equipment and services, unless the latter are significantly cheaper or better in quality, and that the Federal Railways (Bundesbahn) and the Federal Postal system (Bundespost) are almost exclusively oriented towards German supplies and frequently use their monopsonistic market power to discriminate among domestic industries to the benefit of manufacturers located in structurally weak regions.

---

[165] See Dyson, K., *supra* note 144, at p. 48.
[166] E. C. Commission, 13th Report on Competition Policy, at p. 142.
[167] K. Schatz, "La experienca nacionalizadora en Alemania Fedral" in J. Buchanan et al., *El sector publicio en las economias de mercado* (Madrid 1979) at p. 344.
[168] Obviously this would be outlawed by the two Directives on Procurement and furthermore the judgement of the ECJ in the *Irish Souvenirs* case has condemned such practices. (Case 118, Commission v Ireland [1981] E.C.R. 1625).

Given the extent to which the Federal government uses alternative strategies to bolster up or further the interests of the firms in which it participates and the degree to which these firms may be utilised in pursuit of employment, regional and sectorial policy, it would appear that the public sector is used as an instrument of economic management in Germany's "not so market-oriented economy"[169] subject to the caveat that the public sector has been immune from counter-inflation or cyclical policies, The Federal Government remains loyal to the principle of *Tarifautonomie*, i.e. the autonomy of price and wage determination from public regulation.

The new centre right government, pledged to cut the public sector deficit and to return to the market oriented model of economic management, has begun by selling off part of its share in Veba to the public, although as in the BNOC case, the Minister plans to retain a holding sufficient to secure influence on national energy policy matters.[170]

F. Hungary

1. Size and Importance

Table 5: The Structure of Hungarian[171] Industry

	Gross production	Employment
State industry	93.7	83.8
Cooperative industry	5.6	13.4
Socialist industry	99.3	97.2
Private industry	0.7	2.8

The legal position of enterprises in the Hungarian energy sector is quite different from the European experience. Section 8, para 23 of Act I 1972, amending the Constitution of 1949, vests ownership in the state of all mineral wealth, natural resources, as well as major production plant and the mines section and entrusts the management of state property to state enterprises while S7 specifies that the activities of the latter are to be determined by the state's national economic plan.

The private sector is of course small and has been traditionally limited to private plot agricultural production, a large portion of residential construction and some retail trade. Labour market theorists working on the structure of the Hungarian labour market distinguish between the socialised sector – comprising the state or co-operative-regulative aspects of activity within the state and co-operative organisations, and the *second economy* – which is made up of private, semi-legal

---

169 The phrase is borrowed from Donges, J. B., "Industrial Policies in West Germany's 'not so market-oriented' Economy," (1980) 3 *World Economy*, at p. 203.

170 Further sales of Government holdings in VIAG have recently been announced. Financial Times, November 3, 1984.

171 Statistical Pocket Book of Hungary, Budapest 1981.

and illegal activity.[172] In a country beset by shortages of raw materials and suffering from an excess of labour demand, the growth of the second economy at the expense of the socialised sector is hardly desirable.[173]

Domestic energy production was entrusted to two *trusts* until 1980, with the OKGT a 'vertical trust' being responsible for oil and gas production, distribution, importation and trading while the MVMT – the Hungarian Electricity Works Trust, also 'vertical' in nature, is responsible for electricity-production and distribution. Since 1981 the latter has been subject to a public utility services regulation. The Coal Mining Trust went into liquidation in 1980, but the basic regional structure of the coal mining industry remains unaltered.

2. Form and Structure

State enterprises in Hungary have distinct legal personality and, as with their French counterparts, their contracts are governed by private law. The higher organs of the state administration have in theory to respect the autonomy of the enterprise. Each government department supervises the activities of those enterprises for which it is responsible, provides them with initial funds, analyses the results of their operations, and on the basis of this analysis calculates the renumeration of the principal officers of the enterprise. Only in exceptional cases defined by statute may an enterprise be instructed to perform specific economic tasks, for example when the interests of the national economy cannot otherwise be guaranteed.

Management and control of the state enterprises in the energy sector is assured not only in the context of the five year, medium range and annual plans but also, through the supervision of the Ministry of Industrial Affairs. Responsibility for energy was transferred to this newly created Ministry in 1981, following fears that the former sponsoring Ministry – the Ministry of Heavy Industry – had become too autonomous.[174]

3. Developments

It has been pointed out that enterprises in a socialist economy tend to be growth-oriented and create a growing tendency towards excessive demand for all factors of production, including raw materials and labour.[175] In a country with a shortage of labour and seeking to modernise its productive base, this poses serious problems. Labour market policies are aimed at neutralising or eliminating the consequences of this continuous excess demand. The content of the sixth five year plan for

---

172 Semi-legal activity is classified as activity by people who have full-time jobs in certain sectors of the socialised sector, and in particular the service sector, who perform part-time work for a fee in the private sector, e.g. doctors, lawyers, dentisits or who receive tips or goods in exchange for services.

173 M. Marese, "The Evolution of Wage Labour in Hungary," in P. Hare, H. Radice and N. Swaine eds., *Hungary: A Decade of Economic Reform*, (1981 London), at p. 54.

174 I. Dobzi, "Energy Planning and the Energy Situation in a Socialised Planned Economy« in L. Lindberg, *The Energy Syndrome*, (1977, Lexington), 182.

175 I. Gabor and P. Galassi, "The Labour Market in Hungary since 1968" in Hare et al, *supra* note 172.

1980–85 reveals a similar preoccupation for the adverse consequences of increased energy demand. The 1964 third five year plan had stressed the importance of substituting oil for coal, but by 1973 a government report stated that the change of energy consumption and the increased demand for hydrocarbons had progressed at higher than the desirable level.[176] However the objective of modernisation was given priority in the fifth five year plan and hence the growing demand for energy was to be met by increased domestic production. By 1979 it became evident that changes in the energy economy would be required and a comprehensive programme was adapted in the sixth Five Year Plan in 1980.[177] The programme envisaged energy saving, alteration of energy consumption, and changes in the energy supply patterns: all being objectives adopted to a greater or lesser extent by the five European countries under study in 1974–1975.

The growing concern at energy demand levels, combined with the desire to move away from over centralised planning, towards a more decentralised control through *regulated markets* has led to a profusion of legal measures, limiting public sector energy consumption and encouraging rational use of energy in the public sector. It has been suggested that the move away from directive planning has resulted in the appearance of a new form of economic control, namely "economic control and management based on the responsibility for the supply of the enterprise". The Hungarian economy is dominated by monopolistic industries or trusts which increasingly formulate their own plans and targets but which are also increasingly subject to intra-product competition. This could lead to the development of a controlled market mechanism and the break up of large-scale firms in a number of sectors.[178] As a consequence we might expect to see an increase in the number of detailed legal measures, targeted at individual trusts or companies.

G. Conclusions

The above national accounts of the development of public sector management in the past decade would suggest that despite the divergent nature and extent of public ownership within the five Western European countries and despite different traditions of state intervention, there has been an element of convergence in policy goals if not in their realisation. Each government has sought to restore a degree of managerial autonomy to the operations of the public sector, with the aim of allowing it to function in accordance with market criteria. The counterpart to this development in Hungary has been the move away from central planning to the notion of a regulated market. However, as Cassese points out,[179] the price of

---

[176] T. Farkas, "Questions of Hungarian Energy Management," paper read at IIAS seminar, *The Adjustment of the Administration to the Energy Crisis*, 1982, Brussels.

[177] *Ibid.*

[178] I. Schweitzer, "Enterprise Organisation and the Economic Mechanism in Hungary" (1981) 27 *Acta Oeconomica* (3–4) 289. See also A. Harmathy, "Relations Between Economic Regulators and Contractors," (1980) 22 *Acta Juridica Academiae Sueritarium Hungaricae* (3–4) 327.

[179] Cassese, below pp. 239–240.

commercial autonomy is increased independence from government and a possible reluctance to pursue centrally determined objectives.

In the three countries with the most established tradition of public sector management significant changes have been attempted, even if not always realised in the last decade. Such change has taken extreme forms: privatisation in the United Kingdom and nationalisation in France. In Italy the attempt to restructure and restore greater autonomy to the state holding companies in 1977 has failed, but express dissatisfaction with the instrumental use of the public sector in the pursuit of short-term economic goals remains. The United Kingdom has sought to return a major part of the public sector back to the private sector. This policy has affected not only public enterprise, but local government and statutory authorities such as schools and hospitals have been urged by a combination of Ministerial circular and legislation to return certain services such as rubbish collection, cleaning and printing to the private sector. The United Kingdom's privatisation scheme has as far as it affects the energy industry stopped short of "denationalising" those functions of nationalised industries which may be of strategic importance. In this respect it could be argued that the United Kingdom's use of the public sector has moved into line with German and Dutch policy. Public ownership will survive but the government will attempt to avoid utilising firms in an *ad hoc* or haphazard manner. Public enterprise will continue to exist because its very existence is perceived as securing certain policy goals, but its deployment in securing ad hoc macro-economic policy ends will ostensibly be reduced. Where the government seeks to use the public sector as a policy instrument in the pursuit of more specific policy objectives, this would be done in a more strictly circumscribed manner, as envisaged in the recent Treasury proposals.[180]

If practice follows policy we could expect to see an approximation to the Dutch and German model of public sector management. In *quantitative* terms the level of publicly owned enterprise is not dissimilar to that of the United Kingdom, Italy or France but its instrumental use has been quite different. This may in part be due to the legal form of public enterprise in these two countries. As we have noted public sector firms are constituted along the same lines as private companies. Nonetheless even where the state is the majority shareholder, it has on the whole been reluctant to utilise its powers of influence. The autonomy of the firms to pursue commercial goals has largely been assured. There have been occasions where it would appear that the Dutch and German governments have attempted to informally influence the activities of large public firms, but it does not appear that the pressure exerted has been any different from that put upon large private sector companies. The fact that a single enterprise or group of enterprises controls a substantial part of the economy will often mean that it is an effective negotiating partner with government. This remains true whether the enterprise is public or privately owned.

[180] *Supra* note 123.

IV. The Choice of Public Sector Management as a Policy Instrument

A. Introduction

To what extent do the patterns of development of state involvement in the economy outlined above explain the choice of public sector management as an alternative to other forms of policy instrument in the implemantation of energy and manpower policy? To what extent have governments relied on alternative supplementary instruments? From our survey in section III we have identified two distinctive styles of public sector management: a restrained use on the part of Germany and the Netherlands, and a more marked use on the part of Italy and France and to a lesser extent, the United Kingdom. In the following section I will examine the choice of the public sector in pursuance of energy policy and manpower goals in order to determine the extent to which pre-existing styles of intervention have influenced the selection of policy instruments.

B. Energy Policy

As far as energy policy is concerned, a public sector presence can be identified in the major energy markets of all five countries with the exception of nuclear power generation in Germany. In the United Kingdom, France and Italy public sector firms have an absolute or near monopoly of conventional and nuclear electricity generation, natural gas distribution, and coal production. In the Netherlands – Gasunie, a public sector firm, holds a key position as a monopoly wholesale distributor of natural gas. In Germany, public enterprise is involved in each of the different energy markets, but no single enterprise enjoys a national monopoly in energy production or distribution. In the oil production market, each country has a limited public sector presence, with the notable exception of the Netherlands. Howewer no public sector company enjoys a monopoly of oil production or supply in any country. As far as the distribution of petroleum products is concerned, there is some public sector presence in each country, with the exception of the Netherlands once more.

To what extent is this degree of public sector ownership reflected in the choice of energy policy instruments and to what extent are traditions of intervention important?

1. Short-term Energy Policy Objectives
These have been identified as follows:

1. restriction of consumption
2. preservation of the pattern and level of supply
3. stabilisation of prices and profits in energy markets

It would appear from the national inventories that little use of legal measures of public sector management was made in government's attempts to control consumption levels, or to preserve patterns and levels of supply. The relative absence of public sector management may be explained by a number of factors. Firstly the 1973 crisis was primarily an oil crisis. As noted in section III, state participation in the production, supply and distribution of oil products was relatively limited during this period. Secondly, we also noted in section III that national oil companies have traditionally been accorded a considerable degree of autonomy in their commercial operations. Governments predominately relied on unilateral regulation as opposed to public sector management to mitigate the immediate effects of the 1973 oil crisis, and there is no evidence that public sector companies were singled out or required to pursue more onerous distribution policies. The Schwartz Report[181] in France was especially critical of the high profits made by the CFP and Elf during the crisis. Reluctance on the part of governments to single out national oil companies for the performance of certain tasks may be attributed to the perceived need to ensure the efficacy of the operations of these companies on the international oil scene. In order to complete effectively with the oil majors, nationals required similar autonomous status.[182]

Despite this marked overt bias towards unilateral regulation as a policy instrument in the attainment of short-term energy policy goals, the use of public sector management as a means of influencing consumption and supply levels cannot be ruled out. Informal pressure may well be brought to bear on public sector companies to restrict consumption of certain fuels and switch to others: coal production or natural gas production could be increased to match a shortfall in oil supplies. These pressures could easily be exerted without resort to more visible forms of policy instrument. Secondly informal arrangements are often built into international emergency schemes. The International Energy Programme expressly provides, through the institution of the Industry Supply Advisory Group, for informal supply arrangements to be made at company level. National oil companies participate in this Group and may find themselves subject to government pressures in arriving at their allocation policies.[183]

If we move on to consider the arrangements made in each country to put emergency energy legislation in a more permanent footing, including the United Kingdom's Energy Act of 1976,[184] the emergency laws enacted in France in 1974 and 1978, and in Germany in 1974, the powers vested in the executive allow for regulation of all stages of production, importation, distribution and transportation of fuels. These powers have yet to be put to the test, but there seems no reason to suppose that public sector firms will be exempted from them if the experience of 1974 is taken as a guide.

The *stabilisation of prices and profits* in energy markets is an objective which is commonly achieved by public sector management. The use of existing powers to direct national energy corporations to stabilise prices in fluctuating markets can be observed in the United Kingdom, France and Italy, and to a lesser extent, the

---

181 Assemblé Nationale, *Rapport sur les sociétés pétrolières opérant en France.* 1976. (Schwartz Report)
182 Bercusson, below, at pp. 377–378.
183 International Energy Program 1974, Cmnd 5826 (1975) I.L.M.I.
184 Evidence of government's preference in using its public sector as opposed to imposing more general price measures may be gleaned from the various national positions on the Commission's proposal to introduce emergency price control legislation.

Netherlands.[185] These powers have been exercised through a combination of powers granted to Ministers to give policy directions to the public sector firms and powers available under general price regulation mechanisms. The latter set of mechanisms were applied to private and public sector oil companies alike in the period 1974–1979 in Britain and France, and continue to be applied to the activities of all the national energy corporations in Italy. In the Netherlands a maximum price for oil products had been imposed until 1981.[186]

In the two countries which are the largest Western European producers of natural gas – the United Kingdom and the Netherlands – an interesting contrast in the choice of instrument emerges. In order to preserve domestic resources and to discourage exports governments have imposed minimum prices for gas. The British government directed the British Gas Corporation in 1979, 1980 and 1983 to raise its domestic gas tariffs considerably. No special instrument was needed for this. In the Netherlands, however, the *Natural Gas Prices Act 1974* marks a significant departure from previous relations between the Minister of Economic Affairs and Gasunie. Prices and tariffs are usually fixed by consensual agreement, but the 1974 Act confers upon the Minister for Economic Affairs the power to fix minimum prices for the sale of natural gas when the agreed prices, domestic and export, do not properly reflect market values. The Act seems primarily aimed at giving the Minister a "stick behind the door" to control indirectly the domestic contracts concluded between Gasunie (which is 50 per cent state-owned and Vegin (the Association of regional and municipal gas distribution companies). More recently oil producing countries have been concerned to bolster up oil market prices and until March 1985, the government was obliged to provide BNOC with a considerable amount of financial support in order to maintain higher term prices for North Sea Oil.[187]

The *taxation* of the increased profits which have accrued as a result of fluctuating prices has affected public sector and private sector companies alike. Governments have not on the whole tended to fashion new regulatory mechanisms, however, to deal with public corporations: the United Kingdom's Gas Levy Act of 1981 – imposing a special levy on profits resulting from the price increased of 1979 and 1981 – appears to be an exception. The British National Oil Corporation was initially exempt from paying Petroleum Revenue Tax but section 22 of the Finance Act 1979 brought the Corporation within the ambit of the Oil Taxation Act 1975. The increased profits accruing to the Netherlands' gas producing company, NAM, in which the state has an interest, have been recouped by means of a gentleman's agreement.[188]

The ability of governments to use the public sector for a number of different goals is well illustrated by the Italian government's threat to increase the tax on

[185] Staatscourant, July 29, 1981, no. 144.
[186] R. Barents, "Legal Aspects of Dutch Energy Policy," (1983) *Journal of Energy and Natural Resources Law* 160.
[187] Financial Times, March 14, 1985
[188] White Paper no. 15800, XIII no. 93.

natural gas production (amounting to 60 billion a year for ENI) unless ENI took over three struggling textile companies.[189]

In conclusion it must be said that overt legal measures of public sector management have not been a favoured instrument for achieving short-term energy policy goals. As noted above, the 1978 crisis was after all a crisis provoked by a shortage of oil. Public sector firms did not dominate the West European oil markets and in those countries in which national oil corporations were in existence in 1973 – Italy and France – these corporations have always been accorded a high degree of autonomy. Hence their behaviour has not been markedly different from private sector corporations. This may account for the predominance of unilateral regulation of imports and exports of oil and oil products in the 1973–1974 period.[190]

Public sector management appears to have played a greater role in regulating prices and profits but this may partly be explained by the fact that counter-inflation policy and revenue considerations often take precedence over energy policy objectives as far as the public sector is concerned. At the same time it should be noted that *France* only enacted comprehensive powers to control prices in emergency situations in 1977,[191] the earlier Act of 1974 being confined to powers to control supply and distribution. Italy has yet to enact emergency price control powers. The extensive degree of public sector ownership, together with a general-ised system of price regulation applying to the products of public and private companies alike, afford these governments sufficient scope to control and contain price increases. In fact Italy only enacted general emergency powers in respect of supply policy in 1977.[192]

Finally it might be suggested that regulation has been the preferred instrument because governments have sought to produce a *generalised* impact on supply patterns. This point may be illustrated by the nature of the instruments deployed to ensure the maintenance of emergency stocks of fuel. All five Western govern-ments have used unilateral regulation to conform to the requirements of the two EC Directives, which oblige major producers and users to hold 90 days work of reserve stocks.[193] There has only been a restricted resort to public sector manage-ment: in Germany a state guaranteed public law corporation was established in 1978 following protests by 'independent' refiners and 'dependent' refiners, owned by the private oil companies, that the differential burdens imposed on each under a 1975 Act were discriminatory. The creation of the EBV has solved the problem of financing the expensive task of holding reserve stocks.

---

[189] F. Grassini, "The Italian Enterprises: The Political Constraints," in R. Vernon and A. Aharoni eds., *State-owned Enterprises in the Western Economies* (1981, London).

[190] EC Commission: Enquiry into the Behaviour of Oil Companies in the period November 1973 to October 1974.

[191] Law no. 77–804 in J.O.R.F. July 20, 1977, p. 3831.

[192] Law no. 883, November 7, 1977 in Gazz. Uff. Dec. 7, 1977, no. 883.

[193] Council Directive 68/414, O.J. 1968 L308/14. Council Directive 73/282, O.J. 1973 L228/11.

Nonetheless the presence of public sector firms can affect the *content* and *scope* of regulations. In Italy ENI, recognised as the state hydrocarbons company, is required to hold strategic stocks on behalf of the government. The British, German and French governments subsidise coal stocks held by their respective energy utilities, but this is primarily a form of subsidy for the coal industry. Strategic deployment of these stocks is nonetheless possible.

It must also be acknowledged that during an energy shortage government may be seeking to influence the conduct of a wide range of actors. Regulation followed by delegation provides a more efficient method than public sector management which may involve lengthy consultation and negotiation between Minister and management.

The pattern of instrument selection in Hungary is quite different from the five Western countries. The energy crisis of 1973 did not have the same sudden impact on Hungary and that country continues to import the major part of its primary energy requirements from the Soviet bloc. Energy demand continued to grow until 1979 and the general thrust of the first five Five Year Plans was to place emphasis on efficiency and modernisation, including the substitution of coal by hydrocarbons, as opposed to the containment of demand. The first fundamental reappraisal of energy policy occurred with the adoption of the Sixth Plan in 1979. This reappraisal was necessitated not so much by a threat to supplies but by the adverse effects of increased oil prices and inflation.

The gradual impact of the energy crisis together with the generalised system of annual intervention in almost every aspect of the market for energy, would seem to combine to reduce the necessity for the Hungarian government to equip itself with a battery of crisis measures to deal with potential disturbances to its supplies. Most of the measures adopted in Hungary can be described primarily as instruments of *planning* and have not been adopted with a view to, or as a result of *crisis management*. Hence they will be considered in detail below.

2. The Alteration of the Structure of Energy Demand

Legal measures of public sector management are rarely used as an instrument to promote economy of energy use but feature more regularly in the attainment of alteration of energy consumption patterns. This is largely to be explained by the fact that most of the measures recorded in the national inventories under the former heading are directed at consumers rather than producers of energy. Hungary is the exception here: a large number of regulations are targeted directly at the public sector and regulate in some detail a variety of fairly specific activities, including the use of public vehicles and heating temperatures in public buildings, lighting in public buildings and fuel consumption levels.

In Britain it should be noted that a large portion of the £320 million, 4-year energy 'save it' campaign package introduced in 1978 was dedicated to energy saving measures in the public sector. Council houses and other local government buildings, education establishments, National Health Service buildings and the buildings of the Property Services Agency were all included in this programme. Public administration accounts for 6 per cent of energy consumption and it was clearly important for the government to set an example, and that it should be seen to use energy efficiently. New legislation was not required. The £280 million allocated to the public sector was partly an addition to departmental voted expenditure and partly increased loan sanction to the local authorities thus enabling them to contribute to the cost of insulating public sector housing. By way of contrast, Parliament passed the *Homes Insulation Act 1978* which provided for grants towards the cost of basic thermal insulation for *private* homes. Similar developments may have taken place in Germany, the Netherlands, Italy and France, but these have not been reported in our inventories.

It is possible to identify the creation of special para-state bodies in France and Italy as instruments of public sector management. The creation of the Agence Pour les Economies d'Energie (APEE) in France and the ENEA in Italy may be termed instruments of public sector management which will indirectly influence the non-public sectors through the use of information campaigns, subsidies, and "energy audits". These services and financial benefits are provided directly by central government departments in the United Kingdom and the Netherlands and by regional governments in West Germany. The existence of the two public sector agencies in Italy and France may be explained by general preferences within the respective national system. In order to avoid the problem of bureaucratic corruption and inefficiency which besets Italian administration it is not uncommon for governments to create new administrative organisations to circumvent these problems.[194] In France a high profile for energy conservation may have been preferred as "sugar on the pill" in the wake of criticism from some sections of the population on the intensity of the nuclear development programme.[195]

A second reason for the relative absence of visible measures of public sector management in relation to conservation may be that governments are able to use general powers to direct state enterprises to alter the level and structure of their tariffs to encourage conservation in energy uses. This was certainly the motivation behind the UK's instruction to the BGC to increase tariffs in 1979. However where state enterprises are granted relative autonomy in fixing tariffs, conflicts may emerge and more visible legal instruments appear. A good illustration of this process occurred in France. EDF, as we noted in section III above, has traditionally retained a great deal of independence from the state. This has been partly assured by its financial strength and its capacity to diversify. In the early 1960's EDF had embarked on a policy of "Tout électrique" with the aim of converting the nation to electricity by the year 2000. Aided by a battery of subsidiaries specialising in home heating equipment and yet another set of companies offering finance at preferential rates, EDF set about convincing the nation of the benefits of electricity. In 1970 EDF convinced the government that a strong marketing policy to promote the sales of electricity was a national imperative. Through a "contrat du programme" concluded with the Ministers of Industry and Finance in 1971, EDF was given relative autonomy to develop sales.

---

[194] Roversi Monaco, "The Implementation of Italian Energy Policy". Paper presented at colloquium on *The Legal Implementation of Energy Policy,* Florence September 1982.
[195] N. Lucas, *supra,* note 83.

By the mid-70's more than one third of the new homes constructed in France were heated with electricity. The new APEE was not satisfied with the results of this policy and it appeared that EDF's promotional policy induced French households to consume greater amounts of energy. The APEE, backed by the government, requested EDF to cease its publicity campaign, proposed that a temporary tax be levied on any new housing that would be equipped with electrical heating and requested EDF to structure its rates to discourage additional consumption. EDF was eventually obliged to concede defeat on the publicity campaign issue. A parafiscal tax was imposed but reimbursed after a few years. Tariffs did not change and EDF oriented its efforts towards industrial uses of electricity.

Measures aimed at encouraging consumers to switch from one type of fuel to another – usually away from oil to coal or gas, (except in the case of the Netherlands post–1974 and Hungary pre–1979) – are primarily directed at households and industrial users. The favoured instruments here are regulation and subsidy. However public sector electricity utilities may be encouraged to switch away from oil to another energy form. This may be done by less visible forms of public sector management, i.e. by increasing investment funds to the public sector firms in order to allow them to develop alternative forms of generating capacity. Such measures may be linked to the development of domestic energy resources in the case of those countries which produce coal, gas or nuclear energy, and may also be linked to the diversification of supplied of imported energy in the case of countries which are primarily energy consumers.

In order to encourage state-owned utilities to switch from oil to other forms of electricity generation, each country has enacted regulations restricting the construction of new electricity generating plant above a certain capacity. In the Netherlands fuel-switching has been achieved by means of a gentleman's agreement between the Minister of Economic Affairs and the electricity producers. The use of a regulatory instrument might at first glance appear surprising given that Energy or Industry Ministers usually have extensive powers to supervise investment and site planning. In fact the British Secretary of State used such powers to block a CEGB investment in an oil fired plant in 1973. Regulatory powers may however be required to supervise private and industrial self-generators. A substantial proportion of electricity is generated by this category of producers in all five West European countries.

Governments do not seem averse to influencing the tariff structures of public utilities in order to favour certain categories of consumer. We have already referred to the Dutch attempt to favour the horticulture sector and to grant favoured rates to industry located in the less favoured regions. In 1979 and 1980 the British government agreed to hold down the level of industrial gas and electricity tariffs, following pressure from industry.[196] Government intervention in both cases was motivated by industrial as opposed to energy policy considerations.

[196] Select Committee on Energy, Second Report on Industrial Energy Pricing Policy. (1980–81), H. C. 422/I.

While governments might encourage research and development in fuel substitution techniques by subsidies and tax concessions to the private sector, the public sector has tended to receive direct funding for such purposes. We noted in section 3 above that German public sector companies have tended to hold onto the lion's share of a great deal of the Minister for Research and Development's budget. In both the United Kingdom and Germany, the electricity generating industry is 'obliged' by a series of 'informal agreements' to buy domestic coal.

3. The development of nuclear power: here we find that public sector management predominates over all other forms of instrument, with the possible exception of Germany. Measures to develop nuclear energy supplies in the United Kingdom, France and Italy are exclusively targeted at the public sector, and relate predominantly to granting funds to the nuclear sector or to reorganising that sector. As governments have sought to augment the pace of nuclear programmes, public sector agencies which once combined technical and commercial aspects of nuclear energy development have been reorganised with aspects of the commercial functions being either privatised (UK) or, as in the case of France, reorganised so that maximum managerial autonomy is assured. The Italian case reflects the opposite tendency: commercial aspects have been transferred from the private to the public sector, and the latter reorganised in order to promote the acceleration of the nuclear power programme.[197] This development reflects, in part, the government's inability to develop new technology without co-ordinated public sector participation.

The siting of nuclear power plants is controlled through general land use planning legislation in the United Kingdom, France and until recently West Germany. An Italian law of 1975 subjected nuclear plant site procedure to a separate system of planning law, allowing for greater consultation with the regions. In 1982 Germany reformed its planning procedure for nuclear sites, allowing for greater centralisation of powers to grant planning permission.

Germany is also the only country where the development of nuclear power remains in the private sector. Research and development is however heavily subsidised and given the close links between the industry and the Ministry outlined in section III, it would appear that the subsidy instrument provided an effective substitute for public sector management. It should be noted that the nuclear power programmes of Hungary and the Netherlands are still in their formative stages.

Germany is the only country to provide, since 1982, for the maintenance of natural and enriched uranium stocks by a public sector body. In France, the only country under study with significant uranium reserves, the exploration for and exploitation of uranium is regulated by the Code Minier. The CEA has a substantial presence in the various companies engaged in exploration and production and in addition the 'cahiers de charges' impose conditions on producing companies as to the holding of uranium stocks. There appears to be no legal

---

[197] Law no. 151 of May 2, 1983. Gazz. Uff., May 6, 1983 no. 123 and Decree no 82–404 of May 13, 1982 in J.O.R.F., May 14, 1982.

requirement to hold reserve stocks of uranium in the other countries under study, but given the dominance of public sector firms in Britain and Italy and the strategic role in the development of nuclear fuel accorded to ENI, resort to further legal controls may have proved unnecessary.

4. *The Development of Domestic Energy Resources:* here we find an extensive reliance on legal measures of public sector management as the preferred policy instrument. This is of course hardly surprising given the dominance of public sector firms in the various energy markets. Although there is extensive regional public ownership in the coal and electricity industry and, following the 1975 Veba/Gelsenberg merger, a federal public sector presence in the oil industry, we do not find legal measures of public sector management in Germany.

In the United Kingdom, the British National Oil Corporation had been created in 1975 with the aim of securing greater state control over the rate of exploration for and production of North Sea oil, as well as establishing a fully integrated national company capable of furnishing government with a source of expertise and information on the workings of the oil industry. BNOC was accorded participation rights in existing licences and along with BGC was originally allowed to apply for new licences outside the licence rounds.

In 1982 the Oil and Gas (Enterprise) Act privatised the exploration and production, but not the participation functions of BNOC. The former were transferred to Britoil Ltd. and 49 per cent of the shares of this new company were subsequently sold in the following year. Part two of the 1982 Act made provision for the transfer of BGC's onshore and offshore oil fields to a separate company, Enterprise Oil. 100 per cent of the shares of this company have now been sold, but the government has retained a so-called 'golden share', allowing it to prevent shares falling into the hands of foreign companies. The government had previously directed the BGC to dispose of its onshore oil assets, using powers under the Gas Act 1972. The 1982 Act further removed the BGC's monopoly over the supply of gas to certain categories of large-scale user.[198]

Until March 1985 BNOC remained as a state trading corporation whose principal activity was the lifting of participation and royalty oil and its disposal in the national interest. In the decade between 1975 and 1985, it would seem fair to say that the British government attempted to secure control over oil and gas production and development through a mixture of public sector management and regulatory controls in the form of licenses, for private sector and public sector firms alike.

The government may exercise control over production rates by means of the controls imposed on all licensees. Under the conditions attached to the licences, it may delay the start of commercial fields, set rates of production and within strict limits, vary these rates.[199] To date there has been extreme caution about the use of these powers and in fact in only one commercial field, owned and operated by

[198] A. W. Baker and G. H. Daniels., "BNOC and Privatisation (1983) 1 *Journal of Energy and Natural Resources Law* 149.

[199] Petroleum (Production) Regulations 1982, S. I. 1982 No 1000, Sch 5, clauses 14 and 15.

BNOC, has the start up of production been explicitly delayed under these powers.[200]

In the Netherlands, the other major hydrocarbon producing country, state participation in the exploration and production of natural gas was increased by a Royal Decree of 1976. This latter Decree provides for the State's right to take via the publicly owned DSM Aardgas BV, a 50 per cent interest in production under a licence. Under the former decree of 1967 the State only took a 40 per cent interest in offshore licences.

As for onshore gas, although exploitation of onshore gas had since 1963 been assured by the NAM (in which the State held a 40 per cent stake, via DSM), additional regulatory measures to cope with the post crisis adjustments were needed. The 1976 Royal Decree provided for a 10 per cent direct state participation reducing the share of Esso and Shell to 25 per cent each. In addition, by a Royal Decree of 1980, the government appointed a Special Commissioner for Gas, entrusted with renegotiating price and quantity terms in existing long-term export contracts. The NAM had apparently been incapable of achieving this result through its own endeavours.

In the oil consumer countries, legal measures of public sector management take a number of forms. We have already mentioned the rationalisation of Elf in 1976, allowing for greater managerial autonomy. Increased funding was made available to GDF and ENI to develop natural gas production and distribution systems in their respective countries, the development of natural gas being a stated goal of national energy policies in both countries. The position of the coal industry was also reassessed in all three coal producing countries: the United Kingdom, France and Germany. Increased financial provision for higher investment had been made in a series of Coal Industry Acts in the United Kingdom, until 1981. In France a contrat d'enterprise was concluded with CDF, providing for increased managerial autonomy on the one hand and a fixed subsidy per tonne of coal produced. CDF has also been encouraged to develop its overseas mining interests, although no explicit legal measure has been enacted for this purpose. Coal production in West Germany has benefited from increased subsidisation. In a series of three 'electricity from coal' laws, the West German government have provided financial compensation to electricity producers to meet the increased cost of using Community coal as opposed to cheaper, foreign imports. In the United Kingdom and France where both coal production and electricity generation are secured by public sector monopolies, no overt legal measures to encourage the use of coal in electricity production have been recorded. In the United Kingdom an agreement between the NCB and CEGB regulates the price and quantity of coal used for electricity production. The CEGB is the NCB's major customer, and although the CEGB has repeatedly sought permission from the Secretary of State for Energy to increase levels of coal imports, this has not been forthcoming.

In Italy and France, public sector management has been an important instrument in securing the development of alternative energy forms, and in particular

---

[200] For government statements on depletion policy, see H. C. Debates 1974, vol. 882 cols. 648–50, and (1982–83) H. C. 134.

solar, geothermal and hydroelectric energy. Public sector agencies responsible for the promotion of alternative energy forms have been set up in both countries. The Italian ENEA was created in 1982 while the French APEE and COMES, the Commission on Solar Energy set up in 1977, were fused in 1982 to form the APME.[201] The latter has been given increased funds to conduct surveys, promote research and development and provide subsidies to encourage domestic and industrial use of alternative energy forms. In Italy the Law of May 29, 1982 providing for the development of renewable energy forms and the operation of non-oil fired electrical generating capacity allows for greater involvement of the regions in developing alternative energy forms and allows for increased electricity production by private and municipal companies at the expense of ENEL's quasi monopoly on electricity generation.

In fact a number of the Regions have adopted enabling legislation allowing for the provision of grants and subsidies to promote research and development on and use of alternative energy forms. The Law of May 29th, 1982 makes provision for the CIPE to issue directives, after consultation with the ENEA, on the coordination of public sector activity in this field. In Hungary, the Act on the sixth national economic plan makes extensive provision for the development of coal mining and the containment of oil consumption. This includes provisions to finance investment and allows for energy prices to be set in accordance with world market levels.

5. *The Diversification of Imported Supplies:* public sector firms have been accorded an important role in securing this objective. Interestingly, most of this public sector management is non-legal and takes the form of government backing for particular agreements. A qualified exception applies in case of French oil companies. Under the 1928 lois Poincaré, as amended in 1979, public and private companies can only obtain an A3 licence to import pertroleum products into France if they produce a satisfactory supply plan. This supply plan, which provides that 80 per cent of supplies must be secured by long-term contracts concluded with refineries within the EC, must be approved by the special Commission instituted under the 1928 legislation. Both French national oil companies have been encouraged to conclude long-term contracts for the supply of crude oil with producer countries, contracts which the oil nationals regard as financially onerous.

The Italian and French governments have both been active in securing the conclusion of contracts between their national gas corporations ENI and GDF, and the USSR and Sonatrach of Algeria for the supply of natural gas. In both countries the governments have had to contribute financial aid to Algeria in order to secure the deal.

In the Netherlands Gasunie has concluded several contracts for the importation of natural gas, having first secured the permission of the Minister of Economic Affairs. The level and source of coal importation is also covered by non-legal public sector management in France and the United Kingdom. Although there is no formal measure prohibiting coal imports into either country, levels of non-EC

201 Agence pour Matriser l'Energie.

imports are in practice dictated by the need to provide support to the domestic coal industry and hence the electricity producing companies are restricted in their purchases of non-EC coal. In Germany, where a high proportion of coal is consumed in the industrial sector as well as in electricity generation, non-EC coal has been subject to a quota since 1958. The so-called Century Agreement concluded between the coal industry and electricity producers in 1980, and approved by the Federal Government, provides for a gradual increase in the importation of foreign coal, so that despite the 'mixed' form of owernship in these sectors, the style of instrument is similar.

6. *In conclusion* it may be stated that public sector management has been an important instrument in securing energy policy objectives, and in particular long-term objectives relating to alteration of supply patterns. It is important to distinguish the use of legal measures of public sector management, particularly in relation to alteration of supply patterns, from non-legal measures. We have identified a large number of legal measures, largely aimed at restructuring, rationalising or increasing the funds or powers of existing public sector companies. These measures have largely been targeted at the public sector as *object* of policy rather than as instrument of policy transmission, but the initial presence of public sector companies in most of the energy markets may have necessitated institutional reforms or delineation of existing powers and duties in order that wider policy goals could be achieved. Non-legal measures, i.e. measures based on managerial controls, have played an important role in securing the alteration of energy consumption patterns and the related objective of increased diversification of imported energy supplies. In particular we might note the non-appearance of specific legal measures to promote nuclear electricity in France. This would suggest that funds have been made available through normal budgetary allocation procedures. We have also drawn attention to the non-appearance of specific public sector instruments in the field of short-term crisis management measures, and the extent to which public and private, or national and foreign oil 'majors' have been dealt with in a relatively similar manner, so that with the exception of the creation of BNOC, and the Veba merger, most of the measures targeted at the public sector oil companies have also been directed at private oil companies.

In certain cases public sector management has been an alternative to other forms of instrument. For instance, the increased funding to the nuclear and electricity industries in Italy, the United Kingdom and probably France has its counter-part in higher research and development subsidies to the German nuclear sector. In other cases, as with the development of United Kingdom oil and gas reserves, public sector management has been combined with unilateral regulation of the private sector.

C. Manpower Policies

According to our national inventories, there has been little reliance on visible legal measures of public sector management in the Western European countries, and indeed our inventories did not record any legal measures targeted at public sector enterprises in the five Western countries in the pursuit of manpower policies. This is in marked contrast to the situation in Hungary where measures directed to secure the objectives of job maintenance, job creation and manpower adjustment take primarily the form of subsidy instruments directed towards state enterprises, industrial trusts and co-operatives. As we have noted the private sector in Hungary has been traditionally limited to private plot agricultural production, residential construction and the retail trade. The problem of controlling the growth of the secondary economy is addressed by a series of regulatory instruments, requiring permission to undertake a second job to be granted by the first employer.

1. Manpower Adjustment: In the United Kingdom, West Germany, Italy, France and the Netherlands, the limited number of reported legal measures of public sector management are to be found primarily in the field of manpower adjustment, taking the form of training schemes which improve access of potential workers to the labour market, schemes to encourage movement between jobs and schemes to encourage early retirement from the civil service. The nature of public sector management as an instrument to secure manpower adjustment objectives has however changed over time. In the period between 1970 to 1975 the size of the *administrative* public sector increased in each country. At this time we see the proliferation of schemes to expand particular areas of the public service through training schemes in Germany, France and Italy. However in recent years labour market policies and personnel policies in the public sector have become subordinated to the demands of general budgetary policy. In Germany the two restrictive budgetary acts of 1975 and 1981 had severe effects on public sector employment. Although employment in the public sector coninued to increase in Germany after the 1975 budget, the rate of growth slowed appreciably, dropping from 15 per cent to 9 per cent. However this trend was wholly attributable to employment trends in the Länder and municipalities: between 1975 and 1980 the number of full-time federal employees actually declined absolutely by two per cent.[202] This trend at federal level should be reinforced by a series of non-binding collective agreements between the government and the civil servants' union, the OTV. In consequence manpower adjustment in the German public sector is to be secured by the promotion of part-time work schemes. By virtue of the Drittes Gesetz zur Änderung dienstrechtlicher Vorschriften of 1980 public servants may be requested to undertake part-time work for an eight-year period if it is deemed in the public interest. The provisions or this law appear to have been applied mainly at Länder level.[203]

The fate of the Bundesanstalt für Arbeit (BA) job creation schemes in the public sector, first introduced in 1975 and primarily concentrated in the construction industry and later the social services, can be attributed not only to the government's aim of trimming the size of the public sector but also to objections from the

---

[202] D. Weber and G. Nass., "Employment Policy in Western Germany", in Richardson and Honning, *supra* note 78.

[203] Bundesministerium der Finanzen (1981). Personalentwicklung bei Bund, Ländern und Gemeinden 1960–80, in BMF Finanznachrichten. Bonn.

powerful ÖTV. The latter argued that workers on the schemes were being employed to do jobs that ought to have been done by civil servants. By the end of 1982 only 23,000 workers were employed on such schemes, less than half as many as three years previously.[204]

In *France*, although the overall size of the public administrative sector has tended to grow, especially following the nationalisation wave of 1982, increased reliance is placed on the promotion of a shorter working week, job sharing, part-time work, and fixed term contracts. A Decree of 1981 introduced the 39-hour working week in the public sector, the shorter working week only being introduced in the private sector in the following year. Part-time work in the public administration has been encouraged by the provisions of an Act of 1980, and further ordinances issued under the Special Powers Act 1982 allow for civil servants to switch to part-time jobs for a specified period, later returning to full time employment. A further ordinace allows civil servants to retire to part-time work at the age of 55 and to retire completely at 57. (The corresponding figure is 60 in the private sector.) Many of these types of measures have been enacted in the form of 'solidarity contracts' with the private sector. We will compare the legal form of these instruments in section 6 below. It should be noted that many of the earliest provisions for a reduced working week, part-time work and early retirement schemes are to be found in the collective agreement between the state-owned car company Renault and the government in 1973.

We do not find express legal measures for manpower adjustment schemes in the *United Kingdom* but most of the public sector firms and statutory authorities, including local government, health boards and universities have all encouraged early retirement. Hence non-legal measures of public sector management play an important role. Central government attempts to reduce the level of public sector employment in the United Kingdom have been more successful at central departmental level. Between 1979 and 1984, civil service numbers have been cut by 16 per cent, but the staff cuts scheduled for local and statutory authorities have not been achieved at as fast a pace, and indeed employment levels in the National Health Service have increased. In the *Netherlands* early retirement provisions and part-time work schemes have been incorporated in collective agreements between government and public sector employees. While the shorter working week was introduced into the public sector and then generalised to the economy as a whole in *France,* the evidence does not suggest that schemes are introduced into the public sector first as a means of 'experimenting' before transfer to the private sector. Indeed in France, further schemes on early retirement, part-time work and shorter working weeks were introduced simultaneously by the same legal mechanism – the contrat de solidarité. It could be argued that the desire to rationalise public sector employment is the prime objective of the relevant manpower policy measures: the public sector is not a mere indirect instrument for policy transmission to the private sector.

A possible exception in the case of manpower adjustment is *Italy*. Special training schemes, although targeted at public and private firms alike, have tended to place

[204] Weber und Nass, *supra* note 201.

employees in the public as opposed to the private sector. Early retirement has been a problem, not an objective, in the Italian public sector, and a Law of March 27, 1983 has prevented civil servants from retiring after as little as 15 years of service.

2. Job Creation and Job Maintenance: Further problems in assessing the importance of public sector management emerge in any consideration of these two remaining general objectives. It is common to find the creation of new public sector agencies or para-state bodies, endowed with the task of encouraging new jobs in new industries in the private sector. Examples are the National Enterprise Board, Welsh Development Agency and Scottish Development Agency created in the United Kingdom in 1975, the CIASI and CODIS and various interministerial bodies in France in 1975, and the creation of GEPI in Italy in 1971. These bodies may be charged with the promotion and support of new industries in certain sectors of the economy but regional job maintenance considerations may be specified in either the enabling legislation or guidelines issued by the sponsoring Minister, as in the case of the NEB, SDA and WDA. The extent to which these 'buffer' organisations actually succeed in 'picking winners' is open to debate. More often as a result of political pressure, these bodies are obliged to play the role of rescuer as opposed to entrepreneur. The funds placed at their disposal to take equity and make loans are absorbed into rescue operations and there seems little scope for parliamentary control of this process.[205] As we have noted the Italian Law no 675 of 1975 attempted to reform and rationalise rescue operations by public sector companies, in particular by curtailing rescue operations in the North and limiting intervention to southern industries. This law however failed. As the head of GEPI commented, "shutting down a factory was a deadly sin for public enterprise in the Italian economy of the 1970's".[206] As noted in section III, GEPI was entrusted with the provision of managerial and financial support to structurally weak industries which would then be returned to the private sector. In fact all its interventions were in the form of rescue operations. In 1976 for example GEPI refused to step in and take over the ailing firm of Leyland-Innocenti. If the factory had been closed down the workers would have been deprived of their salaries, but if the factory was taken over by the GEPI the workers would have 95 per cent of their salaries met by the Earnings Integration Fund. The Government compelled GEPI to set up IPO, a company formally independent of the GEPI, whose purpose was simply to hire the above mentioned workers. The creation of IPO was a prime example of the fact that GEPI is not free to operate according to the criteria set forth by law, but is subject to obligations imposed by government. The same may have been true of the NEB in the United Kingdom: a great part of the NEB's finances were absorbed through its holdings in Rolls Royce and British Leyland.

---

[205] B. Hindley and R. Richardson, "The United Kingdom: Pulling Dragon's Teeth – The National Enterprise Board," in B. Hindley (ed.), *State Investment Companies in Western Europe*, (1983, London) at p. 263.

[206] Grassini, *supra*, note 188.

It is important to bear in mind the flexibility of this type of public sector instrument: a reorientation of role can occur through political pressure alone and no further visible instruments may be required.

A related point may be made about delegation of powers to regional and local governments in relation to job creation and job maintenance. If state shareholding bodies such as GEPI and the NEB have had their powers de facto redefined by government, at the level of local government the opposite may be true. In the United Kingdom, local authorities have been able to use their statutory discretionary powers to set up Enterprise Boards and provide incentives for job maintenance. Stewart has challenged "the myths of statutory constraint" by central government[207] and in France, Ashford has suggested that local authorities have always had considerable freedom of manoeuvre to develop local economic initiatives.[208] Even before the reforms introduced by the French Decentralisation Law of March 5, 1982 and the subsequent transfer of powers to local authorities to promote job maintenance and job creation schemes, local authorities were active in the manpower policy area. In Italy the failure of traditional policy instruments including takeover and rationalisation by public sector companies has prompted a number of novel responses at the regional level.[209] Regional development corporations have been formed in certain regions in the North of Italy with the aim of easing the impact of the publicly owned state company Finsider's restructuring plan. The regional corporations play a mediating role in transferring jobs between the public and private sectors. Lombardy, the region most badly affected by the world steel crisis, has formalated a comprehensive regional plan, which with the help of EC and European Investment Bank aid, is designed to counteract the impact of the steel crisis by encouraging new investment, retraining for steel workers and the development of infrastructure.[210]

Central-local relations are a complex area which cannot be investigated here, but the capacity of lower tiers of government to mobilise support and resources in the pursuit of manpower policy objectives should not be understood from a 'top-down' perspective, involving a transfer of powers or funds to the lower tiers of government. It is however useful to point to the need to reconsider certain aspects of government "self management" and to contrast strategies adopted by the different tiers of government to those adopted by public sector firms vis-á-vis central government. In *Germany* and the *Netherlands* attention should be drawn to the role of regional public banks and the role of the Dutch Reconstruction Company in co-ordinating regional and sectoral subsidies for job creation or job maintenance.[211]

There are no *overt* legal measures directing public sector firms to shed employees or to protect employees in certain geographical areas or industrial sectors.

[207] J. Stewart (ed.), in *A Half Century of Municipal Progress* (1985, London).
[208] D. Ashford, *British Dogmatism, French Pragmatism* (1982, London).
[209] M. Rhodes and J. Eisenhower: The Politics of Public Sector Steel: From the 'Economic Miracle' to the crisis of the Eighties (1984, mimeo, European University Institute).
[210] *Ibid.*
[211] De Jong and Spierenberg, "The Netherlands," in Hindley, *supra* note 204, at p. 59.

Hungary of course is different. It may be assumed that governments may utilise 'management' powers, by constraining finances or prohibiting or redirecting new investments to achieve these objectives. Public sector firms are obviously an important instrument in maintaining jobs in declining industries. In its thirteenth Annual Report the Commission noted that the size of the public sector has increased in general in the shipbuilding, motor vehicles, textiles and man-made fibres industries. The Commission is concerned about the lack of transparency in the transfer of public funds to these sectors and suspects that much could be caught by the prohibitions on state aid as defined by Article 92 of the Treaty of Rome.[212]

In *France* the public sector's tendency to 'silently nationalise' or absorb private sector companies has proved a useful, indirect method of maintaining jobs in certain sectors. In 1983, the government compelled a subsidiary of the CGE to take over an ailing electro-nuclear firm, contrary to the wishes of both the parent and subsidiary companies.[213] Recently the French government has refused to come to the rescue of the huge heavy engineering company, Creuset-Loire, an indication perhaps that the present government is not prepared to intervene to protect jobs at any cost.

In addition following the nationalisation Law of February 11, 1982, the government has concluded a number of *'contrats de plan'* with the major 'new' nationalised companies. A decree of December 2, 1982 provides the legal basis for these contracts. Each company has signed a contract with its sponsoring department. The contracts cover the firm's medium-term strategy – usually for a period of between three to five years. The contracts tend to be declaratory in nature, expressing the individual firm's commitment to the major objectives of the Ninth Plan, and in particular to the maintenance of employment levels. In return the state guarantees that a certain level of investment will be assured. In addition 'contrats de plan' have been concluded with the traditional 'grandes entreprises nationales', and while the content of the contracts are largely similar to those concluded with the newly nationalised companies, there is more detailed provision for financial contributions by the State.

Commentators have pointed out that for the most part the contracts contain contradictory objectives; a return to healthy finances, the introduction of new technology and modernisation of plant as well as the maintenance of employment.[214] They contrast this with the British situation where public sector concerns such as British Airways or British Rail have only achieved profitability by laying off a large number of workers and by cutting back on services. In addition the consequences of breach of these contracts remain unclear. Indeed the government had been committed under the relevant 'contrat' with the Schneider group to provide funds for its ailing subsidiary, Creusot-Loire, to allow for rationalisation. In addition the government had been committed to re-imburse GDF for the extra costs involved in the purchase of Algerian gas. This compensatory payment was dropped, however from the 1984 budget, leaving GDF with an extra bill of FF 1.4

[212] E. C. Commission, 13th Report on Competition Policy (1984, Brussels) at pp. 11–12.
[213] Chronique (1984) 3 *Revue Française d'Administration Publique* at p. 144.
[214] Chronique, infra.

billion. It is perhaps doubtful that these new contrats du plan will make a significant impact on the nature of public sector management in the pursuit of manpower policy objectives in France. Furthermore, the various heads of the newly nationalised industries have made no secret of the fact that they consider their enterprises overstaffed.

3. *In conclusion*, it must be stressed that for manpower policy, non-legal measures of public sector management are far more important than legal measures. This is in direct contrast to energy policy objectives where we recorded a large number of legal measures. It should also be remembered that although the public sector in Germany is not 'managed' in such a way as to achieve manpower policy goals, we have noted that firms which are at least in part publicly owned have a greater take up of subsidies for job creation or maintenance in specific sectors or regions. This might explain the quantitative and qualitative reliance on the subsidy instrument both in Germany and the Netherlands. Less visible forms of intervention, either through the extension of public sector participation in the economy or by indirectly utilising public sector firms to take up financial benefits obviously have political attractions in France and Italy.

The increased participation of lower tiers of government, even in the absence of express statutory interventionist powers is an important development in the provision of manpower adjustment policies. Detailed research comparing central government 'contrôles techniques' over subordinate levels of government to those controls and pressures exerted over state owned enterprise is surely a field ripe for study. As far as Western European countries are concerned, public sector management can provide an attractive means of attaining goals and objectives which might fall foul of the provisions of the Treaty of Rome and relevant secondary legislation if those objectives were pursued by more overt instrument types. However public take-over of bankrupt private firms remains an expensive procedure and will usually only be used when continued subsidisation fails to maintain jobs.

V. The Operationalisation of Legal Measures of Public Sector Management

Our survey of the selection of public sector managements as a policy instrument in the manpower and energy fields suggests a marked reliance on *legal*, visible measures in the energy field while non-legal, 'invisible' measures appear more frequently in the manpower field. As mentioned in section IV, the public sector has been a politically convenient mechanism for maintaining employment levels and it would be unsurprising to find governments exerting informal pressure, backed up by financial incentives.

At the same time, the prevalence of legal measures targeted at the energy sector provokes the need for further investigation. To what extent are these measures distinct from those targeted at the private sector? To what extent is the private sector used as a model for legal measures of public sector management and vice versa? Secondly, are there major differences in the degree of legalisation of ownership controls in the different countries and does this reflect constitutional constraints? Dealing with the second point, we have noted that many of the legal measures of public sector management involve the transfer of funds to public sector bodies. In the *United Kingdom,* various specific Acts of Parliament secure the transfer of funds to the nuclear, electricity and coal sectors for a fixed number of years. Under ordinary budgetary law, financial provision may be made on a yearly basis only. Augmentation of the 'fondi di dotazione' in Italy has also required separate, non budgetary legislation, but in general funding for the public sector is provided through the annual budgetary legislation in all five Western countries. Loan sanction for individual investment schemes would appear to be required by all public corporations, at least in theory in Britain, France and Italy, although it is the approval of a sponsoring Minister or Committee of Ministers, usually with Treasury agreement which is required. Hence control over public sector finances is often beyond the reach of Parliament, and any influence is *a posteriori* as opposed to *a priori.* This may be contrasted with the provision of subsidies to private firms in conjunction with energy and manpower policy goals. The national inventories reveal a high level of parliamentary participation in the enactment if not in the implementation of subsidy schemes. Most such schemes are either of a temporary nature, of if permanent, require annual budgetary approval. In *Germany* we have mentioned that the subsidy instrument is the preferred means of financing firms in which federal or Länder governments participate, but those subsidy instruments are *generalised* across public and private industry. Subsidy schemes are usually sectoral or regional, although programmes for research and development may identify specific beneficiaires, as in the case of the German Research and Development programme which singles out the private nuclear sector.

Reorganisation or rationalisation of the public sector to secure efficient pursuit of primarily energy as opposed to manpower policy goals has usually taken legislative form. Again constitutional constraints may require the high legal profile of such instruments, particularly where the provision of funding is involved. For example, the British National Oil Corporation was created by an Act of Parliament in 1975. The vesting of assets in a public corporation has been the most characteristic feature of British public enterprise since 1945. While there are no constitutional conventions requiring public ownership of an industry to take the form of a public corporation, this has nevertheless been the pattern of intervention, and thus a high legal profile is assured. In *France* the 'first national-isation' law was successfully challenged before the Conseil Constitutionnel. In its decision of January 16, 1982 the Conseil held that the first law did not make adequate compensation to private shareholders and was hence in breach of Article 17 of the Declaration of the Rights of Man 1789. Furthermore the fact that banks and credit institutions were excluded was in breach of the principle of equality of treatment and finally the Conseil held that the various provisions which endowed management with substantial powers to sell off part of their assets to the private sector was in breach of Article 34 of the Constitution. The second nationalisation law reflected the Conseil's suggested amendments and became law on February 11, 1982. We have already noted that Article 34 was invoked unsuccessfully to challenge the restructuring of the CEA and SNEA.

One should also note that privatisation of some of the assets of the British public corporations has been preceded by the adoption of legal measures, which may be in the form of statutory instruments or Acts of Parliament. The Secretary of State whose department sponsors the relevant enterprise is usually empowered to transfer the assets of the company into his own name. This is usually executed by means of delegated legislation, so that the executive has substantial control over the timing of the transfer of assets and subsequent sale to the private sector. Hence these type of measures have a high legal profile and follow the general pattern of regulation in the United Kingdom. Paradoxically, in *Germany* the Federal Minister of Economics' powers to sanction mergers which allow for the restructuring of industry, hence promoting 'national champions', have a low legal profile: commentators have pointed to the general weakness of the FCO and the courts: "the rights given to the courts and the Federal Cartel Office to act as countervailing institutions are rather modest".[215] Public sector firms which are also exempted from certain provisions of competition law are allowed considerable operative autonomy immunised from challenges by either interest Groups or the FCO. Kaufer and Blankart argue that these firms, backed by political support, can achieve government policy objectives either by "an expansion of the monopoly domain to other product markets or resort to public subsidies".[216]

In conclusion it may be argued for energy policy that measures aimed at changing ownership profiles, restructuring and transferring funds have *a high legal profile* in each of the countries under study, with the possible exception of Germany. In the manpower policy sector, changes in ownership may have a lower legal profile for two reasons: 'buffer organisations' such as the NEB, or the GEPI, may be endowed with powers to participate in private sector companies, or the legal *form* of public enterprise as such may allow for diversification and participation in the private sector. This certainly seems to be the case in Italy and France where 'creeping nationalisation' has been used as an ad hoc instrument. This has not affected the *quantity* of subsidy instruments available to the private sector in either of these countries. Our inventories reveal that subsidy schemes are general in scope and usually of temporary validity. Rescue packages tend to come 'tailor-made' to suit the individual firm and even if expressed to be 'temporary solutions' it is often difficult to return these firms back to the private sector, for both practical and constitutional reasons. As the GEPI experience in Italy demonstrates the 'ownership option' can be an expensive one.

It is perhaps more important to compare the content of legal measures addressed to the public sector with that of measures addressed to the private sector. Can we find any support for our initial hypothesis that in countries where the public sector is small the private sector might operate as a model?

The legal measures addressed to the public sector in pursuit of energy policy and manpower policy objectives in the *Netherlands* seem to conform to the form and content of those addressed to the private sector. Most of the energy policy measures can be classified as consensual agreements, concluded between the

---

[215] Bauer, *supra* note 160.
[216] *Ibid.*

Minister for Economic Affairs and the various public sector companies, in the gas distribution, electricity generation and distribution sectors, the Natural Gas Prices Act 1974 being an exception. However the latter has been used on one occasion and is generally expected to operate as a 'stick behind the door', only being activated in the event of failure to agree on the minimum prices to be charged by Gasunie for domestic supply and exports. In the context of manpower adjustment, the collective agreements concluded are similar in content and form to these concluded in the private sector.

In *Germany*, there is no distinctive style of public sector management. Publicly owned firms are subject to the same regulatory constraints and may have access to the same financial benefits as those in the private sector. However the de facto privileged position of public sector firms may allow them to take advantage of sectoral and regional aid schemes at the expense of private sector firms. In the manpower policy area, the few legal measures addressed to the public sector, in the area of early retirement, do not differ in form from those addressed to the private sector.

In the United Kingdom, most of the legal measures are targeted at the public sector as *object* of energy policy. Given that the electricity, coal and gas public utilities enjoy a monopoly, it is difficult to find a counterpart measure in the private sector. In the area of gas and oil exploration and production where public *and* private firms operate, we have noted an increasing approximation of instrument types. The privileges of BNOC have been removed and BGC's monopoly of supply of gas restricted. Whereas the profits of private sector companies engaged in oil production were subject to the Oil Taxation Act 1975 and its subsequent amendments, BNOC's financial activities were directly controlled. BNOC and the newly privatised Britoil are no longer exempt from these taxation regimes. As we have mentioned, there are few distinct legal measures targeted at the public sector in the manpower field. The National Enterprise Board has been wound up, and a number of firms have been transferred back to the private sector. While it is possible to identify a number of overt legal measures of public sector management in the United Kingdom, these measures are all *specific* in nature, applying to individual public enterprises. Italy and France present a different picture. The first thing of note is that these are the only two countries in Western Europe where measures are addressed to the public sector in *general*. In the three other countries, legal measures are directed at individual public sector enterprises.

In Italy the law no 675 of 1977, and in France the nationalisation law of 1982, decree of June 1983 on the 'contrats de plan' and Law of July 1983 on the democratisation of the public sector are all *general* measures.

By virtue of the 1982 Law and the decree of 1983, the public sector firms conclude contracts with their sponsoring ministry, guaranteeing their commitment to the objectives of the Ninth Plan. The aim is to assure the greater co-operation of the public sector firms in the pursuit of manpower policy objectives, but at the same time guarantee their commercial autonomy. For the private sector similar ends may be achieved by virtue of the Special Powers Act 1982. This Act authorised the French government to issue a series of ordinances on the reduction of working time, increased holiday time, part-time jobs, temporary jobs, fixed labour contracts, reduction of retirement age, limitation of pension rights, youth employment and, most importantly, allow the conclusion of solidarity contracts with the private sector. Eighteen ordinances were issued under this Act. An Ordinance of January 16, 1982 provided for the conclusion of four distinct types of *solidarity contract*, but the form and content of the contractual device is common to public and private sectors. However, it would be difficult to determine conclusively whether the public sector serves as a model for intervention in the private sector. Several of the ordinances issued under the 1982 Special Powers Act have been targeted solely at the public sector, providing for part-time work in and early retirement from various state bureaucracies. The law on the public sector, of July 26, 1983 follows many of the provisions of the 'Lois Auroux' of August 4, 1982 to December 23, 1982. The time-lag between the two laws may of course be explained by a variety of factors, including lack of Parliamentary time. What does appear to be clear however is that the new interventionist mechanisms in the private sector take a similar form and are related in content to those adopted in the public sector.[217]

In Italy intervention has tended to be ad hoc and piecemeal in nature in both the public and private sectors. The device of the decree-law to provide subsidies and wage supplements to the private sector allows for a similar style of ad hoc intervention as the take-over of the assets of failing firms by the state shareholding companies or the public sector institutions such as GEPI. As noted above, attempts at rationalisation have failed.

The extent to which *global* or *general* instruments of public sector management appeared in the French and Italian inventories, as compared to the British preference for specific instruments, targeted at individual firms, is perhaps a reflection of national policy styles. All three countries are traditionally regarded as "interventionist' but the United Kingdom, unlike France and Italy, has never engaged in indicative planning since the abject failure of the early experiments of the mid-sixties. It would therefore appear fair to suggest that there has never been any significant attempt to delineate or determine the role of the public sector firm in any detail[218] or to delegate specific tasks in the context of a sectoral plan. The failure or inability to conceive of a systematic strategic role for public sector firms may explain why, despite the size and economic importance of that sector, there has been no attempt to introduce general legal measures which seek to re-orient or redefine the instrumental role of the public sector. The various French attempts at 'contrats du programme, contrats d'entreprise and contrats du plan' seem to fit into this latter category as does the Italian attempt at rationalisation. The existence of these legal measures appear to represent an attempt, albeit a largely unsuccessful one, to reconcile the conflicts inherent in the instrumental use of the public sector. In particular the tension between the financial autonomy of the firm and its future willingness to pursue governmental objectives. It is perhaps paradoxical that the recent proposals on the future of the United Kingdom nationalised enterprises, if

---

[217] Y. Gaudemet, "Les contrats de solidarité" (1982) *Droit Social* 335.
[218] See National Economic Development Office, *The Role of the Nationalised Industries* (1976, London).

implemented, do envisage a generalised approach to the public sector, and in particular envisage a substantial increase in Treasury controls and a reduction in the scope of activities retained within the public sector.[219] Hence in the British case, the public sector is to be controlled by the traditional financial mechanisms. In France by contrast the various attempts at restating or redefining public enterprise goals through the device of the contract have involved the incorporation of more flexible or particularised *sanctions* to be deployed where the firm fails to achieve stated goals.

Further indication of the limitations inherent in the instrumental use of the public sector in achieving particularised goals is apparent from a brief consideration of the form and content of legal measures addressed to national oil companies. Our inventories have demonstrated the extent to which these companies have been regulated in a manner similar to their private sector counterparts. This sectoral feature of the legal implementation of energy policy cuts across national boundaries and can be explained by the international nature of the oil industry and, as Bercusson emphasises, the enduring dominance of the private multinationals.[220]

VI. Conclusion

The above analysis suggests that the *choice* of public sector management as an instrument of policy is shaped by a variety of factors including administrative tradition, political and ideological traditions, constitutional constraints, and not unimportantly by the nature of the industry itself. As I have stressed throughout this chapter, it is important to distinguish between ownership and management of public enterprises, as the experiences in the oil sector of all five Western states illustrates. Nor is the *potential* for management by hierarchical control a constant factor in any of the five western countries examined. The fortunes of non-oil public enterprises fluctuate, making them more or less amenable to managerial forms of control by central government.

While the choice of public sector management may be a reflexion of the traditions mentioned above, I have also examined the *form* of public sector management and in particular, highlighted the reliance on *visible legal* measures of public sector management in the United Kingdom, France and Italy, especially in the energy sector. This can be contrasted with the relative absence of such measures in West Germany and the Netherlands in this sector and the overall absence of visible legal measures of public sector management in the implementation of manpower policy in all five Western European countries. As we have noted it is primarily as a result of the need for institutional re-organisation in the public sector that visible arms-length instruments are resorted to, especially in the three countries which are traditionally regarded as interventionist. The legal shape which this restructuring has taken has been determined by legal tradition and preexisting legal structures. Public enterprise takes a distinctive legal form in France, Italy and the United Kingdom. Daintith has argued that 'collective interest law'

---

[219] Treasury paper, *supra* note 123.
[220] Bercusson, below at pp. 369–371 and 372–374.

has closely approximated to the goal-oriented, purposive model as opposed to the traditional, conditional private law model of law.[221] Public enterprises have traditionally been set up to perform a number of vaguely-defined tasks. Statutes speak of powers not duties, and it is rare to find mention of explicit sanctions. As Cassese points out,[222] the goals to be served by public enterprise are not always clear but are often fluid. The energy crisis of 1973 precipitated a reassessment of goals and the ability of the public sector to achieve them. Hence amendments and additions to existing legislation have been enacted to incorporate new goals or to enable the public sector to pursue existing goals by more rational means. The public sector is the *object* of these measures, and in particular the relationship between the firm and government is redefined so that goals are stated more clearly and powers and duties allocated in a more precise manner. However, as Cassese emphasises, the inherent tension between the 'public' role of the firm, and the degree of autonomy necessary to enable it to pursue an entrepreneurial role, would suggest the virtual impossibility of delineating roles and specifying goals in a wholly satisfactory manner. Hence restructuring of the public sector, even where pursued by visible legal measures, cannot be equated with regulatory measures targeted at the private sector. Not only is it different in purpose but also its form is dictated by past legal structures.

In the Netherlands and Germany on the other hand, the legal form of the public enterprise as well as the relationship between government and the public sector is more akin to the private sector model. Restructuring does occur, but largely through indirect measures. Whereas British, French and Italian measures take a *directive* form, allocating functions or defining new responsibilities, German and to a certain extent Dutch measures, may be seen as *supportive* or reactive, endorsing a public sector company's initiative. Here reliance has been placed on what we have termed supplementary instruments: competition law and preferential access to subsidies. The importance of the legal *form* of public enterprise re-emerges when we examine the instrumental use of the public sector in the pursuit of manpower policy objectives. Here we noted the absence of *overt* measures of public sector management and a reliance on invisible measures especially in the pursuit of the objectives of job maintenance in all five countries. "Silent national-isations" have been feasible in France and Italy through the mechanism of creating subsidiaries. In the United Kingdom certain rescue operations have taken statu-tory form, involving nationalisation or through the creation of intermediaries such as the National Enterprise Board, but informal directions have been equally important. In Germany preferential access to subsidies and exemption from the provisions of the anti-trust laws have served to protect certain sectors of industry, while in the Netherlands the public sector utilities have been required to grant special tariff rates to certain industries, in the interests of employment protection. While it might be concluded that there is an element of public sector management in all five Western countries, in the two countries where the tradition of interven-tion in the economy has been more limited the reliance on supplementary

[221] Daintith, above at pp. 12–14.
[222] Cassese, below at pp. 239–240.

measures suggests a different type of relationship between the national government and the industries in which it participates. Resort to these measures suggests not only a divergence in political styles but also a preference for non-hierarchical methods of control of state enterprises. In France and Italy on the other hand, extensive intervention in the public and private sectors of the economy has led to an increase in 'command' type measures addressed to both sectors of the economy. Subsidies are only granted, subject to the agreement of the firm (Public or private) to comply with stated conditions. The ability of central government to secure compliance with these conditions may be potentially greater in the public sector, although recent experience in the newly-nationalised sectors in France does not bear this proposition out.

We should however be wary of characterising this type of governmental self-management as necessarily hierarchical, even if the legal measures take that form. As far as energy policy objectives are concerned it is important to examine the process by which goals and targets are formulated. The public energy utilities in France, Italy and the United Kingdom compete for customers, and even in France where the process of indicative planning has met with periods of relative success, goals and targets are often more a reflexion of bargaining than the result of synoptic planning by central government.[223]

The appearance of legal measures of public sector management which were not aimed at the restructuring of the state sector have predominantly involved the transfer of funds from central government. As we have noted increased transfers of funding have usually taken the form of a specific budgetary allocation and may be the counterpart to subsidisation of the private sector. However the presence of this type of legal measure has been confined to the energy sector. In the pursuit of manpower policy objectives 'invisible' measures of public sector management have been preferred, unless a significant transfer of ownership in the enterprise is envisaged. We have argued that the presence of this type of instrument has not affected the quantity of alternative forms of instrument. Subsidies are preferred because they are temporary in nature and are cheaper, in the short run, than takeovers by the public sector. Manpower policies in the public sector have become increasingly subordinated to expenditure containment goals, and governments are hesitant to embark on rescue operations in the interests of job maintenance. Resort to these 'invisible' forms of public sector management is ad hoc in nature. Again the recent French experience would seem to indicate that even where job maintenance and job creation are made express priorities in the new planning contracts, commitment to these goals is not marked. Political expediency as opposed to contractual obligation will be the determining factor.

In conclusion it may be suggested that the choice of public sector management and the 'legal quality' of that instrument has not been shaped by rational policy considerations. Legal measures of public sector management feature in a somewhat haphazard way, dictated by past styles of intervention and pre-existing legal structures rather than by the content of present policy objectives. Non-legal or invisible measures are even more ad hoc in nature, and the potential to mobilise the

[223] Lucas, *supra* note 194.

public sector in the pursuit of policy objectives appears to be constrained less by parliamentary controls over the executive, which appear to be weak and ex post facto in all five Western countries, than by the bargaining power of the firm concerned. Public sector management in Hungary takes the opposite form: the measures are legal in nature, are based on goals stated in the Five Year and Annual Plans, and the appearance of legal measures is systematic rather than sporadic. In the five western countries ownership has not necessarily implied the systematic deployment of hierarchical managerial controls, but resort to other forms of instrument either of a regulatory or supplementary form appears to have been the result of a process of bargaining between central government, public sector firms and the lower tiers of government. The extent to which bargaining between government and public firms and government and private firms diverges is beyond the scope of this paper. Research comparing the participation of public firms in policy formation and implementation with that of the private sector is vital to a fuller understanding of the instrumental role of law in the pursuit of policy objectives.

Appendix 1

Table 1: Electricity – Public Ownership

Country	Organisation	Ownership	Share of Market
UK	CEGB	100% state owned	99% conventional production 100% nuclear production monopoly of distribution
France	EDF	100% state owned	87% of production
	CNR	mixed (state/private)	6% of production
NL	11 producing companies owned by municipal or provincial authorities 94 distribution companies owned by municipal or provincial authorities		
Italy	ENEL	100% state owned	78% conventional production 74% hydroelectric production 100% nuclear production
Germany	RWE	mixed (30% owned by Länder and municipalities)	
	VEW	mixed (state/private)	45% production
	Veba	mixed (state minority share)	30% distribution

Source: T. Daintith and Leigh Hancher, *Energy Strategy in Europe: The Legal Framework* (1986, Berlin) p. 52.

Table 2: Nuclear Energy – Public Ownership

Country	Organisation	Ownership	Share of Market
UK	CEGB	100% state owned	100% production
	BNFL	100% state owned	manufacture of reactors monopoly of research
France	Cogema	wholly owned subsidiary of CEA	monopoly of fuel cycle process
	CEA	100% state owned	research, and control of all nuclear activities
	Framatome	34% owned by CEA	sole French manufacturer of nuclear steam supply system
NL	–	–	–
Italy	Agip Nucleare	100% owned by ENI	monopoly on acquisition of fuels
	Finmeccanica	subsidiary of IRI	sole licensee for PWRs
Germany	RWE	*see* Table 3	largest single producer

Source: T. Daintith and Leigh Hancher, *Energy Strategy in Europe: The Legal Framework* (1986 Berlin) p. 59.

Table 3: Coal – Public Ownership

Country	Organisation	Ownership	Share of Market
UK	NCB	100% state owned	99% monopoly of production
France	CDF	100% state owned	monopoly of production
	ATIC	100% state owned	monopoly of imports
NL	–	–	–
Italy	Agip Carbone	wholly owned subsidiary of ENI	importation of coal
	ENI	100% state owned	monopoly of production
Germany	Ruhrkohle AG	mixed (state/private)	77% of production 16% of production
	Saarbergwerke	100% Federal/Länder owned	
	Rheinische Braunkohle	wholly owned subsidiary of RWE (*see* Table 3)	85% lignite production

Source: T. Daintith and Leigh Hancher, *Energy Strategy in Europe: The Legal Framework* (1986, Berlin) p. 61.

Table 4: Gas – Public Ownership

Country	Organisation	Ownership	Share of Market
UK	BGC*	100% state owned	monopoly of sales until 1982
France	GDF	100% state owned	78% of sales
	SNGSO	wholly owned subsidiary of GDF	22% of sales
	Elf-Aquitaine (SMEA)	70% state owned	96% of production
NL	NAM	mixed (state) minority share)	operates Groningen Concession, can take 40% or 50% participation in offshore production licences
	Gasunie	mixed (50% state share)	monopoly of sales
Italy	ENI	100% state owned	monopoly of onshore production
	SNAM	100% subsidiary of ENI	de facto monopoly of wholesale and industrial distribution
Germany	–	–	–

* BGC was transferred to private ownership in 1986.

Source: T. Daintith and Leigh Hancher, *Energy Strategy in Europe: The Legal Framework.* (1986, Berlin) p. 65.

Table 5: Oil Production – Public Ownership

Country	Organisation	Ownership	Share of Market
UK	Oil & Pipelines Agency	100% state owned	right to acquire (in emergency) 51% of production at market price
	Britoil	mixed (state minority share)	
France	Elf-Aquitaine (SNEA)	70% state owned	
NL	–	–	–
Italy	ENI	100% state owned	exclusive production rights
Germany	–	–	–

Source: T. Daintith and Leigh Hancher, *Energy Strategy in Europe: The Legal Framework* (1986, Berlin) p. 77.

Table 6: Oil Distribution – Public Ownership

Country	Organisation	Ownership	Share of Market
UK	–	–	–
France	Total	subsidiary of CFP	50% finished products
	Elf	subsidiary of Elf-Aquitaine	
NL	–	–	–
Italy	Agip	subsidiary of ENI	34% finished products
Germany	Aral	subsidiary of Veba (mixed with state minority interest)	25% petroleum products

Source: T. Daintith and Leigh Hancher, *Energy Strategy in Europe: The Legal Framework* (1986, Berlin) p. 77.

Appendix 2

Privatisation in Britain 1979–84

Company	Business	Date of sale	Means of sale	Remaining government holding[1]	Net proceeds[2] £m
British Petroleum	Oil	Oct 79	offer 5%	31.7%	276
		Jun 81	rights sale		8
		Sep 83	tender 7%		543
British Aerospace	Aerospace	Feb 81	offer 51.6%	49.4%	43
British Sugar Corporation	Sugar refiner	Jul 81	placing 24%	nil	44
Cable & Wireless	Telecom-munications	Oct 81	offer 49.4%		182
		Dec 83	tender 22%	23.1%	263
Amersham International	Radio-chemicals	Feb 82	offer 100%	nil	64
National Freight Co	Road haulage	Feb 82	management buyout	nil	5
Britoil	Oil	Nov 82	tender 51%	48.9%	627
Associated British Ports	Seaports	Feb 83	offer 51.5%		46
		Apr 84	tender 48.5%	nil	51
International Aeradio	Aviation communica-tions	Mar 83	private sale	nil	60
British Rail Hotels	Hotels	Mar 83	private sale	nil	51
British Gas Onshore Oil Assets (Wytch Farm)	Oil	May 84	private sale	nil	82
Enterprise Oil	Oil	Jun 84	tender 100%	nil	380
Sealink	Harbour and ferry	Jul 84	private sale	nil	66
Jaguar	Cars	Jul 84	offer 100%	nil	297
British Telecom	Telecom-munications	Nov 84	offer 50.2%	49.8%	3,916*
British Technol-ogy Group § and other sales	miscellaneous	–	private sales and placings	–	716

* Gross proceeds. [1] Excluding special share held in some companies. [2] Including part payments not yet received. § Includes sale of 25% of ICL (1979), 100% of Fairey and 50% of Ferranti (1980) and 75% of Inmos (1984).

Source: The Economist, February 23, 1985.

Public Enterprises and Economic Policy: A Comment

SABINO CASSESE

Rome

Contents

I. The Problem Over the Past Centuries, During the Age of Laissez-faire and the Age of Intervention

That public enterprises are instruments of economic policy is an affirmation that has been repeated ever since the existence of public enterprises and economic policy. In the modern era, one only need recall, for example, the 17th century French "manufactures royales" and, in the same century, the Dutch, French and English colonial trading companies. In the 19th century, the state monopolies in France on tobacco and matches and in Italy on salt and tobacco. Another example, in a subsequent period, is the participation of the English admiralty in the Anglo-Persian Oil Company (later to become British Petroleum). These industrial activities of the State had as their objective power or money; the former tied to colonial expansion and defence, and the latter to the need to guarantee income to the State coffers.

The subject then receded into the background because of the influence of the so-called economic laissez-faire policy, throughout Europe, in different periods around the end of the last century and the beginning of the 20th century. Laissez-faire policy, in affirming that the State should not interfere in economic matters, denied rights of citizenship both to economic policy as well as to public enterprise. Historical studies have shown however that this general trend had more influence on intellectual matters than on reality. Public enterprises continued to exist in fact, even though governments pretended to have no interest in them.

Instrumentalisation of public enterprises for the economic policy of governments became once more important with the development of economic interventionism which occurred in many countries at the end of the First World War and during the depression in the 'thirties'. During this period, the principle of symmetrical biconditional connection between economic policies and public enterprise came to the fore; on the one hand, public enterprise is the indispensable instrument of economic policy and, on the other, economic policy is indispensable as a guide for public enterprise.

Why does public enterprise become an indispensable instrument of economic policy? The explanation is to be found in the limitations of regulatory intervention. As a rule, the latter is characterised by conditional norms rather than programmatical or goal-oriented ones (using, with some adaptation, the distinction made by Niklas Luhmann[1] between "Konditionalprogramme" and "Zweckprogramme"). Regardless of how complete is the panoply of so-called indirect intervention instruments (antitrust norms, authorisations, concessions, plans, etc.), they are in conflict with private initiative. The question is how to impose "positive objectives" within this array. Even public financial incentives offered to private industry in the last analysis do not guarantee positive results. For example, these incentives are not able to create private entrepreneurship where it does not exist (clear proof of this is the case of Southern Italy). Regulatory intervention therefore has its limits: it can set down the "rules of the game", but it cannot guarantee the results and consequently the success of economic policy.

These negative reflections on regulatory policies are the starting point of my conceptualisation of public enterprise not only as an instrument, but as a privileged instrument, of government economic policy. Public enterprise, institutionally placed at the service of the State, not only has to follow the "rules of the game" but may also be orientated and directed by the government in order to reach its goals.

As regards the second relationship, the question is why an economic policy is indispensable to public enterprise. If public enterprise is indispensable to economic policy, the absence of the latter would result in a "loss of the objectives" of public enterprise, which would then be placed in the position of having to act without any guidelines. The constitutive laws or statutes of public enterprises alone are not sufficient. They codify a small number of general principles, which may function as general points of reference. Some type/measure of public guidance other than that established by the government is also necessary. In some European countries, there are other reasons in addition to the ones mentioned above. Both general economic policy and global economic planning in the true sense of the word are indispensable for guiding a public enterprise. Public enterprise cannot be guided unless the entire market is orientated at the same time.

As with laissez-faire policy, these rationales must be evaluated with caution.

---

[1] Luhmann's distinction is in Luhmann, N., "Lob der Routine" (1964) 55 *Verwaltungsarchiv*, 1–11.

They have had a large following in cultural and political debates, as well as in guidelines proclaimed by governments, but less success in policies that have actually been implemented.

II. Limits of the Instrumentalisation of Public Enterprise as Regards Economic Policy

The weak point in the concept of public enterprise as an instrument of economic policy is in that which may be called the myth of the transitive quality of "publicness". Governments appoint administrators of public enterprises and have the power to guide activity with directives or other acts. By means of appointment and directives, government guidelines should be absorbed by public enterprises which thus become an instrument of their realisation. However, this effect does not necessarily occur. The following three cases illustrate this point.

First of all, governments do not always have guidelines. For example, in cases of so-called rescue operations, following the depression in the 'thirties', many public enterprises were constituted, without an objective or a precise guideline, simply in order to protect depositors who had entrusted their savings to banks in crisis, which were then rescued. Another example is public enterprises constituted for reasons that were not strictly economic, as for example the case of Renault which was confiscated because its owner was found guilty of collaboration with the Nazis.

In the second place, regulatory intervention usually has a single objective. However, the same cannot be said of public enterprises which are instead multipurpose. Examples of this are public enterprises in the petroleum sector which were founded, for the most part, in order to ensure the supply from abroad of petroleum products or to promote domestic exploration for and production of liquid and gaseous hydrocarbons. Nevertheless, during the 'sixties', when the petrochemical sector went through a period of expansion, petroleum public enterprises developed, in many countries, according to criteria of vertical integration. Petroleum public enterprises thus became chemical companies as well. This occurred not because governments had indicated or imposed this type of development but simply because vertical integration was, in a manner of speaking, dictated by the market. (The major private oil companies had already followed this trend.)

In the third place, public enterprises do not always act as the instrument of economic policy simply because they avoid doing so. An example of this may be found in Italy in relation to investments in the South. In 1957 a law was passed, obliging Italian public enterprises to locate part of their investments in Southern Italy (initially 60 per cent of new investments: the percentage was later raised). At that point, public enterprises reacted in two ways. First of all, they claimed that some of their investments could not be located in the South and were to be exempted from the total. The government accepted this point of view which, in some cases, was reasonable. (How could Alitalia invest in aircraft in Southern Italy?) Then, public enterprises maintained that the obligation of locating investments in the South had to respect the "ceteris paribus" principle. Thus, they were placed in the position of availing themselves of the financial incentives provided by the State for the development of the South. In this case, the regulatory (and therefore general type of intervention) is added to the directive type (provided only for the public enterprises). One may wonder why the second type is provided if it was implemented (only in part, as mentioned above) only on the condition that the former type was also present. The argument of the public enterprises was the following: the government cannot, in order to implement an economic policy of development, force public enterprises to act under less favourable conditions than private companies, thus placing them at a distinct disadvantage. Therefore, public enterprises must have the same access as private companies to incentives for investment in the South. In this way however it is recognised that the directive power given by the law is inadequate to guide public enterprise.

In actual fact, therefore, public enterprise may fail to operate as an instrument of economic policy.

III. Public Enterprises in the Public Service and Manufacturing Sectors

In the two preceding sections, a review of the various approaches to instrumentalisation of public enterprise was attempted and doubts were expressed on the effective instrumentalisation of public enterprise as regards economic policy. Now the problem will be examined in more general terms.

A distinction must be made between public service and manufacturing public enterprises. The former type of public enterprise possesses some common characteristics. Public service public enterprises (electricity in Britain, France and Italy; gas in Britain and France; railways and telephones in most countries, etc.) were usually created following the nationalisation of private utility companies with expropriation of private citizens. As a rule, they operate in one sector only. Usually, their field of operation is established by law, which prevents them from carrying out *ultra vires* activities. In addition, public service public enterprises are monopolies and therefore operate in non-competitive markets. Finally, because of the great number of users, public service public enterprises are organised into networks. When these elements are present, there is usually a close relationship between the instrumentalisation of the public enterprise and the economic policy of the government. Policy is generally defined with precision in the constitutive statute of the enterprise and is directed toward the benefit of the user or consumer in the supply of a service or of terms (price, for example). The objective for which a public enterprise has been founded – and thus the objective of the law – becomes the objective of the enterprise and its management.

Naturally, in the light of technical developments, much may change within a few years. An example of this is developments in telecommunications, where there is a possibility that competition will develop and private companies are emerging.

The situation of public manufacturing enterprises is different. Usually, they do not originate in an act of nationalisation. They are not necessarily single-sector enterprises. They operate in competition and go where the market leads them.

Examples are public enterprises in the automobile industry in France and Italy, Italian and Spanish public banking enterprises, and the publicly-owned steel industry (prior to the crisis) and so on. In the case of public enterprises like these, and in contrast with the monopolistic public enterprise, the objective of the law that constituted the public enterprise and the objective of the public enterprise itself may not coincide. New objectives are added to those of the law, which the public enterprise selects and follows autonomously, precisely because it is an enterprise and hence (according to the point of view of Schumpeter) innovative.

IV. The Instability of the Government-Public Enterprises Relationship in the Competitive Sector

For the reasons cited above, manufacturing public enterprises constitute the basis of a very interesting case history study. Such a study cannot be developed within the confines of this paper; only an interpretative hypothesis may be indicated. The hypothesis is the following: that between the government and public enterprises operating on competitive markets, a vicious circle of actions and reactions comes into being, producing considerable instability in the relationship between these actors. Such actions and reactions are examined below.

We said above that manufacturing public enterprises are created (or taken over) by the government with public objectives, to which are added the objectives produced by the very actions of the enterprise as such. The equilibrium between these two types of objective is often transformed into conflict. Governments attempt to solve this problem in two ways: with directives to public enterprises or with *ad hoc* laws whose content consists of government directives. Often these solutions are worse than the problems because the constraints imposed give rise to confusion regarding responsibility, limit the authority of the public enterprises' management, and produce inefficiency. In any case, public enterprises react by attempting to avoid the adoption of these solutions. This requires governments to intervene with new instruments. These, which may be defined as last-ditch instruments, are of three types: financial, such as an increase in capital; restructuring of the public enterprise, by means of new laws; and use of general regulatory instruments, conforming to the market (such as the "programme contracts" introduced following the Nora Report in France during the years from 1970 to 1977; the control "by cooperation and agreement" proposed by the National Economic Development Council in Great Britain in 1976 and introduced in a 1978 White Paper; the phase, 1957–72, of agreements contracted between the Italian Ministry of State Participation and the Managing Agencies of State Participation).

What need would there be for "programme contracts" if public enterprises were truly always instruments of government economic policy? Why do public enterprises change from being an instrument of government economic policy and become its object? The game of cat and mouse illustrated above sheds light on the contradictions of public enterprise and its relationship with government policy. Public enterprise is an instrument of economic policy, but not to the point of being completely servile to it, and not to the point of losing its nature as an enterprise (namely, its economic self-sufficiency, which permits it to operate on the market).

Not all types of economic policy, therefore, may utilise public enterprise as an instrument. The latter may function as an instrument in anti-monopolistic policy (as illustrated in the pricing policy for ENI petroleum and chemical products in Italy, in the 'fifties'). Public enterprise may pursue a development policy, but only on the terms and within the limits described in our brief review of Italian public enterprises and their investments in the South. It is less likely that public enterprises will implement policies for maintaining employment levels. In order to do so, additional financing from the Treasury, which is usually granted for specific purposes (for example, the Italian experience with the so-called improper burdens)[2] would be required. This financing increases the public enterprise's dependency upon the Treasury and opens the door to further government requests for interventions which are not always economically self-supporting. In this way, another vicious circle is formed, transforming public enterprises from instruments of the government into its auxiliaries.

As mentioned above, this series of actions and reactions produces considerable instability in government policies on the management of public enterprises. For example, in France, from 1930 to 1955 government controls over public enterprises were increased. Later they diminished, and in 1967 the Nora Report proposed granting even greater autonomy to public enterprises. The proposals in the Report, adopted by the Government in 1970, were abandoned shortly thereafter. In Great Britain, the 1967 White Paper adopted the autonomy line: public enterprises were to behave as businesses financed in the marketplace. The 1978 White Paper on the other hand, took the opposite view, whereby public enterprises were considered different from private companies. Then came the Conservative government, which favoured greater autonomy and privatisation.

The subjects covered in this paper require deeper study, not over brief periods of time, but with investigation – possibly through case studies – over periods long enough to allow one to examine the alternation and interweaving of different instruments of economic policy.[3] One is left with the concluding impression that, on the whole, the analysis of public enterprise has hitherto emphasised the adjective at the expense of the noun, thus distorting the analysis of facts.

---

[2] That is, investments which public enterprises are called upon by governments to make but which they do not consider economic. For such investments, Italian public enterprises, especially the State railways and IRI, have requested government to meet the costs on a case-by-case basis.

[3] There is a wide range of literature on public enterprises. The most recent comparative research studies, neither of which has yet been published, are those directed by Henry Parris (Action Society Trust) and by Gerard Timsit (Institut européen d'administration publique).

Part Five

Comparative Legal Systems

The Influence of Legal Systems on Modes of Implementation of Economic Policy

ATTILA HARMATHY

Budapest

Contents

The paper outlines a special aspect of the comparative analysis which is the main subject of the present volume. By way of preliminary, it may be helpful to recall one or two essential points. The basis of the work was a common interest in problems of the use of law as a policy instrument. The aim of the research was not, however, to try to cover the whole field connected with the problems but to make an investigation of two specific areas, analysing in detail the implementation of economic policy. Energy policy and manpower policy were selected for investigation over the period 1973–1982. The laws of the following countries were

examined: France, Federal Republic of Germany, Hungary, Italy, the Netherlands, and the United Kingdom.[1]

This paper sets out to perform the following tasks: first, some general remarks
will be made on the analysis of legal implementation of economic policy;
secondly, the importance of national legal systems will be dealt with as one of the
factors influencing the implementation process; thirdly, the effect of legal systems
on the manner of implementing economic policy in different countries will be
compared.

I. The Analysis of Policy Implementation

The subject matter of the legal implementation of economic policy is closely
connected with a series of theoretical problems. To refer to only two of them, we
can neglect neither questions of economic analysis of regulation on the one hand,
nor the discussion of delegalisation on the other. When examining legal implementation of economic policy we cannot enlarge the field of analysis so as to try
to answer questions pertaining to both the regulation debate and to delegalisation
theory. Nevertheless, the decision on what to examine in the implementation
process, and how, involves taking a position indirectly on questions of regulation
and delegalisation as well.

A. Regulation Theory

The theory of *regulation* has undoubtedly the merit of directing attention to the
costs and benefits of the regulatory process and also to the question of whose
interest regulation serves. It seems, however, to an outsider that there is no
generally accepted conception of regulation in the economic literature. An all-
embracing definition of regulation has been formulated by Stigler who states that
regulation is an attempt by the state to use its legal powers to direct the conduct of
non-governmental bodies.[2] It is evident that this cannot be accepted by lawyers as
the basis for legal research and it is probably also too broad for some economists.

In the theory of regulation there is another somewhat awkward point, as was
shown by Peltzman when he gave an outline of the development of the research
done in this field. As he puts it, the economics of regulation had been focusing on
American institutions. He suggested, therefore, that international comparisons of
regulatory institutions be made and gave as a possible topic market failure in
electricity supply.[3]

The research work under review here has not got the economics of regulation as
its basis, nor does it accept Stigler's nor any other author's definition of regulation.

---

[1] For further details see T. C. Daintith "Law as Policy Instrument: A Comparative Perspective", above at pp. 20–23.
[2] G. J. Stigler, "Comment" in G. Fromm ed., *Studies in Public Regulation* (1981, Cambridge, Mass.) at p. 73.
[3] S. Peltzmann, "Current developments in the economics of regulation" in G. Fromm ed.,
supra note 21 at p. 380.

The different instruments by means of which economic policy is implemented have been considered as legal phenomena and regulation as one of the instruments. Attempts have been made to state the result of the use of instruments but without trying to calculate the costs and benefits. The idea is somewhat similar to that of Peltzman's, namely to examine situations arising when the government intervenes because of market failures and to make comparisons. During the years from 1973 to 1982 there were serious economic difficulties both in the energy and in the employment field and governments had to be very active in trying to eliminate or reduce tension. The question has been put whether the different states were acting in a similar way. In case of either affirmative or negative answers a series of supplementary questions have been posed.[4]

It is rather clear that the above questions are not questions of efficiency and that they do not belong to the field of empirical economic theory where the institutions of social system and political power can be irrelevant.[5] For us the role of these institutions is of vital importance. Nor do we want to leave out of consideration the proposition drawn from the sociological approach to economics that in society there are values which are acted upon independent of cost.[6]

At this point some similarities may be observed between our work and the comparative research organised by Kirschen, some of whose ideas, methods and results have been applied by us. It has been stressed by Kirschen's group that the selection of instruments of state intervention in the economy does not take place simply according to a judgement of their effectiveness but under the influence of institutional and political constraints.[7] The role of these factors and their classification is not the same as in our work, which is probably due in part to the different subject matter (Kirschen's research being an economic analysis of policies while ours is an analysis of legal implementation of policies), and in part to a different approach. Thus, in this paper implementation policy of different states is examined comparing one with another and considering the effect of the institutions of social and political power.

To make a comparison one needs, however, a common denominator on the basis of which the identities and the differences of government reactions can be pointed out. For this research the aims to be achieved by the state in the energy and manpower policy fields have been accepted as the common denominator. The oil shock and in general the energy crisis has made an impact on the economy of each country involved in the research. While the impact was different in degree there were no significant variations as far as the objectives were concerned. Although the importance of one or another objective is not the same in the different countries the same short-term responses to disturbances (restriction of consumption, preservation of supply, stabilisation of prices), the same attempts to alter the

---

[4] See Daintith, above at pp. 20–21.
[5] T. Parsons, *The Social System*, (1966, London–New York) at p. 125.
[6] T. Parsons and N. J. Smelser, *Economy and Society* (1965, New York) at p. 26.
[7] E. S. Kirschen, ed., *Economic Policies Compared* (1974, Amsterdam–Oxford–New York) at pp. 31–32. Among the institutional and political considerations the following factors are mentioned: constraint from abroad, institutional constraint (e.g. the use of public finance and monetary instruments) and ideological constraints.

structure of energy demand and of energy supply, can be found in each of them. In relation to the other countries Hungary was in an exceptional position as a member-state of the Council of Mutual Economic Assistance and getting oil, gas, and electricity within the framework of this market system. Nonetheless the effects of the energy crisis were felt in Hungary, too, albeit in a modified way.

While the energy policy field offers the possibility of comparison there are some fundamental problems in the manpower policy field. In the majority of countries examined there were serious difficulties because of the high level of unemployment. On the contrary, in Hungary it was labour shortages that caused problems. Consequently, it should not be expected that the objectives of job creation, job maintenance and manpower adjustment, important as they were in all those countries suffering from unemployment, would be given priority in Hungary also. It does not mean, however, that the common denominator is completely excluded. In Hungary there are also some regions where some of the objectives have been of some importance (e.g., job creation for peasant women in the country, mainly in the winter months, or manpower adjustment in the steel industry). Thus, the common background element is partly present and a cautious and restricted comparison can take place in the manpower policy field as well.

B. Difficulties of the Ends-Means Approach

It might seem to be obvious that the comparison on the basis mentioned above should proceed by putting an objective, and the instruments and measures implementing it in different countries, side by side thus focusing interest on how the given objective is implemented. This method may be plausible, though the results which it can achieve are of doubtful value. Weber pointed out that undesired side effects are brought about by the legal regulation of the economy where the market plays a major role in economic activity. The side effects may annihilate the aim of the regulation. Therefore, even in a single country, it cannot be stated what the real power of law is when regulating the economy.[8]

I would stress not merely the unpredictability of the results of policy implementation. It is necessary to bear in mind the fact that governments do not have only one policy objective to be implemented. The instruments and means implementing the objectives are not rigidly segregated, each for a separate objective. They are mixed and both the desired effects and the undesired side effects of a single rule are connected with more than one objective. The situation is further complicated if we examine an implementation process as it proceeds over a period of time. After the beginning of the period the position of the government may change and it will then react to new elements, modifying the objectives, or the instruments and measures of implementation, or both. In such circumstances the causal relations in the implementation process will, as Mayntz has explained, be hard to identify.[9]

---

[8] M. Weber, *Wirtschaft und Gesellschaft*, 5. Aufl. besorgt J. von Winckelmann (1972, Tubingen) at p. 197.

[9] R. Mayntz, *Die Interpretation politischer Programme, Theoretische Überlegungen zu einem neuen Forschungsgebiet*, Die Verwaltung (1977, Köln) Bd. 18 at p. 17.

As an example of changes taking place after the acceptance of an objective and measures we can refer to certain events which occurred in the Netherlands. The Netherlands was highly dependent upon Saudi Arabian oil imports during the oil crisis. Parliament voted the government wide discretionary powers. The government made use of the powers and took a series of steps. All motor traffic on Sundays was forbidden, this measure later being replaced by petrol rationing. After a few days rationing was abolished because there appeared to be no real shortage of oil. Parliament investigated the role of oil companies as there were suspicions that they had attempted to use the atmosphere of international oil crisis to obtain high profits.[10] On this occasion the events got wide publicity but in many cases one cannot detect the immediate cause of an instrument, and the objective can only be guessed at. In such cases it is hard to find a firm base for an analysis which seeks to show how the instruments and measures are determined by an objective.

In our study the situation is more complicated in that during the years from 1973 to 1982 elections took place and opposition parties got into power in some countries, and thus changed the instruments, and measures, and reformed the implementation process.

Because of these problems in examining the causal connection between objectives on the one hand and instruments and measures on the other, the paper does not concentrate on these relations but on the general "style of action" of the relevant governments. Objectives will not be forgotten but no effort will be made to point out the correlation between objectives and instruments or measures.

It has been noted that in our research two specific areas have been chosen for analysis. It seems to be a hazardous attempt to compare the "style of action" of different governments in these areas irrespective of general tendencies. The real importance of a phenomenon cannot be evaluated on a strictly limited basis. Therefore, we will try to make the comparison of the symptoms of government action observed in the material gathered by the working group by putting these observations into a larger framework which draws on general literature not restricted in energy and manpower problems. This means a great enlargement of the work to be undertaken and as it is rather difficult to set its limits, we shall only concentrate on a small number of questions.

C. The Legalisation Debate

The examination of the way the state is acting directs our attention to the problems of *legalisation* and *delegalisation*. It is well known that the number of legal rules is growing steadily. Regulation of human behaviour is becoming more and more a state monopoly as social bodies that had created and enforced rules lose importance and, sometimes, disappear. At the same time there seem to be more demands for state intervention in the economy. It has been clearly stated, however, by Weber that although the legal enforceability of private actions in the economy has

---

[10] D. Coombes and S. A. Walkland eds., *Parliaments and Economic Affairs* (1980, London) at p. 219.

grown in principle, the actual power of law over the economy has not increased.[11] It is characteristic of state intervention that the law is mostly "mobilised" by state agencies and not by citizens.[12]

The effectiveness of legal intervention is at least doubtful in cases where public opinion is indifferent to infringements of law. That is one of the reasons why the power of the law has not grown. Governments, being aware of these facts, try to get people involved in implementing an objective instead of imposing rules on people who are indifferent or hostile to the government's aim. The state may work out incentives like tax allowances or transfers of funds for people who co-operate in policy implementation or it may try to reach agreement with enterprises, confederations of employers, and trade unions whose behaviour is important to successful implementation. The latter method is considered as leading to delegalisation. Thus, the statement that the debate on legalisation and delegalisation is also concerned with the possibilities and limits of the law as a policy instrument[13] would appear to be correct.

What has been said above suggests that in our comparative study we should take into consideration the activity of state agencies during the implementation process on the one hand and the behaviour of the addressees, and the social context, on the other.[14] At the same time one should not forget the different instruments of state intervention. There may be several categorisations of instruments but for the purposes of the present paper two groups may be distinguished: the instrument of unilateral regulation, and the instruments by means of which the state tries to get people involved in implementation (incentives, agreements).

II. The Legal System as One of the Factors Influencing Policy Implementation

The legal system is but one of the factors influencing the actions of the state and it is not the most important one. Without attempting a complete list of the factors which decide what kind of actions will be taken by the state, I shall refer only to those few whose role is somehow reflected in dealing with the influence of the legal system.

A. East-West Comparisons

The comparison of legal institutions requires the careful examination of their function and how they are embedded in the social, economic and political

---

[11] M. Weber, *supra* note 8, pp. 196–98, 516.

[12] J. Black "The Mobilization of Law" (1973) 11 *Journal of Legal Studies* 138.

[13] R. Voigt "Gegentendenzen zur Verrechtlichung, Verrechtlichung und Entrechtlichung im Kontext der Diskussion um den Wohlfahrtstaat", in R. Voigt, ed., *Gegentendenzen zur Verrechtlichung, Jahrbuch für Rechtssoziologie und Rechtstheorie*, (1983, Stuttgart) Bd. 9 Opladen at p. 20; G. Himmelmann "Öffentliche Bindung durch neokorporatistische Verhandlungssysteme?" in T. Thiemeyer, C. Bohret, G. Himmelmann, eds., *Öffentliche Bindung von Unternehmen* (1983, Baden-Baden) at pp. 58–59, 64–67.

[14] R. Mayntz, *supra* note 9, at pp. 62–65.

system.[15] The first question to be dealt with here is how the laws of the EEC countries and those of Hungary can be compared. One may note that the differences between economic policies in socialist and capitalist countries have been taken into consideration by Kirschen's group also. However, the differences have been referred to as arising out of the institutional framework, out of economic mechanisms and instruments,[16] and not as having their origin in the social, economic and political system. As their subject matter is different from that of our investigation and given the absence of identical definitions of some basic categories (such as the instruments) it is little wonder that the decisive factors are not the same. However at one point there is a coincidence of factors. A fundamental part of the social and economic system is the *ownership* of the means of production and this same factor has been dealt with by Kirschen as an example of the institutional framework.

The effect of the difference of the system of ownership in Hungary and in the EEC countries examined can be observed if we compare their legal systems as a whole. The difference has a decisive role for the whole field to be regulated or influenced: in Hungary state ownership is dominant and it is operated by state enterprises, in the other countries examined, private ownership and private entrepreneurship prevail even if state enterprises have a considerable role.

The difference in the economic structure has particular consequences in the choice of instruments of implementation. In our research we used the following instrument categories: unilateral regulation of private activity, taxation of private activity, consensual constraint, removal or relaxation of unilateral regulations, other public benefits, public sector management, information.[17] In the EEC countries in the majority of cases the steps to be taken by the state concerned private activity. In some cases it happened that the only addressee of a given measure was the public sector but even in these cases the state usually wanted to influence private activity, too, by means of the public sector. On the other hand, in Hungary, the main aim of the government was to influence the activity of the public sector itself as the private sector does not have any great importance in the national economy.[18] Some of the measures also concerned citizens as consumers of energy or employees but the large consumers and employers are to be found in the public sector and to a lesser extent among cooperatives. The public sector was almost always one of the addressees.

There are, therefore, some difficulties in using the above categorisation of instruments for comparative purposes. Here, the first question is whether the government is going to act as owner or as public authority. In Hungary the government, despite its ownership position, has normally used the legal forms of

---

[15] I. Szabo, "Theoretical Questions of Comparative Law", in I. Szabo and Z. Peteri, eds., *A Socialist Approach to Comparative Law* (1977, Budapest) at pp. 12–13, 38–39.

[16] E. S. Kirschen, *supra* note 7, at p. 291.

[17] See Daintith, above, at p. 51.

[18] The share of the different sectors in the production of the national income is as follows: state-owned enterprises 67.4 per cent, cooperatives 23.1 per cent, private sector 5.1 per cent: *Statistical Yearbook 1983*, (1984, Budapest) at p. 13.

public law,[19] in part because, following nationalisation, state enterprises were considered as public bodies rather than as commercial undertakings. Enterprise activity was seen as a special form of state administration: in many sections of the economy, for example, there was no balance between offer and demand and enterprises played a role in rationing.

In his paper Jarass points out that the instrument of regulation has been more often used in Hungary than in the other countries examined.[20] If this is so, there may be several reasons, one of which is the economic structure just discussed. In several areas the activity of the public sector is regulated in Hungary while there is no similar instrument at all in the other countries or, if there are similar ones, the number of measures is much smaller and control is usually left to market forces. This can be observed, for example, in the field of price regulation or in the limitation of energy consumption in the public sector. In Hungary prices charged by public enterprises for coal, gas, electricity, etc. have been regulated by the government. In other countries the price level was not regulated to the same extent and sometimes the instrument chosen was of a different category, e.g. in the United Kingdom compensation was paid to public bodies for the losses suffered in consequence of their compliance with the national policy relating to limitation of prices (in the form of the instrument of public sector management).[21] Another example may be taken from the Netherlands where the Minister of Economic Affairs issued a circular on electricity price policy and the different electricity companies determined their prices accordingly.[22]

The social and economic systems of the different EEC countries, though similar one to another, are still not quite identical. Nevertheless, it seems to me that they do not need any further comment. Some remarks should be made however about the political factor.

B. Political Factors

The legal system as a whole is under the influence of the *political system*. There are technical elements of the legal system which are neutral in character and which are not affected by the political system. The general rule is still that the political system has a determining effect on the law. The same is true in respect of the style of government actions. Even at a lower level than that of the political system as a whole, we find direct effects exerted by individual political factors upon the choice of instruments and measures. Two examples from the energy policy field may be mentioned here.

[19] It would have been interesting from the Hungarian point of view to make a sub-categorisation within the instrument type of "public sector management" according to the nature of the other instruments (regulation, taxation, etc.) used in relation to the private sector. This sub-categorisation was discussed in the working group but for reasons of simplicity was not adopted.

[20] H. Jarass, "Regulation as an Instrument of Economic Policy", above at p. 93.

[21] See the Statutory Corporations (Financial Provisions) Act 1975 and orders made thereunder.

[22] See K. Mortelmans, Netherlands Energy Inventory, Doc. 7/83 on file at EUI, item 12 NE.81.002.

The first concerns international politics. I refer here to the difference between the EEC countries and Hungary. The states which were members of the EEC (and IEA) made decisions on stockpiling oil and on some other energy emergency rules. Consequently, they were bound to enact national rules in accordance with the international decisions using the instrument of regulation and without much difference in the measures of implementation. In Hungary, a CMEA member country, this question was not raised. Some influence of the national legal systems, however, can be found as far as measures applied by the EEC member states are concerned. In France regulation took place by a decree of the President while in other countries, like the United Kingdom, an Act of Parliament contained authorisation to give directions on stockpiling.

The other example of the effect of political elements is the change in national political life arising from changes in power positions. It has been pointed out that instruments implementing economic policies are not purely technical things, they are not neutral but value-laden, and political parties show preferences for particular types of instruments.[23] The use of the public sector as an instrument implementing the government's objectives shows the truth of this statement. The British Labour Party usually tries to enlarge the activity of the public sector in order to help it realise some of its aims. The politics of the Conservative Party, on the contrary, favour private initiative, free competition and the handing over of some parts of the public sector to private firms. Thus state enterprises were given the task of pursuing government policy in the operation of the North Sea oil and gas fields in the years of the Labour government, while the State's oil exploration and production activities were transferred to a mainly private corporation and the monopoly of gas was dismantled as a result of the Conservative government's policy.[24] Another example of choosing one's instrument according to political conviction is the use of tax allowances by Conservatives and cash grants by Labour governments.[25]

During the period examined political changes took place in France also. The victory of the Socialist Party changed the attitude of the government and the increasing reliance on market forces under the former government was replaced by nationalisation, the greater use of public enterprises by the government, and the increased role of planning.[26] There was change in Hungary too. This did not mean change of government but a new line in economic policy. In the first years of the 1970s a recentralisation tendency prevailed, restricting enterprise autonomy, strengthening regulation and making frequent use of informal directives for guiding the national economy. At the end of the 1970s and in the early years of the

---

[23] F. T. Blackaby, ed., *British Economic Policy 1968–1974* (1978, Cambridge) at p. 7.

[24] Petroleum and Submarine Pipelines Act 1975, Energy Act 1976, Oil and Gas (Enterprise) Act 1982; D. Evans, *Western Energy Policy* (1978, London–Basingstoke) at pp. 89–92; T. C. Weyman-Jones, "The Nationalized Industries", in P. Maunder, ed., *The British Economy in the 1970s* (1980, London) at pp. 199 and 211.

[25] T. C. Daintith, "The Functions of Law in the Field of Short-term Economic Policy", (1976) 92 *Law Quarterly Review* 63.

[26] F. F. Ridley, ed., *Policies and Politics in Western Europe* (1984, London–Sydney) at p. 57.

1980s a series of new political decisions were taken returning to and pursuing the economic reform of 1968, thereby increasing enterprise autonomy and stressing the importance of incentives.

C. The Characteristics of the Policy Field

Another factor, albeit of minor importance, which has an influence on the choice of the instruments and means, is the policy field, in other words the object towards which the action is directed. The social and economic implications of the different objects pose their own requirements as to what kind of action can be taken. Social and economic relations in the energy sector have different features and consequently require different kinds of actions from those in the manpower field.

In the manpower field problems often arise in the contractual relationships between employer and employee, and both sides have their own organisation for representing their interest. It is characteristic of this sector that a special device, that of the collective bargaining agreement, is used, and a special body frequently intervenes to help solve the problems which arise between the two sides. Manpower policy objectives themselves or the decisions giving effect to them often relate to the workers' fundamental rights. Legal rules on manpower policy are therefore generally debated by Parliament and formulated in Acts. Moreover, while the objectives can be grouped into short-term, medium-term and long-term categories they are generally not connected with emergency situations (other perhaps than strikes). In contrast, in the energy sector emergency situations have occurred and have required special measures. When choosing the instrument and means of implementation governments had to bear in mind that there was usually concentration in supply but a very large number of consumers with heterogenous demands (industrial and non-industrial use). In this sphere it often happened that Parliament authorised the Executive to take the necessary steps and undertake a whole range of actions in order to put the policy into practice. To put it briefly and at the risk of simplifying the issue, one could say that in the energy field intervention was to a great extent technical in nature though having some political implications, while on the other hand, manpower problems concerned unemployment and the livelihood of large numbers of people so that the implementation of policy was at the centre of political struggle.

III. The Effects of the National Legal System

A. Functions of the Legal System

When comparing the legal system as a factor with others having an influence on the choice of instruments and measures of policy implementation we can see that the effect of the legal system is of *secondary importance*. It does not affect the direction of government's action but rather the way its steps are taken.

Thus, one might say that the national style of action depends on the legal system but even this statement is not strictly accurate. The influence of the legal system has a double character. On the one hand, the legal system reflects the social, economic and political system of the country. It transmits requirements whose origins can be found in the determinants of the law and not in the law itself. On the other hand, the legal system has its own special features and requirements. It is scarcely possible to find a demarcation line between the effects of the one and of the other kind. This is all the more so in that this second kind of influence is not isolated from the other factors, but intermingles with them, for example with political elements. Nevertheless, if we try to point to differences between the two kinds of effects it may be said that on the side of the legal system as a reflection or transmission mechanism structural questions arise: instruments and measures are to be worked out in such a way that they fit within the given structure of the given legal system, and are in harmony with the constitution and main institutions of the law. On the other side the "internal" demands of the legal system affect rather the style of action of government, encouraging the use of instruments and measures which reflect established habits of legal implementation.

B. Institutional and Instrumental Elements

The statement that the national legal system has no great importance in the implementation process requires to be set in the context of the aim and subject matter of this research, which has concentrated on the legal implementation of economic policy in two specific areas and has sought to gain knowledge of some of the problems of the use of law as an instrument of economic policy.[27] We have already noted how the political or technical emphasis of policy in the areas examined may affect the way implementation proceeds. Another relevant point, stemming from academic discussion of legalisation, is that the law is not homogeneous. Some parts of the law function as legal institutions. These could be characterised as norms of conduct, rules of the game between citizens, or between companies, rules deciding the general framework and the procedures regulating the activity of public bodies. In contrast, other parts of the law can be considered as having an instrumental function as the means of enforcing, executing, implementing some objectives.[28]

This research has not dealt with the differences between these two parts of the law nor with questions particular to the institutional part. The analysis has been carried out in the field of instruments. Instruments, seen as techniques or tools, seem to be more neutral as far as legal traditions and culture are concerned than do institutions, where historical, social and economic conditions play an important role in the formation of their content. In the course of this research the content of the measures has been examined but only as a part of the implementation process. Had the research work focused on law as an institution, on such concepts as ownership, contracts, or executive powers, and not on the law as an instrument of implementation, its results would have been different, and the effect of the national legal system would have appeared more important.

---

[27] See Daintith, above at pp. 3–5.
[28] R. Voigt, *supra*, note 13, at p. 37 with a summary of the discussion.

C. System Influence on Instruments and Measures

Among the hypotheses adopted by the research group to guide its work are some concerning the effect of the national legal system on implementation. It has been hypothesised that rules having constitutional status would be of great importance, as also would rules attaching procedural and other incidents to particular legal forms and techniques. It has been thought, too, that legal culture might dictate or encourage certain implementation devices and that the existence of relevant bodies of substantive law would have some influence on the choice of means of implementation.[29] These hypotheses will not be dealt with in sequence but will be taken into consideration when we follow the elements of the measures of implementation.

The effects of the national legal system can be best found at the level of measures. The kind of influence the legal system has on the choice of instruments is by no means certain. Choosing regulation or granting benefits or imposing taxation depends to some extent on a political style of governing and not on the legal system. There is uncertainty about the role of different factors. The incidence of taxation instruments, for example, is relatively low in the areas we examined. At the same time taxes have an important general role in the economic policy of governments. Taxation seems to be a political problem only in the United Kingdom because of the Conservative Party's commitment to lower taxes. The use of taxes as an instrument is related to the existing burden of taxes, to the people's sensitivity to taxes, to the structure of taxes (for example, the proportion of direct and indirect taxes).[30] One might say that these factors show effects of the legal system. On the other hand, it is doubtful if the proportion of direct and indirect taxes can be qualified as belonging to rules constituting the core of a legal system. Here again the question of the different parts of the law and of the distinction between its institutional and instrumental rules is raised. Because of these doubts we shall not deal with instruments but rather with measures.

D. Constitutional Factors

Measures have been classified according to their scope, validity and source, the nature of the relation they create, their content, and procedural conditions. Some of these classes are interesting as indicators of the legal system.

The constitutional system of a country has a role in deciding at what *level* in terms of source measures are issued. Two main groups of countries can be distinguished. In the first group the proportion of Acts of Parliament is high, in the second group, government decrees are preponderant. Characteristic of the first group are the Federal Republic of Germany and the United Kingdom, of the second, France and Hungary.

In the United Kingdom it is Parliament that has the power to legislate. The government or a minister needs an authorisation through an Act, a delegation of legislative power by Parliament. While delegation of legislative power takes place

---

[29] See Daintith, above at pp. 35–36.
[30] F. F. Ridley, *supra*, note 26, at pp. 189–96.

quite often, parliamentary legislation is nevertheless the norm. Subordinate legislation is to be considered as an extension of the Act under which it is made. In some cases the Crown retains an inherent power to legislate but it is limited both in content and in time.[31]

There is a similar constitutional solution in Germany. Government gets powers to legislate under authorisation given by specific Acts. It has been pointed out by the literature on the German constitution that in the 1960s and 1970s the actual weight of government legislation grew in importance.[32] Still it is stressed that the government decrees do not preponderate among legislative measures.[33]

The French system is quite different from the British and German ones. The rules concerning legislation can be found in the constitution of 1958, which profoundly modified the previous system. As Burdeau put it, the rules of the constitution of 1958 have put aside the hierarchy of legal rules within which the Act of Parliament was at the highest level; its article 34 has enumerated the questions to be regulated by Acts while article 37 has opened all other areas to regulation by decree.[34] Although the Conseil Constitutionnel has enlarged the domain of Acts by its interpretation of the constitutional rules, it has not changed the autonomous character of decrees which are independent of any authorisation given by a specific Act.[35]

The Hungarian constitution does not contain a list of subject matters comprising an exclusive field of parliamentary legislation but in article 35, paragraph 2, it authorises the Council of Ministers to issue decrees and to pass resolutions within the sphere of its functions. There is a hierarchy of legislation in the sense that decrees and resolutions of the Council of Ministers may not be contrary to rules of law and law-decrees. Similarly, the President of the Council of Ministers, its vice-presidents and members may issue decrees in the execution of their duties. These, again, may not be in conflict with the law, law-decrees, or the decrees and resolutions of the Council of Ministers (Article 37, para 3).

It is possible, in both in France and in Hungary, besides the general rules on regulation by the administration, for an individual Act to delegate legislative powers for specified purposes.

E. Economic Planning

The study data show that the proportion of Acts and decrees depends on other factors also. It is characteristic of the legislation of some countries that there are

---

[31] E. C. S. Wade and G. Godfrey Phillips, *Constitutional and Administrative Law* (9th ed., 1977, London) at pp. 49–50 and 235; F. A. R. Bennion, *Statute Law* (1980, London) at pp. 53–56.

[32] E. Benda, W. Maihofer, H. J. Vogel, eds., *Handbuch des Verfassungsrechts* (1983, Berlin–New York) at p. 1123.

[33] *Kommentar zum Grundgesetz für die Bundesrepublik Deutschland, Reihe Alternativkommentare,* (1984, Neuwied–Darmstadt) at p. 784.

[34] G. Burdeau, *Droit constitutionnel et institutions politiques* (16th ed., 1974, Paris) at pp. 521–22.

[35] C. Debbasch, J. M. Pontier, *Les constitutions de la France* (1983, Paris) at p. 272.

Acts formulating general economic policy objectives and defining the measures to
be taken, while in other countries there are no such Acts and consequently, on
each occasion where a measure is to be taken, Parliament deals with the problem.
In the first case the Parliament has a single discussion on economic policy as a
whole. In the second case there is parliamentary scrutiny of specific issues on
several occasions. The difference between the two is related to the legal system.

General questions of economic policy are discussed and enacted in Hungary
and in France in· the form of national economic *plans*. Although the role of
planning was changing during the period examined, as quick changes in international and internal markets made it very difficult or impossible to forecast
economic development over periods of any length, planning nevertheless remained important in some countries and in others, even if relegated to the
background, may have continued to exist under other forms. It is therefore
worthwhile comparing the position taken by the different countries on the
question of planning.

In Hungary, as in other socialist countries, it is a constitutional principle that
the economic life of the country be determined by the state's national economic
plan.[36] Planning in socialist countries is characterised by comprehensive plans,
which are promulgated as Acts of Parliament and are obligatory (though there are
differences among socialist countries as to the circle of addressees). The plan
contains the main aims of both energy policy and manpower policy, while the
details can be found in numerous decrees. The objectives and the guidelines are
binding upon the government. Energy problems were considered so important
that the Hungarian government worked out a special programme for the energy
economy for the period of the five year plan at the time of its adoption.[37]

In France the character of the national plan is different: the plan is termed
"indicative". The content of the plan changed from time to time and it did not
always get to Parliament.[38] The legal significance of the plan has been a topic of
discussion. At first it was considered as a simple programme of the government
but later, when the plan was adopted by Parliament, discussion centered around
the problem of whether the parliament could do anything else but accept the draft
as a whole without any modification.[39] Since the reform of the planning system in
1982 two Acts have been adopted on the national plan, one on the objectives and a
second on the instruments. As the Socialist Government has reaffirmed the role of
planning it cannot be denied that the law on the national plan is binding upon the
executive.[40] Programmes in the energy and manpower fields are parts of the plan

---

[36] Art. 2 of the Act No XX of 1949 as amended by the Act No I of 1972.

[37] Government Resolution No. 1055/1980/XII.24/Mt.h.

[38] Y. Ullmo, *La planification en France* (1974, Paris) at pp. 5–22; H. Jacquot, *Le statut
juridique des plans français* (1973, Paris) at pp. 44–47.

[39] B. Chenot, *Organisation économique de l'Etat*, (2d ed., 1965, Paris) at pp. 145–46;
P. Bauchet *La planification française* (1966, Paris) at pp. 158–73; H. Jacquot, *supra* note
38, at pp. 95–99 and 137.

[40] A. De Laubadère, P. Delvolvé, *Droit public économique* (4th ed., 1983, Paris) at pp.
432–49.

and they are not taken separately to Parliament. It is clear from what has been said above that the economic objectives are fixed by the government even though they are approved by Parliament.

Italy is known as a state which intervenes strongly in the economy. On basis of the constitutional framework planning can be expected to play an important role. After some years of experiments with sectoral programmes the first national plan was adopted by Parliament in 1967. The plan was promulgated as an Act, and was binding upon the executive.[41] It is not clear, however, what kind of role the plans later had. It has been stated that the plan of 1967 was the first and last attempt to have a general plan. Neither the government nor Parliament was able to set general economic objectives and a chaotic situation prevailed in the administration.[42] The lack of general programmes can be observed in energy policy too, where Parliament and the administration dealt with separate problems).[43]

In the Netherlands planning was introduced after the Second World War. The Central Planning Bureau regularly works out one year plans which are presented to parliament for use in budget discussion after their approval by the government. There are medium-term plans, too. Neither the short-term nor the medium-term plans are considered binding. They are only forecasts serving as a basis for negotiations between the government and organisations of employers and employees.[44] There is no doubt, however, that general economic programmes, if any, are drafted under the control of the government, not of Parliament. The Dutch conception of the relation between government and Parliament is dualistic. The government is not regarded as a committee implementing the decisions of Parliament; it exercises the powers deriving from the constitution and legislation and in so doing acts on its own initiative.[45]

In the German Federal Republic the practice of planning never acquired the same importance as in France, though state intervention in the economy was certainly practised by government. There were several reasons for this situation, some of which are worth mentioning. During the Hitler regime a strongly centralised planning system was in operation which directed the economy towards wartime purposes. After the Second World War there was no clear picture of the kind of economic system to be built up and even the Constitution did not contain any direction. It was a few years after the end of the war that the neo-liberal conception was accepted and the economic system began to be characterised as a

---

[41] G. Sacchi Morsiani, *Bericht über die italienische Wirtschaft* (1973, Brussels, Reihe Wettbewerb – Rechtsangleichung) at pp. 12 and 23–25; M. Cappelletti, J. H. Merryman, J. M. Perillo, eds., *The Italian Legal System* (1967, Stanford) at pp. 66–68.

[42] G. Amato, *Die Funktion der Regierung nach dem italienischen Verfassungsrecht, Jahrbuch des öffentlichen Rechts der Gegenwart N. F.* Bd. 29 at pp. 114–15.

[43] D. Coombes and S. A. Walkland, *supra,* note 10, at pp. 165–66.

[44] D. C. Fokkema, J. M. J. Chorus, E. H. Hondius, E. Ch. Lisser, eds., *Introduction to Dutch Law for Foreign Lawyers* (1978, Deventer) at pp. 496–97 and 511–12; P. VerLoren van Themaat, *Bericht über das niederländische Wirtschaftsrecht* (1973, Brussels) at pp. 25–26; R. T. Griffith, ed., *Government, Business and Labour in European Capitalism* (1977, London) at pp. 136–37.

[45] D. C. Fokkema, J. M. J. Chorus et al., *supra* note 44, at pp. 414–15.

social market economy.[46] The most influential representatives of this concept, Eucken and Boehm, worked out the main ideas of the system in reaction to the Nazi regime.[47] Even in Boehm's later works, which influenced legal thinking in Germany to a great extent, it can be seen that he wanted to oppose dictatorship by strengthening the market economy and the freedom of enterprises.[48]

It has been emphasised that there is a direct relationship between decentralisation and division of power in the state, and competition in the economy; competition may need to be maintained by state intervention, too, but without its reaching the level of dirigisme.[49]

As a result of the economic recession in the 1960s, the government had to work out general economic programmes and plans and in 1967 the Stabilitätsgesetz introduced planning. Under the Act there are several plans which do not create a single comprehensive system. The most important are the one-year financial plan (budget), the five-year financial plan and the government programmes presented to Parliament. Neither the five-year financial plans nor the government's programmes can be considered as binding.[50] It is thus understandable that a series of programmes should also be found in the energy policy and the manpower policy fields. The objectives are formulated by the government and though they are discussed in Parliament the programmes as a whole do not seem to be controlled by Parliament.

In the United Kingdom the idea of planning became identified with the physical controls operated by the Labour Government after the Second World War, which were unattractive to public opinion. Thus no attempt was made to introduce comprehensive planning. Later, however, in the 1960s, the "stop-go" policy and other quick changes of policy (often without any strategy) and the success of the planned French economy often changed the climate of opinion in the United Kingdom. In 1961 the Federation of British Industries began to back planning and in 1962 the Conservative Government established the National Economic Development Council "to examine the economic performance of the nation with particular concern for plans for the future".[51] After the election of a Labour government in 1964, the Prime Minister announced that a five year national plan

---

[46] N. Reich, *Markt und Recht* (1977, Darmstadt) at pp. 78–81.

[47] H. P. Ipsen, "Rechtsfragen der Wirtschaftsplanung", in J. H. Kaiser, ed., *Planung*, Bd. III (1968, Baden-Baden) at pp. 85–86; C. Watrin, "Thesen zum Programm der sozialen Marktwirtschaft", in D. Cassel, G. Guttmann, H. J. Thieme, eds., *25 Jahre Marktwirtschaft in der Bundesrepublik Deutschland* (1972, Stuttgart) at pp. 18–19.

[48] F. Boehm, *Freiheit und Ordnung in der Marktwirtschaft*, E. J. Mestmacker, ed., (1980, Baden-Baden) at pp. 58–59.

[49] E. J. Mestmäcker, *Recht und oekonomisches Gesetz*, (1980, Baden-Baden) at pp. 19–21, 29 and 640–43.

[50] K. Konig, H. J. Oertzen, F. von Wagener, eds., *Public Administration in the Federal Republic of Germany* (1983, Deventer) at pp. 71–73 and 177–79; H. F. Zacher, *Bericht über das in der Bundesrepublik Deutschland geltende Wirtschaftsrecht* (1973, Brussels) at pp. 37 and 46.

[51] T. Blackaby, *supra* note 23, at pp. 402–07; P. Maunder, *Government Intervention in the Developed Economy* (1979, London) at p. 142.

would be prepared. At the end of 1965 the plan was presented to and welcomed, but not approved, by Parliament.[52] In 1966 it became evident that the plan targets could not be achieved, and that economic recession and inflation had created a new situation. In 1968 a new medium-term plan was prepared but at the time of its publication it was called merely a planning document and not a plan and it was not discussed by Parliament. After the elections the new Conservative government abandoned planning. Since that time there has been no new general plan. This does not mean, however, that nothing reamins of the attempt at planning. After 1975 the Labour government wanted to extend planning activity but before it could do so the Conservatives were returned to power.[53] Shanks seems to be correct in underlining that on the one hand the implications of national planning had not been thought through and that there was no coherent system of plans prepared by different bodies. On the other hand, the continuity of economic policy was absent as respective governments always wanted to distance themselves from their predecessors.[54]

The special feature of the legal system of the United Kingdom is that though there are no economic objectives defined in general terms for several years that are to be presented to Parliament, the implementation of specific objectives is often introduced as a financial question in Parliament. The basis of this solution is the rule according to which the government may only spend money for the purposes and in the amounts approved by Parliament by way of legislation.[55] This may reflect the traditional English emphasis on the financial aspects of economic problems.[56]

What we have said above seems to correspond with Savy's view that economic decision-making is in the hand of the executive in all countries and that the importance of Parliament is declining.[57] There is a difference, however, among the countries. In countries where five year plans are enacted Parliament may discuss the plan as whole but later it does not have much opportunity to deal with the objectives, with the exception of the opportunity produced by the budget debate. In other countries where medium-term plans are not approved by Parliament, the objectives can be examined, usually in connection with financial questions, and probably in the context of the budget. In the second group there is a greater probability of presenting economic problems repeatedly to Parliament but this is mainly a partial solution to the problem of control. This is particularly so in the United Kingdom.

[52.] T. C. Daintith, *Report on the Economic Law of the United Kingdom* (1974, Brussels) at p. 26.

[53.] T. Blackaby, *supra* note 23, at p. 412; D. Morris, ed., *The Economic System in the U. K.* (1977, Oxford) at pp. 420–22 and 435.

[54] M. Shanks, *Planning and Politics: The British Experience 1960–1976* (1977, London) at p. 91.

[55] T. C. Daintith, *supra* note 52, at p. 14.

[56] I. Jennings, *Cabinet Government* (3d ed., 1959, Cambridge) at p. 317.

[57] R. Savy, M. Fromont, *Les interventions des pouvoirs publics dans la vie économique* (1978, Limoges) Vol. 1 at p. 16.

F. Parliaments and Implementation

A decision on objectives sometimes involves a decision on the related instruments and measures as well, but it is often a separate question. In countries where the plan is approved by an Act some guidelines or directives are formulated with regard to the instruments to be used. Otherwise the implementation is in the hands of the government. Exceptions to this are the cases where the character of the subject matter requires legislation as it is a question defined by the Constitution or other basic laws as belonging to the domain of parliamentary legislation (e.g. regulation of the workers' rights). The Netherlands belong to this group of countries, thought its plan is not enacted and it does not contain principles regarding its implementation.

In the German Federal Republic, Italy and the United Kingdom the respective constitutional systems usually require the government to present propositions to Parliament if it wants to take certain measures. Thus, it is highly probable that Parliament will look into questions connected with instruments and measures of implementation.

As far as the implementation process is concerned it is not of primary importance for Parliaments. Thus, while it can be assumed that Parliament chooses instruments and measures in a great number of cases, if only as a subordinate or accessory element of the problem discussed, the decision is nevertheless more often made by government then by Parliament. If this is true, then the difference between the two groups of states is not so great as it seems to be.

G. Decentralisation

Decentralised decision-making can be found mainly in the Federal Republic of Germany and in Italy. Whether planning will be within the competence of central organs depends on the subject matter chosen for examination. In the Federal Republic the energy sector is usually governed centrally, while a lot of issues relating to manpower policy are decided by the Länder. In Italy it is not clear if there is such difference between the two fields as the regions seem to have quite a large role in both areas.

If we examine decision-making in relation to other aspects of implementation, we find a similar situation. It depends mainly on the subject matter whether we confront a more or less centralised system of decision-making. In this respect Italy and the Federal Republic are not exceptions but reflect the general pattern. In the other countries decision-making seems to be more centralised in energy policy than in manpower policy. Manpower policy problems are, I think, more readily classified into those requiring a national solution and those which may be tackled at regional or local levels. The lower level solutions are often to be found in the competence of different semi-governmental bodies. The project data was not sufficient to formulate any other thesis.

H. The Content of Measures

The content of the measures is classified according to the following main categories: declaratory, imposing duties, granting powers, removing or relaxing general duties, granting exceptions from general duties, transferring funds or property, constituting bodies.[58]

It is particularly interesting, when examining implementation, to see how the state is acting. The juxtaposition of the use of two main categories is of special importance: one of them is regulation, the other, the use of incentives. More than two of the above categories of the content of measures could be examined at this point but some of them can be left out of consideration. The inventories contained only a few items falling under the headings of removing or relaxing general duties and granting exceptions from general duties. Thus two categories remain: the imposing of duties and the transfer of funds or property.

Here again we face general problems and it is certain that the peculiarities of the national systems play only a secondary role. There are several other factors which are more important than the one selected here, and these also have an influence on the legal system. It cannot be excluded that the result of all these factors will be similar although one might expect a different effect if one considered the factors separately. The reason is that the factors are not unique determinants but parts of a mechanism. Let us take the example of France and Germany.

It is widely believed that in France there is a dirigiste state whose government in strong in relation to its parliament.[59] On the other hand, in Germany the social market economy prevails. It might be expected that in France regulation is used while in Germany incentives are preferred. The research material does not support the hypothesis of the existence of a sharp contrast. It is true that there are more regulations in France, showing a greater willingness to use this kind of instrument, or to use measures imposing duties, than in other countries. However, there is a heavy reliance on regulation in each country when implementing short-term objectives and regulation is also encountered in the implementing of medium-term or long-term objectives. The difference of the proportions in different countries are not as great as may be supposed.

In reality the effect of different factors is complex. Without trying to explain the problem in detail I should like to refer to the use of subsidies as an instrument (and at the same time the granting of funds as the relevant category of measures) of implementation. Nowadays subsidies probably have a greater role in Germany than in the other countries, though they cannot be considered as a traditional instrument in that country. It was a surprising event for lawyers when an Act of 1952 provided for a special subsidy system in order to help the reconstruction of some branches of industry. At this time the use of subsidies was rather limited.[60] It was only in the 1960s that a shift occurred in industrial assistance, from granting

---

[58] See Daintith, above, at pp. 52–54.
[59] A. Shonfield, *Modern Capitalism* (1969, Oxford) at pp. 71–87.
[60] H. P. Ipsen, *Öffentliche Subventionierung Privaten* (1956, Berlin–Köln) at pp. 45–50; P. Badura, *Wirtschaftsverfassung und Wirtschaftsverwaltung* (1971, Frankfurt/Main) at p. 49.

aid through erecting trade barriers to the use of subsidies and tax allowances.[61] Though the use of subsidies has long been debated, it still seems to be undecided whether or not the government needs a special authorisation for granting subsidies, specified as to addressees, amount, and objectives.[62] This uncertainty creates a temptation for government to avoid being bound by public law (inevitable in the case of regulation) by applying private law forms of action. The warning of the danger of such a manipulation was given at the time when the use of subsidies become extensive.[63] It could mean that the German government could evade parliamentary control by means of subsidies to much the same degree as can the French government by means of regulation.

Different modes of granting subsidies can be observed in the inventories. In the manpower policy field subsidies are administered by the Federal Institute for Labour and its subdivisions, which also issues the relevant rules in this field. Subsidies administered by this kind of body can be found in other countries also.[64] Other subsidies are approved by Parliament in the framework of the yearly budget. Special techniques have been applied as well: for example, electricity enterprises (probably under informal state influence) made long-term contracts with the coal mines on deliveries of coal whose costs were recompensed by subsidies under a special Act.[65]

It should be noted that subsidies are often used in France as well. It is also usual to give subsidies by means of contracts. The system of "économie concertée" favoured the creation of special types of contracts granting advantages to enterprises helping the government to implement its objectives. The contracts became so fashionable that the denomination of "économie contractuelle" was used.[66] New forms of contracts have been used since the 1960s to implement economic policy objectives and though there is discussion on the problems they give rise to, Fromont's remark calling attention to the fact that there is no legal analysis of subsidies is correct.[67] In the field of energy policy and manpower policy some elements of granting subsidies by means of contracts can be observed. Examples are the so-called "contrat de solidarité" in use since 1982 and the "contrats de programme" which were made with some important enterprises in the energy sector.

These examples of French and German uses of regulation and incentives

---

[61] W. M. Corden, G. Fels, eds., *Public Assistance to Industry* (1976, London, Basingstoke) at p. 92.

[62] H. D. Jarass, "Der Vorbehalt des Gesetzes bei Subventionen" (1984) 3 *Neue Zeitschrift für Verwaltungsrecht* 473–80.

[63] H. P. Ipsen, *supra* note 60 at p. 12.

[64] See for example the activity of the UK Manpower Services Commission, created by the Employment and Training Act 1973.

[65] The so-called "Century Contract": see T. Daintith and L. Hancher, *Energy Strategy in Europe: The Legal Framework* (1986, Berlin), at pp. 89–92, 114–115.

[66] M. Vasseur, "Un nouvel essor du concept contractuel", *Revue Trimestrielle de Droit Civil* 1964. 14.

[67] M. Fromont, "Le contrôle des aides financières publiques aux entreprises privées", *Actualité Juridique Droit Administratif* 1979. 3.

(imposing duties and granting subsidies, transferring funds) may have shown the complexity of the problems and the influence of legal systems. Although the effect of the national legal system is not of primary importance it is still significant. The person who is responsible for drafting a new decree may be most willing to make use of the forms and techniques he already knows. At the same time it is obvious that the style of implementation is different in France and in Germany. The French system proclaims intervention. On the contrary, the German practice reminds one of a remark made by Wieacker in another context when he said that the state's economic activity takes hidden forms in Germany.[68]

I. Agreements and Concertation

Beside incentives, regulation can have another counterpart, too, and this is the use of agreements where one of the parties is the state. The legal character of these agreements is dubious: nevertheless, they are used in many countries. The approach in the United Kingdom seems to be rather different from the other countries.

We have already referred to the French attachment to planning. Planning through coordination of the different interests, with drafts being prepared in the presence of representatives of both employers' and employees' organisations, was something of a myth: it has been pointed out that in reality there is no consensus making, only information.[69] There are, however, other cases in the implementation process where agreements were reached between the state and large enterprises. Reference has often been made to the research undertaken by Friedberg which showed that the partners were at first the state and organisations of enterprises but later the agreements become individualised and so individual firms became the state's partners.[70] The character of some of these contracts was debatable, and there were different opinions on the question whether the agreements had any effect at all. Various new kinds of contracts have been introduced by the national plan or decrees and these have been used in the energy and manpower fields.

Such agreements can also be found in Germany, but little attention has been paid to their use in practice.[71] It has been pointed out that the State, acting in a new way as a co-operating partner with industry, would not enter into a real contractual relationship, which is too rigid for this purpose.[72] Special informal agreements

[68] F. Wieacker, "Das bürgerliche Recht im Wandel der Gesellschaftsordnungen", in E. von Caemmerer, E. Friesenhahn, R. Lange, eds., Hundert Jahre Deutsches Rechtsleben (1960, Karlsruhe) Vol. II at p. 5.

[69] Y. Ullmo, supra note 38 at pp. 80–81.

[70] L. Richer, "L'évolution des rapports entre l'administration et les entreprises privées", Revue de Droit Public 1981. 219.

[71] E. Bohne, "Absprachen zwischen Industrie und Regierung im Umweltschutz" in V. Gessner, G. Winter, eds., Rechtsformen der Verflechtung von Staat und Wirtschaft, Jahrbuch für Rechtssoziologie und Rechtstheorie (1982, Opladen) Bd. 8 at pp. 275–80.

[72] E. H. Ritter, "Der kooperative Staat" (1979) 104 Archiv für Öffentliches Recht, at pp. 275–80.

were reached in the energy policy field with important industries. In the literature reference has been made to the fact that an increasing proportion of these agreements came to be made with individual enterprises rather than enterprise associations, reflecting the trend in France.[73]

In connection with the agreements (Absprachen) a consultation forum was created by the Stabilitätsgesetz. The representatives of the employers' and employees' organisations, and of the Länder, took part in this forum, and had discussions with the state. This forum (which no longer functions) was different in character from the agreements: a broad consensus on State policies, and on likely reactions to them, was aimed at, rather than an exchange of specific undertakings. The tripartite consultation forum system seems to be widely used in the Netherlands and does not simply replace regulation, but functions even in cases when regulation takes place.[74] Agreements are reached in the course of the discussions, but agreements are also used as an instrument of policy outside the consultation system. Such agreements have had a role in the energy sector.

In the UK we find a different situation. Although the idea of "économie concertée" had some influence and tripartite bodies were created in the nineteen-sixties there is no system of agreements. In the Industry Act 1975 the basis was prepared for a kind of state-industry agreement, the so-called "planning agreement", but there was strong opposition to the idea and it was not put into practice.[75]

These different attitudes, and the differences in the legal culture, may explain why informal deregulatory instruments were used in some countries and not in others.

J. Creation of Administrative Bodies

The influence of the legal system can be felt in relation to another content element, that is, the creation of new administrative bodies by measures taken for the implementation of given objectives. In most countries new bodies have been created both in the energy and in the manpower policy field. Two different approaches have been followed. In the first approach, such bodies form part of the State hierarchical administration system. This is, for example, the usual French solution. The second approach is characterised by the fact that the newly created bodies stand outside this system. This is the traditional British approach which had its origins in the eighteenth century. Since the Second World War a number of such new bodies have been created.[76]

---

[73] K. H. Ladeur, "Verrechtlichung der Ökonomie – Ökonomisierung des Rechts" in V. Gessner, G. Winter, eds., *supra* note 71 at p. 84.

[74] P. VerLoren van Themaat, *supra* note 44 at p. 19.

[75] e.g. J. T. Winkler, "Law, State and Economy: The Industry Act 1975 in Context", (1975) *British Journal of Law and Society* 103; T. C. Daintith, "Regulation by Contract: The New Prerogative", in *Current Legal Problems* (1979, London) at pp. 41–64; T. Smith, *The Politics of the Corporate Economy* (1979, Oxford) at pp. 166–69.

[76] E. C. S. Wade and G. G. Phillips, *supra* note 31 at p. 281.

Socialism, Legalisation and Delegalisation

JOHN N. HAZARD
Firenze

Is experience in the Marxian socialist states of Eastern Europe relevant to a study of various trends toward delegalisation and its alternatives in the capitalist oriented Western world? Almost by definition the marxist oriented states have become symbols of what Habermas has called "colonisation of the life world". If a less colourful characterisation is adopted, for example, *"étatisation"* of traditionally private law relationships, the relevance may be made more apparent than under Habermas' formulation, for there is hardly a developed society that has not moved toward *étatisation* since World War II.[1] Eastern European states have attracted attention only because they symbolise the extreme. They are to be found at or near the end of a spectrum extending from non-regulated to fully regulated societies.

Admittedly, inclusion of comparisons of Marxist oriented states in a study focused on aspects of legalisation and delegalisation and their alternatives in the West raises questions of comparability as an aspect of relevance. Since the first Congress of Comparative Law held in Paris in 1900, comparatists have argued that not all legal systems are comparable, except on a meaninglessly high level of generality. At that time comparatists were looking for a method to develop a rationalised higher law through agreement on unification of legal systems.[2] Consequently, if states embodied non-Christian values in their legal systems, they were excluded from the exercise because unification with the Romano-Germanic legal system of continental Europe was not to be anticipated. The English common law system fell under a shadow, although England treasured Christian values, because, as René David once suggested, jocularly, English law was looked upon by Continentals as immature, and even "folkloric." Only one English scholar was included in the assemblage at Paris, Sir Frederick Pollock of Oxford. Representatives of Islamic law were not invited to the table since they would have represented in European eyes a value system that could not be assimilated in any unification attempt.

---

[1] Georges Langrod of the University of Paris was perhaps the first to develop the *étatist* vocabulary in his articles on administrative law.

[2] For the early goals of comparatists, see M. Ancel, "La confrontation des droits socialistes et des droits occidentaux," pub. in Z. Péteri, ed., *Legal Theory – Comparative Law: Studies in Honour of Professor Imre Szabó*. (1984, Budapest) at pp. 18–20.

Attitudes of comparatists have now changed. This volume of essays is proof of this fact, for its editors have included a paper by a Hungarian comparatist, and also this paper by an observer of the impact of socialist thought upon law. Further, René Rodière of Paris in his *Introduction au droit comparé*[3] found room for comparisons between Western and Eastern European laws because he thought it possible to place socialist legal systems in the camp with those developed manifestly to protect Christian values despite the espousal of atheism officially by Communists who create law. In his view the socialist decades had created but a veneer on a millenial experience in Eastern Europe with Christianity. His minimisation of socialist influence on law has been supported by other noted comparatists such as Wolfgang Friedman, Albert A. Ehrenzweig, and F. H. Lawson.[4] All three thought that Marxism had brought about no major alteration in the Christianised Romanist legal principles introduced by the Tsars into their codes from the twelfth century onward.

In spite of this support for comparison between East and West, a scholar must enter upon comparison with care, for Eastern Europeans have argued for decades that their legal system is unique, by which they mean incomparable with Western systems. As recently as 1964 socialist scholars invited to share in editing an International Encyclopedia of Comparative Law entered upon the task reluctantly.[5] They argued that socialist solutions to contemporary social problems were so different from those of capitalist oriented societies that they were beyond useful comparison. They demanded separate volumes of the encyclopedia for the law of East and West. Only by degrees did they allow themselves to be convinced that there were points of comparison to be made in volumes to be edited on the basis of "branches" of law rather than political and economic philosophies.[6]

If the hypothesis can be accepted that comparison of Eastern and Western legal systems can offer food for thought, one can turn to discussion of content of the systems in a systematic way in the "branches" of law on which this volume is focused, namely manpower and energy regulation. The Hungarian contributor warns that, although Hungary regulates manpower and energy matters, there are sharp differences in the problems that have caused regulation by law. He notes that Hungary's participation in the Council for Mutual Economic Assistance (COMECON) has cushioned the shock felt by the West from increases in price by the OPEC countries. Consequently, the Hungarian legislators have not felt the same pressures as Western parliamentarians to multiply laws and regulations in a process of legalisation of a previously scarcely regulated industry so as to promote conservation. Likewise, he sees a difference in legislation on manpower because

---

[3] R. Rodière, *Introduction au droit comparé* (1979, Paris) at p. 30.

[4] W. Friedmann, *Law in a Changing Society* (New York, 1959) at p. 9. A. A. Ehrenzweig, Book Review, (1970) 59 *Calif. L. Rev.* 1005; F. H. Lawson, Book Review, (1953) 21 *Univ. of Chicago L. Rev.* 780.

[5] For an account of the arguments at the editorial conference, see J. N. Hazard, "Socialist Law and the International Encyclopedia," (1965) 79 *Harv. L. Rev.* 278.

[6] For the result of the effort, see *International Encyclopedia of Comparative Law*, Vol. XI (Torts) (1983, Tübingen, The Hague, Boston, London).

Hungary has experienced no lasting unemployment crisis. On the contrary, it suffers a shortage of manpower, and such unemployment as there is has been only temporary, as with peasant women during the winter, or steel workers while production levels are being readjusted. Hungarian law has, therefore, often quite a different role to play in social management than Western law because the factual situation is often different.

Of course, the Hungarian contrasts emerge not only because of differences in factual situations. Both in Hungary and in other Marxist oriented countries there is heavy influence of Marxist thought on how the burden of production should be shared between the private and public sectors. The keystone of the arch of Eastern social organisation is still what Marx said it must be, namely state ownership of the means of production.[7] While this fundamental principle has been relaxed in some Eastern European states, notably Poland, Hungary and Yugoslavia, because of strong popular resistance to major *étatisation* of property ownership and also because of organisational deficiencies in the state owned system, there has been very little concession to private ownership in the USSR and in socialist states that follow its model closely. Legalisation, or *étatism*, has been preserved in the Soviet-style states in spite of claims on the part of some critics that privatisation of some aspects of the process and delegalisation would increase the production of goods and services. This means that generally the private sector is no more than of auxiliary importance as a gap-filler where the public sector has been unable to meet demand. State ownership and centralised state economic planning have remained the fundamental law.[8]

Centralised state economic planning is not, of course, unique to Marxist oriented societies. The West has passed through periods when state planning seemed necessary, as during World War II. In the United States the War Production Board was established by President Franklin D. Roosevelt to direct economic planning. Its officials held the order books of privately owned enterprises producing critical items such as steel, copper, and aluminum. All orders for such items had to pass through those officials. For the less critical items, such as textiles, planning was conducted less directly. The WPB officials issued priorities to would-be purchasers, and these searched for a supplier able to deliver on such a priority. Here was a combination of state planning and private enterprise. During the war, no factories were nationalised, nor were the railroads nationalised as they had been during World War I. The system of planning was designed to leave private owners in control of their sources of revenue, although their control was limited by the orders of the WPB, and their prices were subject to regulation by the Office of Price Administration. Further, government officials monitored their profits from government orders and demanded return of the portion of profits deemed to be excessive.

[7] There is no need to cite the various well-known sources for the proposition, beginning with The Communist Manifesto (1848).

[8] These principles are enshrined in the constitutions of East European states. For the model, see USSR Constitution of 1977, Arts. 10 and 15. For English translation, see W. E. Butler, ed., *Basic Documents of the Soviet Legal System* (1984, New York, London, Rome) at pp. 109–225.

Socialist planners have been reducing the number of items that are rigidly planned in the East. Planning has become "indicative" in that it has been generalised to overall quantities of scarce resources. Yugoslavia has reduced its central planning to cover only expansion of production resources.[9] Ongoing production is the concern of the enterprise directors who obtain their resources through the negotiation of contracts, as if they were the managers of privately owned enterprises functioning in accordance with a civil code. Even the USSR has moved toward a mixed system under which managers of state enterprises obtain resources under two sets of laws: those that may be called planned contract law and those that may be called unplanned contract law.[10] In the planned situation the enterprise manager has no choice of partner on the contract, nor of quantity, nor of specifications. The contract conforms to the planning order, and contributes to the relationship only such detail as packing instructions, delivery instructions and details of specifications not treated by the central planners. In the unplanned situation the enterprise manager makes the law of the relationship through a contract governed by the civil code, just as he would have done had his enterprise been privately owned. Private law is used to achieve public purposes.

Resolution of disputes between enterprise managers over contract negotiation and performance is also now achieved through the use of procedures comparable to those in use in market economies. This was not always so. During the early years of the 1920s when emphasis upon production was of top priority, resolution of disputes between managers of state enterprises was based on expediency rather than determination of fault. In the early 1930s in the USSR a special set of tribunals, called State Arbitration, was created to hear the parties and to issue a decision based upon a negotiated settlement between the managers, and without reference to law. Indeed, lawyers were excluded from the proceedings. There was no procedure for appeals, as speed of resolution was considered more important than any other factor.

For some fifty years this emphasis upon public concerns predominated in the USSR's tribunals. After the People's Democracies were established following World War II, the same attitudes toward performance of state planned contracts prevailed in their tribunals. The notable development of the 1980s has been the emergence of a new basis for judgment in resolution of disputes between state enterprises. The tribunals have been restructured to provide for appeals, and the judges have been instructed to use as a yardstick for resolution of the dispute not expediency but the determination of "fault". Lawyers are expected to represent the parties. The civil codes of the various republics, as extended by Ministerial instructions on the performance of planned contracts, are applied rigorously. In a

---

[9] For a Yugoslav explanation of the system see B. T. Blagojević, "The Self-Management Law or the Law of Self-Management," published in Péteri, *op., cit., supra*, note 2 at p. 25.

[10] For details of the USSR laws on state planning and their application, see J. N. Hazard, W. E. Butler, P. B. Maggs, *The Soviet Legal System: The Law of the 1980's*. (1984, New York, London, Rome) at pp. 109–225.

sense there is developing a private law attitude toward dispute resolution to achieve public ends.[11]

One socialist state has gone far to symbolise the change in approach. Yugoslavia has renamed its State Arbitration so that it now bears the title of "Commercial Court". Its functions have been compared to those of a commercial court in market economies. The change has been facilitated by restructuring of enterprises from the Soviet model in which Ministries name managers and direct much of the activity of the manager. Under the Yugoslav system which is called "self management" the employees and not the state are technically the owners. Their collective, with the addition of a representative of local government, name and dismiss management. The central authorities play a part only when additional investment is required beyond sums available in the enterprise treasury. Expansion is therefore of public concern, but otherwise the enterprise manager and his workers are autonomous in making day to day production descisions. Delegalisation has occurred, at least in the sense that the enterprise decision is not made by a central planning authority through the law of the plan, but within the parameters established by the plan drawn up by management in consultation with the workers concerned.

The Yugoslav enterprise is left free to conduct its business as its management decides. Its aim is to maximise profits for distribution to the owner-employees. This system may lead to the development of parochial rather than nation-wide concerns, for workers are universally concerned primarily with their own wages. The danger of parochialism is recognised, and nation-wide interests are factored into the decision making process through a characteristic Eastern European institution. There are always present among the workers as well as within the enterprise's management council members of the League of Communists, who by definition have the duty to consider national welfare. To the extent that these communists can dissociate themselves from the parochial interests of their non-party colleagues and can exert influence, the interests of the larger community play some part in the routine decisions of every day's production.

The Yugoslav experiment seems to have influenced a structure introduced by the Hungarians by resolution of its Socialist Workers Party/Communist Party in April 1984, extended into law on January 1, 1985.[12] Under the new scheme ownership of medium and large enterprises has passed to the workers, represented by the "Enterprise Council". The Council sets production policy and appoints the general manager. The Hungarians have not localised the decision on management to the same extent as the Yugoslavs, for the selection of a manager has to be referred to the appropriate Ministry for approval. Further, the Hungarian law places representatives of management on the Enterprise Council in equal numbers with those of the workers, while the Yugoslav workers' collective retains the right

---

[11] For the history and functions of State Arbitration tribunals, see W. E. Butler, *Soviet Law* (1983, London) at pp. 114–18.

[12] For a journalistic summary of the Hungarian innovation, see "A Milestone in Management," published in Hungary: Trade and Investment Opportunities. *International Herald Tribune*, 12 June 1985, p. 7.

to dismiss management, subject to the participation of the chairman of the local governing unit in the decision.

For the small firms, defined as those with less than 500 workers, the system corresponds almost exactly to the Yugoslav model. The enterprise is "owned" by the workers represented by their General Assembly. Management is elected and may be dismissed by the workers' collective, and there is no veto in any supervisory body. Of course, the Hungarian Socialist Workers Party/Communist Party members, like the party members in Yugoslavia, are expected to play a part in decision making and to prevent the adoption of decisions that are parochial. Hungarian authors express some question as to whether the manager and his workers can look beyond parochial concerns, but these fears are thought to be groundless because of long experience in the agricultural cooperatives in which the right to make decisions has rested with the cooperatives' members for years without serious manifestations of parochialism.

Incentives to encourge work on the part of the employees of enterprises in all socialist states of Eastern Europe have also undergone change over the years. Prior to 1930 in the USSR, egalitarianism, which has often been held dear by socialists, was applied to the determination of wage structures. Although not all employees were paid at exactly the same level, there was no great variation. The year 1930 became the dividing line, for Joseph Stalin took the view that material incentives were essential to an increase in productivity. He ordered abandonment of egalitarianism, and had his lexicographers define it as a "petty bourgois utopian concept". Thereafter workers were to be paid in accordance with their productivity.[13] Bonuses were introduced for enterprises that exceeded the plan, and individual workers shared in accordance with their productivity in these bonuses. Since that time the piece work system, formerly severely criticised by socialists, has become the rule. Again it is evident that private enterprise techniques have been made to serve a public purpose.

The importance to production of maintaining a measure of private law structures in a socialist oriented system was demonstrated in the People's Republic of China during the turbulent days of Mao Tse tung's "Cultural Revolution". He abolished the general courts, terminated efforts to draft codes of law, closed the law faculties and disbanded the Bar. It was his expectation that social order and economic life could be fostered through application of the ages-old Chinese penchant for mediation of disputes.[14] He placed upon the Communist Party cadres the duty of guiding citizens in resolving disputes, and especially so when the disputes were between state enterprises. Mao's system may be said to have represented total delegalisation of managerial functions and of enterprise trade while retaining a framework of state owned enterprise and collectively organised agriculture.

---

[13] For a review of labour law history, see A. K. R. Kiralfy, "Labor Law Reform Since the Death of Stalin," pub. in D. D. Barry, W. E. Butler, G. Ginsburgs, eds., *Contemporary Soviet Law* (1974, The Hague) at pp. 158–74.

[14] See L. T. Lee, "Chinese Conceptions of Law: Confucian, Legalist and Buddhist," (1978) 29, *Hastings L. Journal* 1307.

There is no need to dwell on the chaotic conditions that resulted from total delegalisation in China. These conditions reached their peak when management of enterprises passed under the control of the untrained youth of the "Red Guard". At the time a specialist on Chinese politics, Professor Franz Schurman of the University of California, predicted that relegalisation would become necessary in the interests of production. In his view managers of state enterprises would not exert their best efforts unless they could be assured that they could operate under approved rules and would not be punished for production failures arising from no fault of theirs. Schurman expected relegalisation to occur to maximise production, and indeed history has proved him right.

With the impetus envisaged by Schurman the entire institutional legal structure has been restored since Mao's death. Courts, prosecutors and Bar have been re-established, law codes have been drafted and promulgated, and law faculties have been recreated.[15] In spite of this post-Mao structural development there has become evident within the last year a counter trend toward delegalisation and privatisation of the production process. Private enterprise in auxiliary services and small industry has been authorised by law, using familiar private law forms to establish through contracts the law governing commercial relations. The result is a mixed economy, with emphasis upon the public sector for basic industry and upon privatisation for goods and services thought to be subsidiary.

Polish reformers are calling for the introduction of a similarly structured mixed economy, but with the introduction of what they see as a critically important political innovation. They doubt that economic reform can be effective so long as a one-party or "dominant party" system is maintained. In their view the Party no longer has the maximisation of production as its first priority. They fear that the leadership is now concerned primarily with retention of power, at whatever cost to the economy. To these Polish reformers Eastern European communist parties have stood Marx on his head, in that, instead of marking the economy the base and political institutions the superstructure the situation is the reverse in that the goal of production is subordinate to the political goal.

If this be so, all institutions will be structured so as to assure the Party's retention of power. There can be no pragmatic evolutionary restructuring of the economy. There can be no extensive privatisation or delegalisation lest there be created a property base for a class that might seek to oust the present holders of power. In short, the Marxist adage that "property ownership equals political power" is so firmly fixed in Eastern leaders' minds that wide scale privatisation and delegalisation are seen as likely to undermine the foundations of a socialist system.

The Polish reformers' proposal raises the question of the current influence of the classical Marxist texts. Do these texts still govern decision making? The 1977 USSR Constitution, and others patterned upon it in Eastern Europe, incorporate

---

[15] For a Chinese view, see W. Jianfan, "Building New China's Legal System," (1983) 22 *Columb. J. Transnat'l. Law* 1. For Western comments, see J. A. Cohen, "China's New Lawyers' law," (1980) 61 *ABA Journal* 1533 and F. H. Foster, "Codification in post-Mao China," (1982) 30 *Am. J. Comp. L.* 395.

the two fundamental principles of Marxist-Leninist ideology, namely the supremacy of the "vanguard party"[16] and the sanctity of state ownership of the means of production.[17]

To be sure, there is some variation on the Soviet one-party model outside the USSR, as for example in Poland where the leading Party has authorised the activity of two additional parties and of a religious "interest" group. This situation might lead outsiders to suppose that the complaints of the Polish reformers are groundless, but such is not the case. These parties are not in competition with the Communists. On the contrary, they are, in the words of the late Stefan Rozmaryn, a Polish jurist, in "perpetual coalition". This means that they agree with the communists not to seek to become the governing party. In return they are given places on the ballot for election to the Sejm and to local councils and some of their candidates are elected. Their function is not to compete but to provide ideas, especially in matters concerning education and the conduct of agriculture.

Even in the USSR where the Communist Party rules alone, there is emphasis upon participation of non-Party persons in the legislative process at all levels of the state structure. Legislative committees have multiplied in the various legislatures to develop programmes with the help of experts so that the Party may have technical advice in formulating high policy. The Party alone makes the final decision, but the support given to the committee system indicates that the Party does not wish to govern directly.

This attitude was evidenced dramatically while a draft of the 1977 USSR Constitution was in discussion. A group of citizens is said to have suggested that the entire state structure be abolished to be replaced by the Communist Party as the maker and administrator of law. The Party's Secretary General, Leonid Brezhnev, berated the proposers saying that their suggestion indicated that they did not understand the Soviet system of government which calls for a vanguard Party to make policy and to assure its adoption at all levels, but places the formal promulgation of law and its execution in the hands of a parallel state structure. Much Party literature explains that the Party must not administer and must not interfere in state administration.Throughout Soviet history there have been periods when this rule was violated, especially during the Khrushchev era of the early 1960's, for he directed Party secretaries to oversee details of administration at the various levels at which they functioned, and he even divided the lower echelons of the Party into industrial and agricultural sectors to facilitate supervision. His scheme was, however, set aside in 1964, and he was himself ousted from power.

Turning now to the focus of this volume, namely manpower and energy policy, one cannot but ask in light of what has been said of the influence of Marxist ideology upon state structures and law generally, whether ideology guides the determination of manpower and energy policy and provides constraints on pragmatic solutions of problems in these areas of concern.

---

[16] USSR Constitution, Art. 6.
[17] *Idem.*, Art. 10.

With regard to manpower policy ideology has provided constraint in pragmatic resolution of some manpower problems. Perhaps the most critical is redundancy created by the introduction of automation into the production process.[18] Ideologically there is no room for redundancy in a socialist system where economic planners are expected to even out the business cycle and transfer resources, including labour, to new type industry as the established industries relinquish workers.

Since automation is inevitable if socialist states are to compete effectively with market economies, there has been emerging evidence that socialist policy makers are trying to find a mechanism which will meet their re-employment needs as redundancy occurs. In the USSR the mechanism is said to be necessary because of a policy initiated in 1965 under which enterprise directors were authorised to make managerial decisions at the enterprise level relating to use of the wage fund allocated to them by the planners in the Ministry to which they were subordinate. The former system, under which targets for employment within the limits of the wage allocation were set by the central authority, permitted no such initiative. Under the 1965 innovation managers could dismiss workers and use the wage fund to increase payment to those remaining when their productivity increased.[19] This meant that the former emphasis upon full employment, even if it meant maintaining staff at levels higher than required by production, was to be abandoned.

The potential for dismissals was great because of what Western business managers call "featherbedding". Western economists have estimated overemployment by computing costs of production in comparison with Western costs, and these costs have been found to be high.[20] In a less scientific way, the overemployment has been estimated by comparing the number of workers employed in turn-key plants constructed in the USSR by United States firms with the number employed in the identically engineered plants used as models. In a conference at Columbia University some three years ago, corporation officers were asked by a panel chairman to raise hands as he called out figures indicating the excessive employment in the Soviet plants. Most hands went up when the chair asked for those noting "double" the number of workers in the Soviet turn-key plant compared to those in the comparable United States plant. But this was not the end. Some officers held up hands to indicate that the Soviet plant employed treble the number of workers, and a few even thought that the number was four times what were needed in the American prototype.

---

[18] This phenomenon has been examined by S. Marnie, "The Releasing of Redundant Production Workers in Connection with Technological Change: A Comparative Study of the USSR and the G.D.R." (unpublished June paper, Department of Economics, European University Institute, 1985).

[19] Resolution of the Central Committee of the Communist Party of the Soviet Union and of the USSR Council of Ministers "On measures to guarantee the future growth in labour productivity in industry and construction," 22 December 1966. Sbornik Postanovlenii SSSR/Collection of Orders USSR/, No. 1 (1967).

[20] This topic is the focus of a forthcoming monograph by Professor David Granick of the University of Wisconsin.

In light of this evidence, it seems likely that Soviet employment levels are higher than in the West. Perhaps it may be because skills have not been developed fully, and more workers are required than would be the case in a more fully developed industrial economy. Perhaps it may be because there is truly overemployment of workers to cover the fact that without "featherbedding" there would be unemployment. The latter conclusion is hard to support in light of complaints that there is a manpower shortage in the USSR. One would expect the release of surplus workers to fill the manpower need, and the 1965 policy decision seems to indicate that the Party leaders have made this their highest priority.

This evidently rational conclusion seems to lie at the basis of some legislation following the 1965 reform. In 1966 there was created in the Council of Ministers of each Republic of the USSR a State Committee for the Utilisation of Labour Resources.[21] These Committees were to establish "departments" at lower levels of the administrative hierarchy. Coordination of all state committees was to be the function at the outset of the State Planning Committee (Gosplan), but in 1976 coordination was transferred to a new All-Union State Committee on Labour and Social Questions (Goskomtrud).[22] The primary duty of the Committees was to determine where labour was required, and to provide a supply of it from the workers released from overstaffed plants.

In the following year, releases multiplied with the introduction in a few industries of an "experiment" under which enterprise directors were authorised to use any funds saved from their overall wage fund allocation to pay to the retained workers a bonus for increases in productivity. Soon thereafter considerable numbers of workers were released. The experiment was held to be successful, and by 1982, 3,300 enterprises were working in accordance with the system. In spite of the opportunity to release unnecessary workers who are then placed in new positions by the committees, there is still "featherbedding". It has been suggested that enterprise directors have been reluctant to utilise their powers because their own salaries are related to the size of the workforce, and also because after the first releases, the wage fund is reduced to meet the new employment level so that there is no continuing fund from which to pay bonuses. It may also be true that in spite of the 1965 high policy decision, local pressures to avoid unemployment are so great that enterprise directors dare not resist them.

Reference to the work of the State Committees on Utilisation of Labour Resources may suggest that workers are moved about by the economic planners without regard to their wishes. This is not, however, permitted by law. Except for a period beginning in 1940 on the eve of the German attack upon the USSR and ending in 1956, workers have been protected by law against compulsory job placement and an enterprise director's refusal to permit voluntary relinquishment of a job. Consequently, although planners have absolute authority over the distribution of raw materials, they have no such authority over human beings. These have to be induced to accept undesirable assignments by methods used in open market systems, namely by material advantage, whether this be better

[21] *Supra* note 19.
[22] Decree of 17 August 1976, Vedomosti Verkhovnogo Soveta SSSR, 1976, items 487–488.

housing than would be available in other regions, or increased wage scales for work in remote regions of the country. Again it is evident that socialist policy makers are not averse to the use of open market methods of inducement when it is necessary to motivate human beings so as to achieve a public purpose.

Dismissal from a job presents a problem for socialists as it does for contemporary private enterprisers, and for the same reasons. Public opinion can no longer be ignored, the more so in a socialistically oriented state where the policy makers' claim to respect depends upon treatment of the workforce in a manner which is generally accepted as "fair." The Soviet Republics' Codes of Labour Law set forth the rules. Essentially they are the same as civil service rules in Western states. Workers may be dismissed for incompetence, unwillingness to perform assigned tasks, reduction in staff, and when a dismissed worker has been reinstated in the job held by his successor. Such contrast as there is between Western and Eastern law is to be found primarily in the role of the trade union. In the USSR management may not dismiss a worker without the consent of his trade union, and this rule is established by the code. In the West the trade union often also plays a part, but as the result of its weight in collective bargaining, not because of statute. In some Western countries, collective bargaining agreements provide for the rules relating to dismissals from private enterprises, and if grievances accumulate to notable proportions because of dismissals, the trade union may call a strike. As this measure of pressure is not available by law to trade unions in socialist oriented states, the attention given by management to the trade unions has to be established by statute if industrial unrest is to be avoided. Delegalisation of labour relations is ideologically unacceptable to socialist policy makers.

Turning now to the allocation of energy, it must be evident at the outset from what has been said about state economic planning that socialists have no compuction against allocating energy as required to perform their economic plan. But not everything is centrally planned, as has been indicated. The planners appreciate that they cannot be aware of all resources throughout the country so they have left decisions on locally produced energy to local authorities, whether in the local government or in local enterprises. This measure of *laissez faire* is authorised in the interest of efficiency in achieving the public purpose of community welfare. Delegalisation springs, therefore, from no ideological position related to the anticipated advantage of preserving a free enterprise system for its own sake or for the enrichment of the private enterpriser.

Looking back over the past sixty odd years of Soviet history and the past thirty years of the history of its socialist neighbours to the West and in Asia, one cannot escape the conclusion that there has been far more utilisation of private law methods to stimulate production than was expected by the founding fathers of the Soviet model. This development has undoubtedly been dictated in large part by pragmatic considerations, but ideology is not dead as a force motivating Eastern European politicians, as some Western sociologists have claimed.[23]

Lenin made at the outset his often quoted statement that after the Russian

[23] See D. Bell, *The End of Ideology – on exhaustion of political ideas of the fifties.* (1950, New York).

revolution all law had become public law,[24] and in a sense this characterisation remains true. There are institutions, such as contracts, in socialist law which resemble private law institutions as they have been used in the West to develop a law of the parties, but these hold overs have no life of their own. They exist because to the law-makers of socialist-oriented states they serve a public purpose. They are revived under contemporary conditions to further the community interest as conceived by those who establish legislative policy.

The prominent pillars of socialist government and law which Lenin introduced in 1917 remain in place. State ownership of the means of production has been seen to be one of those pillars. Although Yugoslav communists, after separation from direct relationships with Soviet leadership in 1948, found it desirable to take dramatic steps to distinguish their system from Stalin's by creating worker-dominated management of enterprises to replace Stalin's bureaucratically dominated enterprises, the result was not a recreation of a delegalised system in the model of the private law. Productive property remained publicly owned, even though managed by the producers themselves rather than by state bureaucrats. Efforts to create incentives like those stimulating private property owners by instructing workers' collectives to use the property as if it were their own have not transformed the legal system. Ownership is still non-private, for no absent owners of capital reap investment rewards. Profits, if any, are distributed among those who actually work in the enterprise, not to distant investors. Hungarian policy makers have been shown to have copied in large part the Yugoslav model although they have been more cautious in severing the umbilical cord attaching the enterprise to the Ministry.

The second prominent pillar to have been left standing is the domination of the policy making function by a political party that cannot be ousted by any constitutional process from power. Of course, the dominant or monopoly party is by no means unique to socialist political systems, for such parties are frequently found in African non-socialist states, and they have been seen in Europe in the not-so-distant past. In spite of the widespread use of this phenomenon to assure retention of political power, the combination of such a party with state ownership of the means of production has become a hallmark of the socialist system, at least for so long as the party concerned is led by men who profess Marxism-Leninism as their inspiration.

Beyond these two pillars of Marxist-Leninist socialism room is left for manoeuvre. In this manoeuvring property ownership rules have been relaxed for the production and enjoyment of consumers' goods in instances where state produc-

---

[24] René David argues that socialist jurists have long misunderstood Lenin, for only a brief part of his letter to his People's Commissar of Justice, Kurskii, was known to jurists until publication of the entire letter in 1964. In the light of the full text. David concludes that Lenin had no intention of speaking of the nature of socialist law in general terms but meant only to indicate that with the introduction of the New Economic Policy it had become necessary to reaffirm the right of the State to intervene in all relationships between men, even when acting as individuals, to assure achievement of socialism. See R. David, *Le Droit Comparé: Droits d'hier, droits de demain.* (1982, Paris) at p. 124.

ers are unable to meet demands. In terms of reference used by other authors in this volume, there has been introduced a measure of privatisation, a measure of delegalisation, in that parties to a legal relationship may make their own law through contract, but it differs from privatisation which occurs primarily for the benefit of owners and only secondarily and indirectly for the benefit of that part of the public thought to prosper from the maximisation of production expected to result from maintenance of a private enterprise system.

Communists have shown themselves sensitive to the need to placate the people they govern. They know what political scientists in the West also know, that there is an economic limit to the resources that may be allocated to retain political power. Communists have studied that limit, and when it has been reached, they retreat, following Lenin's admonition that at times it is necessary to take two steps backward to make one step forward. Lenin was prepared to reprivatise a part of Soviet Russia's economy when he established his New Economy Policy in 1922, but when political control seemed again assured in 1928, Stalin resumed the advance to monopoly, or near-monopoly state ownership. If this swing to the "left" occurs again in Eastern Europe, it will ring the death knell for the concessions of the current decade.

One cannot end without indicating that if the predictions of Marx, Engels and Lenin that the state and law will eventually "wither away" with the achievement of communism come true, socialism in the Marxist-Leninist model will not lead to total legalisation (or, in Habermas' words, to "colonisation of the life world"). On the contrary, there will be no *étatisation*, for the order which *étatisation* was intended to achieve will have entered into the psyche of every individual. With abundance of goods and services sufficient to meet the needs of all, and universal absorption of the communally oriented system of thought revered by socialists, restraint on non-social activity will be lodged in the inner consciousness of every person, and if it is not, it will be the psychiatrist and not the jurist who will be required to "restore the errant person to life".

Soviet philosophers and their socialist colleagues elsewhere continue to profess belief in the ultimate achievement of total delegalisation with the disappearance of the state and its law,[25] but as some have admitted, no emphasis is currently placed upon this aspect of Marxist traditional thought. The thought remains, perhaps, as encouragement to those who have found it necessary at this stage of socialist development to be strict in creating and applying the extreme legalisation which they have felt necessary to achievement of their social goals. Like King Arthur's "Holy Grail" the expectation of "withering" establishes the ideal which stimulates the Knights of the Socialist Round Table to press on.

---

[25] Two Romanian jurists reaffirmed their expectation that law would eventually wither away in a treatise on civil law published in 1980. In doing so they used the French word *déjuridicisation* instead of the usual *dépérissement*. Their choice of word for the Russian *otmiranie* seems close to the English *delegalisation* used in this volume. See Y. Eminescu and T. Popescu, *Les Codes Civiles des Socialistes: Étude Comparative* (1980, Paris).

Part Six

The Time Element

Short and Long-Term Policy Objectives and the Choice of Instruments and Measures

KAMIEL MORTELMANS

Utrecht

Contents

> The most difficult thing in
> government is the attempt to
> view policy as a considered
> whole at any one given time
> Lord Hailsham

I. Introduction

The terms objectives and instruments, key-words in this study, are borrowed
from the means-end dichotomy, analysed by Tinbergen in his "Economic Policy:
principles and design", and elaborated by Kirschen and others in their "Economic
policy in our time".[1] I will return later to the advantages and disadvantages of this
dichotomy.

A. Definitions

The terms objectives and instruments are employed in this paper in the same way
as Kirschen used them: objectives constitute the economic translation of political
aims into concepts which can be quantified; an instrument is the means by which
an objective is pursued. A measure is, in Kirschen's taxonomy, the use of a
particular instrument at a specific moment in time in order to promote one or more
objectives.[2] In this study a measure has another meaning and can be defined as a
legal rule or other Government act with legal consequences. In other words,
measures are acts through which instruments are realised.[3]

As the title of this study indicates, this survey concentrates on the short and
long term character of the objectives on the one hand and the choice of instruments
and measures on the other.

B. Instruments

The different instruments (unilateral regulation, taxation, consensual constraints,
removal of taxation, public benefits, public sector management and information)
frequently acquire their temporal value via the temporal character of the implementing measures. At first sight many instruments appear neutral when viewed in
a temporal perspective. For instance, a unilateral regulation on import restriction
may acquire its long term character through the long term character of the
measures. Even Kirschen, who did not focus on 'legal' measures as such, combines
the instruments with 'law' when he examines the time element of the instruments.[4]
Taking account of the fact that the decision making process varies as between the
many policy instruments – both with regard to the stages through which decisions

---

[1] J. Tinbergen, *Economic Policy: principles and design* (4th revised edition 1963, Amsterdam) reprinted 1975; E. S. Kirschen et al., *Economic Policy in our time*, (1968, Amsterdam).
[2] Kirschen, *supra* note 1 at pp. 11–7.
[3] T. Daintith, "Legal analysis of economic policy", (1982) 9 *Journal of Law and Society*, at
p. 195.
[4] Kirschen, supra note 1 at p. 290.

are reached and the time lags involved at each stage – he distinguishes four categories of instruments.

First, he identifies built-in and entirely automatic instruments, for example progressive taxation. Once the instrument is set in motion through the approval of a tax law, it works continuously without the need for any discretionary instrument and without any time lag.

Secondly, he refers to quasi-continuous instruments where the responsible authority keeps a constant watch on the situation and then applies this type of instrument immediately when action is deemed necessary. An example is the open market operations of the Central Bank.

Thirdly, he discerns instruments giving rise to measures taken by way of explicit decisions of the Executive.

Lastly, he identifies instruments to be approved not only by the Government but also by Parliament, often after a consultation procedure.

Different elements of Kirschen's economic analysis of the instruments, such as discretionary powers, the role of the Government and of Parliament, are central to this legal study. These elements of the decision making process will be analysed in the first part of this paper.

C. The Instrument/Measure Combination

For analytical purposes the instrument chosen and the measure invoked or created are considered in combination in this first part. This approach assumes a harmony of the instrument/measure combination. If the instrument and measure are not adjusted, the realisation of the objective may be jeopardised. Moreover, the analysis of the relationship of the instrument/measure combination with the time element in the objective pursued becomes very difficult.

In practice this non-adjustment happens, either because the procedure whereby an instrument is transformed into a measure is blocked, e.g. a Bill does not become an Act, or because a deregulation process repeals the existing Act. In the first case the instrument does not become operative; in the second case the instrument becomes inoperative or is implemented through private legal ordering (self-regulation) or in a non-legal way (abuse of a dominant position by an undertaking).[5]

This process can be unblocked and may lead, after a lapse of time, to another instrument/measure combination. For instance, a unilateral regulation (long term instrument) concerning early retirement (long term or permanent objective) proposed in a Bill but blocked in Parliament (long term measure) may be revived as part of a collective bargaining agreement (short or mid term measure); a price policy adopted by an undertaking in a dominant position (private ordering) may be forbidden and replaced by a unilateral regulation of the Government (state ordering).

In many cases on the adaptation of the measure, the character of the instrument changes. A collective bargaining agreement does not have the same unilateral and

---

[5] See, B. Bercusson, Economic policy: state and private ordering, below at pp. 359–420.

general character as an Act governing the same subject-matter. This example proves that not any instrument necessarily interlocks with any measure. In other words, not every instrument/measure combination is operational. Seen in a temporal perspective some instruments are not neutral.

D. Plan

The relationship between long and short term policy objectives and the choice of instruments and measures will be examined both from a theoretical and practical perspective.

In the first section, which has a primarily theoretical character, the time element in the objectives and the time element in the instrument/measure combination will be discussed separately. Two parameters will be analysed: the decision making process parameter, borrowed from Kirschen and the content of instrument parameter (ordering or process policy instruments), borrowed from Eucken and Tinbergen. The harmonious instrument/measure combination will be used as a working hypothesis and the temporal perspective of the objectives (short, long or mixed) will be considered as constant and given because it is impossible to analyse all elements (measures, instruments, objectives and time) as variables at the same time.

In the second section, which is more practically oriented, the three constituents of this research (objective, instrument and measure) will be discussed jointly. The starting point is the time factor in relation to the measure. Each category of measures (long term, short term, cyclical, two-level and deficient measures) will be related to the instrument-parameters analysed in the first section, in order to examine which category of measures goes hand in hand with a given time-oriented objective.

These observations have a tentative character. The information on the time element, collected in the national inventories, is not sufficiently detailed to permit general conclusions.[6] The data drawn from the national inventories (Netherlands, United Kingdom, France, Federal Republic of Germany, Italy and Hungary) are used in an exemplificatory way. For the purposes of a balanced comparison recourse is also made to and material is borrowed from sources common to most national reports (European Community Law and GATT-law).

The first and second sections focus mainly on the instrumental characteristics of the relationship between objectives, instruments and measures. In the third section, the choice of measures is linked with legal values in order to give a balanced view of the implementation procedure.

---

[6] On the compilation of national inventories see also Methodological Note, above at pp. 47–55.

II. The Time Element in the Objectives and in the Instrument/Measure Combination

In this section we examine, in turn, the time element in the objectives, in the instrument/measure combination and in the measures.

A. Objectives and the Time Element

Objectives can be divided into two groups: largely short term (conjunctural) and those which are mainly long term (structural). This distinction is not absolute. In practice, objectives may have an ultra-short, short, mid-term, long or permanent nature.[7] However, for analytical purposes the distinction between the two main groups is the starting point and constant factor of this survey.

Nevertheless, two qualifications have to be made. First, an objective can have both short and long term aspects and second, an instrument/measure combination may produce effects which further more than one objective.

1. One Objective – Short/Long Term Aspects

Short term objectives can have long term aspects as well. As Kirschen states, the objective of maintaining full employment is most commonly a short term cyclical problem but Governments also have long term full employment objectives of reducing structural unemployment.[8] A further elaboration is possible. The long term aspects may complement the short term ones; but the long and short term can conflict as well.

This harmonious or conflicting interrelationship may influence the choice of instruments and measures. In order to avoid a conflict, the Government may employ one overall instrument/measure combination such as a general aid scheme covering both short and long term aspects of full employment. On the other hand, the Government can adopt a strict separation between the short and long term aspects of one objective by choosing two different sets of instrument/measure combinations such as an *ad hoc* subsidy scheme administered by the Minister of Social Affairs for the conjunctural aspects of full employment, and legislation concerning vocational training and manpower adjustment for the long term aspects.

2. One Measure – More Than One Objective

One instrument/measure combination may produce effects which further more than one objective. For example, a road speed restriction introduced in a supply crisis in order to achieve an immediate reduction of petrol consumption (short term objective in the energy field) may possibly be retained in a post-crisis period as a measure of energy conservation (long term objective in the energy field) and/or as a permanent measure favouring road safety (long term objective outside the energy field).

As for the first elaboration (one objective, different time aspects), the long and short term objectives of one measure may be complementary or in conflict.

[7] Kirschen, *supra* note 1 at p. 290.
[8] Kirschen, *supra* note 1 at p. 7.

Consequently, difficulties may appear when the Government decides to repeal the measure because the short term objective has been attained, e.g. the immediate reduction of petrol consumption. In that case the long term objective can no longer be attained by the same measure and a new measure has to be approved.

This analysis illustrates the flexibility of the implementation procedure: it is not a motorway, but a network of interconnected streets. Different types of traffic wardensguide the flow. This metaphor of traffic wardens indicates that one or more authorities have to make a *choice,* or conversely, that circumstances may compel these authorities to make a specific choice. A road accident may oblige a traffic warden to indicate another road. A blocked Bill in Parliament may force the government to approve a ministerial order. This *"busy traffic"* metaphor will be corroborated in the next paragraphs, where the decision-making process is analysed and conclusions are drawn from the theoretical analysis, and particularly in the second section.

3. Energy Policy Objectives

The division of the objectives of the energy policy study is temporal. Three objectives (restriction of consumption, preservation of the pattern and level of supply and stabilisation of prices and profits) have a short term character and represent the aims of the Government in the face of supply crisis and disturbances. Five other objectives (energy saving, alteration of consumption patterns, development of nuclear energy supplies, development of nuclear energy supplies, development of other domestic energy) are pursued continuously and have a more structural character. However as illustrated by the *Campus Oil* case, short and long term objectives are sometimes connected.[9]

The temporal division of energy policy objectives in many cases avoids 'one objective – short/long term aspects' conflicts. As appears in the next paragraph relating to manpower policy the situation in this field is entirely different. Nevertheless, as illustrated by the road speed restriction example 'one measure, several objectives' conflicts are possible.

4. Manpower Policy Objectives

The division of policy objectives in the manpower policy study has a substantive character. Unlike the situation in the energy field, the objectives do not have a clear-cut temporal character. Job creation, job maintenance and manpower adjustment objectives have short term as well as long term aspects. For instance, job creation (part-time or seasonal work) combined with manpower adjustment measures (vocational training) may lead in the short and long term to the realisation of the (full) employment objective.

---

[9] In this case the European Court of Justice considered that the Irish government could place an obligation on the importers of petroleum products to purchase certain quantities of petroleum products. These quantities were not only related to the minimum supply requirements in crisis periods (short term objective), but also to the long term contracts which Ireland had entered into so that it might be assured of regular supplies (permanent objective). See Case 72/83, *Campus Oil Limited,* Judgment of 10 July 1984, *Common Market Law Review* 1984, p. 607.

The mixed character of the objectives may induce mixed instruments/measure combinations. Many collective bargaining agreements, for instance, embody job creation for young workers (subsidy schemes) and adjustment measures for elderly people (retirement measures). This analysis is confirmed by the fact that many such measures are included twice in the national inventories.

5. Temporal Character of the Objectives

The comparison between energy and manpower objectives reveals that some objectives have a temporally oriented character, whereas others follow their own substantive dynamics.[10] The presence or absence of a time element in an objective is a very important factor in the decision making process. This problem will be examined in the next section.

B. Theoretical Aspects of the Instrument and Measure Combination

An instrument is the economic means by which the objective is pursued; the measure relates to the act through which an instrument is implemented. Such acts are usually legal in that they are recognisable as formal elements of the legal order, but they need not necessarily be so.[11] A measure may have no formal legal status. An example is the gentleman's agreement between the Dutch Government and Shell/Esso concerning Groningen gas profits.[12]

In order to analyse the instrument/measure combination two different parameters will be used. The first parameter concerns the decision making process: from instrument chosen to measure in operation. The second parameter relates to the content of the instrument/measure combination itself. In this way circularity, implicit in defining instruments by reference to legal measures, can be avoided.[13]

---

[10] N. Luhmann, *Zweckbegriff und Systemrationalität*, (1973, Suhrkamp) at p. 307 observes that in a goal oriented system some subject-matters are more time-oriented than others. "Es gibt für das System mithin zeitlich plastische Umwelten, die ein hohes Maß an Zeitdisposition erlauben und andererseits Umwelten mit einer Eigendynamik, der sich das System anpassen muß, wenn überhaupt sinnvolle Kausalprozesse zwischen System und Umwelt zustandekommen sollen".

[11] Daintith, *supra* note 3 at p. 195.

[12] After the Iran revolution in 1978 the oil price increased provoking large profits for Shell and Esso, shareholders of the NAM, the concession holder of the Slochteren/Groningen gas field. Under pressure of the trade unions and some political parties, the Minister of Economic Affairs concluded a gentleman's agreement with both oil companies with respect to their investment policy. He did not follow the suggestion of the Left to cream off the profits and to use the money for employment purposes, but preferred to leave the private companies free, under the conditions contained in the agreement, to invest. This gentleman's agreement is not published, but its implications are known because the Minister of Economic Affairs is obliged to report regularly to the Second Chamber. In the Federal Republic of Germany similar gentleman's agreements on self-limitation are concluded between the Government and oil companies. See R. Oldiges, "Staatlich inspirierte Selbstbeschränkungsabkommen der Privatwirtschaft", (1973)² *Wirtschaftsrecht* at p. 1.

[13] T. Daintith, Law as a policy instrument: a comparative perspective, above at pp. 23–24.

In this part, no direct reliance will be placed upon the coding of instruments (unilateral regulation, taxation, information and so on) elaborated for this research project. The approach, which takes as its starting point coded instruments, may be essential for other studies, but it has no direct relevance to a time oriented subject-matter. Nevertheless, these instruments may have different *measure related* time horizons: unilateral regulations may have a short or long term character; subsidy measures usually have a short term character; tax systems a long term character. On the other hand, the same instruments may have different *objective related* time horizons: a long term regulation may pursue a short term objective and a short term subsidy measure may strive for a long term objective. The complexity of the time perspective of the instrument related to objectives or measures provides another argument for the introduction of time related instrument parameters. The coding of instruments applied in this research project will only be used in a complementary manner in the second part of this paper.

1. Decision Making Process Parameter

The time element is an important aspect of decision-making, i.e. the process through which instruments are effectuated. In his book *Economic policy in our time* Kirschen analyses in depth the different stages of decision-making.[14] Hopt has developed a comparable but more law-oriented step-by-step approach.[15] Their analysis will be adopted in this study because it is evident that the steps to be taken and the time needed to make an instrument/measure combination operative may influence the degree to which the objective is realised. Timing may in fact play a dominant role in dealing with conjunctural problems.

a) Recognition

The occurrence of a sudden event (Yom Kippour War 1973), a critical development (unemployment) or the gradual emergence of a new idea (new energy resources, need for vocational training) lies explicitly or implicitly at the root of decision making in economic policy. Except in the case of sudden events, the exact starting point in time is difficult to determine.

With regard to short term objectives the recognition stage is of particular importance if the decisions are provoked by the critical development of economic variables (diminishing oil stocks, lack of seasonal workers). Since sanction at this stage consists of assembling statistical information, it is generally only the Executive which intervenes. The time lag for such information will depend on the period to which statistics refer. The most important current indicators are usually

---

[14] Kirschen, *supra* note 1 at p. 265.
[15] K. J. Hopt, "Rechtssoziologische und rechtsinformatorische Aspekte im Wirtschaftsrecht", *Der Betriebsberater,* 1972 at 102. See also H. D. Assmann, Zur Steuerung gesellschaftlich-ökonomischer Entwicklung durch Recht in: Wirtschaftsrecht als Kritik des Privatrechts, Königstein/Ts. 1980, 337: "Recht ist aber auch systemintern mit einem Zeitproblem beschäftigt, wo es um die Nacheinanderschaltung bestimmter Verknüpfungen und die Herstellung und Kontrolle von Handlungsketten geht. Solche Prozeßdimensionen bilden zusammen mit den Strukturen eines Systems die Hauptanknüpfungspunkte rechtlicher Steuerung". Both Hopt and Assmann rely on Luhmann.

published periodically. An information procedure relating to special features is also possible. It may be prescribed as part of a specific measure implementing an objective. The Dutch Prices Act 1961, which confers the power to fix maximum prices for certain goods and services upon the Minister of Economic Affairs, envisages an information procedure relating to the fluctuation of prices as the first step in establishing price orders in a certain field. The UK Fuel and Electricity (Control) Act 1973 embodied a comparable scheme.

An information procedure can be the residue of an instrument/measure combination which was not adopted. The Dutch Natural Gas Prices Act 1974 confers the power to fix minimum prices for the sale of natural gas upon the Minister of Economic Affairs. The proposal to extend the power of the Minister to tariffs and the tariff structures of the local gas companies was not passed by Parliament. Only the duty of these companies to inform the Minister of their tariffs and tariff structures survived.

The recognition stage is not so important with regard to long term objectives. During the decision-making process corrections can be made and feedback mechanisms can be introduced. For instance, if the building of nuclear power stations is pursued (long term energy objective) the location of the stations themselves may be specified at the last moment.

b) Analysis

Once the subject of economic policy is recognised and the objective described, the analysis begins and the right instrument can be chosen.

Short term developments must be analysed very quickly in order to enable the right remedy to be prescribed. In general the Executive is better equipped to monitor conjunctural developments than is Parliament. Special commissions may be established, such as the Dutch National Office for Petroleum Products during the energy crisis of 1973. This office was charged, inter alia, with the preparation of schemes for the rationing of petroleum products.

Long term developments are monitored by Parliament, especially if the objectives pursued have budgetary or politically important implications. The Executive and sometimes interest groups also intervene. The nuclear energy debate in the Netherlands provides an example of the interaction between the Government, Parliament, interest groups and special bodies. This long analytical process may be useful in the realisation of long term objectives, but when it concerns the realisation of a short term objective the analysis by many different groups may be either too late or may hinder quick decision-making.

c) Design of the Instrument/Measure Combination

If the analysis indicates that intervention is necessary, measures are designed for the instrument chosen. This is the *crucial moment* of the decision-making process as examined in this study.

At this stage, the characteristics of the instrument and the measure must, as far as possible, interlock. If, for instance, the economic situation (oil crisis) requires immediate action, instruments and measures must be used which can be executed immediately. In this case a unilateral regulation which has to be translated into an

Act is not effective, as is illustrated by the fact that in many of the countries under review Ministerial orders (Italian Decree of October 6, 1973, Dutch Order of October 19, 1973) were taken to regulate the import and export of certain energy products. The instrument (unilateral short term regulation) and the measure (ministerial order) interlock with each other.[16]

The characteristics of the instrument may influence the characteristics of the measure and *vice versa*. The choice has to be made by policy-makers with an insight into legal techniques. If they choose the wrong combination, there is a risk that the process will be blocked. On the other hand, measures will obey their own legal principles which may sometimes be in harmony, sometimes be contrary to the instrument pursued. Taxation of petrol by ministerial order as a short term energy objective can be implemented very quickly, but may conflict in many countries with the budgetary powers of Parliament. The German tax law of 1964 on light heating oil illustrates this phenomenon. Although this Act has been frequently amended, Parliament reserves its power to impose taxation. France tries to adopt a middle course. Some 'taxes parafiscales' are based on a Décret authorised by Parliamentary legislation.[17] On the other hand direct taxes on the extraction of coal and crude oil are based directly on the Loi de Finances of January 18, 1980.

d) Consultation

In many matters final decisions are only taken after consulting other policy makers or interest groups. Different forms of consultation are possible, from *ad hoc* deliberations to permanent bodies. This consultation can have a highly political character such as the discussion on nuclear energy, which took place from 1981–1984 and was conducted by a Steering Group, established by the Dutch Government. In this case the consultation stage lasted more than three years before an opinion was delivered. This consultation stage is seen, by the opponents of nuclear energy, as the final objective and not as an intermediate one. Therefore they will impose as many delays and uncertainties as possible. For these opponents lengthy delays in approving sites for nuclear power plants serve no purpose other than as a stategy for killing the project.[18]

e) Parliamentary Discussion and Approval

Issues that are controversial, such as nationalisation or privatisation measures in the United Kingdom or the decision on nuclear power stations in the Netherlands, will require a long period for consultation and negotiation between interest groups, the Government and Parliament. Secondly, under the Constitution of many countries, important and politically sensitive issues are left to Parliament. Lastly Parliament plays a very important role in the budgetary procedure.

In general, changes in taxes and expenditure take a long time because Parliament wants to exercise its prerogatives. For instance, it was many months before the

[16] H. Jarass, Regulation as an instrument of economic policy, above at p. 87.
[17] *E.g.* Décret 78.903 concerning 'taxes parafiscales' on certain products, authorised by the Loi d'économie d'énergie of 1974.
[18] L. C. Thurow, *The Zero-sum Society*, (1980, London) at p. 14.

Dutch Investment Account Act 1978 was adopted. Moreover, during the parliamentary procedure the approval of the EEC Commission had to be given, because the measure was considered to be a state aid in the sense of Article 92 of the EEC Treaty.[19] When the urgency of certain measures is accepted, it is possible to shorten the timelag and reach a decision within a matter of weeks. In the Netherlands the implementation orders concerning energy allowances issued under the authority of the Investment Account Act 1978 are put into operation immediately by ministerial order and later ratified by Parliament.

Law has a function to perform on both sides of the budgetary equation. On each side, however, the purpose and result of this intervention is very different. Taxation requires legislative authority. On the spending side, a roughly parallel annual budget cycle is followed. There are, however, differences of substance. Tax laws are micro-economic in form; they specify the rules for determining the tax liability of each transaction. The appropriation side is exclusively macro-economic; there is no reference to volumes or costs per unit. In other words the Appropriation Act *in no way* reflects the important issues and divisions regarding the diversion of public expenditure. These divisions are taken by Ministers; not by Parliament.[20]

Governmental policy is sometimes hindered by the timing of the budget cycle, which involves the concentration of many important fiscal decisions in one period of the year. This means that the delay involved in conjunctural policy through fiscal measures is dependent on the particular time of the year in which the budget is adopted by Parliament. Many subsidies granted in the energy and manpower field are influenced by this cyclical procedure.

Parliament sometimes delegates its powers to the Government, or to other bodies such as the Italian *Comitato Interministeriale dei Prezzi* or the UK Manpower Services-Commission. Due to its presidential regime the French constitution confers authority directly on the Government so that many measures are taken by Décret. Very important or politically sensitive issues are however approved by legislative Act, such as the Clandestine Immigration Act 1980.

Some national legal orders have developed special mechanisms in order to overcome conflicts that may arise between the slow legislative procedure and the necessity for quick action. In Italy a *decreto-legge* permits immediate action of the Government, albeit for only a limited period unless confirmed by Parliament.[21] In Belgium, Parliamentary Acts on 'pouvoirs spéciaux et extraordinaires' enable the Government during a fixed period and for specified subject-matters to modify existant legislation and/or enact new Royal Decrees having the same legal force as

---

[19] See joint cases 91 and 127/83, *Heineken*, Judgment of the Court of Justice of the European Communities of 9 October, 1984, not yet published.

[20] T. Daintith, "The function of Law in the field of short-term economic policy", (1970) *The Law Quarterly Review*, at p. 63.

[21] Decreti-legge – These are issued by the Executive in cases of urgency and necessity but which only temporarily have the force and effect of legislation; that is, if Parliament fails to convert a decree into law within 60 days of its publication, it becomes retrospectively ineffective. See G. L. Certona, *The Italian Legal System* (1985, London) at p. 81.

parliamentary acts. These radical distortions of the division of powers between Government and Parliament are sometimes criticised as being unconstitutional.[22]

f) Execution of the Measures

Once a measure is taken, the stage of its execution begins, but it can take a long time first before an instrument chosen becomes operational and secondly, before the objective is realised.

The time lag involved in this phase may be considerable, *e.g.* the actual spending of funds voted takes time, which is needed for administrative and technical preparations. This is especially the case when special bodies are established. This type of time lag is often used to explain why in certain circumstances conjunctural measures may aggravate the situation rather than mitigate it, as the actual impact of these measures only occurs when the trade cycle has been completed.

The introduction of a new tax system or a new type of direct control takes time, because new bodies have to be created. Pending their creation, transitional measures can be taken. In the Netherlands a transitional order concerning illegal migrant workers was taken attenuating the introduction of the stringent Migrant Workers Employment Act 1978, in operation since November 1, 1979. The same problem appears when a controversial or cost inducing law is introduced, such as the Equal Pay Act. In this case the prejudices of interested parties have to be overcome before practical implementation can take place.

g) International Obligations

Many measures are taken in the implementation of international obligations. Here the process has some international elements.[23] Pursuant to these international obligations, the Member States have to adapt their legislation within a certain time. In this context it is interesting to recall the definition of a directive issued by the EEC institutions. According to Article 189 of the EEC Treaty, a directive (a Community measure) is binding as to the result to be achieved (the Community objective), upon each Member State to which it is addressed, but leaves to the national authorities the choice of forms and methods (the national instrument/ measure combination). The directive explicitly foresees a time table for implementation. In other words, during the same period different national measures will be taken in execution of the same obligation under international law. Clear examples are the IEA and EEC obligations on the stocking of petroleum products. These international law obligations were implemented in the domestic law of the UK by the Energy Act 1976, of Italy by the law of November 7, 1977, of the Netherlands by the Petroleum Products Stockpiling Act 1976, of Germany by the Energiesicherungsgesetz 1975 and of France by the Decret no. 75–67 of 1975.

---

[22] J. Sarot, "La pratique des pouvoirs spéciaux et extraordinaires avant et après 1945," in: W. J. Ganshof van der Meersch, Miscellanea (1972, Brussels) Volume III at p. 293. W. J. Ganshof van de Meersch and A. Vanwelkenhuyzen, "Les tendances actuelles de la répartition des pouvoirs législatives entre le Parlement et le Gouvernement", in: *Rapports belges au VIIIe Congrès international de droit comparé,* (1970, Brussels) at p. 555.

[23] See e.g. EEC Directive no. 75/129 on the approximation of the laws of the Member States relating to collective redundancies.

Certain national measures cannot be executed or must be repealed because of both international law obligations and those arising under European Community legislation. Many subsidies notified to the EEC Commission were ultimately not granted because the proposed aid was considered contrary to the EEC Treaty. On the other hand some existing measures, such as the UK offshore supply interest relief grants have been terminated following pressure from the EEC Commission.

h) Judicial Review

This stage was not included in Kirschen's analysis. In a legal analysis, however, it is necessary to mention judicial review.

When a measure is scrutinised by the judiciary in order to determine the substantive content, long term delays are common although interlocutory proceedings can attenuate the waiting period. In many cases the fight just begins once an objective is enacted into law. To a great extent the time delays and the uncertainty which the process creates have a more adverse effect on the economy than the regulations themselves.[24] Many cases concerning equal opportunities and equal pay, brought before national and European Courts, illustrate this.[25] This last – judicial – hurdle clearly illustrates the impact of law on economic policy.

Test case judgments sometimes "stop the clock". During the time a case is pending before the Court no decisions are taken by the Executive nor Parliament. Once the test case is solved, the pursued objective may (or may not) be realised. If the government or Parliament do not count this bottleneck in their time planning, the timely realisation of an objective may become an illusion.[26]

Sometimes courts may help governments to overcome this problem. In the second *Defrenne* case on equal pay, the Governments of Ireland and the United Kingdom drew the attention of the Court to the possible economic consequences of attributing direct effect to Article 119 of the EEC Treaty, on the ground that such a decision might, in many branches of economic life, result in the introduction of claims dating back to the time at which such effect came into existence. The Court of Justice thereupon limited the direct effect of this equal pay provision *ex nunc*, except as regards those workers who had already brought legal proceedings.[27]

---

[24] Thurow, *supra* note 18 at p. 122.
[25] *E.g.* Madame Defrenne needed to initiate three separate actions before the European Court of Justice, which took in total nearly ten years of procedure before her equal pay claim was resolved. See note 27 *infra*.
[26] Luhmann *supra* note 10 at p. 307, uses the metaphor of an avalanche: "Jede Zeitfestlegung *einer* Handlung im System, ob freiwillig oder unfreiwillig, überträgt sich als Bindung an diesen Zeitpunkt auf andere Handlungen, die mit jener zu koordinieren sind und hat dadurch einen Lawineneffekt, der bei rationaler Zeitplanung im voraus durchkalkuliert werden muß".
[27] Case 43/75, *Defrenne*, Judgment of 8 April, 1976, European Court Reports 1976, at p. 455; D. Wyatt, "Prospective effect of a holding of direct applicability," (1976) 1 *European Law Review*, at 399; W. Van Gerven, "Contribution de l'arrêt Defrenne au développement du droit communautaire", (1977) 13 *Cahiers de Droit européen*, at p. 131.

Delays can also be overcome by the establishment of dispute settlement bodies. As a rule, these bodies, manned by experts, can work in an expedient way.[28]

C. Content of Instrument Parameter

With regard to the instruments of economic policy a distinction is made by Eucken, Tinbergen and others between ordering policy (Ordnungspolitik, Dauerordnung) or qualitative economic policy on the one hand, and process policy (Ablaufspolitik, Lenkungspolitik) or quantitative policy on the other.[29] This distinction has been adapted and amended by political scientists and lawyers.[30]

Ordering policy alters the shape of the framework within which economic activity is carried on, and process policy operates in the free space within that framework. Ordering policy deals with changes in structure, such as a change in the number of taxes. It concerns what can be called 'the constitution of economic life', in particular the distribution and means of control of economic power. In a market oriented economy competition policy is a typical example of ordering policy.

Process policy relates to changes that can be brought about in the values of the instruments of economic policy. This is the least ambitious type of policy, most frequently applied and is used, in particular, to make rapid changes in policy in response to frequently changing economic indicators. Examples are adaptations in government expenditure, tax levels, discount rates and reserve ratios.

This distinction shows that political activity may have different aspects according to the part of the economic sphere which is primarily at issue. The term

---

[28] According to Article 14.3 of the GATT code on Technical Barriers to Trade, "it is the firm intention of Parties, that all disputes under this agreement shall be promptly and expediously settled, particularly in the case of perishable products." See E. Mc Govern, *International Trade Regulation*, (1982, Exeter) at p. 179.

[29] W. Eucken, *Grundsätze der Wirtschaftspolitik*, (1952, Bern/Tübingen) at pp. 254–5; Tinbergen, supra note 1 at p. 7; K. Schiller, "Wirtschaftspolitik", in: Hauptwörterbuch der Sozialwissenschaften, XII, Stuttgart 1965, p. 213; T. Pütz, Zur Typologie Wirtschaftspolitischer Systeme, Jahrbuch für Sozialwissenschaft 1964 at 140; B. De Gaay Fortman, *Theory of Competion Policy*, (1966, Amsterdam) at p. 167.

[30] Daintith, *supra* note 3 at p. 196; P. J. G. Kapteyn, "Outgrowing the Treaty of Rome: from market integration to policy integration", in: Mélanges Fernand Dehousse, (1979, Brussels) vol. 2 at p. 45. K. J. M. Mortelmans, *Ordenend en sturend beleid en economisch publiekrecht*, (1985, Deventer/Netherlands); P. Badura, "Wirtschaftsverwaltungsrecht", in: *Besonderes Verwaltungsrecht*, herausgegeben von Ingo von Münch, (1979, Berlin) at p. 246 and H. Wolff, and O. Bachof, *Verwaltungsrecht I.*, (1974, München) at p. 19 made primarily a distinction between Ordnungsverwaltung, corresponding more or less to ordering policy, Steuerungsverwaltung and Leistungsverwaltung, both corresponding more or less to process policy. This elaboration is not useful in this time oriented study. In my opinion, Ordnungsverwaltung is as a rule translated in durable legal measures and the other policies as a rule in less durable legal measures. See also R. Mayntz, *Soziologie der öffentlichen Verwaltung*, (1978, Heidelberg) at pp. 44–56.

'primarily' needs to be emphasised because economic policies may touch upon order and process at the same time.[31]

This distinction, made by economists, can be related to the scope of legal measures. It illustrates and corroborates the instrument/measure combination. The characteristics of economic policy instruments influence the characteristics of the measure. Competition policy is based on a durable unilateral regulation approved by Parliament, after consultation of social-economic interest groups; price policy is based on short term unilateral regulations taken by the Government, pursuant to enabling powers.

As a rule, ordering policy has a durable character; process policy has a less durable character. In the context of this study the durability of instruments can be related to the measure enacted.

Ordering policy instruments affect the institutional and organisational framework within which the economic process takes place. In general, ordering policy instruments result in rule making. Durable legal measures are laid down governing economic and social relations. The ordering policy measures are thus concerned with the constitution of economic life. Typical examples covered by this research are dismissal laws, equal pay and opportunities acts and competition laws.

Process policy attempts to manage, to steer the economic process itself, by determining the instrument variables. The need for flexibility and quick reaction requires that public authorities have discretionary powers; these measures are mostly taken by the Executive. They have a short term character and are not durable. Examples covered by this research project are job schemes, restriction orders, subsidies, price orders and so on.

However, some process policy measures have a durable character. These measures deal with the powers of the economic authorities to use economic instruments, such as planning legislation, subsidy framework acts, tax laws, laws creating public bodies. Unlike measures of ordering policy, such durable measures cannot be effective as such. They must be followed by other process policy measures, such as subsidy orders, tax tariff measures and orders of public bodies. In other words, *two-level measures* are needed to make an instrument operative. This phenomenon will be examined at the end of this paper.

Concluding this section, Table 1 gives a schematic view of the place of the objectives and of the two parameters dealing with the instrument/measure combination in a temporal perspective. In the next section this schematic view will be used in order to analyse national measures, examined in the national reports on energy and manpower.

[31] De Gaay Fortman, *supra* note 29 at p. 167.

Table 1: Economic Policy

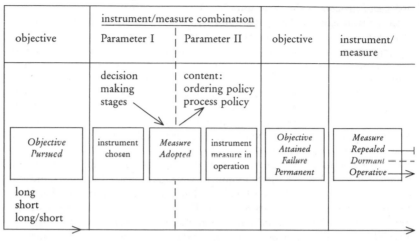

objective	instrument/measure combination		objective	instrument/measure
	Parameter I	Parameter II		
	decision making stages	content: ordering policy process policy		
Objective Pursued	instrument chosen	*Measure Adopted*	instrument measure in operation	*Objective Attained Failure Permanent*	*Measure Repealed —| Dormant — ‑ ‑ Operative —>*
long short long/short				

Time Scale

III. Practical Aspects of the Instrument / Measure Combination

The decision-making model analysed as the first parameter has an ideal-typical character. Only in exceptional cases are the objectives adopted in a coherent way. An example of such an ideal procedure is given in Table 2. As part of the first French National Employment Act the Youth Employment Act no. 77–704 of 5 July 5, 1977 was adopted and extended to new categories, especially women, by the Youth and Women Employment Act no. 78–698 of July 6, 1978.

Table 2: The French Youth Employment Acts 1977–1978

objective	instrument/measure		objective	instrument/measure
Employment short long term	tax exemption	social contribution exemptions	short long term attained??	1) Act of 1977 expired
	Youth Employment Act 1977 no. 77.704			
	quick decision-making	process policy		2) Act of 1978 no. 78–698

Time Scale

The decision making process concerning economic policy instruments and measures in many cases does not follow the chronological path from objective pursued to objective attained without obstacles. Two examples illustrate this.

A. The UK Speed Limits Order 1973

The UK Fuel Control (Modification of Enactment) Speed Limits Order of 1973 extends the powers of the Secretary of State under the Road Traffic Regulation Act 1967 to impose temporary speed limits on the road, so that the power is exercisable in the interest of regulating the use of motor fuel. In this case, the objective is clearly formulated (short term objective), the instrument chosen (unilateral regulation) and the measure adopted quickly because the enabling law was set in operation.This example is illustrated in Table 3.

Comparing Tables 2 and 3 some differences emerge. First, in Table 3, a process policy measure is invoked (Fuel and Energy [Control] Act 1973) enabling the promulgation of another process policy measure (Speed Limits Order 1973). The 1973 Act was a response to emergency and had an initial validity of only one year. In Table 2a process policy measure was adopted with a limited validity (Loi no. 77.704 of 5 July 1977), followed the year after by a comparable measure (Loi no. 78.698 of 6 July 1978). Secondly, in the example outlined in Table 3 two-level measures (legislation and an order) pursue a short term objective whereas in Table 2 single-level measures (legislation) are adopted from time to time in order to pursue mixed objectives (short and long term).

B. The Dutch Nuclear Power Stations Debate

In 1974 the Dutch Government issued a policy statement to the effect that it intended to build three nuclear power stations. Due to parliamentary opposition and civil resistance, the Government did not implement this policy objective but, in order to appease the opposition, proposed in 1978 a Social Discussion on Energy. A Steering Group was established by Royal Decree of 1981. The discussion lasted more than three years. In the meantime no decisions were taken. In this case the objective was clearly formulated (long term energy objective): the instrument was in preparation, but no measure was adopted. Another instrument and another measure were taken instead (Table 4).

This Dutch example illustrates that the original objective (building of nuclear power stations) is pursued via a detour. The main road was temporarily blocked and via another route the original instrument/measure combination was able to re-enter into the right track (U-turn model).

C. "Busy Traffic Situation"

These examples indicate that the Tinbergen approach of coherent policy making, according to a harmonious end and means model, does not always work in practice. This conclusion, drawn from the national inventories, is confirmed by developments in the European Community and other international organisations.

The EEC Treaty embodies various objectives, which are difficult to pursue in a

Table 3: The UK Speed Limits Order 1973

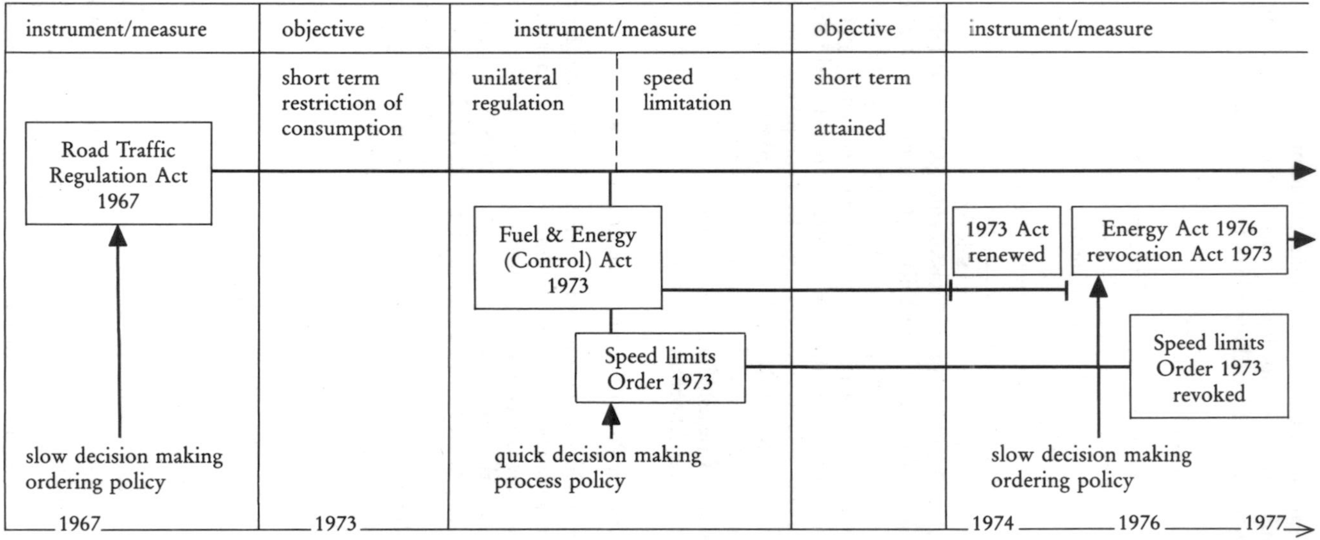

Time Scale

Table 4: The Dutch Nuclear Power Station Debate

objective	instrument/measure	objective	instrument/measure	objective	instrument/measure	objective	instrument/measure
long term alteration of energy supply 1974 8 power stations	in preparation (unilateral regulation) decision-making stopped 1975–77	short term social discussion 1978	information procedure / steering group 1981	information gathered 1984	steering group dissolved 1984	at least 2 power stations end 1984	white paper under examination

Time Scale

harmonious way.[32] Objectives may conflict,[33] objectives are taken for instruments and overt objectives can conceal implicit ones.[34] In order to ensure that objectives were not taken for instruments and vice-versa, economic lawyers introduced the objective-instrument conception (Ziel-Mittel-Konzeption).[35] This objective-instrument relationship leads, in the hand of an active Court, to a teleological method of filling gaps.[36] The European Court of Justice based some landmark judgments on this approach.[37] Moreover in the absence of measures the Courts may fill up provisional lacunae in order to realise objectives.[38]

[32] In case 5/73, *Balkan-Import*, Judgment of 20 October, 1973, European Court Reports 1973, p. 1091, the various objectives of the common agricultural policy, contained in article 39 of the EEC Treaty, were analysed. The Court considered that: "In pursuing these objectives, the Community Institutions must secure the permanent harmonization made necessary by any conflicts between these aims taken individually and, where necessary, allow any one of them temporary priority in order to satisfy the demands of the economic factors or conditions in view of which their decisions are made".

[33] A typical example of conflicting objectives is contained in Article XXIV paragraph 4 of the GATT Agreement, relating to customs unions being excepted from the view that the objectives expressed in this provision (closer integration between the countries parties to such customs unions, while not raising barriers to trade of other contracting parties with such territories) can never be completely reconciled. Much of the increased trade, brought about between the countries involved in economic integration, is likely to be the result of diversion from the trade previously maintained with non-members. See McGovern, *supra* note 28 at p. 203.

[34] *E.g.* A harmonious development of economic activities, one of the objectives of the EEC Treaty, was interpreted by the Community institutions as enabling a common environmental policy. See H. von der Groeben, H. von Boeckh, J. Thiesing, and C. D. Ehlermann, Kommentar zum EWG-Vertrag, (1983, Baden-Baden), volume II, at p. 1610.

[35] N. L. Brown, and F. G. Jacobs, *The Court of Justice of the European Communities*, (1983, London) at p. 256; K. J. Hopt, *supra note* 15 at p. 1020; Assmann, *supra* note 15 at p. 291.

[36] P. Pescatore, "Les objectifs de la Communauté européenne comme principes d'interprétation de la jurisprudence de la Cour de Justice." W. J. Ganshof van der Meersch, in *Miscellanea* (1982, Brussels) vol. 2 at p. 325; See H. H. Hollmann, *Rechtsstaatliche Kontrolle der Globalsteuerung*, (1980, Baden-Baden) at p. 112.

[37.] In case 6/72, *Continental Can*, Judgment of 21 February 1973, European Court Reports, 1973, p. 215 the Court considered that the spirit, general scheme and the wording of Art. 86 of the EEC Treaty as well as the system and objectives of the EEC Treaty must all be taken into account in order to decide if Art. 86 permits a control of mergers of undertakings.

[38] K. J. M. Mortelmans, "Les lacunes provisoires en droit communautaire," *Cahiers de droit européen* (1981, Brussels) at 410. See case 804/79, Commission v United Kingdom, Judgment of 5 May 1981, European Court Reports 1981, p. 1045: "Thus, in a situation characterized by the inaction of the Council and by the maintenance, in principle, of the interim conservation measures in force at the expiration of the period laid down in Article 102 of the Act of Accession, the Decision of 25 June 1979 and the parallel decisions, as well as the requirements inherent in the safeguard by the Community of the common interest and the integrity of its own powers, imposed upon Member States not only an obligation to undertake detailed consultations with the Commission and to seek its

A fortcoming general election may also disturb coherent decision-making. The political calendar can create a great temptation to approve legislation that in the short run might be popular, even if it is inimical to the longer-run economic vitality of a country.[39]

In summary, the temporal relationship between objectives, instruments and measures is complicated. Tinbergen's critics argue that policy is a resultant of decisions rather than one decision.[40] Economic policy decision making is not a logical and coherent process, but a fragmented one. Different bodies ("traffic wardens") intervene at different moments. Feedback is necessary, time related reasons can have priority over substantive arguments[41] and failure in certain cases is inevitable.

It is not surprising, that Kirschen has refined Tinbergen's model.[42] He states that in actual policy-making the described process is not always divided into six stages (recognition, analysis, designing of the measures, consultation, parliamentary discussion and execution). The following interruptions or complications may occur:

(a) The order of the stages is sometimes changed. Consultation may take place before the designing of measures.

(b) Two stages often overlap. In the case of long term objectives the recognition and analysis stages are often merged: initial information having given rise to analysis, the analysis itself may lead to recognition of other relevant information (feedback).

(c) Not all measures have to pass through all stages. Sometimes an act is adopted, sometimes a ministerial order, sometimes both.

(d) The decision-making process sometimes reverts to a preceding phase. As a result of consultation the design of measures may have to be reworked.

(e) The process may be interrupted by outside events, such as changes of government.

Baldwin and Hawkins have made comparable remarks on the nature of legal decision-making. They argue that lawyers and legal scholars have often fallen into the trap of employing a limited conception of decision-making that does violence to the inherent complexity of decisions which are made in a wide variety of legal settings. One result of this is a tendency to see a 'decision' at a particular point in the legal process as an isolated matter, as something logically separable from what

approval in good faith, but also a duty not to lay down national conservation measures in spite of objections, reservations or conditions which might be formulated by the Commission".

[39] E. R. Tufte, *Political control of the Economy*, (1978, New Jersey), at pp. 147–8.

[40] Ch. E. Lindblom, "Tinbergen on policy-making", (1958) 66 *Journal of Political Economy*, at p. 531.

[41] Luhmann, *supra* note 10 at 310: "Eine andere Folge programmierter Zeitplanung liegt in der Verzerrung der Präferenzen, die durch die Vordringlichkeit des Befristeten ausgelost wird. Wenn immer diejenige Handlung vorgenommen werden muß, deren Termin bevorsteht, verliert im Gedränge der Termine die sachliche Wertordnung des Systems an Bedeutung".

[42] Kirschen, *supra* note 1, p. 273.

surrounds it in the processing of cases. This conception in turn tends to lead to a particular view about the control of discretionary powers. Decisions, in short, are seen as simple, discrete and unproblematic as opposed to complex, subtle and woven into a broader process.[43]

This analysis of legal as well as political-economic decision making illustrates the flexibility of the whole process: not a one-track and one-way road, but a network of interconnected streets and motorways, where it is useful to use a *roadmap* in order to relate the time element of the objectives with the time element in the measure. This classification will be examined in the next section.

IV. Classification of the Measures

Both parameters, the first dealing with the decision making process and the second with ordering or process policy, form a useful starting point to classify the measures in a temporal perspective. Five possibilities will be examined.

A. Different Kinds of Measures

1) Long Term Measures
decision making: Executive and Parliament
content: ordering policy

2) Short Term Measures
decision making: Executive (or Parliament)
content: process policy

3) Cyclical Measures
decision making: Executive and/or Parliament
content: process policy

4) Two-level Measures
decision making: (i) Executive and Parliament
                            (ii) Executive
content: (i) process policy/ordering policy
             (ii) process policy/ordering policy

5) Deficient Measures
decision making: blocked
content: – – – –

This classification is used for analytical purposes only. It is clear that one

---

[43] R. Baldwin and K. Hawkins, "Discretionary justice. Davis reconsidered", (1984) *Public Law* at p. 580. See also Hopt, *supra* note 15 at p. 1020 and Assmann, *supra* note 15 at p. 336: "In der zeitlichen Dimension geht es um die Synchronisation verschiedener Zeitebenen bei der Steuerung ökonomischer Prozesse und Überbrückung von Diskontinuitäten in der Entwicklung ausdifferenzierter Systeme. Dies setzt hohe Variabilität des Rechts voraus; andererseits besteht im Recht die Gefahr des Konsistenzverlustes, also der Schaffung von Diskontinuität".

measure can embody short term, long term and two level elements. A Price Act, for example, can contain a short term crisis management system, a permanent working information scheme and enabling powers in order to adopt price orders.

B. Characteristics of the Measures

The classification will be put into practice in the next part of the paper dealing with the relationship between objectives and the choice of instruments and measures, but first the characteristics of each category of measures will be elaborated.[44]

1) Long Term Measures

Long term measures can be defined as measures adopted for a period going beyond a date which is already known, such as the mandate of a government. In the end, long term measures have a permanent character. These measures strive for continuity and legal security. They have a general scope because they do not only aim to give an answer for a present day or known situation, but also for the yet unknown future. Examples are anti-discrimination laws and competition laws. From an examination of their content it is clear that they try to attain ordering policy objectives. Long term measures are approved in a decision making process in which both the Executive and the Parliament intervene.

2) Short Term Measures

Short term measures can be defined as measures adopted for a certain period or as a quick response to sudden events. They do not have a permanent character, and by "legal fiction" they even can have an effect on past situations (retroactivity) or existing situations ("application immédiate").[45] These measures, endowing the Executive with discretionary powers, are specific and flexible because they aim to provide a solution to an existing problem or a response to sudden events. Examples are crisis management measures, subsidies, Central Bank intervention, price measures. They have a process policy character and are adopted as a rule by the Executive or other public bodies.

In many countries the Central Bank operates quietly and selectively in a free space without legal coercion. No hard and fast rules limit the powers of the

---

[44] The characteristics of ordering policy and process policy measures are analysed by Kapteyn, *supra* note 30 at pp. 45–6; E. U. Petersmann, "International Theory and International Economic Law", in: *The structure and process of international law, Essays in legal philosophy, doctrine and theory*, (1983, The Hague) at 230, Mortelmans, *supra* note 30.

[45] P. Delvolvé, "Le principe de non-rétroactivité dans la jurisprudence du Conseil d'Etat", in: Mélanges offerts à Marcel Waline, (1974, Paris) volume 2, at p. 361: "L'éfficacité d'une décision économique est souvent liée à son application immédiate: pour enrayer une hausse des prix, arrêter une perte de devises, relancer l'activité, les mesures prises doivent agir rapidement. En cas de crise, l'urgence en impose la mise en œuvre instantanée. Sans doute des politiques à long terme ont-elles des effects plus profonds, mais aussi plus lents; en attendant qu'ils s'accomplissent, l'administration est incitée à arrêter des dispositions immédiates, applicables à toutes les situations, même constituées dans le cadre de dispositions antérieures".

monetary authorities. The central banks regularly issue recommendations. In Belgium "les pouvoirs de fait" of the Banque Nationale have been consolidated in 1973 by "des pouvoirs de droit". In the Netherlands, gentleman's agreements are concluded but the Bank Law of 1948 foresees a "stick behind the door"-procedure in case the consultation procedure between the Central Bank and the Minister of Finance is unsuccesful.[46] Hard law is, in the words of a Bank of England official responsible for the supervision of the banking system, not suitable as a basis for day to day continuing supervision.[47]

3) Cyclical Measures

Cyclical measures are adopted at intervals, following a previously known (budget cycle) or afterwards perceived (supply crisis) pattern. They can be of an ultra short (open market operations of the Central Bank), short (budget) or long term (planning) character. Regularity is important and not permanency, as is the case of long term measures of flexibility for short term measures. The cyclical measures have a process policy character and are adopted by Parliament and/or the Executive.

4) Two-level Measures

Due to political evolution (role of the Parliament in economic affairs) and for practical reasons (flexibility of governmental action, opposed to the parliamentary procedures), many economic policy objectives are pursued via a two-level approach. Two trends can be discerned (Table 5).

a) First Type

Under the first type principles, sanctions and enabling powers are laid down in an Act having a durable character. The effective or more concrete measures are taken afterwards by the Executive, pursuant to enabling powers. These orders, giving the Executive discretionary powers within the framework set out by the Act itself, have a process policy character.[48] An example is subsidy legislation, leading to specific implementation orders. The basic principles, e.g. concerning the relationship of the aid scheme with the economic policy, dealing with transparency, parliamentary control, are incorporated in the Act itself, whereas the implementation orders fix the amount of the aid and formulate specific conditions. This type is in a certain way a combination of the long term (a) and short term (b) categories. The first level of this type has a long term character and the second level a short term character. But, whereas many long or short term measures work effectively

---

[46] Daintith, *supra* note 20 at pp. 72–75; *Aspects juridiques de l'intervention des pouvoirs publics dans la vie économique.* Brussels 1976, pp. 255–6. *La politique monétaire dans les pays de la CEE, Comité Monétaire,* (1972, Brussels) at p. 285.

[47] Statement quoted by Daintith, *supra* note 20 at p. 74.

[48] E.g. the German Employment Act of 3 June, 1982, dealing with fiscal and other measures for jobs, growth and stability. This Act grants investment aid according to the watering can principle (Gieskannenprinzip). The aid has a not specific character, is widely distributed and does not pursue regional or structural aims. See G. Nicolaysen, in: *Community order and national economic policies,* (1984, Deventer/Netherlands) at p. 90.

Table 5: Two-level measures in the field of state aids

First type

Decision Making Procedure				Judicial Review
first level	Act:	principles	organisation procedure	enabling powers	a) control of principles (e.g. transparency) contained in Act
second level	Implementation Order:	– amount A is granted to undertaking B by minister or Commission C – C has to respect the principles, conditions contained in the Act			AND b) control of general principles of good administration e.g. – proportionality – vested rights

Second type "carte blanche"

Decision Making Procedure				Judicial Review
first level	(Budget) Act:	——	organisation procedure	enabling powers	a) control of general principles of good administration e.g. – proportionality – vested rights
second level	Implementation Order:	– amount A is granted to undertaking B by minister or Commission C – C has wide discretionary powers			OR b) no control at all

without governmental or parliamentary intervention, such as non-discrimination law (long term) or open market operations by the Central Bank (short term), these two-level measures only become effective in combination.

Under the UK Industry Act 1981, the Secretary of State for Industry may make such grants or loans to any body he considers appropriate for the purpose of assisting in the encouragement of young persons and others to take up careers in industry, or in any part of industry, and to pursue appropriate educational courses. The bodies in question must be established by Royal Charter and their members appointed by the Secretary of State.

This two level approach can also work in order to implement ordering policy measures. In many fields Parliament defines the general principles and leaves it to the executive to adopt specific orders or exceptions to these rules. In the UK the Immigration Act 1971 restricts the right of many non-patrials to accept and change employment, but EEC citizens are exempt. This exemption is contained in the Immigration (Revocation of Employment Restrictions) Order 1972. In the Netherlands the activities of self-employed persons in manufacturing are governed by the law on the Establishment of undertaking of 1954, but special conditions on the skill of the trade concerned as well as exemption provisions are contained in Royal Decrees.[49]

b) Second Type

The second type of combination ("carte blanche" measures) has a less elaborate character. The first level measures relate to the powers given by the Parliament to the Executive, or to the establishment of public bodies. The legal status of undertakings and citizens is not influenced directly by this type of measures. Examples are the UK Employment and Training Act 1973 creating the Manpower Services Commission or the Dutch Rationing Act 1939 enabling ministers or local authorities to take emergency measures in crisis situations. In this case, it is up to the Executive to develop and to respect general principles of good administrative behaviour (proportionality, "confiance légitime").

Viewed from the perspective of the division of powers, the Executive has much greater power under the second type. With regard to judicial remedies the judicial control is as rule more extensive in the first type, because the basic principles of the enabling act have to be respected. The behaviour of individual citizen and the Executive is conditioned by principles and guidelines ("signposts") and if the Executive abuses its discretionary powers the Courts may sanction this illegality or render a decision of the Executive inapplicable.[50]

---

[49] In this context see case 115/78, *Knoors,* Judgment of 7 February 1979, European Court Reports 1979, p. 399.

[50] A recent Belgian case illustrates this. Comm. Bruxelles (réf), 20 November 1984, *Etat belge, région bruxelloise c. Société Nationale d'Investissement,* Journal des Tribunaux, 1984, p. 726. "L'article 75 § 1 de la loi (des réformes économiques et budgetaires) du 5 août 1978 n'autorise des aides, autres que celles des lois d'éxpansion économique, qu'aux entreprises en difficulté; la décision de consentir une avance récupérable de 53.000.000 de FB à une entreprise qui n'est pas en difficulté est manifestement contraire à cette disposition". Consequently the aid could not be granted.

c) Deficient Measures

It is useful to include this category as a reminder, in this study, because, as previously stated, not every objective-instrument process leads to (legal) measures. In example is the Dutch nuclear power stations debate. The objective was circumscribed in 1974, the instrument chosen in 1975–1977, but up to now no measures have been taken (see Table 4).

V. Short and Long Term Policy Objectives Related to the Choice of Instruments and Measures

In this section we attempt, in a tentative way,[51] to relate the time element of the objectives to the time element in the measures. The starting point is the classification of the measures mentioned at the end of the preceding section. Each category (long term, short term, cyclical, two level and deficient measures) will be examined in order to determine whether the time element in the measure is appropriate to pursue short term, long term or mixed objectives. At the same time some indication will be given of the kind of instruments used.

A. Long Term Measures

This category concerns measures prepared by the Executive and, as a rule, approved by Parliament. The instrument chosen is in many cases a unilateral regulation. The measures concerned usually have an ordering policy character. They protect certain groups (workers, women, disabled people), they prohibit certain activities (illegal migration) or restrict other activities (energy consumption, energy importation).

Long term measures are appropriate for the realisation of *long term objectives.* Some Acts mentioned in this research project were already in operation before the period under review (1973–1982), such as the UK Disabled Persons (Employment) Act 1944, the Dutch Extraordinary Decree on Labour Relations 1945. Other Acts were adopted in the 1970s, such as the French Disabled Persons Act 1975, or the Italian Act on the location of nuclear power stations 1975.

A good example of long term measures which are suitable as an instrument of realising long term objectives is provided by measures taken pursuant to the timetable foreseen in Article 8 of the EEC Treaty. According to this provision the Common Market was to be progressively established during a transitional period of twelve years (1958–1970). This transitional period was divided into three stages of four years each. Transition from one to another stage was conditioned upon a finding by the EEC Council that the objectives specifically laid down had in part been attained. Consequently, at the end of 1969 a number of Treaty Articles, e.g. relating to the free movement of persons and goods, became self-executing and could be invoked before national courts.[52] In other words, as the objective was

---

[51] On the adequacy of the inventory data for this purpose, see above, at p. 286.

[52] In case 2/74, *Reyners,* Judgment of 21 June, 1974, European Court Reports 1974, p. 631, the Court ruled that, though the basic Community rule on freedom of establishment of

attained, the instrument-measure combination (durable unilateral regulation of governmental activity) became operative from a legal point of view. Due to the progressive case law of the Court of Justice of the European Communities law and economic policy go hand in hand.

The adoption of long term measures to be approved by Parliament is not very suitable as a means of realising *short term objectives*. The Dutch Petroleum Products Stockpiling Act 1976, submitted to parliament in 1971, was adopted too late to be useful in the aftermath of the energy crisis in 1973. However, it was used in the second oil crisis 1977–78. In other words, long term measures are only operable for short term objectives if the measure, in general legislation, is adopted in time. Policy makers and law makers have to be able to anticipate. If not, the measure is not operable, but is available later on. This anticipation mechanism leads frequently to two level measures. However, anticipation is not necessary if "decret-to-legge" or "pouvoirs spéciaux" procedures are available. Italy has used this procedure frequently in the energy field, whereas other countries relied on two-level measures. In Belgium the EEC rules and equal pay, implemented in a Royal Decree of 24 October 1967, were approved very quickly.[53]

Long term measures are appropriate for the realisation of *mixed objectives*, such as road speed limitations (short term restriction of consumption and long term energy conservation) and many manpower objectives (equal opportunities, migrant workers). However, when the Government or Parliament decides to repeal a Decree or an Act because it considers the short term objective attained, the long term objective cannot be attained on the basis of the same measure either. So from a legal-technical point of view it is better to draw up two different sections within one Act or Decree. The UK Employment and Training provided in a separate section for regulations concerning Industrial Training Boards (ITBs). As certain elements within the Conservative Party called for the dismantling of the ITB's, the Employment and Training Act 1981–82 now governs the amended ITB's. The MSC, however, is still governed by the 1973 Act.

Article 52 of the Treaty refers to the enactment of directives by the Council, Article 8 paragraph 7 of the Treaty rendered self-executing the mandate of Article 52 that freedom of establishment be secured, at least to the extent that no implementing measures were necessary to give effect to the national treatment requirement. See Hans Smit and Peter Herzog, *The Law of the European Economic Community*. New York, loose leaf edition, Article 8, I, 73. On the other hand, the timetable foreseen in the Resolution of 22 March, 1971, (O. J. 1971 C 28) on the gradual establishment of an Economic and Monetary Union was not respected. As a result of the deadlock in Community integration two-or-multi-tier integration is envisaged. On the basis of objectives agreed upon by all Member States, some Member States which are able to progress have a duty to forge ahead. Those Member States which have reasons for not progressing will refrain for a definite or indefinite period of time. See European Union, Report by Léo Tindemans to the European Council, Bull. E. C. Suppl. 1/76, p. 20–1; C. Ehlermann, "How flexible is Community law? An unusual approach to the concept of "two-speeds" (1984) *Michigan Law Review* at p. 1201.

[53] G. Piquet, "L'exercise des pouvoirs spéciaux en 1967", (1967) *Revue de jurisprudence du droit administratif et du Conseil d'Etat*, at p. 271.

B. Short Term Measures

This category deals with measures enacted in general by the Executive which possesses broad discretionary powers for rapid action. No, or only short term, consultations are needed and the Parliament rarely intervenes. These measures have a process policy character. They are to the temporary advantage of certain groups in order to restore a lost equilibrum, they can help with teething problems or they can try to remedy unforeseen situations.

The commonly used instruments are unilateral regulations. Subsidies or other public benefits can be given by a minister under his general competences and as far as budgetary means are available, or by another institution (Manpower Services Commission). The instrument of public sector management may also be embodied in short term measures, especially in centrally planned economies. In Hungary the Minister of Finance approves decrees granting each year aid to enterprises which employ workers whose working capacity has changed.

Short term measures are suitable for the realisation of *short term objectives*. The volatility, and susceptibility to frequent change, of economic policy data fits well with unilateral regulations. Subsidies and other public benefits are only suitable for the realisation of short term objectives under certain conditions. These subsidies must be granted for specific ends; *e.g.* "pump priming" purposes, infant industry reasons. In these cases short term objectives and long term ones go hand in hand. A continuing activity (a new industry) is desired, but it is envisaged that a measure to promote it needs to operate only for a short term, after which market forces can take over. Apart from these special situations subsidies are not very appropriate for the realisation of short term objectives: the granting of subsidies depends for its effect on attracting the voluntary co-operation of those concerned which generally takes time. Furthermore subsidies have to be applied for and granted.[54] With long term objectives on the other hand this problem of time is less important.[55]

Short term measures are sometimes favoured in order to realise experiments, such as the Italian regional incentives of 1981 for the exploitation of solar energy and the Dutch urban heating subsidies of 1982. If the experiment is successful, a more permanent scheme may be introduced.[56]

Long term objectives and short term measures may in some circumstances be associated. The alteration of energy consumption patterns or the development of nuclear energy as a rule cannot be realised appropriately by short term measures.

If subsidies are granted for the realisation of long term objectives undertakings receiving them run the risk that this long term objective will not be realised because of a non-approved budget or a change of policy. A general aid scheme incorporated in legislation can in such circumstances give greater legal certainty.

---

[54] J. Hucke, "Implementation von Finanzhilfeprogrammen", in: R. Mayntz (ed.), *Implementation politischer Programme*, (1983, Königstein), Volume II at p. 89.

[55] Jarass, *supra* note 16 at pp. 84–85 D. Von Stebut, Subsidies as an instrument of economic policy, above at pp. 143–144.

[56] Bercusson, *supra* note 5 at pp. 407–408.

For example, the schemes to improve insulation in private homes by way of local authority grants are based on the UK Homes Insulation Act 1978. In these cases, the measures usually fall within the two-level or cyclical measures category.

Short term measures can be helpful as a transitional effort for the realisation of long term objectives. By law Decree no. 4 of 1981 the Hungarian Labour Code was amended and the working week reduced to 42 hours (long term objective, long term measure, ordering policy). A resolution of the Government also adopted in 1981 gave detailed rules concerning the introduction of this Act. This transitional measure did not use the subsidy instrument, but embodied unilateral (but temporarily limited) regulations of private activity.

Another way to reconcile long term objectives with short term measures is possible through sunset legislation.[57] In this case, Parliament or the Government evaluates an Act or Decree after a fixed period of time. This evaluation may lead to new and more effective measures because ineffective measures disappear without renewed parliamentary approval. On the other hand this procedure puts permanent pressure on the legislature: periodical renewal of sunset legislation but without substantive modifications becomes attractive for a parliament in time of trouble and legal inflation ensues. At the same time, the legal quality of this temporary legislation risks being inferior, because in the case of time-limited legislation Parliament does not strive for legal perfection.[58]

Mixed objectives can be realised by short term measures. This phenomenon frequently occurs in manpower policy. Youth employment and employment of other vulnerable groups (women, migrants, elderly people) are in many countries pursued by short term measures, such as vocational training facilities, or retirement premiums. These incentives have merely a short term character. This can partly be explained by the fact that Governments often consider these people as target groups only if extra money is available and if social attitudes tend towards a progressive social policy. In stagnation and crisis periods these groups are the first to be abandoned, so no permanent solutions (long term measures) are adopted.

C. Cyclical Measures

This category concerns measures with a regular or cyclical character. The instruments used are unilateral regulation, information, public sector management, subsidies related to the annually approved budget. The measures adopted take

[57] The national inventories do not give an example of this technique. The EEC Council Regulation no. 2176/84 of 23 July, 1984, on protection against dumped or subsidised imports from countries not members of the EEC, O. J. 1984 L 201/14, illustrates this phenomenon. According to Article 15 anti-dumping or countervailing duties on undertakings shall lapse after five years from the date on which they entered into force or were last modified or confirmed. The Commission shall normally, after consultation and within six months prior to the end of the five year period, publish in the Official Journal of the European Communities a notice of the impending expiry of the measure in question and inform the Community industry known to be concerned.

[58] See Harald Kindermann, "Entwicklungsgrad legistischer Richtlinien des deutschen Sprachraums," in: *Methodik der Gesetzgebung.* (1982, Wien) at p. 222.

different forms such as budget laws, planning laws, private agreements, administrative orders. These measures have a process policy character. They try to respond to periodic events such as commodity price fluctuations, seasonal labour, or they depend on the approval of regularly adopted Acts (budget).

Long term objectives can be realised by cyclical measures if the objective can be attained by repetitive (information and public sector management), gradual (first, research grants for new energy technology; then, development of the project; lastly, construction of a plant) or coherent (planning) processes. The planning approach is favoured by centrally oriented economies such as Hungary and to a lesser extent by France. Many measures have a cyclical character such as the five-year planning system, the yearly approved Hungarian orders of the President of the National Price and Material Office on trade restrictions, or the implementing measures of the French "Pacte national d'emploi".

Short term objectives and cyclical measures fit together only in a limited way. A recurring short term objective, e.g. occasional labour, can be pursued by cyclical measures. Short term measures are preferable when short term objectives have an unforeseen and sudden character, as illustrated by many ministerial orders approved in different countries during the energy crisis of 1973.

Mixed objectives and cyclical measures go hand in hand. Many collective bargaining agreements have short term elements (price compensation, extra leave) as well as long term elements (early retirement schemes, apprenticeship places, working hours). Budget and planning laws also strive for the realisation of mixed objectives.

D. Two-Level Measures

Frequently two different kinds of measures are adopted in order to realise one objective. This two-level approach tries to reconcile the economic policy powers of the Executive with the supervising legislative and budgetary powers of Parliament. By adopting long term legislation Parliament defines the objective, circumscribes the principle and delegates power to the Executive, while the Executive regularly or occasionally tries to cope with the more day to day situations. Frequently the two-level approach embodies the unilateral regulation of private activity. For example, in the UK Energy Act 1976 Parliament defined energy conservation principles and delegated powers to the Secretary of State. Consequently the Secretary of State for Energy adopted orders in this field such as the Passenger Car Fuel Consumption Order 1977. A permanent information procedure and/or public sector management may complete this overall policy.

Two-level measures are not very suitable for the realisation of *short term objectives*. They have the same inconveniences as the long term measures. The approval of the first-level Act takes too much time to enable the objective to be quickly realised. However, once the enabling measure is available, short term response by way of effective administrative measures becomes possible. The UK Energy Conservation Bill 1974, leading to the Energy Act 1976, came too late to be effective in the aftermath of the energy crisis of 1973, but was used regularly in 1976 and 1977 to adopt short term energy orders.

Another procedure can be followed. If sudden events occur, such as an oil crisis, the Executive, in order to cope with an emergency situation, can take refuge in existing enabling laws delegating broad and generally described powers to the Executive (second type of the two level measures). For instance, during the oil crisis in 1973 the Dutch Government chose the Rationing Act 1939 as an enabling measure for short term crisis management measures. In other words, the petroleum boycot in 1973 of the Netherlands by Arab countries and its consequences were considered the cause of a scarcity situation within the meaning of that Act.

The same approach was adopted in the UK where the 1973 oil crisis was managed partly by the enabling emergency laws which originated in wartime regulations.[59] If decision-makers interpret their discretionary powers too widely, the Court may have to adopt a compliant attitude to avoid the annulment of the second-level measure. An example illustrates this. As a result of the increasing influx of foreign currency and short-term speculative capital in the early months of 1971, the Council of Ministers of the EC decided that the measures to be taken immediately should consist in the introduction of a system of compensatory amounts. Consequently the Council adopted a Regulation pursuant to Art 103 of the EEC Treaty which deals with conjunctural policy. The Court of Justice considered that Article 103 was not an appropriate legal basis; but it nevertheless upheld the decision taken by the Council.[60] This Regulation, intended as a process policy answer to a monetary crisis, is still in force. *Ce n'est que le provisoire qui dure!*

Mixed and long term objectives can be attained by two level measures. Automatic instruments such as taxation (or relaxation of taxation) are very appropriate. Once the enabling tax law is set in motion, it works continuously without any discretionary element and without any time lag. The Hungarian

---

[59] Daintith, *supra* note 20 at p. 74, mentions that the United Kingdom Government regulated the minimum rental period for television sets pursuant to the Emergency law (Re-enactments and Repeals) Act, which has its origin in wartime defence regulations.

[60] In case 9/73, *Schluter,* Judgment of 24 October 1973, European Court Reports, 1973, p. 1151, the Court of Justice considered that Article 103 of the EEC Treaty, relating to conjunctural policy, was not an appropriate legal basis to adopt a Regulation on monetary compensatory amounts. The Court considered that the powers contained in Articles 40–43 of the EEC Treaty "conferred for implementing the common agricultural policy do not relate merely to possible *structural* measures but extend equally to any immediate *short term* economic intervention required in this area of production, and that the Council is empowered to resort to them in accordance with the decision-making procedures there set out. However, owing to the time needed to give effect to the procedures laid down in Articles 40 and 43, a certain amount of trade might then have passed free of the Regulations, and this could jeopardize the relevant common organisations of the market". The Court concluded that: "there being no adequate provision in the common agricultural policy for adoption of the *urgent measures necessary to counteract the monetary situation described above, it is reasonable to suppose that the Council was justified in making interim use* of the powers conferred on it by Article 103 of the Treaty". (author's italics added).

Decree of the Minister of Finance of November 1982, which confers tax reductions to undertakings employing home workers, illustrates this mechanism. Other instruments such as conditional subsidies or permissions to be delivered require active intervention by the Executive. For example, the UK Secretary of State for Energy approves, under the Energy Act 1976, proposals concerning the use of coal in energy generating plants.

As for long term measures, the realisation of mixed objectives by way of a two-level approach may cause problems in implementation. If Parliament repeals an Act because it considers that the short term objectives have been attained, the long term objectives may also fall by the wayside. The example relating to speed limits illustrates this. In the United Kingdom the long term powers concerning road traffic were managed under general emergency provisions of the Road Traffic Act 1967. The powers of the Secretary of State for Energy to impose temporary speed limits for energy restriction reasons were included in the Fuel and Electricity (Control) Act 1973. These short term objective powers were revoked by the Energy Act 1976, but the Road Traffic Act 1967 remains in operation. Consequently, the long term objective of safety on the roads can still be attained (see Table 3 above).

E. Deficient Measures

In all the preceding categories instruments were implemented by one or more measures. It is, however, possible that an objective pursued cannot be attained, because of the fact that the instrument has not yet been specified or the measure approved. In the Netherlands a policy statement was adopted in 1974 concerning the building of three nuclear power stations. Due to political opposition no measure has yet been taken (see Table 4). In Germany constitutional obstacles (collective bargaining autonomy of labour unions and employers organisations) limit public intervention in the manpower field. Although national Acts on minimum wages and maximum working hours exist, they are of small importance, because in many cases collective bargaining agreements envisage more favourable regulations.

In this context it is interesting to mention a paradox described by Offe. In his view, while many Anglo-Saxon countries have, in the 1970's, tried to imitate some of the legalistic frameworks adopted by Continental welfare states in the 1950's and 1960's – this has been the case, for instance, in the field of industrial relations – the reverse development seems to have occurred in Germany. That is, the assumption that law is an adequate and effective mechanism for changing situations and actors has been called into question. According to Offe, law is still not flexible and independent enough to deal with the complexity of the social and economic problems processed by the welfare state. As is evident in attempts to regulate production of primary products, such as milk, making a law is often synonymous with making rules that are in need of revision as soon as they are printed. Legal regulation is appropriate for programmes and issues of a medium-range complexity, that is, for events that do not change very rapidly. In other cases, there seems to be a definite limit to the legal form of intervention itself. The law becomes a series of empty and abstract general phrases that have to be interpreted in an *ad hoc,* context-dependent fashion – thereby violating the principle of the rule of law.[61]

This analysis of Offe clearly shows that in rapidly changing situations legal regulations risks becoming a series of empty and abstract general phrases ("carte blanche"-measures) violating the principle of the rule of law. Is this violation permissible or inevitable? This problem can only be examined in a context which links measures with legal values.

VI. The Linkage of the Choice of Measures with Legal Values

The preceding sections have focussed mainly on the instrumental characteristics of the relationship between objectives, instruments and measures. However, a legal evaluation is necessary in order to give a balanced view of the implementation procedure as seen in a temporal perspective. This legal impact is illustrated by the development of the concept of the legitimate expectations (Vertrauensschutz, confiance légitime). When the time horizons of implementation programs are not synchronised, courts may intervene and protect the legitimate expectation of undertakings or citizens.[62] However, this protection is not a compelling principle which always takes priority. It will yield to overriding considerations of public interest.[63] In other words a general principle of law does not always have an absolute character.

Some indications have already been given here of the impact of law on economic policy decisions:
– the characteristics of the instrument may influence the characteristics of the measure and vice versa. Measures will obey their own legal principles which may sometimes be in harmony, sometimes be contrary to the instrument pursued
– the judiciary may block or unblock an implementation procedure
– by legal fiction an instrument/measure combination can have an effect on past situations (retroactivity) or on existing situations.

---

[61] C. Offe, *Contradictions of the Welfare State,* (1984, London) at p. 280.
[62] Assmann, *supra* note 15 at p. 337. See also E. W. Fuss "Der Schutz des Vertrauens auf Rechtkontinuität im deutschen Verfassungsrecht und europäischen Gemeinschaftsrecht" in: *Festschrift zum 70. Geburtstag von Hans Kutscher,* (1981, Baden-Baden) at p. 201.
[63] Case 78/77, *Luhrs,* Judgment of February 1, 1978, European Court Reports 1978, p. 177–78 "It follows from the stated circumstances that Regulation No. 348/76 was adopted pursuant to an *overriding public interest,* which which required that the rules adopted should enter into force immediately. Indeed, the proper functioning of the common market required a measure to restrain a development whereby rising prices and abnormal exports to non-member countries were stimulating each other. Moreover that measure could not surprise trade circles which, even if they had not yet been aware of the abnormal situation, had at all events been warned by earlier Community measures (suspension of customs duties on imports) and by measures already adopted by the Member States which were traditional exporters of potatoes. Consequently the adoption of stricter measures was to be foreseen by prudent and discriminating traders so that in the present case they cannot plead *legitimate expectation".* (Authors italics added).

A. Standards of Legal Excellence

This is not the place to develop a general theory on the linkage of the choice of measures with legal values. However, with the help of Lon Fuller, an attempt will be made to undertake a more systematic approach. In his book Fuller discusses "eight ways to fail to make law": "The first and most obvious lies in a failure to achieve rules at all, so that every issue must be decided on an *ad hoc* basis. The other routes are: (2) a failure to publicise, or at least to make available to the affected party, the rules he is expected to observe; (3) the abuse of retroactive legislation, which not only cannot itself guide action, but undercuts the integrity of rules prospective in effect, since it puts them under the threat of retrospective change; (4) a failure to make rules understandable; (5) the enactment of contradictory rules or (6) rules that require conduct beyond the powers of the affected party; (7) introducing such frequent changes in the rules that the subject cannot orient his action by them; and finally, (8) a failure of congruence between the rules as announced and their actual administration".[64]

These standards deal with the legal value of certain measures. A complete value system has to also include not only non-measure-orientated values, but also constitutional values, such as democracy, and the protection of human rights. However, as the subject matter of this study focuses on measures these underlying values will not be discussed in an explicit way.

Corresponding to the eight routes to failure are eight kinds of legal excellence toward which a system of rules may strive. These standards of legal excellence cannot be realised to perfection. Utopia is not actually a useful target for guiding the impulse toward legality.[65] In other words. Fuller favours a middle course which sometimes involves impairment of some desiderata. He specifies his choice with an example which is illustrative in this context. "It is simultaneously desirable that laws should remain stable through time and that they should be such as impose no insurmountable barriers to obedience. Yet rapid changes in circumstances such as those attending an inflation, may render obedience to a particular law, which was once quite easy, increasingly difficult, to the point of approaching impossibility".[66]

Applying this middle course criterion to this temporally oriented paper, some tentative observations can be made.

B. The Instrument Chosen Linked with Legal Values

If *ordering policy instruments* are used, the implementing legal measures must strive for legal perfection. The rules ought to be clear, consistent with one another, known, and never retroactive. They should remain constant in time, demand only what is possible and give no or only limited discretionary powers to the Executive. There must be effective judicial review.

---

[64] L. L. Fuller, *The Morality of Law*, (Revised edition, 1969, New York) at p. 38.
[65] Fuller, *supra* note 64 at pp. 41–45.
[66] Fuller, *supra* note 64 at p. 45.

If *process policy instruments* are used, some legal desiderata can be neglected. Here a continuing balance must be realised between the instrumental necessities of economic policy, *e.g.* quick response or discrete action, and the standards of legal evaluation. The volatility of policy implies the possession by Government of broad discretionary powers for rapid action, hard to reconcile with law's internal values of stability and consistency and with the demands of the rule of law.[67]

Some measures are not binding and not published, such as the gentleman's agreement between Shell/Esso and the Dutch government. Other measures have an effect on past or existing situations. Most measures are not durable and give the Executive wide discretionary powers, leaving the courts only marginal judicial review.

These broad discretionary powers are not good or bad in themselves. Discretion must be considered in a broader context as part of a complex social, organisational and political process. Discretion is an ambiguous phenomenon.[68] It is really related to power, but because it appears to be concerned with rules as well (the "delegated power"-notion of discretion) it tends to be viewed as a problem of legality or as the lack of a rule bound solution.[69] In other words, discretion forms part of the designing of the instrument/measure combination analysed in the first part of this paper.

The choice – in our study related to a temporal perspective – has to be made by policy makers with legal insight and lawyers with policy insight. Keynes observed that perhaps the most difficult question to determine is how much to decide by rule and how much to leave to discretion.[70] An example illustrates this. If policy makers decide to let the market work and, consequently, they do not grant subsidies, there will be no frequently changing, inaccurately formulated subsidy measures. On the other hand, if they prefer to intervene via subsidies, taxation or other instruments, "bad" law (*i.e.* frequently changing, non-published measures) may be inevitable. The legal measures of the market economy have as a rule a durable character, but the legal measures of the welfare state change frequently in order to achieve variable objectives.[71]

---

67 Daintith, *supra* note 20 at p. 64.
68 Baldwin and Hawkins, *supra* note 43 at p. 599.
69 Z. Bankowski, and D. Nelken, quoted in: Bodwin and Hawkins, supra note 43, at p. 573.
70 Horsefield, J. Keith, *The IMF 1945–1965* (1969, Washington vol. III) at p. 6.
71 Assmann, *supra* note 15 at p. 248: "Das Rechtsgesetz der liberalen Epoche war auf zeitlichen Bestand, auf Dauer angelegt. Gesetze gelten heute nicht mehr ihres Bestandes wegen, sondern gerade aufgrund ihrer Abänderbarkeit im politischen Prozeß; weil Revision und Novellierung von Gesetzen schon bei ihrer Inkraftsetzung mit einprogrammiert werden, können Gesetze zu Mitteln von Reformzielen werden. Die Abänderbarkeit von Gesetzen erlaubt es, Gesetze zu verabschieden, die redistributive Ziele verfolgen, ohne Daueransprüche zu begründen. Gerade weil sie weder auf Dauer noch in ihrer Form auf Konstanz angelegt sind, lassen sich mit ihnen *partikulare Ziele* verfolgen, deren Gesamteinbindung hoch variabel ist".

C. The Measure Adopted Linked with Legal Values

Long term measures and the first level of two-level measures must strive for legal perfection. Short term, cyclical and the second level of two level measures must pursue a middle course. It may, in some instances, be better for an administrative body to resist the temptation to make rules and to concentrate instead on the adjudicative process. Thus, where decisions are taken in a rapidly changing economic sphere, to purport to decide on the basis of outdated rules may help no one.[72] However, decision makers and lawyers have to bear in mind that infringements of the legal standards tend to become cumulative. In Fuller's words: "A neglect of clarity, consistency, or publicity may beget the necessity for retroactive laws. Too frequent changes in the law may nullify the benefits of formal, but slow-moving procedures for making the law known. Carelessness about keeping the laws possible of obedience may engender the need for a discretionary enforcement which in turn impairs the congruence between official action and enacted rule".[73]

D. Evaluation of the Content of the Inventories

When examining the content of the energy and manpower inventories from a temporal standpoint it appears that, as a rule, long term measures which have an ordering policy character are more respectful of the legal values than the short term measures with a process policy character. However, only tentative and general conclusions are possible because the inventories do not give a detailed picture of the legal perfection of each measure.

In this time oriented context, it is interesting to mention the measures taken by the countries under survey in order to stabilise prices and profits in the energy field, especially in the petroleum sector. A broad distinction can be made between three groups of countries.[74] First price regulating countries (Hungary, France and Italy). These countries constantly take short term measures regulating private activity, sanctioned by criminal or civil penalties.[75] Secondly, free market countries (Germany, the United Kingdom since 1979 and the Netherlands since 1982). These countries do not adopt special price measures. They rely upon long term and ordering policy oriented competition rules, although in crisis periods some

---

[72] Baldwin and Hawkins, *supra* note 43 at p. 588. They also argue that: "In certain areas the extreme tendency to indulge in over-inclusive rule-making and the dangers of this (for example, of discrediting the agency and of encouraging rule avoidance by enforcers) may render the enterprise pointless. Policy-making by trial-type adjudication has a number of advantages over rule-making. It is open and flexible; it deals with particulars; it gives opportunities to examine hypothetical instances, and it makes the discussion of alternatives available to those affected by any policy. Again, it cannot be assumed that a discretion limited by rules or standards is necessarily better than one that is less confined but more often exercised and reviewed".

[73] Fuller, *supra* note 64 at p. 92.

[74] E. N. Krapels, *Pricing Petroleum products-strategy for eleven industrial nations*, (1982, New York) at p. XIII.

[75] *E.g.* case 231/83, *Cullet* judgment, of the Court of Justice of the European Communities, of 29 January, 1985, not yet published.

short term and process policy oriented measures can be taken.[76] Lastly mixed economy countries (United Kingdom before 1979, the Netherlands before 1982). These countries followed a short term price policy, but the competent authorities (Price Commissions, Minister of Economic Affairs) did not have the same discretionary powers as the counterparts in price regulating countries.[77]

Conclusion

The relationship between objectives, instruments, measures and the time element has not been easy to analyse. First, although objectives can be divided in largely short term and mainly long term, the distinction is not watertight: one objective can have both long and short term aspects. Secondly, some instruments in general do not have a temporal value as such. They get it via the temporal character of the implementing measure. Thirdly, one instrument/measure combination may produce effects which further more than one objective.

These three observations corroborate the view of political scientists that economic policy making does not work in a coherent and smooth way.

A 'roadmap' has been used in order to relate the time element of the objective with the time element in the measure. Harmonious combinations found, e.g. the realisation of long term objectives through long term measures, short term objectives through short term measures and long term and mixed objectives through cyclical measures. In other cases however the relationship between short and long term objectives and the choice of instruments and measures is not easy. Long term measures, adopted by Parliament, are not very well suited for the realisation of short term objectives, because of the time-consuming decision making process. Short term measures may realise long term objectives, but for the sake of continuity long term measures are to be preferred.

Rules of thumb can be invoked and legal techniques developed to attenuate this disharmony. In this context one rule of thumb has been applied: the distinction between ordering and process policy and their durable, or respectively less durable character. As a rule ordering policy instruments (e.g. competition policy) must be transformed into durable legislation and process policy instruments (e.g. price orders) in less durable administrative action.

---

[76] Krapels, *supra* note 74 at pp. 131–141.

[77] In France a very complicated system of minimum and maximum prices measures exists, see Krapels, *supra* note 74 at pp. 61–66 and the Cullet case, mentioned in note 75. Until 1982, the Netherlands issued maximum price orders. These orders, which were orders applicable to transactions on the Dutch market, were not so effective, e.g. because of the international oriented Rotterdam spot market. Given the surplus of oil on the market, the maximum price order had the effect of pushing the price up. White paper, no. 17100, XIII, nos 119 and 148). Having the choice, either to issue more stringent rules, or to let the market work, the Minister of Economic Affairs withdrew the Petroleum Product price order 1982 (Staatscourant 1982, no. 144). See also Krapels, *supra* note 74 at pp. 86–92.

The most important technique to reduce time lags in decision making is the two-level approach. Enabling laws permits quick reaction once the enabling measures are adopted. Other techniques are transitional measures and sunset legislation. The judiciary, described in the first part of this paper as a possible obstacle, may also unblock a jammed decision making process and formulate principles which are important in solving time-related problems.

The instrumental use of the law, analysed in the first two parts of the paper, gives only one side of the picture. The choice of instruments and measures ought to be linked with legal values.

The application of good law standards gave some indications of the relationship between measures, time and legal values. The choice between long and short term measures, broad or limited discretion, has to be made by policy makers with legal insight and lawyers with policy insight. This other side of the picture also illustrates the impact of law on economic policy.

Jacob Viner defined the special role of the lawyers as follows: "In the ordinary course of events, policy is, of course, ultimately decided not by the technical experts as such, whether they be economists or engineers or political scientists or sociologists, but by the legislators and the responsible executives with the aid of advice by the experts. The excellent formula "The expert *should* be on tap, not on top" would be almost equally valid if it went: "The expert *is* on tap, not on top". This applies no more and no less to the economist than to the other professions – except for the lawyer, who is on tap *and* on top, and omnipresent, omniscient, omnipotent, and omnivorous in addition.[78]

This statement, pronounced in 1939, is too flattering. Nevertheless it clearly illustrates that the design and implementation of economic policy is also the business of lawyers.

[78] J. Viner, "The short view and the long in Economic policy," presidential address at the meetings of the American Economic Association, (30) the *American Economic Review*, 1940, p. 1. Reprinted in: Viner, Jacob, *The long view and the short, Studies in economic theory and policy*, (1958, Illinois) at pp. 109.

Temporal Pluralism and Legal Relativism
Contribution to the Study of De-Legalisation

FRANÇOIS OST

Brussels

Contents

Introduction
  I. Descriptive Approach. Classification of Legal Temporalities
  II. Historical Approach. Articulation of Legal Temporalities
  Conclusions

Introduction

It is no coincidence that the topic of time is of concern to lawyers today. In particular, the question of time could not be avoided by the promoters of the collective research of which the present study is a part. This research, in the field of the managed economy, seeks to pick out alternatives to the de-legalisation which has been induced by increasing awareness of the lack of efficiency affecting legal measures aimed at implementation of ecnomic and social policies.

There can be no doubt that the issue of temporality lies at the heart of this discussion. The fact is that the Welfare State has abandoned the reserve that until very recently characterised the liberal State: government now intends to manage economic, social and cultural change. Accordingly, it can no longer be satisfied with relatively static framework norms defining general standards of conduct (good faith, keeping one's word, obligation to make reparation for damage caused by wrong conduct etc.). Instead of being content to set the ground rules of a game which is for the social actors to play, the State itself intends to intervene in play, though reserving the right to change the rules and the stakes as it goes along. It must further be recognised that the complexity of the game has increased to absolutely unforeseeable proportions, notably because of the globalisation of economic exchange. Thus, the game is increasingly often affected by exogenous shocks (increases in costs of energy or raw materials, as in the major oil crisis of 1974, changes in exchange rates, etc.) which considerably increase the hazards of the undertaking and wrong-foot the most tried and tested strategies. This rise in uncertainty brings about an "endemic instability"[1] which often leads economic

---

[1] A. Jacquemin and B. Remiche, "Le pouvoir judiciaire entre l'opportunité et la légalité

and social actors to sudden reversals in position, especially with a view to shifting new risks onto weaker partners.

There is, then, a twofold reason for the changeability of law in the economic and social areas involved in the managed economy: a deliberate transformation of the role of law in the context of the Welfare State, which ceases to be an arbiter of exchanges in order to orient them in the direction it feels desirable; and an imposed necessity continually to change the strategy adopted so as to react to fluctuations affecting the market and the protectionist reflexes of the operators on it. Governments are thus tempted "to follow the caprices of the economy and to multiply *ad hoc* measures expressed in an inflation of special powers orders, regulations, decrees and other directives".[2]

Condemned to administer the unforeseeable and regulate the haphazard, public economic law is constrained to modify its relationship to time, which inevitably affects its very form. As L. Sfez notes: "the slow, indefinite movement of fixed, mutually corrective, imperative norms is no longer enough. In order to be adapted to a luxuriant, tangled and random economic world, each norm must henceforth carry within itself its own movement, never exhausting its future and the future of those it is addressed to".[3] We thus see the emergence of an "administrative law of uncertainty",[4] made up of "prospective legal acts"[5] (such as plans, programme or research contracts, subsidy agreements, etc.) based more on concertation than command, which impose obligations as to conduct rather than outcome and are ultimately much more determined by the means used than by the ends, which remain largely indeterminate.[6] This set of characteristics, which imply a constant adjustment of the legal obligations entered into by one side or the other, as consultation and concertation expand, available resources are redistributed and objectives being pursued are clarified, has the effect of reinforcing the climate of uncertainty which characterises contemporary economic life.[7] Far from stabilising the market, the law is in turn affected by the precariousness that characterises it.

Hence, according to many authors, the come-back in strength of the theme of withdrawal of law, under the various names that have been given to it: deregulation, dejuridification, de-legalisation, or whatever.

The study by our colleague Kamiel Mortelmans that we have the privilege of discussing here[8] does not however fall within this strategy of withdrawal or disarming of law. It tries rather, in a better defined temporal perspective, to

économiques", in A. Jacquemin and B. Remiche, *Les magistratures économiques et la crise*, (1984, Brussels) at p. 12.

[2] *Ibid.*, at p. 13.
[3] L. Sfez, *L'Administration prospective*, (1970, Paris) at p. 168.
[4] A. Hauriou, "Le droit administratif de l'aléatoire", in *Mélanges Trotabas*, (1970, Paris) at p. 197.
[5] Ph. Chapal, "Recherche sur la notion et le régime des actes juridiques à caractère prospectif", (1968) in *A.J.D.A.*, at p. 323.
[6] On all of this, see L. Sfez, *supra* note 3, at pp. 166–204.
[7] In this sense, see A. Jacquemin and B. Remiche, *supra* note 1, at p. 13.
[8] K. J. M. Mortelmans, *Short and long-term policy objectives and the choice of instruments and measures*, above at pp. 283–321.

improve the processes of legal implementation of economic policies. In the author's own terms, this study reflects the relationship of law and time in an "instrumental" perspective. It seeks to answer the following question: how, on three time scales (short, medium and long-term) can one best adapt the legal measures corresponding to economic instruments aimed at realising the political, economic or social objectives which government sets itself?

On reflection, such an approach is seen to rest on two implicit postulates:

– time is a homogeneous element and is manipulable or programmable;
– law is a mono-functional instrument at the service of government policy.

These postulates are applied by the author without critical discussion, at least in the first two parts of his paper. The fact remains that the author, an alert observer of legal reality, is still forced to record phenomena of resistance by legal form and by the time element to manipulations of which they are the object; dysfunctionalities or perverse effects of the strategies adopted likewiese appear.These include chronological inversion in the ideal rational process of decision-making, irreducible phenomena of contingency or of the outdating of norms by the action of time (a kind of legal entropy), blocking effects of processes applied, at both parliamentary and legal levels and tensions induced by respect for values bound up with legal security or existing rights.

It is our conviction that, if one is properly to measure the scope of these dysfunctionalities, which all belie the instrumentalist approach to law, the validity of the two postulates on which the conception is based should itself be discussed.

Is it so certain that time is a homogeneous, continuous, irreversible, quantitative element, capable of mechanical treatment? Is it really true that legal form is a neutral instrument, which may be mobilised for whatever end the State may assign to it? Against a unidimensional conception of time and of law, we wish in this paper to posit a pluralism of time (which ought then to be written in the plural: time breaks up into multiple competing temporalities) and a relativism of law (which ought then to be free from its identification with the State: the validity of State law is only relative, for it is forced to make compromises with many other factors in the creation of legal norms).

It will be noted in particular that legal reality is a joint resultant, not only of objective state law but also of the subjective rights developed by private initiative and of associative or corporative rights that have emerged from innumerable groups and associations. Moreover, even keeping to law generated by the State, it should nevertheless be seen not only from the viewpoint of its authors, government, but also of those to whom it is addressed, the subjects of law. One would then observe phenomena of dissociation between the legal effectiveness of a measure (a norm issued is applied by the authorities, and abrogated one is no longer so applied) and the sociological effectiveness of the same measure (a norm, issued and applied by the authorities, may be transgressed by the public, while an abrogated norm may continue to survive in behaviour).[9]

---

[9] On this point, see J. Carbonnier, *Flexible droit* (1969, Paris), at pp. 12f.

Thus, causalist perspective models, however complexified they may be (in particular by preferring network causality to linear causality), along with the political and legal action strategies inspired by them, seem to us to be irredeemably doomed to error and failure if they neglect to take account of this radical heterogeneity of both time and law. We would go further: it is the instrumental approach as such that seems to us to be disputable, as liable to ignore values inherent in the legal form itself: in particular, those which involve its relationship to time in a particular direction.[10] This essential point is not overlooked by Mortelmans; and he tries in the third part of his paper to make a legal evaluation of the strategies proposed. These are looked at in the light of the criteria of legality which are constitutive of what the American author Lon Fuller calls the "internal morality of law".[11] The point dealt with by Fuller can be set out as follows: "on what conditions may norms issued by the legislator rightly be termed legal?" A norm may be called legal if it responds, if not totally then as best may be, to eight criteria of legality, in particular generality, stability, non-retroactivity and consistent application by judges and the administration. For this one can see, especially on the basis of the last three criteria, that the relationship between law and time, at least on the liberal rule-of-law model, is far from being indeterminate.

How is one to assess the legal policy of the Welfare State on this basis? Mortelmans thinks he can save it from too much criticism by distinguishing two families of measures. The first, which are long-term and aim at realising structural objectives ("ordering policies") are adopted by the legislature and must meet the criteria of legality set out by Fuller. As for the second, which are short-term and aim only at conjunctural adjustments ("process policies") they are a product of the administration and may depart appreciably from the ideal of legality.

Let us look more closely at this answer. It implies that legality and the values (security, equality and formal liberty) traditionally associated with it are now marginal to the administrative part of normative production which is constitutive of the managed economy. Moreover, it leaves fully open the determination of the respective shares of Parliament and Administration in elaborating the normative framework of the Welfare State. One may wonder in this connection whether administrative rationality is not progressively absorbing the areas which until very recently were part of classical legality. Particularly in the case of double-action measures which combine long-term and short-term norms, it can be seen that, since application of these rules – particularly the determination in the light of socio-economic data of objectives which, in the law, largely remain vague – is entirely concentrated in the hands of the administration, one is dealing with no thing less than a delegation of legislative power to the executive. Thus, D. Loschak was able to call "mystificatory" the legality principle which is supposed to restrain administrative action: it could be analysed "as a sort of provisional and relative self-limitation of the Administration by itself. It is provisional, since the texts

---

[10] On the relationship between instrumentality and morality in the economic sphere, see G. Schrans, The instrumentality and the morality of European economic law, in *Miscellanea W. J. Ganshof von der Meersch*, vol. II (1972) Brussels at p. 383.

[11] L. Fuller, *The morality of law*, (revised edition, 1978 New Haven and London).

rapidly succeed each other in time; and relative because they always allow the authorities that have to apply them a wide measure of discretion, frequently including the power to derogate from the provisions they contain".[12]

Thus, the question that arises – and the issues bound up with the various legal temporalities are no doubt pointers to the reply – is whether today a certain threshold has not been passed, at least in the economic and social measures in connection with which this work invokes the theme of the withdrawal of law. It should in fact be asked whether the changes being made today in legal form are not such that Welfare State law is now law only in name.[13] Is what we are seeing not, at least in tendency, a disintegration of legal form, which would constitute the manifestation of one of the branches of the trilemma mentioned by Gunther Teubner?[14]

Our suggestion for an answer to this question will be twofold. On the one hand, we shall seek to on the basis of our observation of reality to describe, in part I, a variety of legal temporalities. On the other, we shall endeavour to render intelligible the articulations that necessarily arise between the various times of the law; recourse to history, with the periodisation it authorises, will allow us to pick out this architecture of the temporal forms of law (part II). These two developments will each contribute to the illustration of our thesis, which is that the random, provisional and precarious temporality typical of the short-term measures which make up almost all of the law of the managed economy scarcely seem to constitute a truly legal temporality.

I. Descriptive Approach. Classification of Legal Temporalities

This part of the paper is descriptive. The point here is to identify and classify the various temporalities associated with the emergence and development of legal forms. Although the ambition of this initial research remains limited – it will be confined to applying a typology of ideal types of legal times without yet attempting an articulation or an interpretation – it is based on a wish to differentiate the temporality of law which seems to be necessary for at least two reasons.

This effort at relativisation or differentiation is imposed in the first place by the general theme of the research of which this study is a part. On pain of plunging into the crudest political phraseology, the theme of de-legalisation cannot be treated by all-or-nothing methods. Demanding the abolition of law in the economic and social fields, as if law had ever totally occupied these areas, would demonstrate very little sociological sense. A-legalism shares with pan-legalism a common failure to recognise the share of law in social life or the multiple

[12] D. Loschak, "Le principe de légalité. Mythes et mystifications", (1981) *A.J.D.A.*, at p. 392.
[13] D. Loschak, "Mutation des droits de l'homme et mutation du droit – (Les droits de l'homme dans la crise de l'Etat-Providence) (1984)13 special issue *Revue interdisciplinaire d'études juridiques* at p. 77.
[14] "Juridification – Concepts – Limits, Solutions" in G. Teubner ed., *Juridication of Social Spheres* (1987, Berlin).

modalities of intervention by the law itself – a diversity which results from the heterogeneity of its sources, and sometimes from internal struggles among them. It therefore seems much more scientific, in connection with phenomena of legalisation or de-legalisation, to speak of changes in the intensity of legal pressure. Following the indications of Carbonnier, for whom de-legalisation should be understood "not as the absolute vacuum of law, but as more or less considerable reduction in legal pressure",[15] we shall seek to measure the scope of the observable phenomena of escalation or de-escalation of legal control and constraint.

It will likewise be noted that since society – like nature – abhors a vacuum, a certain withdrawal of law will necessarily be reflected by an advance in regulation of some other type: moral principle, usage, or technical norm. Likewise – to stay in the legal field – perhaps the most operational treatment of the theme of de-legalisation ought to consist in finding and interpreting the phenomena of shifts within a given legal system, of the intervention of law in the social, by which we mean both shifts in competences from one legal authority to another, and re-distributions of the specific modalities of intervention. Thus, de-legalisation (less law) does not necessarily lead to de-judicialisation (less judges); quite the contrary, increased responsibilities may be given to the judiciary at the very time when the legislator renounces intervention. Likewise, not all policies of de-penalisation (reduction or suppression of penal sanctions) necessarily imply decriminalisation of the act concerned (suppression of the penal accusation); other sanctions – notably civil or administrative ones – may be applied.[16]

A more refined conception of the various legal temporalities bound up with these multiple forms of intervention of law might thus contribute to a better understanding of the general issue of de-legalisation.

But there is a second reason that makes necessary this attempt to relativise the time of law. This concerns the present state of affairs with the issue of time in general. If one refers to the recent work of an encyclopedic nature (treating the phenomena of time in all the fields of society, thought and action) devoted by K. Pomian to this question, this need for a "stratigraphical" approach becomes obvious: there is a plurality of times, distributed in successive strata, which cannot be reduced to the classical doublets of objective or subjective time, cosmic time and conscious time or whatever.[17]

Nor is it enough to distinguish between the short, the medium and the long term, if justice is to be done to the multiplicity of temporal experience. These three degrees of the arrow of time ultimately do no more than reinforce the classical representation of time, conceived of as a homogeneous flow, as a continuous line traversed by a linear movement, in a single direction and irreversible; a quantitative datum, calculable and masterable like a thing. While such a reductionist

---

[15] J. Carbonnier, *supra* note 5, at p. 21.
[16] On this point, see the excellent study by M. van de Kerchove, "Réflexions analytiques sur les concepts de dépénalisation et de décriminalisation", (1984) 12 *Revue interdisciplinaire d'études juridiques* at p. 31.
[17] K. Polmian, *L'ordre du temps* (1984, Paris).

representation may have led to effective action programmes locally, that does not give it any overall validity.

Be that as it may, the differentiation of time has already been the subject of significant efforts, by both philosophers and scientists.

On the philosophical level, one might mention, after the initial trailblazing of Berson and Husserl, the work of Bachelard on the "dialectics of duration" (understood as a "discontinuous succession of rhythms",[18] of Ricœur, who wrote: "Nowhere do we see a society dedicated to a uni-dimensional time. The gap between temporalities seems to be the law governing not only inter-cultural differences, but also intra-cultural differences."[19] Or again that of Foucault, who sought, in L'Archéologie du savoir, to analyse the history of thought "in a discontinuity which no teleology could reduce a priori".[20]

In science the refutation of the paradigm of a single, continuous time – which nevertheless structures our current representation of time and has led to the production of its various measuring instruments – has today been very largely accomplished. This has not been achieved without a deep crisis – in the sense given this term by Thomas Kuhn in the development of scientific disciplines – similar, for example, to that affecting the various evolutionary theories in biology, geology and paleontology. All these disciplines are based on the postulate that the laws of nature are invariant in the very long term, and therefore that the same causes necessarily have the same effects all along the time line.[21] Against these unitary representations of time, Prigogine can today state: "After more than three centuries, science has again found the theme of the multiplicity of time... Every complex being is consituted by a plurality of times, connected with each other by subtle, multiple articulations. History, whether of a living being or of a society, can never again be reduced to the monotonous simplicity of a single time, whether this time puts its stamp on an invariance or traces the paths of an advance or a degradation."[22]

In the social sciences too, the heterogeneity of the various temporal rhythms is put in perspective from various angles. It is shown that the various forms of collective action, far from presenting only specific durations and rhythms, still mutually commensurable, and identifiable along an overall time line whose objectivity is left undiscussed, involve not only times of their own, but also specific representations of the overall time bound up with particular strategies of

---

[18] G. Bachelard, La dialectique de la duré (new edition 1963, Paris).
[19] P. Ricœur, Le temps et les philosophies, (1978, Paris) at 18. It is well known that Ricœur relates the multiplicity of times to the diversity of ways of symbolising temporal experience. This theme is comprehensively dealt with in his work: Temps et récit, (1893, Paris).
[20] M. Foucault, L'archéologie du savoir (1969, Paris) at p. 264.
[21] For a closely argued refutation of the evolutionist paradigm, see A. Gras, "Le temps de l'évolution et l'air du temps", (1979) Diogène, at p. 68.
[22] I. Prigoginer and I. Sirengers, La nouvelle alliance. Métamorphose de la science, (1979, Paris) at p. 274.

managing it.[23] Thus, for instance, in history, the Annales School well illustrates the complexity of the relationships that link up temporalities of differing nature. The initial postulate of this School in fact lies in rejection of the concept of "overall history", pre-supposing the homogeneous, identical evolution of all elements of society.[24] As Pomian writes: "Today, in the practice of historians, time is no longer conceived of as a uniform flow with phenomena plunged like bodies into a river with a current that carries them ever further off... History has its own time, or rather times, which are intrinsic to the phenomena studied, and take their rhythms not from astronomical or physical phenomena, but from the singularities of these processes themselves."[25] In this line of thought, Le Goff was able to show, in a study entitled "Church time and merchant's time",[26] the difficulty for the merchant class, at the dawn of capitalism, to articulate an economic time founded on speculation and forecasting, the basis for credit, and a theological time which reserved the future for the designs of Providence.

In the field of sociology, there is the remarkable work of G. Gurvitch, who, in an article entitled "The multiplicity of social times", is concerned to show that "social life flows along multiple times, always divergent, often contradictory; their relative unification, bound up with an often precarious hierarchalisation, represents a problem for the whole of society".[27]

The law could not stand aside from this major theoretical movement which would lead to making time strange and alien to lawyers – time, one of the apparently most familiar elements of the "given" on which dogmatics always believes it can complacently base its "constructs". At the end of this downright "epistemological break", time too appeared – like any human experience – as a construct. In the legal sphere, Husserl was the first to seek to pick out the various temporal "styles" revealed by the observation of legal phenomena. In his well-known study, "Recht und Zeit"[28] he establishes an extremely simple temporal typology, based on the vectors of present, past and future. The thesis consists in the affirmation that each of these three constitutive powers of the modern state – the executive, the judiciary and the legislature – is attached specifically to one of these three dimensions of time.

The executive works in the present. The administrator applies the law case by case; he deals with issues in conformity with the law in force, but also in terms of their specific needs, which may where necessary entail amendments to the law. While the Administration is sometimes constrained to look towards the future, it is not incumbent on it to encompass the latter in general norms.

---

[23] In this sense, see D. Mercure, "L'étude des temporalités sociales. Quelques orientations", in (1979) 67 Cahiers internationaux de sociologie at p. 263.

[24] In this sense, F. Furet, "Le quantificatif en histoire", in Faire de l'histoire (1974, Paris), at p. 54.

[25] K. Pomian, "Vème temporalité historique/temps", in La nouvelle histoire, (1979, Paris).

[26] (1960) Annales (May-June) 417.

[27] G. Gurvitch, "La multiplicité des temps sociaux", in La vocation actuelle de la sociologie, vol II (2nd ed. 1963, Paris) at p. 325.

[28] G. Husserl, Recht und Zeit, (1965, Frankfurt am Main).

By contrast, the judge appears as the man of the past. His mission lies in applying the existing law to things that have taken place. His margin of liberty with respect to the will of the legislator seems narrower than the administrator's; moreover, the need for justice and for equal treatment further imply, as far as possible, respect for precedent.

Finally, the legislator's time is the future. For the legislator, the future is open; he may, by general rules, modify social behaviour and thus shape future society.

To these initial analyses one may add the finding that in the modern State the necessary collaboration among the three powers – over and above their separation – means a link, more or less balanced according to the case, among these three forms of temporality. Thus stated, Husserl's thesis seems hard to refute; it would however benefit from being expanded upon and qualified, especially as regards the judge's time. We shall, therefore, attempt to distinguish no less than six different legal temporalities.

The first might be called the *"time of foundations"*. This is the representation of an original, fabulous, sacred and mythical time referring back either to some founding event from which the group takes its birth: divine mandate, social contract or revolution; or to some human nature from which the individual draws inalienable rights. This time of foundation is the time *par excellence* of constitutions which seek to root the foundations of political systems in an unshakeable base. If it is true that every national group forges its unity in some collective myth that the constitutional document has to translate into legal data,[29] then a form of temporality is mobilised which, precisely because it lies outside actual historical time, claims to escape from time itself, to shine in the eternal present of fable. It was Kant who noted that "the origin of supreme power is unfathomable" and that "the source of law must be represented as of divine origin".[30] The content of the particular myth invoked does not matter much; what counts for our proposition is the temporal strategy applied: a suspension of profane time which passes, in favour of the strong time of origins, which has to be revived at each critical stage of social life in order to re-affirm its unity. Everything hapens "as if" the event recounted by the myth then constituted the real origin of the legal order. Questions relating to the historical foundations of this order are thus excluded from view.

In legal discourse there is a strong propensity to use this mythical time, which claims eternity and promises the immutability of the phenomena ascribes thereto. Jacques Ellul noted this point, and explained it by the totalitarian temptation that takes over any society founded upon absolute values.[31] What this representation

---

[29] For an analysis of the foundation myths of the modern State, see G. Burdeau, *La politique au pays de merveilles* (1979, Paris).

[30] E. Kant, *Methaphysics of Morals*, 32: The law must pretend to ignore time and change … Awareness of duration implies an experimental relativism which cannot tolerate political ideology". *Doctrine du droit*, introduction and translation by A. Philonenko (1971, Paris) at p. 201.

[31] J. Ellul, "Aliénation et temporalité dans le droit", in *Temporalité et aliénation* (1975, Paris) at p. 193.

of time totally lacks is an awareness of duration and the changes it makes in the body politic: hence the increasing gap which is liable to arise between the constitutional fable and the political reality.[32] One illustration of this phenomenon can be found in those constitutions which proclaim that they are untouchable, or at least that some of their main provisions are. Thus Article 79 (3) of the Constitution or the Federal Republic of Germany bars any constitutional amendment of the "inviolable and sacred" rights of man or the "federal, democratic and social" order. Likewise, Article 89 (5) of the French Constitution of October 5, 1958 declares that the "republican form of government" is untouchable. History will very often have the better of this pretension[33] which is, be it noted, condemned by the French Constitution of 1793. "A people always has the right to reform and change its Constitution. One generation cannot subject future generations to its laws."[34]

We thus come to an initial form of opposition between two distinct legal temporalities: the time of foundations seeks to curb the long-term time we shall discuss below, right at the point where the latter, in its turn, brings the discourse on origins down in ruins, very often to replace it by, or superimpose on it, some other mythology.

Furthermore, it is necessary to see that it is not only the rulers who invoke this original time with a view to legitimating their power; the ruled also show a propensity to make the rights they are claiming timeless, with the specific aim of guaranteeing them against the powerful. Thus, there is sometimes talk of innate rights, derived from human nature itself; sometimes of acquired rights, a product of social conquest held to be irreversible. In both cases, the individual claims to have untouchable, indefeasible rights. Need it be stressed that these indefeasible rights are no more sheltered from the action of time than are the constitutions that claim to be eternal? Suffice it to recall in this connection Jeremy Bentham's sceptical assessment of the allegedly indefeasible rights proclaimed in the 1789 Declaration of the Rights of Man and Citizen.[35]

---

[32] See F. Perin, "Les dimensions du temps politique", *Langages multiples sur le temps, Cahiers de l'institut de linguistique de Louvain-la-Neuve,* (1981) at pp. 22 and 24: "Le droit doit faire semblant d'ignorer le temps et le changement… La conscience de la durée implique un relativisme expérimental que ne supporte pas l'idéologie politique".

[33] See Delperée, *Droit constitutionnel,* (1980, Brussels), vol. 1 at p. 78. "Constitutions which solemnly proclaim their untouchability are often the most fragile"; the author goes on to cite this opinion of J. Lerbeau, speaking before the National Congress: "If there is no way of making changes to the Constitution, then as soon as opinion turns against it it will either be infringed or despised."

[34] Art. 28 of the Déclaration des Droits de l'Homme et du Citoyen, 24 juin 1793: see L. Duguit, M. Monnier, R. Bonnard, *Les Constitutions et les Principales Lois Politiques de la France depuis 1789* (7th ed., 1952, Paris), at p. 654.

[35] J. Bentham, "Examen de la Déclaration des Droits de l'homme et du citoyen", in *Œuvres de J. Bentham,* translation E. Dumont, (1829, Brussels) at p. 555: "What does reason say on the matter? Reason says that since the public good is the only principle to consult in establishing rights, there is none which need not be maintained as long as it is of benefit to society; none which should not be abolished as soon as it becomes harmful to it".

Very close to this mythical time of foundations is the *intemporal time of legal doctrine*. While this does not lay explicit claim to the origin fable, it is nonetheless deployed in a form of "omnitemporal present", aimed at suggesting the eternal verity of the principles invoked and at sheltering them from any historical context (of enunciation and application) that might relativise their scope.[36] As is well known, the specific style of this doctrine is that of the commentary or the gloss. Starting from a fragment of text, one can, as Legendre has well shown, build up a whole edifice of propositions whose compilation "wipes out the traces of history" in such a way that "the text is offered to the lawyer not as a historical fragment bound up with this or that circumstance, but in an intemporal, mathematical mode".[37] The following important consequence is deduced: the legal texts thereby guaranteed in the ether of pure logical thought cannot disappear; as Legendre goes on to note, "all the accommodations they may be subject to must be understood as implying the lastingness of the textual message, over and above the cheating or compromising of the gloss according to social time".[38] Pomian too has well noted this process of detemporalisation that characterises the treatment of texts, particularly by legal doctrine: "removed from the destructive action of time, the texts appear as existing in a duration which certainly had a beginning and will have an end, but within which no substantial change can be brought about; one recognises here the Thomist definition of the *aevum*".[39]

The third variety of legal temporality might be determined *"instantaneous time"*. The instant in fact plays an important role in legal life, which on analysis appears to be in close solidarity with the mythical time of foundation. It is as if the periodical evocation of the stable foundations of the origins and the emergence of the creative instant of law collaborated to abolish existential duration in favour of an entirely homogeneous legal time.

It is our thesis that legal thought represents the genesis of the binding effect, the *vis obligandi*, as a moment without duration, a pure instant of reason. This thoroughly magical effect assures the legal act of an entirely formal validity which guarantees it against the wear and tear of time. Whether a contract be signed, a law adopted and promulgated, or a judgment delivered in public session, all these various acts that create law come into existence and produce their specific legal effects instantaneously.[40]

---

[36] For an illustration of this effect of the "omnitemporal present" of legal dogmatics, see E. Serverin and S. Bruxelles, "Du judiciaire au juridique: un procès d'avortement dans les revues de jurisprudence", (1979) 53 *Langages* 51 especially at pp. 59–60.

[37] P. Legendre, "L'amour du censeur. Essai sur l'ordre dogmatique" (1974, Paris) at 91; id. Jouir du pouvoir. Traité de la bureaucratie patriote (1976, Paris) at 162: "It is symptomatic that such enormous intellectual output is continuing to grow, in almost total indifference with regard to its own historical nature".

[38] P. Legendre, *supra* note 37, at p. 92.

[39] K. Pomian, *supra* note 25 at p. 257. Saint Thomas distinguishes between three temporalities: *tempus* (succession), *aeternitas* (pure simultaneity), and *aevum* (intermediary between time and eternity).

[40] Though it is true that some delay may come between promulgation of the law and its entry into force, as well as between delivery of a judgment and securing of its execution. Apart

This role of the instantaneous appears very clearly in the classical representations of the social contract, a legal act which, moreover, has the special characteristic of inaugurating the time of foundations. John Locke puts it thus: "When men, in whatsoever number, thus decide to constitute a single community, this very act has the effect of associating them instantaneously, whereafter they form one single body politic."[41] And Jean-Jacques Rousseau: "Instantaneously, instead of the separate person of each contracting party, this act of association produces a moral and collective body."[42]

But what the social contract brings about on the large scale of the nation is brought about by each legal act on the small scale of individual undertakings. It appears in fact, as Hauser has well shown in a recent article, that the conception of freedom in the legal act was, in 1804 and in the classical theory, "instantaneist and elitist".[43] Everything takes place as if the contracting parties decided at a single instant, in which were concentrated all the elements of information and all the factors that condition their freedom. The law apprehends only this moment of reason, leaving in the shade both the pre-contractual period and the duration of actual implementation of the undertakings. It was so, for instance, with the undertaking to marry. While canon law retained a concern for time and for real freedom in promises of marriage, which were carried out in stages, the promises *de futuro* and *de praesenti*, the Civil Code concentrates this whole construction into an exchange of consent which is both solemn and instantaneous. Engagements lose all legal status, and true as it is that "in marriage, let those cheat who can", the flaws that there might be in these actions can scarcely be recognised, since the consent is also reduced to the pure abstraction of the instant. Moreover, the undertaking made – like the matrimonial settlement – is of course not capable of modifications in the future.

Further development was to consist in a certain renewed taking into account of the factor of time, specifically of actual duration, in the formation and development of the conjugal bond. Thus, the new Article 180 of the French Civil Code introduced error as to the essential qualities of the spouse, while the reform of marriage settlements brought the possibility of their amendment.

The same type of analysis might be given of contract. While consensualist theory involves the idea that the formation of the bond of obligation is reduced to the timeless instant – the magic spark where two wills meet – new sectors, like credit law, introduce periods for reconsideration or retraction, which thus bring a little duration to the assistance of abused freedoms. Likewise, at the level of performance of undertakings, the power increasingly widely allowed to the judge to revise contractual provisions and agreed penalties likewise sanctions the emergence of realities lived through in duration.

from the fact that these periods are generally short, as soon as they have elapsed both law and judgment produce their effects, whatever be their degree of effective publicity.

[41] J. Locke, *Deuxième traité du gouvernement civil*, translation by B. Gilson (1977, Paris) at p. 129.
[42] J.-J. Rousseau, *Du contrat social. Ou principes du droit politiquew* (1972, Paris) at p. 76.
[43] J. Hauser "Temps et liberté dans la théorie générale de l'acte juridique", in *Religion, société et politique, Mélanges en hommage à J. Ellul*, (1983, Paris) at p. 503.

These analyses – largely borrowed from Hauser's article cited above – have the merit of simultaneously highlighting the importance of the instantaneous in legal life and the fact of conflict between this temporality and the "long-term" time with which we shall now deal.

"Long-term" time is, in legal discourse, the temporality which is closest to real life; it thus largely escapes qualification by the law. The "long term" has on the other hand recently been rediscovered by the historians of the Annales School. It constitutes, according to Vovelle, "not the quasi-intemporality of myths, but the medium-long duration of a social history defined as unconscious, in Marx's sense that men make history but do not know they are making it". This time, which concerns mentalities more than events, is made up of "blocks of slow history moving within the semi-immobility of a slow-motion time".[44]

This is, in short, a continuous time operating in slow motion. It opens a field for the progressive genesis of customs, the accumulation of precedent, the formation of usage, the crystallisation of practice, the consolidation of *de facto* situations (acquisitive prescriptions). Negatively, this long term destroys evidence, weakens legal agreements and titles, blurs the reasons for the laws and erodes those in force. This customary time is oriented more towards the past than the present, but that does not mean it is immobile. One might say that it brings about the actualisation of the past in the present, while in return this heritage of the past is insensibly modified by contact with current reality. The whole of the process – appeal to tradition, actualisation and progressive transformation – takes place in a collective and largely unconscious manner. It is as if, below the historical time with its rhythm from the accents of great achievements of the will, one could hear the *"basso continuo"* of customary and collective times. This flow of social time within a history of events and a traditional history refers back to the distinction that sets elite culture (the seat of innovation) against popular culture (the seat of resistance to sudden changes). In law one finds an echo of this dichotomy with the superposition of "vulgar" legal system on "official" ones.

Modern legal thought, which for centuries at least has been navigating in a positivist environment and a "promethean" time, which we shall discuss below, gives hardly any room to customary temporality. There is one notable exception, however: the German historical law school. It is known that this school, inspired by Savigny, Hugo, Puchta, Grimm and a few others, was reacting against the rationalism of the *Aufklärung*, the revolutionary spirit and the illusions of the codifiers.[45] Far from proceeding from deductions of an abstract, universal reason, the law, for these others, springs from the popular conscience and evolves with it. It is from the people, conceived of as a natural totality, that the law has emerged, and not from the individual consciousness; thus, this law is essentially national,

---

[44] M. Vovelle "L'histoire et la longue durée", in *La nouvelle histoire, supra* note 25, at p. 317.

[45] On the Historical School of law, see A. Dufour "Rationnel et irrationnel dans l'École du droit historique" (1978) 23 *Archives de philosophie du droit* at p. 147; same author "La théorie des sources du droit dans l'École du droit historique" (1982) 27 *Archives de philosophie du droit* at p. 85.

particular, not capable of universalisation. This means also that it evolves according to a time of its own – the organic rhythm of development of the community. Savigny presented this conception of time very clearly in the editorial to the first issue of the journal launched by the historical law school: "Each epoch creates not its universe for itself, in complete liberty, but only in undissociable relationship with the totality of the past... History is, accordingly, no longer a simple collection of examples, but the only way leading to a true knowledge of our own situation... The historical school maintains that the matter of the law is determined by the totality of the past of the nation, and not in an arbitrary fashion."[46] According to this conception, the law develops in the same way as a language or a game: that is, according to a process of endogenous creation, based on habit and example. This is a truly infinite process of transformation, so that Grimm can write that law and language have in common "equal antiquity and equal youth. Both are based on an ancient, impenetrable foundation, and also on the tendency for ceaseless self-renewal".[47]

Today-after a very long eclipse – this type of representation of legal time might experience a revival of interest in the context of the pluralist theory of law which, by highlighting the limits of legal positivism and State monolithism, at the same time stresses the variety of spontaneous sources of law, secreting specific islets of normativity which evolve at the rhythm proper to the communities that produce them. Sometimes, the specificity may lie only in an attitude of rejection of the rules imposed by the State authority, as was generally the case for the rules relating to personal status imposed by the imperial countries in their various colonies. There then co-exist, in a single territory and a single area, two distinct legal orders that reflect different temporalities: a national regulation oriented towards the future and regarded as progressive, and local customary regulation regarded as conservative.[48]

Whatever the degree of awareness in legal thought of the role played by this "long-term" time, it seems undeniable that it constitutes an essential dimension of legal life.

While customary time has generally been sometimes ignored and sometimes frankly rejected by modern legal thought, the latter has on the other hand never ceased to value the fifth temporality we would like to analyse, which we term *"promethean time"*. Prometheus, as we know, was the demigod who, against the will of Zeus, gave fire to men and taught them the art of metalworking. His action revokes the time of the gods and inaugurates History, which henceforth advances at the rate of progress of human reason. Promethean time is therefore essentially a conscious time, even voluntary, controlled by reason with a view to achieving definite objectives. Just as customary time looked towards the past, promethean

---

[46] F. K. von Savigny "Über den Zweck dieser Zeitschrift", in *Zeitschrift für geschichtliche Rechtswissenschaft*, cited by Dufour, *Rationnel et...*, *supra* note 45 at p. 160.

[47] J. Grimm, Kleinere Schriften, *supra* note at p. 547, cited by A. Dufour, *La théorie des sources... supra* note 45, at p. 101.

[48] For an illustration of this phenomenon, see F. Rigaux, "Le droit au singulier et au pluriel", (1982) 9 *Revue interdisciplinaire d'études juridiques*, at p. 21.

time looks to and is polarised by the representation of the future, which it
constantly actualises in the present. Its privileged reflection in the legal field comes
about through the initiative of the statute. Promethean time is the time proper to
statutes and codifications. A phenomenon like that of codification is nourished
directly from the grand eschatological representations (progress through history).[49] It should be observed in this connection that the writing down of the law,
the registration of the rule in a text, far from favouring, as one might think,
staticity in the solutions, begins a process of constant transformation of them.
While custom reflects an existing state of affairs, statute, at least virtually,
anticipates a possible state of affairs. And in this logic, change itself is valued: the
new law is always held to be better than the old one, which explains why, where
there is conflict, the most recent provision applies.

This promethean temporality is, and this must be strongly emphasised, valued
in modern legal thought by both the natural law and positivist tendencies. From
the point where the source of natural law is sought less in a cosmic harmony than
in the imperatives of practical reason, it is clear that natural law and the positive
law inspired by it are involved in a process of permanent invention. During the
twentieth century, this fact has appeared clearly when natural law has openly been
presented as "historical" or "of variable content". Werner Maihofer defines the
role of natural law in this line of thought: "to keep open, for every order and for
every human decision, the horizon of the human future".[50]

As for legal positivism, whether it finds its source in utilitarianism (the calculus
of pleasure and pain as in Bentham), imperativism (the will of the sovereign, as in
Austin) or normativism (the dynamic structure of the legal order as in Kelsen), it
implies, by hypothesis, this tension towards the future, this constant adaptability
of law.

Most often these various sources of legal thought combine and mutually
support each other: formal legal technique, adaptive in nature, is regarded as
operating in the service of a project for the future guaranteeing collective eman-
cipation.This point of view is put very clearly by François Rigaux: "Positive law",
he writes, "creates values, and if a temporal image is necessary here, the idea of
natural law anterior to the positive law that completes or specifies it must be
replaced by that of the values which the law brings forth in its own unfolding and
which take shape in the future instead of being a heritage from the past... The
fundamental value of law is the forward look. It then becomes otiose to to ask
about its positivity or its legitimacy, since these involve, the first a return to a
mythical origin, and the other a finding of the present, which is to say the most
recent past. If law has a meaning, it is that of offering us a project for a future
society and contributing, by its own methods, to its realisation."[51]

---

[49] On the utopianism inherent in the operation of codification, see C. Varga, "Utopias of
rationality in the development of the idea of codification", in *Law and the future of
society*, A.R.S.P., Beiheft neue Folge, Nr. 11, (1979, Wiesbaden) at p. 27.

[50] W. Maihofer, "Le droit naturel comme dépassement du droit positif", in (1963) *Archives
de philosophie du droit*, at p. 193.

[51] F. Rigaux, *Introduction à la science du droit* (1974, Brussels) at p. 370.

The manifestations in positive law of this organising function, which is instrumental and anticipatory of a legal regulation that is now immersed in a promethean temporality, are innumerable. We shall confine ourselves to mentioning one only, taken from the penal field. It is known that, inspired by the ideas of such thinkers as Beccaria and Bentham, the authors of the modern penal codes have generally favoured the preventive functions of the penalty over its retributive functions. It will appear on reflection that this change in attitude presupposes a radical change in the relationship to time. The retributive penalty aims at redressing a past wrong: the preventive penalty aims at safeguarding the future. Beccaria is quite clear on this: "It becomes clear, he writes, that the object of punishment is not to wipe out a crime already committed... Can the cries of some unfortunate call back in time, which does not return, actions already accomplished? The purpose is then none other than to prevent the culpit from causing new damage to his fellow citizens, and to deter others from following his example."[52] While the retributive penalty exercises an essentially symbolic role with an eye to moral reparation for damage, to the symbolic restoration of a broken equilibrium, or the magical effacement of a defilement of social life,[53] the preventive penalty aims at the correction of the culprit and the dissuasion of his potential imitators. The retributive penalty involves a long-term social time, or a mythical time where the imperative of maintaining established equilibriums within the group is primordial; by contrast, preventive measures presuppose the opening to the future, the malleability of criminal personalities and the adaptability of the public.[54]

Whole sections of modern law thus respond not to the need to reflect and canalise existing states of affairs or established relationships, but to the need to transform these situations and relationships in the light of a definite project of society: one might mention in particular social law, administrative law, consumer law and environmental law.

Finally, we must seek to identify a sixth variety of temporality, perhaps the most specifically legal one. It is rather hard to find a word for: at first sight it might seem to be a time of "alternation between being ahead and being behind", to take up one of Gurvitch's classifications:[55] a time that oscillates between tradition and anticipation, memory and forecast, long-established custom and promethean

---

[52] C. Beccaria, *Traité des délits et des peines*, (new French translated edition 1966, Paris) at p. 93; see also J. Bentham, *Traités de législation civile et pénale*, in *Œuvres...*, *supra*, note 35 at p. 143: "The principal aim of punishments is to prevent similar offences. A matter of the past is nothing but a point; the future is infinite. The past offence concerns only one individual; similar offenses might affect all. In many cases, it is impossible to remedy the ill done; but one may always remove the desire to do ill...".

[53] On this point, see P. Poncerla, "Par la peine, dissuader ou rétribuer" (1981) *Archives de philosophie du droit* at p. 68; see also F. Blondieau and J. Chanteur, e.d., *Rétribution et justice pénale* (1983, Paris).

[54] In connection with the belief in the malleability of the personality, as assumed by the penal policy of rehabilitation, see F. A. Allen, *The Decline of the Rehabilitive Ideal* (1981, New Haven and London) at p. 11.

[55] *Supra*, note 27 at p. 343.

statute. But one will come closer to reality by conceiving this time on the model of the spiral: a cumulative evolution which advances without ever denying itself. We shall therefore speak of *cumulative time,* which characterises a way of change within continuity, of progress imposed upon the inheritance of the past without ever totally replacing it. This temporality seems to us to be the time *par excellence* of the judge, who has sometimes to actualise tradition, to modernise customs and usages, sometimes, on the contrary, to moderate the law's enthusiasm for change. But the inverse position might equally be maintained: as a kind of temporal differential with the function of harmonising the variations of legal rhythms, it might be that the judge would have to anticipate legislative developments that social evolution is making absolutely necessary. This type of image is even tending to multiply today, so that the Husserlian equation between judge and past time seems largely refuted today. Such authors as Jacquemin and Remiche have well described the role of the economic judge, who has to act as a "time switch between the short term of economic advantage and the long term of legislative prescription".[56]

It will have been noted that, by contrast with the five previous temporalities, cumulative time has the special characteristic of bringing about a dialectic among several temporal dimensions. With cumulative time, one may glimpse the architecture or the specific legal organisation of multiple times. There can be seen in it the search for a constant balance between staticity and dynamism, conservation and innovation. Though this time seems to us to be essentially that of the judge – the clearest image of the permanent, gradual, "incremental" production of legality – it nevertheless characterises large areas of the legal system looked at as a whole.

The study of the representation of time underlying the Civil Code and the motives of its authors illustrates this thesis. In the explanatory statement presented to the legislature, Portalis, after regretting "the continual vacillation in the laws for ten years, which has left minds at the mercy of every wind of doctrine and brought about only opposition and resistance", declares that he ought to have forearmed himself "in sketching out the legislative plan that France needs ... both against the spirit of system that tends to destroy everything, and against the spirit of superstition, servitude and idleness that tends to respect everything".[57] Thus, at the very moment when France was giving itself a monument of codification, a symbol of promethean time, its principal architect sets out a prudent conception of time which accepts innovations only in so far as they have been prepared by the evolutions of the past. The manifestations of this conception abound in Portalis's

---

[56] A. Jacquemin and B. Remiche, *Le pouvoir judiciaire entre l'opportunité et la légalité économiques, supra* note 1, at p. 16. This point has likewise been strongly stressed by F. Kuebler, in "Juridification of corporate structures" in G. Teubner ed., *Juridication of Social Spheres* (1987, Berlin) at p. 229: "The courts function more and more often as the forerunners of legislation, which is contenting itself with subsequently converting regulations worked out in the courts into statutory provisions. Sometimes the Courts also intervene when legislative initiatives have failed".

[57] P. A. Fenet, *Recueil complet des travaux préparatoires du Code civil,* vol. VI, (1827, Paris) at p. 57.

writings: "the work would be beyond our powers," he exclaims, "were it to amount to giving this people an absolutely new institution . . ., if one disdained to profit from the experience of the past, and from that tradition of good sense, of rules and of maxims, which has come down to us and which forms the spirit of the centuries".[58]

And again, "leave alone what is good, if one is in doubt of what is better".[59] Moreover, it is impossible to forecast everything in the law: "How can the action of time be tied down? How can one oppose the course of events, or the imperceptible shifting in mores? How can one know and calculate in advance what only experience can show us?".[60]

This is not to say that no change should be made. That would be too paradoxical in embarking on a codification of such scope. One must only take care that "there are no changes to public judgements other than those brought about by the advances of the Enlightenment and by the force of circumstance".[61] Finally – and here the mixed time of the alternation between past and future is in turn related to a third temporality – one must not, maintains Portalis, lose sight of the fact that "rather than change the laws, it is almost always more useful to present the citizens with new reasons for loving them".[62] In that way, the great jurisconsult was recalling the fundamental characteristic of legal rationality, that, whatever be the content of a regulation, it takes its binding force from some "account" relating to the time of foundations, which ought periodically to be recalled.

But apart from Portalis's declaration of intent, it does seem that the Code itself applies this alternating time. The French Civil Code swings, as has often been observed, between a concern for social conservatism and the needs of economic dynamism. The aspiration to lastingness of social relationships and to stability of fortunes is counter-balanced by the desire to leave a field open for private initiative. The technology of time produced in the Code arbitrates between these two antagonistic tendencies. Thus, from a concern for social stability, the authors of the Civil Code "sought to conserve certain long-term contracts such as long leases and ground-rent leases, which allow an increase in the number of property-owners, which is to say of true citizens".

Inversely, the desire not to get in the way of the economic dynamism inherent in the liberal system led to the banning of everything that "might oppose trade, distort the free play of competition, or delay the fortune of the weakest and the impoverishment of those who blunder".[63]

Other illustrations of this cumulative time, or time of alternation and delay, of

---

[58] M. Portalis, "Discours préliminaire", in Locre, *La législation civile, commerciale et criminelle de la France ou commentaire complet des codes français*, Vol. I (1827, Paris) at p. 254.

[59] *Ibid.*, at p. 255.

[60] *Ibid.*, at p. 257.

[61] *Ibid.*, at p. 260.

[62] *Ibid.*, at p. 255.

[63] A. Cabanis, "L'utilisation du temps par les rédacteurs du Code civil", in *Mélanges P. Hébraud*, (1981, Toulouse) at p. 181.

oscillation between memory and forecast, might easily be supplied. Thus, while it is undeniable, as we have sought to show, that the penal policy of prevention is linked with promethean time, it is no less certain that the penal policy actually pursued in our countries during the 19th and 20th centuries seems to sway constantly between prevention and retribution (the latter relating to long-term time and the time of foundations), when it does not simply content itself with simultaneously pursuing both policies, thereby superimposing several temporalities. The image of a legal time that advances spirally, always reintegrating what it seemed to have rejected, then urges itself upon the mind.

What conclusions can be drawn from this typology of legal temporalities?

The first conclusion is the recognition that law is no exception to the rule already widely confirmed in other social fields: the time that they deal with must be considered in the plural. The classification we have just given – which is no doubt not exhaustive – is an illustration of this.

The second conclusion takes us on to the road of interpretation of the phenomena found. There is in fact a point in common that characterises the various temporalities studied: all of them – in different ways and to different extents, to be sure – favour *duration*, as if a certain duration were consubstantial with the legal form itself. The first three times, as we have seen, deploy a strategy of de-temporalisation, which is certainly the best way of lasting: the fabled time of foundations, proper to the constitutional norm, seeks to put itself outside the hazards of the course of history; the omnitemporal present of doctrine puts legal texts into a logical time deprived of any existential attachment; the instantaneous time characteristic of the validity of norms and legal acts seeks to guarantee these against the wear of time that passes.

The long-term time, manifested essentially in custom, usage and general principle, introduces into law the continuity of tradition. As for promethean time – the time of statute and codes – it seeks to bind the future by vast normative projections secreted by eschatological ideologies.

Finally, the cumulative time of case law, to the extent that it brings about a continual adjustment of tradition and change, assures the legal system of stability and continuity, by gradually impressing on it the individual adaptations that become necessary.

Maurice Hauriou was an author who saw clearly this aspiration of law to duration: "Human societies", he wrote, "are hungry for duration. For long they sought it in the past, basing themselves desperately on custom. Following an enormous turn-round ... they now seek it in the future, basing themselves on virtualities".[64] In the same sense, the recent lexical studies of the Civil Code by computer methods show an overgrowth of the vocabulary of conservation, of continuous time, by comparison with ordinary language. Bordeaux, who did these analyses, concludes that they show a conservative, integral time, which he

---

[64.] M. Hauriou, *Principes de droit public* at p. 676, cited in P. Hebraud, "La notion de temps dans l'œuvre du Doyen Maurice Hauriou", in *La pensée du Doyen Maurice Hauriou et son influence* (1969, Paris) at p. 203.

terms "masculine", and reject any manifestation of a split-up, unforeseen time, termed "feminine time".[65]

These last remarks must nevertheless be qualified by pointing out that while the various times of law, and still more the various representations of the time of law, postulate duration, the latter does not always operate in the same direction. Thus, the long duration of custom may very well set up an effect of resistance against the promethean time of statute. In this way the confrontation of different temporalities, their interaction in the real life of law, may in certain cases provoke contingent phenomena which then escape from the attempt to control time made by the social actors and amplified by legal thought.

Furthermore, in the life of law, phenomena of discontinuity are to be noted. The law is a net – as Carbonnier wrote – where the spaces count as much as the material.[66]

As far as time is concerned, this leads to the observation of periods of withdrawal or abstention by the law: like the night, as opposed to the light of day – the night, empty of law, where man, as Carbonnier again writes, returns to the state of nature;[67] likewise the periods of social licence or officially tolerated moral reversal: the Saturnalia of antiquity or the Christian carnival.[68]

These contingencies and these discontinuities do not however alter the profound tendency of the legal form which, as we have seen, implies a minimum of duration, without which neither security nor foreseeability could emerge. This lesson is important: it might well have the effect of placing beyond the sphere of law the phenomena of precarious, random normativity which accompany the implementation of the economic and social policies that the Welfare State feels it must pursue.[69]

II. Historical Approach. Articulation of Legal Temporalities

After the description, the interpretation. One cannot confine oneself to a simple juxtaposition of temporalities, as if every history went its own way. Without falling back into the metaphysical traps of a single history, the attempt must be made to correlate, articulate, arrange in hierarchies, all these times which march to the rhythm of the groups and representations from which they have emerged. It

---

[65] M. Bordeaux, "La grille du temps: approche lexicale du temps des lois (Code civil 1804)", (1979) 53 *Langages*, at p. 115; same author, see also "Quand le temps dévore l'espace: temps et espace, facteurs de normalisation dans le Code civil (1804)" *Religion, société et politique, supra* note 63 at p. 198: "The code banishes the feminine aspect from time: using these antinomic couplets, we may say that is excludes the qualified, the piecemeal, the unexpected, risk and providence, the play of the moment, of novelty, of creation".

[66] J. Carbonnier, *Flexible droit, supra* note 9, at p. 25.

[67] *Ibid.*, at p. 49.

[68] *Ibid.*, at p. 24.

[69] See again Carbonnier (*supra* at p. 115): "The law becomes a procedure of government. Hence those features which are repugnant to true law, but natural to commandments: precipitation, mobility, and also a certain vulgarity of style".

does seem that the only way of avoiding the Scylla of a broken-up, "pointilliste" temporality without falling into the Charybdis of a single, homogeneous time, is to take the path of history itself. That is the essential lesson: time itself is historical. We mean that the necessary hierarchicalisations of various temporalities are themselves a product of history and of the dominances developing within it. There are, therefore, temporal architecture and hierarchical organisation, but these do not have any necessity in the way of the Hegelian march of the absolute Spirit: they too are caught up in history. As Pomian excellently puts it: "The history of time thus unveils itself as a close relation of that of levels of organisation".[70]

The programme for our research is thus traced out: to pick out simultaneously both the history of the temporalities of law and the transformations of levels of organisation of legal forms.

Here too a convenient starting point for reflection can be found in Husserl's essay already mentioned. It will be remembered that the author distinguished between the past time of the judge, the futurist time of the legislator and the present time of the Administration. On this basis, the following periodisation is suggested: as long as the community is anchored in its past, tradition is the source of law, and it is the judge who, quite naturally, acts as its interpreter. The example given is that of the progressive development of Common Law. By contrast, when the community turns towards the future, it is statute which becomes the dominant source of law and, with it, a temporality that tends towards the future. Finally, when the grand schemes of values which bind men to their past or project them into the future weaken, the reign of the present sets in, and with it, the domination of the Administration over the other two powers: legislation can scarcely be distinguished any longer from regulation, while in judges' decision, considerations of appropriateness now fight it out with conclusions of law.[71]

While this presentation may generally be subscribed to, it nevertheless seems essential to put the issues on a wider basis. We shall be helped in doing so from the theory which undoubtedly represents one of the major acquisitions of legal thought of the 20th century, and relates precisely to the level of organisation of the legal order; that is the conception of legal systems as a union of primary rules and secondary rules. It will be recalled that Hart, who laid the foundations for this theory, distinguishes between primary rules, which impose obligations and dictate conducts, and secondary rules which, relating to the former, determine the way in which the primary rules may be identified, decreed, abrogated or amended, and the fact that they have been infringed established.[72] Not content with applying this extremely fertile typology of legal norms, Hart – and here we come to our theme again – suggests that there is a progressive move from simple legal systems made up solely of primary norms to complex legal systems including primary norms and secondary norms.[73]

---

[70] K. Pomian, *supra* note 25, at p. 354.
[71] G. Husserl, *supra* note 28, at p. 63.
[72] H. L. A. Hart, *The concept of law*, translation M. van de Kerchove (1976, Brussels) at p. 119.
[73] **Ibid.**, at pp. 116–119.

However allusive it may be, this notation should enable us to bring about the articulation we are seeking. Accordingly, in the development of normative systems, there would have been a primitive period where, for lack of constitutive authority, the identification of the rules in force, their amendment and the detection and punishment of infringements of them are left to the collective initiative of the members of the group. In a second phase, which not all normative systems, nor even all legal systems, necessarily reach, the group splits up, as it were, with some of its members henceforth acting as authorities, while secondary norms appear. Finally, pursuing this reflection which Hart has not taken to its end, we have to ask how appropriate this representation is for legal systems in our post-modern societies.

There is no doubts that these three stages of structuring of legal systems correspond to particular dominant temporalities. Thus, we maintain that the time proper to simple normative systems made up exclusively of primary norms is the customary time which we have termed long-term time. Complex legal systems, for their part, presuppose a time that is deliberately controlled by legal agents: it would, then, be a promethean time, often tempered, to be sure, by the cumulative time or the time of alternation between advance and delay. Finally, venturing to interpret the most contemporary actuality of our legal systems, we shall put forward the hypothesis that these systems, marked by a very perceptible degradation of legal form because of the break-down of balance in the relationship between primary norms and secondary norms, are today involved in a random temporality – a new phenomena which, while not being without reference to the specific time of technology and science, will call for particular developments in legal matters.

The customary time predominating in simple legal systems we shall scarcely mention, being unable in the limited framework of this study to use the findings of legal ethnology and anthropology on the subject. What should be recalled is that in such a framework those to whom rules are addressed are at the same time their authors and their judges. The changes that affect the norm then operate collectively and unconsciously, as can be seen in the case of rules of etiquette or rules of language. That is no doubt the reason for the impression of staticity to which the contemplation of such systems gives rise, such as, for instance, the system of laws of nature prevailing in the "state of nature" described by such authors as Locke or Kant.

It should further be observed, following Norberto Bobbio, that the move from simple legal systems to complex legal systems is, of course, gradual and progressive, so that the concept of "semicomplex system", bound up with a specific temporality, has to be introduced.[74] A semi-complex normative system is a system that includes only some of the varieties of secondary norms, namely rules of change and not rules of decision, or the other way round.[75] It is of the greatest interest for our discussion to note the temporal consequences of these two cases.

---

[74] On this, see N. Bobbio, "Nouvelles réflexions sur les normes primaires et secondaires" in *La règle de droit*, studies published by Ch. Perelman (1971, Brussels) at p. 18.

[75] Let us recall that in Hart's terminology, rules of change "empower an individual or a body

First hypothesis: a lack of efficiency of the customary system is remedied by reinforcing the system of sanctions. Obedience to the system can apparently no longer be ensured solely through diffuse disapproval of private vengeance; a judge is instituted, to pronounce on breaches of the rule and deliver punishments. This kind of semi-complex system obviously favours the stability of social relationships and the conservation of rules.

Second hypothesis: there is again a gap between the norms in force and social needs, but this time it is remedied by the introduction of rules of change, because customary transformations appear as too slow and uncertain. Authorities are instituted with the power of introducing new rules or amending or abrogating the old ones. In this case, it is obviously the imperative of mutability that is favoured.

From these initial analyses, it appears that a system equipped only with secondary rules on sanctions would be dysfunctional because of the excess of staticity, while a system with only secondary rules of change would be over-dynamic.[76] Thus, most frequently, the transition from simple systems to complex systems takes place gropingly, through the unstable equilibria sought between conservation and innovation, customary time and promethean time. The evolution of public international law over the last few decades could usefully be studied from this viewpoint; one notes there, given the failure of international society to really structure itself and equip itself with common authorities, attempts, generally disappointing, to bring international relationships either under judicial regulation or under general norms adopted in the forums of the international organisations. One has to conclude that international jurisdiction is rejected because it is suspected by some, rightly or wrongly, of reflecting a legal order regarded as too well established, while the binding character of the norms adopted by the major international organisations is rightly or wrongly doubted by others for whom those norms reflect some new legal or economic order regarded as more prospective than effective.[77]

However it may be with these progressive adjustments, the general direction of evolution from simple legal systems to complex legal systems can be understood as the move from a time broadly anchored in tradition to a time broadly oriented towards the future. Linguists today confirm that the grammatical tense that appears latest in the development of languages is the future.[78] But the future, like

---

of people to introduced new primary rules, and to eliminate the old rules"; they likewise confer on "individuals the power of modifying their initial situations vis-à-vis the primary rules"; as for rules of decision, they "empower individuals to resolve with authority the question whether a primary rule has been broken and ... set the sanctions applicable in the event of infringement". (supra note 72 at p. 121).

[76] On this, see N. Bobbio, *supra* note 74, at p. 120.

[77] On the various reasons for dislike of international law-making, see J. Verhoeven, *A propos de la fonction de juger en droit international public, in Fonction de juger et pouvoir judiciaire. Transformations et déplacements,* under the direction of Ph. Gérard, F. Ost and M. van de Kerchove (1983, Brussels) at p. 447.

[78] See G. Jucquois, "Les catégories du temps dans le langage", in *Langages muiltiples sur le temps. Cahiers de l'institut de linguistique de Louvain,* texts edited by P. Watté (1981, Louvain-la-Neuve) at pp. 171 and 181.

the imperative which is also absent from primitive languages, is precisely the "legislative time" *par excellence*, the one that reflects a clear awareness of the rule.[79] It is not that conduct is not regulated in traditional societies: automatisms, rites, religious taboos and prohibitions, usage and custom, certainly provide a tight framework for social life, but not yet any specifically legal regulation.

Furthermore, we must note a feature pointed out by Pomian: the swing from a past-dominated time devoted to the imitation of examples inherited through immemorial custom, to a futurist time which values discovery and invention, presupposes the progressive abandonment of religion, for which the future itself is already programmed, that is to say closed, in favour of science, which day by day constructs an ever more open future.[80] This swing is nevertheless itself extremely slow, and goes through an intermediate stage which might well interest the lawyer at the highest level: this intermediate stage is that of rationalism – half-way between religion and science (thus the whole theme, dear to Rousseau and Bentham, of civil religion, or again the positive religion of Auguste Comte) – represented essentially by legal institutions. We are therefore brought back to complex legal systems.

These complex legal orders are characterised by a dynamic type of equilibrium providing suitable proportions of norms of transformation and rules of sanction. The group resolves no longer to let the evolution of the legal system depend on the spontaneous initiative of its members; henceforth there is a conscious control of the time proper to the system, which inevitably leads to the attempt to control social time through legal regulation. The general direction of the movement is certainly towards the future, which it now claims deliberately to control; but at the same time acquisitions should be consolidated, so that the promethean time is moderated by the cumulative time or the time of alternation. The variety of functions performed by secondary norms well reflects the arbitration thus effected between past and future. But this idea can also be confirmed from another sector of legal thought: the theory of institutions, of which it has rightly been said that in the minds of its protagonists (notably Hauriou and Santi Romano) it had a function equivalent to that of secondary norms in Hart.[81] Specifically, Hauriou never ceased putting forward the institution as the privileged means available to a group for controlling time. "The institution," he wrote, "is an idea of work or of undertaking which is legalised and lasts legally within a social environment".[82] Two dimensions of time are, obviously, involved in this conception. On the one hand, permanence and duration: the institution as a factor of organisation in social life assures it of a coherence and guarantees it against the entropy that threatens every human achievement. But the institution is also a factor of progress and transformation, since it also realises "an idea of work"; it actualises, at the cost of

---

[79] In this sense, see J. Carbonnier, *supra* note 9, at p. 67.
[80] See K. Pomian, *supra* note 25, at p. 294.
[81] On this point, see Bobbio, *supra* note 74, at p. 121.
[82] H. Hauriou, *La théorie de l'institution et de la fondation* at p. 36 cited by P. Hebraud, *La notion de temps dans l'œuvre du Doyen Maurice Hauriou, supra* note 64 at p. 196.

an incessant labour of adaptation to changing circumstances, the "virtualities" of which the social project of the future claims to be the bearer.[83]

It therefore does seem that with the appearance of complex legal systems including secondary norms and institutions, law's relationship to time takes on a new and decisive form. For the first time, the question of placing the legal rule in time becomes a both explicit and legal question. legal systems, now self-regulated, are capable of controlling the duration of validity of their rules and the rhythm of change that is to be imposed on them.

It is again Hart who has most precisely described the capacity of developed legal systems normatively to determine their own placing in time. The thesis forms part of a debate against the imperativist theory of Austin.[84] As is well known, Austin analysed the law as the command of the Sovereign, and its validity rests on the simple habit of obedience of the subjects in his regard. Such a model, maintains Hart, does not meet the needs of a developed legal order. What mechanism can in fact guarantee that orders issued by a new sovereign will be obeyed, before a habit is formed in this sense? Moreover, what phenomena explain that the orders issued by a former sovereign are still in force today, when both this sovereign and the subjects who had the habit of obeying him are dead? The conclusion is inevitable, at least in our legal orders, that the norm already constitutes law even before a habit of obedience has been manifested, just as it still constitutes law vis-à-vis individuals totally alien to the society formed by a dead sovereign and his subjects. Manifestly, the concept of "habit" fails to account either for continuity in the exercise of legislative power or for the permanence of the legal rule. If a new sovereign is obeyed and if a norm outlives its author, this is because in both cases, as Hart explains, a fundamental rule is accepted to determine which people have the right to make law. This secondary rule of recognition "though it must exist today, may in a certain sense be timeless in reference: it may not only be valid for the future and refer to the legislative activity of a future legislator, but also be valid for the past and refer to the activities of a prevous legislator".[85]

One sees what is at stake in this emergence of the secondary rule of recognition: a diffuse, passive temporality characterised by the phenomenon of the habit of obedience is replaced by the deliberately programmed temporality which sustains the empowerment of the authorities. The uncontrollable shifts of the long term, of time as lived through, are replaced by the predictability of the future and the selective conservation of the past. While it is no doubt advisable not to be taken in by this claim of complex legal systems to control time, since the pretension is only partly realised because of the resistance of the other temporalities, and while, moreover, one still has to bear in mind that the very content of the rule of recognition – the determination of the acts that create law and the designation of the competent authorities – may be the object of multiple reconstructions, more or

---

[83] On this interpretation of Hauriou's thought, see A. Brimo "Réflexions sur le temps dans la théorie générale du droit et de l'Etat", in *Mélanges offerts à P. Hébraud* (1981, Toulouse) at p. 158.

[84] *Supra* note 83, at p. 77.

[85] H. L. A. Hart, *supra*, note 72, at p. 85.

less influenced by competing representations of time, that does not mean that one should underestimate the major importance of the relationship to time set up by the complex legal systems.

This point too did not escape Kelsen, who termed "dynamic" the structure of legal orders based on a fundamental norm empowering this or that authority to create law. By contrast with certain ethical systems based on a fundamental norm, from whose content all inferior norms derive, the legal order presupposes a fundamental law that exclusively designates a process of creation of the derived norms. While these ethical systems present a static structure, the legal orders go through a dynamic development, since it is up to the constituted authorities to determine, according to their own will, the content of the inferior norms.[86] This observation entails an important consequence: if it is true that legal orders have a dynamic structure, then "it follows that any content whatsoever can be law".[87] One can understand how this fact favours the mutability of complex legal systems. Whereas in simple legal systems made up of norms of conduct of customary character and not clearly separated from moral and religious imperatives, the significance of a content that is to be respected means a great stability in the rules, by contrast, in a dynamic legal order, the freedom from any foundational content ought in principle to favour very broad initiative on the part of the authorities who create law. Here too the analysis should doubtless be qualified by giving it back a sociological weight which it deliberately rejects: it is clear that multiple condition-ings in fact rarefy the normative production and reduce the field which it could theoretically cover. It is nevertheless the case that mutability is among the principles of our complex legal systems. The determination of the rate at which it seems desirable to introduce changes to the texts raises the problem of transitional law, which we should now look at.

Mutability is a principle of complex systems, we have maintained. This does not mean that any change whatever is assimilable by the social body. Bentham, the great theoretician of the art of legislation, put the problem very clearly. "The goodness of the laws", he maintained, "depends on their conformity with general expectation. It is therefore important to know the course of those expectations well, so as to act in concert with them".[88] And the British reformer goes on to regret that the legislator was not faced with a people of children that the could have shaped as he wished, "as the sculptor does a block of marble".[89] Accordingly – since it must be admitted that a multitude of ancient laws and immemorial usages have already shaped the people's expectations – adjustments are necessary. If it proves that a new law, contrary to present expectations, has to be adopted, it will at least be wise to delay its effects: a generation will not be too long to allow minds to become acclimatised to the new regulation.[90]

[86] H. Kelsen, *Pure Theory of Law*, translation of the 2nd ed by Ch. Eisenmann, (1962, Paris) at p. 258.
[87] H. Kelsen, *supra* note 86, at p. 261.
[88] J. Bentham, *supra* note 35, at p. 81.
[89] *Ibid*. It will be recalled that for his part Rousseau regretted "that men were not, before the laws, what they ought to become through them".
[90] *Ibid*.

Jean Dabin develops this teaching. If one understands that legal creation is a work of prudence, one will admit that positive law is not affected by such great variability as one might have thought. Undoubtedly, normative production is a "wager on the future", but the change will take place only in order to adapt the law to changes in things, in public opinion and in the needs of the public good.[91] One should also bear in mind that "any change in the laws, even if justified in itself, provokes a crisis and consequently an evil".[92] However, when faster changes prove essential, the legislator will do well to provide "certain temporisations or transitional measures in order to attenuate the brutality of the shock".[93]

It is now clear that the promethean temporality, so characteristic of complex legal systems and of the uniterrupted, deliberate process of creation of law which they involve, compromises with the cumulative temporality or the time of alternation between advance and delay. The transitional law, as a complex of secondary norms, reflects the measure of this shifting arbitration.[94]

In this connection, it is clearly too reductive to maintain that the old law's effects cease the day the new law comes into force. Under the rule of the previous legislation, legal situations of all types were set up, certain of whose effects will extend under the rule of the new law, and it is not always desirable or equitable for them to be affected by the latter. If there is no explicit transitional provision, doctrine and case law seek to maintain a balance between, on the one hand, the need for legal security which leads to preservation of acquired entitlements and reinforcement of definitive situations, and on the other, the concern for equality before the law, for unity and progress of legislation, which plead in favour of the immediate application of the most recent regulation. On this basis, some principles of the solution to conflicts of transitional law have been identified, notably by Roubier, in his classic work dealing with transitional law.[95]

The first rule is the non-retroactivity of the new law in respect of definitively accomplished situations. The second, the immediate application of the new law, not only at the creation of situations that arise under its rule, but even to the future effects of situations created under the rule of the old law. The third rule makes exceptions to the second in respect of contracts which benefit from the survival of old law, in order to respect the expectations of the contracting parties and the principle of autonomy of will. This last solution, however, in turn has a derogation – the fourth rule – in cases where the new regulation is one of *ordre public*.[96]

This theory, well balanced in its formulation, was very widely accepted; but it unduly favours legal change, to the extent that it does not retain the concept of

[91] J. Dabin, *Théorie générale du droit* (new ed., 1969, Paris) at p. 309.
[92] *Ibid.*, at p. 310.
[93] *Ibid.*, at p. 312.
[94] On the secondary nature of rules of transitional law, see E. Bulygin, "Time and Validity", in *Deontic logic, computational linguistics and legal information systems*, A. Martine ed. (1983, New York–Amsterdam).
[95] P. Roubier, *Le droit transitoire* (2nd ed., 1960, Paris).
[96] For Belgian doctrine see H. de Page, *Traité élémentaire de droit civil belge*, (2nd ed.,, 1939, Brussels) Vol. I at 277.

"established entitlements". The legal subject is presented as in a "legal situation" which, with the reservation of the maintenance of those of its effects which are definitively established, appears dependent on rules of objective law and exposed to changes in them.[97]

This trend became even more marked over recent decades. In fact, increasingly frequently, the legislator himself intends, through explicit transitional provisions, to regulate the problem of the application in time of the norms that he adopts. One suspects that the result of the process is strengthened support for the principle of immediate application of the new law.

Madame Dekeuwer-Defossez, who has carried out a detailed analysis of "transitional provisions in contemporary civil legislation", proposes the following conclusions: the rapid, widespread application of the new law becomes the common law, so that no distinction is any longer made between the contractual or non-contractual origin of legal situations. "The concern to see reforms felt necessary for social progress promptly applied appears clearly in transitional provisions. Every means imaginable is applied to this effect: the immediate application of the new law, its retroactivity, and the substantive provisions".[98]

It seems, however, that in certain areas which evolve more slowly, like family law, caution has slowed this headlong progression of legislation. Jean Carbonnier, who was closely involved in a series of reforms made in French family law, furnishes several keys to the "legislative strategy" applied in that area. The legislative art, he explains, has become aware of its own limits. "It has learnt to regard the phenomenon of total or partial non-application as natural, and include them in its calculations". Moreover, "it has been understood that legislation does not stop on the day it is promulgated. The archaic conception is finished, whereby the laws were supposed to be shut in on themselves, closed to the future... Modern legislation is a continuous creation".[99]

On the basis of this new sociological realism, the French legislator sometimes adopts "trial laws" whose effectiveness is then assessed after a few years,[100] or sometimes "two-speed laws" which give individuals the choice between various legal models, as is the case in respect of marriage settlements and divorce.[101] In the latter case, the legislator deliberately programmes a form of survival of the old law, for an indeterminate period, which mores and practice will have to define. Thus, at the very moment when the autonomy of the married woman is established, the precaution is nevertheless taken to provide for the legal consequences of the

---

[97] In this sense, see F. Dekeuwer-Defossez, *Les dispositions transitoires dans la législation civile contemporaine* (1977, Paris) at p. 13.

[98] J. Carbonnier, "Tendances actuelles de l'art législatif en France" in *Essais sur les lois* (1979, Paris) at p. 241.

[99] On these "try-out laws", see R. Savatier "L'inflation législative et l'indigestion du corps social" in (1977) *Dalloz*, especially at p. 43.

[100] J. Carbonnier, *supra* note 99, at p. 46.

[101] *Ibid.*, at p. 48; see also at p. 49: "Certainly, this presence of conservative provisions within a reform which wishes to be profoundly innovatory is a flagrant contradiction. Why could French law not this once have chosen to be empirical rather than logical?"

husband's consent to administrative acts by this married woman. In this way, these conscious anachronisms ultimately confer on each generation a statute of its own. It is in fact, Carbonnier concludes, "a hypothesis of sociology that two or more legal generations may co-exist in one and the same society".[102]

Here we explicitly rejoin Bentham's suggestions in his reflections on the "power of the laws over expectations". One will note the flexibility of the legislative procedure described by Carbonnier: here, the placing of the law in a promethean, reforming time is accompanied by an empirical lucidity which allows the text of the law to have deliberately integrated into it procedures of self-control, areas of survival of old norms, provisions that are more suggestions than directives, or even loopholes. All these regulatory provisions allow the social body to adjust gently to the new provisions. The technology of time is no doubt here pushed to its highest degree of refinement. One should not however lose sight of the fact that, whatever the precautions taken to ease the transitions, the whole of the movement is located within an uninterrupted process of reform. And it is clear that the normative process of transformation does not always bother with all those arrangements.

Thus, the French law of November 15, 1976 – interpreting the law of January 3, 1972 which allowed adulterine children to bring an action to establish either their paternity or maternity – declares "the action admissible" without the possibility of any preclusion "even through a decision of justice that has become irrevocable". By this provision, case law is not only condemned for the future, but even in the past. Decisions already given are rendered null. This "super-retroactivity" of the law, using Mazeaud's term,[103] thus strikes a blow simultaneously at the binding authority of *res judicata*, at the independence of the judiciary power and at the principle of non-retroactivity of the laws. Need one recall in this connection Roubier's verdict: "retroactivity of law ... is quite simply the system of legality ridiculing itself"?[104]

On this same line of thought, one must mention the situation prevailing in administrative and regulatory matters. It is not so much the temporal application of regulation of general scope that raises problems: it is agreed that, while they cannot be retroactive, they are instead capable of being abrogated at any moment, and no-one can demand that established norms remain unchanged. A more delicate problem is the abrogation of individual administrative decisions that create law. Against the mutability of such decisions, the principle of their untouchability is sometimes brought up,[105] whereby the overdetermined notion of "established entitlements" reappears. It seems, however, that recent doctrine

---

[102] H. Mazeaud, "L'enfant adultérin et la "super-rétroactivité des lois", (1977) *Dalloz*, at p. 1.

[103] P. Roubier, "De l'effet des lois nouvelles sur les procès en cours", (19, Paris) *Mélanges Maury* at p. 533, Vol. 2.

[104] On this, see B. Jadot "Ordre public écologique et droits acquis" (1983) *Administration publique*, at p. 23.

[105] In this sense, see C. Vedel, *Droit administratif* (5th ed., 1973, Paris) at p. 202; see also C. Cambier, *Précis de droit administratif* (1968, Brussels), at p. 256.

considerably restricts the scope of the principle. To be sure, the administrative authority could not, by bringing about the abrogation of an individual decision, compromise a definitively established situation that has had irreversible effects (building permits, for instance), which would amount to making the abrogation itself retroactive. Moreover, the abrogation measure can be taken only on conditions laid down by law and regulation.[106] But in fact this reservation gives individuals only a very relative guarantee: these conditions are usually set only by administrative regulation, which means that since amendment of the regulations themselves is always possible, the abrogation of particular acts can likewise always be eventually achieved.[107] Altogether, the situation is one much more of a principle of mutability than of untouchability of individual administrative decisions that create law,[108] since the Administration has the task of adapting the legal ordinance to the needs – variable in nature – of the general interest and *ordre public.*

A similar conclusion, moreover, emerges from a study of the position of the user of public services. Need it be recalled that the "law of change", which implies the need for the service to transform itself at the rate of change of the general interest, prevents individuals from availing themselves of an established entitlement to the maintenance of the *status quo* at the moment when they become users?[109] Again, the public service is subject to the principle of continuity, which tolerates no interruption in its functioning, so that things become very clear: the permanence is on the side of the service, and the change on the side of the user.

Several other illustrations might be given of these increasingly precarious legal regulations, characterised by a time which one might term random. In penal law, there are the "sentences of indeterminate length": measures of security or social defence taken in respect of minors held to be "in danger", of abnormal delinquents, of vagabonds, etc. In social security matters, there are regulations subject to constant change; but as Zacher points out, how could there be any social security without a minimum of legal security?[110] As regards state subsidies, there is no security: if the subventions are subject to the system of annual budgets, there is no assurance that they will be renewed in future.

The centre of gravity of legality has thus progressively shifted from the subjects of law to the authorities. While in simple legal systems the convergent conduct of individuals creates the whole of the law, here it is the authorities who monopolise

---

106 In this sense, see J. Carbajo, *L'application dans le temps des décisions administratives exécutoires* (1980, Paris) at p. 131.

107 See J. Carbajo, *supra* note 106, at 226; see also B. Jadot, *supra* note 104, at p. 28: "The rule which it seems should consequently be erected into a principle is rather that of the 'actualisation' of administrative authorisation".

108 J. Riverso, *Droit administratif* (6th ed., 1973, Paris) at p. 419; see also A. Buttgenbach, *Manuel de droit administratif,* (3rd ed., 1966, Brussels), at p. 77.

109 M. F. Zacher, "Juridification of Social Welfare", in G. Teubner ed., *Juridication of Social Spheres* (1987, Berlin).

110 On this, see P. Amselek, "L'évolution générale de la technique juridique dans les sociétés occidentales" (1982) 2 *Revue de droit public et de la science politique en France et à l'étranger,* at p. 281.

the initiative of changing norms. Thanks no doubt to the innumerable resources of secondary norms, the whole process takes place with respect for legality, but if it is true, as has already been pointed out, that this legality itself is at the discretion of the authorities and that, moreover, in some areas the very change is raised to the dignity of "law", it must be admitted that the concession is a slight one. Indisputably, in our contemporary constitutional States, it is hard to resist the feeling that a limit has been reached, or even passed. It cannot in fact be denied that a form of perversion of the relationship to time has entered contemporary legal orders; we link this effect to an imbalance in the relationship of secondary norms to primary norms.

While in a customary context there is a (quasi) absence of secondary rules, and in a modern context there is a kind of balance between primary norms and secondary norms, in a post-modern context there is a movement towards an inflation of secondary rules bound up with the progressive dissolution of primary norms. Not that the primary rules that impose duties or specify prohibitions disappear; on the contrary, they abound. But it is precisely the fact of their proliferation, of their increasingly frequent amendment, and the most often *a posteriori* determination of their content, that make these rules today increasingly less known and internalised.

One may first of all note an astonishing increase of complexity in the rules of recognition allowing identification of the rules in force, which sometimes renders this search for the applicable law haphazard. It will then be noted – and this remark is decisive for what we have to say – that there is an increasingly accelerated rate of amendment, revision or abrogation of texts, which indubitably reflects unbridled use of the rules of change. It has been noted in France that legislation on companies, entirely recast in 1966, had undergone thirteen amendments between 1966 and 1972.[111] In these circumstances, one need not be astonished at failure to adhere to a rule. Cabonnier speaks in this connection of a form of "legal anxiety" due to the fact that "recent, not yet fully rooted law – law not yet thirty years old – represents more than half the applicable law", and the author goes on: "As if that were not enough, many of these new laws change so fast that they have no time to become part of the psychological baggage of individuals".[112]

It will no doubt be said that the rules of sanctions, aimed at ensuring the effectiveness of the primary rules and hence guaranteeing the stabilisation of the legal order, are likewise going through a considerable increase in number. To be sure, no one will deny that the field of penal repression has today considerably expanded: *"Nulla lex sine poena"*, though perhaps one cannot still maintain the converse proposition. One must however agree that these secondary norms of punishment are in turn affected by a considerable lack of effectiveness, a phenomenon which no doubt contributes to an explanation of the popularity of the contemporary theme of de-penalisation. The profileration of repressive norms

---

[111] J. Carbonnier, *Flexible droit*, (4th ed., 1979, Paris) at p. 129.

[112] On this point, see G. Kellens, "Diversification des sanctions" (1983) 1–2 *Aspects particuliers de la réforme du droit pénal, Annales de droit de Louvain*, at p. 180: "Penal law gets lost through multiplying itself".

and the increasingly frequent discrepancies between what they prescribe and the actual possibilities of applying them bring about a multiplication of phenomena of tolerance of transgression.[113]

Such, then, is the imbalance which is progressively arising: intense recourse to rules of change not compensated for by rules of sanction, which are largely ineffective, and rules of identification, which are overcomplex. The transformatory function of the rules of change is no longer sufficiently balanced by the stabilising function of the rules of sanction. Still more serious is the fact that this ineffectiveness of sanction is itself no doubt nothing but an index of a lack of internalisation of models of conduct that one might wish to see adopted by the subjects of law. In other words, there is erosion of the binding character of the primary norms of conduct themselves. The rapid time of secondary norms is no longer meshed with the slower time of conduct and usage.

In this way, unbridled normativism is seemingly leading the constitutional State (made up of primary and secondary laws) up a blind alley: though it is, by comparison with a legal system based only on primary rules, supposed to guarantee certainty, predictability and adaptability to change, it instead leads to ignorance of the rule, to chronic instability and to unpredictability. Leisner has no hesitation in writing in this connection that the modern rule of law is "retroactivity *in potentia* ... a reward for disappointed trust" and that, accordingly, "if there is still calculability in the *Rechtsstaat*, it is far less because of democratic norms than because of the survival of predemocratic structures of custom and practice".[114]

One might be tempted to bring this time of post-modern legal systems together with the social time of technology and science. Can we not see on both sides the same opacity of the future, linked up with its radical openness? Because everything seems possible, nothing is assured, still less because there is no mobilising discourse capable of drawing up some great project for the future.[115] However, the coincidence can only be indirect; it is in fact useless to insist on the difference in nature between legal techniques and the procedures of technology and science. By contrast, if it is true that science and technology function today, as Habermas maintains, as "ideology", then it must be possible to find in present legal rationality the representations inspired by the logic of technological practice.

There does in fact seem to be one dominant representation in the legal field today: the ideology of change itself. From the moment when the law is no longer content to arbitrate social relationships, but seeks to be an agent of social change,[116] it ceases to refer to a general interest conceived in static terms;

---

[113] W. Leisner, "L'Etat de droit, une contradiction" (1976, Paris) *Recueil d'études en hommage à Ch. Eisenmann*, at p. 70.

[114] On this point, see K. Pomian, "La crise de l'avenir" (1980–7, Paris) *Le débat*, at p. 6: "The ideologues seem in our times to have lost the ability to conceive a future that is both plausible and attractive".

[115] On this development, see F. Ost, "Juge-pacificateur, juge-arbitre, juge-entraîneur. Trois modèles de justice", *Fonction de juger...*, *supra* note 77 at p. 19.

[116] In this sense, see J. Chevallier and D. Loschak, *Science administrative*, (1978, Paris) at p. 446, Vol. II.

henceforth it is in terms of dynamic objectives, or prospects, that it will be determined. In these circumstances, the stability and rigidity of the classical rule of law constitute obstacles to be overcome: the law will instead adopt a flexible, adaptable form; it will be called plan, framework-law, enabling law, guideline law. The legal form thus becomes the object of total instrumentalisation in the service of objectives defined by the representatives of other disciplines: economics, management "science", medicine, psychiatry or whatever.[117] Here, the mutability that is part of the principles of complex legal systems is itself placed at the service of a radically evolutionary social normativity.

There has certainly never been so much concern about planning the future – the administration itself is becoming prospective, in Sfez's phrase[118] – but it seems that the intensity of the prospective activity is in inverse relation to the transparency of the future. By privileging the bare idea of progress, conceived of as improved efficiency, increased yield, strengthened utility, one is not yet asking about the goals of this progress, one is not evoking any model of society which, by being largely internalised, would be the only thing capable of assuring some predictability to the future.

Here again, however, one must show restraint: prospective law has not yet stifled the statute, just as the latter has never succeeded in rejecting spontaneous law. The analysis is confined to picking out the normative strata, the superimposition of which, like geological layers, is a function of particular "eras": there is supposed to be the time of custom, peaceful and continuous, the time of the rule, controlled and moderately evolutionary, and finally the time of programme, radically provisional. And just as the arrangement of the landscape may be upset by deep tectonic movements, with the oldest part being brought to the surface, so can social life, in certain areas, be affected by smaller upsets which lead to the first place being given to forms of normativity, and hence of temporality, which hitherto were buried.

Conclusions

The time has come to offer some conclusions to these prefatory reflections.

The first section of this paper offered a classification of observable legal temporalities. No trace was found there of a random temporality. The second section endeavoured to make comprehensible the articulations between these temporalities by placing them in a historical perspective linked with the study of the levels of organisation of legality. In this context, a precarious or random temporality appeared, a recent phenomenon consequent on the imbalance that has arisen in the relationship between primary norms and secondary norms. Accordingly, it is at a time when legal form is undergoing profound alterations – starting with the very considerable reduction in its binding character – that a provisional, precarious or random temporality has arisen.

[117] L. Sfez, "L'administration prospective", *supra* note 3.
[118] In this sense, see D. Loschak, "Mutation des droits de l'homme et mutation du droit", *supra* note 13, at p. 65.

We attribute these imbalances to an undoubtedly excessive instrumentalisation of law, which is thus deprived of any transcendence vis-à-vis the social (while a symbolic distance between rule and power is the very indispensable condition of its authority)[119] and completely in thrall to rationalities which are alien to it, for instance economic or medical ones.

A very clear relationship is thus established between this phenomenon and the theme of de-legalisation. In this case one may indeed speak of de-legalisation through reduced quality: it is, paradoxically, the abundance of law that brings about the perversion of law, just as the inflation of monetary tokens brings about their depreciation, or the pathological multiplication of living cells causes their cancerisation.

This last observation allows one to suggest a few more positive approaches. Instead of giving credit to the demagogic themes of de-regulation or massive disarming of law, it is no doubt better to become more aware of the various levels of intervention of law and to modulate its action in a less unilateral manner.

Thus, for instance, law cannot be reduced to statute, still less to regulation. A certain de-legalisation (abstention from lawmaking) or de-regulation (abstention from regulating) might be accompanied by the recognition of increased responsibilities for the judicial power, which as we have seen could take on an essential role as time switch between the long term of legal principles and the short-term of economic and social appropriateness. A cautiously experimental case-law (itself accompanied by pre-trial judicial intervention in order not to surprise economic and social operators) might subsequently inspire a legislator who would intervene only once the options were clearly established and the means of reaching them clearly identified.

Moreover, the law cannot be reduced to State law. The Welfare State must rediscover the creative potential inherent in legal norms produced by associations and groups. Giving a framework to these groups, promoting concertation and democratisation within them, assigning them some very general objectives and ensuring coordination between them, particularly through setting up negotiating procedures, is the object of the "reflexive" or "procedural" law which is much studied today, and has the double advantage of respecting the rate of development appropriate to social groups while not purely and simply abandoning the social field to the exacerbated struggle of social interests.

It will also be appropriate to rediscover certain precepts of the legislative art. A good law is not necessarily a voluminous law, condemned by its very vastness to undergo repeated amendment. The case of the policy of State subvention of economic sectors in difficulty might constitute an example. Instead of vainly seeking to translate into law subsidy decisions of an administrative nature, i.e. necessarily individual, would it not be better to place two specific obligations on decision-makers: to give reasons for their decisions and to make them public? Are not this publicity, and this invitation to give the issues a full hearing, the best guarantees that the verdict of public opinion can be most efficaciously exercised?

---

[119] See G. Teubner, "Substantive and reflexive elements in modern law" (1983) 17 No. 2 *Law and Society Review* at p. 239.

Ought one not above all to trust its control? Cannot one see that this practice would progressively bring about the establishment of general criteria for subventions, respect for which by the Administration would subsequently enable control through the courts?

Finally, lawyers ought, we feel, to become more aware of the specificity of their field. Everything goes on today as if, at the very time when new and powerful modes of social control are being set up, which compete with, chip away at and sometimes pervert law, lawyers were anxious to treat as legal everything that presents itself as imperative or constraining. To be sure, the legal form is infinitely flexible; it is possible to cast almost any commandment in the form of law. We have even seen totalitarian regimes dressing themselves up in the attributes of the *Rechtsstaat*. But lawyers ought to show more caution. There were commandments before the law, at the time when religious representations ensured social control. Today the scientific norm covers very many sectors of social activity. It is by no means certain that giving the form of legal rule to these technical norms is the way to preserve the values and temporalities associated with legality.

Part Seven

Private Ordering

Economic Policy: State and Private Ordering

BRIAN BERCUSSON
London

Contents

I. Introduction

The questions to be addressed in this paper are three:
  (1) what are the functional equivalents in the private sector of "formal" implementation of economic policy by the State?

(2) to what extent is the decision to use State instruments and measures and the choice of which instruments and measures, a function of private ordering?

(3) what can be learned from the answers to (1) and (2) about the relationship between State regulation and private power?

The research project, of which this paper forms a part, bears the title "Law and Economic Policy: Alternatives to Delegalisation". Many of the papers focus on the policy objectives of the State in the fields of energy and manpower.[1] A great part of the work consisted of gathering together legal *measures,* analysing their characteristics and classifying them as embodying different *instrument* types.[2]

The debate over "delegalisation" or "deregulation" concentrates on the State as an actor and on law, as an emanation of the State, being used as an instrument. The critique of State regulation focusses on the medium – law – and to that extent is neutral of the policy area regulated. The two fields of energy and manpower were selected for study not only for their intrinsic substantive interest, but also because they represented areas of State intervention through law manifest in a variety of measures embodying different instruments of government intervention. There is thus no criticism of the substance of policy here – only of the method of its implementation. Certain policy objectives were selected as common to the countries investigated, and the analysis proceeded on this assumption.

The problems in extending this approach to private actors are self-evident. But if the analysis is neutral as to objectives, then the fact that private actors have different, or even conflicting objectives need not be of concern to the question of functional equivalence. It is, of course, central to my second question – is the choice of State instruments a function of private ordering. The interest of the research lies in the medium through which these non-State actors achieve their objectives – law. They do not have it within their power to enact law in the way the State does: their measures are not legislative, administrative or judicial products as understood in constitutional and administrative law. Nor do their instruments for achieving their objectives possess the formal legal qualities normally attributed to regulation, taxation and so on. But analysis of the legal means they do use to achieve their objectives may reveal parallels with the instrument types and characteristics of measures identified in the study of State economic policy implementation.[3] If so, the application of the critique of (State) "legalisation" to

---

[1] These areas rarely overlap in the literature; hence it was almost a relief to find the article by P. Drouet, "The restructuring of the petroleum refining sector and its social consequences", in (1984) 123 *International Labour Review* 423.

[2] For details of the classification system see the Methodological Note, above at pp. 47–55.

[3] Consider the *Report* by the Commission of the European Communities on the behaviour of the oil companies in the Community during the period from October 1973 to March 1974, which sought "evidence of the existence of agreements between undertakings, decisions by associations of undertakings and concerted practices which might affect, or had affected trade between member states... (and) that major oil companies which occupied a dominant position in respect of a customer might have either restricted their deliveries or imposed prices... (or made) the conclusion of supply contracts subject to the acceptance by the customer of supplementary obligations which were unconnected with

private ordering may prove revealing.[4] The problems with legal implementation of economic policy, particularly those labelled as "legalisation", may arise whether the instruments and measures are those of the State, or are those associated with private processes and outcomes.[5]

That the attacks of the deregulators on State intervention in economic activity can be flexibly adapted to attack private control of economic activity may surprise but should not discourage those dedicated to their task. Enterprising lawyers seeking to devise new principles of "public law" should be encouraged to apply their concepts of accountability, rational discourse and constitutionality to private actors as well as the State.[6] This is scarcely an original proposal. Almost exactly fifty years ago an article in the Columbia Law Review argued: "Those who wield (State) power we have subjected to some sort of responsibility to a democratic electorate, and to various constitutional limitations. Yet much of this recognized political power is not different, in kind or in degree, from much of the power that some individuals and private groups can lawfully exercise against other individuals".[7] This is, perhaps, the one advantage of the unwieldy term "delegalisation" as opposed to the marginally less ugly term "deregulation". For while regulation is normally associated with State functions, most people recognise that the law is as much a powerful tool in the hands of private corporations and associations as in the hands of the State.

Thematically this paper cuts across some of the topics discussed in the companion volume on juridification.[8] While it is not about competition law, the private ordering by cartel or monopoly is examined as the complement of State ordering. Of all private actors, the company or corporation is one of the most important. Private economic actors of great size, with varying qualities of vertical and horizontal integration and with local, national and international presence are to be found in the corporate form. They use their resources as private instruments of

the object of the contracts". Studies, Competition – Approximation of legislation Series No. 26, Brussels, December 1975, at pp. 8–9.

[4] See B. Bercusson, "Legislation and Disorder: State and Private Power" in G. Teubner, ed., *Jurification of Social Spheres,* (1987, Berlin).

[5] This is taking the optimistic view that it will be possible usually to distinguish State and non-State implementation of economic policy. Cf. cases such as the French unemployment benefit administration, of which Gérard Lyon-Caen has said that it is "assez dépourvue d'unité parce qu'elle est le fruit d'une superposition imprécise et successive de couches de sédiments législatifs et conventionnels, au point qu'on ne peut comprendre la situation actuelle sans prendre un peu du recul historique". *Liaisons Sociales* No. 51/83, of 2 May 1983, at p. 10.

[6] See the passionate call for such new principles of public law in I. Harden and N. Lewis, *De-legalisation in Britain in the 1980s,* EUI Working Paper No. 84/125, December 1984; also, by the same authors, "Privatisation, de-regulation and constitutionality: some Anglo-American comparisons", (1983) *Northern Ireland Legal Quarterly* 207. Far from arguing for deregulation, they propose "re-legalisation".

[7] R. L. Hale, "Force and the state: a comparison of 'political' and 'economic' compulsion", (1935) 35 *Columbia Law Review* 149.

[8] G. Teubner, ed., *supra,* note 4.

economic policy directly and indirectly. The sources of private outcomes need be traced deep into the corporate organisation, through mazes of subsidiaries. So while this paper is not about company law, the structure and functioning of companies is a vital element in private ordering. Manpower policy is a good testing ground because, it has been said: "Governments have accepted responsibilities for employment in individual private firms and have developed a whole range of instruments to influence firms' decisions. Equally, firms take on social responsibilities beyond market and profit considerations. Unemployment policy is therefore a good example of the continued erosion of the public/private distinction so evident in other policy areas".[9]

The objectives of manpower policy – job creation, job protection and mobility of labour – are of some importance in both labour and social security law. Trade unions as private actors play a central role in the private ordering of manpower policy. Though this research project, by a self-denying (or self-preserving) ordinance did not investigate social security aspects of manpower policy, the private ordering of manpower policy cannot fail to be related to wider social schemes of income security.

Finally, as will be evident, my paper draws on the concepts and taxonomies developed by Daintith in his paper: "Law as Policy Instrument: A Comparative Perspective",[10] and on Teubner's paper: "Legalisation – Concepts, Aspects, Limits, Solutions".[11] One set of terms which provides a link between the two papers is the notion of a delineation between the "public", the "private" and the "social" (interchangeably, according to taste, the good, the bad and the ugly). For Daintith, regulatory law is State or public law, while for Teubner law may be either public or private, but the scope of both is in danger of intruding on the "social". Confusion can arise when the attempt is made to draw clear boundaries between the public, the private and the social – especially when the word "ordering" is added to each of these terms.

For example, the Italian legal theory known as "ordinamento intersindacale" was developed as a vehicle for understanding Italian labour law at a time when statutory rules concerning labour relations were relatively scarce: "This theory presupposed the existence of a set of rules, over and above those laid down by the state, which took their force from union-management relationships".[12] The relation of these "rules" to State law, the notion that they are an original, non-derivative and non-integrated form of law *parallel* to State law and more or less successfully coordinated with State law is developed and analysed in a recent article drawing on the "structural functionalist" theories of Luhmann: "Using

[9] J. Richardson and R. Henning, "Policy responses to unemployment: symbolic or placebo policies?", in Richardson and R. H. Henning (eds.), *Unemployment: Policy Responses of Western Democracies*, (1984, London), Vol. 8, p. 307 at pp. 313–314.

[10] Above, at pp. 3–55.

[11] In G. Teubner, ed., *supra*, note 8 at pp. 3–48.

[12] G. Giugni, "The Italian system of industrial relations", in P. B. Doeringer (ed.), *Industrial Relations in International Perspective*, (1981, New York) 324 and especially at p. 332.

Luhmannian terminology, one could, therefore, speak of a growing integration between the system of industrial relations and the political system, with the consequence that while the State (traditionally taken as the exclusive subject of the political system) appears as part of the system of industrial relations, trade unions (traditionally exclusive subjects of the latter system) assume a continually clearer position as subjects in the political system".[13] Elsewhere I try to assess the extent to which Teubner's critique of "legalisation" and his proposed solution help to clarify the different realms of public, private and social ordering.[14] This paper focusses on a comparison of the orders of State and private power.

II. Actors v. the State

The starting point of my research required identification of those private actors whose functions in the sphere of legal implementation of economic policy could be argued to be equivalent to those of the State. The sheer multiplicity and variety of actors in the fields of energy and manpower policy is overwhelming. In the area of energy policy, Lindberg highlights the fact that "the power to determine policy decisions and affect outcomes is increasingly dispersed among separate individual actors and ever more complex organizational units", and echoes some critics of "legalisation" when he says this is one of three factors which contribute "in the terms employed by modern decision and organizational theorists... toward policy failure or "overload" in modern industrial societies".[15] Of necessity, there is a case for excluding individual humans, whether workers or consumers, as a focus of attention equivalent to the State. Few, if any, individual humans have the capacity to exercise the instruments of economic policy. Similarly, small and medium enterprises may be very numerous and active in energy and manpower, but taken individually as actors, their impact is relatively negligible.[16] Apart from individual humans, small enterprises and the State, there is still a multitude of other actors. In the energy field, these include, *inter alia*, multi-national oil companies,[17] national oil companies, other nationally organised energy indus-

---

[13] G. Vardaro, "Ordinamento intersindacale e teoria dei sistemi", (1984) *Diritto del Lavoro e di Relazioni Industriali* (no. 21), p. 1 at p. 50.

[14] B. Bercusson, *supra*, note 4.

[15] L. N. Lindberg, "The energy crisis: a political economy perspective", in L. N. Lindberg (ed.), *The Energy Syndrome*, (1977, Lexington) at pp. 10 and 8. Beyond the State, "since energy involves complex international interdependencies, the policymakers of many other nations become *de facto* participants in any nation's energy policy system". Lindberg, "Comparing energy policies: political constraints and the energy syndrome", at p. 336.

[16] Cf. the position in Hungary, where it has been stated: "the organisational structure of Hungarian enterprises is heavily concentrated; contrary to the pattern characteristic in the West, the number of large enterprises is bigger than the number of small enterprises". The Vienna Institute for Comparative Economic Studies, *Mitgliederinformation* 1984/4, at p. 4.

[17] The perception of multinational oil companies (and indeed other multinationals) as powerful actors analogous to States is not uncommon. For example, Senator Frank

tries, cartels of producers,[18] trade associations, national and international joint ventures, consumer organisations and other pressure groups.[19] In the manpower field there are, again, multinational corporations, national companies or groups of companies, employers' associations,[20] trade unions, their confederations/federations, tripartite bodies or joint trade union-employer bodies and various organisations concerned with specific sections of the workforce (youth, women, handicapped, racial groups, immigrants and so on).[21]

The nature of these very different private actors in the selected fields of economic policy implementation may be better understood if they are characterised in terms of various qualities.[22]

Church, opening the hearings of the U.S. Senate Foreign Relations Committee subcommittee on multinational corporations on 30 January 1974: "We are dealing with corporate entities which have many of the characteristics of nations, thus it should surprise no-one that, when we speak of corporate and Government relationships, the language will be that which is appropriate to dealings between sovereigns". Quoted in A. Sampson, *The Seven Sisters*, 3rd impression (updated), (1980, London) at p. 285.

[18] For example, in the 1950s, the German coal barons of the Ruhr operated a cartel whereby all coal produced in the Ruhr (half the Community coal output) was sold by a single sales organisation. To combat this, the French set up a sole purchaser of coal imported to France. The High Authority of the European Coal and Steel Community launched an attack on both monopoly agencies. See. N. J. D. Lucas, *Energy and the European Communities*, (1977, London) at p. 7.

[19] There is a detailed catalogue of actors in the energy field of oil, gas, coal, electricity and nuclear in T. Daintith and L. Hancher, *Energy Strategy in Europe: The Legal Framework* (1985, Berlin), ch. 4.

[20] As to the relation between employers' associations and trace associations, they are both established "to regulate matters of trade and competition by mutual agreement; to seek statutory protection on matters of trade, particularly with regard to imported goods; to erect a united front in dealing with trade unions; to provide services in labor relations and personnel administration; and to contest the passage of social and labor legislation. Where commercial interests were the chief organizational impetus, the outcome was the formation of what is generally referred to as a trade association. By contrast, where the issues centered on the employment relationship, the desire for joint action led to the formation of employers' associations... There were, of course, many instances where a single association served both trade and labour policy objectives". J. P. Windmuller, "Employers' associations in comparative perspective: organisation, structure, administration", in J. P. Windmuller and A. Gladstone, eds., *Employers' Associations and Industrial Relations: A Comparative Study*, (1984, London) at pp. 1–2.

[21] For example, the Community Industry programme in the UK started as a result of initiatives taken in 1971 by a number of voluntary and statutory agencies with a responsibility for the young, who were concerned with the growing number of young people experiencing lengthy periods of unemployment. The programme was run by a National Management Board which included amongst its members representatives of the TUC, CBI, Youth Associations and the Department of Employment. See Research Project, UK Manpower Inventory. Also M. P. Jackson and V. J. B. Hanby, *British Work Creation Programmes* (1982, Kettering) at pp. 17–18.

[22] Cf. the elements in Schmitter's definition of corporatism: "Corporatism can be defined as a system of interest representation in which the constituent units are organised into a

A. Activity in each of the areas of economic policy can be functionally distinguished along an *operational chain:*[23]

   energy – exploration / production / procurement / conversion / distribution / use

   manpower – access to jobs / job creation / training / placement / job maintenance / mobility / exit or job loss.

   The State may intervene in each of these operational functions, but few private actors have the same breadth of coverage.[24]

B. The activity of the private actors in these fields may be *vertically and/or horizontally integrated.* The State can within its structure integrate all the operational functions in energy and manpower policy, i.e. vertical integration. Similarly, within each function, there may be horizontal integration; in energy – distribution of oil, gas, coal, electricity and nuclear energy; in manpower – comprehensive training for all workers in the labour market.[25]

C. The State has a local and a national presence, and also an international dimension in energy and manpower policy. Private actors will vary in their *geographical organisation.*

D. The *links between private actors and the State* can vary in intensity and in their legal nature, e.g. from individual delegated monopolies, joint ventures, concession agreements to more general licensing, restrictive legislation or outright prohibition.

E. In contrast to the usually monolithic and unified constitutional and administrative law of the State, the legal nature of the *internal organisation* of private actors varies considerably, with separate bodies of law affecting companies, trade unions, economic groups, voluntary associations, semi-public enterprises, tripartite organs and so on.

---

limited number of singular, compulsory, noncompetitive, hierarchically ordered and functionally differentiated categories, recognized or licenced (if not created) by the State and granted a deliberate representational monopoly within their respective categories in exchange for observing certain controls on their selection of leaders and articulation of demands and supports". P. C. Schmitter, "Still the century of corporatism?", in P. Schmitter and G. Lehmbruch eds., *Trends Towards Corporatist Intermediation,* (1979, Beverly Hills) at p. 7 and especially at p. 13. These elements are further elaborated on pp. 20–21, which distinguishes "societal" from "state" corporatism.

[23] The energy chain is described in N. J. D. Lucas, "The influence of institutions on the content of energy policy", a paper given to the Colloquium on The Legal Implementation of Energy Policy, EUI, Florence, 22–24 September 1982, (Paper no. 2), at p. 13.

[24] In the case of some private actors, their coverage may exceed that of a particular State, with major consequences for the State's ability to control energy policy. For a comparison, looking to the strength of the multinational oil companies in, for example, exploration and production management, transportation and marketing, see L. Turner, *Oil Companies in the International System,* (3rd ed., 1983, London) at pp. 90–97.

[25] To paraphrase Lucas: State planning with a few large integrated industries will be preferred to planning which requires materials to be obtained from different sources and negotiations to be carried on with multiple and unpredictable actors. *Lucas, supra,* note 23, at p. 129.

The question is posed: do these different qualities of private actors help explain the extent and nature of State intervention in energy and manpower policy?

A. The energy/manpower chain

In the *energy* field, most of the private actors above the individual human level are concerned with those parts of the chain *prior to use*. One study of concentration in energy markets concluded: "(w)ith some possible exceptions, such as bulk users of electricity, such concentration is probably a more important phenomenon among suppliers and transformers of primary energy than among ultimate users".[26] To a large extent this is inevitable since the resources required at earlier stages of the chain are considerable and geography is important. For example, refining capacity in the European Community is concentrated in regions which are advantageous for the receipt of crude oil and onward flow inland of oil products (Rotterdam, Antwerp, the valley of the Seine and near Marseilles), while other regions (e.g. south Germany) have insufficient refining capacity.[27] Many of the large actors prior to use are public corporations or nationalised industries. But private actors are prominent even outside oil. It was said of the French nuclear industry in the mid-1970s: "The ensemble of nuclear activities is controlled by a small number of industrial groups of a 'multimonopolist' character".[28] There are always exceptions: in Germany, if one discounts the coal sector, industry generates one-third of its own electricity demand.[29] And there are some very large consumers: about 25 per cent of oil consumed in the UK is by nationalised bodies ranging from the National Health Service to the Armed Forces and if local authorities and the rest of the public sector entities were included, the figure would be about 40 per cent.[30] Even multitudes of dispersed consumers may occasionally exert organised strength: in Italy it is said that domestic electricity is sold below cost because of political compromises with trade unions which see it as compensating for tax avoidance by the rich;[31] in France it is said that automobile users constitute a powerful pressure group which had some success in opposing speed limits on motorways;[32] and in the Netherlands, associations of cultivators in glasshouses have agreed special tariffs.[33] Nonetheless, "in contrast to the efficient institutional interface of the chains with production, the interface with use is weak and clumsy... energy is generally a low priority of the user and there is no efficient

[26] Daintith and Hancher, *supra*, note 19, at pp. 3–4.
[27] See *Report* of the Commission, 1975, *supra*, note 3, at p. 24.
[28] D. Saumon and L. Puiseux, "Actors and decisions in French energy policy", in *Lindberg* (ed.), *supra*, note 15, at p. 119 and p. 164.
[29] Daintith and Hancher, *supra*, note 19, at p. 50.
[30] L. E. Grayson, *National Oil Companies*, (1981, New York) at pp. 185–186.
[31] Lucas, *supra*, note 23, at p. 18.
[32] Saumon and Puiseux, *supra*, note 28, at p. 152.
[33] K. J. M. Mortelmans, Research Project Comparative Report on Stabilisation of Prices and Profits (on file at EUI), at p. 7.

professional lobby for efficient use. In short there is no energy conservation industry".[34]

In contrast, of the eight energy policy objectives examined in the research project, three are concerned with consumption or use: restriction of consumption, promotion of economy in use and alteration of energy consumption patterns (perhaps also the stabilisation of prices). The argument is that the State focusses disproportionate legal attention on the section of the energy chain where there is least organisation. For major private actors intervene at stages prior to use or consumption, which is highly individualised. This point raises many additional questions. Is it *because* major private actors intervene that there is less State concern at earlier stages in the chain where they are active? Is the absence of organised actors an opportunity for the State to intervene, or does chaos deter such intervention? As to the nature of State intervention, one hypothesis suggested by a comparative report written during the research project was that the government prefers to resort to individual measures concerning a restricted number of important economic entities and takes general measures having an impact on the public at large only later.[35]

In the *manpower* field, the major private actors usually are concerned mainly with one or perhaps two sections of the chain. Employers are concerned mainly with job creation (when expanding) and job loss or workforce reduction (when contracting). Their commitment to other parts of the manpower chain is relatively less. Trade unions are concerned mainly with job maintenance and job losses.[36] The rest of the chain – access, training, placement, mobility – is catered for by private or non-State actors of any size only very sporadically, very often through participation in tripartite institutions.[37] As with energy, it may be that the absence of major organised actors left a vacuum to be filled by the State. For active manpower policies dominate in the areas of training and re-training, placement services and job mobility schemes.[38] Perhaps less that the State was impelled to intervene in these sections of the chain, but that the existence of the vacuum allowed for such intervention more easily.[39]

---

[34] N. J. D. Lucas, chap. VII in G. T. Goodman, L. A. Kristoferson and J. M. Hollander, *The European Transition from Oil*, (1981) at p. 173 and especially at p. 177.

[35] A. Harmathy, Research Project Comparative Report on the Alteration of Energy Consumption Patterns (on file at EUI), at p. 7.

[36] On the trade union's formal role with respect to job losses in Hungary, see G. Garancsy, *Labour Law and Its Termination in Hungarian Law*, (1973, Budapest) at pp. 46–48. Also A. Weltner, *Fundamental Traits of Socialist Law*, (1970, Budapest) at p. 114 (trade union's right to take legal action against persons responsible for infringement of worker's right to work and sue them for damages).

[37] On such trends in France, see M. F. Mauriaux and R. Mauriaux, "Unemployment policy in France 1976–82", in Richardson and Henning, *supra*, note 9, at p. 148.

[38] B. Bercusson, Research Project Comparative Report on Movement between Jobs (on file at EUI), pp. 3 ff.

[39] In extreme cases, private actors may be deliberately excluded, as in the case of the public monopoly of labour exchanges in the Federal Republic of Germany, though the Bundesanstalt für Arbeit may occasionally delegate this function to private welfare

With the beginning of the economic recession in the early 1970s, the aspects of manpower policy to do with job creation, job maintenance and particularly job losses became politically more sensitive. State intervention in these areas became a feature of government manpower policy, which entailed the need to confront or coordinate the actions of employers and trade unions.[40] As Willke observed: "Economic policy is no longer – if it ever was – concerned with influencing or controlling economic variables but has to deal with groups who condition economic outcomes: business groups, labour unions, other political bodies, occupational groups, categories of households (and voters). A heavy element of bargaining and persuasion is therefore involved".[41] The more powerfully organised are the client groups, the more likely it is that consensual rather than regulatory arrangements are adopted. For example, in Italy, the largest union confederation (CGIL) sees itself as representing the working class as a whole (rather than simply its members), and thus works on behalf of the unemployed (those between jobs). The union's power results in negotiated agreements on labour mobility. Contrast the UK, where a weakened trade union movement failed to stop the Conservative Government abolishing many tripartite industrial training boards. Again in contrast, the powerfully organised small business lobby successfully argued for exemption from statutory training requirements.[42] Parallel with State intervention in job creation and protection, trade unions and employers' strategies were affected by their analysis of the economic crisis: "collective bargaining came to distinguish explicitly between dismissals due to conjunctural causes and those due to structural causes, allowing in the former case for interventions in the form of training and in the latter for reductions in hours of work tied to indemnities for partial unemployment".[43]

agencies. J. Malagugini, "Colocamento della mandopera, orientamento e consulenza professionale nella Repubblica federale tedesca", in C. Marazia ed., *Istituzioni e Politiche del Lavoro nella Comunità Europea*, (1981, Roma), 89 at p. 101.

[40] As well as other private actors, see, for exampler, S. Ricca, "Private temporary work organisations and public employment services: effects and problems of coexistence". (1982) 121 *International Labour Review* 141. This is *not* to say that the State was exclusively concerned to *protect* jobs or *create* jobs. Rather, that the economic crisis put employment issues of this kind unavoidably before governments. Some governments saw the solution in creating new jobs, maintaining old ones, protecting threatened ones (as in France post-1981; UK pre-1979). Other governments saw the solution in breaking down job protection by trade unions, or withdrawing job maintenance measures in the form of support for ailing industries or indeed destroying jobs in the public sector (UK post-1979; Federal Republic of Germany post-1982). State measures reflected these different policies and their inter-action with trade unions and employers' policies was obviously significant. For a general survey, see R. B. McKersie and W. Sengenberger, *Job Losses in Major Industries*, (1983, Paris) OECD, E. Yemin (ed.), *Workforce Reductions in Undertakings*, (1982, Geneva) ILO.

[41] G. Willke, in A. Maddison and B. S. Wilpstra eds., *Unemployment: The European Perspective*, (1982, London) at p. 165.

[42] See M. Anderson and J. Fairley, "The politics of industrial training in the UK", (1983) 3 *Journal of Public Policy* 191, at p. 196.

[43] C. Assanti, "Strumenti istituzionali e mercato del lavoro nei paesi della CEE: un

It is argued, then, that the presence of private actors with a history of concern and intervention in the areas of job creation, maintenance and losses shaped State intervention in this area. The State had a much freer hand in other areas of the manpower policy chain where it had traditionally intervened. Similarly, where there was a history of State intervention in the energy chain, this background of interaction with private actors was important.

B. Vertical Horizontal Integration

In the *energy* field, the degree of integration of the private actors which are the concern of this paper varies. In terms of *vertical* integration, at one extreme are the international oil companies which are fully integrated from one end of the chain to the other, from exploration and production through procurement to conversion and distribution.[44] The degree of integration of other major energy sources varies. Gas and electricity are often strongly integrated, coal and nuclear much less so.[45] But there are many variations. For example, the gas regime in the Netherlands provides for the production condession to be granted jointly to the NAM (owned jointly by Esso and Shell) and DSM (State-owned) with an obligation to sell all the gas produced to the NV Nederlandse Gasunie (owned 40 per cent by DSM, 10 per cent by the State and Shell and Esso, 25 per cent each), which domestically sells it to some 140 gas distribution companies and 20 power stations, mostly owned by provinces or councils, which in turn provide gas to the consumers (80 per cent of households are dependent on this source).[46] Barents concluded: "The structure of the electricity and gas supply is thus rather fragmented which constitutes a barrier for direct state influence. Preparations are under way for a large scale horizontal and vertical integration".[47]

There is rather less in the way of horizontal integration, in the sense of actors who combine within themselves the operational functions of different energy

problema aperto", in C. Marazia ed., *supra*, note 39, 15 at p. 24. For a critical analysis of "The notion of structural unemployment", see G. Standing, (1983) 122 *International Labour Review* 137. The author criticises the notion of structural unemployment as "messy and as used by many economists obscure", and says of policies on, for example, training, mobility and placement, that although welcome: "if the unemployment is not 'structural' the emphasis given to the policies may breed resentment and cynicism about their inefficiency among both those for whom they are designed and those reponsible for implementing them" (at p. 150).

[44] "Shell oil was pumped from Shell oilfields into Shell tankers, onto Shell refineries into Shell storage tanks, and through Shell pipelines to Shell filling-stations". *Sampson, supra,* note 17, at p. 24. National oil companies also are often integrated: ENI in Italy; CEP/ Total in France. Full integration of oil companies has been much weakened by host country nationalisations.

[45] Lucas, *supra*, note 23, at pp. 13–15. For example, Gaz de France and Electricité de France are strongly integrated, as is the British Gas Corporation and the Central Electricity Generating Board in the UK. These, of course, are public sector actors.

[46] R. Barents, "Legal aspects of energy policy in the Netherlands", (1983) 1 *Journal of Energy and Natural Resources Law*, at p. 160.

[47] *Ibid.,* at p. 13.

sources. There are national actors (often in the public sector) who horizontally integrate all of one energy source in that country (nuclear, coal) at one or more sections of the chain. But the proliferation of committees, commissions, institutes, councils, associations, agencies, offices, authorities and bureaux charged with coordination and concertation of those active in different energy sources indicates the absence of horizontal integration.[48] Horizontal links between actors in the oil industry are more common, if less publicised. The 1973 oil crisis gave rise to many examples, ranging from communication networks set up by the oil companies in Germany to avoid disturbances of supply, to very close contacts between various companies members of supply pools in the Netherlands, to the London Policy Group consisting of the international oil companies who wished to present a common front to OPEC.[49]

In *manpower*, vertical integration is a function of the sophistication of the firm. As mentioned above, attention of employers is devoted mainly to issues of job availability and job loss. The personnel departments of large firms may concern themselves to varying extents with training, placement, mobility and job maintenance. But the firm's primary concern is not manpower policy, it is wage costs. Labour is a factor of production. Trade unions also reflect traditional preoccupations with job maintenance and job loss (though there may also be concern with training (apprenticeships) and access (the closed shop). To some extent, vertical integration of manpower policy reflects trade union structure. Organisations based on industries, occupations or enterprises will allow more or less scope for integration through the manpower chain. In a fascinating account of the 1975 Volkswagen Redundancy Scheme, Streeck points out how the proposed closure of one plant might have been acceptable to the company's works council, but that "the political imperatives of industrial unionism" made such a closure unacceptable to the industrial metalworkers' union (IGM).[50] In France, the different ideologies of the CGT, CFDT and FO do not preclude considerable similarity in their structures and organisations: industry-based rather than craft-based. Each has a structure part horizontal (geographical) and part vertical (industrial) with about 30–40 federations and 90 union departments.[51]

Horizontal integration of manpower policy is a function of industrial concentration and trade union structure. Monopolistic employers and industrial trade unions could provide an integrated manpower policy. Fragmented industries and

---

48 Conversely, governments may encourage competition between fuel industries; for example. the UK Fuel Policy Paper of 1967 discussed in J. H. Chesshire *et al.*, "Energy policy in Britain", in *Lindberg* (ed.), *supra*, note 15, 33, at pp. 45–46.

49 On Germany and the Netherlands, see *Report* of the Commission, 1975, *supra*, note 3, at pp. 52–53; on the London Policy Group, *Sampson, supra*, note 17, at pp. 234 ff.

50 W. Streeck, *Industrial Relations in West Germany: A case study of the car industry*, (1984, Berlin) ch. 5, at 68. Cf. Hungarian labour law theory in which collective agreements at the enterprise level are between the enterprise on one side and a collective of workers and employees on the other. L. Nagy, *The Socialist Collective Agreement*, (1984, Budapest) at pp. 114–115.

51 IDE-International Research Group, *Industrial Relations in Europe*, IIM Papers, Berlin, 1979, chapter X (The French Industrial Relations System), at p. 14.

unions cannot. One report of a series of case studies of manpower policy in enterprises in the UK found that "in none of our case studies have the companies relied on the employers" organisation in carrying out policies of radical change".[52] Windmuller found that most of the time the employers' confederations are industry associations (the vertical structure), although in some countries, such as Italy, regional groups (the horizontal structure) were the more important constituents.[53]

The energy crisis of the 1970s in Western Europe was primarily a function of dependence on oil. The private actors in the oil sector are predominantly vertically integrated oil companies. There was much evidence of cooperation between them, at times institutionalised to a point which raises the prospect of horizontal integration. For example, in the Netherlands, the chairman of the Liaison Committee for the Oil Industry was asked by letter from the Minister to direct service stations and oil companies to reduce sales.[54] In the UK, in October 1973, the Department of Trade and Industry set up an Oil Emergency Group which was charged with coordinating government action. At the same time, the Oil Industry Emergency Committee was convened, consisting of representatives of the principal oil refining and marketing companies, to deal with supply difficulties.[55] The Commission's report on the period concluded: "Whether in the case of actual joint ventures, exchanges of refining capacities or transfers of products, the large companies are linked by an extensive network of relationships which, even if there are good historical and economic reasons for them, constitute none the less a factor in strengthening their solidarity and consolidating their position".[56] Where the multinationals led, the national oil companies were not loath to follow: in July 1976 five European companies (CFP, ENI, Veba, SNEA and Petrofina) addressed a joint memorandum to the Commission seeking its approval for their coordinating exploration, production, refining and marketing policies.[57]

State attempts to intervene in the functional operations of the oil energy chain were not effective in the face of the extensive vertical and horizontal integration of

---

[52] E. Jacobs, S. Orwell, P. Paterson and F. Weltz, *The Approach to Industrial Change*, Anglo-German Foundation for the Study of Industrial Society Research Paper B 0179/1E, 1978, at p. 76. Cf. the exception in the printing industry, where the Newspaper Publishers' Association played an important part. The case study of the UK National Coal Board and National Union of Mineworker's comprehensive structure of consultation at all levels demonstrates the potential for integration of manpower policy (at pp. 38–42).

[53] Windmuller and Gladstone (eds.), *supra*, note 20, at p. 9. An impressive analysis of horizontal and vertical integration of national trade union movements is by J. Visser, *The Position of Central Confederations in the National Union Movement*, EUI Working Paper No. 102, 1984. He also develops a third dimension: organisational concentration (cf. below: internal organisation).

[54] Research Project, Netherlands Energy Inventory (on file at EUI).

[55] *Report* of the Commission, 1975, *supra*, note 3, at p. 49.

[56] *Ibid.*, at p. 152.

[57] Grayson, *supra*, note 30, at p. 17.

the oil companies.[58] It would seem likely that the same would apply to other integrated supply chains. To the extent that the chain is not integrated, e.g. nuclear, where production of fuel, construction of reactors, conversion to electricity and distribution may be divided among different actors, the vulnerability of the sector to State intervention may be increased.[59] On the other hand, the disorganised nature of the actors may deter government intervention.[60] If government does intervene, the instruments used will reflect the institutional structure of the private actors – hence the proliferation of "gentleman's agreements" where large integrated actors are involved.[61]

As regards manpower policy, the main thrust of State intervention since the early 1970s has been in job creation, job maintenance and job losses. To the extent that employers did not integrate vertically through the manpower chain, there was scope for State intervention. For example, in training, the State could exploit the gap in employers' policies to promote extensive training schemes which became by-words for job creation. On the other hand, where trade unions had a strong interest in training (e.g. apprenticeship schemes) such intervention was more difficult.

The degree of horizontal integration by private actors also conditioned State intervention. Where a union organises across an entire industry (seamen, acting, printing) or area, and controls the labour market, State intervention becomes much more fraught. The process of State intervention in a contracting industry where the union is poised to fight job losses will differ from where the industry is only weakly organised. Similarly on the employers' side, where a few employers monopolise the jobs in a particular sector, State intervention in the event of job losses will differ from where there is a multitude of small employers (contrast steel and textiles).[62]

C. Geographical Organisation

By and large, the economic policy objectives pursued in energy and manpower are national, sectoral or local in scope. This despite the fact that the crises in energy and manpower that began in the 1970s were to a large extent international in origin

[58] The head of government relations of Shell commented: "if the supply had been in the hands of minor non-integrated and state companies we would have seen acute contention between consumers and direct confrontation between consumers and producers". Quoted in Sampson, *supra*, note 17, at p. 277.

[59] See, for example, E. H. Hubert, "Regulation of the siting of nuclear and conventional electricity generating plant", a paper given to the Colloquium on The Legal Implementation of Energy Policy, EUI, Florence, 22–24 September 1982, (Paper no. 10) (on file at EUI), which contrasts the multitude of actors involved and the existence of a single French Ministry (at pp. 13–17).

[60] Civil servants "will tend to avoid projects involving many parties with diverse, ill-comprehended motives because the negotiating costs are high, monitoring is difficult and assessment uncertain". Lucas, *supra*, note 23, at p. 21.

[61] See L. Hancher, Research Project Comparative Report on the Management of Short-Term Energy Disturbances (on file at EUI), at pp. 12, 18, 25.

[62] These and other sectors are examined by McKersie and Sengenberger, *supra*, note 40.

– the disruptions in oil supply and the changes in the international division of labour.[63]

In the *energy* field, the oil industry is dominated by multinational companies.[64] This fact alone raised the issue of potential clashes of interest between these companies and national energy policies, which were a focus of attention in the aftermath of the 1973 crisis. Much of the history of national energy policy in Western Europe consists of dealings with multinational oil companies and promotion of "national champions" in that sector. State intervention in oil policy is, therefore, likely to be determined in the type of instrument used by the fact that the major private actors are multinationals. Comparison of State intervention where the actors are national or local should demonstrate this. Actors in the gas, electricity, coal and nuclear sectors are mainly national organisations, often with substantial State participation. This allows them to be manipulated by a variety of instruments, partly because of their congruency with State structures. International actors break with this pattern. The increasingly international nature of the energy chain, not only in oil, but also in gas, nuclear energy and even the coal trade, makes an assessment of the adequacy of "national" instruments and measures of State policy even more imperative.

There is much to be learned from the experience of the oil producing States which have long grappled with the problems of energy policy and multinationals. A recent book cites the view, expressed by a British M.P. in the 1975 House of Commons Debate on the Petroleum and Submarine Pipelines Bill, that adequate control over the operations of petroleum development is possible through the exercise of regulatory powers.[65] This view is criticised on the basis that "no matter how stringently or extensively applied the control (regulatory) from *without* is it is not enough. Control from *within* is ... essential".[66] Effective participation is hampered by lack of expertise, but even more so is regulation "since the regulatory

---

[63] As put in one report: "The overall effects on employment of competitive imports from developing countries are relatively small compared with other variables which affect employment levels in the EEC. However, problems do arise from the fact that the negative effect on employment caused by changes underway in the international division of labour is concentrated on certain categories of workers, firms and regions, whereas the positive effects (in terms of employment and consumers' revenue) are spread more widely". Commission of the European Communities, D-G for Development, *The European Economic Community and Changes in the International Division of Labour,* January 1979, at p. 3.

[64] As Sampson points out, however, referring to Exxon and Shell: "the fact remained that their shareholders were predominantly American and British; and their boards represented only their own country – and a small segment of that". On the other hand, he quotes a top U.S. anti-trust official to the effect that "Anti-trust has become much more an international problem. And it is often hard to know the genuine nationality of a big company... What nationality is Aramco now?". *Supra,* note 17, at pp. 200 and 292.

[65] K. Hossain, *Law and Policy in Petroleum Development: Changing Relations between Transnationals and Governments.* (1979, London/New York), at p. 136.

[66] H. S. Zakariya, "New direction in the search for and development of petroleum resources in the developing countries", (1976) 9 *Vanderbilt Journal of Transnational Law* 545 at p. 552; quoted in *Hossain, ibid.,* at p. 137.

agency is not as closely involved with operations nor does it have the same access to technical and financial information as government representatives involved in a venture in which the government is a participant".[67]

The inadequacies of instruments such as regulation and taxation gave rise to participation via *joint ventures,* pioneered as a new form by ENI. These can take the form of equity joint ventures, under which a joint stock company is established, in which each partner owns 50 per cent of the equity, with various formal mechanisms for resolving any deadlock. Another form extensively adopted is the contractual joint venture (joint structure), where the partnership is not constituted into a joint stock company, and thus does not assume a separate corporate identity. Rather, the relations between the parties are governed by the terms of the partnership contract. Nonetheless, management of the venture is entrusted to a non-profit making joint stock company, with parity of representation on the board of directors. Various special features have developed over time, e.g. the "carried interest system", whereby the government can acquire an equity interest if a commercial discovery is made (exploration being at the risk and expense of the company). The company is said to "carry" the government's interest during the exploration phase. The "carried interest" formula was introduced into the North Sea region by the Netherlands in 1967.[68] The development of joint ventures involves the setting up of new actors to pursue policy objectives in the energy field.

Finally, the existence of *local* actors active in the energy chain can affect State policy. It is interesting to note the extent to which energy organisational structures parallel State structures, so that energy law follows the pattern of constitutional and administrative laws. Lucas distinguished centralised forms of control (France and Italy) and localised forms (Germany). But, as he says, it is the gaps in these structures which are revealing. That in France, cogeneration and district heating schemes are the exclusive possession of those areas which have retained autonomous control of electricity sales and distribution.[69] It has been pointed out already how fragmentation in electricity and gas supply in the Netherlands (9 provincial and 5 municipal electricity companies deliver 70 per cent of total electricity; the rest by some 82 small public distribution companies) constitutes a barrier for direct State influence.[70] In Italy, the law of 1962 which reserved to the ENEL the monopoly of electricity activities exempted from nationalisation enterprises run by local authorities at the time when the whole sector was being nationalised, which raised the prospect of integration via collaboration agreements, a restraint on centralised administration.[71]

---

[67] *Hossain, supra,* note 65, at p. 137: "The 'inner workings' of an operation are more likely to reveal themselves to government representatives involved in the operations, than to government inspectors functioning under the regulatory framework"; at p. 175.

[68] *Ibid.,* generally, at pp. 120–138 on joint ventures.

[69] Lucas, *supra* note 23, at pp. 36–37. He points to the same phenomenon in Italy and concludes that one of the characteristics receptive to such planning is that the municipality be involved in energy distribution – at p. 38.

[70] Barents, *supra,* note 46, at p. 13.

[71] F. A. Roversi-Monaco, "Legal aspects of energy policy in Italy", a paper given to the

The multinationals' role in *manpower* policy is highlighted by the widely acknowledged inadequacy of States in dealing with job losses when they pull out, and the multitude of inducements offered by States to multinationals promising job creation. To some extent at least the international division of labour results from the investment by these multinationals outside Western Europe, with resulting transfer of jobs outside the States' jurisdiction.[72] Trade unions have been similarly incapable of meeting the challenge. The geographical organisation of national and local employers is important particularly in its relation to the regional policy aspects of States' manpower policies which seek a particular geographical distribution of jobs.[73] This becomes increasingly so as local authorities become more active in manpower policies, and where the State's major manpower agencies use locally based institutions.[74]

The geographical organisation of trade unions is also significant, if not on the international level where they are not in the same league with multinational employers.[75] On the one hand, the Italian trade unions perceived the ever

Colloquium on The Legal Implementation of Energy Policy, EUI, Florence, 22–24 September 1982 (Paper no. 5).

[72] One illustration of the importance of multinational corporations is the Scottish case: by 1975 in Scotland, U.S. owned firms accounted for 14% of total Scottish manufacturing employment, and a further 3% was in foreign companies from other countries (not including England) – a total of 108,200 people. By 1980, this had fallen to 80,457, a net loss of about 30,000 jobs. S. Henderson, C. Baldry, N. Haworth and H. Ramsay, "Multinational closure and the case of Massey-Ferguson, Kilmarnock", (1984) 15 *Industrial Relations Journal,* No. 4, 17.

[73] For example, there is a long-standing system of selective regional and industrial assistance in the UK. This continues even under the nominal banner of deregulation, as is commented by one observer of the development of the concept of enterprise zones: "The (enterprise zone) concept has moved in essence from being an experiment in de-planning to a package of incentives for industry to locate in particular areas". G. Jordan, "Enterprise zones in the UK and USA: ideologically acceptable job creation?", in Richardson and Henning, *supra,* note 9, p. 125 at p. 146.

[74] On the increasing role of local authorities in manpower policy after the reforms of 1982, see J.-P. Muret, C. Neuschwander, H. Sibille, *L'Economie et les Emplois,* (1983, Paris) The role of local authorities in the UK can be seen, for example, in the Job Creation Programme introduced in October 1975. When the programme ended in December 1978, over 15,000 projects had been approved, of which the majority were sponsored by local authorities (64%), with voluntary organisations/charities (10%) and other public bodies (8%) prominent. Only 2% were sponsored by private companies. See D. Metcalf, *Alternatives to Unemployment: Special Employment Measures in Britain,* (1982, London) at pp. 19–20; Jackson and Hanby, *supra,* note 21, at pp. 18–20; *Incomes Data Services,* Study No. 173 (July 1978), p. 14. On the use of local institutions by the Manpower Services Commission in the UK and the Bundesanstalt für Arbeit in the Federal Republic of Germany, see J. B. Carruthers, *Labour Market Services in Britain and Germany – Employer and Trade Union Participation,* Anglo-German Foundation for the Study of Industrial Society, Monograph Series B 0779, 1979.

[75] On the legal implications, Gérard and Antoine Lyon-Caen, *Droit Social International et Européen,* (5th ed., 1980, Paris) at pp. 130–138.

increasing gulf between the industrialised and unionised North and the industrially weak and poorly organised South as one of their greatest problems, and used their political and industrial influence to further policies aimed at reducing this gap, as in collective agreements with FIAT and Montedison in 1975 which included guarantees that the companies would invest in the South.[76] On the other hand, in the UK, movement of workers can be inhibited when unions are geographically based, membership is mandatory and changing jobs also means changing union membership. Hence Treu's call for "parallel" institutions of government labour market policy to complement those of the trade unions.[77]

D. Links Between Private Actors and the State

Despite the overlap with another paper considering the public sector in legal implementation of economic policy,[78] it is worth reiterating here how major actors in the energy and manpower fields can assume a highly ambiguous legal character. In the energy field, there are the joint ventures by way of the "carried interest" formula already mentioned in the Netherlands,[79] with State participation, Italian "enti di gestione" being public agencies holding shares in joint stock companies which receive policy directives (e.g. ENI and IRI), the power of the French atomic energy commission to buy controlling shares in companies and, of course, the stake of the UK government in British Petroleum, to mention but a few. Then there are the multitude of direct and indirect arrangements for the formal and informal control of national energy corporations, ranging from direct Ministerial control, to formal independence subject to theoretical powers of veto and influence via appointments and the old boy network.[80]

Given the extensive links between private actors in the energy field and the State

---

[76] P. Lange and M. Vanicelli, "Strategy under stress: The Italian union movement and the Italian crisis in developmental perspective", in P. Lange, G. Ross and M. Vanicelli, *Unions, Change and Crisis: French and Italian Union Strategy and the Political Economy, 1945–1980*, (1982, New York) at 95 at pp. 150–160. The authors state that these agreements were more symbolic than practical; that virtually no investments in the South ensued from them.

[77] T. Treu, "Azione legislativa, controllo sindacale, problemi del mercato del lavoro", in Treu *et al.*, *Per Una Politica del Lavoro*, 1979, at p. 47 at p. 57.

[78] L. Hancher, "The Public Sector as Object and Instrument of Economic Policy", above pp. 165–236.

[79] *Supra*, at 18, established by the Continental Shelf Mining Act of 23 September 1965 (Mijnwet Continentaal Plat); Research Project, Netherlands Energy Inventory.

[80] For a detailed account of the many forms of public enterprise, see the chapters on Italy, France and the UK in W. G. Friedmann (ed.), *Public and Private Enterprise in Mixed Economies*, (1974, New York). M. Forster emphasises the power of the Secretary of State in the UK to appoint the management as having considerable policy significance; "Legal implementation of energy policy in the UK", a paper given to the Colloquium on The Legal Implementation of Energy Policy, EUI, Florence, 22–24 September 1982 (on file at EUI), at p. 15. Grayson refers to the "informal elite links among the anciens of the grandes écoles" as affecting relations between national oil companies and government in France; *supra*, note 30, at p. 19.

in the five West European countries, the position in Hungary is not as different as would be the case in other areas of economic policy. Until 1968, the organisation of the energy economy corresponded to the general system of economic control and management – it was fundamentally centralised. With the transition from energy scarcity to energy surplus, certain changes occurred to decentralise, not so much in the planning process as in the implementation of the central plan. For example, in energy turnover, administrative restrictions and forced channels of distribution were ended. The realisation of the planned targets was to be achieved using other means of economic regulations: "With the exception of concepts related to prospective development, the significant part of decisions on energetics have for all practical purposes been shifted to the enterprise spheres of authority".[81] The attempt to reduce the rate of growth in energy demand in the 1970s, however, led to an increase in the degree of centralisation.

In manpower, there is much less in the way of participation by the State in private actors. However, assistance by the State to ailing enterprises may take the form not only of loans, but also of purchase of equity capital. Thereafter, the political importance of participation is often appreciated when it precludes the "private" partner from adopting plans involving job losses.[82] The public sector itself, of course, accounts for a high proportion of national employment.

A third link between private actors and the State arises which is different from either State participation inside the actor or control from outside the actor. This is where the State recognises or licences or creates the actor to carry on activities or perform functions within the policy area.

The actor thus has a degree of private autonomy from the State: within the terms of its "licence" or "charter" it may be free of regulation; or the absence of formal State participation or representation, and the predominance of private actors in its structure, gives it a quasi-private character.

Energy and manpower are particularly rich areas for such actors. In manpower they range from the Equal Opportunities Commission and Manpower Services Commission in the UK, to the Bundesanstalt für Arbeit (Federal Employment Institute) in Germany, to the Agence Nationale pour l'Emploi and l'Association Nationale pour la Formation Professionelle des Adultes in France.[83] Interesting questions arise when comparison is made between these and similar bodies in the energy sphere – the national oil companies or other national energy corporations.

---

[81] I. Dobozi, "Energy planning and the energy situation in a socialist planned economy lacking energy: a study of Hungary", in Lindberg (ed.), supra, note 15, p. 173 at p. 198, which also lists the "means of regulation". He concludes: "The new system of economic control and management, introduced in 1968, has made it possible for socialist market relations to play a greater role together with direct contacts and agreements between producers and consumers" (at pp. 202–203) (author's emphasis).

[82] For an illustration of when foreign State participation in joint ventures with Massey-Ferguson may have had the effect of forcing closure of operations in Scotland (where the operations were not the subject of such restrictions) when the company got into financial difficulties, see Henderson et al., supra, note 72.

[83] For recent reforms in the French public employment services, see Liaisons Sociales, No. 5485 of 17 May 1984: "Mise en place du service public de l'emploi".

It is not the purpose of this paper to explore the different qualities of these actors, much conditioned by their different operating environments (e.g. the tendency of national oil companies to ape the multinationals; the tendency of manpower institutions to be tripartite in organisation). The factor to be highlighted is that the *existence* of the actor, or its functions or competences, is owed to the State. Whether this fact in itself is significant is difficult so say. It does mean that actors so created are to some extent at the mercy of their creator: the conditions which obtain at their creation can be changed or their competences be encroached upon.[84] Whether the fact that their legal origins are characterised by "private constitutional" documents helps to understand their nature and relevance to economic policy implementation is a question which may find its answer in the different public constitutional laws of the countries studied.[85]

---

[84] The rise in unemployment with the recession of the 1970s has, the British Manpower Services Commission acknowledged, "very substantially changed the nature of the Commission's role; though it is essentially about employment rather than unemployment, the Commission could not avoid being affected and concerned by the increasing levels and incidence of unemployment". MSC, *Review of Services of the Unemployed*, March 1981, para. 1.1. This change in role has been accompanied by changes in the MSC's constitutional competence; for example, the removal of its exclusive power to recommend establishment or abolition of Industrial Training Boards by the Employment and Training Act 1981. See annotations to the Industrial Training Act 1982 in the *Encyclopedia of Labour Relations Law* (general eds.: B. A. Hepple and P. O'Higgins). Similarly, the Bundesanstalt für Arbeit complained about government interference by way of manpower programmes which "would have been more appropriate to incorporate... in the Bundesanstalt's budget". See Bundesanstalt für Arbeit, *Employment Policy in Germany: Challenges and Concepts for the 1980s*, (1980, Nürnberg) (translated from a German edition of 1979).

[85] For example, a primary illustration is the 1949 Constitution of the Federal Republic of Germany, which in Art. 12 grants "the freedom of the citizen to choose his work". This legal support for a free market in labour precludes, for example, placement services from assuming a regulatory character of compulsion (for an exception: recruitment of handicapped workers). A similar article in the Italian constitution (Art. 4: Right to Work) led to a dispute between those supporting State against trade union control of employment services in 1949, which was decided in favour of the former. See J. Malagugini, "Collocamento della mandopera, orientamento e consulenza professionale nella republica federale tedesca"; and E. Siniscalchi, "Il sistema italiano di collocamento", in Marazia, *supra*, note 39, respectively, p. 89 at p. 90; and p. 163 at p. 165. *A propos* the problem of defining "public enterprise", Daintith observes: "A spectrum of legal possibilities is normal: at one end, the enterprise is organised as a department of central, regional or local government; at the other, under the same forms as private enterprise; in the centre, as a legally independent body of a kind specifically designed for the carrying on of public activities". He concludes: "despite the heavy reliance of all mixed economies on public enterprise as an instrument for the achievement of a variety of economic purposes, it has signally failed to attract to itself a comprehensive and coherent set of legal attributes. In the legal, if not the economic organisation of the State, public enterprise has been a sharer of the attributes of other, more firmly grounded institutions: of the Government Department, of the concessionnaire, of the public utility, of the limited company". T. C. Daintith, "Competition between public and private enterprise", in

A second major category of such State "chartered" actors is where associations are so recognised, licenced or created. In the case of associations, Schmitter distinguished societal from state corporatism with respect to recognition by differentiating "between recognition granted as a matter of political necessity imposed from below upon public officials and that granted from above by the state as a condition for association formation and continuous operations".[86] The ambivalence here is well illustrated in the manpower area with regard to workers' organisations, as in the tensions between works councils and industrial unions in the Federal Republic of Germany, the attempt by the Industrial Relations Act 1971 to restrict recognition of British trade unions to registered organisations, and the notion of "most representative trade unions" in France.[87] In both manpower and energy, corporations are major actors, yet there is some debate, in the UK at least, about the extent to which companies are a creature of the State, or whether associations of capital owners adopted the company form as a matter of convenience.[88] The implications of this debate for the use of company law as an instrument of State policy are obvious.[89]

General Reports to the 10th International Congress of Comparative Law, Budapest, 1981, p. 845 at p. 847 and p. 870.

[86] *Supra*, note 22, at p. 21.

[87] In West Germany, Streeck points to the 1972 amendments to the Works Constitution Act: "by simultaneously improving the unions' access to the statutory representation system (works councils) and strengthening the latter as an effective representative of the workforce, the 1972 amendment... amounted to a massive organizational support by the state for the unions in adapting their basic structures to new conditions and requirements without endangering the stability of industrial unionism". W. Streeck, "Organizational consequences of neo-corporatist cooperation in West German labor unions", in G. Lehmbruch and P. C. Schmitter, *Patterns of Corporatist Policy-Making*, (1982, Beverly Hills, London) at p. 9 and especially at pp. 50–51. On the British experience, see B. Weekes, *et al.*, *Industrial Relations and the Limits of Law*, (1975, Warwick). On the French law of "most representative" Unions, see M. Forde, "Trade union pluralism and labour law in France", (1984) 33 *International and Comparative Law Quarterly* 134; and for a complaint by a small French union, see J. Menin, "La rapport Auroux tue la pluralisme syndical", *Droit Social*, April 1982, at p. 278. For a brief review of the problems of a legal system identifying certain parties as having exclusive competence to make collective agreements on behalf of workers (as in France, the Netherlands, and the Federal Republic of Germany only trade unions can be party to collective agreements though in fact other bodies are as well), and a contrast with the absence of restrictions on parties competent to make collective agreements on behalf of employers, see G. C. Perone, *The Law of Collective Agreements in the Countries of the European Community*, Document V/40/82 – EN, Commission of the European Communities, at pp. 6 ff.

[88] The public joint stock company hardly existed outside banking and transport before the last quarter of the century (E. J. Hobsbawm, *Industry and Empire*, (1976, London) at p. 215. It only entered industry and multiplied after 1880 (T. Kempner, K. MacMillan and K. H. Hawkins, *Business and Society*, (1974, New York) at p. 32. See for further arguments along these lines, G. M. Anderson and R. D. Tollison, "The myth of the corporation as a creation of the state", (1983) 3 *International Review of Law and Economics* 107.

[89] For a consideration of the role of company law as an instrument of labour policy, see B.

In sum, the links between private actors and the State can range between relative autonomy and total subordination. In a specific area of policy, the pattern may be one of State control of the numbers of actors, their fields of operation and their competences, and this, as will be argued later, is an instrument of economic policy implementation of considerable interest.[90]

E. Internal Organisation

This could be called the "private constitutional law" of the actors I am concerned with in energy and manpower; to adapt the title of an article by Kahn-Freund: the impact of private constitions on economic law.[91] The argument is that State law can determine the internal legal organisation of complex private actors. The economic behaviour of these actors is affected by their internal legal organisation. Hence, the direction of economic policy may be shaped by the State through its control of the internal legal organisation of powerful private actors.[92] This goes beyond the view which looks to State regulation of the framework of interaction *between* actors.[93] Rather it looks to inter-action between elements *within* the organisation/actor.

Energy actors provide an excellent setting for the testing of this argument. This is because of the prevalence of that particular actor – the joint venture. There are two types of joint venture that could be looked at, the inter-company joint venture and the company-government joint venture. Herman provides a chart of 2,755 joint ventures by oil companies *inter se*, over half of which involved a collective investment of ten million US dollars each.[94] He quotes a study which concluded

Bercusson, "Workers, corporate enterprise and the law", in R. Lewis (ed.), *Labour Law in Britain*, (forthcoming).

[90] Teubner amplifies Schmitter's distinction as follows: "In societal corporatism, the limitation of number, the singularity and the compulsory character of the collectives are due to social processes, through competition, cooptation, social pressures and inter-organizational arrangement. In contrast, state corporatism creates these elements by deliberate government restriction, state-imposed eradication of multiplicity and through means of law". G. Teubner, *Industrial Democracy Through Law? Social Functions of Law in Institutional Innovations.* EUI, Florence 1983 (mimeo, on file at EUI), at pp. 18–29.

[91] O. Kahn-Freund, "The impact of constitutions on labour law", (1976) 35 *Cambridge Law Journal* 240.

[92] G. Teubner, *Juridification,* in Teubner, *supra* note 4, EUI, Florence, 1985, at p. 72: "...the well considered design of internal organizational structures... the major function of such reflexive internal structures would be to replace interventionist state control by effective internal control".

[93] Though to the extent that the State establishes institutional frameworks for coordination of private actors, these institutions – given certain qualities – could themselves be called actors, their public or private capacity being subject to whether their origin or function is linked to, and the larger framework within which these institutions operate could be called, society.

[94] E. S. Herman, *Corporate Control, Corporate Power,* (1981, Cambridge) at pp. 206–208. Grayson, *supra,* note 30, devotes an entire chapter to such relationships between the national oil companies and the oil multinationals (chapter 11): CFP and the BP Connec-

that "joint ventures are a form of interfirm linkage used to reduce competitive and buyer-seller interdependence, to establish, in Cyert and March's terms, a 'negotiated environment'".[95] The common concern of the parties to the venture, however, remains limited to the furthering of their private economic interests. For the purposes of the view that such organisational arrangements could be shaped to further State economic policies, the company-government joint venture is more salient.[96]

Hossain gives an account of various legal mechanisms in the field of petroleum development: equity joint ventures, contractual joint ventures, production sharing contracts, service contracts, and so on. He concludes:[97]

> It is possible, and indeed advisable, to extract certain mechanisms contained in one form, and to incorporate them in another, or to replace a less effective mechanism contained in one by a more effective one drawn from another. The above survey has shown how most of the agreements have been developed and strenghthened, through a process of "cross-fertilization", which has led to the emergence of "hybrids" – thus for example, the features of joint ventures have been grafted on to concessions, and to production-sharing contracts, and various provisions designed to ensure rapid and effective exploration under one system, have been readily incorporated in another.
> The task of establishing a good legal framework involves not the mechanical imitation of standard precedents, but the imaginative and resourceful putting together in a package of mechanisms which have proved to be the most effective to secure certain general objectives, while safeguarding certain specific interests in each distinct phase of operations.

The key to success in the company-government joint venture is, in Herman's phrase, "the mobilization of equivalent or greater power".[98] Proposals to structure the internal organisations of private actors in the energy field must, therefore, have a clear perspective on where power lies *within* the organisation, and must bring to bear sufficient State power to shape that organisation's structure so as to ensure that specified economic policies are furthered.[99] This is a daunting task, not least because the legal concepts and institutions of company law which purport to

tion, SNEA and the Caltex Connection, ENI and the Exxon (Esso) Connection, VEBA and the Mobil and BP Connections, BNOC and what is to be the BP, Esso and Shell Connection? See also the chart on ownership links between the majors and the major crude oil producing countries in the Middle East prepared for the U.S. Senate Hearings on Multinationals, reproduced in Sampson, *supra*, note 17, at p. 182 ("The Dance of the Sisters"). Herman states: "oil company joint ventures link together the major producers on a scale that is unduplicated in any other industry" at p. 205.

95 Herman, *ibid.*, at p. 211.
96 States may control the behaviour of private joint venture partners *inter se* (e.g. interest reallocation) via licence terms. See T. C. Daintith and G. D. M. Willoughby, *United Kingdom Oil and Gas Law* (2nd ed.), (1984, London/New York), Part I, chapter 8, paras. 1–803/4.
97 Hossain, *supra*, note 65, at pp. 175–176.
98 Herman, *supra*, note 94, at p. 294.
99 Herman is pessimistic of the prospects in the U.S.: "It is easy to conjure up proposals for altering corporate power structures; it is quite another thing to get such proposals enacted in forms that retain any bite". Indeed, he puts forward the advantages of straightforward

Brian Bercusson

govern corporations which are the principal organisations in the energy field are often not only inadequate, they are positively misleading.[100] The major private actors in the energy field are the multinational oil companies and "one can safely say the principal legal form of the multinational enterprise is simply an aggregate of variously organized companies, incorporated... under a variety of legal systems, but controlled centrally by a parent company, and thus forming a single economic unit".[101] What the author of this formulation emphasises, however, is that "of all the essential or possible criteria one might mention, the one that is absolutely crucial and common to every form of multinational enterprise – and correlative with the obvious propensity to have a considerable collection of foreign branches and affiliates – is: central direction".[102] Centralised control together with "the very great flexibility which large groups are permitted in the organisation of their affairs and the extent to which their formal legal structures differ from their practical managerial organisation" make taming the giant corporation a formidable task.[103]

The focus on centralised direction lies at the heart of Herman's view of "strategic position" (the occupancy of top positions in large companies with diffused owership) as the basis of control of the corporation.[104] He analyses the various routes whereby strategic position may be obtained and the reasons for its importance as a power base. But neither of these gives much comfort to those who seek a solution in structural reforms.[105] The elusive qualities of power and its

regulation: "There is also a tendency to underrate the corporation's ability to absorb news instructions, offices, and individuals with special responsibilities, without effect – whether by cooptation, obstruction, tokenism, public relations efforts, or otherwise. Externally imposed rules may be effective, even in the face of conflicting corporate interests, if the rules are clear, simple, and virtually self-enforcing (the number of minority group members to be hired by a particular date, the number of scrubbers of a certain type to be installed per stack)". *Ibid.*, at pp. 293–294.

[100] Herman is particularly scathing about the role of the board of directors in U.S. corporations; *ibid.*, at pp. 30–48.

[101] C. Day Wallace, *Legal Control of the Multinational Enterprise*, (1982) at p. 18.

[102] *Ibid.*, at p. 20. Cf. C. Tugendhat, *The Multinationals*, (1971, London): "the subsidiaries are supposed to put the wider interests of the company as a whole above their own... The parent secures this commitment through a variety of means. But it exercises its most constant influence on its subsidiaries through its control of the overall company structure and the planning function, which between them determine the flow of investment funds" at p. 126.

[103] The quotation is from T. Hadden, *The Control of Corporate Groups*, London, Institute of Advanced Legal Studies, 1983, at 5. He too concludes, however, that "effective regulation of the affairs of complex groups is likely to require rather less emphasis on disclosure and rather more on the regulation of the internal structures which such groups are permitted to adopt" at p. 6. Cf. R. Nader *et al.*, *Taming the Giant Corporation*, (1976, New York).

[104] Herman, *supra*, note 94, at pp. 26–29.

[105] Herman is dismissive of Christopher Stone's proposals: "It is naive to assume that corporate behaviour may be finely tuned through external intervention"; *ibid.*, at p. 293.

control in the modern corporation may, however, succumb to the mobilisation of labour as a power where shareholders, governments and directors have failed. Unlike these others, labour is a power organised *both* within and outside the corporation.

Here, conveniently, there may be lessons to be learned from the manpower policy area. For example, there is the prevalence of the tripartite formula in manpower policy institutions. Heretofore, the tripartite principle has been expressed primarily on bodies external to the company. The Report of the Bullock Committee on Industrial Democracy in the UK attempted to apply that principle to company boards with its famous $2 \times + y$ formula.[106] If ever worker directors have any impact, it is most likely to have been on issues to do with manpower.[107] A recent study of manpower policy decisions within multinational corporations in the UK demonstrated that different types of decisions tended to be taken at different levels (e.g. decisions on numbers employed were made primarily by the parent company/registered headquarters in 22 out of 30 cases, whereas recruitment of management staff was decided mainly by the UK subsidiary in 24 out of 30 cases).[108] This has implications for the insertion of employee organs with specific powers in defined circumstances. For example, a new French law of March 1984 requires companies in economic difficulties to communicate this fact and other information to the comité d'entreprise, which may examine it with the assistance of experts of its choice and may demand the nomination of an expert to report on management's operations.[109] The works councils in German companies have long had the power of co-determination on manpower issues under the Works Constitution act 1972.[110] Streeck has analysed "the organisational consequences of neo-corporatist cooperation in West German labour unions"; what is needed is an analysis of its consequences for the internal organisation of companies. By breaking down the functions of corporations and organising countervailing power

But cf. G. Teubner, *Corporate Responsibility as a Problem of Company Constitution*, EUI Working Paper No. 51, 1983.

[106] Report of the Committee of Inquiry on Industrial Democracy (chairman: Lord Bullock), Cmnd. 6706, January 1977.

[107] There is a detailed account of the manoeuvres within the Volkswagen company on manpower policy which focuses in particular on the effects of the particular composition of the company's supervisory board in Streeck, *supra*, note 50, at pp. 67–74.

[108] J. Hamill, "Labour relations decision making within multinational corporations", (1984) 15 *Industrial Relations Journal* No. 2, at p. 30.

[109] Loi No. 84–148 of 1 March 1984 (O.J. 2.3.84); see *Liaisons Sociales* No. 5476 of 18 April 1984.

[110] For example, section 92: "(1) The employer shall inform the works council in full and in good time of matters relating to manpower planning including in particular present and future manpower needs and the resulting staff movements and vocational training measures and supply the relevant documentation. He shall consult the works council on the nature and extent of the action required and means of avoiding hardship". Text given in Streeck, *supra* note 50, at 166. A recent court decision extended their involvement to issues concerning the installation of new technology, see *European Industrial Relations Review*, No. 124 (May 1984), at p. 9.

units to be inserted into the structure, it may be possible to decentralise the company and reduce the power of those having strategic positons.[111]

By way of conclusion, it is worth noting that the two major private actors in the manpower area – companies and trade unions – are said to share with the State the constitutional quality of democracy (shareholder/union democracy). This quality, when applied to the State through constitutional and administrative law, imposes various restraints on State action.[112] Labour law has used administrative law standards (e.g. rules of natural justice) to resolve problems of discipline both within trade unions and within enterprises in the UK.[113] Company law is also not immune, as the perennial debates over majority shareholder rights and the protection of minorities indicate. But these are exceptions. For the most part there is a marked absence of such "public law" standards applicable to private actors' transactions. The absence of such constraints on what are mainly private property transactions may be a key factor in the decisions of States to implement economic policy through "dominium" rather than "imperium".[114] The interplay of private interest and public policy *within* private organisations and the overarching concept of democracy provide a fascinating matrix for analysis of legal implementation of economic policy.

III. Processes v. Instruments

The development and application of a typology of instruments of economic policy implementation by the State is a major feature of the research project. As Daintith says in his paper: "[the instrument typology's] basic concepts are equally relevant to private power holders, who may also deploy a range of resources in order to

---

111 This differs from Stone's views of external directors representing public and other interests, since the emphasis is on labour's role as a countervailing power *within* the company. An analysis of the recent French labour law reforms concluded: "one might find in the Auroux laws an outstanding example of that 'reflexive' law (citing Teubner) which has begun to be put forward as a solution to some of the problems of the role of law in complex, heterogeneous, modern societies. Avoiding both the characteristic inequities of laissez-faire and the arbitrariness and crudeness of the direct regulatory response to the inadequacy of laissez-faire, reflexive law would confine the State's role where possible to providing a structural basis for the coordination of interaction among social subsystems. It would shape procedures for participation and communication within and among these structures, rather than prescribing goals or taking responsibility for substantive outcomes". M. A. Glendon, "French labour law reform 1982–1983: the struggle for collective bargaining", (1984) 32 *American Journal of Comparative Law* 449, at p. 484.

112 The "State action" doctrine in U.S. law embodies the issue of whether private implementation of economic policy is sufficiently akin to State action to allow for the imposition of constitutional restraints. See, for example, P. Brest, "State action and liberal theory: a casenote on *Flagg Brothers v. Brooks*"; and F. I. Goodman, "Comment" in (1982) 130 *University of Pennsylvania Law Review* 1296 and 1331.

113 B. A. Hepple and P. O'Higgins, *Encyclopedia of Labour Relations Law*, 1972, Part 1, paras. 1A-035-040, and paras. 1-389-391/1.

114 T. C. Daintith, "Legal analysis of economic policy", (1982) 9 *Journal of Law and Society*, p. 191 at pp. 214–216.

change the relative costs of behaviour by others".[115] In this part of the paper, I want to pursue the application of this instrument typology to the behaviour of the private actors discussed above in the energy and manpower policy fields.

A reflection of this type of private implementation of economic policy is to be found where State instruments *incorporate* private ordering (actors, processes or outcomes) into the formal instrument or measure, or even abdicate expressly in favour of informal private ordering. Another indication of the way formal State implementation could shade off into informal private implementation is to be found in certain aspects of State intervention examined in the national inventories compiled by the research project. For example, there are less formal acts of government (circulars, advice); there exist and operate bodies, the "public law" character of which is diffused by their independence from formal State machinery; the State may act through bilateral but not legally binding relationships; the State may issue declarations of policy, without more, or impose duties without sanctions, or undertake to consult, inform or even obtain the approval of private bodies.

The typology of instruments of economic policy used by States which was developed by Daintith for the research project includes: unilateral regulation and removal or relaxation of regulations; taxation and the removal of taxation or the granting of tax exemptions; consensual constraints; public benefits; public sector management; and information.[116] The questions this part of the paper addresses include: what are the functional equivalents of these instruments in the private sector, and what are the implications for State instruments of the use by private actors of equivalent instruments (e.g. will the State use its instruments; when will it use its instruments; which instruments will it use).[117]

To understand the concept of "instruments" as applied to the behaviour of private actors, it is helpful to recapitulate the two concepts used by Daintith in developing his typology: *relative costs* and *resources.*[118] As to relative costs, the proposition is that the behaviour of the actors to be influenced by the instruments of government policy involves a *choice* by each actor between the relative costs of different courses of action.[119] Further, it is emphasised both that there is almost invariably such a choice in practice, but also that the effect of a government instrument in altering the relative costs and therefore choices is imprecise. Hence,

---

[115] T. C. Daintith, *Law as Policy Instrument: A Comparative Perspective,* above, at pp. 40–44.

[116] For full details see above at pp. 25–33 and the Methodological note at p. 51.

[117] For example, it has been noted that in the U.S. and Japan, there are State controlled strategic reserves of oil, whereas in Europe (UK excepted), it is the companies themselves which maintain the stocks, with government cooperation and backing. G. P. Levy, "The relationship between oil companies and consumer State governments in Europe", (1984) 2 *Journal of Energy and Natural Resources Law* p. 9 at p. 15.

[118] Daintith, *supra,* note 114, and above, at p. 28.

[119] Problems of identifying all the factors to be costed, of the degree to which different actors will be aware of or consider various cost factors, of assigning weights to each factor and the assignment of different weights by different actors – these will be left aside for the moment.

this combination of freedom of choice plus imprecision in government impact on choice create together the problems of legal implementation of economic policy with which the research project is concerned. The second concept is that of resources of the State: force, wealth and respect, possessed in varying degrees by different governments.

Prima facie, there seems nothing to prevent the application of these concepts to private actors. The concept of relative costs can easily be adapted to (for it originated in) an economy in which private actors as well as the State participate. The concept of resources can also be applied – though the relative weights of force, wealth and respect may be different for private actors from those of the State.

Two points further will help illuminate the discussion of specific instruments which follows. First, the possibility of there being no choice is considered, but thought by Daintith to be rare. Considered in the context of a particular area of economic activity – energy (or a particular sector, gas, oil, electricity and so on) or manpower (availability of work, or a particular kind of work, in a particular place) – the element of choice may be considerably reduced more frequently than not. Secondly, the notion of resources in the abstract, and their use by government or other actors, becomes much clearer when one considers specific resources in specific areas of policy. The use by the State of force in maintaining the criminal law, the use by monopolistic enterprises of their wealth in the energy industry, the use by organisations of workers of respect and loyalty in manpower policy indicates how the distribution of resources varies and how the significance of different resources to different actors in different policy areas also varies. Both the concepts of choice between relative costs and resources available to actors are flexible in their applications to different circumstances in different fields of economic policy.

A. State v. Private Regulation

The concept of unilateral regulation by the State, following Daintith's analysis, implies the restriction of choice (to compliance or non-compliance) through the application or threat of force. The use of force (as one of the resources available to an actor) is often accounted an attribute of the State; indeed it is said to possess the "monopoly" of force or violence. The effect of force or the threat of it on freedom of choice is not, however, such as to totally eliminate it. Nor does it achieve necessarily precise results in the sense of disappearance of non-compliant behaviour. In sum, State regulation allows for possible choice and does not stipulate precise results.

Private actors in the fields of energy and manpower do not normally rely on force. They do, however, possess other resources – wealth and respect – which enable them to similarly restrict the choices of others and increase the relative costs of certain courses of action to the extent that courses of action dictated by these private actors become overwhelmingly the norm, despite the theoretical freedom of choice and imprecision of calculable results. Indeed, by way of analogy to the State, to the extent that they possess a monopoly of wealth or respect, their control over choices made is akin to that of the State. The focus on monopolistic control as a characteristic of regulation is reflected, for example, by Breyer when he considers the role of antitrust laws: "When critics contrast regulated with unregulated marketplaces, they typically think of 'workably competitive' markets – markets that are free of private restraint as well as of governmental regulation".[120] One need not look too far in the energy field: "The impetus for growth is very strong in the oil industry... Growth is required not only to realize economies of scale, but to exercise control over the social, political and economic environment in which the firm operates".[121]

The two monopolies, of force and of wealth, coexist, but it is their occasional confrontations which reveal much of the nature of regulation. State regulation may impinge on an area controlled by a private actor or actors. These private controls may be banned or restricted or controlled or changed. In a clear case of private control (whether by monopoly or unequal bargaining power in a marketplace) *State regulation is equivalent to private deregulation.*[122] In particular, antitrust or competition law is a State instrument of private deregulation.[123] The actions taken by private actors to avoid the rigours of competition law amount to the *private removal or relaxation of regulation* of areas of economic activity.[124] Conversely, State removal or relaxation of regulation is often the signal for private regulation.[125] Paradoxically, the exception occurs when these two spheres of

---

[120] S. Breyer, *Regulation and Its Reform*, (1982, Cambridge, Mass.) at p. 157. Also Herman, *supra*, note 93, at pp. 173–174: "the 'old regulation' (OR) is usually characterised by detailed controls over the most strategic business variables, notably prices charged, allowable entry, and services that may (or must) be rendered. These are the variables that private cartels seek to control but are prevented from doing (at least in flagrant ways) in the United States by the antitrust laws".

[121] Grayson, *supra*, note 30, at p. 250. Leaving aside the seven sisters, VEBA is the largest company in the Federal Republic of Germany; CFP and SNEA are first and third in France; ENI is second in Italy.

[122] "The relation between the regulator and the firms affected by regulation is adversarial. In part, this is because the regulator must lead the industry to perform in a way different from that dictated by the incentives of the unregulated market". Breyer, *supra*, note 120, at p. 6. Daintith provides a fascinating glimpse of the strangely inverted case of regulation by the State of the "regulatory" practices of its own monopolies, when he describes UK controls on the practice of public corporations by way of "full-line forcing", preferences, cross-subsidisation and price cutting. "Public and private enterprise in the UK", in Friedmann (ed.), *supra*, note 70, at p. 195 at pp. 250–262.

[123] *Pace* Breyer, *ibid.*, who sees anti-trust as different in aims and method from classical regulation; at pp. 156–157. Conversely, it has been remarked that collective agreements can be a form of deregulation of State law, in that they may relax the stringency of statutory requirements. L. Hancher, Research Project Comparative Report on exit from the labour market, at p. 13 (on file at the EUI).

[124] Though "(t)he antritrust laws cannot effectively deal with tacit collusion or oligopolistic behaviour – the behaviour of several firms in a concentrated industry that do not agree to certain anticompetitive behaviour but over time informally take actions with the same effect". Breyer, *ibid.*, at p. 173.

[125] Examples are easy to find: in the Federal Republic of Germany, electricity supply undertakings made demarcation agreements (demarkationsvertrage) to determine zonal

private and State regulation are congruent – public corporations or State regulated industries. Then relaxation of the one (State regulation) may lead to removal of the other (private monopoly) – i.e. open competition.

The State is a unique actor. Equally unique to the case of private regulation, however, is the fact that a number of actors may combine or organise or jointly deploy their resources so as to exercise regulation of an area. Hence, unlike State unilateral regulation, in the case of private use of the instrument there may be bilateral or multilateral regulation: two or more actors combine or agree on a set of controls for an area of economic activity. The oil industry, again, seems to have developed the most sophisticated mechanisms and stimulated the more exotic metaphors. Sampson quotes many, including one which describes the combination of the major oil companies with the independents as "'oligopoly with a fringe': or more picturesquely as being like roses growing on a pergola. The major companies, having together constructed their pergola, had an interest to maintain its stability, and they could tolerate quite well the intrusion of the roses, which indeed made the structure look more attractive".[126]

It need hardly be pointed out that such private regulation is not limited to the energy field but is also prevalent in the manpower field, if not on such a global scale as in the oil industry. The different qualities of the major private actors in manpower, as elaborated above, affect their capacity to "monopolise" the manpower chain. A major cleavage is obviously between *unilateral regulation* by either employers of workers' organisations of one or more parts of the chain (access to work, mobility, exit and so on), and *bilateral regulation* through collective bargaining. Broadly speaking, the employer has an initial monopoly of power within the enterprise.[127] Its scope will be determined by the size of the enterprise, which may embrace a large segment of or even all of an industry and a substantial proportion of the national workforce. Its unilateral exercise may be constrained by the presence of organisations of workers, and the enterprise's manpower policy may be regulated bilaterally.[128] Similar regulation, unilateral,

monopolies and when the Gesetz gegen Wettbewerbsbeschränkungen was passed in 1957, the electricity industry was exempted from the operation of competition policy. Daintith and Hancher, *supra*, note 19 at p. 51. In the UK, the Energy Act 1976 makes provision for the temporary suspension of competition law during an emergency so as to allow restrictions as to price and conditions of supply. Forster, *supra*, note 80, at pp. 5–6. Sampson gives a vivid account of the meetings of the oil companies' representatives in New York in January 1971 while officials of the anti-trust division waited to consider drafts of agreements for clearance; *supra*, note 17, at pp. 229–230.

[126] Sampson, *supra*, note 17, at p. 160. Other phrases include "oligopolistic interdependence" (p. 186), "bilateral monopoly" (after OPEC, p. 251), and, of course, many times "conspiracy"; for example, in the anti-trust action against Exxon, Mobil, Socal, Texaco and Gulf in 1953: "The objective of the conspiracy was market stabilisation; its essential terms were market division and price fixing". Quoted at p. 140.

[127] Whether this is solely a consequence of wealth, or a delegation of force, or "latent" force, in that interference can be met by force, is a question to be deferred.

[128] For example, the UK case studies of manpower changes examined in Jacobs et al., *supra*, note 52, conclude: "that the means invariably chosen to deal with the problem was an attack on labour costs, usually involving a rundown in manpower. It confirms that

bilateral or multilateral, may occur through negotiations at sectoral, regional or national levels.

It is not difficult to assemble a catalogue of illustrations of the private regulation of policy in the fields of energy and manpower. Here a few will suffice. Perhaps the most obvious are those cases where there is an express delegation or concession by the State to a private body of regulatory authority.[129] For example, the group of laws in France which make the petroleum sector a public monopoly delegated to private enterprise. As Grayson puts it: "By using the systems of delegated monopoly the government had given a clear lead to the industrialists to organize the industry as they saw fit, once the overall framework was established by the government".[130] Another illustration is the coal protection policy of the German government in the late 1950s. As Grayson describes it, there was "a short-lived (1958–59) effort to regulate the oil 'invasion' by having the principal domestic and foreign firms in coal and oil form a coal/oil cartel, followed by a temporary successful effort to encourage the oil companies into voluntary acceptance of a scheme limiting the growth of heavy and light fuel oil supplies to certain annual percentage rates. Finally laws were passed...".[131] In manpower, the clearest instance of such delegation is the widespread recognition of professional bodies (lawyers, doctors, nurses, architects, pharmacists and so on) with monopolistic controls over access, placement, training and mobility within occupational spheres.

The literature on energy and manpower contains innumerable cases of private actors exercising controls over substantial areas of policy. The Commission's report on the 1973–74 crisis described how the oil companies attempted to prevent filling stations giving priority to regular customers, and how control by the companies of distribution led to the closure of independent petrol stations.[132] Bilateral regulation of manpower issues through collective agreements ranges from reduction in working time (by May 1, 1984 over 100 agreements in 88 occupational groups had been signed in France covering about 5,533,000 workers), to individual and collective dismissals (the national inter-confederal agreements of 1965 in Italy) to the closed shop in the Dutch printing industry where employers' association members will not employ non-unionists and union members will not work for non-association firms.[133]

> change is determined by management according to its particular circumstances and that
> as yet neither government measures nor collective bargaining have created the systematic
> approach that could make the processes of industrial change more predictable and
> consistent" at p. 10.
> [129] See Turner's characterising of oil companies at "agents" or "transmission belts" for
> governments; *supra*, note 24, at pp. 118–120.
> [130] Grayson, *supra*, note 30, at 34. Cf. in Italy, the ENEL is usually described as an
> administrative monopoly rather than a de facto or de jure one. G. Quadri, *Diritto
> Publico dell'Economia*, (1977, Bologna) at pp. 80–81, quoted in Hancher, *supra*, note
> 19, at p. 14.
> [131] Grayson, *ibid.*, at p. 149.
> [132] *Report* of the Commission, 1975, *supra*, note 3, at pp. 52, 146.
> [133] On the French agreements, see *Liaisons Sociales*, No. 101/84 of 26 September 1984, at p.

The problem remains of clarifying the relation between private regulation and State regulation. To a great extent, the balance depends on how much accumulation and use of resources is permitted by either the State or private actors. The greater the allowance for private agglomerations of wealth or respect, the greater the degree of private regulation. The issue of whether there *should* be "deregulation" of private monopolies by State regulation becomes one of policy: are the objectives of public policy served by these monopolies. The question of whether there *will* be deregulation of private power is linked to the political balance of power, in which private monopolies may be expected to wield their power against "deregulation" of private power and, occasionally, for deregulation of State power when it conflicts with their interests.[134] In the case of energy, these conflicts are less likely to occur because governments, by and large, accept the validity of the economic judgments made by the powerful private actors.[135] In the case of manpower, the trade unions have not been so fortunate. A recent article summarises the position: "West German Employment Policy: Restoring Worker Competition".[136]

B. Taxation v. Private Pricing

Taxation as an instrument of government has an ambiguous character. Imposition of a tax may have little to do with a desired change of behaviour. Taxes are a revenue source for States as well as an instrument for affecting behaviour. So, for example, when governments impose petroleum taxes, their objective may not be so much a restriction on production or consumption as an attempt to raise more revenue.[137]

2; on the Italian inter-confederal agreement, E. Ghera, *Diritto del Lavoro*, 1983, p. 282; on the Dutch printing industry closed shop, Windmuller and Gladstone, *supra*, note 20, at p. 20.

[134] As the Commission of the European Communities commented: "The Commission has found that in all countries operating price controls the oil companies exerted pressure on governments in order to have prices adjusted ..."; *supra*, note 3, at p. 59. Ultimately, of course, the companies may simply pull out, as Shell and BP did in Italy. The rest, it is said, simply "create market shortages and threaten more severe disruptions until the Interministerial Committee for Prices conceded enough temporarily to satisfy the companies". Lucas, *supra*, note 23, at p. 8. C.P. Kindleberger, in considering the relative power of multinational corporations and governments looks to size of company assets, the degree to which the company originates and its management is resident in the country the government controls, and suggests that the bargaining strength of companies relates to their relative positions of monopoly. Cited in Turner, *supra*, note 24, at pp. 19–20. Cf. in manpower, the British trade unions' successful campaign against the Industrial Relations Act 1971.

[135] As Lucas says, however, "they are least successful when issues become highly politicised"; *supra*, note 34, at p. 174.

[136] W. Sengenberger, (1984) 23 *Industrial Relations*, no. 3, at p. 323.

[137] The view of one study was that "the period since 1967 has been characterised by increasing government interventions in the affairs of the nationalised fuel industries in the interests of the balance of payments and anti-inflation policies". J.H. Chesshire *et al.*,

Once taxation is perceived as putting a price on an activity, its private analogue is clear – the price policies of private actors can be used in similar ways to the tax policies of the State. Insofar as price policies are intended as income generators, they have their parallel in State revenue raising. Where the purpose is to encourage or discourage activity, then pricing policy can be an intrument of economic policy which may achieve equivalent effects to the use by the State of taxation.[138] A study of the respective roles of regulation and prices in France, Germany and Italy with regard to energy policy between 1973–77 concluded that prices had played the dominant role in achieving results.[139]

The instrument of pricing policy is less obvious in manpower. But it ultimately implies the imposition of a cost on others for the adoption of a particular manpower policy. Payment of subscriptions by trade union members, for example, could be said to be a tax or price imposed by the union for, inter alia, manpower services provided.[140] Similarly with employers' organisations; for example, membership in the Dutch employers' association in the printing industry (KVCO) was compulsory in that sector and it maintained a Mutual Guarantee Scheme financed by a mandatory levy on members.[141] More often, however, the tax or price is imposed by workers and their organisations on employers, and vice versa. Manpower policies imposing a price on employers include overtime rates or shift premia, redundancy or severance payments, reductions in hours without reduction in pay and various mobility benefits. These, and many other union manpower policies impose costs on the employer which will affect behaviour. Conversely, employers also impose costs through manpower policies; for example through lower rates of pay for trainees, or encouraging self-employment of workers in the "hidden" economy. Other manpower pratices by employers, such as short-time working, impose costs on governments (tax revenue lost) and social insurance institutions (short-time or unemployment benefits) as well as the individual workers affected.[142] Other actors in the manpower area also charge for services; for example, private employment agencies.

"Energy policy in Britain: a case study of adaptation and change in a policy system", in Lindberg (ed.), *supra*, note 15, at p. 33 at p. 47.

[138] For a hybrid, since 1975 Holland has had an air pollution levy – Heffingbrandstoffen luchtverotreinigung – invoiced to household purchasers by the gas distribution companies in the same way as VAT, but in the case of industrial customers it is incorporated into the tariff structure. Hancher, *supra*, note 19, at p. 96.

[139] A. Baudet, *Bilan des politiques d'economie de l'énergie dans 3 pays: RFA, France et Italie (1973–77)*, cited in P. Pringuet, "Legal aspects of energy policy in France", a paper given to the Colloquium on The Legal Implementation of Energy Policy, EUI, Florence, 22–24 September 1982 (Paper no. 6), at pp. 21–22.

[140] Streeck has observed in the West German labour movement a change to a "service organisation, based on market-like relationships"; *supra*, note 77, at p. 65. Similarly in France: G. Adam, "L'Institutionnalisation des syndicats, esquisse d'une problématique", *Droit Social*, November 1983, p. 597. The Italian trade unions resist this tendency, see M. Regini, *I Dilemmi del Sindacato*, 1981, at pp. 198–202.

[141] W. van Voorden, "Employers' Associations in the Netherlands", in Windmuller and Gladstone, *supra*, note 20, pp. 202 at 216–219.

[142] L. Reyher, M. Koller, E. Spitznagel, *Employment Policy Alternatives to Unemployment*

In the energy field, a useful illustration of pricing as a flexible "taxation" instrument is the practice of transfer pricing: "the term... applies indiscriminately to all pricing for the transfer of goods within one corporate group or enterprise, and... the term itself is strictly neutral, though usually used in a pejorative sense denoting artificially manipulated intra-enterprise pricing".[143] The uses to which this instrument can be put by multinationals or groups of companies are described by Tugendhat who emphasises how much subsidiaries are at the mercy of headquarters in the matter of financial transfers and adds: "the companies' ability to manipulate transfer prices enables them to get around even the most severe restrictions, at least partially (by) varying the prices paid by subsidiaries to each other in their transactions".[144] Transfer pricing may be used to run down the reserves of subsidiary X by instructing it to sell at low prices to other subsidiaries and instructing those others to raise their prices as regards purchases by subsidiary X. By reducing the profits of X, headquarters can justify its high prices to outsiders. Conversely, by helping subsidiary Y through transfer pricing (allowing it to buy from other subsidiaries at low prices), headquarters may enable Y to cut prices to outsiders and compete more effectively in a particular market. The oil companies are ideally situated, given their extensive vertical integration, to use this instrument. The Commission commented on the scope for manipulation by oil companies of the true costs of extraction and hence of the prices they could charge associated companies.[145]

Insofar as transfer pricing is *internal* to the groups of companies that practise it, it is not an "instrument" in the fullblooded sense as it does not affect others. Of course, these internal effects can have substantial impact on States, for example, on the balance of payments and on tax revenues, and thus indirectly affect others.[146] As direct instrument, however, transfer pricing has its effect ultimately on the prices the various subsidiaries charge for specific products in specific markets. This ability of a company to shift its prices using internal transfers is the index of its ability to affect the behaviour of outsiders: "The manipulation of transfer prices is one of the most flexible tools in the hands of a multinational company. If handled with care and discretion there is a wide range of uses to which it can be put".[147]

The relation between private pricing and State taxation policies comes into sharpest relief in the shape of price controls – a form of compulsory relaxation or

---

    in the Federal Republic of Germany, Anglo-German Foundation for the Study of Industrial Society, 1980, at pp. 176–179.

[143] Wallace, *supra,* note 101, at p. 128.

[144] Tugendhat, *supra,* note 102, at p. 169 and chapter 10 generally.

[145] *Report* of the Commission, 1975, supra, note 3, at pp. 84–94.

[146] Its use to minimise tax liability is one of its primary functions, according to Tugendhat, *supra,* note 102, at p. 170; Wallace, *supra,* note 101, chapter VII; Sampson, *supra,* note 17, at p. 217: "tax avoidance is the critical element in the oil companies' financial power...". Cf. the "ring-fence" policy of the UK government described in J. B. Skinner, "Oil and gas policy – the part played by tax considerations", *International Bar Association,* Sydney, 1978, at p. 172.

[147] Tugendhat, *ibid.*

removal of private taxation. Price controls often involve close cooperation between companies and governments in the fixing of tariffs which clarifies the proximity of the functions of pricing and taxation as instruments. For example, in the Netherlands a private law agreement of 1963 between the Gasunie (50 per cent publicly owned) and the State gave the Minister for Economic Affairs the power to approve the price of natural gas. Fears as to depletion led to the decision to use pricing policy as the instrument to slow down consumption. A 1974 law brought the pricing policy of the Gasunie under State control (thought not that of local gas companies). Barents concludes: "natural gas prices to be paid by consumers more or less reflected the market value through periodical negotiations between both (distributors and producers) under close control of the Minister. The existence of the Act, however, significantly determined the result of these negotiations... natural gas prices have been brought up to the price level of fuel oil".[148]

Conversely, removal or relaxation of State taxes allows for greater flexibility in companies' pricing policies; in other words, it strengthens private power. An illustration is to be found in the selective retail price support given by the oil companies to outlets selling their petrol. By October 1975, about 50 per cent of aggregate petrol sales in the UK were subject to some form of selective support, in the form of rebates or allowances. At the end of 1974 the oil companies sought increased prices for petroleum products and, under pressure from the UK government, the increases were loaded disproportionately onto petrol. What followed is described as follows: "In response the refiners increased rebates in new solus contracts and introduced rents and rebates for tenants and licensees. This form of temporary selective support had several advantages for wholesalers: it was more flexible, could cover geographical variations in the intensity of competition, and it could be withdrawn at the discretion of the companies whereas scheduled wholesale prices could only be increased with the approval of the Prices Commission".[149] In the manpower field, government taxation may complement private

[148] Barents, *supra*, note 46, at p. 166. Cf. the 1977 Italian system of administered prices (set by the government and imposed on the companies) and supervised prices (set by the companies and notified to the government). This system collapsed in 1980 and a new system was introduced based on a comparison of ex-refinery revenues in Italy with ex-refinery revenues in other countries. The French system is described as having had four types of price controls: liberté controlé, liberté contractuelle, liberté conventionnelle and programmation des prix industriels, as well as perhaps a fifth liberté surveillé. Daintith and Hancher, *supra*, note 19, at p. 87 (Italy) and p. 86 (France). ENI also priced its plentiful and cheap gas supplies in relation to alternative and more expensive fuels and made immense profits. *Grayson, supra,* note 30, at p. 118.

[149] Document: Petroleum Products-UK, prepared by L. Hancher for the Research Project, (on file at EUI), p. 6. For another example: the UK government ordered the Inland Revenue to grant tax concessions to Esso and Shell on ethane gas from the North Sea to be used to feed a giant petrochemicals plant at Mossmorran in Scotland (otherwise the government feared the companies would pull out). ICI's petrochemicals complex on Teeside used expensive gas, rendered even more so relative to the Mossmorran plant's gas by virtue of the concession on tax. ICI won a court order that the tax concession was illegal in putting too low a taxable value on the Mossmorran gas. *Guardian*, 26 January 1985, p. 18.

manpower pricing policy (as when there is tax exemption for privately agreed severance payments) or it may combat private manpower pricing policy (as when measures are taken to ensure the taxation of workers hired as "self-employed" by employers).

The relation between State taxation policy and private pricing policy is a function of the objectives each is designed for. These objectives are often mixed – both revenue or income generation and other policy objectives can be pursued. The use by the State of taxation as an instrument depends on whether the revenue objective is important. If not, then the use of private pricing may, in certain circumstances, be an alternative. Conversely, the policy objective of the State's taxation (revenue raising or other) may conflict with the private actor's objectives (income generation or otherwise) and provoke counter pricing policy measures. The conflict may lead to a failure of State policy, or some degree of control of private pricing policy.

C. Consensual Constraints v. Private Bargaining

The notion of consensual constraints is normally clear when this instrument is used by governments. Regulation as an instrument for affecting relative costs is a clear-cut alternative: the behaviour of large and unorganised groups may be best controlled by regulation (or, perhaps, general subsidy schemes) whereas small groups and organisations can be dealt with more individually, under consensual arrangements.[150] In the case of private consensual constraints, however, there is an important distinction to be maintained. As elaborated above, the notion of *regulation* by private actors involves not the use of force, but of wealth and respect to secure the desired changes in the behaviour of others.[151] The *legal form* through which these private actors implement their regulation is different from that of the State. Almost invariably it takes the form of bargaining leading to agreements between the regulator (often a large private actor, be it trade union, oil company, multinational or other large organisation) and the regulated (a relatively much weaker party).[152] The regulatory nature of consensual constraints where the State is a party has not gone unnoticed. In the case of the UK licensing regime in the North Sea, it was commented: "While the licences granted under the present regulations undoubtedly have a contractual form, i.e. they consist of an assignment of certain valuable rights, over a specified period of time by the Crown, in return for annual payments, at the same time the arrangements have a strong regulatory character... these licences are far more regulatory than contractual in character".[153] The notion of bargained constraints as a legal form of regulation

---

[150] See Daintith, above, at p. 40.

[151] *Above*, pp. 386 ff.

[152] The notion of regulation by consensual agreements is well brought out by Daintith in speaking of the State: the threat of force is used to increase costs both through regulations (including prohibitions) and through taxes, both through unilateral imposition of regulations and their consensual acceptance. Above at pp. 30–31.

[153] L. Hancher, "Post-crisis energy legislation in Britain", February 1981, a paper prepared for the Research Project, at p. 5.

should no longer trouble us; the mystique of freedom of contract has long since been exposed.[154]

Hence, when I speak of the instrument of consensual constraint as used by private actors, I do not refer to that area of regulation where worker parties accept terms dictated by powerful actors through their resources of wealth (e.g. a monopoly of a supply of an energy source) or respect (e.g. a craft union). Rather, the instrument of consensual constraint is expressed in bargained agreements by powerful actors with other powerful actors – resulting in consensual constraints mutually imposed on the actors agreeing. So defined, the instruments of private regulation and consensual constraint may be manifested in the same activities. For example, when two or more powerful organisations bargain and agree on a set of mutually binding constraints, the effect of which is also to control the activities of numerous other (usually weaker) actors. The latter is regulation, albeit multilateral regulation rather than unilateral as when done by the State; the former is the instrument of consensual constraint by powerful actors.[155]

There is no room here to do more than hint at the variety of private consensual arrangements. Those in the energy field are notorious.[156] In manpower, the

---

[154] As put by the Webbs, "What particular individuals, sections, or classes usually mean by 'freedom of contract' . . . is freedom of opportunity to use the power that they happen to possess; that is to say, to compel other less powerful people to accept their terms. This sort of personal freedom in a community composed of unequal units is not distinguishable from compulsion"; S. and B. Webb, *Industrial Democracy*, 1897, 1920 ed., at p. 847. And cf. their very full footnote 2 on p. 656: "It is interesting to find this situation clearly seen by an unknown French writer of 1773: 'Partout où il y a de très-grandes propriétés, et par conséquent, beaucoup de journaliers, voici comment s'établit naturellement le prix des journées: le journalier demande une somme, le propriétaire en propose un moindre; et comme il ajoute *je puis me passer de vous plusieurs jours, voyez si vous pouvez vous passer de moi vingt-quatre heures*, on sait que le marché et bientôt conclu au préjudice du journalier". – *Éloge de Jean Baptiste Colbert*, par Monsieur P. (1773, Paris), at p. 8. Three years later Adam Smith remarked that "in the long run the workman may be as necessary to his master as his master is to him, but the necessity is not so immediate" (*Wealth of Nations*, [1776, London] Book I, ch. viii, p. 30 of M'Culloch's edition). Du Cellier (*Histoire des Classes Laborieuses en France*) observes that "the struggle in the labour market too often takes place, not between two equal contracting parties, but between a money-bag and a stomach" – at p. 324. "In the general course of human nature", remarked the shrewd founders of the American Constitution, "power over a man's subsistence amounts to a power over his will" (*Federalist*, No. lxxix). This is no less so in the energy field: the Commission of the European Communities commented in 1975: "Large numbers of enterprises have long-term contracts covering varying proportions of their requirements with this or that large international company. Are these enterprises independent or not? In concluding these contracts are they not giving up their freedom of source of supply by the very act whereby they seek to secure their supplies?" *Report* of the Commission, 1975, *supra*, note 3, at p. 141.

[155] For further elaboration of this point, see below at p. 406.

[156] The "Red Line" and "Achnacarry" or "As Is" agreements of July–August 1928, the further "Memorandum of Principles" of 1934, the secret "participants' agreement" on Iranian oil of 1954, the secret "offtake agreements" restricting production in the Middle

impact of collective agreements is considerable. Rather than catalogue these, what
follows is an exposition of issues which arise from a consideration of State and
private consensual constraints.

In terms of a comparison of consensual constraints between the State and
private actors, and those between two or more private actors, there is not much
difference by way of the process or instrument itself. In each case a determining
factor will be the resources each party brings to bear. There will occur, and it
would be very interesting to assess, differences in outcomes where the resources
brought to bear by the parties are different in kind: in one case force (the State), in
other cases wealth or respect or combinations of these. Whether wealth or respect
can prevail against force, or wealth can prevail over respect is often at the heart of
the bargaining process that leads to consensual constraints, for example, in the
case of industrial conflict over manpower issues.

In terms of the relation between consensual constraints involving the State and
those exclusively between private actors, a third variation on the theme has proved
to be of considerable interest. This is where the bargaining between the two
private actors is constrained by the State – either as to its procedure or as to the
substantive parameters of any agreement (often called neo-corporatist arrangements). These arrangements are particularly evident in the tripartite character of
many manpower policy institutions. They are a hint that the separation of private
and State instruments of economic policy can be questioned, a point to be pursued
later.

There is also the problem of the extent to which private bargaining may
determine whether and how the State will intervene. Breyer considers the
alternative of bargaining with reference not to State consensual constraints, but to
State regulation.[157] His observations, however, are valid in considering whether
the State will intervene by way of consensual constraint. The advantages of
bargaining which he identifies include participation, both by the organisations
involved and within the organisations (internal trade-offs), decentralisation of
decision-making reflecting the structures of the private actors, and reduction of
enforcement problems given the consensus between the parties. But he also
highlights weaknesses which may be conducive to State intervention: bargaining
may fail to lead to agreement, there may be an imbalance of power or indeed one
side may not be organised at all, and the interests of third parties not represented
may be affected: "In sum, bargaining may work well when the strength of the
parties is roughly equivalent; when decentralization, compromise, and the rank-
ing of priorities is important; when the effect upon non-represented parties is not
significant; and when agreement itself and not its precise substantive details is of
particular importance".[158] The deficiencies of bargaining indicate both whether
and how the State may intervene: to put pressure on the parties to agree
(sometimes called the "stick behind the door"); to redress the balance of power or

East, the "Libyan producers' agreement" of 1971, and so on. See, for details of these,
Sampson, *supra*, note 17, at pp. 84, 89–90, 93, 145, 184 and 230.
[157] Breyer, *supra*, note 120, at pp. 177–181.
[158] *Ibid.*, at p. 179.

provide organisational incentives (e.g. by providing resources); and by securing third party interests (e.g. by fixing the substantive parameters of the parties' agreement or establishing tripartite institutions).

Conflict between private agreements and State economic policy emerges with clarity in the field of competition or anti-trust law. Insofar as a State does seek to enforce competition, agreements between major actors which inhibit competition – "in restraint of trade" – will be unlawful. Insofar as the parameters of what is lawful or unlawful are vague or differ from country to country, there exists an element of uncertainty about the legitimacy of private consensual constraints as an instrument of economic policy implementation. On the other hand, State intervention by way of consensual constraints may equally encounter difficulties, perhaps primarily political rather than legal.[159] It may be that the State would prefer the private actors to agree rather than incur the political and legal costs of intervention.[160]

D. Public v. Private Provision of Benefits

The inventories compiled in the course of the research project revealed that the instrument of public benefit provision, particularly subsidies, was very frequently used by governments to achieve their objectives in both the manpower and energy fields. Private actors, however, may be expected to be less likely unilaterally to dispense money, goods or services as a means of achieving their objectives. A closer look at the benefits distributed by the State, however, does reveal parallels with practices in the private sector. An example is the enormous sums of money often allocated by States to semi-independent actors in the public sector. As Grayson says: "We might expect that government assistance should be easy to identify; after all, one should be able to recognise a subsidy when one encounters it. Alas, the realities are much more complicated. It is not altogether clear whether... a particular measure represents government support or the sound business practice of a prudent owner".[161] For example, the government may inject capital funds to support a public corporation in a way comparable to that extended by a conglomerate to one of its companies or an enterprise to one of its divisions.

Two lines of analysis may help to understand the use by private organisations of financial or other assistance as an instrument of economic policy implementation. They are to do with the structure of the actor or organisation, and its ideology.

---

[159] Much of the exercise of "dominium" will be by way of consensual constraint, and insofar as this is less subject to legal restraint it is more open to political attack. See Daintith, *supra*, note 114.

[160] The shift of emphasis in labour law towards collective bargaining as an instrument of State policy has been marked particularly recently in France; see A. Supiot, "Les syndicats et la négociation collective", *Droit Social*, January 1983, at p. 63. For a view which sees in this a reflection of delegalisation, A. d'Harmant François, "La de-legificazione del diritto del lavoro: alcuni reflessioni", (1983) 57 *Il Diritto del Lavoro* 165.

[161] Grayson, *supra*, note 30, at p. 234, from which the example which follows is taken – p. 235.

As to structure, where the actor is an association, for example, a trade union or a business association, or is closely linked with other actors, as in a group of companies or a union confederation, it is likely that benefit provision will be used as an instrument for achieving the actor's policy, by dispensing benefits internally to members or associates. The implementation of economic policy requires not only the inducement of outsiders to change their behaviour, it also requires the inducement of insiders to mobilise their support for the actor's policy.[162] The internal distribution of benefits may not be equal or even equitable, for example in the case of transfer payments within groups of companies or dividend policy within a company, where practices may weigh more heavily on some members than others. Illustrations in the manpower field include redundancy selection, seniority lists and demarcation rules.

As regards outsiders, the provision of benefits by private actors is recognisable in the form of discriminatory practices. For example, in the form of specially low prices for fuel to certain customers, discount rates and "rebates".[163] Or in using the high profits available at one end of the energy chain, e.g. crude oil production, to subsidise sales of petrol at the other end of the chain.[164] Or in using the large gas production profits resulting from the rise in crude oil prices to cross-subsidise downstream activities.[165] In the area of manpower, employers may offer bonuses or ex gratia payments to employees who retire early or accept mobility or undergo training. Hungary offers an interesting illustration with widespread implications. One of the most effective manpower measures an employer can take is to pay high wages, thus attracting and retaining employees: effectively subsidies to secure a high quality workforce. This point is developed in a study of the Hungarian labour market which highlighted the growth orientation of economic units because, for example, the degree of an enterprise's influence on the central

---

[162] State aids also have this ambivalent nature, as evidenced by numerous instances of *post facto* payments made to energy corporations to compensate them for their "voluntary" adherence to government policies on price restraint.

[163] For example, a private agreement of 1 May 1981 between the Gasunie and landbouwschap provided a preferential tariff charged to glasshouse growers for natural gas. Research Project, Netherlands Energy Inventory. In the Federal Republic of Germany, special contracts between large-volume users and electric utilities provide for special pricing; IEA, *Energy Policies and Programmes of IEA Countries*, (1982, Paris) OECD, p. 171. As to rebates, in the UK, the Court of Appeal held that a solus agreement will become an unreasonable restraint of trade whilst a petrol company discriminates against a particular garage in its support during a price war (*Shell UK v. Lostock Garage* [1976] 1 Weekly Law Reports 1187); Research Project, UK Energy Inventory. In September 1976, the five "European" oil companies – CFP, SNEA, ENI, Veba and Petrofina – requested the EEC to forbid all oil companies to grant discounts; *Grayson, supra,* note 30, at p. 231.

[164] Sampson, *supra,* note 17, at p. 125, who explains the tax benefits accruing to the oil companies by this practice.

[165] Grayson, *supra,* note 30, at p. 240 points out this advantage possessed by some of the oil multinationals. This, and the example referred to in note 151 may also be *internal* distribution of benefits, depending on whether the distributor is independent or integrated with the oil company. In any event, the customers benefit from the subsidy.

planning system was above all a function of its size; and "one of the most important characteristics of enterprise behaviour in relation to growth is to retain labour and therefore to try to increase personal incomes".[166]

The second line of analysis concerns the ideology of the actor. Even when governments distribute largesse, there is often an element of mutuality which makes such "subsidies" appear more in the nature of constraints.[167] By analogy, business organisations are not normally expected to give away their property. In British company law this is enshrined in the rule that gratuitous payments will be *ultra vires* unless the objects of the company expressly provide for such payments or they are intended to benefit the company.[168] The ideology of the welfare State providing benefits is not matched by a corporate welfare ideology in the private sector. Indeed, the drift in certain countries appears more towards the adoption of a "business" ideology by the State parallel to that of the private business sector.[169]

There do exist private actors, charitable or non-profit organisations, which regularly provide services of various kinds or encourage certain kinds of behaviour in the manpower or energy fields. Trade unions are an interesting hybrid. In some countries the unions consider themselves very much a service organisation for their own members. The provision of benefits is construed strictly as a contractual obligation paid for by the member's subscriptions. In other countries the union movement sees itself in a societal role as representing the working class, and therefore provides services despite non-payment of subscriptions.[170]

---

166 I. Gábor and P. Galasi, "The labour market in Hungary since 1968", in P. G. Hare, H. K. Radice and N. Swain (eds.), *Hungary: A Decade of Economic Reform*, (1981, Glasgow), at p. 41, and especially at pp. 44–45.

167 For example, the "solidarity contracts" in France which subsidise employers who create jobs (mainly through early retirement – see *Liaisons Sociales*, No. 101/83 of 25 August 1983) include a requirement that the employer keep the level of employment steady for a least one year. See D. Frank, R. Hara, G. Mignier and O. Villey, "Enterprises et contrats de solidarieté de préretraite-démission", (1982) 13 *Travail et Emploi* (July–September) p. 75 at p: 86. Cf. a similar development under the UK Youth Opportunities Programme (a training scheme); B. Bercusson, Research Project Comparative Report on Movement between Jobs, at p. 9.

168 *Hutton v. West Cork Railway* (1883) 23 *Chancery Division Reports* 654 (Court of Appeal); and see generally, A. J. Boyle and J. Birds, *Company Law*, (1983, London) at pp. 68–72. *A propos* manpower policy, consider now section 719 of the Companies Act 1985 in the UK which states that the powers of a company shall be deemed to include a power to make provision "for the benefit of persons employed or formerly employed by the company or any of its subsidiaries, in connection with the cessation or the transfer to any person of the whole or part of the undertaking of that company or that subsidiary" (notwithstanding that the exercise of this power is not in the best interests of the company – section 719 [2]!). On the "interests of the company", see the Note by Lord Wedderburn of Charlton in (1983) 46 *Modern Law Review* 204.

169 Cf. Grayson's comment that, nothwithstanding their protests, the oil multinationals welcomed the national oil companies because of the number of their non-financial objectives, which inhibited their financial performance. *Supra*, note 30, at p. 14.

170 But see the comments in note 140 *supra*.

The relation between provision of benefits by private actors and that by the State is similar to that traced above with respect to other instruments. The more private actors subsidise an activity, the less the need for the State to do so. The low level of such private provision in the energy field does not make for much overlap. An important exception, which impinges also on manpower policy, is that area of State policy concerned with social services and welfare. The diminution in the role of the welfare State has given the provision by private organisations of equivalent benefits a greater prominence, and governments withdrawing from these areas use such private charitable provision as one justification for withdrawal. Where State policy conflicts with the private provision of benefits, there may be attempts to curtail it.[171]

E. Public v. Private Sector Management

The concept of public sector management in the instrument typology developed for the research project preceded the consideration of resources (force, wealth, respect), the use of which is central to the other instruments of State implementation of economic policy. The concept of public sector management was based on the distinction between *direct* action – when government has immediate control of activities and resources – and *indirect* action – when government operates on the actions and decisions of actors outside government. The concept of direct control was essential to "the whole phenomenon of 'public sector management', understood as comprising both governmental self-management in the strict sense of direct, hierarchical control, and the distinctive application of policy instruments to public sector bodies outside central government".[172]

The latter aspect of public sector management – the existence of separately constituted public bodies which may be subject to varying degrees of public control – is said to be distinctive from the way external private bodies may be controlled by government. The instrument of public sector management may be qualitatively different from those of either government control over private actors, or that of private actors' control.

The equivalent in the private sphere of public sector management, thus defined, is evident, but needs be precisely understood. First, there is the use by private actors of their *direct* control over resources. This is distinct from their *indirect* use of these resources to affect others. The latter is characterised as, for example, regulation – whether the form this instrument takes when government uses it, or that which it assumes when private actors exercise the power their monopolistic position gives them. The former allows for private actors to use their often very extensive "direct hierarchical control" over persons and property to achieve economic objectives.

The difference can be demonstrated in the manpower area by the contrast between control over *external* labour markets (which could be *regulated* by a

---

171 For example, discriminatory employment or trading practices (see the case mentioned in note 163 *supra*). Interesting cases are those of trade union strike pay and political contributions by companies.

172 Daintith, above, at p. 27.

union's hiring hall or an employer's monopoly of hiring), and *internal* labour markets (union protective practices and employer personnel policies).[173] Illustrations of the latter can be found, for example in company policies on working time. A recent study described various adjustments to working time open to employers with substantial manpower implications: increasing available labour through overtime and temporary workers, putting workers on short time or offering unpaid leave, using part-time workers and introducing flexibility, and so on.[174] In Hungary, the power of enterprises to reclassify their administrative and clerical workers as manual workers enabled them to evade State measures restricting the employment of the number of workers in administrative and clerical jobs.[175] In the energy field, private sector management is evinced by the efforts of energy conservation by various very large firms.[176]

The counterpart in the private sphere of those "separately constituted public bodies" controlled in various ways by the State needs also to be considered. Certain obvious parallels exist, for example, the relation between a company and its subsidiaries, or between the members of a group of associated or linked companies allows for various kinds of direct controls.[177] Again, the relations between various organisations of workers (workplace, union, federation, confederation) may be direct and hierarchical or more complex, depending on internal constitutional patterns and the requirements of laws on trade union structures. Organisations of employers may themselves control, or be controlled by members in their use of resources. In sum, the variety of public laws of different countries concerning the management by governments of the public sector is mirrored in the laws governing the private sector's diffusion of centralised power within groups of companies, organisations of workers and other associations.[178]

---

[173] For an account of union-management practices, see P. Jacobs, *Dead Horse and the Featherbird,* Center for the Study of Democratic Institutions, California, 1962. Dead horse is the type set by printers on the "lobster shift" (off-hours) which is not used but consigned to the "hell box" (to be turned into hot lead. again). The featherbird is the superfluous airman who warms a chair in the pilot's cabin.

[174] *Working Time in Britain and West Germany,* a summary by A. Lapping of studies by the Trade Union Research Unit, Ruskin College, Oxford, *et al.;* Anglo-German Foundation for the Study of Industrial Society, 1983, at p. 15. In the area of job creation, it was estimated that among the companies studied, the average increase in numbers employed after a 10% cut in working time was likely to be between 1.9%–3.7%, depending on the method adopted (p. 69).

[175] Gábor and Galasi, *supra,* note 166, at pp. 50–51.

[176] For examples in the UK, *Energy saving: the fuel industries and some large firms,* Department of Energy. Energy Paper No. 5, 1975.

[177] F. Wooldridge, *Groups of Companies: The Law and Practice in Britain, France and Germany,* Institute of Advanced Legal Studies, London, 1981; R. R. Pennington and F. Wooldridge, *Company Law in the European Communities,* (1982, London).

[178] Illustrations of the uses made of these laws for private energy and manpower policies are numerous. For example, the allegation that in France companies use subsidiaries and various contract mechanisms to evade the 1973 laws on dismissal (*Liaisons Sociales,* No. 154/83 of 21 December 1983, at p. 2); the use by the National Coal Board in the UK of a subsidiary to adopt a pricing policy which operated to the detriment of a competitor

The exercise by the State of its direct hierarchical control over its own resources does have much in common with the private sector's similar controls. But there are differences which derive from the constitutional and administrative laws concerned with State activities, which differ from the private laws on use of resources by private actors. Consideration of these factors led Daintith to conclude that: "the difference between large private organisations and State organisations, both in terms of internal structure and of relations with other economic actors, is sometimes hard to perceive, and their relations with each other are hard to classify in terms of any public/private dichotomy. This process of assimilation and interpenetration of public and private suggests at least that it may sometimes be appropriate for laws changing existing private rights to be structured according to public law criteria, and vice versa".[179] To the extent that the two spheres of public and private are governed by similar legal principles, the question becomes paramount: are there still differences in the *values* upheld by the public and private spheres; and if so, which of the different underlying values is to prevail in the common legal principles?[180] The significance of this issue can be judged by one illustration in the manpower area. Access to work is subject to very different legal regimes in the public and private sectors. In the former, there is usually a rigorous set of rules establishing what purport to be objective standards for the assessment and evaluation of applicants who are selected after advertisement and open competition. In the private sector, apart from legal provisions related to race, sex, national origin and so on, there is rarely any legal control over an employer's discretion in hiring. The public and private law principles, therefore, embody completely different approaches to access to work. Any approximation will necessitate a choice between the values enshrined in each approach (rational criteria v. subjective preference).

(Research Project, a paper on UK Coal Production and Distribution, prepared by L. Hancher, at pp. 10–12, discussing *National Carbonising Co. Ltd. v. EC Commission* (1975) *Common Market Law Reports* 457); the use of the major holding company, with capital from General Motors, Standard Oil of California and Firestone, which in the 1930s and 1940s gained control of 46 transit systems in 45 American cities and required the local transit companies to purchase vehicles, fuel and supplies exclusively from the investors and replace or expand rolling stock solely with petrol or diesel powered vehicles effectively replacing urban streetcar systems with bus lines (account given in K. P. Erickson, "The political economy of energy consumption in industrial societies", in R. M. Laurence and M. O. Heisler eds., *International Energy Policy*, (1983, Lexington) at p. 113 and especially at p. 118. For further illustrations of the use and significance of structures in the oil companies of France and the Federal Republic of Germany, see Grayson, *supra*, note 30, at pp. 28, 51, 56, 75–79, 83, 121, 150–151, and 153.

[179] Daintith, above at p. 19 (footnotes omitted).

[180] "It is the accountability to, and control by, the Government that is the most distinct feature of, and the principal justification for, the constitution of a particular industry or service as a public enterprise. Although there is much talk nowadays of the social responsibilities of private business, and, in particular, of the major corporations... the principal business of private enterprise remains the making of profits for which the corporation is responsible to its shareholders". W. G. Friedmann, "Public and private

F. Information, Advertising and Public Relations

The use of information as an instrument of economic policy in the private sector is more highly developed that what most States have been able to devise. Use of information by private actors may be considered under two headings: its use vis-à-vis the State, and its use vis-à-vis other actors.

As regards other actors, the use of information comes under the rubric of advertising or public relations – major industries in themselves and ones which are infinitely more highly developed in the private than in the public sector, evident when governments hire agencies to do their public relations work. For example, Electricité de France created subsidiaries in association with French private industry to influence consumer use of electricity, launched an aggressive commercial campaign and published a magazine extolling the virtues of electricity as a source of heat for homes, commerce, industry, agriculture, swimming pools, and so on.[181] Information in the manpower field will be used by trade unions, employers and their associations to influence members and non-members to support the policy espoused by them. Information itself is a resource. Maintaining exclusive possession is a powerful instrument of, for example, manpower policy, as workers combatting closures have found to their cost.[182] When the OPEC embargo of October 1973 was imposed, it was the oil companies' control of information which enabled them to reallocate supplies to Holland "trying both to obey Arab instructions and to fulfil long-term contracts".[183]

As used by private actors vis-à-vis the State, information can have considerable power, as the influence of lobbyists and press campaigns attests.[184] Exclusive control of information by private actors can be an even more valuable instrument of economic policy vis-à-vis governments. An illustration is given in the Commission's report: Platt's Oilgram is a daily oil price recording and reporting service based in New York, the quotations of which are taken into consideration by governments when determining prices for oil products. The basis of the pricing service consists of the acquisition of information, the majority of which is obtained from major oil companies.[185]

enterprise in mixed economies: some comparative observations", in Friedmann (ed.), *supra*, note 80, p. 359 at p. 382.

181 See N. J. D. Lucas, *Energy in France: Planning, Politics and Policy*, (1979, London) at p. 37. For the opposition this provoked, see Saumon and Puiseux, *supra*, note 28, at pp. 153–154.

182 See, for example, the accounts of management secrecy in the case studies of closures in the UK in Jacobs *et al.*, *supra*, note 128, and in Henderson *et al.*, *supra*, note 73.

183 Sampson, *supra*, note 17, at p. 274.

184 For example, in the UK effective lobbying by private motorists, road haulage contractors, motor car manufacturers and oil companies contributed to a major programme of motorway construction in the late 1950s, J. H. Chesshire et al., *supra*, note 48, at p. 41. In France, a press ampaign by a "cabal" of the nuclear construction industry was linked to their preference for a particular contracting practice which gave them most of the responsibility. Saumon and Puiseux, *supra*, note 28, at pp. 145–146.

185 *Report* of the Commission, 1975, *supra*, note 3, at pp. 119–120; as to the Commission's reservations, see p. 158.

These examples illustrate the relation of State and private use of information as an instrument of economic policy. Where private actors dominate a policy area, their control over essential information is a powerful weapon to counter State policy they oppose. It was in part to gain access to information that many national oil companies were established, or joint ventures with government participation made mandatory for multinationals' activities.[186] Even where information is equally available to government and to private actors, sophistication in advertising and public relations is an important factor in the success with which information is used. A privately owned press, often a subsidiary in a multinational's empire, is often a valuable ally in disputes with governments.

IV. Private Outcomes v. State Measures

The functional equivalents of State legal *measures* in the private sphere are the *outcomes* of the processes/instruments utilised by private actors. The coding of legal measures developed by Daintith for the purposes of the project looks to such factors as scope, temporal validity, source, nature of relation created, substantive content and procedural conditions; and is derived from and applicable to State emanations.[187] The outcomes this paper is concerned with are *private law* outcomes. The coding of State legal measures reflects the public character of the *actor* concerned (the State and its branches) – as in the coding "source", which refers to Parliament, the judiciary, and so on. Other aspects of the coding reflect the *instruments* used by the State – as in the coding "nature of the relation created": regulation is reflected in unilateral relations, consensual constraints in bilateral.[188]

The problem of analysis of the characteristics of private legal outcomes through a coding system for private outcomes is made difficult because of the variety of different private actors, analysed in Section II. The differences in the public laws of States made Daintith speculate "that demands of the national legal system are perhaps a stronger determinant of the shape of legal measures than are the characteristics of the instruments they implement, and that these demands are diverse enough to make all measures from a given system resemble each other more than they resemble the measures from each other system operationalising the same instrument".[189] The differences in the *private* law that affects the outcomes

---

[186] Forster described how under the UK Petroleum and Submarine Pipelines Act 1975, which created BNOC, it was envisaged that licences granted to oil companies would include options by BNOC to acquire 51% of production and that BNOC should sit on field development and operating committees: "These advantages and its access to information about all the development being undertaken made the Corporation (BNOC) not only the largest trader of North Sea Oil by 1979, but also the most knowledgeable operator. On the return of the Conservative Government in 1979, BNOC ceased to sit on operating committees on fields where it had no equity interest". *Supra*, note 80, at pp. 25–26.

[187] See the Methodological Note, above, at pp. 52–54.

[188] Daintith, above, at p. 53. Correspondences between other instruments and the qualities of measures are more difficult to establish.

[189] *Ibid.*, at p. 34.

of the activities of differently constituted private actors in different countries makes the compilation of a general taxonomy a formidable task. I have not attempted this. What I have done is to examine one category of outcomes in the energy and manpower fields which recurs across different countries. This is scarcely comprehensive, but in a paper of this kind, more would be too much. For the purposes of this research, the more important questions are whether the outcomes examined affect whether the State intervenes, and if so, in which ways. In particular, whether these outcomes of private processes are acceptable per se, are capable of incorporation (if so desired) into State legal measures, and if unacceptable, what measures of the State can prohibit, reverse or amend them.

The private outcome to be examined here is the *agreement* between two or more actors. This outcome is also a legal measure of State economic policy implementation, a result of the instrument "consensual constraints". As a State measure, however, its qualities are usually rather limited. Following Daintith's coding, it is almost invariably individual rather than general in scope, and creates bilateral relations. In contrast, the agreement has a much wider role to play in private implementation of economic policy. An agreement can be the outcome of the private processes *both* of regulation and of consensual constraint (private bargaining). By definition, the agreement implies a consensus as to a course of conduct, or abstention, between the parties. But in the realm of private economic policy implementation, agreements are, and may be perceived primarily as, instruments governing the relations between the parties and third parties. The agreement's function may not be only to regulate relations between the parties, though that may be its only function in many cases. It may also regulate a field of economic activity – manpower or energy – in which the parties have resources (wealth or respect), especially when their influence is monopolistic. Illustrations are not difficult to find. A comparative study of collective agreements concluded: "The contents of a collective agreement are traditionally subdivided into the obligatory or bilateral part and the normative part; the first determines the rights and obligations of the parties (usually trade unions and employers' associations) to a collective agreement; the second is intended to affect parties to individual contracts of employment, creating rights and obligations for parties other than those who made the collective agreement. This important distinction is accepted ... in France, the Federal Republic of Germany, Italy ... Netherlands".[190] In Hungary, the Minister of Labour and the Central Council of Hungarian Trade Unions issued guiding principles for 1976–1980 relegating the regulation of certain manpower issues to collective agreements.[191] In the energy field, the Netherlands is particularly rich in such "gentleman's agreements". For example, all companies which undertake refining in Holland are represented on the Olie Contact Com-

---

[190] Perone, *supra* note 87, at p. 25. On the UK, see P. Davies and M. R. Freedland, *Kahn-Freund's Labour and the Law*, (3rd ed., 1983, London) chapter 6, at pp. 158 ff. (2. The Collective Agreement as Contract; 3. The Collective Agreement as a Code).

[191] Nagy, *supra*, note 50, at pp. 91 ff. But according to Art. 8, Section 3 of the Hungarian Labour Code the collective agreement can differ from another rule concerning labour relations only insofar as the rule allows it.

missie, established in 1950, one of the functions of which is to formulate joint propositions on maximum prices for submission to the Minister of Economic Affairs.[192] The electricity companies cooperate through the so-called "Arnhem institutions". For example, each company participates in a company (SEP Ltd.) established in 1949 which owns a national grid and annually produces the Electriciteitsplan which contains binding agreements between the companies on electricity supply, installations and the grid.[193]

In the next section, I will examine certain characteristics of private agreements, as an exemplar of private outcomes, following the taxonomy set out by Daintith in his coding of State measures.

A. Scope

A private agreement may be *individual* in scope, insofar as it is a product of private bargaining between two actors. However, given that there may be a number of actors party to the agreement, there is the possibility not only of individual, but also of *multiple* application. Insofar as the agreement is intended to regulate an area of economic activity in which the parties are powerful actors, then its scope may be *general* – to this area of activity. Agreements thus have the quality of being at once general – as to the area of activity, yet also limited insofar as the parties to the agreement may not control the whole area, albeit they control a substantial part of it. The scope of regulation by a private agreement may be not individual, nor general, but, to borrow a word from contemporary labour market theory – segmented or sectoral. The agreement regulates activity in a defined segment of economic activity.[194]

The scope of private regulation by agreement can be varied very flexibly. It may be limited deliberately to affect only a strategically selected area, or to govern specified actors' behaviour, and it may be expanded or contracted as the parties agree (or are constrained to agree by changes in the balance of bargaining power).[195] This flexibility may be contrasted with the greater rigidity of State

---

[192] *Report* of the Commission, 1975, *supra*, note 3, at p. 46. The companies represented are Shell, Esso, BP, Chevron, Texaco, Mobil, Gulf, CEP and Petrofina.

[193] The "Arnhem institutions" are described in Barents, *supra* 46. There is occasionally a surprising tendency to seek parallels between the energy and labour relations/manpower fields where agreements are being negotiated. For example, Sampson, *supra* note 17, draws a parallel between oil policy and labour negotiations: "the danger is that, as in union agreements, it will be the consumers and the outsiders that will suffer"; at p. 328. He also quotes a Dutch Shell director as saying about negotiations with producing countries: "It was like labour unions, when they've agreed about wages, they go for co-determination"; at p. 245.

[194] This is not the argument as to non-compliance by a part of the persons covered – a factor inherent in regulation whether State or private. Perone, *supra*, note 87, expresses this as follows: "Freedom to determine the field in which a collective agreement is to apply constitutes one of the most characteristic expressions of trade union independence, since this is the way in which it displays the various types and dimensions of the collective interests which spontaneously emerge"; at p. 33.

[195] An illustration is the industry agreement in France between oil refiners relating to market

regulation (though non-regulatory instruments of the State can be very flexible). Indeed, the selective application of State regulation may be precluded by constitutional or administrative law standards which prohibit discriminatory treatment. Interesting questions arise when the application of these standards is attempted to private agreements.[196]

B. Temporal Validity

An agreement may be permanent or temporary. But its very quality as a private outcome of bargaining allows for a degree of fluidity. As a matter of mutual constraint, the parties may not specify its duration, but leave it indefinite. In its capacity as a regulatory measure, the effect of the agreement on others may be specified in its duration by an agreement which is indefinite as regards the parties' own relationship. It is of interest that some countries exercise statutory control over the period of validity of collective agreements, while others leave the parties maximum freedom.[197]

The temporal validity of an agreement has implications for its qualities as an instrument of economic policy. The parties have to trade off security against flexibility. Long duration gives the agreement more of a planning or regulatory character, but may prevent the parties from reacting to changing events. Two cases in the energy field illustrate this. In one case, an Italian company had concluded supply contracts on a long-term basis to secure adequate supplies of crude oil, and had to suffer the consequences of price escalation clauses in the contract after 1973. A second company purchased supplies from time to time and was thus able to avoid the regulatory effects of price escalation clauses.[198]

Another account of the effects of the 1973 crisis puts it somewhat differently in describing the plight of "the many smaller companies which had been relying either on the Rotterdam market or on more or less formalised supply arrangements with various crude-surplus majors. As the latter found they had to concentrate on supplying their own affiliates and those outside clients with whom they had binding contracts, these companies with marginal arrangements were faced with the possibility of being without any crude oil at all".[199] The trade-offs encountered in private regulation are not dissimilar to certain dilemmas of State

position, refining capacity and import authorisation. This made it possible to expand only by merger, not competition. The entrance into the market of a new actor, not party to the agreement, caused Esso to take the initiative in 1964 in breaking up the arrangement. Grayson, *supra*, note 30, at p. 79.

[196] An illustration is the decision of the European Court of Justice in *The Commission of the European Communities v. UK* (1984) *Industrial Cases Reports* 192, which held the UK to be contravening the equal pay provisions of the Treaty of Rome by reason that non-binding collective agreements were not affected by the UK implementing legislation.

[197] Perone, *supra*, note 87, at p. 34. Statutory restrictions, he notes, are present in France and the Netherlands, while in the Federal Republic of Germany, UK and Italy the parties are free to specify the agreement's duration.

[198] *Report* of the Commission, 1975, *supra*, note 3, at p. 96.

[199] Turner, *supra*, note 24, at p. 130.

implementation of economic policy. For example, an analysis of UK employment policy noted the relatively high number of temporary measures. It concluded that there was no one explanation for this, but mentioned that many schemes were seen as pilot projects only testing different ideas and that changes of government brought about new ideas.[200]

C. Source

The source of a State measure may be the constitution, Parliament, central government, other territorial authorities, judicial decisions, other regulatory bodies, European Community and international organs (following the Daintith taxonomy). Where the instrument used by the State is consensual constraint, the measure which ensues is an agreement between the State and another actor or actors. The actors may, of course, be private bodies. They could, therefore, also be considered as "sources" of the measure. The difference in the case of private agreements is that all the sources of the agreement, unless the State is also a party, are private. This applies whether the agreement is an outcome of the regulatory or the bargaining process.

That a private body can be perceived as a joint source of State economic policy implementation (when there is a State/private body agreement) reinforces the case for characterising purely private implementation of economic policy as a parallel to State action.[201] Involvement of private actors in State implementation of economic policy raises the possibility that the State could play a junior role in any agreement.[202] Indeed, the State could abstain from any active involvement in the area covered by the agreement; policy implementation would be the responsibility of the private body. For example, the conservation policy of the Federal Republic of Germany includes voluntary agreements between industry and government for the purposes of reducing energy consumption.[203] In State-to-State contracts, the governments set principles and perhaps details of the agreement, but "it is then the practice that one or more oil companies are selected to implement the contract and are left to do so under the government's control".[204] The lesser the role of the State

---

[200] J. Moon, "Policy change in direct government responses to UK unemployment", (1983) 3 *Journal of Public Policy* 301. The study also pointed to the government's need to continually be *doing* something about a growing problem.

[201] Cf. the repeated emphasis on the dominance of private law in Dutch energy policy. See Barents, *supra*, note 46.

[202] Again, in Holland the profits of Shell and Esso on natural gas sales provoked calls for closer control of the use of these profits, the result of which has been only gentleman's agreements between the companies and the State as to future investments. Barents, *ibid.*, at p. 166.

[203] W. Birner, "Legal aspects of energy policy in West Germany", a paper given to the Colloquium on The Legal Implementation of Energy Policy, EUI, Florence, 22–24 September 1982, (Paper no. 9) (on file at EUI), at p. 10 (automobile industry, electrical appliance industry).

[204] Levy, *supra*, note 117, at pp. 17–18. Cf. the analogy with the French "contrats de programme" between, for example, EDF and the government, one clause of which reads: "The State will carry on the policy now initiated and designed to reduce the

in such agreements, the more economic policy is under the control of private actors, despite the ostensible authorisation of the State. The extent of policy implementation by the State through private actors, particularly where control by powerful private bodies looms large in comparison with the role of the State, is scrutinised by those concerned with "neo-corporatism".

In accordance with the Daintith taxonomy, the identification of the source of an agreement (the State or a private actor) is only the first step. The coding then seeks out the internal component of the actor which is the source of the particular measure. Such an analysis, in the case of State measures, serves to identify which part of the State is particularly involved with the aspect of economic policy under examination. A similar exercise in the case of private actors making agreements would be extremely complex, given the multiplicity of actors and their different constitutional structures – even within a single country, let alone in different countries.[205] Insofar as private actors fall into categories that can be identified in different countries: companies, trade unions, associations of employers, cartels and so on, common elements might be sought. But the degree of homogeneity in, for example, company structures and trade union organisations differs from country to country. It is not possible always to know which organ within a company will take the decision on a manpower issue.[206] The structure of a trade union may allow for different and overlapping competences of district, national, sectoral and workplace organisations.[207] In energy, the predominance of multinational corporations in the oil industry does not provide a simple legal structure which allows for identification of the organ responsible for an agreement. The problems of secrecy seem to be pervasive.[208] Even if one could formulate a model

administrative and technical control so that EDF will be able to take advantage of the freedom normally pertaining to enterprises of the competitive sector, so far as it is consistent with the proper functioning of a public service". R. Drago, "Public and private enterprise in France", in Friedmann, *supra*, note 80, at p. 3, and especially at p. 29.

[205] That the exercise is still an important one is emphasised by Breyer: "The internal ordering (of bargaining actors) is important, for the individual members of each group, whether a union, a firm, or some other organization, have different needs and objectives". *Supra*, note 120, at p. 177.

[206] Thus J. D. Reynaud has pointed out the extreme centralisation of management control in France: "With the same technology and in similar conditions, German and French firms have neither the same number of levels, nor the same number of people in those levels, nor the same wage differentials between levels". "Industrial relations research in France: 1960–1975: a review", in Doeringer (ed.), *supra*, note 12, at p. 252.

[207] The problems of conflicts between collective agreements negotiated at different levels by different organs of the trade union are the subject of perennial debates in labour law. For example, in Italy, *Rapporti tra Contratti Collettivi di Diverso Livello*, AIDLESS, Annuario di Diritto del Lavoro, No. 15, 1982. In France, as to reduction in hours, see A. Supiot, "La réduction conventionnelle de la durée du travail", (1981) *Droit Social*, p. 448 at p. 454.

[208] As put by one authority: "It seems incontestable that the rate of supply was subject to some sort of controlled planning... but there is no evidence at all that control was exercised in any centrally co-ordinated manner". E. Penrose, quoted in Sampson, *supra*,

for this one type of actor, it is not clear that this would be helpful. Wallace states: "the real structure of the (multinational enterprise) cannot be ascertained by merely examining its legal form . . . the legal structure, basically designed for cash-flow and tax purposes, in accordance with governmental regulations, is not always an accurate reflection of the true distribution of management and control functions".[209] Similarly with manpower organisations, as put by Windmuller with regard to employers' associations: "Nor should one assume that the formal structure of decision-making, as embodied in bylaws and other documents, invariably corresponds to actual practice. There are bound to be power centers and pressure groups existing informally and operating through informal channels to supplement and sometimes to bypass the formal structure, particularly in situations involving relations with unions or governments".[210]

In sum, identifying the source within the private actor or actors making the agreement presents serious difficulties. The solution by way of investigating formal legal structures is inadequate, as legal structure does not necessarily reflect the decision-making mechanisms of the organisation. The parallels with bureaucratic decision-making in State administrations are obvious and raise the prospect of a reformation of the internal structures of large organisations using public law principles. There remains, of course, the problem of determining *which* public law principles.

D. Nature of Relation Created

The agreement may, in its quality as a "bargained outcome" or "consensual constraint" create bilateral or multilateral relations between the parties to it. In its quality as "regulator", however, it would be unilaterally determining the courses of action of those whose choices were dictated by the parties' monopoly of resources.

E. Substantive Content

The substantive content of an agreement can be varied, as is demonstrated by Daintith's coding of State measures: it may be declaratory; impose, remove or relax, or grant exemptions from duties; grant powers; transfer funds or constitute other bodies. The impact of these will fall on different parties depending on

---

note 17, at p. 148. Or, as Sampson put it in another context where the oil companies were trying to hold back production and the OPEC countries were trying to push it up in the mid-1960s: "It was clear that in the midst of the glut the companies were agreeing between themselves to hold back production. However, the producing governments could not discover exactly how they were taking their decisions, and their arrangements were carefully shrouded"; at p. 180.

209 C. Day Wallace, *supra*, note 101, at p. 17. For example, the 50% shareholding of the UK government in BP did not allow for it to control the company's behaviour during the 1973 crisis; see the account of the confrontation between Edward Heath and Sir Eric Drake of BP in Sampson, *ibid.*, at p. 276.

210 Windmuller, in Windmuller and Gladstone, *supra*, note 20, at p. 14.

whether the agreement is a consensual constraint between the parties alone, or whether it is to have a regulatory effect in a specified field.[211]

An interesting set of problems arises with agreements which purport to impose duties. In Daintith's coding, measures having this content are further analysed in terms of the *sanctions* applicable for breach of the duties. This aspect of bargained outcomes is not problematic where the agreement is legally binding, in which case legal penalties will be available,[212] The problem of sanctions arises, first, with regard to non-legally binding agreements which nonetheless impose duties on the parties; and secondly, with agreements which purport to have a regulatory effect on third parties.

As to non-legally binding bargained outcomes, the concept of sanctions would have to include not only legal, but also other sanctions. These are well-known in the area of industrial relations: manpower agreements which are violated lead to a variety of forms of industrial action by unions or to management crack-downs which have a penalising effect.[213] Such sanctions may not succeed in restoring the *status quo ante*, but this is not invariably the case where legal sanctions are available.

As to regulatory agreements, their effect on third parties raises the problem of enforcement against those third parties who ignore the rules laid down in the agreement. In some cases, for example, the normative part of a collective agreement binding on members of the employers' association and trade union members, sanctions for breach may be provided by the law in the form of civil actions by the third parties or administrative enforcement.[214] In other cases, the

---

[211] An example of the former in the energy field is the Dutch cooperative, the Interim Central Petroleum Storage Organisation (ICOVA), created in 1978 to hold oil stocks, where running costs are met by levies imposed on members of the cooperative; Levy, *supra*, note 117, at p. 15. An example of the latter in the manpower field is the so-called "Bridlington" agreement in the UK whereby trade unions affiliated to the Trades Union Congress agree to refuse to accept into membership a member of another union without first inquiring into the applicant's status with other Unions: Hepple and O'Higgins, *supra*, note 84, Part 1, para. 1A–O43. For an illustration of such a refusal, see K. W. Wedderburn, *The Worker and the Law*, (2nd ed., 1971, London) at pp. 463–464.

[212] Thus, in all countries of the European Community, save the UK (Trade Union and Labour Relations Act 1974, section 18), collective agreements are considered to be legally binding as contracts between the parties.

[213] For a less well known but interesting example, see the account of the discipline attaching to violations of agreements by members of employers' associations *inter se;* generally, Windmuller, in Windmuller and Gladstone, *supra*, note 20, at pp. 19–20; and in particular in the Federal Republic of Germany, R. F. Sunn, "Employers' associations in the FRG", p. 169 at p. 193, and in the Netherlands, W. van Voorden, "Employers' associations in the Netherlands", p. 203 at p. 219.

[214] The normative effect can be provided for by statute (Netherlands, France, Federal Republic of Germany), or it can be derived from case law (Italy). Cf. the UK, where normative effect is a function of contractual consent of workers and employers. Perone, *supra*, note 87, at p. 30. For administrative enforcement of collective agreements by labour inspectorates (Italy, France), see p. 40. On supervision and enforcement of collective agreements in Hungary, Nagy, *supra*, note 50, Part 4, pp. 201 ff.

sanctions will reflect the resources which give the parties their regulatory capacity. So where the parties to an agreement, for example in the energy field, possess a monopoly of the production or supply or distribution of a product, they will be able to use this to penalise third parties who do not comply with the system laid down in the agreement.[215] In the case of manpower policy, where the employer or trade union controls the supply of jobs or labour, those who will not comply with the agreement may be forced out of the particular sector, or out of the labour market altogether.[216] The contrast between regulatory agreements which rely on the regulators to enforce it and those which rely on the regulated to enforce it parallels a situation encountered with respect to State measures. The reliance on third party, rather than State enforcement, is to be found in the job maintenance area, but not in the energy conservation area because "there is a high degree of congruence between individual interests in job security and a state policy of job maintenance, and a high capacity for effective enforcement of individual worker rights based on trade union support, both of which factors are absent in the energy sector".[217]

A special case of enforcement of regulatory agreements is where the agreement is co-opted by a State measure and enforced using State machinery as well. The most prominent illustration is the process of "extension" of collective agreements to cover entire sectors of industry or regions. The relation between State measures and regulatory agreements throws up some interesting sidelights on the notion of "legalisation". A French commentator noting the future incorporation of a collective agreement on occupational training into statute form spoke of it as being "legalised".[218] Conversely, in Hungary, one study which looked at three collective agreements showed that each followed closely and referred constantly to the

---

[215] For example, by withholding supplies from individuals who do not respect an agreed system of rationing. See L. Hancher, Research Project Comparative Report on Management of Short-Term Energy Disturbances (on file at EUI), at p. 23.

[216] As, e.g., where trade unions and employers agree a compulsory retirement scheme for the workforce. Employees who refuse to accept this will be dismissed, and in the UK their claims for unfair dismissal fail because, as one judge put it: "the whole basis of good industrial relations... is that agreements arrived at between the employing authorities... and the trade unions in question ought to bind everybody... it can only lead to industrial anarchy if individual branches or individual members of a trade union are entitled to opt out and to avoid the consequences of a decision democratically arrived at in an overall national connotation". *Nelson and Woolett v. The Post Office* (1978) *Industrial Relations Law Reports* 548 (Employment Appeal Tribunal), at p. 550, para. 15, per Mr. Justice Kilner Brown.

[217] T. C. Daintith, Research Project Comparative Report on Maintenance of Employment (on file at EUI), at p. 13.

[218] *Liaisons Sociales*, No. 146/83 of 7 December 1983, p. 1. Presumably, the fact that the 1966 French law on training found its implementing provisions not in a ministerial decree but in a collective agreement – the 1970 inter-industry agreement – would, therefore, be "delegalisation". *Reynaud, supra*, note 192, at p. 259. The 1983 collective agreement on training has now, in part, been transformed into statute; *Liaisons Sociales* No. 5460 of 7 March 1984.

Hungarian Labour Code and applicable decrees "with negative consequences for the readability and comprehensibility of the text of the agreement".[219]

F. Procedural Conditions

Procedural conditions for the making of agreements are one of the ways in which the constraints or regulations imposed by private actors can be controlled. At least three sets of procedural conditions are possible. First, if there is an obligation to inform, consult, obtain the approval of or go through a special procedure involving State authorities before coming to an agreement there is thereby exercised a degree of public control over the behaviour of private bodies. For example, on November 20, 1981, German companies contracted for long-term imports of Soviet gas, a contract approved in principle by the federal government.[220] After 1973 in France, light and heavy fuel oil was subject to a price system called "régime de cadre de prix" which required trading associations to submit the price lists for each category of product to enable the authorities, if they objected, to defer their entry into effect.[221] With regard to marketing oil in France during the late 1950s and early 1960s, Grayson says: "with a certain degree of governmental approval, the major companies completed 'industry agreements' on three of the major products".[222] Under the gentleman's agreement between Esso and Shell and the Dutch government, Parliament has to be informed.[223]

Secondly, apart from this public external control, there are the procedural conditions prescribed *internally* by the actors' constitutions. The conditions which precede the entering into of agreements by certain organs of the company, or trade union or association may provide some degree of constraint on such agreements. This can arise from externally prescribed procedures as well as internal constitutional protections laid down by the members or shareholders or constituent bodies. Apart from general procedures, individual members may have the power to prevent certain agreements being concluded; for example, minority shareholders, dissident trade union members, constituents of a federal association, and so on.

Finally, in the case of agreements purporting to regulate the behaviour of third parties, private outsiders may have the power to forestall such regulation by invoking, for example, restraint of trade doctrines, or other public policy precluding regulation generally or a particular instance of it. Workers may complain of procedure agreements which deny them fair representation by unions before employers; members of minorities may complain about discriminatory agreements; consumers may complain about a standard of service or a quality of product. Ultimately, the power of a regulatory agreement may be undermined, of

---

[219] B. Cardini and G. Lipschitz, *Il Nuovo Codice del Lavoro della Republica Popolare Ungherese*, (1981, Rome) at p. 85.

[220] *IEA, supra,* note 163, at p. 176.

[221] *Report* of the Commission, 1975, supra, note 3, at p. 102.

[222] Grayson, *supra,* note 30, at p. 237.

[223] K. J. M. Mortelmans, *supra,* note 33, at p. 10.

course, by informal means breaking down the monopoly of resources controlled
by the parties to the agreement (discovery of new sources of energy; changes in
labour markets).

V. Private Actors, Processes and Outcomes: Some Conclusions

Heretofore, I have been concerned to describe and analyse the functional equivalents in the private sector of State instruments of implementation of economic
policy, and to hint at the relationship between State and private instruments. Four
possible relationships could occur:

  (i) private policy implementation is consistent with State policy, and the State
      does not intervene;
 (ii) private policy implementation clashes with State policy, but still the State
      does not intervene;
(iii) private policy implementation is consistent with State policy, but the State
      still intervenes; and
 (iv) private policy implementation clashes with State policy, and the State does
      intervene.

Options (i) and (ii) both result in State non-intervention. By definition this is
difficult to chart. Only by reference to the pronouncements of public authorities
can one assess (and then only tentatively) the extent to which private policy
implementation is being deferred to either willingly (because it promotes the
State's policy) or unwillingly (because the State cannot or will not do anything to
counter the private policy).

An illustration of the ambivalent quality of State non-intervention is to be
found in the so-called "stick-behind-the-door" instrument of policy implementation. In the Netherlands, for example, the Natural Gas Prices Act of December
19, 1974 confers upon the Minister of Economic Affairs the power to fix minimum
prices for the sale of natural gas when the agreed prices do not properly reflect its
market value. It has only been used once. Rather, it operates as an indirect control,
a "stick behind the door" of the Minister through the power to approve the gas
price contracts between the Gasunie and the distributors.[224] Another example: in
March 1976, the UK government announced that export of crude oil should be
restricted to a third of the total produced and that at least two-thirds should be
refined in the UK. This was based on the voluntary acquiescence of the oil
companies, but with the threat of direct measures in the background.[225] In the
Federal Republic of Germany, agreements are encouraged by the government
between the electricity industry and enterprises in order to exploit the waste
energy of industry, in the knowledge that the government could enact stricter

---

[224] Wet aardgasprijzen, Research Project, Netherlands Energy Inventory. As Barents says:
"An important feature of public law … is to function as a 'stick behind the door'"; *supra*,
note 46, at p. 174.
[225] Hancher, *supra*, note 154, at pp. 2–3.

rules.[226] Again in the UK, the government has warned that failure by industry to establish adequate voluntary manpower training institutions will lead to the re-establishment of statutory Industrial Training Boards. In France, the oil sector was incorporated into energy planning, though the oil companies displaced indigenous coal much faster than provided for in the Plans. Lucas comments: "The government had the means to prevent this displacement, but did not use them. The companies operated with the complicity of the government achieving objectives desirable to both sides while Le Plan was used as a public avowal of an intention to pursue politically popular protection of coal".[227]

The research project uncovered a multitude of methods used by States to stimulate or repress private activity without formal legal intervention using a policy instrument. Planning itself is such an instrument, since it inherently involves a preference for a few large predictable actors (oil, nuclear) over policies involving many less predictable actors (coal with its labour force).[228] The "broad social discussion" on nuclear power in the Netherlands is another informal instrument of energy policy.[229] Forster highlights the options by way of hearings v. enquiries, adversarial v. investigative proceedings, which allow the UK government to shape the choice between informal or legal instruments of policy.[230] During the 1973–74 crisis, the government of the Federal Republic of Germany "did not find it necessary to introduce any law or regulation concerning quantities and prices of oil products. The difficulties which nevertheless arose in connection with supplies were solved through close contacts between the public authorities and the oil companies".[231]

Options (iii) and (iv) both reflect State intervention. Option (iv) is of central importance to the project: whether the State intervenes to achieve economic policy objectives where the behaviour of private actors conflicts with these objectives, and how it does so, using which instruments to change the behaviour of those actors. Option (iii) is also of the greatest interest: when private instruments may not directly clash, but the State nonetheless intervenes. This is the situation referred to by Daintith: "The self-regulation phenomenon is one of deliberate and explicit organisation or ratification by the State of a diffusion of economic power".[232]

The research project identified many instances of deliberate incorporation or use by States of private actors, processes or outcomes as instruments of economic policy. In energy policy, for example, Germany and the Netherlands encouraged the oil companies to form stock holding cooperatives.[233] In State-to-State contracts, the governments set the principles and then in practice one or more oil

[226] Research Project, German Energy Inventory (on file at EUI).
[227] Lucas, *supra*, note 23, at p. 5.
[228] Lucas, *supra*, note 18, at p. 129.
[229] Barents, *supra*, note 46.
[230] Forster, *supra*, note 80, at p. 21.
[231] *Report* of the Commission, 1975, *supra*, note 3, at p. 51.
[232] Daintith, above at p. 33.
[233] Levy, *supra*, note 117, at p. 15.

companies are selected to implement the contract.[234] For instance, in the Netherlands, the Gasunie-Norway agreement of 1975 was a private contract involving a
consortium of German, Belgian and French companies with Norway for the
import of gas from Norway, subject only to the approval of the Minister of
Economic Affairs. During the 1973–74 crisis, a State office, the Rijksbureau was
set up by a Ministerial decision of November 13, 1973 to organise the country's
supplies of oil products. It consisted of experts seconded from oil companies.[235]

Manpower policy also offers many examples. In the Netherlands, all dismissals, individual and collective, need the sanction of the director of the local
employment office (GAB), who must act in consultation with his advisory
committee of trade union and employer representatives. In 1976, a reform of the
unemployment benefit system enabled older workers over 57½ to receive unemployment benefit until age 65 (effectively early retirement). At the time of the
reform, the Minister of Social Affairs inssued a circular to employment offices
stressing that older workers should not be over-represented as a consequence in
selection for redundancy. Nevertheless, as one study put it: "the directors of the
GABs found themselves increasingly confronted with dismissal plans which had
been drawn up in consultation with the Works Councils (and also normally
following negotiations with the trade unions involved) which did indeed make
such selective dismissals. Because of the manner in which these plans are drawn up
they are, of course, acceptable to the advisory committee of the GAB, and thus it
is very difficult for the director to refuse to consent to them".[236] In the UK, there
are a number of statutory provisions which expressly refer to or incorporate
collective agreements: requiring, for example, the employer in selecting employees for redundancy to adhere to any "customary arrangement or agreed procedure"; allowing for collective agreements to replace statutory provisions on
dismissal, on lay-off pay and on redundancy payments[237] In the Federal Republic
of Germany, employment offices must ensure that all collective agreements are
respected in any placements made by them.[238] In Italy, the recent "Accordo" of 22
January 1983 between unions, employers and the government contained an
undertaking to redefine the rules on inter-company mobility in accordance with
collective bargaining experience.[239]

The intertwining of State and private instruments does not lend itself to any
simple explanation of why a given area of economic policy is selected by the State

---

[234] *Ibid.*, at pp. 17–18.
[235] Research Project, Netherlands Energy Inventory (on file at EUI).
[236] *Report* of the Commission, 1975, *supra*, note 3, at p. 55.
[237] B. Casey and G. Bruche, *Work or Retirement? Labour market and social policy for older
workers in France, Great Britain, the Netherlands, Sweden and the USA*, (1983, London)
at pp. 60–61. The result is effectively to undermine the provision in the general dismissal
law which purports to extend extra protection to older workers threatened with
dismissal because of their subsequent greater difficulty in finding work.
[238] Employment Protection (Consolidation) Act 1978, section 59 (b) and also sections 65, 18
and 96. See C. Bourn, "Statutory exemptions for collective agreements", (1979) 8
Industrial Law Journal 85.
[239] Malagugini, in Marazia, *supra*, note 39, at p. 99.

for intervention or which instruments of State policy implementation will be adopted and how these will relate to existing private actors, processes and outcomes. It would have been gratifying to have been able to present a general theory. I have contented myself at this stage with occasional observation of possible tendencies only.[240] The purpose of the preceding portion of this paper has been more to demonstrate the parallels between State and private implementation of economic policy. For much of the debate over "delegalisation" has, it is submitted, ignored these parallels. And insofar as the deficiencies of "regulation" or "legalisation" or "juridification" are to be found not only in the qualities and characteristics of State instruments and measures, but also where private actors engage in parallel processes which result in similar outcomes, then the critique of these deficiencies must embrace areas of private as well as State implementation of economic policy. Insofar as issues of "legitimacy" and "efficiency" are germane to State implementation of economic policy, they must also be addressed when powerful private actors implement *their* economic policies.[241] It is to these questions that I turn in another contribution to this research.[242] In concluding this paper, I will address questions more pertinent to the subject of this volume: State implementation of economic policy and its implications for private ordering.

A major assumption on which the research project proceeded – the identification of economic policy *objectives* of the State – was the starting point of my conclusions. So long as comparison was limited to the *instruments* and *measures* used, parallels could be sought in the realm of private ordering. It is when the question of "consistency" or "clash" of public and private policy *objectives* arises that the lines not only curve, they appear to intersect or distance themselves at random, as numerous examples illustrate.

Nonetheless, this contrast of policy objectives presumes at least that the implementation of economic policy by States is *affected* in some way by private policy objectives, even though the precise interrelationship is very difficult to disentangle, given the myriad of instruments/processes and measures/outcomes. Again, this notion of State implementation of policy objectives (through instruments and measures) being affected by private policy objectives operates conversely as well: private implementation of policy objectives (processes and outcomes) is affected by State policy objectives.

---

[240] The text is in T. Treu, *Il Patto contro l'Inflazione*, (1984, Bologna) at p. 203, Art. 9 (d). For a general account of preceeding practice on this, see F. Guarriello, "La disciplina legislativa e contrattuale della mobilità interaziendale", (1982) 1 *Rivista Italiana di Diritto del Lavoro* 289. For a general catalogue of recent labour market instruments, many of which involve unions and employers, see F. Strati, "Strumenti nazionali e regionali per le politiche del lavoro", (1984) *Rassegna Sindacale Quaderni*, No. 106, p. 43.

[241] See above, pp. 367, 371–380, 384, 386–390, 393–394, 396–397, 399–403, 406–407, 412.

[242] Issues of efficiency are well-worn topics in the literature. Those on the legitimacy of private economic orderings also have a respectable lineage. For recent treatments of the issue, P. C. Schmitter, *Democratic Theory and Neo-Corporatist Practice*, EUI Working Paper No. 74, 1983; and the symposium on the public/private distinction in law reported in (1982) 130 *University of Pennsylvania Law Review* 1289–1608.

More importantly, however, it was conceded much earlier [243] that the assumption as to the definition of common State policy objectives was not applicable to the private sphere, where various major actors have different, or even conflicting objectives. Major private actors must relate not only to a potentially antagonistic or friendly State (enemy or ally) in terms of policy objectives, but also (and perhaps more importantly) to other major private actors who may be enemies or allies (e.g. competitors or customers). Whereas the State deals with major private actors through the single framework or matrix of a public (constitutional/administrative) law system, major private actors operate through this system (in relation to the State), but also, and primarily (in relation to other private actors) through a private law system. In the case of economic policy, the private law system operates in the context of an economy characterised by varying degrees of market imperfection – as both energy and manpower vividly illustrate.

It might be said that to speak of "private" economic policy objectives is misleading in that it overlooks the pressures of the market which constrain the ability of any single actor to unilaterally implement policy objectives. But once market imperfections are acknowledged, there is room for the exercise of private power to achieve private objectives. The position is not much different from that of the State – the subject of a notional political market place which nonetheless leaves room for the determination of objectives which may oppose those of many, even most private actors, and which allows even for a "national" interest of the State itself.

The very market which may condition the exercise of private power is shaped by the rules and institutions of private law – just as public (constitutional/administrative) law shapes the political system in which the State seeks to achieve its objectives. I am not concerned here to distinguish private and public law. On the contrary, my argument is that the study of the legal implementation of economic policy by the State cannot be separated from the study of the law governing the economic relations between private actors. Illustrations are legion: State regulation through the imposition of duties may rely on private enforcement mechanisms; State taxation may be defeated by private financial arrangements; State benefits will have a differential impact on different private actors' ability to apply successfully, and so on.

Some instruments of State economic policy implementation may allow to private actors a wide capability to continue to pursue private objectives (within the further limits of their ability due market constraints). Other instruments may impose severe restrictions on the freedom of action of private actors – not only vis-à-vis the State, but also vis-à-vis other private actors. To some extent it may be possible to analyse individual measures (and even differentiate instrument types) in light of their tendency or ability to restrict private inter-actions. Illustrations would include government contracts with clauses determining manpower or energy policies of private contractors (hiring of specified numbers and descriptions of employees; use of specified energy-saving techniques); regulations which prohibit certain manpower practices (e.g. the closed shop, or control the private

[243] *Above*, pp. 360–361.

activity of energy supply or distribution); public benefits which encourage the hiring of special categories of manpower or installation of energy efficient equipment; information on certain employment markets or energy sources, and so on.

Two hypotheses may be postulated:

I. It seems that the greater the degree of State control over private transactions, the less likely it is that private actors will be able to pursue their objectives in a way which clashes with State policy. Conversely, those State instruments which facilitate or promote private transactions may be used to support the private pursuit of objectives consistent with State policy.

II. In a sense, since the existence of a perfect market constrains private actors from the uninhibited pursuit of private objectives (which are contrary to market forces), the State may encourage market conditions where private objectives clash with State policy, and allow for market imperfections where these encourage private behaviour consistent with State policy.

Hypothesis I seems more likely to be manifested in regulatory or instrumental law – direct control over the substance of private transactions to prohibit or restrict those which clash, and support those which are consistent with State policy. Hypothesis II seems more likely to take the form of "reflexive" law,[244] setting a framework determining the permitted degree of competition, of freedom for private actors to enter into private transactions. But, as is argued elsewhere, this boundary between regulatory and reflexive law is difficult to maintain.[245]

To summarise: the implications of State legal implementation of economic policy for private ordering can be stated as follows:

1. Private objectives may be consistent or clash with State policy objectives.
2. State instruments and measures may restrict or encourage private processes and outcomes.
3. Assuming State objectives are stipulated, one must:
   A. determine whether (and if so which) private actors' objectives are consistent or clash with them;
   B. use those instruments/measures which:
      (i) restrict private ordering to control the processes and outcomes of those actors whose objectives clash;
      (ii) promote private ordering to support the processes and outcomes of those actors whose objectives are consistent.
4. Insofar as competitive markets operate to inhibit the pursuit of autonomous private objectives, State instruments/measures may promote competition where private ordering clashes with State policy, and may control competition where private ordering is consistent with State policy.

---

[244] See G. Teubner, "Juridification: Concepts, Aspects, Limits, Solutions", in Teubner ed., *supra*, note 4; see also Teubner, "Substantive and reflexive elements in modern law", (1983) 7 *Law and Society Review* 239.

[245] B. Bercusson, "Legalisation and Disorder: State and Private Power", in Teubner ed., *supra*, note 4.

The paradox in this summary lies in the apparent conflict between restraining competition (promoting private ordering consistent with State objectives) and promoting competition (to control clashes of private ordering with State objectives). Competition is the context of private ordering which is manipulated to control major private actors hostile to the State, whereas imperfect markets are used to assist those who are friendly.[246] Classical economists are doubtless spinning in their university chairs. But the paradox is only a apparent one. For it is premised on the presence, indeed the dominance, of the State and *its* objectives in economic policy. None of the propositions apply where State objectives are subordinated to private ordering. In the event of State intervention being relegated in this way (as by the "deregulators"), private objectives predominate, and reliance is placed on the workings of the market to control these.

This is fine in theory. But market imperfections in both energy and manpower have reached levels where few can deny their existence, least of all politicians. States have been compelled to intervene. Indeed, it is asserted that certain objectives (such as those posited by the research project) are important and even prevail over private objectives. In that event, the issue of State intervention and private ordering requires attention, and the propositions put forward should be considered. The State, like the market, is no longer *deus ex machina*. But, unlike the market, it has become *deus in machina*. If it is unsuccessful in using private ordering to achieve its objectives, it may become the *machina*.

---

[246] A study of the legal implications of controlling major private actors and markets as a method of implementing State economic policy in the sphere of low pay and incomes policies is B. Bercusson, *Wage Determination: Instrumentalist and Neo-Corporatist Approaches*, Paper presented at the European University Institute Colloquium "Law and Economic Policy – Alternatives to De-Legalisation", mimeo, 1985.

Authors' Biographical Sketches

BERCUSSON, BRIAN, Professor of Law; born 1947; LL. B. 1969, London; LL. M. 1970, McGill University; Ph. D. 1974, Cambridge University; Research Fellow of Christ's College, Cambridge 1973–1977; Teaching Fellow, Osgoode Hall Law School, York University, Toronto, 1973–74; Lecturer in Laws, Queen Mary College, London University, 1978–1983; Senior Lecturer 1983; Professor of Law European University Institute 1986–; Jean Monnet Fellow, European University Institute, Firenze, 1983–84. *Author:* Fair Wages Resolutions, 1978; (with C. D. Drake), The Employment Acts 1974–1980, 1981; Legislation Editor of the Encyclopedia of Labour Relations Law.

CASSESE, SABINO, Professor of Law; born 1935; Doctor's Degree University of Pisa and Scuola Normale Superiore, Pisa, 1956; Assistant Professor, Universities of Pisa and Rome, 1957–61; Associate Professor, University of Urbino, 1962–70; Professor and Dean, University of Urbino, 1970–73, Professor of Law, University of Naples, 1973–74; Professor of Public Administration, Scuola Superiore della Pubblica Amministrazione, 1974–82; Professor of Law, University of Rome, 1982. *Author:* Partecipazioni pubbliche ed enti di gestione, 1962; I beni pubblici, 1969; Cultura e politica del amministrativo, 1971; La formazione dello Stato amministrativo, 1974; Il sistema amministrativo italiano, 1983.

DAINTITH, TERENCE, Professor of Law; born 1942; M. A. Oxford University, 1968; Barrister, Lincoln's Inn, 1966; Associate in Law, University of California at Berkeley, 1963–64; Lecturer in Constitutional Law, University of Edinburgh, 1964–72; Professor of Public Law, University of Dundee, 1972–83; Director, Centre for Petroleum and Mineral Law Studies, University of Dundee, 1977–83; Professor of Law, European University Institute, Florence, 1981–87; Professor of Law and Director, Institute of Advanced Legal Studies, University of London, 1988. *Author:* The Economic Law of the United Kingdom, 1974; (with G. D. M. Willoughby) United Kingdom Oil and Gas Law, 1977, 2nd ed. 1984; (with L. Hancher) Energy Strategy in Europe: The Legal Framework, 1986; (with S. Williams) The Legal Integration of Energy Markets, 1987. *Editor:* Journal of Energy and Natural Resources Law (Vol. 1, 1983–); The Legal Character of Petroleum Licences, 1981; (with G. Teubner) Contract and Organisation, 1986.

FROMONT, MICHEL, Professor of Law; born 1933; Doctor in Law of the University of Paris, 1958; Agrégé of the Faculties of Law, with specification for public law and political science, 1962; Professor at the University of the Saar, 1962–66; Professor at the University of Dijon, 1966–75; Associate Professor at the University of Freiburg-im-Breisgau, 1975–76; Professor and Director of the Institute for Comparative Law of Dijon 1976. *Author:* Rechtsschutz gegenüber der Verwaltung in Deutschland, Frankreich und den Europäischen Gemeinschaften, 1967; Le droit économique français, 1973; Les recours contre les actes administratifs dans les Etats des Communautés européennes (en collaboration avec J. M. Auby), 1971; Introduction au droit allemand (en collaboration avec A. Rieg), Tome I, Les fondements 1977; Tome II, Le droit public et le droit pénal, 1984; Les grands systèmes de droit contemporains, 1987. *Editor:* L'intervention de l'Etat dans la vie économique, Institutions es politiques (en collaboration avec Savy), 1978; Les instruments juridiques de la politique foncière des villes, 1978; Le régime juridique des plus-values et moins-values foncières dues à l'urbanisation, 1984; Les compétences des collectivités territoriales en matière d'urbanisme et d'équipement (Europe occidentale), 1987.

HANCHER, LEIGH, Lecturer in Law; born 1956; LL. B. University of Glasgow 1978, MA in Socio-Legal Studies, University of Sheffield 1979; Researcher, European University Institute 1980–1983; Lecturer in Commercial and European Law, University of Warwick 1983–1987. Senior Research Fellow, Institute for International Energy Law, University of Leiden 1987. *Author:* (with T. C. Daintith) Energy Strategy in Europe: The Legal Framework, 1986; (with M. Moran) Capitalism, Culture and Regulation, forthcoming 1988.

HARMATHY, ATTILA, Professor of Law; born 1937; Doctor juris Budapest University 1959; diploma of the Faculté internationale de droit comparé, Strasbourg 1967; candidate of legal sciences 1972, doctor of legal sciences 1981; research officer of the Institute for Legal and Administrative Sciences of the Hungarian Academy of Sciences since 1962 (head of department 1973–1986, deputy director 1986–); lecturer at the Budapest University Faculty of Law since 1959, docent 1974, Professor 1982–; head of Roman Law department 1982–1983, head of civil law department 1986–1987. *Author:* Felelösség a közremüködöért (Liability for subcontractors), 1974; Szerzödés, közigazgatás, gazdaságirányitás (Contract, state administration, state intervention in the economy), 1983. *Coauthor:* A gazdaság jogi szabályozása (Legal regulation of the economy), ed. Gy. Kálmán, 1979 (Also published in Chinese), A Polgári Törvénykönyv magyarázata (Commentary on the Civil Code), ed. Gy. Eörsi-Gy. Gellért, 1981; and papers in English, French, German and Russian.

HAZARD, JOHN N., Nash Professor Emeritus of Law, Columbia University. Visiting Professor of Law, European University Institute 1984–85. Member of the New York Bar. Deputy Director, USSR Branch, Foreign Economic Administration, USA Government 1941–45, Adviser on State Trading, US Dep't of State 1945–46. *Author:* Communists and Their Law (1969), Managing Change in the USSR (1983), The Soviet System of Government (1957 and subsequently 5 editions), etc.

JARASS, HANS D., Professor of Law; born 1945; Referendar Munich 1970; LL. M. Harvard (USA) 1972; Dr. jur. Munich 1974; Assessor Munich 1974; Assistant Professor of Law Munich 1974–1977; Habilitation in Law Munich 1977; Professor of Public Law, Berlin 1978–1982; Professor of Public Law, Bochum 1972–. *Author:* Executive Information Systems and Congress, 1974; Politik und Bürokratie als Elemente der Gewaltenteilung, 1975; Die Freiheit der Massenmedien, 1978; Wirtschaftsverwaltungsrecht, 2. ed. 1984; Die Freiheit des Rundfunks vom Staat, 1981; Bundes-Immissionsschutzgesetz, 1983; Konkurrenz, Konzentration und Bindungswirkung von Genehmigungen, 1984; Neuordnung des Rundfunks, 1986; Anwendung neuen Umweltrechts auf bestehende Anlagen, 1987; Umweltverträglichkeitsprüfung bei Industrievorhaben, 1987.

MAYNTZ, RENATE, B. A. at Wellesley College (USA), doctorate in sociology at the Free University of Berlin, honorary doctorates from the universities of Uppsala and Paris. She has held chairs at the Free University in Berlin and the Hochschule für Verwaltungswissenschaften in Speyer. She has taught at Columbia University and the New School for Social Research in New York, at the University of Edinburgh, at the FLASCO (Facultad Latino-Americana de Cienzas Sociales), Santiago de Chile, and at Stanford University. Before becoming Director of the Max-Planck-Institut für Gesellschaftsforschung, Cologne, she held a chair at the University of Cologne and was Director of the Institut für Angewandte Sozialforschung.

MORTELMANS, KAMIEL, Professor of Law; born 1946; A. B. 1966, J. D. 1969, Special Licence Degree in European Law, 1970, agréation de l'enseignement supérieur, University of Ghent (Belgium); Assistent University of Ghent, 1970–1971; Lecturer in European Law at the Europa Institute of the University of Leyden (The Netherlands), 1971–1977; Legal Secretary to President of the European Court of Justice, Luxembourg, 1977–1982; Senior Lecturer in Economic and European Law, University of Leyden, 1982–1984; Professor of Law (Economic and European Law), Europa Institute, University of Utrecht (The Netherlands), 1984–. *Author:* De invloed van het Europees Gemeenschapsrecht op het Belgisch economisch recht (The Influence of European Community Law on Belgian Economic Law), 1978; Ordenend en sturend beleid en economisch publiekrecht (Ordering and Process Policy in Public Economic Law), 1985; Gedifferentieerde integratie en het Gemeenschapsrecht (Two-tier Integration and Community Law, 1985 (with J. J. Feenstra). *Editor:* Handboek van de Europese Gemeenschappen (Handbook of the European Communities), 1983; Restructuring the International Economic Order, The Role of Law and Lawyers, 1987 (with P. van Dijk, F. van Hoof and A. Koers).

OST, FRANÇOIS, Professor of Law, born 1952; Director of the faculties of Law at the Saint-Louis University Brussels 1982 –; Editor of the "Revue interdisciplinaire d'études juridiques" and member of the editorial board of the "Revue Droit et Société". *Author:* Droit mythe et raison, Bruxelles, 1980 (avec J. Lenoble); Bonnes mœurs, discours pénal et rationalité juridique, Bruxelles, 1981 (avec M.

van de Kerchove); Jalons pour une théorie critique du droit, Bruxelles, 1987 (avec M. van de Kerchove). *Editor:* Fonction de juger et pouvoir judiciaire. Transformation et déplacements, Bruxelles, 1983 (avec Ph. Gérard et M. van de Kerchove); Actualité de la pensée juridique de Jeremy Bentham, Bruxelles, 1987 (avec Ph. Gérard et M. van de Kerchove).

VON STEBUT, DIETRICH, Professor of Law; born 1936, Dr. jur. Hamburg 1971, Dr. jur. habil. Munich 1977, Professor of Civil Law, Labour Law, Commercial Law, Procedural Law, Freie Universität Berlin 1978 –. *Author:* Geheimnisschutz und Verschwiegenheitspflicht im Aktienrecht, 1972 (Maintenance and Obligation of Secrecy in Company Law), Der soziale Schutz als Regelungsproblem des Vertragsrechts, 1982 (Legal Implementation of Social Protection by Contractual Law).

STEWART, RICHARD B., Professor of Law; born 1940; B. A. Yale University 1961; M. A. Oxford University 1963; Ll. B. Harvard University 1966; Law Clerk to Mr. Justice Stewart, Supreme Court of the United States, 1966–67; Private practice, Washington D. C., 1966–71; Assistant Professor of Law, Harvard University, 1971–1975, Professor of Law 1975–1983, Byrne Professor of Administrative Law 1983 –; Special Counsel, U. S. Senate Watergate Committee 1973; Visiting Professor of Law, University of California, Berkeley, 1979–80, University of Chicago 1986–87. *Author:* Environmental Law & Policy (2nd ed. 1978) (with J. Krier); Administrative Law and Regulatory Policy (2nd ed. 1985) (with S. Breyer); Integration Through Law: Enviromental Protection Policy (1985) (with E. Rehbinder).

Index